W9-ABR-909

THE THEOLOGY
OF CHRISTIAN PERFECTION

ANTONIO ROYO, O.P., AND JORDAN AUMANN, O.P.

THE THEOLOGY OF CHRISTIAN PERFECTION

THE PRIORY PRESS DUBUQUE IOWA

IMPRIMI POTEST: J. E. MARR, O.P., S.T.M., PRIOR PROVINCIAL
IMPRIMATUR: +ALBERT CARDINAL MEYER, ARCHBISHOP OF CHICAGO, 5 · 7 · 1962

 PRINTED IN THE UNITED STATES OF AMERICA
LIBRARY OF CONGRESS CARD NO. 62-17314

TABLE OF CONTENTS

TABLE OF CONTENTS

V THE LIFE OF PRAYER

The present volume is offered to the English-reading public as a definitive work on the theology of Christian perfection. It is not merely a translation but the adaptation and revision of an original Spanish work entitled Teologia de la Perfeccion Cristiana, *first published in 1954. Since that time it has gone through four editions and sold many thousands of copies.*

The principal author, Father Antonio Royo, O.P., has won wide renown in his native Spain as a preacher. For some ten years he has taught ascetical and mystical theology at St. Stephen's in Salamanca, where he received the doctorate of theology at the Pontifical Faculty. In that time he has emerged as one of the outstanding theologians in Spain. A clear and incisive intellect which can penetrate to the depth of the most difficult theological questions is coupled with a clarity and simplicity of style which makes him easily understood by all. His literary output is impressive. Besides his frequent contributions to theological reviews, the following works have already been published or are in the process of preparation and soon to be released: Theology of Salvation, Moral Theology for the Laity, Theology of Charity, *and* Jesus Christ and the Christian Life. *He is likewise the founder of the Preacher's Institute at the Pontifical Faculty at Salamanca.*

At Salamanca, Father Royo soon discovered the pressing need for a manual of spiritual theology which would avoid the two extremes of excessive abstraction and undue emphasis on the experimental and casuistic methods. His first intention to compile a textbook for seminarians was soon discarded in favor of a manual which would be suitable for the educated laity as well as for priests, religious and seminarians. The present volume, then, will serve admirably as a textbook of ascetico-mystical theology in seminaries, where the professor will know how to select the sections of the book which have immediate reference to the specialized study of asceticism and mysticism. But the book as a whole will be of invaluable benefit to all those who need a more detailed explanation of the principles upon which the theology of Christian perfection is based and to those who seek detailed applications of those principles in the preaching of retreats, the guidance of souls, and the direction of their own lives.

Father Jordan Aumann, O.P., has prepared the original Spanish edition for publication in English. He has changed the order of the chapters, summarized and adapted certain sections, and rewritten some of the material in view of the English-reading public.

Like Father Royo, a doctor in theology from the Pontifical Faculty at St. Stephen's in Salamanca, Father Aumann is the founder of the Institute of Spiritual Theology and also the founding editor of the Cross and Crown Series of Spirituality. His many works and translations and his public lectures and extensive retreat work have earned him a justified reputation in America.

INTRODUCTION

One of the first problems which arises in the study of any science is the question of terminology. The study of the theology of Christian perfection is no exception. Although the traditional concept of theology is a remarkably unified one, by the middle of the seventeenth century the study of Christian perfection had not only become a well-defined branch of theology, but it was further divided on the basis of new distinctions introduced at that time. Moreover, from the seventeenth century to the present day the differences between the various schools have become so pronounced that they have led to theological conclusions which are in no sense compatible.

The result has been what one would expect: there is no uniformity of terminology among theologians when they treat of the science of Christian perfection. Even when the same terms are used, they are often understood in different ways by different theologians. Such a situation makes it a prime necessity to define one's terms carefully and to indicate clearly the scope of this branch of theology.

TERMINOLOGY

What we designate as "the theology of Christian perfection" has been called by various names throughout the history of theology. Some have called it simply *spirituality* (Pourrat, S.S., Viller, S.J.); others have referred to it as *spiritual theology* (Heerinckx, O.F.M.), *spiritual life* (Le Gaudier, S.J., Schrijvers, C.SS.R.), *supernatural life* (de Smedt, S.J.), *interior life* (Meynard, O.P., Mercier, Tissot), or *devout life* (St. Francis de Sales). But the terms most commonly used throughout the history of spirituality have been *ascetical* and *mystical,* although these words do not have the same connotation for all the theologians of Christian perfection.

Ascetical and mystical

The word "ascetical" comes from the Greek verb meaning to exercise or train, and it had special reference to athletic training. In his epistles St. Paul makes frequent references to the Christian as an "athlete," one who strives, struggles and trains. In the primitive Church the "ascetics" were those who took public vows, especially of chastity, and led an austere life. Origen and St. Athanasius make reference to such persons.

But the word itself came into common Latin usage only in a later period. The first to use the term seems to have been a Polish Franciscan named Dobrosielski, who wrote in 1655. After the middle of the seventeenth century the word was used by Scaramelli in contradistinction to mystical. Giovanni Battista Scaramelli, S.J. (1687-1752), wrote his *Direttorio ascetico* and his *Direttorio mistico* in an attempt to show that the ascetical life is not essentially ordained to the mystical life and that acquired forms of prayer do not necessarily predispose the soul for infused contemplation.

The word "mystical" means hidden and was commonly used among the ancient Greeks to designate religious truths which were as yet unknown to the uninitiated. The word *mysterium* is found in the Septuagint version of the Book of Daniel and also in the Deutero-canonical books. In the New Testament it is found especially in St. Paul, who uses it in three different senses: 1) as a secret of God pertaining to the salvation of man; 2) as the hidden or symbolic sense of a narration or description; 3) as anything whose activity is hidden or unknown.

Yet the adjectival form "mystical" is not found in the New Testament nor in the apostolic Fathers. It was introduced in the third century, and with the passage of time it assumed three different meanings: 1) a liturgical sense, to signify something that pertains to religious cult; 2) an exegetical sense, to signify a typical or allegorical interpretation, distinct from the literal interpretation; 3) a theological sense, of which we shall now speak.

The expression "mystical theology" appears in the fourth century in the writings of Marcellus Ancyranus and again in the fifth century in the writings of Marcus Eremita. It was to appear later in the famous *De mystica theologia* by the pseudo-Dionysius. As used by the last-mentioned author, the phrase was meant to designate an immediate and experimental knowledge of God, superior to that knowledge acquired through reason or from ordinary faith.

Still later, and until the middle of the seventeenth century, the distinction was made between *practical* mystical theology and *speculative* mystical theology. The first was the result of infused contemplation, and the second was the result of scientific study. Thus Gerson wrote the two treatises: *Theologia mystica speculativa* and *Theologia mystica practica* (1706). The term "speculative mystical theology" was then extended to embrace the entire science of the spiritual life, from the first infusion of grace to its full flowering in the mystical life. This is represented in such authors as Henry Herp, O.F.M., Philip of the Holy Trinity, O.C.D., Anthony of the Holy Ghost, O.C.D., and Thomas A. Vallgornera, O.P. But when the term "ascetical theology" was introduced in the seventeenth century, mystical theology was again restricted to the study of infused contemplation and the extraordinary graces of the spiritual life.

Modern uses

In view of the historical development of this terminology, it is not surprising that there is no unanimity among modern theologians in the use of the words ascetical and mystical. That very fact, however, makes it important for students of the theology of the spiritual life to understand the terminology of an author before accepting or rejecting his doctrine. Modern authors will generally fall into one of the following classifications in their use of the words ascetical and mystical:

1) The terms are used interchangeably to designate the entire field of the theology of the spiritual life (Aureliano a SS. Sacramento, O.C.D.; Murawski; Rouet de Journel, S.J.; Louismet, O.S.B.).

2) Ascetical theology should treat of the purgative, illuminative and unitive ways so far as man progresses in them with the assistance of ordinary grace; mystical theology pertains to the extraordinary gifts and states which constitute infused contemplation or those *gratiae gratis datae* which sometimes accompany infused contemplation (Poulain, S.J.; Denderwindeke, O.F.M.Cap.; Farges; Naval, C.F.M.; Richstatter, S.J.; Pourrat, S.S.; Zimmerman, S.J.; von Hertling, S.J.).

3) Ascetical theology pertains to the theory and practice of Christian spirituality as far as the threshold of infused contemplation; mystical theology pertains to the practice of the spiritual life from the night of the senses to mystical marriage (Tanquerey, S.S.).

4) The purgative and illuminative ways pertain to ascetical theology; the unitive way belongs to mystical theology (Saudreau; Zahn; Krebs).

5) The distinction between the ascetical and the mystical ways is based on the predominance of the virtues (ascetical) and the predominance of the operations of the gifts of the Holy Ghost (mystical). The gifts, working *modo divino,* predominate in the mystical life; the virtues, working *modo humano,* predominate in the ascetical life (Arintero, O.P.; Garrigou-Lagrange, O.P.; Joret, O.P.; Schrijvers, C.SS.R.; Masson, O.P.; Menéndez-Reigada, O.P.; Osende, O.P.).

6) Although fundamentally in agreement with the previous interpretation, others base the distinction upon the activity or passivity of the soul so far as it operates by its own efforts under the virtues (active and ascetical) or under the influence of the Holy Ghost working in the soul (passive and mystical) (Cayré, A.A.; Mutz; Valensin).

THE THEOLOGY OF CHRISTIAN PERFECTION

Since there is as yet no generally accepted term to designate the science of Christian spirituality, we prefer to call it simply *the theology of Christian perfection.* This title has the advantage of expressing three basic points which are not clearly expressed in any of the other titles: 1) that this is a true theological science and a branch of the one theology; 2) that its proper object and purpose is to expound the theological doctrine of Christian perfection in all its amplitude and extension; 3) that there is no previous persuasion or assumption concerning such disputed questions as the necessity of infused contemplation for perfection, the dichotomy between asceticism and mysticism, the unity or duality of ways to perfection, etc.

Since theology is essentially one by reason of the identity of its formal object in all its branches, it necessarily follows that all the parts of theology are intimately interrelated. Therefore, it should not seem strange that the theology of Christian perfection derives from dogmatic theology those grand principles of the intimate life of God which are shared by man through grace and the beatific vision: the doctrine of the indwelling of the Trinity in the souls of the just; reparation by Christ, the Redeemer of the human race; the grace of headship in Christ; the sanctifying efficacy of the sacraments; and other principles which are the foundation of Catholic dogma. Cardinal Manning spoke truly when he said that dogma is the source of true Christian spirituality.

But even more intimate is the relation between moral theology and the theology of Christian perfection. As one of the great modern theologians has said,[1] it is evident that moral theology and ascetico-mystical theology have the very same formal object *quod*. The reason for this is that the moral act by essence, which is the act of charity toward God, is also the primary object of ascetico-mystical theology. Hence between "moral theology" and "the theology of Christian perfection" there is only a modal or accidental difference, since moral theology considers the act of charity in all its aspects, as incipient, proficient and perfect. Thus "casuistic" moral theology is concerned primarily with incipient charity and treats of the lawful and unlawful, or of that which is compatible or incompatible with this initial charity; "ascetical" moral theology insists principally on proficient charity, accompanied by the exercise of the other infused virtues; and "mystical" moral theology treats primarily of perfect charity under the predominating influence of the gifts of the Holy Ghost. Nevertheless, there is no exclusive division between any of these parts of theology; it is merely a question of the predominance of certain activities which are common to all these parts.

"Therefore, they are in error who wish to establish an essential difference between moral theology and ascetico-mystical theology by reason of the primary object, just as they would be in error who would attempt to make a specific distinction in the psychology of the infancy, adolescence and maturity of the same man."[2]

---

[1]Cf. J. M. Ramírez, O.P., *De hominis beatitudine* (Matriti: 1942), I, n. 85.

[2]Cf. Ramírez, *loc. cit.*

"Pastoral theology" is that part of theology which teaches the ministers of the Church, according to revealed principles, the manner in which they are to care for the souls confided to them by God. It is an eminently practical science and is closely related to the theology of Christian perfection, since one of the principal duties of the pastor of souls is to lead them to perfection. It differs from the theology of Christian perfection inasmuch as the perfecting of souls constitutes one of the partial objects of pastoral theology, while it is the proper and exclusive object of the theology of Christian perfection.

SUBJECT MATTER

At first glance, and interpreting the title of this branch of theology in a strict sense, it would seem that it should be limited to a study of the questions that pertain to Christian perfection itself or the things that immediately lead to it. But it would be an error to limit the field of spiritual theology to this extent. Since it is closely related to dogmatic and moral theology, it necessarily embraces a much wider field. In order to justify this amplitude of subject matter, we need only turn to the authority of the eminent theologian, Reginald Garrigou-Lagrange, O.P.:

> Theology is the science of God. We distinguish between natural theology or theodicy, which knows God by the sole light of reason, and supernatural theology, which proceeds from divine revelation, examines its contents, and deduces the consequences of the truths of faith.
>
> Supernatural theology is usually divided into two parts, dogmatic and moral. Dogmatic theology has to do with revealed mysteries, principally the Blessed Trinity, the Incarnation, the Redemption, the Holy Eucharist and the other sacraments, and the future life. Moral theology treats of human acts, of revealed precepts and counsels, of grace, of the Christian virtues, both theological and moral, and of the gifts of the Holy Ghost, which are principles of action ordained to the supernatural end made known by revelation.
>
> Modern theologians have often exaggerated the distinction between moral and dogmatic theology, giving to the latter the greater treatises on grace and on the infused virtues and gifts, and reducing the former to casuistry, which is the least lofty of its applications. Moral theology has thus become, in several theological works, the science of sins to be avoided rather than the science of virtues to be practiced and to be developed under the constant action of God in us. In this way it has lost some of its pre-eminence and is manifestly insufficient for the direction of souls aspiring to intimate union with God.
>
> On the contrary, moral theology as expounded in the second part of the *Summa theologica* of St. Thomas keeps all its grandeur and its efficacy for the direction of souls called to the highest perfection. St. Thomas does not, in fact, consider dogmatic and moral theology as two distinct sciences; sacred doctrine, in his opinion, is absolutely one and is of such high perfection that it contains the perfections of both dogmatic and moral theology. In other words, it is eminently speculative and practical, as the science of God from which it springs.[3] That is why he treats in detail in the moral part of his *Summa* not

[3]Cf. *Summa,* I, q. 1, aa. 2-8.

only human acts, precepts and counsels, but also habitual and actual grace, the infused virtues in general and in particular, the gifts of the Holy Ghost, their fruits, the beatitudes, the active and contemplative life, the degrees of contemplation, graces gratuitously bestowed, such as the gift of miracles, the gift of tongues, prophecy and rapture, and likewise the religious life and its various forms.

Moral theology thus understood evidently contains the principles necessary for leading souls to the highest sanctity. Ascetical and mystical theology is nothing but the application of this broad moral theology to the direction of souls toward ever closer union with God. It presupposes what sacred doctrine teaches about the nature and the properties of the Christian virtues and of the gifts of the Holy Ghost, and it studies the laws and conditions of their progress from the point of view of perfection.

To teach the practice of the highest virtues and perfect docility to the Holy Ghost and to lead to the life of union with God, ascetical and mystical theology assembles all the lights of dogmatic and moral theology, of which it is the most elevated application and the crown.

The cycle formed by the different parts of theology, with its evident unity, is thus completed. Sacred science proceeds from revelation contained in Scripture and tradition, preserved and explained by the teaching authority of the Church. It arranges in order all revealed truths and their consequences in a single doctrinal body, in which the precepts and counsels are set forth as founded on the supernatural mystery of the divine life, of which grace is a participation. Lastly, it shows how, by the practice of the virtues and by docility to the Holy Ghost, the soul not only arrives at belief in the revealed mysteries but also at the enjoyment of them and at a grasp of the profound meaning of the word of God, source of all supernatural knowledge, and at a life of continual union with the Blessed Trinity who dwells in us. Doctrinal mysticism thus appears as the final crown of all acquired theological knowledge, and it can direct souls in the ways of experimental mysticism. This latter is an entirely supernatural and infused loving knowledge, full of sweetness, which only the Holy Ghost by his unction can give us and which is, as it were, the prelude of the beatific vision. Such is manifestly the conception of ascetical and mystical theology which has been formulated by the great masters of sacred science, especially by St. Thomas Aquinas.[4]

This being so, there can be no doubt that the theology of Christian perfection coincides in a certain manner with the field of the one theology. In its experimental and descriptive aspect it should take the soul as it is found at the beginning—even if it be in the state of mortal sin—and teach it the way to be followed, step by step, to the heights of Christian perfection. This is the way in which St. Teresa of Avila understood the spiritual life. At the beginning of her *Interior Castle* she speaks of "paralyzed souls who live in great danger" and the ugliness of a soul in mortal sin, and then discusses the seven mansions which lead to the transforming union.[5]

---

[4]Reginald Garrigou-Lagrange, O.P., *Christian Perfection and Contemplation,* tr. by Sister M. Timothea Doyle, O.P. (St. Louis: 1945), pp. 12-14.

[5]Cf. *Interior Castle,* First Mansions, Chaps. 1-2.

We do not mean by this that the theology of Christian perfection should begin with a discussion of the conversion of the sinner who is far removed from any practice of religion or who lives as an unbeliever or pagan. We believe, with Joseph de Guibert, S.J.,[6] that the study of the conversion of the sinner belongs to religious psychology (if one treats of its modes, effects and motives), to pastoral theology (if one treats of the means to attain the conversion of the sinner), and to missiology (if it is a question of the conversion of the infidels and pagans). But bearing in mind the possibility of sin, even mortal sin, in a pious soul which sincerely aspires to perfection, we believe that a complete treatise of the spiritual life should embrace the entire panorama of this life, from its beginning (the justification of the sinner) to its ultimate crowning in the high grades of union with God.

DEFINITION

We can now attempt a definition of the theology of Christian perfection. Let us first see some of the definitions that have already been proposed by various authors.

According to Garrigou-Lagrange, O.P., ascetico-mystical theology is nothing other than the application of moral theology to the direction of souls toward ever more intimate union with God. It presupposes whatever sacred doctrine teaches concerning the nature and properties of the Christian virtues and the gifts of the Holy Ghost, and it studies the laws and conditions of the soul's progress in view of perfection.[7] This part of theology, says the same author, is a development of the treatise on the love of God and of the gifts of the Holy Ghost and has for its end the explanation of the applications which derive from them and lead souls to divine union.[8]

According to de Guibert, S.J., spiritual theology may be defined as the science which deduces from revealed principles what the perfection of the spiritual life consists in and the manner in which man as *viator* can tend to it and attain it.[9] A. Tanquerey, S.S., states that this science has as its proper end the leading of souls to Christian perfection. Differentiating between ascetical and mystical theology, he holds that the former is that part of the spiritual science which has as its proper object the theory and practice of Christian perfection from its beginnings to the threshold of infused contemplation, and the latter has for its object the theory and practice of the contemplative life from the first night of the senses and quietude to the mystical marriage.[10] For J. Schrijvers, C.SS.R., the science of the spiritual life has for its object

---

[6]*The Theology of the Spiritual Life,* tr. by Paul Barrett, O.F.M. Cap. (New York: 1953), n. 6.

[7]Cf. *op. cit.,* Chap. 1, a. 1.

[8]Cf. *The Three Ages,* tr. by Sr. Timothea Doyle, O.P. (St. Louis: 1947), I, p. 10.

[9]Cf. *op. cit.,* n. 9.

[10]*The Spiritual Life* (Westminster: 1948), nn. 3, 10, 11.

the orientation of all the activity of the Christian to supernatural perfection.[11] P. Naval, C.F.M., defines mysticism in general as the science which has for its object Christian perfection and the direction of souls toward that perfection.[12]

All the definitions given are substantially in agreement and differ only in minor details. By taking what is common and best from all of them and adding the experimental aspect of the mystical state, we can formulate the following definition: The theology of Christian perfection is that part of sacred theology which, based on the principles of divine revelation and the experience of the saints, studies the organism of the supernatural life, explains the laws of its progress and development, and describes the process which souls are wont to follow from the beginning of the Christian life to the heights of perfection.

Explanation

We say that the theology of Christian perfection is a part of sacred theology in the sense that it is based on the principles of divine revelation, for it would not be theology at all if such were not the case. Theology is nothing more than the deduction of virtually revealed truths from revealed data by means of reason enlightened by faith. As one modern theologian has stated it, theology is the *explicatio fidei,* or the development of the data of faith.[13]

The theology of the spiritual life also makes use of the experience of the saints, thus manifesting that there are two distinct but harmonious aspects of this branch of theology, one subordinate to the other. The basic element is revealed data and the virtualities contained in that revelation. This is what makes it true theology. But it is not licit to prescind entirely from the experimental element of which the mystics give testimony, for then one runs the risk of formulating an *a priori* system which turns its back on reality. This experimental aspect is entirely subordinate to the theological, to the extent that the theologian will reject an experimental datum which is not in accord with the *certain* data of theology.[14] Nevertheless, it is beyond any doubt that this experimental aspect is of great importance and is indispensable for a complete picture of the supernatural life, its laws and vicissitudes, could not be explained sufficiently by the theologian who lacks the testimony of those souls who have lived this life in its fulness. We believe, therefore, that any definition of the theology of the Christian life would be incomplete if it did not incorporate this experimental element which constitutes to a great extent the material for the investigation of the theologian.

We further state that this branch of theology studies the organism of the supernatural life, and this is the first thing that the theologian should do

[11] *Principles of the Spiritual Life,* a. 1.

[12] *Curso de teología ascética y mística,* n. 1. Cf. Garrigou-Lagrange, *The Three Ages,* Vol. II, p. 653.

[13] Cf. Marín-Sola, O.P., *La evolución homogénea del dogma católico* (Madrid: 1952), p. 812.

[14] We underline the word "certain" in order to forestall any rash and hasty interpretation on the part of speculative theologians.

before he passes on to study the growth and development of that life. In this section the theologian should restrict himself almost exclusively to the data of revelation, because it is only on this firm basis that he can establish the solid principles of the Christian life, which do not depend on the variety of experiences of individual souls or the opinions of particular schools of theology.

Spiritual theology then studies the laws of the growth and development of the supernatural life. Once the characteristics of the supernatural organism have been explained, it is necessary to investigate the progressive growth of that life until the soul reaches the summit of perfection. The theological element, based on revealed truths, still conserves its importance here and is again used almost exclusively, rather than the appeal to experimental data.

Then this theology describes the process which souls will follow from the beginning to the end of Christian perfection. Theology is both a speculative and a practical science, although as a unity it is more speculative than practical.[15] But the theology of Christian perfection has many aspects which bear directly and immediately on the practical. It does not suffice to know the principles of the supernatural life and the theoretical laws of its growth and development; it is necessary also to examine in what manner this evolution and growth is developed in practice and the paths by which souls actually travel in their journey to perfection. And while it is true that God acts in a variety of ways upon souls and that in this sense each soul may be said to follow a path that is proper to itself, there can be found in the midst of this variety certain common characteristics which enable the theologian to point out the basic steps along which the soul is wont to journey toward perfection.

For this part of the theology of Christian perfection, the descriptive and experimental data are absolutely indispensable. The theologian should study them attentively and contrast them with theological principles in order to formulate the theoretico-practical laws which the spiritual director can apply to each soul according to the dictates of prudence. And this applies not only to certain stages in the struggle for perfection but to the entire journey, although the theology of Christian perfection aims especially at the great heights of perfection which souls ought to attain. So important is this aspect that, since *res denominatur a potiori,* our science derives its title from the ultimate goal, which is Christian perfection.

Necessity of this science

Having seen the definition of the theology of Christian perfection, it should be immediately evident that this study is of extraordinary importance. Nothing is so important or excellent for man as that which will teach him the path and the means to intimate union with God, his first beginning and last end. It is true that only one thing is necessary, namely, the salvation of one's soul, but only in heaven will we be able to appreciate the great difference between

[15]Cf. St. Thomas, *Summa,* I, q. 1, a. 4.

salvation attained in its lowest grade and the highest and fullest measure which is the salvation of the saints. These latter will enjoy a much higher degree of glory and will glorify God in a much higher measure for all eternity. Hence there can be no object more noble or more deserving of study than that which constitutes the essence of the theology of Christian perfection.

The necessity of this study is manifest, especially for the priest as director and guide of souls. Without a profound knowledge of the speculative laws of the Christian life and of the practical norms of spiritual direction, he will travel blindly in the sublime mission of leading souls to the summit of perfection. Thereby he will contract a grave responsibility before God if he should frustrate the possible making of a saint. For that reason the Church has legislated for the establishment of chairs of ascetico-mystical theology in all the higher institutions of learning for the diocesan and regular clergy.[16]

But even for the faithful the study of this branch of theology is most useful. Observe the importance which the Church has always placed on spiritual reading. Few things so stimulate and arouse the desire for perfection as contact with those books which can open new horizons and explain methodically and clearly the road to intimate union with God. The knowledge of these ways facilitates and complements spiritual direction and can assist in supplying for it in those cases, not infrequent, when souls lack a director. Bearing in mind the needs of such souls, we shall in the course of this book frequently descend to practical counsels and details which would not be necessary in a book directed exclusively to priests and spiritual directors.

In approaching the study of spiritual theology one should above all possess a great spirit of faith and piety. The relationship between theory and practice is so intimate in the study of these matters that he who does not possess a vital faith and intense piety will not be able to judge correctly concerning the speculative principles of this science. Speaking of theology in general, St. Thomas says: "In the other sciences it is sufficient that a man be perfect intellectually, but in this science it is necessary that he also be perfect affectively, for we are to speak of great mysteries and explain wisdom to the perfect. But each one is wont to judge things according to his dispositions; thus he who is dominated by anger judges in a very different manner during his seizure of anger than when he is calm. Therefore, the Philosopher says that each one seeks his own end in those things to which he is particularly inclined."[17]

It is also necessary to take into account the intimate relations of this part of theology with dogmatic, moral and pastoral theology. There are certain fundamental points of doctrine which we shall simply recall but whose perfect knowledge demands a deep study of those branches of theology where they

[16] Cf. *A.A.S.*, XXIII (1931), p. 271.
[17] *In Epist. ad Hebr.*, cap. 5, lect. 2.

are treated in their proper place. In no other science as in theology does that famous axiom of Hippocrates have such significance: "The doctor who knows nothing more than medicine does not even know medicine." One must know well all theology and the auxiliary sciences in order to direct souls, and among these auxiliary sciences rational and empirical psychology and the somatic and psychic pathology of the nervous system and mental illness hold a prominent place.

METHOD OF STUDY

Since the theology of Christian perfection is a part of the one theology and is intimately related to dogmatic and moral theology (from which it derives its fundamental principles) and since it contains much that is practical and experimental (for it outlines for us the concrete norms for leading souls to the height of perfection), the method to be employed in its study must be at once strictly theological—positive and deductive—and experimental and inductive, substantiated by experience and the observation of facts. The exclusive use of one of the two methods leads to grave inconveniences.

The descriptive and inductive method, if used exclusively, leads to the following defects: 1) It ignores the fact that spiritual theology is a branch of the one science of theology and converts it into a part of experimental psychology. 2) It cannot constitute a true science, for although it does offer certain material on which a science could be constructed, as long as it does not investigate the causes of the phenomena studied and the laws which govern such phenomena there can be no science properly speaking. To assign causes and laws it is indispensable to resort to the principles from which the deductive method takes its start. Without this, the director would have to move in the narrow and confusing field of casuistry and be liable to many perplexities and errors. 3) There is a great risk of placing too much importance on phenomena which, however spectacular, are secondary and accidental in the Christian life. This would be prejudicial to that which is basic and fundamental, such as sanctifying grace, the virtues and gifts. In fact, one of the staunchest defenders of the descriptive and inductive method, while admitting theoretically the truth of the doctrine on the gifts of the Holy Ghost, has gone so far as to say that this doctrine is "little less than sterile for spiritual directors."[18] On the other hand, many modern theologians maintain that only the doctrine on the gifts of the Holy Ghost can solve the principal problem of spiritual theology, namely, of determining what pertains to the order of sanctifying grace and enters into its normal development, and what pertains to the *gratiae gratis datae,* which are properly extraordinary and beyond the ordinary exigencies of grace.[19]

---

[18]A. Poulain, S.J., *The Graces of Prayer* (St. Louis: 1928), Chap. 6, n. 19.

[19]Reginald Garrigou-Lagrange, O.P., *Christian Perfection and Contemplation,* p. 10.

The exclusive use of the analytic or deductive method offers the following difficulties: 1) It tends to overlook the fact that the great principles of the theology of Christian perfection should be orientated to the direction of souls and should therefore be contrasted or correlated with the facts of experience. It would be a grievous mistake to be content with the theological principles of St. Thomas without paying any attention to the admirable descriptions of mystical experience given by such eminent authorities as St. John of the Cross, St. Teresa of Avila, St. Catherine of Siena and others. 2) There is the danger of admitting as incontestable, truths taken *a priori* which do not actually agree with experience and are not confirmed by facts, thus establishing a lamentable dichotomy between theory and practice, which would have dire results in the direction of souls.

It is therefore necessary to make use of both the inductive and deductive method, or the analytic-synthetic method, which is both rational and experimental. One must study above all the revealed doctrine as found in Scripture, tradition and the magisterium of the Church. Then one must determine, by a deductive method, the nature of the Christian life, its supernatural organism, its growth, the laws which govern it, the essence of Christian perfection, what pertains to the normal development of sanctifying grace by an intrinsic necessity and what is extraordinary, etc. At the same time, it is necessary to observe the facts of experience, collect the data from mystics themselves who have lived these truths, examine the tests, trials, struggles, difficulties, methods used for attaining sanctity, results obtained, etc. With all this in mind, one will be careful to distinguish the essential from the accidental, the ordinary from the extraordinary, that which is absolutely indispensable for the sanctification of a soul and that which is variable and adaptable to different temperaments, circumstances, states of life, etc. Only in this way can one give norms and rules of direction which are precise and exact, not following certain *a priori* principles or certain variable casuistic norms, but concluding from solid theological principles and the actual experience of mystics and the direction of souls. Such is, in our opinion, the only legitimate method to be employed in the study of this branch of theology, and to this end we shall endeavor to develop this book.

SOURCES OF THIS SCIENCE

Having shown the method to be followed, we are led logically to discuss the various sources for the study of the theology of Christian perfection. They can be reduced to two general classes: theological and experimental.

The inspired books offer the fundamental principles upon which the theology of Christian perfection should be established. There one finds the speculative doctrine on God and man which is the foundation of all the spiritual life. Scripture speaks to us of the nature and attributes of God, his intimate life, the processions of the divine Persons, the Incarnation, the Redemption, incorporation with Christ, sanctifying grace, the infused virtues, the gifts of the Holy Ghost, actual inspirations, the sacraments, the *gratiae gratis datae,* etc. It also speaks to us of the final end or goal of the Christian life, which is the beatific vision in glory. At the same time, it instructs us concerning the precepts which pertain to the substance of Christian perfection and the counsels which enable one to reach perfection more readily. Moreover, we find in Scripture the sublime examples of the patriarchs and prophets of the Old Testament and those of Christ, Mary and the disciples in the New Testament. And if anything were to be lacking in our rich arsenal as regards the formulas of prayer, there is given to us the rich source of the psalms, hymns, doxologies and the *Pater Noster* as a nourishment for our interior life. There can be no doubt that Sacred Scripture is the principal source for the theology of Christian perfection, as it is for all the branches of theology.

THEOLOGICAL SOURCES

Sacred Scripture

Tradition and the magisterium

Another primary source for the theology of Christian perfection, which completes and supplements Sacred Scripture, is tradition and the magisterium of the Church. It is known that the testimony is authentically preserved and promulgated by the teaching of the Church, either in its solemn magisterium (dogmatic definitions, the symbols and confessions of faith) or in its ordinary magisterium which is exercised principally by the teaching and preaching of the pastors of the Church throughout the entire world and by the practice of the Church in her liturgy, the writings of the Fathers, the unanimous consent of theologians, the Roman Congregations under the vigilance of the Supreme Pontiff, and the unanimous consent and sense of the faithful.

Reason and faith

Although the fundamental principles of the theology of Christian perfection have been revealed by God and accepted by faith, human reason is not a stranger to sacred science but is an absolutely indispensable auxiliary, since it is necessary to deduce the conclusions which are virtually contained in the revealed principles. This cannot be done without the exercise of reason under the light of faith. Moreover, it is necessary to confirm the revealed truths by showing that there is nothing in them that is contrary to the demands of reason. In each theological problem one must state the question, make the truths of faith more intelligible by means of analogies and comparisons, reject the arguments of the incredulous by means of arguments of reason, etc. The theologian cannot prescind in any way from the light of reason, although his fundamental argument must always be taken from the authentic sources of divine revelation.

In addition to these three primary sources, common to all theology, the theologian who attempts to construct a theology of Christian perfection must also take account of other sources which are more proper to this part of theology which treats of perfection.

Writings of the saints

Apart from the descriptive value of these works, they also have a special value conferred on them by the fact that the Church has canonized the authors and sometimes has declared them doctors of the Church. Hence the spiritual writings of certain saints have an incalculable value for the theology of Christian perfection: St. Augustine, St. Bernard, St. Thomas Aquinas, St. Bonaventure, St. John of the Cross, St. Francis de Sales, St. Alphonsus Liguori, etc. Next to these doctors, one must place the writings of the great experts in the life of prayer, such as St. Gertrude, St. Brigid, St. Catherine of Siena, and above all, St. Teresa of Avila, of whom the Church prays liturgically that "we may be nourished with the celestial pabulum of her doctrine."[20] Nor can the theologian limit himself to the study of those mystics who have been raised to the altars of the Church. There is a veritable treasury of spiritual teaching in the works of pseudo-Dionysius, Cassian, Hugh and Richard of St. Victor, Eckhart, Tauler, Blessed Henry Suso, Ruysbroeck, Gerson, Dionysius the Carthusian, Thomas à Kempis, Walter Hilton, Blosius, Louis of Granada, Francis of Osuna, Bernardine of Laredo, John of the Angels, Chardon, Louis of León, Alvarez de Paz, Alphonsus Rodríguez, Surin, Scaramelli, Olier, Berulle, Faber, Weiss, Marmion, Arintero, etc.

Hagiography

The lives of the saints also offer valuable descriptive material for the study of the Christian life and place before our eyes models for imitation. Among these works the autobiographies are of special value or those biographies written by a saint on the life of another saint (e.g., the autobiographies of St. Teresa of Avila and St. Thérèse of Lisieux, or the life of St. Francis of Assisi by St. Bonaventure).[21]

---

[20]However, such writings should be genuine and critically certain. As a rule it is safer to read the works that are instructive rather than personal letters or ardent exhortations, where exaggeration may easily creep in. Those works which have won the special approbation of the Church (St. John of the Cross, St. Teresa of Avila, St. Thérèse of Lisieux, etc.) and those which have been universally used by the faithful through the centuries (*Imitation of Christ*) are always safer than those which have a merely negative approbation or appeal to only a few. The words of St. Bonaventure are worth noting in this regard: "Si quaeras quomodo haec fiant, interroga gratiam, non doctrinam; desiderium, non intellectum; gemitum orationis, non studium lectionis; sponsum, non magistrum; Deum, non hominem; caliginem, non claritatem; non lucem, sed ignem totaliter inflammantem" (*Itinerarium mentis ad Deum,* cap. 7, n. 6).

[21]The spiritual theologian must read the lives of the saints with a critical judgment. The ancient lives of the saints and even some of the second lessons of the Breviary are not as historically exact as would appear at first glance.

History of spirituality

This is another important source of information for the theology of Christian perfection. Although Christian spirituality, like the grace on which it is founded, is basically the same in all ages and countries, it is helpful to see the application of the principles of spirituality throughout the centuries and to study the tendencies and schools of spirituality in order to avoid errors and illusions and to stress those means which experience has demonstrated to be more efficacious for the sanctification of souls. It also enables the theologian to discover the common basis of spirituality in all the various schools and to distinguish what is nothing more than the particular tendency of a given school. History is the teacher of life, and perhaps in no other branch of history can we be better instructed.

Psychology of religion

This source is subsidiary and of much less importance than the others, since the principles of Christianity differ radically from all other religions. Nevertheless, it is helpful to contrast the phenomena of the Christian religion with those of pagan religions which answer a basic need in man's psychological structure. Thus one can study with interest and profit the states of consolation and desolation, the ascetical and purgative practices, etc.[22]

EXPERIMENTAL SOURCES

These sources comprise, not only those which come from one's own experience and the experience of others, but the material offered by the physio-psychological sciences, which is necessary for the correct evaluation and interpretation of many of the phenomena which occur in the spiritual life, especially in the mystical state.

Psychology

The first teaches us the functioning of the internal and external faculties, the formulation of ideas, the laws of the affective and emotional life, the nature of the human soul as the substantial form of the body, the interrelation between body and soul, etc. Experimental psychology complements the principles of rational psychology by means of the data of experience and experiment and an analysis of the phenomena of normal and abnormal or pathological subjects. The study of morbid states, whether physical or psychic, is of capital importance for distinguishing between the supernatural, the preternatural or diabolical, and the natural and pathological. It is evident today that many of the phenomena which were formerly attributed too readily to supernatural or diabolical influence must now be attributed to pathological states. Hence this source is of great importance for determining the causes of visions, locutions, aridity, consolations, etc.

Personal experience

No other source of information can replace entirely one's own experience if he is to judge correctly the ways of God. This is evident from the unsuccessful attempts of many rationalists to judge the cases of mystics and saints. Not

[22]Cf. J. Maréchal, S.J., "Essai sur l'étude comparée des mysticismes," in *Revue des Quest. Scientifiques*, 1926, and *Etudes sur la psychologie des mystiques* (Paris: 1937), Vol. II, pp. 411-83.

being Christians themselves, they lack the light of faith and therefore find it impossible to comprehend the supernatural, which is the foundation of the Christian life. Nor does it suffice to possess grace in its lowest or minimum degree if one wishes to judge the mystics and the ways of union with God. Certain things can be understood only by those who have a spiritual affinity for those things. Hence the principle repeated so often by St. Thomas Aquinas: "Each one is wont to judge according to his own dispositions."[23] In the same sense Báñez wrote: "In identical circumstances he will be more learned in theology who possesses charity than he who does not possess it, because without charity one does not possess the gifts of the Holy Ghost united to faith, which illumines the mind and gives understanding to the little ones."[24]

Experience with souls

To one's experience we must add the association with, and direction of souls. He who wishes to know the ways of God cannot be content with a theoretical study of the mystical life nor even with his own personal experience, though he be a saint of the first rank. Not all souls ascend to the height of perfection by the same path or with the same ascetico-mystical practices. It is not enough, therefore, to know one particular path; one must be conversant with the greatest possible number. And although this knowledge will necessarily be incomplete—for it is not possible to know the ways of all the souls that attain perfection—nevertheless, by a constant observation of the various ways by which God leads souls, the theologian will learn two important facts: 1) not to hold for particular ways or methods as the only proven or possible ways of perfect union with God, and 2) to respect the initiative and movement of God, who leads each soul by a special way to the summit of perfection.

DIVISION

There is no more uniformity in the division of the theology of Christian perfection than there is in its terminology. But the confusion is understandable when one considers that the subject matter is so ineffable and there are so many questions that overlap. It is generally more difficult to establish the proper order of a practico-speculative science.

While we readily admit that the ascetical and the mystical phases are two distinct aspects of the spiritual life, as are the active and the passive phases, we deplore the division of spiritual theology into these two parts. In practice the life of the Christian striving for perfection usually oscillates between the ascetical and active phase and the mystical and passive phase; therefore, it seems to be more in keeping with the facts of reality not to make a division of the theology of Christian perfection along those lines.

Moreover, there is the danger of falling into the error of postulating two different perfections: the one ascetical and the other mystical. Therefore, in

[23]Cf. *In Epist. ad Heb.*, cap. 5, lect. 2.

[24]*In Iam,* lect. 4, ad 2am confirmationem, arg. 2.

the desire to preserve and safeguard the unity of theology as well as the unity of the way to Christian perfection, we choose rather to present first the doctrinal principles upon which the theology of Christian perfection rests (PART I), then to consider Christian perfection itself (PART II), the negative aspect of growth in Christian perfection (the struggle against sin, the world, the flesh and the devil: PART III), the principal positive means of supernatural growth (PART IV), including the life of prayer (PART V), and certain secondary means, both internal and external (PART VI); we shall conclude our work with a discussion of mystical phenomena (PART VII).

DOCTRINAL PRINCIPLES

I

1: THE END OF THE CHRISTIAN LIFE

The consideration of purpose is the first thing required in the study of any dynamic work. And since the Christian life is essentially dynamic and perfectible—at least during our present state of wayfarers upon earth—it is necessary that we should know where we are going and what is the end we hope to attain. For that reason St. Thomas begins the moral part of his *Summa theologiae*—man's return to God—with a consideration of the ultimate end.

Two ends can be proposed for the Christian life or, if one prefers, one end with two distinct modalities: the absolute or ultimate end and the relative or proximate end. We shall examine each separately.

THE GLORY OF GOD

The classical definition of glory is: *clara notitia cum laude*. This definition expresses something extrinsic to the one who is the subject affected by glory; yet in a less strict sense we can distinguish a double glory in God: the intrinsic glory which springs from his intimate divine life, and the extrinsic glory which proceeds from creatures.

Intrinsic glory

The intrinsic glory of God is that which he procures for himself in the bosom of the Trinity. The Father, by way of an intellectual generation, conceives a most perfect idea of himself: his divine Son or his Word, in whom is reflected his life, his beauty, his immensity, his eternity and all his infinite perfections. As a result of their mutual contemplation, there is established between these two divine Persons—by way of procession—a current of indescribable love, an impetuous torrent of fire, which is the Holy Ghost. This knowledge and love of himself, this eternal and incessant praise which God showers upon himself in the incomprehensible mystery of his interior life, constitutes his *intrinsic glory,* which is rigorously infinite and exhaustive and to which no created being nor the entire universe can contribute absolutely anything. It is the mystery of the inner life of God in which he finds an intrinsic glory that is absolutely infinite.

God's external glory

God is infinitely happy in himself and has no need whatever of creatures. But God is love,[1] and love is communicative. God is the infinite good, and goodness tends to diffuse itself. As the philosophers say: *Bonum est diffusivum sui.* Here is the reason for creation. God desired to communicate his infinite perfections to creatures, thereby intending his own *extrinsic glory*. The glorification of God by creatures is therefore the ultimate reason and supreme finality of creation.[2]

The explanation of this could not be more clear, even to the light of reason deprived of the light of faith. It is a philosophical fact that every agent acts for an end, especially an intellectual agent. Therefore, God, the first and most intelligent of all agents, must always act for some end. But the attributes of God and all his operations are not distinct from his divine essence, they are identified with it. Therefore, if God had intended in the creation of the universe some end distinct from himself, he would have had to refer and subordinate his creative action to that end—for every agent puts its operation at the service of the end which is intended—and hence God himself would have subordinated himself to that end, since his operation is himself. Consequently, that end would have been above God; that is, God would not be God. It is therefore absolutely impossible that God intended by his operations any end distinct from himself. God has created all things for his own glory; and creatures cannot exist but in him and for him.[3]

---

[1]Cf. Jn. 4:16.

[2]St. Thomas beautifully expresses how God, by his intrinsic and extrinsic glory, unites in himself the most perfect plenitude of all possible happiness: "Whatever is desirable in whatsoever beatitude, whether true or false, pre-exists wholly and in a more eminent degree in the divine beatitude. As to contemplative happiness, God possesses a continual and most certain contemplation of himself and of all things; and as to that which is active, he has the governance of the whole universe. As to earthly happiness, which consists in delight, riches, power, dignity and fame . . . he possesses joy in himself and all things else for his delight; instead of riches, he has that complete self-sufficiency which is promised by riches; in place of power, he has omnipotence; for dignities, the government of all things; and in place of fame, he possesses the admiration of all creatures" (*Summa,* I, q. 26, a. 4).

[3]Cf. St. Thomas, *Summa,* I, q. 44, a. 4. In order to understand the finality of creation, it should be noted that God works for an end not only *ex parte operis* but also *ex parte operantis*; not, however, as creatures do, for the desire of some end or goal which they do not yet possess, but simply for the love of the end which he already possesses actually in himself, which is nothing other than his goodness identified with his own essence. For that reason, St. Thomas says (*De potentia,* q. 3, a. 15, ad 14) that the communication of goodness is not the ultimate end, but the divine goodness itself, for love of which God desires to communicate it; for God does not work for his goodness as desirous of that which he does not possess,

This does not presuppose a transcendental egoism in God, as some impious philosophers have dared to say; this is the apex of generosity and disinterest. God did not seek his own utility in creation, for he could add nothing at all to his own personal happiness and perfection; but he sought only to communicate his goodness. God knew how to organize things in such a way that creatures would find their own happiness by glorifying God. For that reason St. Thomas says that God alone is infinitely liberal and generous. He does not work because of any need, as if seeking something that he lacks, but only out of goodness, to communicate to creatures his own overflowing happiness.[4]

Sacred Scripture is filled with expressions in which God demands and exacts his own glory: "I am the Lord, this is my name; my glory I give to no other nor my praise to idols" (Is. 42:8). "For my own sake, for my own sake, I do this; why should I suffer profanation? My glory I will not give to another" (Is. 48:11). "Listen to me, Jacob, Israel whom I named! I, it is I who am the first, and also the last am I" (Is. 48:12). "'I am Alpha and Omega, the beginning and the end,' says the Lord God, 'who is and who was and who is coming, the Almighty'" (Apoc. 1:8).

ULTIMATE END OF THE CHRISTIAN LIFE

Thus the glory of God is the end and purpose of all creation. Even the incarnation of the Word and the redemption of the human race have no other finality than the glory of God: "And when all things are made subject to him, then the Son himself will also be subject to him who subjected all things to him, that God may be all in all" (I Cor. 15:28). For that reason, St. Paul exhorts us not to take a single step which will not lead to the glory of God: "Therefore, whether you eat or drink, or do anything else, do all for the glory of God" (I Cor. 10:31). For we have been predestined in Christ in order to become a perpetual praise of glory for the Blessed Trinity: "As he chose us in him before the foundation of the world, that we should be holy and without blemish in his sight in love. He predestined us to be adopted through Jesus Christ as his sons, according to the purpose of his will, unto the praise of the glory of his grace, with which he has favored us in his beloved Son . . . for the praise of his glory" (Eph. 1:4-6, 14). Everything must be subordinated to this finality. Even the soul's salvation and sanctification must be sought for the greater glory of God. Our own sanctification and salvation cannot become our absolute ultimate end; even they must be

---

but as desirous of communicating that which he already possesses. He does not operate for the *desire* of the end, but for *love* of the end. "The entire universe with all its parts," says St. Thomas, "is ordained to God as to its ultimate end, in the sense that in all its parts it reflects the divine goodness by a certain limitation and for the glory of God" (*Summa,* I, q. 65, a. 2). Cf. also Ramírez, *op. cit.,* I, nn. 932-38.

[4]Cf. *Summa,* I, q. 44, a. 4; q. 19, a. 2, ad 3.

sought only because our happiness consists in the eternal praise of glory of the Blessed Trinity.[5]

Such is the ultimate and absolute end of the entire Christian life. In practice, the soul that aspires to sanctify itself must place as the goal of all its striving the glory of God. Nothing whatever should be preferred to this, not even the desire of one's own salvation or sanctification, which must be considered in a secondary place as the most efficacious means of giving glory to God. One must seek to resemble St. Alphonsus Liguori in this, of whom it was said that he had in his head nothing else but the glory of God, and one must take as a theme or motto the standard of the Society of Jesus as enunciated by St. Ignatius Loyola: *"Ad majorem gloriam Dei."* All the saints adopted this attitude, following the teaching of St. Paul, who gave this axiom to the Corinthians: "Do all for the glory of God" (I Cor. 10:31).

Hence the sanctification of one's own soul is not the ultimate end of the Christian life. Beyond this is the glory of the Blessed Trinity, which is the absolute end of all that exists. And although this truth is so fundamental for those who comprehend the divine transcendence, it nevertheless does not appear to dominate the lives of the saints until rather late, when the soul is transformed through love in the unity of God, when in the transforming union the soul is fully identified with God. Only Christ and Mary, from the first moment of their existence, realized this glorification of God which is the terminus of all sanctity on this earth. Nothing should so preoccupy the soul which aspires to sanctity as the constant forgetfulness of self and the intention to do all for the greater glory of God. At the summit of the mount of perfection, St. John of the Cross has printed the words: "Here on this mount dwell only the honor and glory of God."

SANCTIFICATION

After the glory of God, and perfectly subordinated to it, the Christian life has for its end or goal the sanctification of one's own soul. This is tantamount to saying that all Christians are called to sanctity or the perfection of the Christian life, at least by a remote and sufficient call, although in various degrees, according to the measure of their predestination in Christ.[6] The testimony of Sacred Scripture is clear and unmistakable on this point: "You,

[5]For a more ample explanation of this doctrine, see M. M. Philipon, O.P., *The Spiritual Doctrine of Sister Elizabeth of the Trinity* (Westminster, Md.: 1955).

[6]Cf. I Cor. 10:31.

therefore, are to be perfect, even as your heavenly Father is perfect" (Matt. 5:48); "called to be saints" (Rom. 1:7, 8:28; I Cor. 1:2); "for this is the will of God, your sanctification" (I Thess. 4:3).

But when we speak of man's sanctification or perfection, we must necessarily make a distinction, because of the double state or condition of man. Since man's sanctification and perfection are a participation in the divine sanctity and perfection, they will be measured by the degree of man's union with God. But man's union with God will be realized perfectly only in glory when, through the beatific vision, he possesses and enjoys forever the goodness, truth and beauty of the triune God. As a wayfarer here on earth, because of the soul's obediential potency to an ever increasing influx of grace and charity, a man can grow in perfection indefinitely. Death alone will put a definitive limit to any further growth in grace and charity.

Man's ultimate beatitude, says St. Thomas, is his supreme perfection.[7] But when we apply the term "perfection" to a soul in glory and to a wayfarer, the term is an analogous one, and therefore the analogates are essentially diverse. Nevertheless, if we know what constitutes man's union with God in glory, we can deduce what constitutes that union with God in the state that precedes glory, for the selfsame entity whereby man merits glory is the principle of his spiritual life here on earth.

Perfection in glory

The Angelic Doctor tells us that beatitude or perfection in glory requires two conditions: the total perfection of the one who is beatified and a knowledge of the good possessed.[8] These conditions are actually verified in the happiness of the blessed because, as Pope Benedict XII declares: "The souls of the just see the divine essence by an intuitive, face-to-face vision, with no creature as a medium of vision, but with the divine essence immediately manifesting itself to them, clearly and openly."[9] And the Council of Florence stated: "Souls immediately upon entrance into heaven see clearly the one and triune God as he is, one more perfectly than another, depending on their merits."[10]

But since the divine essence takes the place of the intelligible species for the intellect of the blessed, the intellect needs something over and above its own natural powers in order to enjoy the beatific vision. This is actually the light of glory (*lumen gloriae*), the need for which is upheld by the Council of Vienne, which condemned the opposite opinion.[11] The nature of the *lumen gloriae* is not defined, but according to Thomistic teaching it is a created quality divinely infused into the intellect whereby it is intrinsically

[7]Cf. *Summa,* I-II, q. 3, a. 2 and ad 4.
[8]Cf. *ibid.,* I, q. 26, a. 1.
[9]Constitution *Benedictus Deus;* Denz. 530.
[10]Decree for the Greeks; Denz. 693.
[11]Cf. Denz. 475.

perfected and elevated.[12] As infused charity vitalizes and supernaturalizes the will, so the *lumen gloriae* supernaturalizes and elevates the intellect, and both somehow arise from sanctifying grace, which is infused into the essence of the soul.

Perfection of wayfarer

What, then, is the difference between the perfection of the wayfarer and the perfection of the blessed in glory? The union of the blessed with God in glory presupposes three distinct elements in the souls of those who enjoy the beatific vision: sanctifying grace, charity and the light of glory. Here the two conditions for beatitude are fulfilled: by means of the light of glory, the soul knows the good that it possesses; by reason of the plenitude of its charity, it is completely transformed by grace.[13] If, therefore, we wish to know the elements that are required for the perfection of the wayfarer, we need only ask which of the above-mentioned elements are common to both the just soul on earth and the blessed in heaven.

What remains for the perfection and sanctification of man as a wayfarer? Not the light of glory, but the other two elements: sanctifying grace and charity. Indeed, the soul is called just and perfect precisely because it participates to some degree in the very life of God through sanctifying grace and is able to be united with God in the bond of supernatural charity. In glory there is the clear and unobstructed facial vision of God, but here on earth the soul has only the dim (but supernatural) knowledge of faith and the certain (but not infallible) confidence of hope. And since sanctifying grace, as we shall see, is the principle from which all our supernatural actions proceed, it is evident that sanctifying grace is, as St. Thomas states, the beginning of glory in us.[14] And, finally, since St. Paul tells us that faith and hope will pass away but charity will not pass away,[15] we can see that the elements which effect our union with God here on earth are nothing other than those two realities which will last forever: grace and charity.

The plan

Since the theology of Christian perfection is concerned with the sanctification of man as a wayfarer and studies the supernatural organism of the spiritual life in order to discover the laws of growth in perfection, we shall now consider the supernatural organism and its faculties or powers and then proceed to investigate the nature of Christian perfection and the mystical state.

[12]Cf. St. Thomas, *Summa,* I, q. 12, aa. 5-7; I-II, q. 5 a. 6, ad 2.
[13]Cf. St. Thomas, *ibid.,* II-II, q. 24, a. 8; *Suppl.,* q. 93, a. 3.
[14]Cf. *ibid.,* II-II, q. 24, a. 3, ad 2.
[15]Cf. I Cor. 13:10-13.

2: SANCTIFYING GRACE

Man is a mysterious being, composed of body and soul, of matter and spirit, intimately united to form one nature and one person. It has been said of him that he is a little universe or microcosm,[1] a synthesis of all creation. He has existence, as do inanimate things; he is nourished, reproduces and grows, as do plants; he knows sensible objects and is moved toward them by the sense appetite or passions and has locomotion, as do animals; and like the angels, but in a much lower degree, he can know the immaterial under the aspect of truth and his will can be drawn to the rational good. The mechanism and function of all these vital powers, in the triple order of vegetative, sensitive and rational, constitute the natural life of man. These three manifestations of his natural life are not superimposed one on the other by a kind of juxtaposition, but they compenetrate each other, are co-ordinated and mutually complement one another, to lead to the one end or goal of the natural perfection of the whole man.

There is nothing in man's nature which postulates or exacts, either proximately or remotely, the supernatural order. The elevation to this order is a totally gratuitous favor of God which infinitely transcends all the exigencies of nature.[2] Nevertheless, there is a close analogy between the natural and the supernatural orders, for grace does not destroy nature but perfects and elevates it. The supernatural order constitutes a true life for man and has an organism which is similar to the natural vital organism. As in the natural order we can distinguish four basic or fundamental elements in human life—the living subject, the formal principle of life, the faculties or powers, and the operations of those faculties—so also we find similar elements in man's supernatural organism. The subject is the soul, the formal principle of supernatural life is sanctifying grace, the faculties are the infused virtues and the gifts of the Holy Ghost, and the operations are the acts of those virtues and gifts. We have here in outline or summary the elements which we shall consider in the succeeding chapters.

---

[1] St. Gregory, *Hom. 29 super Evang.* (M.L. 76: 1214).

[2] Cf. Denz. 1001-07, 1009, 1021, 1023, 1079, 1671.

FORMAL PRINCIPLE OF THE SUPERNATURAL LIFE

The human soul is a spiritual substance which is independent of matter in its being and its operations, although while it is in the body it makes use of bodily powers for the exercise of certain functions. But the soul is not a complete substance, nor can the soul alone properly be called a person. The ego or the person is not the body alone nor the soul alone, but the composite which results from the substantial union of the two.

We know from reason and from sound philosophy[3] and also from the teaching of the Church[4] that the soul is the substantial form of the body. By reason of this substantial informing of the body by the soul, man has the being of man, of animal, of living, of body, of substance, and the very fact of existence. Consequently, the soul gives to man his essential grade of perfection and communicates to the body the same act of being by which the soul itself exists.[5] But the soul is not immediately operative.[6] As a substance, it is given to us in the order of being, but not in the order of action or operation. Like every created substance, it needs faculties or powers for operation, and in the case of the human soul these powers are the intellect and the will, which emanate from the essence of the soul, although they are really distinct from the soul and from each other.[7]

Such is the subject in which our supernatural life resides. Grace, which is the formal principle of that supernatural life, is rooted in the very essence of the soul in a static manner. The virtues and gifts, which are the dynamic elements in the supernatural organism, reside in the human faculties or powers precisely to elevate them to the supernatural order.

We have said that sanctifying grace is the formal principle of our supernatural organism, as the spiritual soul is the formal principle of our natural vital organism. As an accidental participation in the very nature of God, grace elevates us to the status of children of God and heirs of heaven. "We are sons of God," exclaims St. Paul. "But if we are sons, we are heirs also: heirs indeed of God and joint heirs with Christ" (Rom. 8:16-17). And in his famous sermon before the Areopagus he insists that we are of the race of God: "We are the offspring of God" (Acts 17:29). This same expression is

[3]Cf. St. Thomas, *Summa,* I, q. 76, a. 1.

[4]Council of Vienne; Denz. 481.

[5]This is thesis 16 of the 24 theses proposed by the Sacred Congregation of Studies as norms of sound doctrine. Cf. *A.A.S.*, VI (1914), pp. 383 ff.

[6]Cf. St. Thomas, *Summa,* I, q. 77, a. 1.

[7]Cf. *ibid.,* aa. 1-3, 6.

re-echoed by St. Thomas when he comments on the words of St. John, *ex Deo nati sunt*: "This generation, since it is of God, makes us sons of God."[8]

NATURE OF GRACE

Sanctifying grace can be defined: a supernatural quality, inhering in the soul, which gives us a physical and formal participation, although analogous and accidental, in the very nature of God precisely as God. Let us examine more closely the elements of this definition.

Quality

A quality is an accident which modifies or disposes a substance. Four species of quality are usually distinguished: if a substance is disposed well or badly in regard to itself, we have the qualities of *habit* and *disposition*; if the substance is disposed for action or operation, we have the qualities of *potency* and *impotency*; if the substance is disposed to receptivity, we have the qualities of *passion* and *passible quality*; and if the substance is disposed to quantity, we have the qualities of *form* and *figure*.

It should be evident at once that sanctifying grace cannot pertain to any of the last three species of quality, for grace is not ordained directly to operation, as are potency and impotency, nor is it a bodily accident, as are passion, passible quality, form and figure. By elimination, therefore, sanctifying grace must pertain to the first species of quality, and within that species it pertains to habit and not to simple disposition, since it is a quality that of itself is permanent and difficult to remove.

Supernatural

Grace is clearly supernatural, as the formal principle of our supernatural life; it is that which elevates us and constitutes us in this order. As supernatural, it far excels all natural things, transcending all nature and making us enter into the sphere of the divine and uncreated. St. Thomas has said that the minimum degree of sanctifying grace in one individual is greater than the natural good of the entire universe.[9]

Inhering in the soul

That grace inheres in the soul is denied by those Protestants who hold for extrinsic justification, but it is a truth of faith defined by the Council of Trent.[10] St. Thomas bases the distinction between human love and divine love on the theological principle: "The love of God infuses and creates goodness in things."[11] In us, love is born of the good object, real or apparent; but God creates goodness in an object by the mere fact of loving it. And since love finds complacence in that which is similar to itself, the grace by

---

[8]*Comment. in Evang. Joan.* 1:13.

[9]Cf. *Summa,* I-II, q. 113, a. 9, ad 2.

[10]Canon 11 on justification: "If anyone say that men are justified only by the imputation of the justice of Christ or simply by the remission of sins, thus excluding the grace and charity which are infused in hearts by the Holy Ghost and inhere in them, or that the grace by which we are justified is simply the favor or benevolence of God, let him be anathema." Cf. Denz. 821.

[11]Cf. St. Thomas, *Summa,* I, q. 20, a. 2.

which God loves us with the love of a friend elevates us in a certain manner to his level and deifies us, so to speak, by means of a formal participation in the divine nature. "It is necessary that God alone deify by communicating his divine nature through a certain participation of likeness."[12] Briefly, God loves with an absolutely supernatural love the man who is pleasing to him, but since the love of God is the cause of that which he loves, it follows that he must produce in the man who is pleasing to himself the reason for that supernatural goodness, namely, grace.[13]

Participation

Participation is nothing other than the assimilation and inadequate expression in an inferior thing of some perfection existing in a superior thing. St. Thomas says in this regard that that which is totally a determined thing does not participate in that thing but is identified with it; that which is not totally a thing, but has something of that thing, is properly said to participate in it.[14]

Participation may be *moral* or *physical*. Physical participation is divided into *virtual* and *formal*, and formal participation may be *univocal* or *analogous*. The following examples should clarify the meaning of this division. The members of a corporation or association participate *morally* in its good or evil reputation; the moon participates *physically* in the light of the sun; flowers and fruits are *virtually* contained in the tree that will produce them and even in the seed from which the tree grows; animality is participated *formally* by men and brutes. If the physical participation refers to subjects that participate in the same thing and in the same way, as humanity is predicated of all men in the same sense, we have *univocal* participation; but if the participation refers to subjects in a different manner or proportionally, as being is predicated of God, the angels, men, animals, plants and inanimate things, we have an *analogous* participation.

Bearing in mind the foregoing distinctions, we may say that sanctifying grace gives us a physical, formal, analogous and accidental participation in the divine nature. That it makes us participants in the divine nature is a truth constantly repeated in Sacred Scripture. St. Peter says, for example: "He has granted us the very great and precious promises, so that through them you may become partakers of the divine nature" (II Pet. 1:4). The liturgy also proclaims this fact when it sings in the Preface for the feast of the Ascension: "He ascended to heaven to make us participants in his divinity." And how persuasively St. Leo speaks of this truth when he says: "Recognize your dignity, O Christian, and having been made a participant of the divine nature, do not desire to return to the baseness of your former condition."[15]

---

[12]*Ibid.*, I-II, q. 112, a. 1.

[13]*Ibid.*, q. 110, a. 1; *De veritate*, q. 27, a. 1.

[14]Cf. *Metaphys.*, I, lect. 10.

[15]*Sermo* 21 (M.L., 54: 192).

But it is necessary to examine the manner in which sanctifying grace confers a participation in the divine nature. God is not like creatures, for he and he alone is being by his very essence, while all creatures are being by participation. Nevertheless, creatures are in some way similar to God, because as every agent produces something similar to itself, it is necessary that there be some likeness of the agent in the effect which it produces.[16] But it cannot be said that creatures are like God by reason of a communication of form according to genus and species, but only according to a certain analogy, because God is being by essence, while creatures are being by participation.[17] Hence there are three classes of creatures which imitate God analogically and are like him in some respect:

1) *Irrational creatures,* which participate in the divine perfection so far as they have being. This likeness is so remote that it is called a trace or vestige.[18]

2) *Rational creatures,* which, so far as they are gifted with intelligence, represent the perfections of God in a more express and determined manner. For that reason they are called the natural image of God.

3) *Souls in the state of grace,* which are united with God by the love of friendship and therefore imitate him in a much more perfect manner. For that reason they are called the supernatural image of God.

Physical and formal

But in order to be perfect, does the image of God as author of the supernatural order require a physical and formal participation in the very nature of God? Undoubtedly yes. Apart from the fact that this is a truth which is verified in revelation, there are theological arguments to support it. First, the operations proper to a superior nature cannot become connatural to a lower or inferior nature unless the latter participates in some way in the former, because as a thing is, so it acts, and its effects cannot be greater than the cause. But some of the operations proper to God—such as the beatific vision, beatific love, etc.—are in some way connatural to man through grace. Therefore, it is evident that man, through grace, in some way participates physically and formally in the very nature of God.

Secondly, from grace springs an inclination to God as he is in himself. Now every inclination is rooted in some nature and reveals the condition of that nature. But an inclination to the divine order cannot be rooted in a nature of an inferior order; it must be rooted in a nature which is divine, at least by participation. Moreover, this participation must be physical and formal, since the inclination proceeds physically and formally from that participation.

---

[16]Cf. St. Thomas, *Summa,* I, q. 4, a. 3.
[17]Cf. *ibid.,* ad 3.
[18]Cf. St. Thomas, *In I Sent.,* dist. 3, q. 2, aa. 1 f.

Thirdly, the infused virtues are the faculties of supernatural operations in us, but it is evident that, since operation follows being, a supernatural operation which proceeds from the soul presupposes in the soul the presence of a supernatural nature, and this can be nothing other than a physical and formal participation in the nature of God himself.

And let no one say that through the power of an actual grace a sinner can realize a supernatural act without the need of sanctifying grace in his soul. This objection does not invalidate our argument, since we are speaking of an act which proceeds from the soul connaturally and without violence, and not of a forceful impulse to second act without passing through the proximate habitual dispositions.

Analogous and accidental

It now remains for us to examine in what sense this physical and formal participation of the divine nature is accidental and analogous. *Analogous* participation signifies that the divine nature is not communicated to us univocally, as the Father transmits it to his Son by way of the natural eternal generation or as the humanity of Christ subsists in the divinity. Man does not become God through grace, neither by natural generation nor by the hypostatic or personal union nor by any pantheistic union of our substance with the divine substance, but by an analogous participation in virtue of which that which exists in God in an infinite manner is participated by the soul in a limited and finite manner. The iron cast into the furnace retains the nature of iron and merely takes on the properties of fire; the mirror which captures the image of the sun does not acquire the nature of the sun but merely reflects its splendor. In like manner, says St. Leo, "the original dignity of our race lies in the fact that the divine goodness shines in us as in a resplendent mirror."[19]

The reason for the *accidental* participation of the divine nature through grace is clearly explained by St. Thomas: "Every substance constitutes either the nature of the thing of which it is the substance or it is a part of the nature, as matter and form are called substance. And because grace is above all nature, it cannot be a substance or a substantial form, but it is an accidental form of the soul. Hence what is substantially in God becomes accidental in the soul which participates in the divine goodness."[20]

Moreover, the Council of Trent expressly teaches that habitual grace inheres in the soul of man.[21] But that which inheres in another is not a substance but an accident, as we learn in philosophy. Nor does this in any way lessen the dignity of grace, for as a supernatural accident, by its very essence it infinitely transcends all created or creatable natural substances. Let us not

[19]*Sermo* 12 (M.L. 54: 168).

[20]*Summa,* I-II, q. 110, a. 2, ad 2.

[21]Canon 11 on justification; Denz. 821.

forget the words of St. Thomas, to the effect that the good of grace in one individual surpasses the good of nature in the entire universe.[22]

In the nature of God precisely as God

Not all theologians admit that we share in the nature of God precisely as God, but it is the teaching of the best interpreters of the Thomistic school, such as Cajetan, Ledesma, del Prado. The principal arguments are as follows:

a) Grace is the connatural principle of the operations which reach God himself under the formal aspect of deity. Therefore, grace, as the principle of these operations, must necessarily participate in the divine nature precisely as divine, that is, under the formal aspect of deity.

The antecedent of this argument is undeniable; all supernatural love and knowledge have God himself as their object under the aspect of his deity. Such is the case with faith, charity, the beatific vision; they are fixed directly on God as he is in himself, whether it be through the veil of faith or in the clear light of the facial vision. The consequence is a necessary conclusion from the fact that grace is the root principle of the theological virtues.

b) The supernatural participation could not otherwise be distinguished from a merely natural participation. The natural participation in the divine nature is also a formal participation, because man, as an image of God, understands, loves, etc., and is intellectual by nature as is God. Therefore, the divine, formally as such, must be the differential note between the natural and the supernatural.

c) In order to transcend all nature and constitute the supernatural, the supernatural form which is grace must be either God himself or something which touches God under the formal aspect of his deity, for this alone transcends all nature. But grace is not God himself, as is evident, and hence it must necessarily be something which touches God precisely under the formality of his deity. In other words, it is a participation of the divine nature precisely as divine.

These arguments seem to us to be entirely conclusive. Of course, one should not think that through grace we participate in the divine nature in such a way that it is communicated to us in the same way that it is communicated to the second Person of the Blessed Trinity by the Father, or as the humanity of Christ subsists in the divinity through the hypostatic union with the Word. Nor is the participation through grace to be understood in a pantheistic sense, for we are referring to a participation that is accidental and analogous. St. Thomas says that "grace is nothing other than a certain participated likeness of the divine nature."[23] Taking the intimate nature of God as an exemplar, sanctifying grace is a perfect imitation which is effected in us by divine infusion. In virtue of this infusion, anterior to any operation of the intellect or will, there is conferred on the soul a physical and formal perfection which is real and supernatural and which is formally in God in an eminent degree. In this way there is produced in the soul a special likeness to God which infinitely transcends that which is had in the purely natural order as an

---

[22]Cf. *Summa,* I-II, q. 113, a. 9, ad 2.

[23]*Ibid.,* III, q. 62, a. 1.

image of the God of nature. By reason of this intimate likeness to the divine nature as divine, man becomes an offspring, as it were, of God. He becomes God's son by adoption and forms a part of the family of God. Such is the sublime grandeur to which we are elevated by grace.

THE SUBJECT OF GRACE

This question must be resolved in view of another question concerning the distinction between grace and charity. The theologians who deny the distinction between grace and charity state that grace resides in the will as in its proper subject.[24] Those who affirm the real distinction between grace and charity place charity in the will and sanctifying grace in the very essence of the soul.[25] The following arguments are offered in proof of the second opinion.

a) The regeneration of man is effected by sanctifying grace. But regeneration primarily affects the essence of the soul rather than the faculties, because the generative action terminates in the essence. Therefore, grace resides in the essence of the soul.[26]

b) Spiritual accidents which pertain to being inhere in the substance of the soul, while those which pertain to operation inhere in the faculties. But sanctifying grace confers on the soul a supernatural being, while charity is ordained to operation. Therefore, sanctifying grace should inhere in the very essence of the soul, and charity in one of the faculties, namely, the will.

c) "Every perfection of the faculties of the soul has the nature of a virtue."[27] But sanctifying grace does not have the nature of a virtue nor is it ordained by its nature to operation.[28] Therefore, sanctifying grace is not a perfection of the faculties of the soul but of the very essence of the soul. For this reason theologians speak of sanctifying grace as a static perfection and of the virtues as dynamic perfections in the spiritual life.

EFFECTS OF GRACE

Having examined the nature of sanctifying grace and the subject in which it inheres, it remains for us to discuss the effects of grace in the soul of the just. The first effect of sanctifying grace is to give us that participation in the divine nature of which we have already spoken. This is the root and foundation of all the other effects which flow from sanctifying grace.

Principal effects

Among the other effects, those three hold a place of pre-eminence which are mentioned by St. Paul in his Epistle to the Romans: "Now you have not received a spirit of bondage so as to be again in fear, but you have received a spirit of adoption as sons, by virtue of which we cry: Abba! Father! The

---

[24]For example, Peter Lombard, Henry Ghent, Scotus, Durandus, Bacon and Biel.

[25]For example, St. Thomas, Giles of Rome, Capreolus, Medina, Soto, Suárez, Valencia, the Salmanticenses and the majority of modern theologians.

[26]Cf. St. Thomas, *Summa*, I-II, q. 110, a. 4, *sed contra.*

[27]*Ibid.*, a. 4.

[28]*Ibid.*, a. 3.

Spirit himself gives testimony to our spirit that we are the sons of God. But if we are sons, we are heirs also: heirs indeed of God and joint heirs with Christ" (Rom. 8:15-17). Fortified by this sublime passage, let us examine the three principal effects produced by sanctifying grace.

1. *Grace makes us adopted sons of God.* To be a father, it is necessary to transmit to another being one's specific nature. The artist who makes a statue is not the father of the work but only the author. On the other hand, the "author of our days" is truly our natural father because he truly transmits to us, by way of generation, his own human nature.

Is it a natural filiation of God which is communicated to us by sanctifying grace? By no means. God the Father has only one Son according to nature: the eternal Word. Only to him is there transmitted eternally, by an ineffable intellectual generation, the divine nature in all its plenitude. In virtue of this natural generation the second Person of the Blessed Trinity possesses the selfsame divine essence of the Father and is God as fully as the Father is God. Therefore, Christ, whose human nature is hypostatically united with the Person of the Word, is not the adopted son of God, but the natural Son in all the rigor of the word.[29]

Our divine filiation through grace is of a different kind. It is not a question of a natural filiation but of an adoptive filiation. But it is necessary to understand this truth correctly in order not to form a deficient concept of this great dignity. Adoption is the gratuitous admission of a stranger to a family. He is henceforth considered as a son and is given a right to inheritance of the family goods. Human adoption has three requisites: a) on the part of the subject there must be human nature, for there must be a likeness of nature with the adopting father; one cannot adopt a statue or an animal; b) on the part of the one adopting there must be gratuitous love and free election, for no one has the right to be adopted and no one has an obligation to adopt; c) on the part of the goods or possessions, there must be a true right to the inheritance of the adopting father—otherwise the adoption would be purely fictitious.

Now sanctifying grace confers on us a divine adoption which not only fulfills all these conditions but goes far beyond them. Purely human or legal adoption is ultimately reduced to a legal fiction, entirely extrinsic to the nature of the one adopted. It confers on the one adopted, before human society, the rights of a son, but without infusing in the adopted the blood of the family, and hence without causing any intrinsic change in the nature and personality of the adopted son. On the other hand, on adopting us as his sons, the one and triune God[30] infuses sanctifying grace in us, which gives

[29]Cf. St. Thomas, *ibid.*, III, q. 23, a. 4.

[30]Cf. *ibid.*, I, q. 45, a. 6; III, q. 23, a. 2.

us a mysterious real and formal participation in the divine nature itself. It is an intrinsic adoption which places in our souls, physically and formally, a divine reality which makes the blood of God circulate in our souls. (We speak metaphorically to capture a sublime truth.) In virtue of this divine infusion, the soul shares in the very life of God. It is a true generation, a spiritual birth, in imitation of natural generation, and it reflects, analogically, the eternal generation of the Word of God. As St. John says explicitly, sanctifying grace not only gives us the right to be called sons of God, but it makes us such in reality: "Behold with what manner of love the Father has bestowed upon us, that we should be called children of God; and such we are" (I Jn. 3:1).

2. *Grace makes us true heirs of God.* This is an inevitable consequence of our divine adoptive filiation. St. Paul says expressly: "If we are sons, we are heirs also" (Rom. 8:17). How greatly this adoption through grace differs from legal and human adoption! Among men the sons inherit only at the death of the father, and the inheritance is less as the sons are more numerous. But our Father will live for all eternity, and we shall possess with him an inheritance which, in spite of the number of inheritors, will never diminish or lessen. For this inheritance is basically infinite. It is God himself, one in essence and three in persons, the principal object of our inheritance as adopted sons. "I am your shield; your reward shall be very great," God said to Abraham (Gen. 15:1), and he says the same to every soul in grace.

The beatific vision and the enjoyment of God which accompanies it are the principal part of the heritage which belongs, through grace, to the adopted sons of God. There will be communicated to them in addition all the riches of divinity, all that constitutes the happiness of God himself, a joy without end. Lastly, God will place at our disposition all extrinsic goods, such as his honor, his glory, his dominions. This will cause the soul ineffable happiness, which will completely satisfy all its aspirations and longings. And the soul will receive all these benefits and gifts under the title of justice. Grace is entirely gratuitous; but once possessed, it gives us the capacity to merit heaven under the title of justice. For the operation of a being follows its essence or nature, and the value of a work comes primarily from the dignity of the person who performs the work. And since grace is a divine form which inheres in the soul of the just, any supernatural action of which grace is the root and principle bespeaks an intrinsic relation to glory and carries with it a title to the same. Grace and glory are situated on the same plane and they are substantially the same life. There is between them only a difference of grade or degree. It is the same life in its initial or terminal stage. The child does not differ specifically from the mature man; he is an adult in potency. The same thing is true of grace and glory, and thus St. Thomas states that "grace is nothing other than the beginning of glory in us."[31]

[31]*Ibid.*, II-II, q. 24, a. 3, ad 2.

3. *Grace makes us brothers and co-heirs with Christ.* This relation derives immediately from the two already mentioned. The reason, as St. Augustine points out, is that he who says "our Father" to the Father of Christ, what shall he say to Christ but brother?[32] By the very fact that sanctifying grace communicates to us a participation in the divine life which Christ possesses in all its plenitude, it necessarily follows that we become his brothers. He desired to be our brother according to his humanity, in order to make us his brothers according to his divinity, "that he might give us a share in his divinity."[33] St. Paul states that God has predestined us "to become conformed to the image of his Son that he should be the firstborn among many brethren" (Rom. 8:29). It is evident that we are not brothers of Christ in nature, nor are we sons of God by the same form that he is such. Christ is the firstborn among many brothers and also the only-begotten of the Father. In the order of nature he is the only Son; but in the order of grace and adoption he is our elder brother, as well as our Head and the cause of our salvation.

For this reason, the Father deigns to look upon us as if we were one thing with the Son. He loves us as he loves his Son; he looks on Christ as our brother and confers on us the title to the same heritage. We are co-heirs with Christ. He has the natural right to the divine heritage, since he is the Son who was constituted heir of all, for which reason he made the world.[34] For that reason "it became him for whom are all things and through whom are all things, who had brought many sons into glory, to perfect through sufferings the author of their salvation. For both he who sanctifies and they who are sanctified are all from one. For which cause he is not ashamed to call them brethren, saying: 'I will declare thy name to my brethren; in the midst of the church I will praise thee'" (Heb. 2:10-12). Therefore, the brothers of Christ must share with him the love and heritage of the heavenly Father. God has modeled us on Christ; with Christ, we are sons of the same Father who is in heaven. All this will be effected by realizing the supreme desire of Christ: that we be one with him as he himself is one with the Father.[35]

OTHER EFFECTS

The foregoing are the three principal effects of grace, but they are not the only effects. The others are as follows:

4. *Grace gives us supernatural life.* The physical and formal participation in the very nature of God, which constitutes the essence of sanctifying grace, infinitely transcends the being and exigencies of every created nature, human or angelic. By it, man is elevated not only above the human plane but even

[32]*In Joan.*, tr. 21, n. 3 (M.L. 35: 1565).
[33]Preface of the Ascension.
[34]Cf. Heb. 1:2.
[35]Cf. Jn. 17:21-24.

above the angelic nature. He enters into the plane of the divine, is made a member of the family of God, and begins to live in a divine manner. Grace, consequently, has communicated to him a new type of life, infinitely superior to that of nature; it is a *supernatural* life.

5. *Grace makes us just and pleasing to God.* As a physical participation in the divine nature, grace necessarily gives us a sharing in the divine justice and sanctity, since all the attributes of God are really identified with his own essence. Therefore, sanctifying grace is absolutely incompatible with mortal sin, which presupposes the privation of that justice and sanctity. Hence grace makes us just and pleasing to God, as he contemplates in us an irradiation of his divine beauty and a reflection of his own sanctity.

The Council of Trent teaches this when it states that the justification of the sinner through sanctifying grace "is not merely the remission of sins but also the sanctification and interior renovation of man by the voluntary reception of grace and the gifts, by which man is changed from unjust to just and from an enemy into a friend." A little farther on, the Council adds that the unique formal cause of that justification is "the justice of God, not that which makes him just, but that which makes us just; or rather, that which, given by him, renews us interiorly and makes us not only to be reputed as just but that we should be called such and should be such in very truth."[36]

6. *Grace gives us the capacity for supernatural merit.* Without sanctifying grace, the most heroic natural works would have absolutely no value toward eternal life.[37] A man who lacks grace is a corpse in the supernatural order, and the dead can merit nothing. Supernatural merit presupposes radically the possession of the supernatural life. This principle is of the greatest importance in practical life. How much suffering and pain, which could have extraordinary value in the eternal life, are completely sterile and useless because the soul lacks sanctifying grace? While a man is in mortal sin, he is radically incapacitated for meriting anything at all in the supernatural order.

7. *Grace unites us intimately with God.* United as we are with God in the natural order through his divine conserving power, which makes him truly present to all creatures by his essence, presence and power,[38] sanctifying grace increases this union to an ineffable degree and transforms and elevates it to an infinitely higher type of union. By reason of this new union, God is really present in the just soul as a friend, and not merely as creator and conserver, establishing a mutual exchange of love and friendship between the soul and God and a kind of mutual transfusion of life. "God is love, and he who abides in love abides in God, and God in him" (I Jn. 4:16). A more intimate union

---

[36]Decree on justification, Chap. 7; Denz. 799.

[37]Cf. I Cor. 13:1-3; St. Thomas, *Summa,* I-II, q. 114, a. 2.

[38]Cf. St. Thomas, *ibid.,* I, q. 8, aa. 1-3.

with God cannot be imagined, apart from the personal or hypostatic union which is proper and exclusive to Christ. The ultimate grades of development which grace can attain in this life and even the indissoluble union proceeding from the beatific vision in heaven are not substantially different from the union which is established between God and a soul that has been justified by grace even in its minimum degree. There is a difference of degree among these types of union, but they are all the same substantial order.

8. *Grace makes us living temples of the Trinity.* This is a consequence of what we have just said, and Christ himself revealed this truth to us when he said: "If anyone love me, he will keep my word, and my Father will love him, and we will come to him and will make our abode with him" (Jn. 14:23). It is the uncreated reality, rigorously infinite, which sanctifying grace brings with it. We shall study this mystery of the indwelling of the Trinity in the following chapter. For the moment, having studied the static principle of our supernatural life, let us consider the role of actual grace in that life. It is not our intention to enter into the disputes which for centuries have divided the schools of theology concerning the nature and function of the various actual graces. We shall limit ourselves to a summary discussion of those points which pertain in a particular manner to spiritual theology.

ACTUAL GRACE

ITS NATURE

Actual graces may be defined as those which dispose or move in a transient manner for doing or receiving something in regard to eternal life. Ordained by their nature to the infused habits, they serve to dispose the soul to receive those infused habits when it does not yet possess them, or to put them into operation when it already possesses them. Actual graces are received into the faculties of the soul, sometimes elevating them so that they can produce indeliberate supernatural acts—as happens with operating grace (*gratia operans*)—and at other times to produce them in a deliberate manner (co-operating grace—*gratia co-operans*).

Actual graces cannot be reduced to any determined species since they are transitory qualities communicated by God and impressed on the faculties of the soul after the manner of transient movements or passions. Each actual grace is reduced to the species of habit or act which it moves, for example, to faith, hope, etc. From these general notions we can readily discern the differences between actual and habitual grace:

1) Habitual graces (sanctifying grace, the infused virtues and the gifts of the Holy Ghost) are permanent qualities or habits which produce

effects in a continual and indefectible manner in the subject in which they reside, namely, the essence of the soul or the faculties of the soul. Actual graces are fluid and transient movements whose final effect is often frustrated.

2) Habitual graces are limited to disposing for action (radically or proximately, depending on whether one speaks of grace itself or the virtues and gifts). Actual graces prompt and produce the act itself.

3) The virtues and the gifts have a restricted area which affects determined faculties or determined objects and operations. Actual graces extend to the entire supernatural life and all its operations.

NECESSITY OF ACTUAL GRACE

Actual graces are absolutely necessary in the dynamic supernatural order. It is impossible for a purely natural impulse to put the infused habits into operation, since the natural order cannot determine the operations of the supernatural order. Nor is it possible that the supernatural powers actuate themselves, because a habit can be actuated only by the power and action of the agent which caused it, and in regard to the infused supernatural habits only God who produced them can put them in motion. The action of God in this respect is as necessary as is the influence of a being already in act to reduce a potency to act. Absolutely speaking, God could develop and perfect sanctifying grace, which is infused into the essence of our soul, simply and solely through actual graces, without infusing any supernatural operative habits into the faculties. But this would be a kind of violence. On the other hand, God could not develop sanctifying grace without using the actual graces, although he has given us the infused supernatural habits, since those habits could not be reduced to act without the previous divine motion which in the supernatural order is nothing other than an actual grace. Every act of an infused virtue and every operation of the gifts of the Holy Ghost presupposes a previous actual grace which has set that virtue or gift in motion, although not every actual grace infallibly produces an act of virtue (e.g., a sufficient grace rejected by a sinner). The actual grace is nothing other than the divine influence which has moved the infused habit to its operation.

DIVISION OF ACTUAL GRACE

Theologians through the centuries have drawn up lengthy lists of distinctions between the various actual graces. We list only the principal ones.

1) *Operating grace* and *co-operating grace.* Operating grace is that in which the movement is attributed only to God; the soul is moved but does not move itself. Co-operating grace is that in which the soul is moved and moves at the same time. This is the manner of speaking of St. Augustine and St. Thomas.[39]

[39]Cf. St. Augustine, *De gratia et libero arbitrio,* cap. 17; St. Thomas, *Summa,* I-II, q. 111, a. 2. This fundamental division is of great importance in spiritual theology. Co-operating grace is proper to the workings of the infused virtues, in

2) *Gratia excitans* and *gratia adjuvans.* The first impels us to act when we are dormant or static; the second assists or aids us in the act once we are moved to perform it.

3) *Prevenient grace, concomitant grace* and *consequent grace.* The first precedes the act of man by disposing or moving the will; the second accompanies the act by concurring with man in producing the effect; the third bespeaks a relation to some anterior effect produced by some other grace.[40]

4) *Internal grace* and *external grace.* The first intrinsically aids the faculty and concurs formally in the production of the act; the second influences only extrinsically, moving the faculty by means of the objects which surround it (e.g., by the examples of Christ and the saints).

5) *Sufficient grace* and *efficacious grace.* Sufficient grace impels us to work; efficacious grace infallibly produces the act itself. Without the first, we cannot act; with the second, we act freely but infallibly. The first leaves us without any excuse before God; the second is an effect of his infinite mercy.[41]

As can be seen, these divisions of actual grace can easily be reduced to operating and co-operating grace. The *gratia excitans* and *gratia preveniens* are really operating graces; *gratia adjuvans* and *gratia subsequens* are co-operating graces; and sufficient grace and efficacious grace will be either an operating or a co-operating grace, depending on the particular situation in which they are given. But all these graces are transitory qualities which move the faculties of the soul to supernatural acts, either deliberate or indeliberate.

FUNCTION OF ACTUAL GRACE

Actual graces have three functions: to dispose the soul for the reception of the infused habits of sanctifying grace and the virtues, to actuate these infused habits, and to prevent their loss. A word on each function.

We say that actual grace disposes the soul for the reception of the infused habits either when the soul has never possessed them or when the soul has lost them through mortal sin. In the latter case actual grace carries with it a repentance for one's sins, the fear of punishment, confidence in the divine mercy, etc.

Actual grace also serves to actuate the infused habits when they are already possessed, together with sanctifying grace (or without it, as in the case of unformed faith and hope). This actuation, presupposing the possession of

---

which operation the soul is aware that it moves itself, with the help of God's grace. Under the influence of operating grace, on the other hand, which is proper to the gifts and eminently contains co-operating grace, the soul perceives that it is moved by God, letting itself be acted upon by him. Hence the relative passivity which is characteristic of the mystical state.

[40]Cf. St. Thomas, *ibid.,* I-II, q. 111, a. 3.

[41]Cf. Salmanticenses, *Cursus theologicus, De gratia,* dist. 5, n. 180.

sanctifying grace, carries with it the perfecting of the infused virtues and, consequently, the increase and growth of the supernatural life.

The third function of actual grace is to prevent the loss of the infused habits through mortal sin. It implies a strengthening in the face of temptations, an awareness of special dangers, mortification of the passions, inspiration through good thoughts and holy desires, etc.

It is evident, therefore, that actual grace is a priceless treasure. It gives efficacy to sanctifying grace and the infused virtues and gifts. It is the impulse of God which places our supernatural organism in operation and prevents us from forgetting that our soul, in the state of grace, is the temple of the Blessed Trinity.

3: THE INDWELLING OF THE TRINITY

The indwelling of the Blessed Trinity in the soul of the just is one of the truths most clearly revealed in the New Testament,[1] which insists again and again on this sublime truth. This is evident from the following texts selected at random:

"If anyone love me, he will keep my word, and my Father will love him, and we will come to him and make our abode with him" (Jn. 14:23).

"God is love, and he who abides in love, abides in God, and God in him" (I Jn. 4:16).

"Do you not know that you are the temple of God and that the Spirit of God dwells in you?" (I Cor. 3:16-17).

"Do you not know that your members are the temple of the Holy Spirit, who is in you, whom you have from God, and that you are not your own?" (I Cor. 6:19).

"For you are the temple of the living God" (II Cor. 6:16).

"Guard the good trust through the Holy Spirit, who dwells in us" (II Tim. 1:14).

Scripture uses various formulas to express the same truth, namely, that God dwells in the soul in grace. This indwelling is attributed to the Holy Spirit, not because there is any special presence of the Holy Ghost which is not common to Father and the Son,[2] but by reason of an appropriation, since this is the great work of the love of God, and the Holy Ghost is essential love in the bosom of the Trinity. The Fathers of the Church, and especially St. Augustine, have written beautiful tracts on the indwelling of the Trinity in the souls of the just.

---

[1]Although there are certain vestiges of this revelation in the Old Testament, the full revelation of the mystery was reserved for the New Testament.

[2]Certain theologians (Lessius, Petau, Thomassinus, Scheeben, etc.) held this opinion, but the majority of theologians teach the contrary doctrine, which is deduced from the data of faith and the teaching of the Church. Cf. Denz. 281, 703; Froget, *The Indwelling of the Holy Ghost in the Souls of the Just,* pp. 58 ff.

THE INDWELLING

ITS NATURE

Theologians have written much and disputed much concerning the nature of the indwelling. We shall enumerate the principal opinions sustained by various authors, without attempting to settle a question which only secondarily affects the object and finality of our work.

1) According to Galtier, the indwelling consists formally in a physical and loving union between God and the soul. This union is effected by sanctifying grace, in virtue of which the one and triune God is given to the soul and is substantially and personally present to the soul, making it share in the divine life. Grace is like a seal on fluid matter, and for the permanence of the seal on such matter it is necessary that the seal be impressed constantly; so, in like manner, if grace—which is the assimilative impress of the divine essence in the soul—is to remain in the soul, it is necessary that this divine nature be physically present to the soul.[3] This interpretation is rejected by many theologians because it does not seem to differentiate the indwelling from the common mode of God's existence *per essentiam* in all created things.

2) Other theologians have interpreted the teaching of St. Thomas as if he had placed the formal cause of the indwelling in supernatural knowledge and love, independently of the presence of immensity, that is, exclusively in the intentional presence. Suárez tried to complete this doctrine by that of the supernatural friendship which charity establishes between God and the soul and which demands, according to Suárez, the real presence and not only the intentional presence of God in the soul, and in such wise, he says, that by the power of this friendship God would really come to the soul even if he were not already there by any other title (e.g., the presence of immensity).[4] But this explanation has not satisfied the majority of theologians, because friendship, since it pertains to the affective order, does not offer a sufficient explanation for the formal presence of the divine Persons. Love as such does not make the beloved to be physically present, for it is of the purely intentional order.

3) One branch of the Thomistic school, following John of St. Thomas,[5] interprets St. Thomas in the sense that, presupposing the presence of immensity, sanctifying grace, through the operations of knowledge and love which proceed from faith and charity, is the formal cause of the indwelling of the Trinity in the souls of the just. According to this opinion, knowledge and love proceeding from

[3]P. Galtier, S.J., *La habitation en nous des trois Personnes* (Rome: 1949), pp. 217-40.

[4]Suárez, *De trinitate,* 12, 5, 13.

[5]John of St. Thomas, *Cursus theologici,* in Iam. q. 43, dist. 17.

faith and love do not constitute the presence of God in us but, presupposing that God is already in the soul by the presence of immensity, the special presence of the divine Persons consists in supernatural knowledge and love or in the operations which proceed from grace. This theory, much more acceptable than the preceding, seems nevertheless to encounter an insuperable difficulty. If the operations of knowledge and love proceeding from grace were the formal cause of the indwelling of the Trinity, the indwelling would have to be denied to those baptized before the use of reason, to the just souls during sleep, to those who are not actually performing acts of knowledge and love, even though they be in the state of sanctifying grace. To this difficulty, the proponents of the theory reply that even in such cases there would be a certain permanent presence of the Trinity by reason of the possession of the virtues of charity and faith, which are capable of producing that presence. But this reply does not satisfy some theologians, because the possession of those virtues would give only the faculty or power of producing the indwelling and, as long as they were not actually operating, we would not have the indwelling properly speaking.

4) Other theologians propose a blending of the first and third theories to explain the divine indwelling.[6] According to them, the divine persons are made present in some way by the efficacy and conservation of sanctifying grace, since this grace gives a formal and physical participation in the divine nature as such and therefore gives also a participation in the intimate life of God. Yet these theologians are careful to preserve intact the certain theological principle that in the works *ad extra* God works as one and not as triune. Since the Trinity is present to the soul in some way through sanctifying grace, the just soul enters into contact with the Trinity by the operations of knowledge and love which flow from grace itself. By the production of grace, God is united to the soul as principle; by the operations of knowledge and love, the soul is united to the divine Persons as the terminus of those same operations. Hence the indwelling of the Trinity is both an ontological and a psychological fact: ontological by reason of the production and conservation of grace, psychological by reason of supernatural knowledge and love.

Perhaps none of the theories offers an adequate explanation of the divine indwelling. But what is important for our purposes is not so much the nature or mode of the indwelling as the fact of the indwelling, and concerning this, all theologians are in accord.

PURPOSE OF THE INDWELLING

Let us now investigate the finality or purpose of the divine indwelling, which is of much more importance in spiritual theology. There are three purposes for the indwelling of the Trinity in the souls of the just: 1) to make us share

[6]Cf. S. González, *De gratia,* n. 212, in *Sacrae Theologiae Summa* (Madrid: B.A.C., 1953), III, p. 611.

in the divine life; 2) to make God the mover and rule of our actions; 3) to make God the object of fruition by an ineffable experience.[7]

Sharing divine life

When we say that God dwells in our souls as in his temple, we are expressing a truth which is supported by two famous passages in St. Paul,[8] but we must take care not to imagine that God's presence in us is like that of the Eucharist in a tabernacle, inert and with only a spatial relationship to the tabernacle. The presence of God in the just soul is infinitely superior to this; we are living temples of God, and we possess the three Persons in a vital manner.

To acclimate ourselves to this mystery, it is well to recall that sanctifying grace is the "seed of God,"[9] which engenders us and makes us live a new life, the participated divine life by which we are called, and are, sons of God.[10] This doctrine of our divine filiation is constantly repeated in the pages of Scripture, as is that of the divine indwelling, to which it is closely related. What does God do when he dwells in a soul? Nothing other than to communicate himself to that soul, to engender it as his son, which is to give it a participation in his nature and his life. And that generation is not verified, as is human generation, by a transient action through which the son begins to be and to live independently of the father from whom he receives his origin, but it presupposes a continued act of God as long as the soul remains in his friendship and grace. If God were for one instant to withdraw his conserving action from all the things which he has created, they would at that same instant return to the nothingness from which they came.[11] Similarly, if God were for an instant to withdraw his conserving action from grace in the just soul, grace would cease to exist and the soul would cease to be a child of God. Through grace, the soul is constantly receiving from God its supernatural life, as the embryo in the womb of the mother is constantly receiving life from the mother. For this reason did Christ come into the world, that we might live by him, as St. John says,[12] and Christ himself says that he came that we might have life and have it more abundantly.[13] Now we can see why St. Paul says: "It is now no longer I that live, but Christ lives in me" (Gal. 2:20).

Hence our divine adoptive generation has some similarity with the eternal generation of the Word in the bosom of the Father, and our union with God

---

[7]Cf. J. Menéndez-Reigada, O.P., *Los dones del Espíritu Santo y la perfección cristiana* (Madrid: 1948), cap. 1; Chardon, O.P., *The Cross of Jesus* (St. Louis: 1959), II, Chaps. 1-9; M. M. Philipon, O.P., *The Spiritual Doctrine of Sister Elizabeth of the Trinity* (Westminster, Md.: 1947).

[8]Cf. I Cor. 3:16-17; 6:19.

[9]Cf. I Jn. 3:9.

[10]Cf. I Jn. 3:1.

[11]Cf. St. Thomas, *Summa,* I, q. 104.

[12]Cf. I Jn. 4:9.

[13]*Ibid.*

through grace is somewhat similar to that which exists between the Word and the Father through the Holy Ghost. No theologian would ever have dared to say this, were it not for the sublime words of Christ, spoken at the Last Supper:

> Yet not for these only do I pray, but for those also who through their word shall believe in me, that all may be one, even as thou, Father, in me and I in thee; that they also may be one in us, that the world may believe that thou hast sent me. And the glory which thou hast given me, I have given to them, that they may be one, even as we are one: I in them and thou in me; that they may be perfected in unity, and that the world may know that thou hast sent me, and that thou hast loved them even as thou hast loved me.[14]

The Son is one with the Father by the unity of nature; we are one with God by the formal and physical participation of his own divine nature, which participation is nothing other than sanctifying grace. The Son lives by the Father, and we live by participation in God. He is in the Father and the Father is in him;[15] we are also in God and God is in us.

Thus it is through grace that we are introduced into the life of the Trinity, which is the life of God, and God dwells in us and communicates his divine life to us. And it is the three Persons who dwell in us, since it is not the property of any one Person in particular to engender us as sons of God, but it is an action common to the Three. They are in the just soul, all three Persons, engendering that soul supernaturally, vivifying it with their life, introducing it, through knowledge and love, to the most profound relationships. Here the Father engenders the Son, and from the Father and the Son proceeds the Holy Ghost, thus realizing in the soul the sublime mystery of the triune unity and the one Trinity, which is the inner life of God Himself.

The Holy Ghost as mover and ruler

Life is essentially dynamic and active. We know the existence of a vital form and its nature by the activity which proceeds from it. Since grace is a divine form, its actuation must also be divine; this is an intrinsic exigency of grace as a formal participation in the nature of God. To live the divine life is to operate in a divine mode.

This is precisely the function and finality of the gifts of the Holy Ghost, as we shall see. Human reason illumined by faith, which is the rule of the infused virtues, is a mover of relatively little power, a rule too lowly for the lofty operations which attain God as he is in himself. It is true that the theological virtues have God as their immediate object, and God precisely as he is in himself, but as long as they are subject to the rule of reason (even reason enlightened by faith), they must be accommodated to the human mode which is necessarily impressed upon them, and hence they cannot develop fully the immense virtuality which is theirs. This is the reason invoked by St. Thomas

[14]Jn. 17:20-23.
[15]Cf. Jn. 14:10.

to prove the necessity of the gifts of the Holy Ghost, which perfect the infused virtues by communicating to them a divine modality and place them on a level which is strictly supernatural, as is required by the very nature of grace and the infused virtues. Under the influence of the gifts, human reason is more acted upon than acting, and the resulting acts are materially human but formally divine. Only in this way can we ultimately live in all its plenitude the divine life received through grace.

Whence it is evident that the divine motion of the gifts is very distinct from the divine activity found in the infused virtues. In the divine movement of the infused virtues, the full responsibility of the action is man's, as immediate cause and mover, and for that reason the acts of the virtues are entirely our own because they come from us, from our reason and free will. True, they are always under the motion of God as First Mover, without whom no act of any kind can proceed from a potency either in the natural or the supernatural order. But in the case of the gifts, the divine motion is utterly different. The unique mover is God, who places the gifts in operation, while man is limited to receiving the divine movement and seconding it with docility, without offering any resistance and without modifying it or changing its direction. Therefore, the acts which proceed from the gifts are divine in the way that the melody which a musician plays on his instrument is materially from the instrument but formally from the musician who plays it.[16] Nor does this in any way diminish the merit of the soul which seconds the divine motion by its docility; for in spite of the fact that the Holy Ghost is the unique mover, the soul adheres with all its power of free will to the divine motion, although many times it simply lets itself be led without offering any resistance. The passivity of the soul under the activity of the gifts is a relative passivity—that is, with respect to the initiative of the act, which belongs exclusively to the Holy Ghost. But once the divine motion is initiated, the soul reacts actively and associates itself intensely with the act with all the vital power of which it is capable and with all its free will. Thus the divine initiative, the relative passivity of the soul, the vital reaction of the soul, the exercise of free will and the supernatural merit of the action are blended and mutually complement each other. Through the divine motion of the gifts, the Holy Ghost dwelling in the soul takes the reins of our spiritual life. It is no longer human

[16]The gifts of the Holy Ghost do not convert man into an instrument in the strict sense, but only in a wide sense. He is an instrument so far as he is moved by God, but he retains his secondary principal causality. If man were an instrument in the strict sense, the act of the gift would cease to be a vital act, for it is proper to a vital act that it proceed from a vital principle and that it operate by its own proper form. Hence it must be concluded that the gifts of the Holy Ghost and human reason elevated by grace concur in the production of the act of the gift as two principal causes which are total and *per se* subordinated causes. Cf. Ramírez, *op. cit.*, III, n. 287.

reason which rules and governs but the Holy Ghost, who acts as the rule and mover of our acts, putting the entire supernatural organism in motion until it attains its full development.

Object of fruition

It is a fact testified by the mystics that in the most profound center of their souls they experienced the august presence of the Blessed Trinity working intensely in them.[17] "I used unexpectedly to experience a consciousness of the presence of God," says St. Teresa, "of such a kind that I could not possibly doubt that he was within me or that I was wholly engulfed in him."[18] Again, she writes that the Trinity reveals itself, in all three Persons, and that the soul "perceives quite clearly, in the way I have described, that they are in the interior of her heart."[19]

The number of texts from the mystics could be multiplied indefinitely.[20] This divine experience of contemplative souls is so clear that some of them, through this experience, came to know the mystery of the indwelling of the Trinity even before they had heard anything about it.[21] Actually, the experience of the mystics is a verification of the lofty teachings of theology. St. Thomas, writing as a theologian, makes the following startling statement: "By the gift of sanctifying grace, the rational creature is perfected so that it can freely use not only that created gift but even enjoy the divine Person himself."[22] And in the same place he writes: "We are said to possess only what we can freely use or enjoy; and to have the power of enjoying the divine Person can only be through sanctifying grace."[23]

Here in all its sublime grandeur is the most intimate purpose of the indwelling of the Trinity in our souls. God himself, one in essence and three in persons, becomes the object of an ineffable experience. The divine Persons are given to us that we may enjoy them, to use the amazing expression of the Angelic Doctor. And when this experimental joy reaches the culmination of the transforming union, the souls that have reached this summit are unable to, and do not wish to, express themselves in the language of earth. They prefer to taste in silence that which in no way could be explained to others. As St. John of the Cross says:

> Wherefore the delicacy of the delight which is felt in this touch is impossible of true description,[24] nor would I willingly speak of it lest it should be supposed that it is no more than that which I say. There are no words to ex-

---

[17]Cf. St. John of the Cross, *The Living Flame,* Stanza 1, n. 3.
[18]*The Life,* chap. 10.
[19]*Interior Castle,* Seventh Mansions, Chap. 1.
[20]Cf. A. Poulain, S.J., *The Graces of Prayer* (St. Louis: 1928), Chap. 5, nn. 2-48.
[21]Cf. Philipon, *op. cit.,* Chaps. 1 and 3.
[22]*Summa,* I, q. 43, a. 3, ad 1.
[23]*Ibid.,* a. 3.
[24]St. John is here speaking of the substantial touches of God, which is the culminating point in the mystical experience of the divine indwelling.

> pound such sublime things of God as come to pass in these souls; the proper way to speak is for one that knows them to understand them inwardly and to feel them inwardly and enjoy them and be silent concerning them. . . . This alone can be said of it with truth, that it savors of eternal life. For although in this life we may not have perfect fruition of it, as in glory, nevertheless this touch, being of God, savors of eternal life.[25]

In these sublime heights, where the soul experiences the divine indwelling in an ineffable manner, what the soul knew and believed through faith it now experiences as if by sight and touch, as St. Teresa explains:

> So that what we hold by faith the soul may be said here to grasp by sight, although nothing is seen by the eyes, either of the body or of the soul; for it is no imaginary vision. Here all three Persons communicate themselves to the soul and speak to the soul and explain to it those words which the gospel attributes to the Lord, namely, that he and the Father and the Holy Ghost will come to dwell with the soul which loves him and keeps his commandments.[26]

This experimental knowledge of God, although substantially the same, is infinitely superior in its mode to that which we have of him through reason enlightened by faith. St. Teresa exclaims: "Oh, God help me! What a difference there is between hearing and believing these words and being led in this way to realize how true they are!"[27] The reason for this inequality and difference between the knowledge of faith and experimental knowledge is clear:

> The mystical or experimental knowledge of God has for its real object God himself, who is manifested to us through faith in an ideal manner, one in substance and three in persons. Faith tells us that there are three distinct persons in God in one essence. With that we have a supernatural knowledge of God as he is in himself, but this knowledge does not surpass the ideal order. But by the mystical experience, which makes this ideal object palpable, the object of faith and the object of experience are totally identified.
>
> I have in mind a fruit which is said to be very tasty, but I have never eaten it. I know that it is a tasty fruit because he who told me does not deceive me. This is God as known by faith and possessed by charity (*fides ex auditu*). But I put the fruit to my mouth and begin to eat it, and then I know by experience that it was true what they told me of its sweetness and savor. This is God as known by mystical experience.[28]

MYSTICAL EXPERIENCE

Before terminating this discussion of the indwelling of the Trinity, we would like to point out an important conclusion which will shed great light on one of the most disputed questions in spiritual theology. From all that we have said, one can readily deduce that the mystical experience is the normal end or terminus of the divine indwelling in the souls of the just. Every soul in the

---

[25] *The Living Flame,* Stanza 2, n. 19.

[26] *Interior Castle,* Seventh Mansions, Chap. 1.

[27] *Loc. cit.*

[28] Menéndez-Reigada, *op. cit.,* Chap. 1.

state of grace is a mystic in potency, and every potency begs to be reduced to act. If one does not yet experience the presence of God within his soul (and this is what constitutes the most characteristic phenomenon of the mystical state from a psychological point of view), it is not because he does not yet possess all the infused elements which are indispensable for this experience, nor because God prevents this passage to the mystical experience, but simply and solely because he has not yet totally detached himself from the things of earth, he has not yet overcome the obstacles which prevent this ineffable experience, he has not yet spread his wings to soar to lofty things, he has not yet given himself fully and unreservedly to God to let him work these marvels in the soul. This is precisely the teaching of St. Teresa:

> Remember, the Lord invites us all; and since he is Truth itself, we cannot doubt him. If his invitation were not a general one, he would not have said: "I will give you to drink." He might have said: "Come, all of you, for after all you will lose nothing; and I will give drink to those to whom it pleases me." But since he said "all," without any condition, I am sure that none will lack this living water unless they stop on the way.[29]

After such explicit testimony from St. Teresa, which is nothing less than a confirmation from the field of experience of the theological principles on the divine indwelling, would it not be ridiculous to ask whether all are called to the mystical state? Whether this enters into the normal development of grace? Whether it is licit to desire the mystical state? Whether there is one or many ways to union with God? A contemporary theologian points out:

> This stupendous phenomenon [of the indwelling of the Trinity], whose reality is guaranteed by Sacred Scripture, is it something mystical or ascetical? Is it the patrimony of some few souls or the common heritage of all the children of God? How petty our divisions and distinctions appear in the face of these sublime realities which faith teaches! The fact of the mission of the divine Persons unifies all the phases of the Christian life from baptism to the spiritual matrimony. . . . The gift of the divine Persons is not something peculiar to the ascetical or the mystical phase nor even to the higher stages of the mystical state (the *awareness* of the divine indwelling may be, but not the gift itself). The divine Persons are given to all who live in the state of grace.[30]

---

[29] *The Way of Perfection,* Chap. 19; cf. also St. John of the Cross, *The Living Flame,* Stanza 2.

[30] S. Lozano, O.P., *Vida santa y ciencia sagrada* (Salamanca: 1942), Chap. 6, pp. 68, 72; cf. also St. Thomas, *Summa,* I, q. 43, aa. 3, 6.

4: THE INFUSED VIRTUES

There is a perfect analogy between man's natural organism and his supernatural organism. Man's soul is not immediately operative by its proper essence but operates through its faculties or powers of intellect and will, which emanate from the soul as from their proper root. The same thing occurs in regard to the supernatural organism. Sanctifying grace, which is, as it were, the soul or essence of the supernatural organism, is not immediately operative. It is not a dynamic but a static element, for it is not a perfection in the order of operation but in the order of being. The reason is that, although grace itself is an accident and not a substance, it nevertheless acts as a substance in the supernatural order and, like all substances, it requires faculties or powers in order to operate. These faculties or powers are infused by God in the soul together with grace itself, from which they are inseparable.[1] Some of these supernatural powers are nothing other than the infused virtues and the gifts of the Holy Ghost.[2]

THE VIRTUES THEMSELVES

EXISTENCE AND NECESSITY

The existence and necessity of the infused virtues follows from the very nature of sanctifying grace. Grace is a divine seed which by its nature seeks growth and development until it reaches full perfection. But since sanctifying grace itself is not immediately operative (although it is so radically as the remote principle of all our supernatural operations), it follows that grace

[1]With the exception of faith and hope, which can subsist without sanctifying grace in an uninformed or non-vital manner.

[2]For the reader who desires a more profound treatment of the theology of the virtues in general, we suggest the Latin manuals of moral theology by Prümmer, Merklebach or Fanfani, who interpret the teaching of St. Thomas Aquinas very accurately; or, in English, *The Christian Life*, edited by F. L. B. Cunningham, O.P. (Dubuque: 1959).

demands and postulates certain immediate principles of operation which flow from grace itself and are inseparable from it. If this were not the case, man would be elevated to the supernatural order only as regards his soul but not as regards his operative powers. And although, absolutely speaking, God could elevate our faculties to the supernatural order by means of continual actual graces, this would produce a violence in the human psychological structure by reason of the tremendous disproportion between the purely natural faculty and the supernatural act to be effected. And such violence could not be reconciled with the customary suavity of divine providence, which moves all things according to their natures. From this we deduce the necessity of certain supernatural operative principles so that man can tend to his supernatural end in a manner that is perfectly connatural and without violence.

As St. Thomas points out:

> It is not fitting that God should provide less for those he loves, that they may acquire supernatural good, than for creatures whom he loves that they may acquire natural good. Now he so provides for natural creatures that not merely does he move them to their natural acts, but he bestows on them certain forms and powers which are the principles of acts, in order that they may of themselves be inclined to these movements, and thus the movements whereby they are moved by God become natural and easy to creatures. . . . Much more, therefore, does he infuse into those he moves toward the acquisition of supernatural good certain forms or supernatural qualities whereby they may be moved by him sweetly and promptly to acquire eternal good.[3]

THEIR NATURE

The *infused virtues* may be defined as operative habits infused by God into the faculties of the soul to dispose them to function according to the dictates of reason enlightened by faith.

Operative habits

"Operative habits" is the generic element of the definition, common to all natural and supernatural virtues.[4] From the psychological point of view, an operative habit is a quality, difficult to remove, which disposes the subject to function with facility, promptness and delight. It gives the subject facility for operation because every habit is an increase of energy in relation to its corresponding action; it gives promptness because it constitutes, so to speak, a second nature in virtue of which the subject quickly gives himself to action; and it causes delight in the operation because it produces an act which is prompt, facile and connatural.

Infused by God

"Infused by God" is a radical difference between the infused and acquired virtues.[5] The natural or acquired virtues are engendered in man by means of repeated acts. The only cause of the supernatural or infused virtues is the divine infusion; hence their name, "infused virtues." And we say that they are

[3]*Summa,* I-II, q. 110, a. 2.
[4]Cf. St. Thomas, *ibid.,* I-II, q. 55.
[5]Cf. *ibid.,* q. 63, a. 4, *sed contra* and ad 3.

infused by God into the faculties of the soul because we are speaking of operative habits that are immediately ordained to action. Their purpose is to supernaturalize the faculties by elevating them to the order of grace and making them capable of performing supernatural acts. Without them, or without the actual grace which supplies for them (as in the case of the sinner before justification), it would be impossible for man to perform an act of supernatural virtue, as it is impossible for an animal to perform an act of intelligence. Here again is evident the close similarity and analogy between the natural organism and the supernatural organism. As St. Thomas says: "As from the essence of the soul flow its powers, which are the principles of deeds, so likewise the virtues, whereby the powers are moved to act, flow into the powers of the soul from grace."[6]

Reason illumined by faith

The principal element of specific differentiation between the acquired and the infused virtues is that by reason of the formal object. The infused virtues dispose the faculties to follow the dictate or command, not of simple reason, as do the acquired virtues, but of reason illumined by faith. The motives of operation for the acquired virtues are simply and solely natural motives; the motives for the operation of the infused virtues are strictly supernatural motives. Hence the great abyss that separates the one from the other set of virtues by reason of the formal object, which is the most characteristic element of the specific difference in the definition.

But how are the infused virtues united with the natural faculties or powers to constitute with them one principle of operation? To answer this question it is necessary to bear in mind that the infused virtues are meant to perfect the natural faculties or powers by elevating them to the supernatural order. Consequently, the supernatural virtuous act will proceed from the union of the natural faculty with the supernatural virtue which perfects it. As a vital act, it has its radical power in the natural faculty, which the infused virtue essentially completes by giving it the power for a supernatural act. Hence every supernatural act springs from the natural faculty or power precisely as informed with the supernatural virtue, or from the natural faculty which has been raised to the supernatural order. The radical power, for example, is the intellect or will; the formal proximate principle of action is the corresponding infused virtue.

Difference between virtues

The teaching of St. Thomas is that the infused moral virtues are essentially distinct, by reason of their formal object, from the acquired moral virtues. These latter virtues, however heroic and perfect, could grow indefinitely and never attain the formal object of the infused virtues. There is an infinite difference between temperance according to Aristotle, regulated by right reason alone, and Christian temperance, which is regulated by reason enlightened

[6] *Ibid.*, q. 110, a. 4, ad 1.

by faith and by supernatural prudence. The magnificent article on this point in the *Summa theologiae* manifests the lofty idea which St. Thomas has of the infused virtues as compared with the acquired virtues.[7]

The infused virtues are inspired and regulated by the teaching of faith concerning the consequences of original sin and our personal sins, the infinite grandeur of our supernatural end, the necessity of loving God more than self, the need to imitate Christ, which leads us to self-abnegation and renunciation. None of this is attained by pure reason, even by a Socrates, an Aristotle or a Plato. With good reason does St. Thomas say that the specific difference between the acquired and infused virtues is evident by reason of their formal objects:

> The object of every virtue is a good considered as in that virtue's proper matter; thus the object of temperance is a good with respect to the pleasures connected with the concupiscence of touch. The formal aspect of this object is from reason, which fixes the mean in these concupiscences. Now it is evident that the mean that is appointed in such concupiscence according to the rule of human reason is seen under a different aspect from the mean which is fixed according to the divine rule. For instance, in the consumption of food, the mean fixed by human reason is that food should not harm the health of the body nor hinder the use of reason; whereas according to the divine rule it behooves man to chastise his body and bring it under subjection (I Cor. 9:27) by abstinence in food, drink and the like. It is therefore evident that infused and acquired temperance differ in species; and the same applies to the other virtues.[8]

Nor does it change matters to object that habits are known by their acts and the act of infused temperance is identical with that of acquired temperance (namely, the moderation or control of the pleasures of touch) and that therefore there is no specific difference between them. St. Thomas answers this objection by conceding the identity of the material object but insisting on the specific and radical difference by reason of the formal object: "Both acquired and infused temperance moderate desires for pleasures of touch, but for different reasons as stated: wherefore their respective acts are not identical."[9] Therefore, according to the teaching of St. Thomas, the infused virtues differ from the acquired virtues, not only by reason of their entitative elevation, but also by reason of their formal object, which makes them substantially superior to the acquired virtues.[10]

---

[7]*Ibid.*, q. 63, a. 4.

[8]*Loc. cit.*

[9]*Ibid.*, ad 2. The identity of the acts is purely material and not formal, as St. Thomas insists: "Although the act of the acquired and the infused virtue is materially the same, it is not the same formally" (*In III Sent.*, dist. 33, q. 1, a. 2).

[10]For further study on this point, see Garrigou-Lagrange, *The Three Ages,* I, pp. 57-65; Froget, *The Indwelling of the Holy Ghost in the Souls of the Just,* pp. 197-202; Arintero, *The Mystical Evolution,* Vol. I, pp. 204-215.

Potencies or habits

Let us now see into what category we are to place the infused virtues. Are they potencies or habits? Properly speaking, the infused virtues do not fit exactly into either category, although they are more habits than they are potencies. They have something of a potency so far as they give a power in the dynamic supernatural order, but they are not potencies strictly and formally speaking. And this for various reasons:

1) the potencies can be moved to their acts and can acquire habits, and if the infused virtues were true potencies, they would be able to acquire new habits, which is a contradiction, for they would then be acquired and infused at the same time;

2) the potencies are indifferent to good and evil, but virtues cannot act evilly;

3) the potencies as such do not increase in intensity (for example, the intellect, as a potency or power, does not itself increase, although its knowledge may increase), but the infused virtues do admit of an increase of intensity.

Hence the infused virtues belong more to the category of habits than to potencies.

But the infused virtues also lack something of the perfect definition of habits, since they do not give complete facility in operation, which is characteristic of true habits. They confer, it is true, an intrinsic inclination, ease and promptness for good, but they do not give an extrinsic facility because they do not remove all the obstacles to good, as is evident in the case of the converted sinner who experiences great difficulty in the performance of good because of his past acquired vices, in spite of the fact that he has received, together with sanctifying grace, all the infused virtues. St. Thomas distinguishes very clearly between the facility which proceeds from custom and that which proceeds from the strong inhesion regarding the object of virtue. The first is not conferred by the infused virtues from the first instant of their infusion into the soul, but they do confer the second. "Facility in performing the acts of virtue can proceed from two sources: from custom (and the infused virtue does not give this facility from its beginning) and from a strong inhesion as regards the object of the virtue, and this is found in the infused virtue at its very beginning."[11]

The reason why the infused virtues do not fit exactly into either of these categories—potencies and habits—is because supernatural entities cannot properly be placed in natural categories any more than God can, of whom they are a kind of participation. Nevertheless, they can be reduced more or less and by a certain analogy to natural categories. Thus sanctifying grace, as a spiritual and permanent accident, is reduced to the species of quality as an entitative

[11] *In IV Sent.*, dist. 14, q. 2, a. 2, ad 5; *De virtutibus,* a. 10, ad 15.

habit, and the principles of supernatural operation are reduced to the species of quality as operative habits, although they do not have all the characteristics of these habits.[12]

INFUSED VIRTUES

Natural and supernatural

The principal differences between the natural and supernatural, or the acquired and infused virtues are the following:

By reason of their essence. The natural or acquired virtues are habits in the strict sense of the word. They do not give the power to act (for the faculty has that already), but they give facility in operation. The supernatural or infused virtues give the power to act supernaturally (without them it would be impossible, apart from an actual grace), but they do not always give facility in operation.

By reason of the efficient cause. The natural virtues are acquired by our own proper acts; the supernatural virtues are infused by God together with sanctifying grace.

By reason of the final cause. By means of the natural virtues man conducts himself rightly in regard to human things and performs acts in accordance with his rational nature. The supernatural virtues, on the other hand, give man the ability to conduct himself rightly in regard to his condition as an adopted son of God, destined for eternal life, and to exercise the supernatural acts proper to the divine nature by participation.[13]

By reason of the formal object. In the natural virtues it is the good according to the dictate and light of natural reason which is the rule or formal object; in the supernatural virtues it is the good according to the dictate and supernatural light of faith or conformity with the supernatural end.

From the foregoing distinctions it is evident that the infused virtues are specifically distinct and extraordinarily superior to the corresponding acquired or natural virtues.

PROPERTIES OF INFUSED VIRTUE

There are four properties which the infused virtues have in common with the acquired natural virtues: 1) they consist in the mean or medium between the two extremes (except for the theological virtues, and even these do so by reason of the subject and mode); 2) in the state of perfection they are united among themselves by prudence (and the infused virtues by charity also); 3) they are unequal in perfection or eminence; 4) those which imply no imperfection perdure after this life as to their formal elements.[14]

Besides these characteristics, let us review the characteristics or properties which are exclusive to the infused virtues.

---

[12]Cf. Merkelbach, *Summa Theologiae Moralis,* I, n. 619.
[13]Cf. St. Thomas, *Summa,* I-II, q. 63, a. 3.
[14]Cf. *ibid.,* qq. 64-67.

1) *They always accompany sanctifying grace and are infused together with grace.* This doctrine is common among the theologians, although it is not exactly defined by the Church.

2) *They are really distinct from sanctifying grace.* It suffices to recall in this respect that grace is an entitative habit infused into the essence of the soul, while the infused virtues are operative habits infused into the potencies, which are really distinct from the soul.[15]

3) *They are specifically distinct from the corresponding acquired natural virtues.* This has been demonstrated above.

4) *We possess the supernatural virtues imperfectly.* We shall explain this more fully in the tract on the gifts of the Holy Spirit. This particular characteristic has great importance in solving the question of the mystical state and Christian perfection.[16]

5) *They increase with sanctifying grace.* This is clear from Scripture and the teaching of the Church. St. Paul writes to the Ephesians: "Rather are we to practice the truth in love, and so grow up in all things in him who is the head, Christ" (Eph. 4:15). To the Philippians he says: "And this I pray, that your charity may more and more abound in knowledge and discernment" (Phil. 1:9). And he prays for the Romans "that you may abound in hope, and in the power of the Holy Spirit" (Rom. 15:13). St. Peter writes: "Grow in grace and in the knowledge of our Lord and Savior Jesus Christ" (II Pet. 3:18). Following the lead of the apostles, the Church asks in the liturgy for an "increase of faith, hope and charity."[17]

6) *They give us the intrinsic power for supernatural acts but not the extrinsic facility for those acts.* We have already seen this fact, which explains why the repentant sinner experiences great difficulty in the practice of the virtues opposed to his former vices. It is necessary that these difficulties be overcome by the infused virtues, aided by the acquired virtues. The acquired virtues cannot assist the infused virtues intrinsically, of course, because the natural habit of the acquired virtues is absolutely incapable of intrinsically perfecting the supernatural habit of the infused virtues. But they can render such assistance extrinsically by removing the obstacles or the perverse inclinations and the disordered concupiscence. When these obstacles are removed, the infused virtues begin to work promptly and delightfully.[18]

7) *They all disappear, except faith and hope, by mortal sin.* The reason for this is that the infused virtues are like properties flowing from sanctifying

[15]Cf. *ibid.*, q. 110, a. 4, ad 1.

[16]Cf. *ibid.*, q. 68, a. 2.

[17]Collect, Thirteenth Sunday after Pentecost.

[18]Cf. St. Thomas, *De virtutibus in communi*, a. 10, ad 14.

grace. Hence when grace is destroyed they also are destroyed. Only faith and hope can remain, and they in an unformed and imperfect state, as the last effort of the infinite mercy of God so that the sinner may be more easily converted.[19] But if a man sins directly against either of these two remaining virtues, they also are destroyed, and the soul is then deprived of every trace of the supernatural.

INFUSED VIRTUES

8) *They cannot diminish directly*. This diminution could be caused only by venial sin or by the cessation of the acts of the corresponding virtue, for mortal sin does not diminish but destroys the infused virtues. But they cannot be diminished by venial sin because this, a deviation from the path which leads to God, leaves intact the tendency to the supernatural ultimate end which is proper to the infused virtues. Nor can they be diminished by the cessation of the acts of the virtues, for as infused virtues they were not acquired by the repetition of acts, and they cannot be lessened or diminished by the cessation of acts. Nevertheless, the infused virtues may be diminished indirectly by venial sins so far as these sins stifle the fervor of charity, impede progress in virtue, and predispose to mortal sin.[20]

DIVISION OF THE INFUSED VIRTUES

Some of the infused virtues ordain the faculties to the end or goal, and others dispose them in regard to the means. The first group are the theological virtues; the second group are the moral virtues. The first correspond, in the order of grace, to the principles of the natural order which direct man to his natural end; the second correspond to the acquired virtues of the natural order which perfect man in regard to the means. Once again the close similarity and analogy between the natural and the supernatural orders are evident.

THEOLOGICAL VIRTUES

Existence

The existence of the theological virtues seems to be clearly stated in Sacred Scripture, as is evident from several texts of St. Paul. "The charity of God is poured forth in our hearts by the Holy Spirit who has been given to us" (Rom. 5:5); "without faith it is impossible to please God" (Heb. 11:6); "there abide faith, hope and charity, these three; but the greatest of these is charity" (I Cor. 13:13). In the Council of Trent, the Church stated in equivalent formulas that man receives with sanctifying grace the other gifts of faith, hope,

[19]Cf. Council of Trent, canon 28 on justification (Denz. 838); also see Denz. 1407, St. Thomas, *Summa,* I-II, q. 1, a. 4.

[20]Cf. St. Thomas, *ibid.,* q. 24, a. 10.

charity, etc.[21] Since the acts are not infused, it must be concluded that reference is here made to permanent habits or the infused virtues. Nevertheless, the question as to whether this doctrine has been expressly defined by the Church is disputed among theologians. Vega, Ripalda, Suárez and Pope Benedict XIV say that the doctrine has been defined, and they refer to the Council of Trent for verification; but Soto, Medina and Báñez hold that Trent did not expressly define the doctrine, although it did state the doctrine equivalently. Consequently, this doctrine is at least a truth *proxima fidei*. Billot says that it is a most certain theological conclusion. As to the rest of the theologians, no ancient or modern theologian has ever denied the existence of the theological virtues except Peter Lombard. The Master of the Sentences erred in this matter; he identified charity with the Holy Ghost and thus destroyed it as a virtue.

The existence of the theological virtues is postulated by the very nature of sanctifying grace. Since grace is not immediately operative, it requires operative principles to grow and develop to perfection. Among these principles, some must refer to the supernatural end (theological virtues), and others must refer to the means which lead to that end (moral virtues). This argument takes its force principally from the suavity of the workings of divine providence, made known to us through revelation.

Nature

The theological virtues are operative principles by which we are directed and ordained directly and immediately to God as our supernatural end. They have God himself as their material object and one of his divine attributes as their formal object. Since they are strictly supernatural, only God can infuse them into the soul, and their existence can be known only through revelation.[22]

Number

There are three theological virtues: faith, hope and charity. The reason for this number is that by these three immediate union with God is realized perfectly. Faith enables us to know and unites us with God as First Truth; hope makes us desire him as the Supreme Good for us; charity unites us to him by the love of friendship, so far as he is infinite goodness in himself. There are no other aspects of union with God, for although the divine perfections are infinite, they cannot be attained by human acts except under the aspect of truth (by the intellect) and goodness (by the will). And only this latter admits of a twofold aspect, namely, good for us (hope) and goodness in itself (charity).

That the theological virtues are distinct among themselves is something beyond doubt, since they can actually be separated. Faith can subsist without hope and charity (as in one who commits a mortal sin of despair without losing his faith); charity will perdure eternally in heaven, separate from faith and hope, which will have disappeared;[23] and finally, in this life faith and hope can

[21]Decree on justification, Chap. 7 and canon 11; Denz. 799, 800 and 821.
[22]Cf. St. Thomas, *Summa,* I-II, q. 62, a. 1.
[23]Cf. I Cor. 13:8.

subsist without charity, as always happens when one commits a mortal sin which is not directly opposed to faith or hope. It is evident that in all these instances faith and hope remain in the soul in an unformed or non-vital state, since charity is the form of the virtues, and for that reason they lack the proper and true reason of virtue.[24]

Their order

One can distinguish two orders: the order of generation and the order of perfection.[25] By the order of generation or of origin the first is to know (faith), then to desire (hope), and lastly to attain (charity).[26] Although this gradation is by reason of acts, that by reason of the habits is the same: faith precedes hope and hope precedes charity, since the intellect precedes the will and imperfect love precedes perfect love.

According to the order of perfection, charity is the most excellent of the theological virtues ("And the greatest of these is charity"—I Cor. 13:13) because it is the one that unites us most intimately with God and the only one of the three that perdures in eternity. As to the other two, Medina and Báñez say that *in se,* as a theological virtue, faith is more excellent than hope because it bespeaks a relation with God in himself while hope presents God to us as a good for us, and also because faith is the foundation of hope. On the other hand, hope is more closely related to charity, and in this sense it is more perfect than faith.

Their subject

According to the doctrine of St. Thomas, which is held by the majority of theologians, faith resides in the intellect, and hope and charity in the will.[27] Among the mystics, St. John of the Cross, in spite of the fact that he is Thomistic in his doctrine, places the virtue of hope in the memory. This is undoubtedly because he followed the division used by many of the ancient mystical theologians who spoke of a threefold spiritual faculty: intellect, memory and will, and more especially because this was a convenient division for explaining the purification of the memory in the mystical state.

MORAL VIRTUES

Existence

The existence of the infused moral virtues was denied by numerous ancient theologians (Scotus, Durandus, Biel), but today it is admitted by almost all theologians, in accordance with the doctrine of St. Augustine, St. Gregory and St. Thomas. The basis of this doctrine is to be found in Scripture. Thus in the Book of Wisdom we are told that nothing is more useful in the life of a man than temperance, prudence, fortitude and justice. "If one loves justice, the fruits of her works are virtues, for she teaches moderation and prudence, justice and fortitude, and nothing in life is more useful for men than these"

[24]Cf. St. Thomas, *Summa,* I-II, q. 65, a. 4.

[25]Cf. *loc. cit.*

[26]We refer to a priority of nature and not of time, for all the infused virtues are infused into the soul simultaneously.

[27]Cf. *Summa,* II-II, q. 4, a. 2; q. 18, a. 1; q. 24, a. 1.

(Wisd. 8:7). St. Peter, immediately after speaking of grace as a participation in the divine nature of God, states: "Do you accordingly on your part strive diligently to supply your faith with virtue, your virtue with knowledge, your knowledge with self-control, your self-control with patience, your patience with piety, your piety with fraternal love, your fraternal love with charity" (II Pet. 1:5-7).

In these and other texts we have the scriptural basis which was later elaborated by the Fathers and theologians to give us a body of doctrine which is perfectly organized and systematic.[28] It is true that the Church has not expressly defined anything in this question,[29] but today the doctrine on the existence of the infused moral virtues is so general among Catholic theologians that one could not deny it without manifest temerity.

We have already indicated the reason for the existence of the infused moral virtues when we spoke of the infused virtues in general and the theological virtues in particular. The theological virtues are demanded by the very nature of grace so that it can be dynamically orientated to the supernatural end; the moral virtues are demanded by the theological virtues, in turn, because to be ordained to the end requires a disposition to the means. The relation which the moral virtues bespeak with the theological virtues in the order of grace is the same as the relation between the acquired natural virtues and the acts of synderesis and rectitude of the will.[30]

Nature

The infused moral virtues are habits which dispose the faculties of man to follow the dictate of reason illumined by faith in relation to the means which lead to the supernatural end. They do not have God as their immediate object—and in this they are distinguished from the theological virtues[31]—but the honest good distinct from God; yet they rightly ordain human acts to the supernatural end, and in this way they are distinguished from the corresponding acquired natural virtues.[32]

The means which are regulated by the infused moral virtues refer, in a certain sense, to all the acts of man, including (at least on the part of prudence) the very acts of the theological virtues, in spite of the fact that these virtues

[28]Cf. Rom. 8:5-6, 8:15; I Cor. 2:14; Jas. 1:5.

[29]Nevertheless, there are insinuations sufficiently clear in the magisterium of the Church. Thus Pope Innocent III speaks of faith, charity and the other virtues in infants (Denz. 410). Pope Clement V teaches as most probable the opinion which states that at baptism there are infused into infants grace and the virtues (Denz. 483). The *Roman Catechism* of St. Pius V teaches that through baptism there is infused into the soul grace and "the noble cortege of all the virtues" (II, *De sacr. bapt.*, cap. 2).

[30]Cf. St. Thomas, *Summa,* I-II, q. 63, a. 3.

[31]*Ibid.*, q. 62, a. 2.

[32]*Ibid.*, q. 63, a. 4.

are superior in perfection to the moral virtues.[33] For although the theological virtues, considered in themselves, cannot be excessive, and in this sense they do not consist in the mean or medium as do the moral virtues,[34] they can nevertheless go to excess in the manner of our operation, and it is that manner or mode which falls under the moral virtues. So it is that the moral virtues must be numerous, because there are so many ways in which the faculties can operate and these must be regulated in view of man's supernatural end.

Number

St. Thomas establishes a fundamental principle of distinction for the moral infused virtues: "For every act in which there is found a special aspect of goodness, man must be disposed by a special virtue."[35] Accordingly, there will be as many moral virtues as there are species of honest objects which the appetitive faculties can discover as means leading to the supernatural end. St. Thomas studies and discusses more than fifty moral virtues in the *Summa theologiae,* and perhaps it was not his intention to give us a complete and exhaustive treatment.[36]

However, since ancient times it has been the custom to reduce the moral virtues to four principal ones, namely, prudence, justice, fortitude and temperance. They are expressly named in Sacred Scripture, as we have already seen, and are called the virtues most profitable for man in this life.[37] They were also known to the ancient philosophers—Socrates, Aristotle, Plato, Plotinus, Cicero, etc. Among the Fathers of the Church, St. Ambrose is apparently the first to call them cardinal virtues.[38] The scholastic theologians unanimously subdivided the moral virtues on the basis of the four cardinal virtues.

---

[33]Cf. *ibid.,* q. 58, a. 3; q. 66, a. 6.

[34]Cf. *ibid.,* q. 64, a. 4; II-II, q. 17, a. 5, ad 2.

[35]*Ibid.,* II-II, q. 109, a. 2.

[36]The classification of the infused moral virtues made by St. Thomas in his *Summa* is surprisingly similar to the Classifications of the acquired natural virtues which were made by the ancient philosophers such as Socrates, Aristotle and Plato. The philosophers deduced their classifications from a close and penetrating analysis of human psychology. The theologians base their classification on two fruitful principles, namely, that grace does not destroy nature but perfects and complements it, and that God can have no less providence in the supernatural order than in the natural order. As a result, they establish almost a perfect parallelism between the natural and the supernatural orders. This does not mean, however, that there cannot be more infused moral virtues than those which have been enumerated by the theologians.

It is a different matter when treating of the theological virtues. Being strictly supernatural and having no parallel in the natural order or among the acquired virtues, the philosophers ignored them completely. Their existence is known only through divine revelation. In this revelation, however, it is expressly stated that the theological virtues are no more than three in number (I Cor. 13:13).

[37]Cf. Wisd. 8:7. "Moderation" is called "temperance" explicitly in the Douay version.

[38]*Expositio in Lucam* (M.L. 15:1738).

CARDINAL VIRTUES

Nature

The name "cardinal" virtues is derived from the Latin word *cardo,* the hinge of a door. The reason is that on these basic virtues hang all the moral life of man. St. Thomas maintains that these virtues can be called cardinal from two points of view: in a less proper sense, because they are certain general conditions or characteristics necessary for any virtue (in every virtue should shine forth prudence, justice, fortitude and moderation); more properly, so far as they pertain to the special matters in which principally shines forth the general material of the given virtue.[39]

Hence the cardinal virtues are in fact special virtues, not merely genera of virtue which contain or comprise all the other virtues.[40] Consequently, they have their own proper matter, which is constituted by those objects in which those general conditions of all virtue shine forth to a maximum degree. It is true that all the virtues should participate in some way in those four general conditions, but it does not follow from this that every type of discretion will be produced by prudence, all rectitude by justice, all firmness by fortitude and all moderation by temperance. These virtues are those which effect those conditions in a principal manner and, as it were, by antonomasia, but they do not do so exclusively. Other virtues also share in these qualities, although to a lesser degree.

The principality of the cardinal virtues is demonstrated precisely in the influence which they exercise over their neighboring and subordinated virtues, which are like participations derived from the principal virtues, which communicate to the other virtues their mode, their manner of being and their influence. These are called *potential parts* of the cardinal virtue; their role is to function in secondary matters, reserving the principal matter for the corresponding cardinal virtue.[41] The influence of the principal virtue is manifest in the subordinated virtues: he who has conquered the principal difficulty will more easily conquer the secondary one.

In this sense each one of the cardinal virtues can be considered as a genus which contains beneath itself the integral parts, the subjective parts and the potential parts. The integral parts refer to those useful or necessary complements which ought to concur for the perfect exercise of the virtue. Thus patience and constancy are integral parts of fortitude. The subjective parts are the various species subordinated to the principal virtue. Thus sobriety and chastity are subjective parts of temperance. The potential parts are those other annexed virtues which do not have the full force and power of the principal virtue or are ordained to secondary acts. Thus the virtue of religion is annexed to justice because it has to do with rendering to God the cult that is due, al-

[39] *Summa,* I-II, q. 61, a. 4.

[40] This is the teaching of Seneca, Cicero and St. Augustine.

[41] Cf. St. Thomas, *Summa,* II-II, q. 48.

though this cannot ever be done perfectly, because one cannot realize in this matter the condition of equality which is required for strict justice.[42]

But does the principality of the cardinal virtues over the other virtues pertain also to their intrinsic excellence? Evidently not, for religion and penance are more excellent virtues than justice, since their object is more noble. Humility pertains to temperance, but is a more excellent virtue as a *removens prohibens* for all the other virtues.

Nevertheless, it is necessary to preserve the principality of the cardinal virtues as hinges of the others, and they perform their function in a more perfect manner than do the other virtues. Thus commutative justice has more of the reason of justice than do religion or penance; the matter or object of any annexed virtue may be more excellent than that of the principal or cardinal virtue, but the mode of the cardinal virtue is always more perfect.

Number

That there are precisely four cardinal virtues can be proved by various arguments:

By reason of the object. The good of reason, which is the object of virtue, is found in four ways: essentially in reason itself and by participation in the operations and passions, while among the passions there are those which impel to acts contrary to reason and others which withdraw from what reason dictates. Hence there should be a virtue which safeguards the good of reason itself (prudence), another which rectifies external operations (justice), one which goes against the passions which depart from the dictate of reason (fortitude), and one which refrains the disorderly impulses of passion (temperance).[43]

By reason of the subject. There are four potencies of man capable of being subjects of the moral virtues, and in each one of them there should be a principal virtue: prudence in the reason, justice in the will, fortitude in the irascible appetite, and temperance in the concupiscible appetite.

As a remedy against the four wounds of original sin. Thus against ignorance of the intellect is placed prudence; justice is necessary against the malice of the will; against the weakness of the irascible appetite fortitude comes into play; and for the disorder of the concupiscible appetite is the remedy of temperance.

We reserve for a later discussion the treatment of the virtues in particular. For the time being, however, we offer the following schemata of the moral virtues, as treated in the *Summa,* grouped around the principal or cardinal virtue to which they are related. We shall also point out in passing the gift of the Holy Spirit, the fruit of the Holy Spirit, the beatitude which corresponds to the various virtues, and the vices which are opposed to the various virtues.

---

[42]Cf. *loc. cit.*

[43]*Ibid.,* I-II, q. 61, a. 2.

PRUDENCE (II-II, q. 47)

A) INTEGRAL PARTS

- a) considered in itself
  - regarding the past: *memory* (q. 49, a. 1)
  - regarding the future: *understanding* (a. 2)
- b) in its predispositions
  - regarding others: *docility* (a. 3)
  - regarding self: *sagacity* (a. 4)
    reasoning (a. 5)
- c) its right use
  - regarding the end: *foresight* (a. 6)
  - regarding circumstances: *circumspection* (a. 7)
  - regarding obstacles: *caution* (a. 8)

B) SUBJECTIVE PARTS OR SPECIES

- a) for governing oneself: *monastic prudence*
- b) for governing others (prudence of government)
  - in a ruler: *regnative prudence* (q. 50, a. 1)
  - in the subjects: *political prudence* (a. 2)
  - in the family: *domestic prudence* (a. 3)
  - in war: *military prudence* (a. 4)

C) POTENTIAL PARTS (q. 57, a. 6)

- a) for right counsel: *eubulia* (q. 51, aa. 1-2)
- b) for judging according to common rules: *synesis* (a. 3)
- c) for rightly departing from common law: *gnome* (a. 4)

CORRESPONDING GIFT OF THE HOLY GHOST: *counsel* (q. 52, aa. 1-3)

CORRESPONDING BEATITUDE: *mercy* (a. 4)

CONTRARY VICES

- a) manifestly contrary (q. 53)
  - *imprudence* (aa. 1-2)
    - *precipitation* (a. 3)
    - *inconsideration* (a. 4)
    - *inconstancy* (a. 5)
  - *negligence* (q. 54)
- b) false prudence (q. 55)
  - *prudence of the flesh* (aa. 1-2)
  - *craftiness* (a. 3) . . . . .
    - *guile* (a. 4)
    - *fraud* (a. 5)
  - *excessive solicitude* (aa. 6-7)

JUSTICE (II-II, q. 58)

A) INTEGRAL PARTS (q. 79)

a) *do good* (i.e., the good due to another)

b) *avoid evil* (i.e., the evil harmful to another)

B) SUBJECTIVE PARTS OR SPECIES

a) toward the community: *legal justice* (q. 58, aa. 5-6)

b) individually (particular justice)
- of ruler to subjects: *distributive justice*
- among private persons: *commutative justice*

C) POTENTIAL PARTS (q. 80)

a) lack of equality
- toward God: *religion* (q. 81; also *penance* after sin)
- toward parents: *piety* (q. 101)
- toward superiors: *observance* (q. 102)
  - *dulia* (q. 103)
  - *obedience* (q. 104)
- for benefits received: *gratitude* (q. 106)
- for injuries received: *just punishment* (q. 108)

b) lack of strict debt:
- regarding truth: *veracity* (q. 109)
  - in promises *fidelity* (q. 110, a. 3, ad 5)
  - in word and deed: *simplicity* (q. 109, a. 2, ad 4; q. 111, a. 3, ad 2)
- association with others: *affability* (q. 114)
- for moderating love of wealth: *liberality* (q. 117)
- for departing for just cause from letter of the law: *equity* (q. 120)

CORRESPONDING GIFT OF THE HOLY GHOST: *piety* (q. 121, a. 1)

CORRESPONDING BEATITUDE: *meekness* (a. 2)

VICES CONTRARY TO JUSTICE

A) Against justice in general: *injustice* (q. 59)

B) Against distributive justice: *respect of persons* (q. 63)

C) Against commutative justice:

- a) in deed
  - against persons
    - *murder* (q. 64)
    - *mutilation* (q. 65, a. 1)
    - *flagellation* (a. 2)
    - *imprisonment* (a. 3)
  - against things: *theft* and *robbery* (q. 66)
- b) in word
  - in judgment
    - on the part of *judges* (q. 67)
    - on the part of the *accused* (q. 68)
    - on the part of the *guilty* (q. 69)
    - on the part of *witnesses* (q. 70)
    - on the part of *lawyers* (q. 71)
  - outside of judgment
    - *contumely* (q. 72)
    - *defamation* (q. 73)
    - *murmuring* (q. 74)
    - *derision* (q. 75)
    - *cursing* (q. 76)
- c) in voluntary exchanges
  - *fraud* (q. 77)
  - *usury* (q. 78)

D) Against the potential parts of justice

- a) against religion
  - *superstition* (q. 92)
  - *undue worship* (q. 93)
  - *idolatry* (q. 94)
  - *divination* (q. 95)
  - *vain observance* (q. 96)
  - *tempting God* (q. 97)
  - *perjury* (q. 98)
  - *sacrilege* (q. 99)
  - *simony* (q. 100)
- b) against piety
  - *impiety* (q. 101, prologue)
  - *excessive love* (q. 101, a. 4)
- c) against obedience: *disobedience* (q. 105)
- d) against gratitude: *ingratitude* (q. 107)
- e) against just punishment
  - *cruelty*
  - *excessive indulgence* (q. 108, a. 2, ad 3)
- f) against truth
  - *lying* (q. 110)
  - *simulation* and *hypocrisy* (q. 111)
  - *boasting* (q. 112)
  - *irony* (q. 113)
- g) against friendship
  - *adulation* (q. 115)
  - *spirit of contradiction* (q. 116)
- h) against liberality
  - *avarice* (q. 118)
  - *prodigality* (q. 119)
- i) against equity: *legal pharisaism* (q. 120, a. 1, ad 1)

FORTITUDE (II-II, q. 123)

A) ITS PRINCIPAL ACT: *martyrdom* (q. 124)

B) NO SUBJECTIVE PARTS (q. 128) because of its determined matter.

C) INTEGRAL AND POTENTIAL PARTS*

- a) regarding action
  - as to the end: *magnanimity* (q. 129)
  - as to means: *magnificence* (q. 134)
- b) regarding resistance
  - against present evils
    - *patience* (q. 136, aa. 1-4)
    - *longanimity* (a. 5)
  - in the exercise of virtue
    - *perseverance* (q. 137, aa. 1, 2, 4)
    - *constancy* (a. 3)

CORRESPONDING GIFT OF THE HOLY GHOST: *fortitude* (q. 139, a. 1)

CORRESPONDING BEATITUDE: *hunger and thirst for justice* (a. 2)

CONTRARY VICES

- a) to fortitude itself
  - *timidity* or *cowardice* (q. 125)
  - *impassibility* (q. 126)
  - *audacity or rashness* (q. 127)
- b) to magnanimity
  - *presumption* (q. 130)
  - *ambition* (q. 131)
  - *vainglory* (q. 132)
  - *pusillanimity* (q. 133)
- c) to magnificence
  - *meanness* or *niggardliness* (q. 135, a. 1)
  - *wastefulness* (a. 2)
- d) to patience
  - *insensibility*
  - *impatience*
- e) to perseverance
  - *inconstancy* (q. 138, a. 1)
  - *pertinacity* (a. 2)

*These are the same: *integral* parts pertain to dangers of death; *potential* parts pertain to lesser dangers.

TEMPERANCE (II-II, q. 141)

A) INTEGRAL PARTS

a) *shame* (q. 144)

b) *honesty* (q. 145)

B) SUBJECTIVE PARTS OR SPECIES

a) regarding nutrition
- in food: *abstinence* (q. 146)
- in drink: *sobriety* (q. 149)

b) regarding procreation
- temporarily: *chastity* (q. 151)
- perpetually: *virginity* (q. 152)

C) POTENTIAL PARTS

a) regarding delight of touch: *continence* (q. 155)

b) against anger: *meekness* (q. 157)

c) against rigor of punishment: *clemency* (q. 157)

d) modesty
- in esteem of self: *humility* (q. 161)
- in desire for knowledge: *studiosity* (q. 166)
- in bodily movement: *bodily modesty* (q. 168, a. 1)
- in games and diversions: *eutrapelia* (q. 168, a. 2)
- in dress and adornment: *modesty in dress* (q. 169)

CORRESPONDING GIFT OF THE HOLY GHOST: *fear of the Lord* (q. 141, a. 1)

CORRESPONDING BEATITUDE: *poverty of spirit* (q. 19)

CONTRARY VICES

a) against temperance in general
- *insensibility* (q. 142, a. 1)
- *intemperance* (q. 142, aa. 2-4)

b) against abstinence: *gluttony* (q. 148)

c) against sobriety: *drunkenness* (q. 150)

d) against chastity: *luxury* (qq. 153-54)

e) against continence: *incontinence* (q. 156)

f) against meekness: *anger* (q. 158)

g) against clemency: *cruelty* (q. 159)

h) against humility: *pride* (q. 162)

i) against studiosity: *curiosity* and *negligence* (q. 167)

j) against bodily modesty: *affectation* and *rusticity* (q. 167)

k) against eutrapelia: *foolish mirth* and *excessive austerity* (q. 168, aa. 3-4)

l) against modesty of dress: *excessive adornment* (q. 169)

5: THE GIFTS OF THE HOLY GHOST

In general usage, a gift signifies anything that one person gives to another out of liberality and with benevolence.[1] We say "out of liberality" to signify that on the part of the giver a gift excludes any notion of debt or obligation, not only in justice but in gratitude or any other kind of debt. And we say "with benevolence" to signify the intention of the giver to benefit him who receives the gift gratuitously.

The exclusion of all debt of justice or gratitude is necessary by reason of the gift; otherwise there would be no way of distinguishing between a gift and a reward or recompense. Likewise, there should be no need of any compensation or recompense incurred on the part of the one who receives the gift. We are not treating here of a *do ut des* situation but of a completely gratuitous bestowal which exacts nothing in return. A gift is something unreturnable, as St. Thomas says, quoting Aristotle.[2] Nevertheless, the notion of a gift does not exclude gratitude on the part of the one receiving the gift; even more, it sometimes demands the good use of the gift, depending on the nature of the gift and the intention of the giver, as when one gives something in order that the receiver be perfected by its use. Such are the gifts which God bestows on his creatures.

The first great gift of God is the Holy Spirit, who is the very love by which God loves himself and loves us. It is said of the Holy Ghost in the liturgy of the Church that he is the Gift of God.[3] The Holy Ghost is, therefore, the first gift of God, not only as substantial love in the intimate life of the Trinity, but as he dwells in us through the divine mission.

From this first gift proceed all other gifts of God. In the last analysis, whatever God gives to his creatures, both in the supernatural and in the natural order, is nothing more than a completely gratuitous effect of his liberal and

[1]According to A. Gardeil, O.P., in his article on the gifts of the Holy Ghost in the *Dictionnaire de théologie catholique,* a gift is "the gratuitous and benevolent transfer of the ownership of something to another person."

[2]Cf. *Summa,* I-II, q. 68, a. 1, obj. 3.

[3]Cf. *Veni Creator.*

infinite love. In a wide sense, whatever we have received from God is a "gift of the Holy Ghost," but this expression may have various specific meanings:

1) In a wide sense, the gifts of the Holy Ghost are all those gifts of God which do not include that first gift which is the Holy Spirit himself; for example, the natural gifts given by God to his creatures.

2) In a less wide sense, they are the gifts which, without necessarily including that first gift nor presupposing that the soul must be in the state of grace and charity, pertain nevertheless to the supernatural order. Such gifts are principally the *gratiae gratis datae,* actual prevenient graces, servile fear of God, supernatural attrition and unformed faith and hope.

3) In a more proper sense, they are gifts of the Holy Ghost which include the first great gift of God and presuppose or place the soul in the state of grace and friendship with God. For example, sanctifying grace, charity, faith and hope informed by charity, the infused moral virtues, the seven gifts of the Holy Ghost.

4) In the formal and most proper sense, the gifts of the Holy Spirit are those which we are now to study in particular, namely, the seven gifts of the Holy Ghost.[4]

THE GIFTS THEMSELVES

EXISTENCE The existence of the gifts of the Holy Ghost can be known to us only through revelation, since they are supernatural realities which completely transcend the light of natural reason. St. Thomas begins with this supposition in the treatise on the gifts of the Holy Ghost in the *Summa theologiae,* and says that in the doctrine on the gifts we should follow the mode of speaking as found in Sacred Scripture, where they are revealed to us.[5] Let us first investigate the scriptural foundation for the existence of the gifts, and then we shall briefly examine the doctrine of tradition, the magisterium of the Church, and the teaching of theologians.

Sacred Scripture The classical text of Isaias is usually quoted as the scriptural foundation for the doctrine on the gifts of the Holy Ghost: "And there shall come forth

[4]This division is based on the following doctrine of St. Thomas: "Although all natural and gratuitous gifts have been given to us by God through love, which is his first gift, nevertheless, Love himself is not given to us in all these gifts but only in the gift which is a likeness and participation in that love, namely, the gift of charity" (*In I Sent.,* dist. 18, a. 3, ad 4).

[5]Cf. *Summa,* I-II, q. 68, a. 1.

a rod out of the root of Jesse, and a flower shall rise up out of his root. And the spirit of the Lord shall rest upon him: the spirit of wisdom, and of understanding, the spirit of counsel, and of fortitude, the spirit of knowledge, and of godliness. And he shall be filled with the spirit of the fear of the Lord" (Is. 11:1-3). This text is clearly Messianic and properly refers only to the Messias. Nevertheless, the Fathers of the Church and the Church herself have extended the meaning to the faithful of Christ in virtue of the universal principle of the economy of grace which St. Paul enunciated: "For those whom he has foreknown he has also predestined to become conformed to the image of his Son, that he should be the firstborn among many brethren" (Rom. 8:29). From this it is inferred that whatever perfection is found in Christ, our Head, if it is communicable, is found also in his members united to him through grace. And it is evident that the gifts of the Holy Spirit pertain to communicable perfections, if we bear in mind the need we have of them. Hence, since grace is so prodigal in supplying for those things which are necessary, and at least as prodigal as nature itself, we may rightly conclude that the seven spirits which the prophet saw descend and rest upon Christ are also the patrimony of all those who are united to him in charity.[6]

In addition to this text, which the Fathers and the Church have interpreted as a clear allusion to the gifts of the Holy Ghost, authors are wont to cite other texts from the Old and New Testament.[7] We shall omit them, not only because it is not our task here to investigate the true meaning of these texts, but because it seems evident that the use of most of those scriptural texts can lead to nothing but conjectures. It must be admitted that the doctrine on the gifts of the Holy Spirit in Sacred Scripture rests almost exclusively on the text from Isaias, although that text, explained, confirmed and clarified by

[6]The text from Isaias offers no few exegetical problems. P. F. Ceuppens, O.P., made a study of this problem and offered the following conclusions: 1) The gifts really exist and proceed from Yahweh, for the spirit of Yahweh in the Old Testament is not the person of the Holy Ghost but God himself. But since in the New Testament the work of grace is ascribed in a special manner to the Holy Ghost, gradually in patristic theology the Holy Ghost was acknowledged as the author of the gifts. 2) The gifts were conferred on Christ after the manner of habits; but no mention is made in Isaias of the conferral of these gifts on the members or the faithful of Christ. 3) Although the real distinction between the gifts and the infused virtues is nowhere mentioned in Isaias, nevertheless a vestige of the distinction may perhaps be found in the repetition of the word "spirit." 4) It is not explicitly taught either in Isaias or in any other place in Scripture that there are seven gifts of the Holy Ghost. This doctrine was only perfectly expounded in the time of the Scholastics. Cf. *Angelicum,* VI (1928), pp. 525-38.

[7]These are the principal texts cited: Old Testament—Gen. 41:38; Exod. 31:3; Num. 24:2; Deut. 34:9; Judg. 6:34; Ps. 31:8, 32:9, 118:120, 144, 142:10; Wisd. 7:28, 7 and 22, 9:17, 10:10; Sirach 15:5; Is. 11:2, 6:1; Mich. 3:8. New Testament—Lk. 12:12, 24:25; Jn. 3:8, 14:17, 26; Acts 2:2, 38; Rom. 8:14, 26; I Cor. 2:10, 12:8; Apoc. 1:4, 3:1, 4:5, 5:6.

the Fathers of the Church, the magisterium of the Church and scholastic theologians, gives us a firm foundation for the existence of the gifts of the Holy Ghost, not only in Christ, but in each of the faithful in the state of grace. Some theologians believe that the double existence of the gifts is formally revealed in Scripture;[8] others maintain that it is at most a certain conclusion which is *proxima fidei.*

Fathers of the Church

Both the Greek and the Latin Fathers have treated extensively of the gifts of the Holy Ghost under various titles. Among the Greek Fathers the outstanding names are St. Justin, Origen, St. Cyril, St. Gregory Nazianzen and Didymus. Among the Latins, the primacy in this question goes to St. Augustine and St. Gregory the Great, and to a lesser degree to St. Victorinus, St. Hilary, St. Ambrose and St. Jerome.[9] In St. Thomas we find a synthesis and complete summary of their teaching.

Magisterium of the Church

Only one council of the Church speaks expressly of the seven gifts of the Holy Ghost, affirming them of Christ: the Roman Synod held in 382 under St. Damasus.[10] Whether or not the Council of Trent referred to the gifts is still disputed and nothing can be said for certain.

The teaching of the Church is much clearer in the liturgy. In the hymn *Veni Creator* reference is made to the sevenfold gift of the Holy Ghost: *Tu septiformis munere digitus paternae dexterae.* In the Sequence of the Mass for Pentecost the Holy Ghost is asked for his seven gifts: *Da tuis fidelibus in te confidentibus sacrum septenarium.* In the hymn for Matins of the same feast we read: *Solemnis urgebat dies quo mystico septemplici orbis volutus septies signat beata tempora.* And in Vespers another reference is made to the gifts: *Te nunc Deus piisime vultu precamur cernuo illapsa nobis caelitus largire dona Spiritus.*

In the administration of the sacrament of confirmation the bishop prays with hands extended over the faithful to be confirmed: *Emitte in eos septiformem Spiritum Sanctum Paraclytum de caelis. Amen. Spiritum sapientiae et intellectus. Amen. Spiritum consilii et fortitudinis. Amen. Spiritum scientiae*

---

[8]P. Aldama, S.J., believes that the existence of the gifts of the Holy Ghost is not a conclusion elaborated from one premise of faith and another premise of reason, but that it is a conclusion which follows from two formally revealed truths, namely, the existence of the gifts in Christ as the Messias (Is. 11:2) and the statement of St. John that Christ is full of grace and truth and that we all share in that plenitude (Jn. 1:14-16). (Cf. "Los dones del Espíritu Santo," *Revista Española de Teología,* XI [1949], p. 5.)

[9]For a more detailed study of the scriptural and patristic foundations for the doctrine on the gifts, consult Gardeil, "Dons du Saint Esprit," in *Dictionnaire de théologie catholique,* col. 1728 f; Ferrero, *Los dones del Espíritu Santo* (Manila: 1941).

[10]Cf. Denz. 83.

et pietatis. Amen. Adimple eos spiritu timoris tui. . . .[11] Hence the Church, in the solemn moment of the administration of a sacrament, recognizes and applies to each of the faithful the famous Messianic text from Isaias.

The *Catechism of the Council of Trent,* which enjoys great authority among theologians, says that "from these gifts of the Holy Ghost . . . we derive the rules of Christian living, and through them are able to know whether the Holy Ghost dwells in us."[12] In all the Catholic catechisms throughout the world there is a section which treats of the gifts of the Holy Ghost. Lastly, Pope Leo XIII, in his admirable Encyclical *Divinum Illud Munus,* of May 9, 1897, recalls and makes his own the testimony of Catholic tradition on the existence, necessity, nature and marvelous effects of the gifts:

> More than this, the just man, that is to say, he who lives the life of divine grace and acts by the fitting virtues as by means of faculties, has need of those seven gifts which are properly attributed to the Holy Ghost. By means of these gifts the soul is furnished and strengthened so as to be able to obey more easily and promptly his voice and impulse. Wherefore these gifts are of such efficacy that they lead the just man to the highest degree of sanctity; and of such excellence that they continue to exist even in heaven, though in a more perfect way. By means of these gifts the soul is excited and encouraged to seek after and attain the evangelical beatitudes which, like the flowers that come forth in the springtime, are signs and harbingers of eternal beatitude.[13]

Theologians

On the question of the existence of the gifts of the Holy Ghost, the teaching of theologians interests us only as a witness to the tradition of the Church, since they could not create a doctrine which treats of supernatural realities. The theology of the gifts underwent a slow and laborious development through the centuries, but its existence was always universally admitted by all, except for rare exceptions. Today there is no theologian who denies the existence of the gifts of the Holy Ghost, although there is still great discussion concerning their nature and function.

Conclusion

In general, we may conclude with respect to the existence of the gifts of the Holy Ghost, backed by the solid support of Scripture and the testimony of tradition, that we can be absolutely certain of the existence of the gifts of the Holy Ghost in all souls in the state of grace. Even more, there are some theologians of great authority who maintain that the existence of the gifts of the Holy Ghost is an article of faith.[14] Although the Church has not expressly

---

[11] *Rituale Romanum,* c. 9, n. 3.

[12] *Catechism of the Council of Trent* (New York: 1923), Part I, Article VIII, "The Seven Gifts."

[13] Reprinted from the *Tablet* (London) by the America Press (1938), p. 15.

[14] Among them, John of St. Thomas, the greatest of the commentators on the doctrine of Aquinas on the gifts of the Holy Ghost. He says that it is not only *de fide* that these gifts were in Christ and were supernatural, but that it is *de fide* also that these gifts are given to us and are supernatural. Cf. *Cursus theologici,* in I-II, disp. 18, a. 2, n. 4 (Paris: 1885), VI, p. 583.

defined this point, if we consider the constant teaching of the Fathers of the Church through the centuries, the mind of the Church in her liturgy and in the administration of the sacraments, the unanimous consent of theologians, and the sense of all the faithful throughout the world, it would seem that one has sufficient basis for saying that this is a truth of faith proposed by the ordinary magisterium of the Church. Those who would not dare to say this much will at least affirm that it is a theological conclusion that is most certain and *proxima fidei.*

NUMBER OF THE GIFTS

This is another question which is greatly disputed among exegetes and theologians. There are two principal difficulties involved: 1) in Sacred Scripture the number seven is classically interpreted to signify a certain indefinite plenitude; 2) in the Masoretic text of Isaias only six gifts are enumerated, for the gift of piety is not mentioned.

Modern exegetes are inclined to think that the text of Isaias refers to an indefinite plenitude. It is the plenitude of the qualities of government which pertain to the Messias as king.[15] The Fathers and the scholastic theologians, however, insist on the number seven, and on the basis of the sevenfold gift they establish their classifications and parallelisms with the infused virtues. St. Thomas dedicates an ingenious article in his *Summa theologiae* to justify this number.[16]

What are we to think of all this? In our opinion, one should conclude as follows. First of all, it is true that in Scripture the number seven is often used to designate an indefinite plenitude, and perhaps this is the meaning of the passage in Isaias. But one cannot draw from this any conclusive argument against the fact that there are seven gifts of the Holy Ghost. Actually, plenitude may be completely undetermined, and thus mean an indefinite number which is not known exactly; or it may be restricted to a definite number and thus express all the possible realities. According to the interpretation of the Fathers, the teaching of the Church (in her liturgy, in the administration of the sacraments, and in papal encyclicals), and the unanimous consent of theologians, the plenitude expressed by Isaias should be taken in this second sense. Hence, as the sacraments are seven in number and in them is to be found the plenitude of the graces which God grants to men *ex opere operato,* so the gifts of the Holy Ghost, as seven distinct habits, comprise the plenitude of the movements of the divine Spirit which are communicated to us through those gifts.[17]

---

[15]Cf. Ceuppens, *art. cit.,* pp. 526-27.

[16]Cf. *Summa,* I-II, q. 68, a. 4.

[17]This explanation is proposed by Aldama in the *Revista Española de Teología, art. cit.,* p. 26, and in *Sacrae Theologiae Summa* (Madrid: 1956), III, p. 730.

Secondly, as regards the Masoretic text which enumerates only six gifts, nothing can be concluded against the existence of the gift of piety. Various explanations have been offered for this omission in the text,[18] but whatever the reason, it is certain that the gift of piety is mentioned in the Vulgate (which is substantiated by a declaration of the Church which states that there are no dogmatic errors in this version),[19] in the version of the Septuagint, in patristic tradition, in the official teachings of the Church, and in the unanimous teaching of theologians. To prescind from this enormous weight of authority because of certain textual obscurities in the Masoretic text would seem to be excessive. Many things formally revealed in Sacred Scripture did not appear in their fulness except through the interpretations of the Fathers and the magisterium of the Church. Such seems to be the case with the gift of piety. Whatever the text of Isaias, St. Paul marvelously describes that reality which theology recognizes as the gift of piety when he writes to the Romans: "For whoever are led by the Spirit of God, they are the sons of God. Now you have not received a spirit of bondage so as to be again in fear, but you have received the spirit of adoption as sons, by virtue of which we cry: 'Abba! Father!' The Spirit himself gives testimony to our spirit that we are sons of God" (Rom. 8:14-16).

THEIR NATURE

St. Thomas studies the metaphysical nature of the gifts of the Holy Ghost by asking whether they are habits,[20] in order to determine the proximate genus in the essential definition of the gifts. The reply is in the affirmative, and theologians of all schools hold for the same response, with a few notable exceptions. Hugh of St. Victor says that the gifts are like seeds of virtue, a certain preparation for them, after the manner of first movements and aspirations of the soul.[21] Vázquez says that the gifts are actual movements and not habits.[22] Cardinal Billot, who introduced so many innovations in his treatise on the infused virtues, instead of admitting that the gifts are habits, identifies them with actual graces which do not necessarily presuppose the presence of habits in the soul and can be received even by sinners.[23]

Against all these opinions, and in accordance with the doctrine of St. Thomas, we hold the following proposition: *The gifts of the Holy Ghost are strictly supernatural or per se infused habits.*

---

[18]See Ferrero, *Los dones del Espíritu Santo* (Manila: 1941).

[19]Cf. Council of Trent, Sess. IV (Denz. 785); Vatican Council, Sess. III (Denz. 1787).

[20]Cf. *Summa,* I-II, q. 68, a. 3.

[21]Cf. *De sacramentis,* II, p. 13, cap. 2 (M.L. 176: 526).

[22]Cf. *In III,* dist. 44, c. 2, n. 7.

[23]Cf. L. Billot, S.J., *De virtutibus infusis,* q. 68.

That they are strictly supernatural or infused *per se* is evident. Their intimate nature (the formal *quod* and formal *quo* objects in scholastic terminology) transcends completely (*simpliciter*) the powers of nature, so that they cannot be acquired by human efforts. Therefore, either the gifts do not exist or they are necessarily infused by God. The arguments are as follows:

From the teaching of Sacred Scripture. Speaking of the Holy Spirit, the Lord stated: "He will dwell with you, and be in you" (Jn. 14:17). But the Holy Ghost is not in men without his gifts; the gifts also dwell in men, and hence they are not acts or transitory movements but true habits.[24]

By analogy with the moral virtues. The moral virtues dispose the faculties of the soul to follow the rule of reason; therefore, they are habits. The gifts of the Holy Spirit dispose the faculties of the soul to follow the movement of the Holy Ghost; therefore, they also are habits. The gifts of the Holy Ghost fill the same role with respect to the Holy Ghost as the moral virtues do with respect to reason.

By reason of the necessity of the gifts for salvation. The gifts are necessary for salvation; therefore, they must be in the soul permanently, and hence they are habits. That they are necessary for salvation is demonstrated by St. Thomas, as we shall see later. That gifts of this kind are habits is proved by the authority of St. Gregory, who says: "By those gifts without which one cannot obtain life the Holy Ghost always dwells in all the elect, but he does not always dwell by his other gifts."[25]

Psychological argument. The dispositive qualities by which men are habitually moved or can be moved by a principal mover are the habits. But the gifts by definition are dispositive qualities by which man is habitually moved or can be moved by the Holy Ghost. Therefore, the gifts are habits. The major is clear; it expresses the difference between a habit and a simple disposition. The minor follows from the very nature of that kind of motion which is an inspiration of the Holy Ghost, which is proper and characteristic of the gifts.

Against this doctrine, which is of capital importance in the Thomistic synthesis, various difficulties can be raised. Their solution will enable us to see more clearly the nature of the gifts.

First difficulty

There is no reason to multiply things without necessity. But for a man to be moved by the inspiration or instinct of the Holy Ghost an actual grace suffices. Therefore, the gifts are not habits but actual graces.

Response. We concede the major but distinguish the minor. Actual grace is sufficient on the part of the principal mover, we concede; it is sufficient on the part of the soul, we subdistinguish: actual grace suffices where the

[24]Cf. *Summa,* I-II, q. 68, a. 3. This habitual character seems implicit also in Isaias when he says that the spirit of the Lord "shall rest" (*et requiescet*) upon Christ.
[25]Cf. *Moralia,* II, cap. 56 (M.L. 75: 598).

motion is not produced in the manner of a habit, we concede; it suffices where the motion is produced after the manner of a habit, we deny. Therefore, in virtue of these distinctions, we deny the consequence and nexus. We explain as follows: The movement of grace can be considered in two ways: 1) so far as it proceeds from the Holy Ghost, and thus every movement of the Holy Spirit in man can be called and is an actual grace; 2) so far as this movement is received in the soul, and this requires another distinction: a) so far as it is a certain impulse or illumination generically considered which could be granted even to sinners; b) as a special movement so that the soul must have some disposition to receive it and to be moved promptly and easily under its influence. And this again can happen in two ways: i) to be moved in a human manner, according to the rule of reason enlightened by faith (and for this we have the infused virtues); ii) to be moved in the manner of the movement itself, that is, in a divine or superhuman manner, and for this we need the habits of the gifts of the Holy Ghost.

From this it can be seen that Billot incorrectly identifies the movement of the gifts with actual grace. With all due respect, we must reject his theory for the following reasons:

1) Actual grace is required for every act of virtue, even the most imperfect; but the movement of the gifts is not required for every act of virtue. Therefore, they are two distinct things.

2) Actual grace is given even to sinners so that they will be converted; but the movement of the gifts presupposes the state of grace, from which the gifts are inseparable. Therefore, the two cannot be identified.

Second difficulty

The ultimate disposition already corresponds to the form; but the ultimate disposition to receive the movement of the Holy Spirit corresponds to the movement itself. Therefore, the gifts are not required as habits.

Response. It is necessary to distinguish. The ultimate disposition for receiving the movement of the Holy Spirit will correspond with the movement itself *in actu secundo,* we concede; *in actu proximo primo,* we subdistinguish: the disposition produced by the Holy Ghost will be possessed in the form of a habit by infusion, we concede; in the form of an act, we deny. And we explain: Potency bespeaks a relation to act in four ways:

1) *radically,* and in this sense it is nothing other than the nature itself of the subject-agent—in our case the human soul—in which the power or faculty is rooted;

2) *as ordained to the first remote act (actu primo remoto),* and this is the nature endowed with the potency or faculty (for example, the soul endowed with intellect and will);

3) *as ordained to the first proximate act (actu primo proximo),* and this is the nature, not only endowed with the power or faculty, but also with

the habits and dispositions, acquired or infused, to work promptly, with ease and with delight;

4) *as ordained to the second act (actu secundo)*, and this is the very operation or movement of the faculty in question.

Now the disposition for this last operation is certainly bestowed by the movement itself, and is the last disposition. Only in this sense is it said that the ultimate disposition corresponds to the form. In the objection, 3) and 4) were confused. Whence, one can see how violent would be the motion of the Holy Spirit without the habits of the gifts. It would be absolutely possible, but it would be a violent movement for the soul because the soul would have to leap from the *actus primus remotus* (2) to the *actus secundus* (4) without passing through the *actus primus proximus* (3).

Third difficulty

When the motor power of the agent is infinite, no previous disposition is required for movement; but the motor power of the Holy Spirit is infinite. Therefore, previous habits are not necessary in the soul for it to be moved by the Holy Ghost.

Response. We have already admitted that, absolutely speaking, the Holy Spirit could directly move the powers of the soul without the necessity of the habit of the gifts. But this is not the ordinary manner of divine providence, which always works sweetly and desires that men dispose themselves freely to receive the divine inspirations and movements. This question must be resolved on the basis of the fact that the gifts exist—a fact we believe established beyond all doubt. It is not a question of what the Holy Ghost could do, but of what he has done in reality.

The reason for the infusion of the supernatural habits is to make the divine movements connatural, as it were, to the sons of God. God does not wish that the acts of the virtues of the supernatural order be less perfect—even in the mode of their production—than the works of the natural order which proceed from the acquired habits. Let us not forget that man, though moved by God in the supernatural order, is also moved by his own free will; and even though under the movement of the gifts of the Holy Spirit he is led in a much more passive manner than under the influence of the infused virtues, he always remains endowed with free will and never ceases entirely to be an agent, even under the action of the Holy Ghost. For that reason also he must be perfected by the habitual qualities of the gifts.

Fourth difficulty

Man receives from the gifts of the Holy Ghost a perfection which renders him readily moved by the same Spirit; but so far as he is moved by the Holy Ghost, man is converted, in a certain way, into a mere instrument of the Holy Ghost. Therefore, the gifts of the Holy Spirit are not habits, because it is not fitting for an instrument to be perfected by a habit but only the principal agent.[26]

[26] Cf. St. Thomas, *Summa,* I-II, q. 68, a. 3, obj. 2.

Response. This reason is valid for the instrument that is completely inert, which does not move itself, but is moved (as a brush or hammer). But man is not such an instrument; he is moved by the Holy Spirit in such wise that he also moves himself, so far as he is endowed with free will. Therefore, he does need a habit.[27] Whence it follows that the gifts of the Holy Ghost are not purely active habits nor purely passive habits, but rather passive-active. In relation to the divine movement they are receptive or passive habits, but with respect to the vital reaction of the soul they are active habits. To summarize, as man by the acquired virtues is disposed to be readily and easily moved by the dictate of simple natural reason for his naturally good acts, and by the infused virtues to be moved by reason enlightened by faith to supernatural acts in a human mode or manner, so by the gifts of the Holy Spirit the just man is connaturalized, so to speak, for the acts to which he is moved by a special instinct or impulse of the Holy Ghost in a divine or superhuman manner.[28]

GIFTS AND VIRTUES

Until the time of St. Thomas it was not settled whether the gifts were really distinct from the infused virtues or whether there was only a rational distinction between them. But thanks to the marvelous synthesis of Aquinas, the real, specific distinction between the virtues and the gifts has been established. It is true that some theologians will still raise a discordant note, especially among the Scotists, but there are so few exceptions in modern theology that it can be said that the opinion is now unanimous among theologians.

In spite of certain variations in expression, the doctrine of Aquinas is the same in all his writings.[29] He begins by listing certain erroneous opinions and answering them. 1) The gifts are not distinguished from the virtues. But if this be so, why are certain virtues called gifts and others not? 2) The gifts perfect reason; the virtues perfect the will. That would be true if all the gifts were intellectual and all the virtues were affective; but such is not the case. 3) The virtues are ordained to good operations; the gifts are ordained to resist temptation. But in fact the virtues also offer resistance to temptations. 4) The virtues are ordained *simpliciter* to operation; the gifts are ordained to conform us with Christ, and especially in his passion. Yet Christ himself impels us to be conformed to him in humility, meekness and charity; and these are virtues, not gifts.

Having rejected the errors, St. Thomas proceeds to explain the positive doctrine. In the first place he cites St. Gregory, who distinguishes perfectly

---

[27]Cf. *Summa,* I-II, q. 68, a. 3, ad 2.

[28]Cf. J. B. Gonet, O.P., *Clypeus theologiae Thomisticae,* tract. III, *de virtutibus et donis,* disp. I, a. 1, § 1.

[29]Cf. *Summa,* I-II, q. 68, a. 1; *In III Sent.,* dist. 34, q. 1, a. 1; *In Isaiam,* cap. 11; *Ad Gal.,* cap. 5, lect. 8.

the seven gifts from the theological and cardinal virtues. The gifts are represented by the seven sons of Job; the theological virtues are represented by his three daughters; and the cardinal virtues are represented by the four corners of the house.[30] The exegesis of St. Gregory may be dismissed as ingenious, but there can be no doubt of his conviction that the gifts are distinct from the virtues—the point St. Thomas wished to prove. St. Thomas then states that, if we consider simply the name "gifts," we cannot find any difference between the infused virtues and the gifts because they are all gifts received gratuitously from God:

> For that reason, in order to distinguish between the gifts and the virtues, we must be guided by the manner in which Sacred Scripture expresses itself, for we find that the term used there is "spirit" rather than "gift." For it is written thus (Is. 11:2-3): "The spirit of wisdom and of understanding shall rest upon him"; from which words we are clearly given to understand that these seven are there set down as being in us by divine inspiration, and inspiration denotes motion from without.
>
> But it must be noted that in man there is a twofold principle of movement; one within him, namely, the reason, and the other extrinsic to him, namely, God. . . . Now it is evident that whatever is moved must be proportionate to its mover; and the perfection of the mobile as such consists in a disposition whereby it is disposed to be well moved by its mover. Hence the more exalted the mover, the more perfect must be the disposition whereby the mobile is made proportionate to its mover. Thus we see that a disciple needs a more perfect disposition in order to receive a higher teaching from his master. Now it is evident that human virtues perfect man according as it is natural for him to be moved by his reason in his interior and exterior actions. Consequently, man needs yet higher perfections whereby he can be disposed to be moved by God. These perfections are called "gifts," not only because they are infused by God, but also because by them man is disposed to become amenable to the divine inspiration, according to Is. 50:5: "The Lord God hath opened my ear, and I do not resist; I have not gone back." Even the Philosopher says . . . that for those who are moved by divine instinct there is no need to take counsel according to human reason, but only to follow their inner promptings, since they are moved by a principle higher than human reason. This, then, is what some say, namely, that the gifts perfect man for acts which are higher than acts of virtue."[31]

Differences

There is no need to add any commentary to this clear exposition of the doctrine, but we shall investigate further the reasons for the specific difference between the virtues and the gifts. To do this, we need only list the common characteristics of the virtues and the gifts and then point out their differences.

The principal common properties are the following:

1) They are generically the same because both are operative habits.

2) They have the same efficient cause, namely, God, and therefore they are both infused *per se* and are totally supernatural.

---

[30]Cf. St. Gregory, *Moralia,* I, cap. 27 (M.L. 75: 544).

[31]*Summa,* I-II, q. 68, a. 1.

3) They have the same subject *in quo*: the human faculties.

4) They have the same material object (*materia circa quam*): all moral matter.

5) They have the same final cause (remote end): the supernatural perfection of man, incipient in this world and consummated in the world to come.

The following are the differences between the virtues and the gifts:

First

1) *By reason of the motor cause.* As habits, the virtues and the gifts have the same efficient cause, namely, God, the author of the supernatural order. But the motor cause or principle is completely distinct. In the virtues it is human reason (for the infused virtues, reason illumined by faith and under the previous motion of God through an actual grace). The gifts, on the other hand, are under the motor principle of the Holy Ghost, who moves the habits of the gifts as his direct and immediate instruments. For that reason the habits of the infused virtues can be used when we please, presupposing an actual grace, but the gifts of the Holy Spirit are actuated only when he wishes to move them.

Second

2) *By reason of the formal object.* As is known, the formal object is that which properly specifies an act or a habit. Habits and acts may have in common the same two extrinsic causes (efficient and final) and even the same material cause (which is a generic element and not specific), but if they differ by reason of their formal object, the habits must be classed as specifically distinct, though they agree in all other respects. This is precisely what happens with the infused virtues and the gifts of the Holy Ghost. They have, as we have seen, the same efficient cause, final cause and material cause, and yet their specific difference is evident by reason of the distinction between their formal objects.

The formal object may be considered under a double aspect: a) that by which the act is constituted in its proper nature and is distinct from every other act by reason of a determined aspect or reason (*objectum quo; ratio sub qua*); b) that which is a terminus of the act or habit under the precise aspect of being (*objectum quod*). For example, the act of stealing has for its formal constitutive object (*objectum quo*) the taking of something which is another's—it is this which is its formal cause and essentially constitutes this act an act of stealing. The formal terminative object of this act (*objectum quod*) is the object taken, the thing of another as such. Let us now apply these notions to the questions of the gifts and the infused virtues.

The terminative formal object (objectum formale quod). The terminative formal object of human acts, considered as moral, is the honest good, in contradistinction to the useful or delightful good which, as such, cannot be a norm of morality. Under this aspect the gifts do not differ from the virtues, for both tend to the honest good. But this honest good has two aspects, depending on whether it comes under this dictate of reason illumined by faith or the rule of the Holy Ghost. But this aspect falls into the area of the *formal quo* object or the *ratio sub qua,* which is the properly differentiating element and specifying element.

The constitutive formal object (objectum quo). The formal object *quo* or *ratio sub qua* is totally distinct in the infused virtues and in the gifts. In the infused virtues the proximate and immediate rule is human reason enlightened by faith, so that an act is good if it is in accord with this dictate and evil if it departs from it. In the gifts, on the other hand, the proximate and immediate rule of action is the Holy Spirit himself, who directly governs and moves the gifts as his instruments, impressing on them his direction and causing the acts to be produced for divine reasons which surpass even the level of reason illumined by faith.

Thus the acts of the gifts proceed from a formal motive which is completely distinct. This argues for a specific distinction between the gifts and the virtues, for habits are specified by their acts and acts are specified by their formal objects. Hence specifically distinct objects evoke specifically distinct acts, and these latter correspond to specifically distinct habits.

Third

3) *By reason of the human and divine mode.* This difference necessarily follows from the foregoing. An operation must be of the same mode as the motor cause which impels it and the norm or rule to which it is adjusted. Since the infused virtues have man as their motor cause and reason illumined by faith as their rule, they necessarily impress their acts or operations with a human mode. On the other hand, and for the same reasons, since the gifts have as their motor cause and as their rule or norm the Holy Ghost, their acts must be vested with a mode which corresponds to their motor cause and norm, namely, a divine or superhuman mode.

From this third difference flow two conclusions of exceptional importance in ascetical and mystical theology: 1) the radical imperfection of the infused virtues by reason of the human mode of their operation and the inevitable necessity that the gifts come to their aid to give them a divine mode of operation, without which the infused virtues can never reach full perfection; 2) the impossibility of an operation of the gifts of the Holy Spirit in a human mode or manner, whereas their divine mode is precisely an element of specific differentiation between the virtues and the gifts. An operation of the gifts *modo humano* would be a contradiction.

Fourth

4) *By reason of human will and divine will.* We can use the infused virtues when we wish, but the gifts of the Holy Spirit operate only when he wishes. These latter habits are not under our control as regards use, and the reason is clear. All the habits which are under the control of reason are subject to our will as to their exercise because they are our

acts in every sense of the word.[32] But the gifts are habits which confer on the soul only the facility to be moved by the Holy Ghost, who is the unique motor cause in those operations; the soul can do no more than co-operate in these operations or movements, though it does so consciously and freely, by not placing any obstacle and by seconding the impulse of the Holy Spirit with its own docility.

In the actuation of these habits, we do no more than dispose ourselves (for example, by restraining the tumult of the passions, affection for creatures, distractions and phantasms which impede God's action, etc.), so that the Holy Ghost can move us as and when he pleases. In this sense we may say that our acts are the dispositive causes for the actuation of the gifts. That is what St. Teresa of Avila means when she says: "The first kind of prayer I experienced which seems to me supernatural I should describe as one which cannot, in spite of all our efforts, be acquired by industry or diligence; but we can certainly prepare for it, and it must be a great help if we do."[33] It is therefore necessary that the subject dispose himself so that the gifts may operate in him, not by a proper and formal disposition (for that is conferred by the gifts themselves), but by ridding oneself of the impediments (*sicut removens prohibens* or *causa per accidens*) to the end that this docility to the Holy Spirit can become real by passing into action and not be merely potential by the simple possession of the gifts of the Holy Ghost. Moreover, in a certain sense our actions can also be a meritorious cause for the actuation of the gifts, although in a remote manner, in the sense that by our supernatural acts we can merit the increase of grace, of the infused virtues, and of the gifts of the Holy Spirit as habits. And in the measure that the gifts of the Holy Ghost grow in perfection, they will be more readily actuated and will operate with greater intensity and will, in turn, conquer and resist more easily the obstacles or impediments, much as fire more quickly consumes dry wood than wet wood. But however great the degree of habitual perfection which the gifts may attain in us, their actuation will always be entirely beyond the scope of our powers and free will. The Holy Spirit will actuate them when and as he wishes, and we shall never do so of our own account.

Fifth

5) *By reason of activity and passivity.* This difference also follows from the first difference between the virtues and the gifts. In the exercise of the infused virtues, the soul is fully active; its acts are produced in a human manner or mode, and the soul is fully conscious that it works

[32]It goes without saying that our actions are always under the divine premotion, and in the case of the infused virtues an actual grace is required for their exercise.

[33]Cf. *Spiritual Relations,* Relation V.

when and how it pleases. The soul is the motor cause of its own acts, though always under the general divine motion of an actual grace. The exercise of the gifts is entirely different. The Holy Spirit is the unique motor cause of the gifts, and the soul passes to the category of a simple recipient, though conscious and free. The soul reacts vitally on receiving the motion of the gifts, and in this way we preserve freedom and merit under the operation of the gifts, but the soul merely seconds the divine motion, whose initiative and responsibility belong entirely to the Holy Ghost. And the action of the gifts will be the more pure and perfect as the soul succeeds in seconding the divine motion with greater docility, without trying to divert it by movements of human initiative, which would be to impede or obstruct the sanctifying action of the Holy Ghost.

It follows from this that the soul, when it feels the action of the Holy Ghost, should repress its own initiative and reduce its activity to seconding the divine movement. It is passive only in relation to the divine agent; but it can be said that the soul works also that which is worked in it, it produces what is produced in it, it executes what the Holy Spirit executes in it. It is a question of activity received,[34] of an absorption of the natural activity by a supernatural activity, of a sublimation of the faculties to a divine order of operation. And this has absolutely nothing to do with the sterile inactivity of Quietism.

Such are the principal differences between the infused virtues and the gifts of the Holy Ghost. The first two establish the radical and specific differences between the virtues and the gifts; the other three are no more than logical consequences of the first two.

MODE OF OPERATION

The next question which merits our attention is the possibility of a double mode of operation in the gifts of the Holy Ghost. The question has been answered in the affirmative by a few theologians who oppose the common theological teaching.[35] The only reason we treat of the matter is because some have tried to quote the authority of St. Thomas as holding for the double mode of operation.

The thought of St. Thomas on this question is clear: he has repeatedly affirmed that one of the most characteristic notes of difference between the

---

[34]Cf. St. Thomas, *Summa,* II-II, q. 52, a. 2, ad 1.

[35]Father Crisógono de Jesús Sacramentado (*Compendio de ascética y mística* [Avila: 1933], pp. 21-24; *San Juan de la Cruz, su obra cientifica y literaria* [Avila: 1929], I, pp. 115-17) mentions the following in support of his doctrine: Cardinal Billot, Nicholas of Jesus-Mary, Joseph of Jesus-Mary and Denis the Carthusian. As far as we can see, only Joseph of Jesus-Mary states explicitly that there is a double mode of operation for the gift of wisdom.

virtues and the gifts is their distinct mode of operation.[36] The distinct mode of operation is necessitated intrinsically by the distinct formal objects and the distinct rules or measures which are followed. The virtues operate in a human manner or mode, following the rule of reason enlightened by faith; the gifts operate in a divine manner or mode under the impulse of the Holy Ghost. How, then, could anyone affirm on the authority of Aquinas that the gifts could also operate in a human manner or mode?[37]

But even prescinding from the authority of St. Thomas, which is definitive in spiritual theology,[38] and examining the matter objectively, it seems clear to us that it is impossible to defend a human mode of operation in the gifts of the Holy Ghost. In the first place, it would be superfluous and would multiply things without necessity. Why should we postulate a human mode of operation for the gifts when we have at our disposal the activity of the infused virtues? Are they not supernatural *quoad substantiam* and do they not operate *modo humano?* Then why multiply entities without necessity?

Moreover, the fact that the gifts have a formal object and a motor cause which are divine makes it impossible for the gifts to operate in a human mode. St. Thomas states clearly: "The mode of a thing is taken from its measure. Hence the mode of operation is taken from the rule or measure of the action. Therefore, since the gifts are meant to operate in a divine mode, it follows that the operations of the gifts are measured by another rule than the rule of human virtue, which is the divinity participated by man in such a way that he does not operate humanly but as God by participation. Therefore, all the gifts share in this measure of operation."[39]

[36]Especially in his *Commentary on the Sentences,* St. Thomas insists on this fundamental distinction: "The gifts are distinguished from the virtues in this, that the virtues perform their acts in a human mode and the gifts in a superhuman mode" (*In III Sent.,* dist. 34, q. 1, a. 1). "[The gifts] are above the virtues so far as they act in a superhuman mode" (*ibid.,* ad 1). "Therefore, since the gift does not surpass the virtue except by reason of its mode" (*ibid.,* ad 5). "It is not necessary that the gifts be more perfect than the virtues as regards all conditions, but according to their mode of operation which is above the human mode" (*ibid.,* dist. 35, q. 2, a. 3). "The gift transcends the virtue in this, that it operates in a superhuman mode, which mode is caused by a higher measure than the human measure" (*ibid.,* dist. 36, a. 3). Cf. also *ibid.,* q. 1, aa. 2 and 3.

[37]As to the objection that St. Thomas wrote his *Commentary on the Sentences* as a young man and therefore this does not necessarily represent his mature thought, the same doctrine is taught in the *Summa theologiae.* De Guibert contended that St. Thomas changed his teaching, but he was answered definitively by Garrigou-Lagrange. Cf. F. Joret, O.P., in *Bulletin Thomiste,* I (1925), pp. 245-248. For St. Thomas' teaching in the *Summa,* see I-II, q. 68, a. 2, ad 1; II-II, q. 139, a. 1; I-II, q. 69, a. 3; see also *De caritate,* a. 2, ad 17.

[38]"Asceticae mysticaeque theologiae capita si quis pernosse volet, is Angelicum in primis doctorem adeat oportebit," Pope Pius XI, *Studiorum ducem, A.A.S.,* XV (1923), p. 320.

[39]*In III Sent.,* dist. 34, q. 1, a. 3, resp.

The reason for the error on the part of those who favor a human mode of operation for the gifts is their belief that the mode of the gifts' operation is something accidental and does not affect their intimate nature. They do not seem to realize that it is a question of an essential mode, imposed by the formal constitutive object of the very essence of the gifts, which is the divine rule to which they are accommodated.[40] Consequently, to deprive the gifts of this essential divine mode is to destroy the gifts. If the formal reason of being of the gifts is the adjustment to the divine rule or measure, one cannot deprive the gifts of this mode of operation without incurring a contradiction. Either the operation of the gifts is adjusted to this divine rule or it is not. If it is adjusted, we have the divine mode of operation; if it is not adjusted, it cannot be an act of the gifts, because it lacks the formal constitutive (*objectum formale quo* or *ratio sub qua*) for the gifts.

In the second place, if the gifts of the Holy Spirit could have an operation in the human mode, this operation would be specifically distinct from its operation in the divine mode. But it is elemental in philosophy that two specifically distinct operations argue by ontological necessity for two specifically distinct habits, for habits are distinguished by their operations and these latter are distinguished by their objects.[41] But if the gifts are habits, and could have an operation in the human mode specifically distinct from the operation in a divine mode, it would inevitably follow that one and the same habit had two acts that are specifically distinct. To admit this, it would be necessary to reject the most fundamental principles of philosophy.

The reason for the confusion in this second argument is the inability to distinguish between the material object and the formal object of a habit.[42] It is true that one and the same habit may treat of many material objects which are specifically distinct. For the act of theft it is immaterial whether one steal a loaf of bread, a watch or a sum of money. These things are specifically distinct, but they all constitute the same material object of the act. The formality of these things, that which specifically constitutes theft, is that they are the property of another. Thus one and the same habit may produce many acts which are materially distinct if considered in their physical entity, but are not at all distinct if considered in their moral entity and formally. The formal object must always be one because it is the formal object which specifies a habit. To give food to the hungry or to clothe the naked are materially distinct acts, but formally they are both the result of the one habit or virtue of mercy. The

[40]Cf. St. Thomas, *loc. cit.*

[41]A diversity of objects according to species causes a diversity of acts according to species and consequently a diversity of habits" (St. Thomas, *Summa,* I-II, q. 54, a. 1, ad 1).

[42]"In the distinction of potencies or habits the object is not to be considered materially but in its formal aspect as differing specifically or even generically" (St. Thomas, *Summa,* I-II, q. 54, a. 2, ad 1).

material object does not bespeak any relation to the habit, but only the formal or constitutive object.[43]

Final argument

As a final argument, let us reduce the contrary position to a practical conclusion. Any actuation of the gifts of the Holy Spirit which would destroy the nature and finality of the gifts is theologically absurd. But the actuation of the gifts in a human mode would destroy the nature and finality of the gifts. Therefore, it is theologically absurd.

According to the doctrine of St. Thomas (and this is a point admitted by all the schools of theology) the gifts of the Holy Spirit are supernatural habits which, moved by the direct and immediate impulse of the Holy Ghost as his instruments, have as their finality the perfection of the infused virtues. There is no disagreement or discussion among theologians on this point. But the operation of the gifts in a human mode would destroy the supernatural nature and finality of the gifts.

First, it would destroy their nature, for if the gifts of the Holy Spirit could operate in a human mode, it would follow logically and inevitably that in that human modality we could actuate the gifts at will, with the help of ordinary grace; for the human mode of operation, even when it touches the supernatural, is connatural to us; it does not transcend the rule of reason enlightened by faith. But if a habit with two specifically distinct operations is unintelligible in philosophy, an actuation of the gifts of the Holy Spirit produced by man himself with the aid of ordinary grace would be a monstrosity in theology. All theologians admit the impossibility of our actuation of the gifts at our own good pleasure; in each case there is required a special impulse of the Holy Spirit independent of all human initiative. This requires that the gifts be direct and immediate instruments of the Holy Ghost.

But there is more. If the gifts could operate in a human mode, in that human modality they would cease to be direct instruments of the Holy Spirit and would become instruments of man or of the soul in grace, as are the infused virtues.

Secondly, according to St. Thomas the gifts have as their finality the perfection of the acts of the infused virtues. But an operation of the gifts *modo humano* would be completely incapable of attaining this end, especially as regards the theological virtues, in whose perfect development Christian perfection consists. For the theological virtues, as St. Thomas teaches,[44] are in themselves more perfect than the gifts, and if they need the gifts to attain full perfection, the reason lies in the fact that, since all the infused virtues are actuated *modo humano,* it is necessary for this human element to disappear and be replaced by the divine and totally supernatural mode conferred by the

[43]Cf. St. Thomas, *ibid.,* a. 4.
[44]Cf. *Summa,* I-II, q. 68, a. 8.

gifts, the mode which enables the virtues to operate mystically. Only then will the infused virtues produce perfect acts, completely divine, as befits their supernatural nature. But if the gifts worked in a human mode, they would contribute nothing to the perfection of the virtues. Their acts would continue to be imperfect and in a human mode. Hence, however we look at the question, it is evident that the gifts of the Holy Spirit do not have and cannot have anything but a superhuman and divine mode of operation. This their nature demands as direct and immediate instruments of the Holy Ghost.

NECESSITY OF THE GIFTS

We shall here establish three propositions of which the first is the most important in mystical theology.

First proposition

The gifts of the Holy Spirit are necessary for the perfection of the infused virtues.

The general argument is simple and clear. The gifts are necessary for the perfection of the infused virtues, if these have certain defects which cannot be corrected by themselves but only under the influence of the gifts. But this is precisely the case with the infused virtues. Therefore, the gifts are necessary for the perfection of the infused virtues.

The major premise is evident. If the virtues cannot of themselves correct certain imperfections which accompany them and if these imperfections disappear under the activity of the gifts, it is evident that the gifts are necessary for the perfection of the infused virtues. What must be proved is the minor premise.

Above all, we should not forget that the infused virtues are habits, and it is necessary to examine the types of imperfection which can be found in habits and see which of these, if any, are found in the infused virtues. There are five principal sources of imperfection in any given habit:

1) When a habit does not attain its complete material object. Such is the case of the student of theology who has not yet studied certain tracts. He knows something of theology and he has the habit of theology, but incompletely and imperfectly.

2) When the habit lacks the intensity by which it should attain its object. E.g., the student who has gone over an entire assignment, but superficially and carelessly.

3) When the habit is weakly rooted in the subject (e.g., through lack of sufficient use).

These three imperfections are found in the infused virtues but can be corrected by the virtues themselves. They do not need the influence of the gifts to be extended to new objects, to increase in intensity, or to multiply their acts.

4) By reason of an intrinsic imperfection, essential to the habit itself. This occurs, for example, in the habit of faith (*de non visis*) and hope (*de non*

possessis). Neither the virtues themselves nor the gifts can correct these imperfections without destroying the virtues themselves.

5) Because of the disproportion between the habit and the subject in which it resides. This is precisely the case with the infused virtues. The infused virtues are supernatural habits, and the subject in which they are received is the human soul, or, more exactly, its powers and faculties. But according to the axiom, *quidquid recipitur ad modum recipientis recipitur,* the infused virtues, on being received into the soul, are degraded, so to speak, and acquire our human mode of operation, because of their accommodation to the psychological operations of man. This is the reason why the infused virtues, in spite of being much more perfect in themselves than the corresponding acquired virtues, do not give us the facility in operation which we obtain from the acquired virtues. This is clearly seen in the sinner who repents and confesses after a life of sin; he could easily return to his sins in spite of having received all the infused virtues with grace.

Now it is evident that if we possess imperfectly the habit of the infused virtues, the acts which proceed from them will also be imperfect unless some superior agent intervenes to perfect them. This is the purpose of the gifts of the Holy Ghost. Moved and regulated, not by human reason, as are the virtues, but by the Holy Ghost, they bestow on the virtues, and especially the theological virtues, that divine atmosphere which they need in order to develop all their supernatural virtuality.[45]

This necessity is also seen from the formal motive which impels the act of the infused virtues. As long as the object or motive does not surpass human reason, even enlightened by faith, it will always be an imperfect motive—even though materially the act is the same as that of the gift of the Holy Ghost. This does not mean that the infused virtues are imperfect in themselves; on the contrary, they are most perfect realities, strictly supernatural and divine. In fact, the theological virtues are more perfect than the gifts of the Holy Ghost.[46] But we possess them imperfectly by reason of the human modality which inevitably attaches to them because of their accommodation to the natural psychological functions under the control of simple reason enlightened by faith. Hence the imperfection of the infused virtues is not in themselves, but in the imperfect mode with which we possess them. From this flows the necessity for the gifts of the Holy Spirit to come to the aid of the infused virtues, disposing the faculties of our soul to be moved by a superior agent, the Holy Ghost, who will actuate them in a divine mode, in a mode completely proportioned to the most perfect object of the infused virtues. Under the influence of the gifts, the infused virtues will be, so to speak, in their proper *milieu.*

---

[45]Cf. St. Thomas, *Summa,* I-II, q. 68, a. 2.

[46]Cf. *loc. cit.*

DOCTRINAL PRINCIPLES

Of all the infused virtues, those which most need the aid of the gifts are the theological virtues, in which Christian perfection essentially and principally consists when they have reached their full development. By their very nature they demand the divine mode of the gifts. These virtues give us a participation in the supernatural knowledge which God has of himself (faith) and of his very love of himself (charity), and make us desire him for ourselves as our supreme good (hope). These lofty objects, absolutely transcendent and divine, are necessarily constrained to a modality that is human as long as they remain under the rule and control of reason, even though enlightened by faith. They demand, by their own divine perfection, a regulation or rule which is also divine—that of the gifts. This is the argument used by St. Thomas to prove the necessity of the gifts for salvation: "But as regards the supernatural end, to which reason moves man so far as it is somehow and imperfectly informed by the theological virtues, the motion of reason does not suffice unless it receive in addition the prompting or motion of the Holy Spirit, according to Rom. 8:14: 'Whoever are led by the Spirit of God, they are the sons of God.'"[47]

This argument is also valid for the infused moral virtues. Although they do not transcend the rule of reason as regards their immediate objects (since they do not refer immediately to the supernatural end but to the means to the end), they are ordered to a supernatural end and receive from charity their form and their life in that transcendent order.[48] Therefore, to be perfect, they must receive a divine mode which will adapt and accommodate them to this orientation to the supernatural end. Therefore, the gifts embrace all the matter of the infused virtues, both theological and moral.[49]

Objections

We shall complete this proposition by answering the principal objections. First objection:

How can the gifts perfect the theological virtues when they are inferior to the theological virtues?[50]

Response: They cannot perfect the theological virtues intrinsically and formally but only extrinsically, by remedying the imperfection of the subject in which the virtues reside. The gifts elevate the subject to the divine plane which is proper to the theological virtues and thus give man a full and perfect possession of them. They eliminate the human mode of operation and bestow a divine mode. Hence the gifts do not perfect the theological virtues as such, but the faculties in which those virtues reside. It follows from this that the gifts are necessary for Christian perfection. Without them, the infused virtues, especially the theological, could develop in all their virtuality but would always remain imperfect in their operations—not by any defect

[47]*Loc. cit.*

[48]St. Thomas, *Summa,* I-II, q. 65, a. 2; II-II, q. 23, aa. 7, 8.

[49]*Ibid.,* I-II, q. 68, a. 4.

[50]Cf. *ibid.,* a. 8.

of the virtues, but because of the subject in which they reside. In this sense the theological virtues have a special need of the corresponding gifts, because their inherent supernatural perfection demands a divine modality which only the gifts can bestow.

Second objection:

In order that the infused virtues be developed and perfected, it is sufficient that their acts be produced with ever increasing intensity. But this can be effected by an actual grace, independent of the gifts. Therefore, the gifts are not required for the perfection of the virtues.

Response: Actual grace, accommodating itself to the human mode of the infused virtues, will make them develop in the line of this human modality, but for them to rise above this human modality (which will always be an imperfect mode) and to acquire the divine modality which corresponds to the essence of the infused virtues, there is required a new habit capable of receiving directly and immediately the movement of the Holy Ghost. This human reason can never achieve even under the impulse of an actual grace.[51]

Third objection:

But cannot the Holy Spirit directly produce in the infused virtues the divine mode of operation without recurring to the gifts?

Response: If we admit that the Holy Ghost would exert violence on the rational creature and make it depart from its connatural mode of action without first bestowing on it the necessary dispositions for receiving a higher modality, the answer is yes. But if otherwise, the answer is no. This is the reason so often alleged by St. Thomas to prove the necessity of the infused virtues: the suavity and facility of divine providence, which moves all things according to their proximate dispositions, natural or supernatural. For the rest, this objection has to be answered in view of the doctrine on the existence of the gifts of the Holy Ghost, which we have already demonstrated.

We conclude, therefore, that the gifts of the Holy Spirit are necessary in order that the infused virtues reach their full perfection and development, and this opinion is commonly admitted by all the schools of Christian spirituality. Now let us consider the second proposition, which is much more difficult to prove, although of less importance for mystical theology.

Second proposition

The gifts of the Holy Ghost are necessary for salvation.

The Angelic Doctor expressly asks this question and answers in the affirmative. In order to prove his answer, he emphasizes the imperfection with which we possess the infused virtues, as we explained in the preceding proposition.

> The gifts are perfections of man by which he is disposed to be amenable to the promptings of God. Hence in those matters where the promptings of

[51]Cf. John of St. Thomas, *Cursus theologici,* in I-II, disp. 18, a. 2.

reason is not sufficient and there is need for the prompting of the Holy Spirit, there is consequently a need for a gift.

Now man's reason is perfected by God in two ways: first, with its natural perfection, namely, the natural light of reason; secondly, with a supernatural perfection, the theological virtues. And though this latter perfection is greater than the former, the former is possessed by man in a more perfect manner than the latter; for man has the former in his complete possession, but he possesses the latter imperfectly, because we know and love God imperfectly. But it is evident that anything that possesses a nature or a form or a virtue perfectly can of itself work according to them (although not excluding the operation of God, who works interiorly in every nature and in every will). But that which possesses a nature or form or virtue imperfectly cannot of itself work unless it be moved by another. Thus the sun, which possesses light perfectly, can shine of itself; but the moon, which has the nature of light imperfectly, sheds only a borrowed light. Again, a physician who knows the medical art perfectly can work by himself, but his disciple, who is not yet fully instructed, cannot work by himself unless instructed by him.

Accordingly, in matters subject to human reason and directed to man's connatural end, man can work through the judgment of his reason; and if a man receives help even in these things by way of special promptings from God, it will be out of God's superabundant goodness. Therefore, according to the philosophers, not everyone who had the acquired moral virtues had also the heroic or divine virtues. But in matters directed to the supernatural end, to which reason moves insofar as it is in a manner and imperfectly informed by the theological virtues, the movement of reason does not suffice, unless there be present in addition the prompting and movement of the Holy Ghost. This is in accord with Rom. 8:14: "Whoever are led by the Spirit of God, they are the sons of God"; and in Ps. 142:10 (Douay) it is said, "Thy good Spirit shall lead me into the right land," because no one can ever receive the inheritance of that land of the blessed unless he be led and moved thither by the Holy Ghost. Therefore, in order to accomplish this end, it is necessary for man to have the gifts of the Holy Ghost.[52]

To many theologians this doctrine has seemed excessive, but that is because they confuse the question *de jure* with the question *de facto*. As a matter of fact, many are saved without any operation of the gifts of the Holy Ghost, but never without the habits of the gifts.[53] But this is completely *per accidens* and in no way compromises the general thesis. In the development of the Christian life the actuation of the gifts, more or less intense, is morally and sometimes physically necessary in order to preserve grace, and in this sense

---

[52]*Summa*, I-II, q. 68, a. 2.

[53]For example, baptized infants who die before the use of reason are saved without the operation of the gifts but not without possessing them as habits. The same is true of those who repent at the hour of death and die immediately after, and those who live a lukewarm life (without any actuation of the gifts) but die in the state of grace. The virtues can perform acts imperfectly without the assistance of the gifts, and if no difficult occasions arise which demand the aid of the gifts, this suffices for salvation, although it will be *quasi per ignem*, as St. Paul says (I Cor. 3:15).

the actuation of the gifts would be necessary for salvation. Such is the case of the martyr; either he makes a heroic act of fortitude in giving his life for his faith (which can scarcely be realized without the help of the gift of fortitude to make this most difficult act possible), or he commits a mortal sin by apostatizing. There are many other cases in which one must perform a heroic act of virtue or lose sanctifying grace. The reason is given by St. Thomas: the insufficiency of human reason, enlightened by faith, to lead us to the supernatural end without obstructions.

But there is still another reason, based on the corruption of human nature as a consequence of original sin. The infused virtues do not reside in a sound nature but in a nature inclined to evil, and although the virtues have sufficient power to conquer all temptations opposed to them, they cannot *de facto* overcome some of them without the help of the gifts, especially those violent temptations which arise unexpectedly. In those circumstances in which resistance or a fall are a decision of the moment, a man cannot depend on the slow deliberation and discursus of reason but must act quickly, as if by a supernatural instinct, that is, under the influence and movement of the gifts of the Holy Ghost. Without this movement of the gifts, a fall is almost certain, granted the vicious inclination of human nature wounded by original sin. It is true that these situations are not usually frequent in the life of a man, but it does not follow from this that the gifts of the Holy Spirit are not necessary for salvation, even though they may not be necessary for each and every salutary act.

Third proposition

The gifts of the Holy Ghost are not necessary for each and every salutary act.

This question seems to have arisen in modern times by reason of a false interpretation of the doctrine of St. Thomas as stated in the *Summa,* I-II, q. 68, a. 2, ad 2. There are some who hold for the necessity of the gifts for every salutary act,[54] and they base their opinion on the citation which follows: "By the theological and moral virtues man is not so perfected in relation to the supernatural end that he does not always need to be moved by the instinct of the Holy Ghost." But what St. Thomas seems to mean here is that man is not so perfected by the theological and moral virtues that he does not need, at times, to be inspired by the interior Master. The word *semper* can have two meanings: always and in every instant (*semper et pro semper*), and always but not in every instant (*semper sed non pro semper*). Undoubtedly, St. Thomas is using the word in the second sense. We admit that the text is obscure and difficult to translate, but the thought of the Angelic Doctor is clear if we keep in mind the general context of the article as a whole and the doctrine of the *Summa.* The following are the proofs of the proposition as stated:

[54]Among the authors who hold for the necessity of the gifts for every salutary act are Lehmkuhl, Cardinal Manning, Gaume and Pierrot.

DOCTRINAL PRINCIPLES

1) St. Thomas says in this article that the gifts are necessary because without them we know and love God imperfectly. Then without the gifts we do know and love God—even though imperfectly. Therefore, the gifts are not necessary for every salutary act.

2) Without the gifts, human reason cannot avoid all folly, ignorance and other defects (cf. *loc. cit.,* ad 3). But the fact that it cannot avoid all defects implies that human reason can avoid some. Therefore, the gifts are not necessary for every act of virtue. On the other hand, it is certain that one can perform a supernatural act of faith with the help of an actual grace and without any help from the gifts. Such is the case of a Christian in the state of mortal sin, who has lost the gifts of the Holy Spirit together with sanctifying grace and charity and can nevertheless make acts of supernatural faith under the impulse of an actual grace.[55]

We conclude, therefore, that the gifts are not necessary for each and every salutary act, but they are necessary in the general course of life for perfect acts and to conquer certain grave and unexpected temptations which could put one's salvation in jeopardy.

RELATIONS OF THE GIFTS

AMONG THEMSELVES

St. Thomas studies the mutual relations of the gifts in three articles of his *Summa,* in which he asks whether the gifts are conveniently enumerated in the famous text of Isaias;[56] what is the connection of the gifts;[57] and what is the order of dignity or excellence among the gifts.[58]

Enumeration

Basing his answers on the authority of Isaias 11:2, St. Thomas finds the enumeration of the gifts a fitting one. In the body of the article he sets up a parallelism between the moral virtues and the gifts and concludes that in all the faculties of man which can be principles of human acts the gifts of the Holy Spirit must correspond with the virtues. It should be noted, however, that St. Thomas changes his mind in the II-II when he treats of the classification of the first four gifts,[59] and also assigns corresponding gifts to the theological virtues, something he had not done in the I-II, where the classifi-

[55]On this question see A. Gardeil, O.P., in the article "dons" in the *Dictionnaire de théologie catholique,* col. 1779.

[56]*Summa,* I-II, q. 68, a. 4.

[57]*Ibid.,* a. 5.

[58]*Ibid.,* a. 7.

[59]Cf. q. 8, a. 6., where St. Thomas expressly states that he has changed his opinion.

cation is made only by analogy with the intellectual and moral virtues.[60] His definitive classification is as follows:

- in reason
  - to penetrate the truth: *understanding*
  - to judge rightly
    - of divine things: *wisdom*
    - of created things: *knowledge*
    - of practical conduct: *counsel*
- in the appetitive power
  - in relation to others (God, parents, country): *piety*
  - in order to oneself
    - against fear of danger: *fortitude*
    - against disorderly concupiscence: *fear of the Lord*

Their connection

St. Thomas proves there is a connection among the gifts of the Holy Spirit by pointing out that, as the virtues perfect the faculties of the soul to enable them to be governed by reason, so the gifts perfect those faculties to enable them to be governed by the Holy Ghost. But as the Holy Spirit is in us through sanctifying grace and charity, it follows that he who is in charity possesses the Holy Ghost together with his gifts. Therefore, all the gifts are connected with charity, as the moral virtues are all united in the virtue of prudence. Without charity, it is not possible to possess any of the gifts; nor is it possible to lack them if one has charity.

Their excellence

As it appears in the Vulgate, the enumeration of the gifts is as follows: 1) wisdom; 2) understanding; 3) counsel; 4) fortitude; 5) knowledge; 6) piety; 7) fear of the Lord. St. Thomas says that Isaias places wisdom and understanding as the first *simpliciter*; but counsel and fortitude are placed before the others because of the matter which they treat and not because of their principles and their acts. By reason of their proper acts, the gifts would be classified as follows:

- in the contemplative life
  - wisdom, understanding, knowledge, counsel — corresponding to the intellectual virtues
- in the active life
  - piety, fortitude, fear of the Lord — corresponding to the moral virtues

[60]This does not mean that in the I-II the gifts are not considered to be related to the theological virtues; on the contrary, St. Thomas expressly states that "all the gifts pertain to these three virtues, like certain derivations from the aforesaid virtues" (q. 68, a. 4, ad 3), but he prescinds from them in making his classification. For that reason he corrects himself in the II-II.

As regards the matter treated, the ordering is that of Isaias, with the following distribution:

- regarding arduous things
  - wisdom
  - understanding
  - counsel
  - fortitude
- regarding common things
  - knowledge
  - piety
  - fear of the Lord

GIFTS AND VIRTUES

In Article 8 which follows the treatment of the relations among the gifts themselves, St. Thomas inquires whether the virtues are to be preferred to the gifts. He answers with a distinction. The gifts are more perfect than the intellectual and moral virtues, but the theological virtues are more perfect than the gifts. His argument is simple. With respect to the theological virtues which unite man to the Holy Ghost, his mover, the gifts are what the moral virtues are with respect to the intellectual virtues, which perfect reason as the motor principle of human acts. Consequently, as the intellectual virtues are more perfect than the moral virtues which they regulate and govern, so the theological virtues are more perfect than the gifts which they regulate.[61] But if we compare the gifts with the other virtues, intellectual and moral, the gifts are more perfect, for they perfect the faculties of the soul to follow the impulse of the Holy Spirit, while the virtues perfect the human reason or the other faculties to follow the impulse of reason. It is manifest that to the more perfect motor principle correspond more perfect dispositions in the one moved.

The following conclusions follow from this particular article:

1) The gifts are to the theological virtues what the moral virtues are to the intellectual virtues.

2) The theological virtues are more perfect than the gifts because they have God himself as their immediate object, while the gifts refer only to docility in following the inspirations of the Holy Ghost. But the gifts are superior to the intellectual and moral virtues because through them we are ruled by the Holy Spirit, whereas through the virtues we are ruled by reason.

3) By the gifts the faculties of the soul are perfectly prepared and disposed to follow the impulses of the Holy Ghost.

4) The intellectual and moral virtues precede the gifts in the order of generation or disposition, because if man is well disposed to follow the dictates of reason, he is prepared and disposed to receive the divine motion of the gifts.

[61]Cf. *Summa,* I-II, q. 68, a. 4, ad 3.

St. Thomas studies the beatitudes and the fruits of the Holy Ghost at great length,[62] but we shall limit ourselves to summary observations. This will suffice for our purpose, but not on that account is the reader dispensed from a careful study of the beautiful text in the *Summa*. We shall first consider the fruits, which are more perfect than the gifts but not as perfect as the beatitudes.

GIFTS AND FRUITS

When the soul corresponds with docility to the interior movement of the Holy Ghost, it produces acts of exquisite virtue which can be compared to the fruit of a tree. Not all the acts which proceed from grace have the characteristic of fruits, but only those which are mature and exquisite and possess a certain suavity or sweetness. They are simply acts which proceed from the gifts of the Holy Ghost.[63]

They are distinguished from the gifts as the fruit is distinguished from the branch and the effect from the cause. They are also distinguished from the beatitudes in the degree of perfection, the beatitudes being more perfect and more finished than the fruits. Therefore, all the beatitudes are fruits, but all the fruits are not beatitudes.[64] The fruits are completely contrary to the works of the flesh, since the flesh tends to sensible goods, which are beneath man, while the Holy Spirit moves us to those things which are above.[65]

As regards the number of the fruits, the Vulgate enumerates twelve. But in the original Pauline text only nine are mentioned: charity, joy, peace, longanimity, affability, goodness, faith, meekness and temperance. St. Thomas says, in full agreement with St. Augustine,[66] that the Apostle had no intention of enumerating all the fruits but wished only to show what type of fruits are produced by the flesh and what are produced by the Spirit; hence he mentions some of them by way of example. Nevertheless, St. Thomas adds, all the acts of the gifts and the virtues can in some way be reduced to the fruits enumerated by the Apostle.[67]

BEATITUDES

Still more perfect than the fruits are the beatitudes. They signify the culmination and definitive crown of the Christian life on earth. Like the fruits, the beatitudes are acts and not habits.[68] Like the fruits, they flow from the virtues and the gifts,[69] but they are such perfect acts that we must attribute them

[62]Cf. *Summa*, I-II, qq. 69, 70.

[63]Yet they are not exclusively from the gifts, since they may also proceed from the virtues. According to St. Thomas, those virtuous acts in which the soul finds spiritual consolation are fruits of the Holy Spirit. Cf. *Summa*, I-II, q. 70, a. 1, ad 1; a. 2.

[64]Cf. *ibid.*, I-II, q. 70, a. 2.

[65]*Ibid.*, a. 4.

[66]Cf. *loc. cit.*, a. 3, ad 4; a. 4.

[67]Cf. *loc. cit.*

[68]*Ibid.*, q. 69, a. 1.

[69]*Loc. cit.*, ad 1.

more to the gifts than to the virtues.[70] In spite of the rewards which accompany them, they are an anticipation of eternal beatitude here on earth.[71]

In the Sermon on the Mount, our Lord reduces the beatitudes to eight: poverty of spirit, meekness, tears, hunger and thirst for justice, mercy, purity of heart, peace and persecution for justice' sake.[72] We may also observe that the number is a mystical number which indicates something without limits. St. Thomas dedicates two articles to the exposition of the eight beatitudes and their corresponding rewards. The following is a brief summary and schema of the relationship among the virtues, gifts and beatitudes as set down by St. Thomas.[73]

	Virtues	*Gifts*	*Beatitudes*
Theological	Charity	Wisdom	Peacemakers
	Faith	Understanding	Pure of heart
		Knowledge	Those who weep
	Hope	Fear	Poor in spirit
Moral	Prudence	Counsel	The merciful
	Justice	Piety	The meek
	Fortitude	Fortitude	Hunger and thirst for justice
	Temperance	Fear (secondarily)	Poor in spirit

The eighth beatitude (persecution for justice' sake) is not listed because, as the most perfect of all, it contains and embraces all the others amidst the greatest difficulties and obstacles.[74]

DURATION OF THE GIFTS

The question is whether the gifts terminate with this life or whether they remain in glory. St. Thomas answers the question with a distinction. Considered in their essence, that is, so far as they perfect the faculties of the soul to follow the movements of the Holy Ghost, the gifts remain in glory in a most perfect manner, since in heaven we shall be completely docile to the movements of the Holy Spirit and God will be our all in all, as St. Paul says.[75] But if we

---

[70] *Ibid.*, q. 70, a. 2.
[71] *Ibid.*, q. 69, a. 2.
[72] Cf. Matt. 5:3-10.
[73] Cf. *Summa*, I-II, qq. 68-69; II-II, qq. 8, 9, 19, 45, 52, 121, 139 and 141, ad 3.
[74] *Ibid.*, I-II, q. 69, a. 3, ad 5.
[75] Cf. I Cor. 15:28.

consider the matter of the gifts, it will disappear in part, because in heaven there no longer exists such matter nor is there any reason for it to exist. For example, the gift of fear will be changed to reverential fear before the greatness and immensity of God, and the same thing, *mutatis mutandis,* will happen to those gifts which pertain to the active life, which will have ceased in heaven.[76]

From this article we should note especially: 1) Man is moved more perfectly by the gifts as he more perfectly subjects himself to God. In glory we shall be moved most perfectly by the gifts because we shall be most perfectly subjected to God. 2) The active life terminates with the life on earth;[77] therefore, the works of the active life will not be matter for the operations of the gifts in heaven, but all of those gifts will be preserved in their proper acts as referring to the contemplative life, which is the life of the blessed.

SUMMARY

The gifts of the Holy Ghost are seven supernatural habits, really distinct from the infused virtues, by which man is disposed fittingly to follow in a prompt manner the direct and immediate inspiration of the Holy Spirit in a mode which is superior to the human mode of operation and toward an object or end which the virtues (*hic et nunc*) cannot attain by themselves. For this reason the gifts are necessary for salvation. The gifts are more perfect than the intellectual and moral virtues but not as perfect as the theological virtues from which they are derived and by which they are regulated. They are connected among themselves and with charity in such wise that he who possesses charity possesses all the gifts, and he who does not have charity cannot possess any of the gifts. The gifts will perdure in glory in a most perfect manner. The gifts of wisdom and understanding are the most perfect. The others can be ordered in various ways, according to whether one attends to their proper acts or the matter which they treat. The habitual and perfect rule of the gifts prevails when the soul is habitually and perfectly subject to God. The gifts produce certain exquisite acts called the fruits of the Holy Ghost and certain works which are still more perfect and are called beatitudes.

We reserve a detailed study of each of the gifts for a later part of this work, where we shall be able to give it a more practical and concrete orientation. It suffices here to point out that with the gifts the supernatural organism is complete. Sanctifying grace is the principle and foundation of this organism, the infused virtues its faculties or powers, and the gifts of the Holy Ghost are instruments of perfection in the hands of the divine Artist.

[76]St. Thomas, *Summa,* I-II, q. 68, a. 6.
[77]Cf. *loc. cit.,* obj. 3.

6: SUPERNATURAL GROWTH

Leaving for a later treatment the discussion of the particular means for growing in perfection, we shall here discuss the fundamental laws of the growth of the supernatural organism of sanctifying grace, the virtues and the gifts of the Holy Ghost. Can sanctifying grace increase and develop in us? What is the efficient cause of this increase? What are the laws which govern the growth of the supernatural organism? How is this growth effected? We shall answer these questions in the form of definite conclusions.

FIRST CONCLUSION

Sanctifying grace is meant to increase and develop in our souls.

The proof of this conclusion can be stated simply. Sanctifying grace is, according to St. John (I Jn. 3:9), the seed of God. This seed is sown in the soul in the sacrament of baptism. Therefore, by its very nature, sanctifying grace is meant to increase and develop in the soul.

SECOND CONCLUSION

God alone is the efficient cause of the increase of our supernatural life.

Any living thing that has not yet reached its full perfection and development can, under normal circumstances, grow and increase until it attains that plenitude. In the natural order our bodily organism increases and grows by its own proper development, that is, it evolves by its natural powers and is increased by the incorporation of new elements of the same order. Our supernatural life cannot grow in this way. Grace is by its nature static and inert, and it must grow in the way in which it was born. But grace is born in us through a divine infusion; therefore, it cannot increase except by new divine infusions. Our natural powers would strive in vain to increase grace; they are completely impotent to effect any increase, even with the help of actual grace. Only from without can the soul receive new degrees of that divine being which is grace, and only God can produce those degrees of grace in the soul.

We can see the same truth from another point of view. Habits cannot be actuated—and consequently they cannot develop and be perfected—except by the same principle that caused them. But grace, the infused virtues and the gifts are supernatural habits caused by God alone. Therefore, only God can actuate them and increase them.

Hence the action of God is the principal efficient cause of the growth of the supernatural life. The soul in grace can merit that increase under certain specified conditions, as we shall see, but as to the increase itself, only God can cause it.[1] It is clear that the action of God as the direct and immediate cause of the increase of the infused habits is not arbitrary, but is subject to the laws and conditions which the divine will has designed to determine and establish.

SUPERNATURAL GROWTH

3) *Ordinarily, the increase of grace is produced in two ways: ex opere operato by the sacraments, and ex opere operantis by supernatural meritorious acts and by the impetratory efficacy of prayer.*[2]

THIRD CONCLUSION

Let us examine each of these elements separately: the sacraments, merit, and prayer.

THE SACRAMENTS

It is a truth of faith that the sacraments instituted by Christ confer grace *ex opere operato,* that is, by their own intrinsic power, independently of the subject.[3] The Council of Trent specifically states: "If anyone says that through the sacraments of the New Law grace is not conferred *ex opere operato,* but that faith alone in the divine promise suffices to obtain grace, let him be anathema."[4]

Let us recall briefly the theological doctrine on the sacraments. It is of faith that the sacraments of the New Law contain and confer grace on all those who receive them worthily. As the Council of Trent says: *"omnibus non ponentibus obicem."*[5] Baptism and penance confer the first infusion of grace; the other five sacraments confer an increase of the grace already possessed. For that reason

[1]Cf. St. Thomas, *Summa,* I-II, q. 92, a. 1, ad 1.

[2]On the sacraments, see the Council of Florence, Decree for the Armenians (Denz. 695 and 698) and the 6th canon on the sacraments of the Council of Trent (Denz. 849); on good works, the Council of Trent, Decree on Justification, Chap. 10 (Denz. 803) and canons 24 (Denz. 834) and 32 (Denz. 842); on prayer, see St. Thomas, *Summa,* II-II, q. 83, aa. 15-16.

[3]It is understood, of course, that this is true as long as no obstacle is placed to the reception of grace (cf. Council of Trent, Sess. VII, canons 6 and 7; Denz. 849-50). In other words, the subject must have the proper dispositions for the worthy and fruitful reception of a sacrament. The sacraments of the living require the state of grace; the sacraments of the dead require supernatural attrition.

[4]Sess. VII, canon 8 (Denz. 851).

[5]*Loc. cit.*

the first two sacraments are called sacraments of the dead; the other five are called sacraments of the living, since they presuppose supernatural life in the soul. Nevertheless, at times the sacraments of the dead may produce an increase of grace *per accidens,* and the sacraments of the living may sometimes confer the first infusion of grace *per accidens.* This would happen in the case of those who receive the sacraments of baptism or penance when they are already justified by charity or perfect contrition, or in those who, in good faith and with supernatural attrition, receive a sacrament of the living without knowing that they are in mortal sin.[6]

In equal circumstances, the sacraments produce a greater or less infusion of grace according to the greater or less dignity of the sacrament.[7] The reason for this is that a more noble cause produces a more noble effect. We say "under equal conditions," however, because an inferior sacrament received with a greater intensity of fervor may produce a greater grace than a sacrament of greater dignity received with little devotion. One and the same sacrament will produce the same degree of grace in all who receive it with identical dispositions, but will produce greater grace in those who have better dispositions.[8]

The last two conclusions are very important in practice. Sometimes too much insistence is placed on the *ex opere operato* effect of the sacraments, as if that were the only effect or as if everything depended on that exclusively. One should not lose sight of the fact that in the reception of a sacrament the effect *ex opere operato* is conjoined with the effect *ex opere operantis* or with the dispositions of the one who receives the sacrament.[9] Therefore, in practice

[6]Cf. St. Thomas, *Summa,* III, q. 72, a. 7, ad 2; *In IV Sent.,* dist. 9, q. 1, a. 3; dist. 23, q. 1, a. 2.

[7]That some sacraments have greater dignity than others has been expressly confirmed by the Council of Trent, Sess. VII, canon 3 (Denz. 846).

[8]Cf. St. Thomas, *Summa,* III, q. 69, a. 8. The Salmanticenses conclude from this doctrine that not only does he receive a greater grace who receives a sacrament with a more intensive disposition, but *a fortiori* he who receives it with a more perfect but less intensive disposition. For example, if two people in the state of grace receive Communion, one with an attrition of four degrees and the other with a contrition of two degrees, the latter receives greater grace because contrition, although in the given case more weak, is a more perfect disposition than attrition, although the attrition was more intense. Cf. Salmanticenses, *De sacramentis in communi,* dist. 4, n. 127.

[9]We should not forget that the Council of Trent, speaking of the justification of the sinner (Decree on Justification, Chap. 7), refers to the supernatural dispositions of the recipient as a fundamental element for determining the degree or measure of that justification: "We are truly called and are just, receiving justice within us, each one according to his own measure, which the Holy Spirit distributes to each one as he wills (I Cor. 12:11), and according to each one's disposition and co-operation" (Denz. 799). This occurs in the first justification, and *a fortiori* it will occur in the sacraments of the living, which presuppose in the soul the elements necessary for supernatural merit *de condigno.*

it is of great importance that the recipients of the sacraments make a careful preparation and cultivate an intensity of fervor. The example of the vessel and the fountain is classical. The amount of water contained in the vessel depends not only on the fountain but also on the size of the vessel. The vessel of our soul is widened by the intensity of our fervor or devotion.

SUPERNATURAL MERIT

This is a most important question in the spiritual life. St. Thomas studies it at great length in various parts of his works, and in the *Summa theologiae* he dedicates an entire question (I-II, q. 114) of ten articles to the subject. We shall summarize his doctrine here.

Nature and kinds

Merit signifies the value of an act which makes it worthy of a reward. "*Actio qua efficitur ut ei qui agit, sit justum aliquid dari.*"[10] There are two types of merit: condign merit (*de condigno*), which is based on reasons of justice, and congruous merit (*de congruo*), which is not founded on justice or even pure gratitude, but on a certain fittingness by reason of the act and a certain liberality on the part of him who recompenses. Thus the agent has a strict right (*de condigno*) to the wage which he has merited by his act, while the person who has done us a favor is entitled (*de congruo*) to our grateful recompense. Condign merit is further divided into merit in strict justice (*ex toto rigore justitiae*) and not of strict justice (*ex condignitate*). The first requires a perfect and absolute equality between the act and the reward, and in the supernatural order this type of merit is proper to Jesus Christ exclusively. The second presupposes only an equality of proportion between the good act and the reward, but because God has promised to recompense those good acts, the reward is owing in justice.[11] Moreover, some theologians further divide congruous merit into fallible congruous merit (if it bespeaks an order to a reward solely on the title of fittingness) and infallible conguous merit (if to this fittingness is added a promise by God to bestow the reward).[12]

Elements of merit

Man cannot, by his natural powers alone, produce acts that are meritorious for eternal life.[13] No one can merit supernaturally except in virtue of a free gift of God; hence merit presupposes grace.[14] But so far as it proceeds from

[10]Cf. St. Thomas, *In IV Sent.*, dist. 15, q. 1, a. 3, ad 4.
[11]Cf St. Thomas, *Summa,* I-II, q. 114, a. 1.
[12]Cf. V. Zubizarreta, O.C., *Theologia Dogmatico-Scholastica* (Bilbao: 1937), III, n. 304.
[13]Cf. St. Thomas, *Summa,* I-II, q. 109, a. 5.
[14]Cf. *ibid.*, q. 114, a. 2.

grace, the meritorious act bespeaks an order to eternal life through a merit based on justice.[15] It is of faith that the just man can by his good works merit an increase of grace and, consequently, an increase of the infused habits (the virtues and the gifts of the Holy Spirit) which accompany grace, as well as eternal life and an increase of glory. Thus canon 32 of the Decree on Justification of the Council of Trent expressly states: "If anyone say that the good works of the justified man are the gifts of God in such a way that they are not also the good merits of him who is justified; or that, by the good works which are done by him through the grace of God and the merit of Jesus Christ (whose living member he is), the one justified does not truly merit increase of grace, eternal life and the attainment of that eternal life (if he dies in grace), and even an increase of glory: let him be anathema" (Denz. 842).

Merit always presupposes liberty, and where there is no freedom there can be no merit or demerit. But a free act, if ordered to God, can be meritorious. "Our acts," says St. Thomas, "are meritorious so far as they proceed from free will moved by God through grace. Whence every human act that falls under the freedom of the will, if related to God, can be meritorious."[16]

It does not matter for merit—at least *per se*—what type of act is performed; what matters is the motive and manner of doing it.[17] Whence it follows that a materially insignificant act performed with ardent charity solely to please God is of itself much more meritorious than a great deed realized with less charity or for a less perfect motive. For that reason supernatural merit is especially evaluated by the virtue of charity. The intensity of the love of God with which an act is performed determines the degree of merit. The merit of the other virtues depends on the greater or less influence which charity has in the production of their acts. "Eternal life consists in the fruition of God. But the movement of the soul toward the fruition of the divine good is the proper act of charity, through which all the acts of the other virtues are ordained to this end, since all the other virtues are imperated by charity. Therefore, the merit of eternal life pertains in the first place to charity and secondarily to the other virtues so far as their acts are imperated by charity."[18]

There is yet another reason: the acts performed under the impulse of charity are more voluntary because they proceed from love. For that reason also they are more meritorious. "It is likewise evident that what we do out of love we do with the greatest voluntariness. Whence also on the part of the voluntariness

[15]Cf. *ibid.*, a. 3.

[16]*Ibid.*, II-II, q. 2, a. 9.

[17]Cf. St. Thomas, *De veritate,* q. 24, a. 1, ad 2: "Opus meritorium a non-meritorio non distat in quid agere, sed in qualiter agere."

[18]St. Thomas, *Summa,* I-II, q. 114, a. 4.

which is required for merit it is evident that merit pertains especially to charity."[19]

Increase of charity

In order that the actual growth or increase of charity be effected, a more intense act is required than the habit which is actually possessed. "Charity does not actually increase by any act of charity whatever. But any act of charity disposes for an increase of charity, so far as by an act of charity a man becomes more prompt to continue working through charity, and as this disposition increases, the man breaks forth in a more fervent act of charity through which he strives to grow in charity, and then charity is actually increased."[20] This more intense act logically presupposes a previous actual grace which is also more intense.

Notice the practical importance of this doctrine. If properly understood, it is one of the most efficacious means of combatting slothfulness and tepidity in the service of God. Without acts which are constantly more fervent, our supernatural life can become practically paralyzed (at least on the score of supernatural merit, since other laws govern the sacraments) even when we live in the state of grace and perform many good works, but with tepidity and indifference. An example will clarify this point. With the increase of grace and the other infused habits, something occurs which is similar to an increase on the scale of a thermometer. If a thermometer, which now registers 72 degrees, is to register 76 or 78 degrees, it is necessary that the surrounding air or water rise to that degree. If there is no rise in the surrounding element, the thermometer will not register an increase. The same thing occurs in regard to the increase of the habits. Since this increase is nothing more than a greater radication in the subject, it is impossible that an increase be effected without a more intense act. To use another simile, this more intense act is like the more powerful stroke of the hammer which drives the nail of the habit more deeply into the soul.

But must we then conclude that remiss acts, those performed with tepidity, indifference and with less intensity, are of no value whatever in the supernatural life? We must answer with a distinction. As regards the essential increase of the degree of grace which is actually possessed and of the degree of essential glory in heaven, those acts are completely sterile and useless. The degree of grace does not increase nor does the degree of glory in heaven, which corresponds to the degree of grace on earth. Nevertheless, these acts serve two purposes: first, the soul will not become cold and thus predispose itself for mortal sin which would rob it of grace,[21] and secondly, the soul gains

[19]*Loc. cit.*

[20]*Summa,* II-II, q. 24, a. 6.

[21]Note that this coldness refers only to the dispositions of the soul and not to the degree of grace formerly achieved, which never diminishes but can only be destroyed completely by a mortal sin. Short of mortal sin, the degree of grace already attained never diminishes.

by them in heaven an increase of accidental glory, which is, as Báñez says, the reward of a created good and not of an infinite good.[22]

Objects of merit

No one can merit the first grace for himself, nor final perseverance, nor the grace to rise again from a serious fall.[23] But one can merit the first grace for another, although only by a merit *de congruo*.[24] The reason for the first three assertions is based on the theological axiom that the principle of merit does not fall under merit. This is evident as regards the first assertion, because without grace one cannot merit grace; otherwise the natural would have a claim on the supernatural, which is absurd and heretical.[25] As to final perseverance, it is an infallible effect of predestination to glory, which is totally gratuitous. And the third assertion is also evident, because the nature of merit depends on the supernatural divine motion, which would be cut off by the grave sin. The reason why one can merit the first grace for another is pure congruence. Since the just man and friend of God does God's will, it is reasonable, according to the laws of friendship, that God should comply with man's desire for the salvation of another.

No one, however just and perfect, can merit for himself the actual efficacious graces by a strict or condign merit, but we can all merit them by congruous merit: infallibly by prayers which have the proper qualifications, and fallibly by good works. The reason for the first statement is the famous axiom cited (the principle of merit does not fall under merit), for the actual graces conservative of grace pertain to the same grace as a principle of merit.[26] The reason for the second statement is the divine promise to grant us infallibly whatever is necessary for our salvation if we ask for it in prayer that is humble, confident and presevering.[27] Our simple good works do not have this special promise, given in view of prayer, and for that reason their merit is only congruous and fallible. If God grants it, it will be out of pure mercy,

[22]Cf. *In IIam IIae*, q. 24, a. 6.

[23]Cf. St. Thomas, *Summa*, I-II, q. 114, aa. 5, 9, 7.

[24]Cf. *ibid.*, a. 6.

[25]Cf. the condemnation of the contrary assertions of Bàius (Denz. 1021, 1023, 1024, 1026), Frohschammer (Denz. 1671), etc.

[26]Cf. St. Thomas, *Summa*, I-II, q. 114, a. 9. In this regard John of St. Thomas says: "Principium meriti non potest cadere sub meritum; sed auxilium et motio divina qua aliquis movetur a Deo ut non succumbat tentationibus nec gratiam interrupat per peccatum tenet se ex parte principii meriti quia auxilium et motio est principium operandi, et in hoc solum consistit quod moveat ad opus; igitur non potest cadere sub meritum." "Conservatio est continuatio primae productionis . . . unde qui mereretur auxilia continuativa gratiae, seu perseverantiam, consequenter mereretur ipsam continuationem principii meriti, quod est gratia secundum quod se tenet ex parte Dei moventis ad conservandum. . . . Quod probat non posse sub meritum cadere motionem divinam, non quamcumque, sed quatenus est conservativa gratiae quae est principium merit." Cf. *Cursus theologici*, in I-II, q. 114, a. 9, nn. 1 and 4, and the Salmanticenses on the same article, nn. 89-109.

[27]Cf. Matt. 7:7; Jn. 16:23.

since the works do not merit it of themselves, nor has he promised to give it to us in view of good works.

The difficulty encountered in the performance of a work does not increase the merit of the work, except perhaps indirectly and *per accidens* as a sign of greater charity in undertaking the work. Merit is determined by the goodness of the work in itself and by the motive which impels us to perform the work. As St. Thomas points out: "The good is of much greater importance for the basis of merit and virtue than is the difficult. Whence it does not follow that whatever is more difficult is more meritorious, but only that which, besides being more difficult, is also better."[28]

The reason is that the principle of merit is in charity. Therefore, it is more meritorious to perform easy works with a great degree of charity than to accomplish very difficult works with a lesser degree of charity. Many lukewarm souls carry a great cross with little merit, while the Blessed Virgin, with her ardent charity, merited more by her simplest and smallest acts than all the martyrs together in the midst of their torments.

Temporal goods can also be merited *de condigno,* so far as they are useful for gaining eternal life.[29]

Necessary conditions

The necessary conditions of merit are outlined below:

- CONDIGN
  - On the part of the work
    - a *positive* act[30]
    - a *morally good* act
    - a *free* act (without freedom the act would not be human and voluntary)
    - a *supernatural* act (proceeding from grace and charity)
  - On the part of the one meriting
    - that he be a *wayfarer* (in the next world one cannot merit)
    - that he be *just* and a *friend* of God
  - On the part of God
    - the *acceptance* of the work for the reward which he has promised
- CONGRUOUS
  - Strict—same as above
  - Broad—same as above, *except*
    1) state of grace[31]
    2) promise on part of God as rewarder.[32]

[28]*Summa,* II-II, q. 27, a. 8, ad 3; cf. I-II, q. 114, a. 4, ad 2; II-II, q. 123, a. 12, ad 2; q. 155, a. 4, ad 2; q. 182, a. 2, ad 1; q. 184, a. 8, ad 6.

[29]Cf. St. Thomas, *Summa,* I-II, q. 114, a. 10.

[30]Cf. *ibid.,* q. 71, a. 5, ad 1: "Meritum non potest esse sine actu sed peccatum potest esse sine actu." The omission of an evil act is not meritorious as such.

[31]Cf. St. Thomas, *Supplementum,* q. 14, a. 4.

[32]This promise is necessary for merit which is infallible, but not for merit *de congruo* which is fallible.

Revival of merit

Merits which are destroyed by mortal sin revive and are of value for an eternal reward when the sinner is restored to sanctifying grace. But according to the more probable opinion, merit does not always revive in the same degree as was possessed before the mortal sin, but according to the actual dispositions of the subject when he recovers sanctifying grace, and this will be either in an inferior, an equal or a greater degree.[33]

Note well the great practical importance of this doctrine. It is a pure illusion, besides being a grave imprudence, for the sinner who sins with the greatest of ease to think that after the sin he can recover everything he has lost by means of penance. Apart from the fact that God could deny him the grace of repentance (without which it would be absolutely impossible for him to leave his state of sin), it is likely that he will rise from his sin with a degree of sanctifying grace which is less than he previously possessed. It is very difficult for one to make a more intense act of repentance with powers that have been weakened by sin. This presupposes an actual grace which is more intense than that by which he made himself unworthy through the commission of sin.

PRAYER

St. Thomas assigns four distinct values to prayer: satisfactory, meritorious, impetratory and a certain spiritual delight. While we are most interested in pointing out the impetratory value of prayer, we must first say a word about the other three values.

EFFECTS

The satisfactory value of prayer is evident. It is clear not only from the fact that it always presupposes an act of humility and subjection to God, whom we have offended by our sins which are rooted in pride, but also because prayer springs from charity, the source of all satisfaction for sin. Finally, a prayer well made is of itself a difficult task for imperfect souls, by reason of the attention and firmness of will which it requires; hence it is also satisfactory as regards the difficulty involved.[34] The Council of Trent expressly mentions the satisfactory value of prayer.[35]

Like any other act of supernatural virtue, prayer receives its meritorious value from charity, from which it springs by means of the virtue of religion,

[33]Cf. St. Thomas, *Summa,* III, q. 89, a. 5 and ad 3.
[34]Cf. *ibid.,* II-II, q. 83, a. 12.
[35]Cf. Sess. XIV, can. 13; Denz. 923.

of which it is a proper act. As a meritorious act, prayer is subjected to the conditions for any other virtuous act and is ruled by the same laws. In this sense prayer can merit *de condigno* whatever can be merited in this way as long as the proper conditions are fulfilled.[36]

The third effect of prayer is a certain spiritual delight of the soul. This effect is produced by the mere presence of prayer—as St. Thomas says, *praesentialiter efficit.*[37] But in order that prayer actually produce this spiritual delight, attention is absolutely necessary; spiritual delight is incompatible with distractions, voluntary or involuntary. For that reason, ecstatic prayer, in which the attention of the soul is the greatest possible by reason of the concentration of all one's psychological energies on the object contemplated, carries with it the greatest delight that can be attained in this life. And it is natural that this should be so. Prayer nourishes our intellect, arouses our sensibility in a holy manner, and stimulates and strengthens our will. It is truly a *refectio mentis* which by its very nature is meant to fill the soul with sweetness.

PRAYER AS PETITION

But it is the impetratory value of prayer which interests us most as an element of increase and development of the Christian life independent of merit. Let us first see the principal differences between the meritorious and impetratory aspects of prayer. As a meritorious act, prayer implies a relation of justice in regard to a reward; its impetratory value implies a relation simply to the mercy of God. As meritorious, it has an intrinsic efficacy for obtaining a reward; as impetratory, its efficacy rests solely on the promise of God. The meritorious efficacy is based above all on charity; the impetratory value is based primarily on faith. The object of merit and of impetration is not always the same, although sometimes these two aspects may coincide. Let us now examine the question of the infallible efficacy of prayer.

FOURTH CONCLUSION

Prayer, when it fills the requirements, infallibly obtains what is asked in virtue of the promises of God.

This thesis is definitely *de fide,* based as it is on innumerable significent scriptural texts:

> Ask, and it shall be given you; seek, and you shall find; knock, and it shall be opened to you. For every one who asks, receives; and he who seeks, finds; and to him who knocks it shall be opened (Matt. 7:7-8). And all things whatever you ask for in prayer, believing, you shall receive (Matt. 21:22). And whatever you ask in my name, that will I do, in order that the Father may be glorified in the Son. If you ask me anything in my name, I will do it (Jn. 14:13-14). If you abide in me, and if my words abide in you, ask whatever you will and it shall be done to you (Jn. 15:7). Amen, amen I say

[36]Cf. St. Thomas, *Summa,* II-II, q. 83, a. 7, ad 2; a. 15.
[37]*Ibid.,* a. 13.

to you, if you ask the Father anything in my name, he will give it you. Hitherto you have not asked anything in my name. Ask, and you shall receive, that your joy may be full (Jn. 16:23-24). And the confidence that we have towards him is this, that if we ask according to his will, he hears us. And we know that he hears whatever we ask; we know that the requests we make of him are granted (I Jn. 5: 14-15).

It is impossible to speak more clearly or with more insistence. The divine promise regarding an answer to prayer stands out in full certainly in the sources of revelation. But what conditions are required that prayer infallibly obtain and fulfill the divine promises? St. Thomas assigns four of them to which all the others which are listed by other authors can be reduced: that one pray for himself; that one pray for that which is necessary for salvation; that one pray piously; and that one pray with perseverance.[38] Let us examine each of these conditions in particular.

First condition

The reason that one must pray *for himself* is that the granting of a divine grace always demands a subject who is properly disposed, and it may be that one's neighbor is not disposed to receive that which is asked in prayer. On the other hand, he who prays for himself, if he does it fittingly, is by that very fact disposed to be heard. If it were otherwise, his prayer would not be true prayer at all. This is not to say, however, that prayer for others is always inefficacious. On the contrary, it often obtains what is asked; but we cannot have infallible certainty of an answer because we cannot be certain of the dispositions of the person for whom we pray. We may ask God that he dispose our neighbor for a certain effect through his infinite mercy, but God has not promised this to anyone and therefore we cannot obtain it infallibly.

Second condition

One must pray *for those things necessary for salvation.* This means anything at all which in any way is necessary or useful for salvation. As such it falls under the infallible impetration of prayer. Hence we can impetrate by prayer the growth or increase of the infused virtues and of the gifts of the Holy Ghost, and even those things which cannot in any way be merited. It is evident from this that the area of impetration is much wider than that of merit. Thus by impetration one can petition actual efficacious grace in order not to fall into a grave sin or to perform some salutary act or even the gift of final perseverance which is infallibly connected with eternal salvation. The Church, under the guidance of the Holy Ghost, frequently begs in the liturgy for these graces which no one can merit in the strict sense of the word.

Third condition

One must pray *piously,* and by this word St. Thomas refers to all the conditions which are required on the part of the individual who prays—humility, confidence, attention and petition in the name of Christ. Some authors include all these subjective conditions under the heading of the state of grace, without which, they say, no one can pray piously. But they are mistaken. St. Thomas

[38]Cf. *ibid.*, a. 15, ad 2.

raises this very objection, and this is his solution: "The sinner cannot pray piously in the sense that his prayer is informed by the supernatural habit of the virtue of piety, which he lacks, but he can pray piously in the sense that he can ask for something that pertains to piety, just as he who does not have the habit of justice may nevertheless desire something that is just. And although the prayer of the sinner is not meritorious, it can nevertheless have an impetratory value, because merit is based on justice, while impetration is based on pure gratuity or liberality."[39]

Consequently, although the state of grace is undoubtedly most fitting for the infallible efficacy of prayer, it is not absolutely necessary. It is one thing to demand a wage that is due in justice, but it is something quite distinct to beg for an alms. In the second case, no other titles are necessary but one's need. What is always necessary, however, is the previous impulse of an actual grace, which can be given and actually is given to sinners.

Fourth condition

The prayer must be made *with perseverance.* The Lord repeated time and again the necessity of perseverance in prayer until we obtain what we ask. Recall the parable of the friend who came to beg for bread (Luke 11:5-13), of the evil judge and the importunate widow (Luke 18:1-5), the moving episode of the woman of Cana who insisted in spite of an apparent rebuff (Matt. 15:21-28), and the sublime example of Christ himself, who frequently spent the whole night in prayer and in Gethsemane prayed in great anguish to his heavenly Father (Luke 6:12; 22:44).

Such are the conditions for the infallible efficacy of prayer. In practice, however, we obtain many things from God without fulfilling all these conditions because of the superabundance of the divine mercy. But if we do fulfill all the conditions, we shall infallibly obtain, by reason of the divine promise, even those graces which we could not merit in an absolute sense.

GROWTH OF THE SUPERNATURAL ORGANISM

FIFTH CONCLUSION

By the worthy reception of the sacraments, by the performance of works which are supernaturally meritorious, and by the impetratory efficacy of prayer, the infused habits all increase at the same time, and this increase is effected by a greater inherence or radication in the subject.

The reason for the simultaneous increase of all the supernatural habits—sanctifying grace, the virtues, and the gifts of the Holy Spirit—is that they all have an intimate connection with grace and charity. For that reason, the in-

[39] *Ibid.*, a. 16, ad 2.

crease of grace effects a corresponding increase in the entire supernatural organism. As St. Thomas says, it is comparable to the simultaneous growth of the fingers of the hand.[40]

The reason why this increase consists in the greater radication of these habits in the subject is that the very nature of grace, the virtues and the gifts require it. As inherent forms or supernatural habits, they can increase only in intensity. The subject participates more and more in this form by a greater radication of the form, which results in a greater facility and intensity in the operations which proceed from it.[41]

First consequence

Two important conclusions follow from this doctrine. The first is the impossibility that an infused virtue could be perfect by itself alone, that is, without others being perfect also. United as they are among themselves and rooted in grace, from which in a certain manner they flow and to which they are ordained, and having charity as their form, when some of them increase by a more intense act, they draw with them the entire supernatural organism. In other words, there is an increase in grace, which is the principle of the virtues, in charity, which is the form of the virtues, and in all the other virtues and gifts which are inseparably connected with grace and charity.

However, although the increase of one virtue is accompanied by an increase in all the other supernatural habits, it does not follow that there is likewise effected an increase in the facility in the use of those other virtues or gifts. The facility depends on the repetition of the acts proper to a particular virtue. The other virtues, although perfectly developed as supernatural habits, will find in practice (or at least can find in practice) certain difficulties which proceed from extrinsic impediments or contrary dispositions remaining in the subject because of former evil actions.[42] For that reason a saint may encounter a certain resistance and difficulty in the practice of a virtue which he never had the occasion to exercise, in spite of the fact that he possesses the supernatural habit of the virtue perfectly.[43]

Second consequence

The second conclusion, derived from the first, is that for the growth of the habit of the virtues it is not necessary to practice all of them. Even those virtues which are not exercised because of the lack of opportunity are increased by the exercise of the other virtues. For example, a mendicant saint

---

[40]Cf. *ibid.*, I-II, q. 65; q. 66, a. 2; q. 68, a. 5. Notice the singular importance of this doctrine in ascetical and mystical theology. The growth of grace and charity implies the growth of all the infused virtues and the gifts of the Holy Spirit as habits. It is therefore impossible that charity should reach a state of relative perfection without the gifts having increased in the same degree and being actuated with greater frequency and intensity, so that the soul is normally introduced into the full mystical state.

[41]Cf. St. Thomas, *Summa,* I-II, q. 52, a. 2; II-II, q. 24, a. 5.

[42]Cf. *ibid.*, I-II, q. 65, a. 3, ad 2.

[43]Cf. *ibid.*, ad 3.

cannot practice the virtue of magnificence, for this requires the expenditure of great wealth in the service of God or for the benefit of one's neighbor for the glory of God. Nevertheless, he can and does possess the habit of this virtue in a perfect state and is disposed to practice it at least *in preparatione animi*, as the theologians say, if the possibility should arise.

NORMAL DEVELOPMENT

We terminate this brief review of the development of the Christian life by distinguishing between that which is ordinary or normal and that which is extraordinary or abnormal in this development. We understand by the *normal* development of sanctifying grace the evolution of its intrinsic virtualities, the expansion and increase of its dynamic elements (the infused virtues and the gifts of the Holy Ghost) under the corresponding divine motion. Whatever the infused virtues and the gifts of the Holy Spirit can attain by their simple actuation under the divine movement evidently pertains to the normal development of sanctifying grace. On the other hand, that must be considered *abnormal* and extraordinary which by its very nature is not contained in the intrinsic virtualities of grace under its double aspect of static and dynamic.

Such, it seems to us, is the sense in which ascetical and mystical authors, whatever the school to which they belong, should understand these expressions. Those who deny the universal call to the mystical state allege, in proof of their opinion, that the mystical state is outside the exigencies of grace,[44] whereas whatever would be within the exigencies of grace would be completely ordinary and normal in its development.

But for the time being we are interested simply in defining our terminology. Later we shall demonstrate that the mystical state does fall perfectly within the exigencies of grace and is for that reason the normal and ordinary path to sanctity for all souls in grace.

[44]Cf. Crisógono de Jesús, O.C.D., *Compendio de Ascética y Mística*, (Avila: 1933), Part III, c. 1, a. 1, p. 159.

CHRISTIAN PERFECTION

II

1: CHRISTIAN PERFECTION

Having examined the nature and organism of the supernatural life and having defined the fundamental laws of its growth to perfection, let us now see in what perfection consists. After a brief introduction on the concept of perfection in general, we shall explain the nature of Christian perfection, its obligation for all Christians, its principal degrees, its possibility, and its relationship with the difficult problem of predestination. At the same time we shall examine complementary questions.

PERFECTION IN GENERAL

The word "perfection" comes from the Latin word *perficere,* which means "to make completely," "to terminate," or "to finish." From this comes the word "perfect," which signifies "that which is completed or finished," and the word "perfection," which signifies the quality of being perfect. A thing is said to be perfect when it has all the being, all the reality which is due to it according to its nature. A blind man is physically imperfect because he lacks the use of a faculty which is due to human nature; but the lack of wings does not signify any imperfection in man, because man by his nature is not meant to fly.

The etymological meaning of the word perfection gives us a clue to the authentic real definition. The very word "perfection" is an analogous term, and this allows for the true use of the word in several different senses. It could not be otherwise, because perfection is a transcendental concept which can be applied to all things that exist, in view of the philosophical axiom, "a thing is perfect so far as it is in act" (*unumquodque in tantum est perfectum in quantum est in actu*). But an analogous concept derives its ultimate meaning and significance, not from its lowest application, but from its primary and principal analogate. The reason for this is, as St. Thomas points out,[1] that in the concrete order the analogy of proper proportionality virtually contains the analogy of attribution. In other words, the analogy by which being is predicated of God and of creatures is formally the analogy of proportionality and

---

[1] *In I Ethic.,* lect. VII, in fine.

virtually the analogy of attribution.[2] The important conclusion which follows from this is that in the concrete order all analogous perfections imply either a dependence upon the one source or an ordering to the one goal and, moreover, analogous perfections admit of degrees of more or less which are essentially dependent on one another. Thus God, who is pure act, is being in all its actual plenitude and is perfection by essence. In reality he is the only absolutely perfect being; all other perfections are denominated by his perfection; and all other perfections are in some way or other a participation in his absolute perfection.

Although the term "perfection," taken in the abstract, is an analogous and transcendental concept, as soon as we speak of a particular type of perfection or descend to the concrete order we immediately leave the realm of the transcendental and arrive at that of the predicamental. Hence as soon as we begin to discuss Christian perfection we are dealing with a predicamental perfection. And that is not all. Analogous terms are predicated of things that are essentially diverse and only accidentally the same. This means that when we define Christian perfection we must break the term down into its elements and find the one to which that term most properly refers. We shall, therefore, review St. Thomas' division of perfection as he applies it to the spiritual life, in order to discover the nature of Christian perfection properly speaking, and the way in which the term "perfection" applies to the various aspects of Christian perfection.

St. Thomas states that anything is perfect insofar as it is in act and imperfect insofar as it is in potency.[3] Then, in his commentary on Aristotle's *Metaphysics*,[4] he says that there are three different ways of using the term "perfection": when a thing lacks nothing due to its nature; when there is neither excess nor defect as regards its powers of operation; and when it has attained its proper goal or end. He further clarifies this division when he states that perfection is threefold: 1) when a thing is constituted in its proper being (*perfectio in esse*); 2) when it also possesses the faculties required for its perfect operation (*perfectio in operatione*); and 3) when it attains to something else as its end or goal (*perfectio in assecutione finis*).[5] Again, he sometimes speaks of perfection in slightly different words, specifying as "first perfection" that according to which a thing is substantially perfect by reason of its form, and as "second perfection" the attainment of the end. But the end or goal which constitutes second perfection may be either an operation

---

[2]According to J. Ramírez, O.P., in the concrete order every analogy of proportionality is annexed *per accidens et in obliquo* to an analogy of attribution. Cf. *De analogia*, p. 75.

[3]*Summa*, I-II, q. 3, a. 2.

[4]Cf. lib. V, cap. 18.

[5]*Summa*, I, q. 6, a. 3.

as such (as the end of the violinist is to play the violin) or something distinct that is attained through an operation (as the end of a builder is to construct a house). But the first perfection is the cause of the second because the form of a thing is the principle of its operation.[6]

From what we have seen thus far as regards perfection, it is apparent that first perfection is identical with substantial perfection or perfection *in esse;* second perfection may be either the operation itself or the attainment of some goal distinct from the agent. Note that St. Thomas does not place perfection *in operatione* as a middle state between perfection *in esse* and perfection *in assecutione finis;* he states only that sometimes perfection consists merely in an operation and sometimes it consists in the attainment of an extrinsic goal. Nor does this mean that both types of perfection may not be found in one and the same agent. Thus man's formal beatitude consists in the perfection *in operatione* which is the beatific vision; and man's objective beatitude consists in the perfection *in assecutione finis* which is God. We can see from the foregoing why St. Thomas maintains that beatitude and perfection are synonymous terms.[7]

But we have not yet finished with the divisions of perfection. In the first chapter of his treatise, *De perfectione vitae spiritualis,* as well as in the *Summa,*[8] St. Thomas divides perfection into perfection *simpliciter* and perfection *secundum quid.* The former comprises that which belongs to the very nature of a thing (an animal is perfect *simpliciter* if it possesses all that is required for its animal life); the latter perfection is accidental in relation to the formal and substantial perfection (an animal is perfect *secundum quid* as regards its blackness or whiteness, its size, etc.). Lastly, St. Thomas speaks of that which constitutes perfection essentially or *per se* and that which constitutes perfection instrumentally, depending upon whether perfection consists in charity operating according to the precepts or according to the evangelical counsels.[9]

THE NATURE OF CHRISTIAN PERFECTION

We are now in a position to apply the various members of the division of perfection to Christian perfection, but before doing so, it is necessary to recall that the term "perfection" is an analogous term and will not apply to each

[6]*Ibid.,* q. 73, a. 1.
[7]Cf. *ibid.,* q. 26; I-II, q. 3, aa. 1-2.
[8]*Ibid.,* II-II. q. 184, a. 1, ad 2.
[9]*Ibid.,* a. 3.

and every element of the division with equal rigor. This should be evident from the division itself as well as from the notion of analogy.

From the various distinctions already given, we can list three general headings under the notion of Christian perfection: 1) perfection *simpliciter* (the perfection due a Christian as raised to the supernatural order); 2) perfection *secundum quid* (the perfection which is accidental to the proper perfection of the Christian); and 3) instrumental perfection. Under perfection *simpliciter* we have first perfection (which is also called perfection *in esse* or substantial perfection) and second perfection (which consists either in an operation or in the attainment of an end).

It now remains to identify the various elements of Christian perfection according to the foregoing division of perfection. As regards first perfection (perfection *in esse;* substantial perfection), it is common teaching that it consists in *sanctifying grace,* since sanctifying grace is the very soul of the supernatural life and is therefore due to a Christian in the supernatural order. As to second perfection, we have the testimony of Scripture as well as common theological teaching that second perfection *in operatione* is *charity,* either in its elicited act or as imperating the other virtues. Second perfection *in assecutione finis* is likewise charity, since charity is the virtue which unites us directly with God as our supernatural end.[10] Perfection *secundum quid* comprises the elicited acts of the supernatural virtues other than charity, and *instrumental perfection* is found in the evangelical counsels. Let us now amplify these statements by stating and explaining the theological conclusions which logically follow from them.

FIRST CONCLUSION

Christian perfection consists especially in the perfection of charity.

We do not mean to say that Christian perfection consists integrally and exclusively in the perfection of charity, but that charity is its principal element, its most essential and characteristic element. In this sense we must say that the measure of charity in a man is the measure of his supernatural perfection, in such wise that he who has attained the perfection of the love of God and of neighbor can be called perfect in the truest sense of the word (*simpliciter*), while he may be only relatively (*secundum quid*) perfect if he is perfect only in some other virtue.[11] This second type of perfection is impossible in the supernatural order, granted the connection of the infused virtues with grace and charity.[12] Understood in this way, the present conclusion seems to many

[10]Cf. St. Thomas, *Summa,* II-II, q. 184, a. 1.

[11]"He is perfect *simpliciter* in the spiritual life who is perfect in charity; but he is perfect *secundum quid* in regard to anything else that pertains to the spiritual life" (St. Thomas, *De perfectione vitae spiritualis;* cf. *Summa,* II-II, q. 184, a. 1, ad 2).

[12]Cf. *ibid.,* I-II, q. 5.

theologians to be a conclusion which is *proxima fidei* because of the evident testimony of Sacred Scripture and the unanimous consent of tradition.[13]

Proof of the thesis

From Sacred Scripture. This is one of the truths which is most often repeated in Scripture. Christ himself tells us that upon the love of God and of neighbor depends the whole Law and the prophets (Matt. 22:35-40; Mk. 12:28-31). The texts from St. Paul are very explicit and abundant. Here are a few of them: "But above all these things have charity, which is the bond of perfection" (Col. 3:14); "love is the fulfillment of the Law" (Rom. 13:10); "so there abide faith, hope and charity, these three; but the greatest of these is charity" (I Cor. 13:13). Even faith, according to St. Paul, receives its value from charity: "For in Christ Jesus neither circumcision is of any avail, nor uncircumcision, but faith which works through charity" (Gal. 5:6). The other virtues are nothing without charity (I Cor. 13:1-3).

From the magisterium of the Church. This same doctrine has been amply commented upon and developed by the Fathers of the Church[14] and has been sanctioned by the magisterium of the Church. In the bull *Ad conditorem* of John XXII, one reads the following words: "Since the perfection of the Christian life consists principally and essentially in charity, which is called the bond of perfection by the Apostle (Col. 3:14) and which unites or joins man in some way to his end . . . ."[15]

Theological argument. The proof given by St. Thomas is that the perfection of a being consists in the attainment of its ultimate end, beyond which there is nothing more to be desired. But it is charity which unites us with God, the ultimate end of man. Therefore, Christian perfection consists especially in charity.[16]

The fundamental reason which St. Thomas gives is clarified by an examination of the nature and effects of charity. Charity alone unites us entirely with God as the ultimate supernatural end. The other virtues prepare or intiate that union, but they cannot terminate and complete it, since the moral virtues are limited to the removal of the obstacles which impede us in our progress toward God and they bring us to him only indirectly, by establishing the proper order in the means which lead us to God.[17] As regards faith and hope, they certainly unite us with God, since they are theological virtues, but they do not unite us with God as the absolute ultimate end or as the Supreme Good who is infinitely lovable in himself—the perfect motive of charity. They

[13] Cf. J. de Guibert, S.J., *The Theology of the Spiritual Life* (New York: 1953), n. 50.

[14] Cf. Rouet de Journel, S.J., *Enchiridion asceticum* (ed. 3), nn. 89, 687, 734, 787, 789, 1262, 1314, etc.

[15] Cited by J. de Guibert, S.J., *Documenta ecclesiastica christianae perfectionis studium spectantia* (Rome: 1931), n. 266.

[16] Cf. *Summa,* II-II, q. 184, a. 1.

[17] Cf. *ibid.,* I-II, q. 63, a. 3, ad 2.

unite us with God as the First Principle from whom there come to us the knowledge of the truth (faith) and perfect happiness (hope). Charity regards God and unites us to him as the end; faith and hope regard God and unite us to him as a principle.[18] Faith gives us a knowledge of God which is necessarily obscure and imperfect (*de non visis*), and hope is also radically imperfect (*de non possessis*), while charity unites us with God in a perfect manner even in this life by giving us a real possession of God,[19] and by establishing a current of mutual friendship between him and ourselves.[20] For that reason, charity is inseparable from grace, while faith and hope are compatible, in some way, even with mortal sin (unformed faith and hope).[21] Charity presupposes faith and hope, but it surpasses them in dignity and perfection.[22] Beyond all doubt, therefore, charity constitutes the very essence of Christian perfection; it presupposes and includes all the other virtues—without charity, these are lacking in value, as St. Paul expressly teaches.[23]

Correct understanding

Nevertheless, it is necessary to understand this doctrine correctly in order not to fall into lamentable error and confusion. From the fact that Christian perfection consists especially in charity, it does not follow that the role of the other virtues is purely accidental or that they do not form any part of the essence of Christian perfection. The word "especially" does not mean totally, nor should one confuse the metaphysical essence of a thing with its physical essence.[24] The metaphysical essence of Christian perfection is constituted by the simple perfection of charity, to be sure; its physical essence, which is total or integral, demands all the other infused virtues in the same degree of perfection as charity.

We must not forget that the moral virtues, and with greater reason faith and hope, have their proper excellency even when considered in themselves, independently of charity. For although all the acts of the Christian life can and should be *commanded* by charity, many of them are nevertheless acts *elicited* by the other infused virtues. It is evident that there can be a diversity of degrees of perfection in the manner of producing the elicited act of any virtue, even prescinding from the greater or lesser influence which imperating charity may have had on it. As a matter of fact, when the Church wishes to

---

[18]Cf. *ibid.*, II-II, q. 17, a. 6.

[19]Cf. *ibid.*, I-II, q. 66, a. 6.

[20]Cf. *ibid.*, II-II, q. 23, a. 1.

[21]Cf. *ibid.*, q. 24, a. 12 and ad 5; I-II, q. 65, a. 4.

[22]Cf. *ibid.*, II-II, q. 23, a. 6.

[23]Cf. I Cor. 13.

[24]In scholastic philosophy, one understands by the metaphysical essence of a thing that which is conceived as the first and most knowable property of that thing and the source or principle of all its other perfections. By the physical essence is understood the conjunction of all the properties and perfections which belong to a thing in the real order.

judge the sanctity of a servant of God in view of possible beatification, she does not consider charity only but also the exercise of the other virtues to a heroic degree. This means that the infused virtues are integral parts of Christian perfection.

SECOND CONCLUSION

Christian perfection consists integrally in the elicited act of charity and in the acts of the other infused virtues imperated by charity which are of precept.[25]

Preliminary notions

It is necessary to distinguish in the Christian virtues what is of grave precept, what is of light precept, and what is of counsel. So far as something is of *grave precept* it is *per se* essentially connected with charity, in such a way that without it charity itself would cease to exist because of a mortal sin which the transgression of a grave precept implies. As to the *light precept,* a thing is required, not for the very essence of charity, but for its perfection, since the perfection of charity is incompatible with a voluntary venial sin which follows the transgression of a light precept. But in a matter of pure *counsel,* a thing is only accidentally related to charity and perfection, since acts of pure counsel do not affect the substance of charity nor its perfection.

We must also note that the act of the infused virtues can be considered in two ways: in itself (the elicited act) and as imperated by charity. An act of humility performed precisely as an act of humility is an elicited act of that virtue. The same act performed for the love of God is an elicited act of the virtue of humility and at the same time an act commanded by the virtue of charity. So too, the essence of a thing can be taken in two senses: in the abstract or as regards its formal principle (metaphysical essence), and in the concrete or integrally (physical essence).

Finally, perfection can be considered either habitually (*in actu primo*) or actually (*in actu secundo*). The first is substantial or radical perfection; the second is accidental perfection or perfection *simpliciter.* For the first type of perfection the simple state of grace suffices; for the second, there is required a notable degree of development of the active principles which emanate from grace.

In view of the foregoing distinctions, we say that actual perfection (perfection *simpliciter* and *in actu secundo*) consists essentially (in the sense of the physical or integral essence), not only in the elicited act of charity itself (the metaphysical essence), but also in the acts of the other infused virtues; not in themselves (in this sense they are only secondary or accidentally related to perfection), but precisely as they are imperated by charity and are of precept.

Proof of the thesis

1) Since Christian perfection cannot be considered as a simple form but must be considered as a moral whole integrated by the conjunction of those conditions which perfect the life of the Christian, we are evidently dealing with

[25]Cf. P. M. Passerini, O.P., *De statibus hominum . . . ,* in q. 184, a. 1.

a plenitude which presupposes the perfect submission or rectification of our entire moral life. But this total rectification is not achieved by charity alone, which refers only to the end; it also presupposes the complete rectification of the means which are ordained to that end, by subjecting and rectifying the disordered passions which place obstacles and difficulties to the act of charity. Hence it follows that the acts of all the other infused virtues—whose precise work is that of above-mentioned means—form a part of the very essence of Christian perfection considered in a physical or integral manner.

2) Christian perfection, as St. Thomas teaches,[26] consists essentially in the precepts and not in the counsels. Nonetheless, since in addition to charity many other virtues fall under the precepts, we must conclude that they also must enter into the essential concept of Christian perfection. In the areas ruled by infused virtues there are a great many matters which fall under precept, some gravely and others lightly. Only by the fulfillment of the grave duties is the existence of charity possible; only when those duties which bind lightly are fulfilled is its perfection possible. Thus initial charity is incompatible with any mortal sin, perfect charity with venial sin—and this necessarily presupposes the practice of the infused virtues in those matters which are prescribed, gravely or lightly. The virtuous acts which are purely of counsel are simply excluded from this necessary minimum, although these also are most useful and to a certain extent they may even be necessary.

3) Only in this way can we justify the expressions of Sacred Scripture which attribute an essential role to the acts of the other virtues, such as faith, obedience, patience, humility, etc. This follows likewise from the practice of the Church in the beatification of the servants of God, which requires heroism in all the Christian virtues and not only in charity. Nevertheless, one must not lose sight of the fact that the acts of the other infused virtues pertain to the essence of Christian perfection, not in themselves (in this sense they pertain to it only secondarily and accidentally), but so far as they are imperated by charity, which is the form of all the other virtues.[27] The proper function of charity as the form of all the virtues is to direct and ordain the acts of all the virtues to the ultimate supernatural end, even those of

[26]Cf. *Summa,* II-II, q. 184, a. 3.

[27]Cf. St. Thomas, *Summa,* II-II, q. 23, a. 8. By saying that charity is the form of all the virtues, we do not mean that it is the intrinsic and essential form, as Durandus and certain Scotists imagine, but that it is the extrinsic and accidental form, as St. Thomas teaches. He uses the word *effective.* We can distinguish in the infused virtues three different informative principles: one radical, which is habitual or sanctifying grace, which is, as it were, the root of all the other infused habits; another essential or intrinsic, which is the proper specific form of each virtue in particular; and still another extrinsic or accidental form, which is charity, which ordains and directs the virtues to the supernatural end. Only in this third sense is it said that charity is the form of all the other virtues.

faith and hope, which without charity would be unformed although they would still retain their proper specific form.[28]

In what way does charity exercise this command over the other infused virtues in relation to the supernatural end? Is it a mere external impulse from without? Or does it communicate something to them of its own proper virtuality? Obviously it is necessary to reject the doctrine which makes charity the intrinsic and essential form of all the other virtues. It is impossible that it should be such, since all the virtues would be essentially the same thing as charity, unless we were to admit the absurdity that one virtue could have two distinct substantial forms.[29] But neither should one think that the impulse of charity toward the supernatural end is purely exterior to the act of the other virtues. By reason of this impulse, the acts of the other virtues receive from charity in a passive manner a real intrinsic mode through which both the acts themselves and the virtues from which they flow are perfected.[30]

---

[28]Cf St. Thomas, *loc. cit.*: "In morals the form of an act is taken chiefly from the end. The reason for this is that the principle of moral acts is the will, whose object and form, so to speak, are the end. Now the form of an act always follows from a form of the agent. Consequently, in moral matters that which gives an act its order to the end must needs give the act its form. But it is clear that charity directs the acts of all other virtues to the last end and, as a result, also gives the form to all other acts of virtue; and it is precisely in this sense that charity is called the form of the virtues, for these are called virtues in relation to 'informed' acts."

[29]St. Thomas expressly states that charity is called the form of the other virtues, not because it is their exemplary or essential form, but by way of an efficient cause (*loc. cit.*, ad 1). Cajetan makes the profound comment that charity not only informs effectively because it directs and ordains—this is common to every director—but because a certain passive participation in its direction and ordination is, as it were, the form which constitutes the other acts as virtuous *simpliciter*.

[30]Charity informs not only the acts of the other virtues but the virtues themselves as habits, as St. Thomas expressly teaches in *De veritate,* q. 14, a. 5, ad 9. Properly speaking, charity informs the act of the virtue, but by consequence it informs the habit of the virtue. The following explanation is given by the Carmelites of Salamanca: "Cum aliquis actus attingit aliquem finem, nequit non dicere verum ordinem, sive habitudinem realem ad talem finem; ergo quando actus virtutis inferioris ordinatur ad finem caritatis illumque attingit, nequit non importare verum ordinem et realem habitudinem ad talem finem: cumque hujusmodi ordo non conveniat actui virtutis inferioris ex propria ratione, sive ex parte virtutis proximae a qua elicitur, opus est quod illum participet ex influxu caritatis, cui per se convenit illum finem attingere. . . . Insuper actus virtutis inferioris ratione ordinis ad Deum ultimum finem consequitur valorem adaequatum ad merendum vitam aeternam de condigno. Sed hic valor non est ens rationis, nec denominatio extrinseca, sed aliquod praedicatum reale; ergo ordo, quem actus virtutis inferioris habet ex motione caritatis ad ejus finem est aliquid reale: cumque talis ordo non pertineat ad speciem praedicti actus, sequitur esse aliquid sibi intrinsece superadditum" (*De caritate,* dist. 7, n. 49).

It is evident that if there were no matter capable of being directed to the end, the directive form of charity would have nothing to inform and could not be exercised. Charity would have to be limited exclusively to its own proper act. Consequently, we must conclude that Christian perfection is not a simple form but a moral plenitude constituted principally by the act of charity and secondarily by the acts elicited by the other virtues under the impulse of charity, which directs them to the ultimate supernatural end.

THIRD CONCLUSION

Christian perfection increases in the measure that charity produces its own elicited act more intensively and imperates the acts of the other virtues in a manner that is more intense, actual and universal.

This concluson has two parts which we shall examine separately. First, Christian perfection increases in the measure that charity produces its proper elicited act more intensively. We prescind here from the question of whether the infused habits increase only by a more intense act or even by remiss acts. According to St. Thomas, it is evident that they increase only by a more intense act; he affirms this expressly in regard to charity.[31] But our conclusion would be true even if we followed the opposite opinion concerning the increase of charity, for if any act of charity is capable of increasing the habit of charity, *a fortiori* the more intense acts of charity would also increase it. Since we have already seen that Christian perfection consists especially in the perfection of charity, it is obvious that, in the measure that this virtue produces its elicited act with greater intensity, there is produced a greater increase of Christian perfection itself. In this sense it is certain that the degree of sanctity coincides with the degree of love. To a greater love of God and neighbor corresponds always a greater degree of holiness.

But apart from its elicited act, which constitutes the essence of Christian perfection, charity, as the form of all the virtues, should imperate and direct the acts of all the virtues to the ultimate supernatural end. For that reason we must add the second part of our conclusion, namely, that Christian perfection will be greater as charity imperates the acts of the other infused virtues in a manner that is more intense, actual and universal.

In a more intense manner. This is a simple application and corollary of the doctrine which we have just explained regarding the elicited act of charity.

More actual. Whether the merit of a supernatural act requires the virtual influence of charity or whether the habitual influence suffices

[31]"Charity does not actually increase by every act of charity, but each act of charity disposes for an increase of charity so far as one act of charity disposes a man to be more prompt to act again out of charity; and as this aptness increases, a man breaks forth in an act of more fervent love by which he strives to increase in charity, and then charity actually increases" (*Summa,* II-II, q. 24, a. 6).

is a question disputed among theologians, but it is evident and admitted by all that the most perfect influence of charity is the actual influence. Consequently, in the measure that the imperating power of charity over the virtues is more actual, the acts elicited by those virtues will be more perfect, since the motive of charity is more perfect and more meritorious than that of all the other virtues. There is a great difference between an act which is performed simply for the proper and specific motive of a given virtue, such as humility, and that same act performed for the love of God, which is the perfect motive of charity.

More universal. It would never be possible that the *actual* influence of charity should imperate *all* the human acts of a man in this life. The Council of Trent has defined that no one can absolutely avoid all venial sins during his whole life unless by a special privilege, which does not seem to have been granted to anyone except the Blessed Virgin.[32] Therefore, there is no doubt that certain acts will be produced, namely, venial sins, which are in no way informed by charity. But in the measure that the acts informed or imperated by charity are more numerous and extend to a greater number of virtues, the integral perfection of the Christian life will be increased more and more.

FOURTH CONCLUSION

The perfection of the Christian life is identified with the perfection of the double act of charity—primarily in relation to God and secondarily in relation to one's neighbor.

It is elementary in theology that there is only one virtue and one infused habit of charity, by which we love God for himself, and our neighbor and ourselves for God.[33] All the acts which proceed from charity, whatever be their terminus, are specified by the same formal *quo* object, namely, the infinite goodness of God considered in itself. Whether we love God directly in himself or whether we love our neighbor or ourselves directly, if it is a question of the true love of charity the formal motive of this love is always the same: the infinite goodness of God. There cannot be any true charity for our neighbor or ourselves if it does not proceed from the supernatural motive of the love of God, and it is necessary to distinguish carefully this formal act of charity from any inclination toward the service of our neighbor which is born of a purely human compassion or any other purely natural motive. This being so, it is evident that the increase of the infused habit of charity will provide a greater capacity in relation to the double act of charity. The capacity of loving God cannot be increased in the soul without a corresponding increase in the same degree of the capacity for loving one's neighbor. This truth constitutes the central argument of the sublime first epistle of St. John, in

[32]Canon 23 on justification; Denz. 833.

[33]Cf. St. Thomas, *Summa,* II-II, q. 23, a. 5; q. 25, a. 12; q. 26, aa. 1-4.

which he clearly explains the intimate connection and inseparability of these two loves.

Nevertheless, in the exercise of love there is an order which is demanded by the very nature of things. By reason of this order the perfection of charity consists primarily in the love of God, infinitely lovable in himself, and secondarily in the love of neighbor and ourselves for God. And even among ourselves and our neighbors it is necessary to establish an order which is based on the greater or lesser relation to God of the goods in which one shares. Hence one must love his own spiritual good in preference to the spiritual good of his neighbor, but he must prefer the spiritual good of his neighbor to his own material good.

The reason for this order or scale of values is, as St. Thomas explains, because God is loved as the principle of the good on which the love of charity is based; man is loved with a love of charity so far as he directly shares in that same good. It is therefore evident that one must first of all love God, who is the source of that good, and secondly oneself, who shares directly in that good, and lastly one's neighbor, who is a companion in the sharing of that good.[34] But since the body shares in beatitude only by a certain redundance from the soul, it follows that as regards the participation in beatitude the soul of our neighbor is closer to our soul than our own body, and therefore we must place the spiritual good of our neighbor before our own corporal good.[35]

FIFTH CONCLUSION

Christian perfection consists in the perfection of affective and effective charity; primarily in affective charity and secondarily in effective charity.

It is necessary to distinguish carefully the two modes of exercising charity. This is the way in which St. Francis de Sales explains it:

> There are two principal exercises of our love of God: one affective and the other effective or active, as St. Bernard says. By the first we are attached to God and to everything that pleases him; by the second we serve God and we do whatever he commands. The former unites us to the goodness of God; the latter makes us do the will of God. The one fills us with complacence, benevolence, aspirations, desires, longings and spiritual ardors, so that our spirit is submerged in God and blended with him. The other places in us the firm resolution, the decided intention and the unswerving obedience by which we fulfill the mandates of his divine will and by which we suffer, accept, approve and embrace whatever comes from his divine will. The one makes us take pleasure in God; the other makes us please God.[36]

Since Christian perfection will be greater in the measure that charity produces its elicited act more intensively and imperates the acts of the other virtues in a more intense, actual and universal manner, it is evident that per-

[34] Cf. *ibid.*, q. 26, a. 4; q. 184, a. 3.
[35] Cf. *ibid.*, q. 26, a. 5.
[36] *Treatise on the Love of God,* Chap. 6.

fection depends primarily on affective charity and only secondarily on effective charity. The reasons are as follows:

1) Unless the influence of charity informs the soul in some way, the internal or external acts of any acquired virtue, however perfect they may be in themselves, have no supernatural value, nor are they of any avail in relation to eternal life.

2) The supernatural acts which proceed from an infused virtue and are realized with a movement of charity which is weak and remiss have a meritorious value which is equally weak and remiss, however difficult and painful the acts may be in themselves. We should not forget that the greater or lesser difficulty of an act does not of itself add any essential merit to the act. Merit depends exclusively on the degree of charity with which the act is performed, although difficulty may accidentally cause some increase of merit by reason of the greater impulse of charity which ordinarily will accompany the act.[37]

3) On the other hand, the acts of any infused virtue, however easy and simple in themselves, have a great meritorious value, if performed with a more intense movement of charity, and are of the highest perfection. Thus the slightest action performed by Christ, the simple acts of cooking and housecleaning done by Mary in the house at Nazareth, had a value incomparably greater than the martyrdom of any saint.

4) The same conclusion follows from the fact that Christian perfection consists especially in the proper or elicited act of charity (affective charity) and only integrally in the acts of the other virtues imperated by charity (effective charity).

Nevertheless, subjectively or *quoad nos,* the perfection of divine love is better manifested in the practice of effective charity; that is, in the practice of the Christian virtues for the love of God, especially if it is necessary for that exercise to overcome great difficulties, temptations or obstacles. Affective love, although more excellent in itself, is often subject to great illusions and falsification. It is very easy to tell God that we love him with all our powers, that we desire to be martyrs, etc., and then fail to observe silence, which costs a great deal less than martyrdom, or to maintain, with an obstinacy mixed with self-love, a point of view which is incompatible with that plenitude of love which has been declared. On the other hand, the genuineness of our love of God is much less suspect when it impels us to practice silently and perseveringly, in spite of all obstacles and difficulties, the painful and monotonous duties of everyday life. Christ himself teaches us that a tree is known by its fruits (Matt. 7:15-20) and that they will not enter the kingdom of heaven who

[37]Cf. St. Thomas, *Summa,* II-II, q. 27, a. 8, ad 3; *III Sent.,* dist. 30, a. 3 and a. 4, ad 3; *De virtutibus,* q. 2, a. 8, ad 4.

merely say, "Lord, Lord," but only they who do the will of his heavenly Father (Matt. 7:21). This same truth is taught in the parable of the two sons (Matt. 21:28-32).

SIXTH CONCLUSION *For its complete expansion and development, as is required by Christian perfection, charity must be perfected by the gift of wisdom.*

This is a simple application of the general doctrine of the necessity of the gifts for the perfection of the infused virtues. Without the influence of the gifts, the infused virtues operate according to the rules of natural reason illumined by faith, according to a human mode. Since they are in themselves supernatural and divine habits, the infused virtues demand by their very nature an exercise in a divine or superhuman mode, a quality which properly corresponds to them as supernatural habits. As long as the gifts of the Holy Ghost do not impart to these virtues that divine mode which should be characteristic of them and which they lack of themselves[38] (since they are subjected to the control and rule of natural reason illumined by faith), it is impossible that the infused virtues should attain their perfect expansion and development.

While this is true of all the infused virtues, it is especially true of charity. Being a most perfect virtue in itself, indeed the most divine and excellent of all the virtues, charity demands by a kind of inner necessity the divine atmosphere of the gifts of the Holy Ghost in order to give all that it is capable of giving. The rule of human reason, even when illumined by faith, is insufficient to give charity that divine modality. Natural reason is infinitely removed from the supernatural order and is absolutely incapable, not only of producing it, but even of having any claim on the supernatural order.[39] And even when raised to the supernatural order by grace and illumined by the light of faith, the soul still exercises the infused virtues in a human mode under the control of human reason which, under the ordinary movement of grace, is the operator of the virtuous habit and must of necessity impress upon it its own human modality. In order that charity have a divine modality, it is necessary that human reason cease to be the rule and operator of the habit and that the habit itself be converted into a passive subject which receives without resistance the divine modality of the gifts which proceeds from the Holy Spirit himself. Only under the influence of the gift of understanding (which without destroying faith gives it an intense penetration of the super-

[38]Such is the express doctrine of St. Thomas: "The gifts are distinguished from the virtues in this, namely, that the virtues perform acts in a human mode, but the gifts above the human mode" (*In III Sent.,* dist. 34, q. 1, a. 1).

[39]As the Church teaches against the Pelagians and Semi-Pelagians; cf. XVI Council of Carthage (Denz. 101 ff.), Council of Ephesus (Denz. 126 f.), II Council of Orange (Denz. 174 ff.).

natural mysteries)[40] and especially under the influence of the gift of wisdom (which makes the soul taste divine things by a certain mysterious connaturality)[41] will charity reach its full expansion and development in the measure required for Christian perfection.

It follows from this as an inevitable consequence that the mystical state is necessary for Christian perfection, since the essential characteristic of the mystical state consists precisely in the actuation and predominance of the gifts of the Holy Ghost. There is not and cannot be any perfection or sanctity which is purely ascetical and based on the human mode of the infused virtues. It is necessary that the human modality which characterizes the infused virtues be replaced by the divine modality of the gifts; and this is the mystical state in the technical and strict sense of the word.

SEVENTH CONCLUSION

Charity can increase indefinitely in man as a wayfarer; consequently, Christian perfection has no definite terminus in this life.

In proving this thesis, St. Thomas states that there are three ways in which the increase of any form may have a limit or terminus.[42] The first is on the part of the form itself, when it has a limited capacity beyond which it cannot advance without the destruction of the form itself. The second is by reason of the agent, when it does not have sufficient power to continue increasing the form in the subject. And a third is on the part of the subject, when it is not susceptible of a greater perfection.

But none of these three manners of limitation can be attributed to charity in this life. Not on the part of charity itself, since in its proper specific nature it is nothing other than a participation in infinite charity, which is the Holy Spirit himself. Not on the part of the agent, who is God, whose power is infinite and therefore inexhaustible. And not on the part of the subject in which charity resides—the human will—whose obediential potency in the hands of God is likewise without limit, so that in the measure that charity increases, the capacity of the soul for a further increase is likewise enlarged. Therefore, charity encounters no limitation in its development as long as man is on this earth, and it can for that reason increase indefinitely.[43]

It will be quite different in heaven. There the soul will have reached its terminus and at the moment of its entrance into heaven its degree of charity will be permanently fixed according to the measure of the intensity it has attained up to the last moment on earth. It is true that even in heaven charity could increase indefinitely as regards the three points we have just enumerated,

[40]Cf. St. Thomas, *Summa,* II-II, q. 8, a. 1.
[41]Cf. *ibid.,* q. 45, a. 2.
[42]*Ibid.,* q. 24, a. 7.
[43]This doctrine was officially stated by the Church in the Council of Vienne; cf. Denz. 471.

since in heaven the nature of charity does not change, the power of God is not diminished, nor is the obedential potency of the creature limited. But we know with certainty that charity will not increase in heaven because it will have been fixed in its degree or grade by the immutable will of God and because the time of meriting will have passed.[44]

EIGHTH CONCLUSION

Christian perfection consists essentially in the precepts and secondarily or instrumentally in the counsels.

St. Thomas invokes the authority of Sacred Scriptures to prove this doctrine.[45] We are told in Deuteronomy (6:5): "You shall love the Lord, your God, with all your heart, and with all your soul, and with all your strength." Again in Leviticus (19:18) it is stated: "You shall love your neighbor as yourself." On these two precepts, says the Lord, depends all the Law and the prophets (Matt. 22:40). Therefore, the perfection of charity, in which Christian perfection consists, is demanded of us by precept.

Moreover, St. Thomas argues, we know that Christian perfection consists *per se* and essentially in charity: principally in the love of God and secondarily in the love of neighbor. But both the love of God and the love of neighbor constitute the first and the greatest of all the commandments. Therefore, Christian perfection consists essentially in the precepts. This is confirmed by the authority of St. Paul: "The end of the gospel is charity" (I Tim. 1:5), for it is evident that no limit of any kind is placed in the end but only in the means for attaining the end. Thus the doctor does not place any limit to the health that he wishes to give to the sick, but he does place a limit on the medicine which he administers to that end.

St. Thomas continues by proving that perfection consists secondarily and instrumentally in the counsels. All of them, as he says, are ordained to charity, as are the precepts, but in a different way. The precepts are ordained to remove those things which are contrary to charity, in union with which charity could not exist; the counsels are restricted to the removal of the obstacles which impede the facile exercise of charity, although these things are not totally contrary to charity. It is evident from this that the counsels are not essential for Christian perfection but are only instruments for attaining Christian perfection.

From this magnificent doctrine important practical conclusions can be drawn, especially concerning the obligation of all Christians in regard to Christian perfection. For it is evident that if Christian perfection consists principally in

[44]Such is the common teaching of all theologians. There is no express definition of the Church on this point, but it is clearly taught by the ordinary magisterium of the Church, repeated by all the Fathers of the Church, and definitively incorporated in theology by all the schools. Cf. St. Thomas, *Summa,* I, q. 62, a. 9.

[45]*Ibid.,* II-II, q. 184, a. 3.

the precepts—which means that no Christian whatever is exempt from them—it follows that every Christian, whatever his state or condition, is obliged to aspire to perfection. We are not treating here of a counsel, but a precept, and it therefore obliges all.

The counsels do not oblige all Christians, but all Christians ought to sanctify themselves by the conscientious fulfillment of the precepts and by the affective practice of the counsels, which means the spirit of the counsels. It is necessary to distinguish between the *effective* or material practice of the evangelical counsels (poverty, chastity and obedience), which is not universally obligatory, and the *affective* practice or spirit of the counsels, which obliges everyone. The first is usually verified by public vows (as in the religious state); the second affects all Christians regardless of their state in life. No one is obliged to take a vow of poverty, obedience or chastity, but all are obliged to practice those three virtues in a manner that is compatible with each one's state in life.

It is also necessary to keep in mind that, in addition to the traditional evangelical counsels, there are many other particular or private counsels which proceed from interior inspirations of the Holy Spirit and pertain to works of supererogation (a greater practice of prayer, a greater spirit of sacrifice, greater detachment from worldly things, etc.). Although they do not properly constitute a true precept, these counsels represent a particular invitation or a concrete manifestation of the will of God for a particular soul, and they cannot be ignored without committing an act of infidelity to grace, which is difficult to reconcile with the complete and integral concept of Christian perfection.

THE OBLIGATION OF PERFECTION

This question has already been resolved in the previous conclusion, of which it is nothing more than the logical consequence. If Christian perfection does not consist in the counsels but in the precepts, it follows that it is of obligation for all, since the precepts bind all Christians. But it is well to examine more carefully the whole problem and to complete the picture with its complementary details and secondary questions.

THE GENERAL OBLIGATION

All Christians are obliged to aspire to Christian perfection. We say all Christians in order to signify that the obligation to aspire to perfection is not restricted to priests and religious. They are obliged *a fortiori* by their priestly ordination or by religious profession, but the fundamental obligation regarding perfection stems from the very nature of grace, which is received as a seed at the reception of baptism and by its very nature demands an increase. We are treating, therefore, of an obligation which is common to all Christians by reason of their baptism in Christ.

They are *obliged,* and not simply "invited," although this obligation admits of varying degrees, as we shall see when we distinguish the various classes of persons. The obligation is to *aspire* or *strive.* By this we mean that one is not obliged to be already perfect at the beginning of the Christian life or even at any determined moment in that life, but simply to aspire positively to Christian perfection as an end which one seriously proposes to reach.

The Christian perfection to which we refer is not simply the radical perfection or perfection in first act (which would signify simply the preservation of the state of grace) but perfection *simpliciter* or in second act. This presupposes the eminent development of the entire supernatural organism of sanctifying grace, the infused virtues and the gifts of the Holy Ghost.

Proof of the thesis

We prove this thesis from various sources:

From Sacred Scripture. Let us listen to the words of Christ himself: "You therefore are to be perfect, even as your heavenly Father is perfect" (Matt. 5:48). These words were pronounced by Christ in the Sermon on the Mount, which was addressed to all men. This has been the unanimous teaching of the Fathers of the Church.

The apostles insist on the commandment of the divine Master. St. Paul says that God has chosen us in Christ, "that we should be holy and without blemish in his sight" (Eph. 1:4). He says likewise that we must struggle "until we all attain to the unity of faith and of the deep knowledge of the Son of God, to perfect manhood, to the mature measure of the fulness of Christ" (Eph. 4:13). It is the will of God that we all sanctify ourselves: "This is the will of God, your sanctification" (I Thess. 4:3). St. Peter desires that we be holy, in imitation of God, who is holy: "As the One who called you is holy, be you also holy, in all your behavior; for it is written, 'You shall be holy, because I am holy'" (I Pet. 1:15-16). And in the Apocalypse we read that no one can be considered so perfect that he cannot be more perfect: "He who is just, let him be just still; and he who is holy, let him be hallowed still" (Apoc. 22:11).

The Fathers of the Church. This doctrine is so well attested to by tradition that it would be a simple matter to give variety of texts. The famous axiom, so often cited by the Fathers of the Church, "He who does not go forward on the road of God falls back," clearly expresses the necessity of constantly progressing in the way of Christian perfection at the risk of falling back and of compromising one's salvation.

Magisterium of the Church. The definitive teaching of Pope Pius XI in his encyclical on St. Francis de Sales will serve as ample proof from the Church's teaching. "Let no one judge," says the Holy Father, "that this obligation pertains only to a select few and that all others are permitted to remain in an inferior grade of virtue. They are all obliged to this law, absolutely and without exception."[46]

Theological argument. When St. Thomas teaches that perfection consists in the precepts, he implies that charity, with all its grades and modes, including that of heaven, is of precept for everyone. Charity is not commanded of us in any determined limit or degree beyond which it would be merely a matter of counsel, but it is commanded in all its extension: "With all your heart, and with all your soul and with all your strength" (Deut. 6:5; cf. Matt. 22:37). Of all the spiritual elements in the Christian life, charity alone has the role of end or goal. Not only is charity the end of all the other precepts, which are given to us the better to fulfill this end, but it is also an end for us because by charity we are united to God, our ultimate end and our supreme perfection. Now when one treats of the end or goal, it is not possible to point out a determined measure; and here in the question of Christian perfection this is much less possible than in any other instance, because we are treating of the supreme end which shares in a certain way in God's own infinity.[47]

A very important conclusion follows from this doctrine, and with it we are able to solve the objections which may be brought against it. The perfection of charity is commanded as an end or goal to which one must tend and not as the immediate material which must be practiced at once.[48] The difference is enormous. If the perfection of charity were commanded as something to be possessed at once, all who are not perfect would be in a state of mortal sin because of the transgression of a grave precept. On the other hand, as St. Thomas explains,[49] since perfection is commanded as a goal or end, he does not transgress the precept who has not yet reached full perfection, as long as he travels toward perfection and actually possesses charity at least in a minimum degree—which consists in not loving anything more than God, against God or as much as God. Only he who has not reached this lowest grade of perfection gravely violates the precept to strive for perfection.

It is clear that one must not go to the opposite extreme. The fact that one does not violate the precept as long as he possesses the substantial perfection of charity in its lowest degree does not mean that he is not obliged to travel continuously toward the full perfection of charity. For the precept aims at this full and complete perfection, not as the immediate material but certainly as an end to be sought. Consequently, he who consciously and deliberately resolves not to progress further but to be content with the lowest perfection (simply the state of sanctifying grace) would undoubtedly violate the precept

[46]Pius XI, *Rerum Omnium,* Jan. 16, 1923, *A.A.S.,* XV (1923), p. 50.

[47]Cf. St. Thomas, *Summa,* II-II, q. 184, a. 3.

[48]Cf. Cajetan, *Commentaria in Summam theologicam,* II-II, q. 184, a. 3; Passerini, *op. cit.,* q. 184 a. 3, nn. 70, 106, etc.

[49]*Loc. cit.,* ad 2.

of striving for perfection. But what type of sin would he commit who acts in this way? It depends on his state and condition in the mystical body of Christ.

OBLIGATION OF PRIESTS AND RELIGIOUS

In order to resolve the question, it is necessary to keep in mind the following principles:[50]

1) All Christians are obliged to love God above all things and, consequently, to tend to perfection at least in a general manner by using the means offered them in their state of life.

2) In addition to this general obligation, the religious contracts a special obligation by reason of his religious profession, which obliges him to strive for perfection properly speaking by the practice of the evangelical counsels in the manner determined by his rule and constitutions.

3) The diocesan priest, although he is not in the canonical state of perfection, is obliged, in virtue of his priestly ordination and his ministerial office, to tend to perfection properly speaking and to surpass in perfection the non-clerical or lay religious.[51]

Keeping these principles in mind, we can answer the question concerning the type of sin a person would commit who consciously and deliberately decides not to strive for a higher perfection. If that person is consecrated to God by religious vows he would undoubtedly commit a mortal sin. St. Alphonsus Liguori expressly teaches this,[52] and it is a conclusion which logically follows from the very nature of things. For a religious would thereby be guilty of a grave fault regarding the essential duty of his state in life, which is precisely to strive for perfection.[53]

The same thing is true, *mutatis mutandis,* regarding the diocesan priest. The priest also is especially obliged to strive for Christian perfection. He is not *de jure* in the state of perfection as is the religious, but by reason of the lofty dignity of the priestly functions there is required of him a sanctity which is much higher even than that of the lay religious. "The worthy exercise of orders," says St. Thomas, "requires, not any kind of goodness, but excellent goodness, so that as they who receive orders are set above the people in the degree of order, they may also be above them by the merit of holiness."[54]

---

[50]Cf. R. Garrigou-LaGrange, O.P., *The Priesthood and Perfection* (Westminster, Md.: 1955), Chap. 1; A. Tanquerey, S.S., *The Spiritual Life* (Westminster, Md.: 1948), nn. 353-406.

[51]Cf. St. Thomas, *Summa,* II-II q. 184, a. 8.

[52]"The religious sins mortally who firmly resolves not to strive for perfection or not to be concerned with it in any way" (*Theologia Moralis,* IV, n. 16).

[53]Cf. St. Thomas, *Summa,* II-II, q. 166, a. 1, ad 3 and 4; *Codex Iuris Canonici,* cc. 487 and 593.

[54]*Suppl.,* q. 35, a. 1, ad 3.

Let us now see what St. Thomas says regarding lay religious: "If, however, the religious is also without orders, as is the case of religious laybrothers, then it is evident that the pre-eminence of orders excels in the point of dignity, since by holy orders a man is appointed to the most august ministry of serving Christ himself in the sacrament of the altar. For this requires a greater inward holiness than that required for the religious state. . . . Hence, other things being equal, a cleric who is in holy orders sins more grievously if he does something contrary to holiness than a religious who is not in holy orders."[55]

Presupposing this doctrine, it is easy to establish our conclusion. If the lay religious who seriously neglects his striving for perfection sins mortally, as St. Alphonsus teaches, and if in similar conditions the secular priest who neglects his obligations sins even more seriously than the lay religious, it follows that the transgression of the precept of perfection (if it is a conscious and deliberate transgression) constitutes a mortal sin for the diocesan priest.[56]

OBLIGATION OF THE LAITY

It is quite another matter with the laity. They also are obliged to strive for Christian perfection—not by reason of any special obligation as are the religious and the priest, however, but because of the general obligation contained in the first commandment. By reason of this principle, in order that a lay person be free of any grave transgressions of the general precept concerning perfection, it suffices that he possess charity in its minimum degree.[57] This involves using the means that are necessary not to lose charity and not disdaining or excluding perfection positively;[58] and this, in turn, supposes in practice a certain tendency for perfection and the exercise of certain works of supererogation.[59] This would not suffice for the priest or religious, since

[55]*Summa,* II-II, q. 184, a. 8.

[56]It should be noted, however, that (according to the more probable opinion) the special obligation of striving for perfection, both as regards the priest and the religious, is identified with that of worthily fulfilling the various duties of the priestly or religious life, and these of themselves are efficacious for leading them to the heights of perfection. By reason of the precept of perfection they are obliged to fulfill those duties more and more perfectly, following upon the growth of charity. And charity should increase until death, as St. Thomas teaches (cf. *Summa,* II-II, q. 24, aa. 7-8).

[57]"One does not transgress the precept if one does not attain to the intermediate degrees of perfection, provided one attain to the lowest" (St. Thomas, *Summa,* II-II, q. 184, a. 3, ad 2).

[58]If one were to exclude positively and by contempt the obligation to strive for perfection, it is certain that even a lay person would sin mortally against the precept of Christian perfection (cf. St. Thomas, *Summa,* II-II, q. 186, a. 2, ad 2).

[59]It is common doctrine, as stated by Suárez in the following words: "It could scarcely be morally possible that a person, even a lay person, could have the firm resolution never to commit a mortal sin, without by that very fact performing some work of supererogation and having the intention, either formally or virtually, of doing so" (*De religione,* IV, I, cap. 4, n. 12).

they are obliged to strive for perfection not only by the general obligation which is common to all Christians but also by a special obligation proceeding from religious profession or priestly ordination. The general obligation could be fulfilled by those minimal dispositions which we have spoken of regarding the laity, but they would be lacking in their special obligation which binds them as religious or as priests.

CHOOSING THE BETTER GOOD

This question is much more complex than it would appear at first glance. By gathering together certain principles from different parts of the writings of St. Thomas, we can reconstruct his thought on the matter.

1) In answering an objection, St. Thomas points out that one would transgress the precept of charity if, satisfied with possessing the substantial perfection of charity in its lowest state, he would disdain the higher grades and the total perfection of charity.[60]

2) But it is not enough simply to avoid the rejection of Christian perfection. To fulfill the precept it is necessary to desire to reach perfection. "The perfection of charity is twofold," says St. Thomas. "There is an external perfection which consists in exterior acts as signs of the interior dispositions (for example, virginity and voluntary poverty), and to this perfection (which is the proper material of the counsels) no one is obliged. But there is an internal perfection of charity which consists in the interior love of God and of neighbor . . . and to this perfection all are obliged to tend, although they do not as yet possess it actually. In a word, if one does not wish to love God more than he loves God, he does not in any way fulfill the precept of charity."[61]

3) Is it then necessary always to aspire to the more perfect and to practice it in reality? "It is necessary to make a distinction," St. Thomas says. "The greater good can be considered as the matter of action or as the object of love. We are not obliged to the greater good on the level of action, but we are obliged to it on the level of love. The reason is simple. Every rule of action demands a determined and precise material. But if one were obliged to practice the greater good, he would be obliged to that which is undetermined. Therefore, as regards external actions, since we cannot be obliged to that which is undetermined, neither are we obliged to the greater good. But on the level of love we are obliged to the greater good in all its extension."[62]

In the first quotation St. Thomas stated that one may not disdain perfection; in the second quotation he stated that one must desire perfection; and in the third quotation he teaches that one must love the greater good. Does this mean that the aspiration to the more perfect is limited to a simple affective

---

[60]Cf. *Summa,* II-II, q. 186, a. 2, ad 2.

[61]Cf. *In Epist. ad Heb.,* 6:1.

[62]Cf. *In Evang. Matt.,* 19:12.

and sentimental tendency, to a pure romanticism on the plane of love, without ever reaching the energetic and definitive "I will"? Let us turn again to the Angelic Doctor: "The will is not perfect unless it be such that, given the opportunity, it realizes the operation. But if this prove impossible, as long as the will is so perfected as to realize the operation if it could, the lack of perfection derived from the external action is simply involuntary."[63]

This principle gives us the key to the true solution of the problem. The interior will is not a true will if, when the occasion offers itself, it is not translated into works or action. Consequently, one could not say that interiorly he loves the greater good or the more perfect if, given the opportunity to practice it, he fails to do so without a reasonable cause. The reason given by St. Thomas to prove that we are not obliged to the more perfect in the level of action is that no one is obliged to the uncertain and undetermined. There are so many things that we could do each day which are more perfect than the things that we actually do. But since they are so numerous, so uncertain and so indefinite, we cannot be obliged to practice them, nor is there any fault in omitting them and using that time in performing actions which in themselves are less perfect. But if it should happen that a better good presents itself to us as a particular and specified good, and after taking account of all the circumstances of place, time, obligations of one's state, etc., it is presented to us as the better good here and now, we are no longer dealing with something which is merely objectively or materially the more perfect, and therefore undetermined and uncertain, but with that which is subjectively and formally more perfect, and therefore concrete and determined. Presented in this form, as a definite and concrete good, we are obliged to practice that good under pain of resisting grace. And to resist grace without a reasonable cause (and this would never happen if it is a true inspiration from the Holy Ghost) cannot fail to constitute a fault, at least an imperfection, if one does not wish to admit a true venial sin. In the majority of cases it will be a culpable negligence and therefore a venial sin. In these cases it is evident that this would suffice to justify the doctrine of the obligation to do the more perfect or to choose the better good when it is presented here and now in view of all the circumstances. To say otherwise would be to maintain that the Holy Spirit authorizes us to commit culpable negligence.

This leads us to examine briefly the concept of imperfection, with which we shall complete our discussion of the obligation to strive for Christian perfection.

CONCEPT OF IMPERFECTION

There are two theological opinions on moral imperfections. The first opinion holds that there are no positive imperfections distinct from venial sin, that is, that all positive imperfections are true venial sins. The second opinion

[63]*Summa,* I-II, q. 20, a. 4.

maintains that venial sin and imperfection (even positive imperfection) are two distinct things, or that there are imperfections which of themselves are not venial sins.[64]

Generally speaking, imperfections imply the omission of a good act which is not of precept but simply of counsel or the remiss performance of an act of precept, that is, the performance of an act with a lesser degree of fervor than that of which the agent is capable. What is to be thought of this question? It seems to us that the truth can be found in a synthesis which would gather together the valid arguments for either opinion.

In theory it seems to us that it cannot be denied that there is a difference between venial sin and positive imperfection. For example, if one possesses the habit of charity with an intensity of 30 degrees, but performs an act of only 20 degrees of intensity, he has performed a remiss act and has on that account committed an imperfection. But it is not lawful to say that by that very fact he has committed a venial sin. Venial sin is evil, but the imperfect act performed is good, even though it is less good than it could have been. Nor does it suffice to say that we are obliged to practice that which here and now seems to us to be the more perfect and that, as a consequence, to fail to do the better act and to do the less perfect without sufficient motive would cease to be a good act. In this case, together with the imperfection which proceeds from a less perfect act, there would have to be a venial sin of imprudence, sloth, lack of charity, etc.

But the good imperfect act does not cease to be good simply because it is imperfect. When one recites the rosary or some other voluntary prayer, he is performing a good action, although it may perhaps be accompanied by venial sins which proceed from voluntary distractions. On the other hand, one would have to say that the venial sin totally corrupts the good act and makes it evil, in which case it would be better not to pray than to pray imperfectly, and this is obviously absurd. One must not confuse what is less good in itself with that which is evil in itself, nor that which is less good for us here and now with that which is evil for us here and now. The lesser good is not an evil, nor is the lesser evil a good. We must not confuse good and evil nor precepts with counsels.[65]

---

[64]The first opinion is held by Passerini, Billuart, Hugueny, Vermeersch, etc.; the second opinion is held by Lugo, Salmanticenses, Garrigou-Lagrange, Cathrein, etc. Cf. Jordan Aumann, O.P., "The Theology of Venial Sin," in *Proceedings of the Catholic Theological Society of America,* X (1955), 74-94; J. C. Osbourn, O.P., *The Morality of Imperfections* (Washington, D.C.: Thomistic Studies, 1943).

[65]The transgression of a grave precept is a mortal sin and the transgression of a light precept is a venial sin, while the transgression of a simple counsel is an imperfection. To identify imperfection with venial sin would be equivalent to a denial in the practical order of all classes of counsels.

In spite of all this, it is very difficult in practice to decide the distinction between less generosity and actual negligence or sloth. In the majority of cases there will be true negligence, imprudence, sloth or a lack of charity, and, therefore, a venial sin. It is true that the accompanying venial sin does not compromise the goodness of the imperfect act, but it is something which is connected with the act, and for that reason there is an obligation to avoid it. But apart from this obligation, if we perform the imperfect good act, the act itself does not cease to be good in itself, although it be less good than it could have been and is accompanied by certain venial sins which proceed, not from the act itself (which would be a contradiction), but from the evil dispositions of the subject. There is an obligation to avoid the imperfection by reason of these adjacent sins and not by reason of the less perfect act which is in itself a good and not an evil.[66]

In this way the two opinions concerning moral imperfection can be harmonized. No one is authorized to commit imperfections; he should avoid them at any cost. But the obligation to avoid them does not follow from the fact that an imperfection as such is evil, but because it is almost always accompanied by other evils, such as venial sin, which one is bound to avoid.

RELATED QUESTIONS ON PERFECTION

THE GRADES OF PERFECTION

Since perfection consists formally in the perfection of charity, the grades of the one and the other will coincide. Therefore, to speak of the grades of Christian perfection is to speak of the degrees of charity.

In asking the question concerning the various degrees of charity, St. Thomas uses the classical division which is based on the three ways or stages of the

[66]Cardinal Mercier distinguishes mortal and venial sin as follows: "Mortal sin is the repudiation of the ultimate end. Venial sin is the fault of a will which does not depart completely from the end but deviates from it.

"Imperfections are not opposed to the end nor do they depart from it, but they merely are a lack of progress in the direction of the end.

"Venial sin is the failure to do a good which could and ought to be done; it is, therefore, the privation of a good and for that reason it is an evil, since evil by its definition is the privation of good.

"Imperfection is the non-acquisition of a good, the simple absence of a good, the negation of a good; and hence, in a strict sense, it is not an evil.

"That a man does not have wings is not an evil (physical), but it is simply the absence of a good. That a man does not have eyes is the privation of an organ which he ought to have, and this is an evil (physical).

"These same notions are applicable to the moral order." (Cf. Cardinal Mercier, *La vie intérieure, appel aux âmes sacerdotales.*).

spiritual life: purgative, illuminative and unitive, but he modifies the terminology in order to use terms which are more closely related to the virtue of charity. For him, as for St. Augustine, charity admits of three degrees: incipient, proficient and perfect.[67] He quotes the well-known text of St. Augustine: "As soon as charity is born, it takes food; after taking food, it waxes strong; and when it has become strong, it is perfected."[68] These are the three grades which correspond to the beginners, the proficient and the perfect.

In proving the thesis, St. Thomas returns to an analogy with the natural order which he frequently employs. In the physical and psychological growth and development of human life one can distinguish three basic stages: infancy, adolescence and maturity; these are characterized by the appearance and exercise of vital activities which are more and more perfect. Something similar occurs in the growth of charity. Although one could distinguish in this growth an indefinite number of degrees, all growth and increase can be summarized under the three fundamental grades we have given.

> The various degrees of charity are distinguished according to the different pursuits to which man is brought by the increase of charity. For at first it is incumbent on man to occupy himself chiefly with avoiding sin and resisting his concupiscences, which move him in opposition to charity. This concerns beginners, in whom charity has to be fed or fostered lest it be destroyed. In the second place, man's chief pursuit is to aim at progress in good, and this is the pursuit of the proficient, whose chief aim is to strengthen their charity by adding to it. Man's third pursuit is to aim chiefly at union with and enjoyment of God, and this belongs to the perfect, who desire to be dissolved and to be with Christ.
>
> In like manner we observe in local motion that at first there is withdrawal from one term, then approach to the other term, and, thirdly, rest in this term.[69]

One must not overlook the fact that these three stages of charity are nothing more than divisions which characterize in a general way the infinite variety of aspects in the Christian life. The path of the supernatural life is a winding path, and its stages offer a variety of transitions and levels which will differ with each individual. We must never think that these three basic stages are so many self-contained compartments and that those who are at a given time in one stage will never participate in the activities of another stage.[70]

Sometimes this happens in a transitory manner, as when a soul in the purgative stage experiences *per modum actus* the graces of the illuminative stage. It frequently happens that God gives to souls in one stage of the spiritual life the graces which are proper to another stage or even to the perfection of charity. Likewise, on the path of the advanced it may happen that there are obstacles and difficulties which proceed from the evil inclinations of human

[67]Cf. *Summa theol.*, IIa IIae, q. 24, a. 9.

[68]*In Ep. I Joan.*, Tr. 5, n. 4 (P. L. 35: 2014).

[69]*Summa,* II-II, q. 24, a. 9.

[70]Cf. St. Teresa, *Interior Castle,* Chap. 2, nn. 8 and 12.

nature or there may be greater or less impulses toward the summit of Christian perfection. In a word, in the age of the perfect it may be necessary to return to the struggles against evil inclinations and to the practice of certain virtues which are not as deeply rooted as the individual had thought. Human psychology is too complex to enable us to place these things in a rigid framework.[71]

POSSIBILITY OF PERFECTION

This is a question which is intimately connected with the material we have already discussed. The doctrine which states that charity can increase indefinitely in this life is certainly sublime, and it appeals to the infinite aspirations of generous souls; but it seems to imply a very serious contradiction. If, however much it may increase, charity never reaches its terminus in this life, it would seem necessary to conclude that true Christian perfection is impossible, because one could not imagine a degree of charity which is so perfect that it could not be more perfect.

This difficulty did not escape the attention of St. Thomas. He himself asks the question in two distinct places in his *Summa theologiae,* first in relation to charity, and secondly in relation to man.[72] By summarizing the doctrine of these two articles, we shall be able to solve the question regarding the limit of Christian perfection and the attainment of the perfection of charity in this life.

St. Thomas establishes the thesis of the possibility of perfection by using a proof from authority. The divine law cannot command the impossible; but Christ commands us to be perfect as our heavenly Father is perfect (Matt. 5:48); therefore, it is certain that perfection is attainable in this life:

> The perfection of the Christian life consists in charity. But perfection implies and presupposes a certain universality, since, as the Philosopher says, that is perfect to which nothing is lacking. Hence we may consider a threefold perfection. One is absolute, and answers to a totality not only on the part of the lover but also on the part of the object loved, so that God be loved as much as he is lovable. Such perfection as this is not possible to any creature, but is competent to God alone, in whom good is wholly and essentially.
>
> Another perfection answers to an absolute totality on the part of the lover, so that the affective faculty always actually tends to God as much as it possibly can; and such perfection as this is not possible so long as we are on the way, but we shall have it in heaven.
>
> The third perfection answers to a totality neither on the part of the object loved nor on the part of the lover as regards his always actually tending to God, but on the part of the lover as regards the removal of obstacles to the movement of love towards God, in which sense Augustine says, "Carnal desire is the poison of charity; to have no carnal desires is the perfection of charity." Such perfection as this can be had in this life, and in two ways. First, by the removal from man's affections of all that is contrary to charity, such as mortal

[71]Cf. J. Arintero, O.P., *The Mystical Evolution,* I, 16-24.

[72]Cf. *Summa,* II-II, q. 24, a. 8; q. 184, a. 2.

sin; and since there can be no charity apart from this perfection, it is necessary for salvation. Secondly, by the removal from man's affections, not only of whatever is contrary to charity, but also of whatever hinders the mind's affections from tending wholly to God. Charity is possible apart from this perfection, for instance in those who are beginners and in those who are proficient.[73]

Consequently, to be perfect in this life requires the exclusion of anything that impedes the totality of the affective movement toward God. At first glance, it would seem that St. Thomas is content with requiring very little, but if one penetrates the meaning of his words, it becomes evident that he is referring to a sublime perfection. The totality of the affective tendency toward God excludes not only venial sin but all deliberate imperfections or voluntarily remiss acts. It demands that the soul work to its full capacity. It does not mean a constant and ever actual manner of operation, which is not possible in this life, but the habitual tendency to the practice of the more perfect, excluding, so far as human weakness permits, the voluntary imperfections and remiss acts.

It does not follow from this that, if there exists the slightest voluntary imperfection, one could not be said to be free of all defects and, consequently, he could not be said to be perfect.[74] Christian perfection does not demand this much. Otherwise it would be completely impossible to attain perfection in this life, granted the misery and weakness of fallen human nature. Even in the heights of perfection there are voluntary faults and failures, as can be proved in the lives of the saints, and theologians who admit the confirmation in grace of those souls who have attained the transforming union are accustomed to make the reservation that this confirmation refers only to mortal sins and not to venial sins, and much less to voluntary imperfections. As St. James (3:2) states: "In many things we all offend," and St. John adds: "If we say that we have no sin, we deceive ourselves, and the truth is not in us"

---

[73]*Summa,* II-II, q. 184, a. 2.

[74]This is the teaching of Father Crisógono, O.C.D. (*Compendio de Ascética y Mística,* 41), who, upon examining the negative element of perfection—the absence of voluntary imperfections—says that this element must be identical in all perfect souls. The absence of defects must be absolute and universal. There can be a difference in the degree of charity in two perfect souls, without either of them ceasing to be perfect, but there cannot be admitted any difference whatever in the absence of voluntary defects. All perfect souls must be equally exempt from deliberate defects; the slightest defect would destroy perfection because there would no longer be the absence of defects.

We cannot admit this doctrine. It is *de fide* that in this life we cannot avoid all venial sins except by a special privilege, as was enjoyed by the Blessed Virgin (Denz. 833). Much less, therefore, is it possible to avoid all voluntary imperfections. Therefore, one must conclude either that perfection is not possible in this life or that certain voluntary imperfections (and even venial sins) are not incompatible with the state of perfection. The truth of the matter is that even the greatest saints committed venial sins and moral imperfections.

(I Jn. 1:8). The reason is that, even when the faculties and powers of the transformed soul are habitually ordained to God, they cannot be so in such a perfect manner that they will never be distracted or will never become attached to created goods and thereby commit certain imperfections or venial sins. Only the beatific vision completely exhausts the capacity of the soul and thereby prevents it from the slightest deviation or distraction to anything other than God. Even the slightest imperfection is impossible in heaven, but on earth it is impossible to avoid all imperfection.[75]

It is clear that these imperfections and venial sins do not cause the transformed soul to descend from its lofty state, because they are transitory actions which leave no trace in the soul and are rapidly consumed by the fire of charity. They are like drops of water which fall into a blazing fire and are evaporated in an instant; they even cause the fire to burn more brightly, because on encountering something contrary to itself the act of charity comes forth with greater force to destroy it.

PERFECTION AND GOD'S WILL

Christian perfection cannot consist in the *absolute* perfection of charity, either on the part of the object loved (since God is infinitely lovable) or on the part of the subject in the sense of an ultimate grade of charity possible in this life (since there is no such grade). There can be no terminus to the charity of the soul on earth, but it can increase indefinitely, as we have already seen. Neither can there be any degree of charity which fills perfectly the soul's capacity for charity, since St. Thomas teaches that each new increase of charity enlarges the capacity of the soul, whose obediential potency is limitless.[76] Therefore, if the degree of charity which constitutes perfection is not limited by the nature of charity itself, by its relation to its proper object, or by its relation to the subject, what is it that determines the degree of charity for each soul?

No other answer is possible but the free will of God. We are dealing now with one of the most hidden aspects of divine predestination. God distributes his graces among creatures in various degrees and without any other determination but his own free will, as St. Paul teaches.[77] These are the mysteries which escape the powers of human reason (cf. Rom. 11:33), but so far as we are able to understand these things, the most profound reason for the diversity of graces is that which St. Paul teaches in his marvelous doctrine on the Mystical Body: "But to each one of us grace was given according to the measure of Christ's bestowal. . . . And he himself gave some men as apostles,

[75]Cf. St. Thomas, *Summa,* I-II q. 4, a. 4; Suárez, *De Beatitudine,* dist. 10, sect. 1; Billuart, *De Ultimo Fine,* dist. 2, a. 4, § 2.

[76]Cf. *Summa,* II-II, q. 24, a. 7, ad 2.

[77]Cf. I Cor. 12:11. St. Thomas teaches the same doctrine in regard to charity; cf. *Summa,* II-II, q. 24, a. 3; III, q. 7, a. 10.

and some as prophets, and others again as evangelists, and others as pastors and teachers, in order to perfect the saints for a work of ministry, for building up the body of Christ, until we all attain to the unity of the faith and of the deep knowledge of the Son of God, to perfect manhood, to the mature measure of the fulness of Christ" (Eph. 4:7, 11-13).

There can be no doubt about this. According to St. Paul, the unequal distribution of graces has a finality which pertains to the totality of the Mystical Body of Christ. Here we touch one of the most profound mysteries of our faith: our predestination in Christ. It could be said that the God of predestination did not take into account, when effecting man's predestination, anything else but that immense reality of Christ in his personal and in his mystical aspect. Everything else disappears before the gaze of God, if it is lawful to use such language. And precisely because everything is subordinated and orientated to Christ, it is necessary that there be in the members of Christ a "disordered order," a harmonious dissonance, if one may speak in this paradoxical language, for the purpose of achieving the supreme beauty, the great symphony of the whole.[78] If we add to this the fact that the formation of the Mystical Body of Christ is not the ultimate purpose of creation, but that the whole Christ—both Head and members—is subordinated to the glory of God, the supreme finality, the *alpha* and *omega* of the works of God *ad extra,*[79] we shall have gathered together in its essential lines the marvelous plan of our predestination in Christ, the only one that can give us some notion of the purpose of the inequality with which God distributes his graces among the sons of men. Only when we see God face to face in the beatific vision shall we see perfectly harmonized the will of God and man's freedom, the inalienable rights of the Creator and the meritorious co-operation of the creature.

REQUISITES FOR PERFECTION

If we must grant the inequality of the distribution of graces, is there any way in which we can verify the degree of perfection and charity determined by God for a particular soul? In no way. Since there is neither on the part of the creature nor on the part of grace itself any title which would require a determined degree of perfection, it follows that it is utterly impossible to verify that degree, or even to conjecture what it might be. It depends entirely and exclusively on the free will of God, which cannot be known except by divine revelation.

---

[78] Cf. St. Thomas, *Summa,* I, q. 47, a. 1; I-II, q. 112, a. 4.

[79] "For all things are yours, whether Paul, or Apollos, or Cephas; or the world, or life, or death; or things present, or things to come—all are yours, and you are Christ's, and Christ is God's" (I Cor. 3:22-23). "And when all things are made subject to him, then the Son himself will also be made subject to him who subjected all things to him, that God may be all in all" (I Cor. 15:28).

Nevertheless, while leaving these undeniable principles intact, we can still propose four important conclusions:

> *First Conclusion: Christian perfection, to which all are called, presupposes an eminent development of grace.*

This first statement can be amply demonstrated from divine revelation. The words of Christ, "You therefore are to be perfect, even as your heavenly Father is perfect," presuppose a lofty ideal which is of itself inaccessible to man since it pertains to an exemplar that is infinite. This ideal, without limits of any kind, is presented by the Lord to all men.

Another argument from Scripture can be taken from the words of Christ in his Sermon on the Mount, when he enunciated the beatitudes, for these presuppose an eminent perfection.[80] Therefore, the sanctity which Christ proposes to all as an ideal to be attained presupposes an eminent development of grace, even to the lofty perfection of the beatitudes.

In addition to the arguments from Sacred Scripture, this fact is evident from the analogy with natural life, which requires a complete development of all its virtualities and powers before it can be called perfect. In the supernatural order, as in the natural order, the weak and undeveloped is imperfect.

Grades of perfection

How can we correlate these data of revelation and of natural reason with the teachings of St. Paul on the different grades of perfection to which God predestines us "according to the measure of Christ's bestowal"? To resolve the difficulty it is necessary to distinguish carefully between the call and predestination itself. They are not the same thing, as neither are the antecedent will of God and his consequent will. The antecedent will corresponds to the call to perfection; the consequent will pertains to that which produces predestination.

Here we have the key to the solution of the problem. It is a fact that God does not predestine all of us to one and the same degree of perfection, as he does not predestine all souls to glory. Predestination cannot be frustrated by the creature since it follows from the consequent will of God, which nothing can resist. It is also a fact of daily experience that many Christians die without having reached Christian perfection. Indeed, some die impenitent and showing the signs of reprobation. Does this mean that they were not called by God to perfection or to eternal life? Not at all. To hold this would be an obvious error in regard to perfection, and it would be close to heresy in regard to eternal life. St. Paul expressly tells us that God desires the salvation of all men: "Who wishes all men to be saved and to come to the knowledge of the truth" (Tim. 2:4). This same teaching has been repeated

[80]Cf. St. Thomas, *Summa,* I-II, q. 69.

in various councils of the Church[81] and is the unanimous doctrine of all Catholic theologians. As regards the universal call to perfection, although it is not expressly defined, it is evident from the sources of revelation and is unanimously accepted by all the schools of Christian spirituality.

Then how can one explain the undeniable fact that many Christians die without having attained Christian perfection? Indeed, some even die with all the appearances of eternal condemnation. The key to this solution lies in the distinction which we have just given, namely, the distinction between the call and predestination and between the antecedent and the consequent will of God. Prescinding from the problem of the predestination to glory (which is not the purpose of our study but can be resolved with the same principles that we are going to lay down) and confining our investigation to the universal call to Christian perfection, the solution seems to us to be as follows.

It is certain that we are all called to the highest degree of sanctity and perfection in a *remote* and *sufficient* manner by the *antecedent* will of God. But in a *proximate* and *efficacious* manner, as an effect of the *consequent* will of God (to which predestination in the concrete order and with all the individual circumstances pertains), each one of the predestined has a degree of perfection assigned by God, and to this degree of perfection the degree of glory to which he has been destined will correspond.[82] In practice, only those who are predestined to the summit of perfection will infallibly reach that degree, since the consequent will of God cannot be frustrated by the creature.[83] Those who are not predestined to the heights of perfection will, as a matter of fact, resist that remote and sufficient call to perfection. In other words, *de jure,* remotely, sufficiently and according to the antecedent will of God, all are called to Christian perfection and to all are given sufficient graces to obtain it if they do not place any obstacle to grace and if they freely co-operate with the divine action. But *de facto,* proximately, efficaciously and according to the con-

[81]Here, for example, are the words of the Council of Carisiacum (853) against Gottschalk and the predestinationists: "Deus omnipotens omnes homines sine exceptione vult salvos fieri, licet non omnes salventur. Quod autem quidam salvantur, salvantis est donum; quod autem quidam pereunt, pereuntium est meritum" (Denz. 318). The Council of Valence also states that if a man is not saved it is not because he could not be saved but because he would not (Denz. 322). This question is not expressly defined, but it is certain doctrine for Catholic theologians, and cannot be denied without temerity and probably without an error regarding the true faith. Cf. Denz. 794 ff., 1096, 1380, 1382.

[82]St. Thomas says that each rational creature is led to beatitude by God in such a way that he is also led by divine predestination to a definite degree of beatitude. Consequently, when that degree is reached, he cannot pass to a higher degree. Cf. *Summa,* I, q. 62, a. 9.

[83]Cf. *ibid.,* q. 19, a. 6.

sequent will of God, all souls are not predestined to Christian perfection. It is one thing to be called and it is another thing to be selected, as we read in the gospel: "For many are called, but few are chosen" (Matt. 20:16; 22:14). This is the profound mystery of divine predestination and election, which no created intellect could ever comprehend in this life.[84]

Call to perfection

This tremendous mystery in no way compromises our conclusions that we are all called to Christian perfection and that this perfection is the eminent development of the initial grace received in baptism. The majority of Christians die without reaching Christian perfection, but does this mean that they were not called to perfection? Not at all. They were not called in a proximate and efficacious manner by the consequent will of God because in this case they would have attained it infallibly, since the consequent will of God is accompanied by the efficacious actual graces which will not be frustrated by the creature (although the creature does not thereby lose his freedom). But it is beyond doubt that they were called to perfection remotely and sufficiently according to the antecedent will of God, as is evident from revealed doctrine and the unanimous teaching of all the schools of Christian spirituality.

According to this antecedent will which, according to theologians, is a serious, sincere will (although by man's fall it may fail to produce its ultimate effect), God called those Christians who die imperfect to an eminent perfection of grace and charity, yet differing in degrees. The antecedent will, we repeat, is a serious will to which there corresponds a deluge of sufficient actual graces for reaching that degree of eminent perfection. It is not God's fault if imperfect Christians have resisted those sufficient graces and have not reached the eminent degree of perfection that they could have reached *de jure*. It would be completely immoral to demand of God that he sanctify all, whether or not they co-operate with his divine action. The same could be said in regard to the other problem concerning our eternal salvation. God sincerely desires that all men should be saved, and, consequently, he gives to all sufficient graces for salvation, even to the most primitive savage. But God cannot and should not save one who stubbornly resists grace by abusing the privilege of his liberty. A universal salvation of all men without exception, whether good or evil, would lead inevitably to two terrible consequences: either the human will is not free (nor, then, is it responsible), or it is licit to turn against God.

It is evident, therefore, that all are called to Christian perfection as all are called to eternal salvation. Many souls will not reach perfection and some souls will not be saved, but the fault will be entirely theirs for having resisted voluntarily the sufficient graces which, when used, would have brought

[84] As St. Augustine says: "Quare hunc trahat, et illum non trahat, noli velle dijudicare, si non vis errare" (*Super Joan.* 6:44, tr. 26; P.L. 35: 1607).

them the efficacious graces to lead them to the height of perfection or the door of salvation.[85]

This problem is not concerned with the greater or lesser number of those souls who actually attain Christian perfection, but only the *de jure* exigencies of grace itself. The fact that some human beings do not live beyond infancy does not in any way compromise the general call of all to maturity, and this is true both in the natural and in the supernatural order. Christian maturity or Christian perfection supposes always an eminent development of sanctifying grace with relation to the initial grace which all receive equally at baptism, as St. Thomas teaches.[86]

Without that eminent degree, eternal salvation is possible, but Christian perfection is in no way possible in the sense usually given to this word by theologians.

Second Conclusion: Christian perfection always presupposes the perfection of the infused virtues.

This is an obvious corollary from the nature of perfection itself, which consists precisely in the full development of the infused virtues, and especially of the virtue of charity. Therefore, either there will be no Christian perfection, or it will have to be on the basis of the perfect development of the infused virtues. This doctrine is so clear and evident that no one denies it; it would be useless to insist further.

Third Conclusion: Christian perfection always requires the passive purfications.

According to St. John of the Cross (and as is evident from facts of daily experience in association with souls), "However much the beginner in mortification exercises himself in controlling his actions and passions, he cannot ever control them perfectly until God mortifies the soul passively through the purification of the night."[87] We shall return to this question when we treat in detail of active and passive purification.

Fourth Conclusion: Christian perfection necessarily implies the mystical life.

This proposition is nothing more than a conclusion which follows from the previous two. The argument or proof could not be more simple. In addition

---

[85]There are many places in Scripture in which it is stated that God does not wish the condemnation of anyone but that it depends entirely on the perverse will of men. Cf. Ezech. 13:11; Is. 45:22; I Tim. 2:4; II Pet. 3:9.

[86]Cf. *Summa,* III, q. 69, a. 8. We are speaking of the baptism of infants, who receive the sacrament with exactly the same dispositions, and not of the baptism of adults, who will receive more or less initial grace according to the dispositions with which they receive the sacrament.

[87]*The Dark Night,* Bk. I, Chap. 7, n. 5.

to the fact that the passive purifications, according to the unanimous teaching of all the schools, pertain to the mystical order, the infused virtues cannot attain their perfection until they come under the influence of the gifts of the Holy Spirit and are actuated in a divine manner. It is in this way that the actuation of the gifts of the Holy Spirit constitutes the very essence of the mystical state and the mystical act. Therefore, the perfection of the virtues and, by consequence, Christian perfection are impossible outside the mystical state.

2: THE MYSTICAL STATE

We are now to discuss one of the most fundamental questions in the theology of Christian perfection, perhaps the most important of all from a theoretical point of view. We are firmly convinced that most controversies on the mystical question arise from not having come to any agreement on the terminology to be used. The central problem is to come to an understanding concerning the content of the question, for all the questions which have arisen are completely dependent on the definition of the mystical state. Hence the mystical question should be investigated in the light of theological principles. The argument from authority (usually quotations from the mystics themselves) has been greatly abused and has not led to any practical result, nor will it ever solve the problem, because this type of argument is completely incapable of offering a solution or a basis of agreement. The data of mystical experience are vague and lack precision because they are ineffable; they cannot give us the light that is indispensable for solving this problem.

TEXTS OF THE MYSTICS

To prove our point, we cite the following texts from St. John of the Cross and St. Teresa, which have been quoted countless times by authors of various schools, even though the texts have at times seemed contradictory.

> For not all those who walk of set purpose in the way of the spirit are brought by God to contemplation, nor even half of them; why, he best knows.[1]
>
> And here it behooves us to note the reason why there are so few that attain to this lofty state of the perfection of union with God. It must be known that it is not because God is pleased that there should be few raised to this high spiritual state, for it would rather please him that all souls should be perfect! But it is rather that he finds few vessels that can bear so high and lofty a work.[2]
>
> And so it does not follow that, because all of us in this house practice prayer, we are all perforce to be contemplatives. That is impossible; and those of us who are not would be greatly discouraged if we did not grasp the truth that contemplation is something given by God, and, as it is not necessary for salvation and God does not ask it of us before he gives us our reward, we

[1]St. John of the Cross, *The Dark Night,* Bk. 1, Chap. 9.

[2]St. John of the Cross, *The Living Flame,* Stanza 2.

must not suppose that anyone else will require it of us. We shall not fail to attain perfection if we do what has been said here.[3]

Remember, the Lord invites us all, and since he is truth itself, we cannot doubt him. If his invitation were not a general one, he would not have said: "I will give you to drink." He might have said: "Come, all of you, for after all you will lose nothing by coming; and I will give drink to those whom I think fit for it." But as he said we were all to come without making this condition, I feel sure that none will fail to receive this living water unless they cannot keep to the path. May the Lord, who promises it, give us grace, for his Majesty's own sake, to seek it as it must be sought.[4]

As is evident, it is impossible to establish any solid conclusion on the basis of texts taken from the mystics themselves. The first quotations seem to be clear in denying the universal call to the mystical state. However, the last quotation could not be more decisive in favor of that universal call. If we had no other criterion of investigation than these texts, what would we be able to conclude?[5] If this is true of the two greatest names in mystical theology, the two who have most accurately described the mystical state, what conclusion could we reach if we were to quote abundant texts from other mystical authors? Side by side with a series of selected texts which seem to prove one thesis, one could usually place another series which would give abundant proof of the contrary opinion.

THEOLOGICAL PRINCIPLES

For that reason we prefer a rigorously theological method. Only in this way can we establish a firm basis which is capable of withstanding any attack. The data from the mystics themselves will always be read and studied with great interest and veneration, but only so far as they are compatible with the certain truths which are deduced from the principles of theology. Any statements which are at variance with these theological truths will have to be rejected *a priori,* regardless of their author, since it is impossible that one truth should contradict another and still proceed from the one source of

[3]St. Teresa, *The Way of Perfection,* Chap 17.

[4]*Ibid.,* Chap. 19.

[5]As a matter of fact, St. Teresa herself states: "In this last chapter I seem to have been contradicting what I had previously said, as, in consoling those who had not reached the contemplative state, I told them that the Lord had different roads by which they might come to him, just as he also had many mansions. I now repeat this: His Majesty, being who he is and understanding our weakness, has provided for us. But he did not say: 'Some must come by this way and others by that.' His mercy is so great that he has forbidden none to strive to come and drink of this fountain of life" (*The Way of Perfection,* Chap. 20).

As regards St. John of the Cross, anyone who reads him objectively can see that the intention of the saint is to lead the soul to the heights of mystical union with God, and that is not possible without passing through the passive purfications, which are definitely mystical in nature. Consequently, for St. John of the Cross, Christian perfection is not possible without mysticism.

eternal truth in whom there can be no contradiction. If one must choose between a certain theological conclusion and a contrary statement from mystical experience, one will have to choose the first, because the theological principle from which the conclusion follows has its ultimate basis in divine revelation. To do otherwise would be to fall victim to all types of illusions.[6]

Following the criterion which has been established, let us attempt to define with exactitude and theological accuracy the constitutive element of the mystical state. This will give us the key to the solution of all the other problems which are nothing more than consequences and corollaries of this basic question.

THE STATE OF THE QUESTION

Before formulating our thesis and giving the proof, we shall examine the actual state of the question. We shall select the opinions of those theologians who are most representative among modern authors of the various schools of spirituality, limiting ourselves to theologians and speculative authors of the mystical life to the complete exclusion of the mystics themselves. In recent times theologians have begun to study these questions by using modern methods of critical investigation, and in this respect their opinion is often superior to that of the ancient theologians. Many of the theologians whom we shall mention have made profound studies of the history of the theology of Christian mysticism, and they are for that reason in a better position to tell us what should be understood by the mystical state.

There is a great variety of definitions among modern authors, but through them all one can perceive a basis of common agreement concerning the constitutive element of Christian mysticism. They dispute at great length as to whether mysticism is necessary for Christian perfection and about many other questions related to this one, but as regards the nature of mysticism they are for the most part in agreement. Many identify mysticism with infused contemplation, which is not quite exact, but in any case, since infused contemplation is the mystical act par excellence, their words express clearly the concept which they have formulated concerning mysticism.

Although for convenience's sake we group together the authors of the same religious order, this does not mean that all the authors of the same order are in complete agreement.

Benedictines

For the Trappist abbot of the monastery of Notre Dame de Grâce, Dom Lehodey, mystical prayer is passive contemplation, which is manifestly super-

[6]Cf. Aumann-Greenstock, *The Meaning of Christian Perfection,* pp. 22-23.

natural, infused and passive. In this passive contemplation God makes himself known in the soul in an ineffable manner through a union of love which communicates to the soul peace and repose which overflow to the senses.[7]

Dom Columba Marmion does not treat expressly of mysticism in any of his writings. But we know from the testimony of his biographer and intimate friend, Dom Thibaut, that the great Benedictine spiritual writer considered infused contemplation as the normal but gratuitous complement of the spiritual life.[8]

According to Dom Huijben, the essence of mysticism consists in a confused perception of the very reality of God which is sometimes an awareness of God's proximity, sometimes of his presence, or again of his action, or his very being, depending on whether the mystical experience is more or less profound.[9]

Dom Anselm Stolz maintains that the awareness of the presence of God and of his operation in the soul is essential to the mystical life. The mystical life is a transpsychological experience of the immersion of the soul in the current of the divine life, and this immersion is effected in the sacraments, especially in the Eucharist. For Dom Stolz mysticism is the plenitude of the Christian life, and as such it is not something extraordinary, nor is it a second path to sanctity which is trod only by the chosen few. It is the path which all ought to travel, and if souls do not reach this point in their Christian life, they will be forced to despoil themselves of all the obstacles by a purification in the life to come in order to prepare themselves for union with God in the beatific vision.[10]

In his work on mysticism Dom Cuthbert Butler investigates the mystical doctrine of the primitive Church in the West and offers certain definitions of contemplation and the mystical life which were drawn from different treatises on mysticism by the Fathers. For them, contemplation implied an intellectual intuition, direct and objective, of transcendent reality; a conscious relationship with the absolute; the union of the soul with the absolute, so far as is possible in this life; the experimental perception of the presence and being of God in the soul.[11]

For Dom Louismet mystical theology belongs to the experimental order. It is a phenomenon which takes place in every fervent soul, and it consists simply in the experience of a soul on earth which has succeeded in tasting God and seeing how sweet he is.[12]

---

[7]*The Ways of Mental Prayer* (trans. by a monk of Mt. Melleray; Dublin: M. H. Gill, 1930), Part 3, Chap. 4.

[8]Cf. *L'Union avec Dieu*, ed. R. Thibaut, O.S.B. (Paris: 1934).

[9]Cf. "La Terminologie Mystique," *La Vie Spirituelle*, XXIV (Aout-Septembre, 1930), *Supplément*, pp.[20]-[26].

[10]Cf. *The Doctrine of Spiritual Perfection* (St. Louis: Herder, 1938).

[11]Cf. *Western Mysticism* (New York: Dutton, 1932).

[12]Cf. *Divine Contemplation for All* (New York: Kenedy, 1922).

Father Gardeil places the question of the mystical experience by asking whether in this life we can touch God by an immediate contact and enjoy an experience of him that is truly direct and substantial. The saints maintain that we can, and their descriptions of the prayer of union, ecstasy and spiritual marriage are all filled with this type of a quasi-experimental perception of God within ourselves.[13]

Father Garrigou-Lagrange distinguishes between doctrinal mysticism, which studies the laws and conditions of the progress of the Christian virtues and of the gifts of the Holy Spirit in view of perfection, and experimental mysticism, which is a loving and savory knowledge, entirely supernatural and infused, which the Holy Ghost alone can give us by his unction and which is, as it were, a prelude to the beatific vision.[14]

For Father F.-D. Joret infused love is the essential element of the mystical state. This infused love is frequently preceded by an infused light passively received in the soul, but it is not absolutely necessary.[15]

Father Arintero maintains that the constitutive element of the mystical life consists in the predominance of the gifts of the Holy Spirit and that the mystical life is nothing else but the conscious life of grace, or a certain intimate experience of the mysterious touches and influences of the Holy Ghost.[16]

Father Ignatius Menéndez-Reigada places the essence of the mystical state in the life of grace lived in a conscious manner and characterized especially by the actuation of the gifts of wisdom and understanding through which one begins to be conscious of the fact that he possesses God and is united with him.[17]

Father Marceliano Llamera holds that the mystical life is the life of grace under the rule of the Holy Ghost through his gifts; the constitutive element of the mystical life is the actuation of the gifts; the mystical act is an act of the gifts; the mystical state is the permanent or habitual activity of the gifts in the soul. The mystical state is characterized by the passivity of the soul, which is acted upon by God. Every Christian soul in the state of grace is radically a mystical soul; the mystic in act is that soul which lives the life of the gifts. Every soul is called by a general law to the mystical life and can and should aspire to it. In the ascetical life there may be frequent interventions of the gifts; in the mystical life there may be ascetical intervals. Mystical contemplation is a loving and prolonged intuition of God infused in the soul by the Holy Spirit through the gifts of understanding and wisdom. The normal or ordinary mystical graces are those which actuate the gifts of the Holy

[13]Cf. *La Structure de l'Âme et l'Expérience Mystique* (Paris: 1927).

[14]Cf. *Christian Perfection and Contemplation* (trans. by Sr. M. Timothea Doyle, O.P.; St. Louis: Herder, 1937).

[15]Cf. "Pour Fixer la Terminologie Mystique," *La Vie Spirituelle,* XXI (Novembre, 1929), *Supplément,* pp. [91]-[101].

[16]Cf. *The Mystical Evolution* (trans. by Jordan Aumann, O.P.; St. Louis: Herder)

[17]Cf. *Los Dones Del Espíritu Santo,* pp. 2-78.

Ghost; the extraordinary graces are those which surpass the activity of the gifts, and although they are not necessary for the mystical state, they are not always *gratiae gratis datae* or for the good of one's neighbor, but may also sanctify the soul which receives them.[18]

Carmelites

Father Gabriel of St. Mary Magdalen believes that the mystical state is characterized by infused contemplation, which is the most essential act of the mystical state. He is convinced that mysticism enters into the normal and ordinary development of the life of grace.[19]

Father Chrysogonus of Jesus in the Blessed Sacrament does not give his exact thought concerning the constitutive element of mysticism, but we can gather his teaching from various elements. Mysticism is for him the development of grace through operations which surpass the exigencies of grace itself, in other words, by extraordinary means. The mystical state is essentially constituted by infused knowledge and love. Infused contemplation is an affective intuition of divine things which results from a special influence of God on the soul.[20]

For Father Claudius of Jesus Crucified, mystical theology is the intuitive knowledge and love of God founded in the negation of all natural light of the intellect, through which the intellect perceives an indescribable goodness and being which is truly present in the soul.[21]

The Teresian Congress held in Madrid in 1923 formulated the following statements as the authentic Carmelite doctrine concerning contemplation: 1) Infused contemplation is the mystical operation par excellence. 2) This contemplation is the experimental knowledge of divine things produced supernaturally by God in the soul, and it represents the most intimate union between the soul and God which is possible in this life. 3) It is, therefore, the ultimate ideal and culminating step of the Christian life in this world for souls that are called to mystical union with God. 4) The state of contemplation is characterized by the increasing predominance of the gifts of the Holy Ghost and the superhuman mode with which all good actions are executed through the activity of the gifts. 5) Since the virtues find their ultimate perfection in the gifts and since the gifts reach their perfect operation in contemplation, contemplation is the ordinary path of sanctity and habitually heroic virtue.[22]

[18]Cf. "El Problema Místico," *Teologia Espiritual,* I (1957), pp. 33-69.

[19]*Études Carmelitaines,* April, 1933; "L'Union de Transformation dans la Doctrine de Saint Jean de la Croix," *La Vie Spirituelle, Supplément,* March, 1925.

[20]*Compendio de Ascética y Mística* (Salamanca: 1933).

[21]Cf. *Revista Española de Teología,* I (1940), 598.

[22]Cf. *El Monte Carmelo,* May, 1923, 211. As is evident, these statements reflect Thomistic teaching on the mystical state. However, not all Thomists would accept the third conclusion as stated, since it seems to restrict the call to the mystical state. Neither would all Thomists admit that infused contemplation is the culmination of the gifts of the Holy Spirit for each and every mystic, for infused contemplation is not the only mystical operation.

Father de Maumigny defines infused contemplation as a simple and loving gaze on God by which the soul, suspended in admiration and love, knows and tastes God experimentally, amidst a profound peace which is the beginning of eternal beatitude.[23]

Jesuits

According to Father Poulain, the mystical state is especially characterized by recollection and union. The basic difference in the mystical recollection is that the soul does not merely recall God or think of him, but it has an experimental intellectual knowledge of God. It truly experiences that it is in communication with God.[24]

For Father de la Taille, contemplation comes from love; it is a loving gaze. And what distinguishes this love from the love implied in every act of faith? It is not its perfection or its intensity, for the love of the contemplative could in this respect be less than that of the ordinary Christian. But this love is a love which is *consciously infused.* The mystic has the consciousness of receiving from God a "ready-made" love. The origin of contemplation is in this love which is passively received and in the consciousness of this passivity which swoops on the intelligence and carries it above itself toward the sovereign good to which it attaches it in a dark light.[25]

Father J. V. Bainvel maintains that the mystical state is constituted by the consciousness of the supernatural in us.[26]

Basing his opinion on the testimony of the mystics themselves, Father J. Maréchal believes that infused contemplation involves a new element which is distinct from the normal psychological operations and from ordinary grace, namely, the immediate intuition of God by the soul.[27]

According to Father de Guibert, the soul experiences the presence of God in itself during the act of contemplation. Formerly it knew the indwelling and the action of God indirectly through faith; now it has an actual experience of these things. This direct and experimental perception of God is general and confused; it does not bring new lights or new knowledge, but it is a profound and simple intuition. The will is drawn to God by a simple and direct movement. The soul receives all this in a passive manner, and it can neither achieve it by its own efforts nor retain it as long as it pleases.[28]

---

[23]Cf. *Practice of Mental Prayer* (New York: Kenedy, 1915).

[24]Cf. *The Graces of Interior Prayer* (trans. by Leonora Yorke-Smith; St. Louis: Herder, 1911).

[25]This analysis is given by J. V. Bainvel, S.J., in his introduction to the 10th edition of Poulain's *Des Grâces d'Oraison* (Paris: 1922), p. lxxvi.

[26]Cf. *Revue Ascétique et Mystique,* January, 1923.

[27]*Studies in the Psychology of the Mystics* (trans. by R. Thorold; London: Burns, Oates and Washbourne, 1927).

[28]Cf. *The Theology of the Spiritual Life* (trans. by Paul Barrett, O.F.M. Cap.; New York: Sheed and Ward, 1953), Part 7.

Father Schrijvers, C.SS.R., maintains that contemplation is essentially a knowledge and love produced directly by God in the intellect and will through the gifts of the Holy Ghost. All true contemplation is necessarily infused.[29]

Other authors

For Father Cayré, A.A., mysticism involves the following elements: 1) a certain awareness of God produced by God himself; 2) God is perceived as dwelling in the soul; 3) the mystical experience is completely distinct from any kind of sensible consolation.[30]

Father Lamballe, Eudist, quotes the definition by St. Francis de Sales (*Treatise on the Love of God,* Bk. VI, Chap. 3): "Contemplation is nothing other than a loving, simple and permanent attention to divine things."[31]

Father Naval, C.F.M., teaches that mysticism consists in an intuitive knowledge and an intense love of God received by divine infusion, that is, through extraordinary means of divine providence.[32]

Monsignor M. J. Ribet defines the mystical act as a supernatural and passive attraction of the soul for God, proceeding from an illumination and inflammation which precede reflection and surpass human efforts.[33]

Monsignor Saudreau points out a twofold element in every mystical state: a superior knowledge of God and an intense love which the soul could never attain by its own powers.[34]

Father Tanquerey, S.S., considers that mysticism pertains to the contemplative life and embraces all the phases of the spiritual life from the first night of the senses to the spiritual marriage. He describes contemplation as a simple, affective and prolonged vision of God and divine things, a vision which is an effect of the gifts of the Holy Ghost and a special actual grace which makes us more passive than active.[35]

Monsignor F. X. Maquart summarizes his conclusions as follows:

> If one admits, with the Thomistic school, the *intrinsic* efficacy of actual grace, the nature of the mystical life is easy to explain. Since theologians are unanimous in recognizing the mystical life in a certain vital passivity of the soul, the Thomists, in seeking the cause of this passivity, will find it in the intrinsic development of grace itself. Their doctrine on the efficacy of actual grace gives them the right to do so. If grace is by its very nature efficacious, it is required for every act of the life of grace. And since sanctifying grace and the habits which accompany it (the virtues and gifts) give only the *power* of working supernaturally, the will must be moved *in actu secundo* by an efficacious actual grace.

---

[29]Cf. *Les Principes de la Vie Spirituelle* (Paris: 1938).

[30]Cf. "Pour Fixer la Terminologie Mystique, *La Vie Spirituelle,* XXIII (Juin, 1930), *Supplément,* pp. [131]-[141].

[31]Cf. *La Contemplation* (Paris: 1911).

[32]Cf. *Curso de Teología Ascética y Mística.* (1914; Latin edition, 1919).

[33]*La Mystique Divine* (3 vols.; 1879).

[34]Cf. *L'État Mystique* (2nd. ed., 1921).

[35]Cf. *The Spiritual Life* (Westminster, Md.: Newman, 1948).

On the other hand, the defenders of efficacious grace *ab extrinseco,* that is, by the action of the will, teach in conformity with their doctrine that habitual grace and the virtues suffice. How could it be otherwise? If efficacious grace is nothing other than the actual *sufficient* grace which gives the *posse agere,* to which is added the co-operation of the will, whoever possesses an infused habit which gives him this *posse agere* needs absolutely nothing else for operation except the intervention of the will. But since, according to the Molinist theory, the efficacy of grace proceeds from the will, there cannot be in the normal economy of the life of grace a state in which the vitally operating soul would be passive; the mystical life is thus excluded.[36]

Jacques Maritain considers the mystical state to be the flowering of sanctifying grace and to be characterized by the predominance of the exercise of the gifts of the Holy Ghost. It is not possible to discern the exact moment at which the mystical state begins, but any Christian who grows in grace and progresses to perfection, if he lives long enough, will reach the mystical state and the life of habitual predominance of the activity of the gifts of the Holy Ghost.[37]

Summary

After investigating the various opinions of theologians concerning the essence of mysticism, one fact is very evident: as a psychological fact, mysticism is an experience or awareness of the divine. Practically all theologians agree on this point, in spite of the fact that definitions of mysticism have been formulated by authors of schools that are completely distinct and even contradictory on certain fundamental points. Mysticism is a passive and not an active experience because—and here also there is a general agreement among theologians—only the Holy Spirit can produce this experience in us by the influence and actuation of his gifts.

THE ESSENCE OF MYSTICISM

It is no easy task to attempt a complete psychological and theological synthesis concerning the essence of mysticism, and yet we believe that such a synthesis can be stated with all theological precision in the following thesis:

[36]Cf. "Pour Fixer la Terminologie Spirituelle," *La Vie Spirituelle,* XXII (Janvier, 1930), *Supplément,* pp. [34]-[41]. We do not subscribe to the final conclusions of Monsignor Maquart regarding the Molinist position on the mystical state, for even those theologians who defend the theory of efficacious grace *ab extrinseco* will require the concursus of God in the action of the creature and hence would not exclude the possibility of a mystical state or mystical acts.

[37]Cf. "Une Question sur la Vie Mystique," *La Vie Spirituelle,* VII (Mars, 1923), pp. 636-50 ff.; with Raïssa Maritain, *Prayer and Intelligence* (trans. by A. Thorold; New York: Sheed and Ward, 1934); *The Degrees of Knowledge* (trans. under the supervision of Gerald B. Phelan; New York: Scribners, 1959). Maritain is one of the few authors to define clearly the distinction between mysticism and infused contemplation.

The essential constitutive of mysticism is the actuation of the gifts of the Holy Ghost in the divine or superhuman manner which ordinarily produces a passive experience of God or of his divine activity in the soul.

EXPLANATION OF THE TERMS

Let us examine carefully the various terms of the thesis. In the first place, when we say "essential constitutive," we are not referring to any external characteristic or psychological manifestation to distinguish mysticism from non-mysticism, but we are speaking of the essential note which intrinsically constitutes mysticism.

Actuation of the gifts

When we say that it consists in "the actuation of the gifts of the Holy Ghost in a divine or superhuman mode," we mean that the mystical experience is itself the effect of the actuation of the gifts, which work in a divine manner. This is a most certain conclusion which has been admitted by all the schools of Christian spirituality.

This actuation of the gifts constitutes the very essence of mysticism. Whenever a gift of the Holy Ghost operates, there is produced a mystical act which is more or less intense according to the intensity of the activity of the gift. And when the actuation of the gifts is so frequent and repeated that it predominates over the exercise of the infused virtues, which operate in a human manner—characteristic of the ascetical state—the soul has entered fully into the mystical state. This is always relative, of course, since the gifts never operate, even in the great mystics, in a manner which is absolutely continuous and uninterrupted.

The actuation of the gifts in a divine manner is the primary and essential element of mysticism, and for that reason it is never lacking in any of the mystical states or mystical acts. The experience of the divine is one of the most frequent and ordinary manifestations in the activity of the gifts, but it is not absolutely essential. It can be lacking; and, as a matter of fact, it is lacking during those nights of the soul and other passive purifications which are nevertheless truly mystical.[38] What can never be lacking is the superhuman manner in which the soul practices the virtues as a natural effect of being acted upon by the gifts of the Holy Ghost. There are many degrees of this

[38]To say with Father de Guibert, S.J. (*The Theology of the Spiritual Life*, n. 405) that the nights pertain to mysticism "inasmuch as these states are a preparation for infused contemplation or inasmuch as the soul is passive both in these states and in infused contemplation" is merely to offer a facile argument in order to save the opinion that the experience of the divine is the essential element of mysticism. But this is manifestly contrary to the teaching of St. John of the Cross and all previous tradition, which has always considered the nights of the soul to be essentially mystical. Neither can we admit the opinion of those who consider the experience to be a secondary but essential element of the mystical state. What is essential, even secondarily, can never be lacking; but the experience of the divine is lacking in the nights of the soul.

superhuman mode of action, and they will depend on the greater perfection of the soul and the greater or less intensity with which the gift is actuated, but this mode of action is always verified when the soul operates under the influence of the gifts. The prudent and experienced spiritual director who observes the reactions of the soul can readily discover the operation of the gifts even in those situations, such as the nights of the soul, in which the soul seems far from God. The lack of the experience of the divine during the dark nights makes it impossible to designate the experience of the divine as the essential note of mysticism.[39]

Ordinarily produces

On the other hand, in the midst of the sufferings which cause a feeling of the total absence of God, the soul continues to practice the virtues to a heroic degree and in a manner that is more divine than ever. Its faith is most vivid, its hope is superior to all hope, and its charity is above all measure. Hence it is evident that the only mystical element which is never lacking, even in the terrible nights, is the superhuman activity of the gifts, which is very intense in the periods of passive purgation. If, however, we exclude those nights and any other phenomenon of purification, then we may affirm that the experience of the divine is the most ordinary and frequent effect of the activity of the gifts of the Holy Ghost. The actuation of the gifts, in other words, "ordinarily" produces a passive experience of God or of his divine activity in the soul.

Experience of the divine

The awareness of the divine is also one of the most radical differences between the mystical state and the ascetical state. The ascetical soul lives the Christian life in a purely human manner and has no awareness of this life other than by reflection and discursus. The mystic, on the other hand, experiences in himself, except in those cases mentioned, the ineffable reality of the life of grace. The mystics are, as de Grandmaison says, the witnesses of the loving presence of God in us. How beautifully St. Teresa speaks of this when she treats of the lofty communication of the Trinity to the soul that is transformed by grace:

> What we hold by faith, the soul may be said here to grasp by sight, although nothing is seen by the eyes, either of the body or of the soul, for it is no imaginary vision. Here all three Persons communicate themselves to the soul and speak to the soul and explain to it those words which the gospel attributes to the Lord, namely, that he and the Father and the Holy Spirit

---

[39]Cf. St. Teresa, *Interior Castle,* Bk. IX; *The Life,* Chap. 20. As St. John says: "What the sorrowful soul feels most in this condition is its clear perception that God has abandoned it and, abhorring it, has cast it into darkness, and this is for the soul a serious and pitiful suffering for it to believe that God has abandoned it. . . . Because truly when this purgative contemplation is most pressing, the soul feels very keenly the shadow of death and the lamentations of death and the pains of hell, which consist in the soul's feeling itself to be without God and chastised and rejected and unworthy of him and that he is angry with it, all of which the soul feels in this condition, and what is more, it seems to the soul that this condition will last forever" (*The Dark Night,* Chap. 6).

> will come to dwell with the soul which loves him and keeps his commandments. O, God help me! What a difference there is between hearing and believing these words and being led in this way to perceive how true they are. Each day this soul wonders more, for she feels that they have never left her and perceives quite clearly, in the way I have described, that they are in the interior of her heart, in the most interior place of all and in its greatest depths.[40]

It is true that mystical communications are not always as lofty as this, but they always produce (except in the passive purifications) an experimental awareness of the life of grace. To hear and to believe this is characteristic of the ascetic. To understand in an expenmental and ineffable manner—this is the privilege of the mystic. The reader will recall the remarkable case of Sister Elizabeth of the Trinity, who actually experienced the indwelling of God in her soul before ever hearing anyone speak of this mystery.[41]

Passivity

Passivity is another typical note. The mystic has a clear awareness of the fact that what he is experiencing is not produced by himself. He is restricted to receive an impression produced by an agent completely distinct from himself. He is under the passive influence of an experience which he did not cause and which he cannot retain for a second longer than is desired by the one who produces it.[42]

If we read attentively the descriptions written by those who have been favored by heaven, we shall soon discover amid many varied factors this constant basis of their mysticism. It appears always and above all as an experience which is perceived by a kind of psychological passivity of love which dominates their whole life. The mystics have an impression, more or less sensible, concerning an intervention which is foreign to them and which arises nevertheless from the depths of their being to unite them in a movement to God and a certain fruition of God.[43]

It is a psychological fact admitted by all the schools as a typical note of the mystical experience that the soul is passive during this experience. Even in the most ancient treatise on mysticism, *De Divinis Nominibus* by the pseudo-Areopagite, one can find a famous expression, *patiens divina,* which was repeated by all theologians and masters of the spiritual life as the characteristic note of the mystical state. It is evident that we are referring to a relative passivity, that is, only in relation to the principal agent who is the Holy Ghost, for the soul reacts in a vital manner to the movement of the Holy Ghost." As St.

---

[40]*Interior Castle,* Seventh Mansions, Chap. 1.

[41]Cf. M. M. Philipon, O.P., *The Spiritual Doctrine of Sister Elizabeth of the Trinity* (trans. by a Benedictine of Stanbrook Abbey; Westminster, Md.: Newman, 1955), Chap. 1.

[42]Cf. St. Teresa, *The Life,* Chap. 15.

[43]Cf. F. Joret, O.P., *La Contemplation Mystique d'après Saint Thomas d'Aquin* (Paris: Desclée, 1927), 103.

Teresa says, "the will consents," by co-operating with the divine action in a free and voluntary manner. And thus liberty and merit are preserved under the activity of the gifts.

Of the divine

Sometimes the soul experiences God himself dwelling within the soul in a most clear manner; at other times it is God's divine action perfecting the soul which is experienced. The soul would say that it feels within the very depths of its spirit a kind of contact with the brush of the divine artist as he draws the portrait of Christ in the soul. The soul thinks of that stanza of the *Veni Creator* in which reference is made to the *digitus paternae dexterae* (in the Dominican liturgy, *dextrae Dei tu digitus*) which is the Holy Ghost.

But how do the gifts of the Holy Spirit produce this passive experience of the divine, and why do they cease to give this experience during the passive purgations? The answer is simple. The mystical experience is produced through the gifts because of their divine or supernatural mode of operation. But the infused virtues, even the theological virtues, operate under the rule of reason or in a human manner; hence it is impossible that they could produce the experience of the divine.

It is the constant teaching of St. Thomas and theologians of all schools that the union of the soul with God, begun essentially through sanctifying grace, is actuated and perfected by the acts of supernatural knowledge and love, that is, by the exercise of the infused virtues, principally of faith and of charity.[44] But the infused virtues, although supernatural as regards their essence, are not supernatural in their manner of operation. This is not because they do not demand a divine modality (which is the only one proportioned to their supernatural nature), but because of the imperfect manner in which they are possessed by a soul in the state of grace, as St. Thomas explains.[45] When separated from the influence of the gifts, the infused virtues must act in a human mode or manner, following the rule of reason, although always under the influence of an actual grace which God denies to no one.[46] Hence we say that it is within our power, with the help of actual grace, to put these virtues into practice whenever we wish to do so. Although supernatural in their essence, these acts are produced in our connatural human manner, and for that reason they do not give us nor can they give us any passive experience of the divine. The soul has no more awareness of those actions than the simple psychological awareness which one has while actually performing the acts. The mystical experience is absolutely outside the realm of this type of activity and awareness.

[44]Cf. *Summa,* III, q. 6, a. 6, ad 1; *De Caritate,* q. 2, ad 7.

[45]*Summa,* I-II, q. 68, a. 2.

[46]Actual efficacious grace is a gift of God which no one can merit strictly, but God offers this grace to us to assist us in fulfilling the duty of each moment. Cf. Garrigou-Lagrange, *The Three Ages of the Interior Life,* I, p. 90.

THE MODE OF THE GIFTS

The nature and function of the gifts of the Holy Ghost is far different. As we have already seen, the gifts are supernatural, not only in their essence, but even in their manner or mode of operation. They are not subject to the movement and control of human reason as the infused virtues are, for the Holy Spirit himself directly and immediately moves the gifts to operation. Therefore, although the gifts are essentially inferior to the theological virtues, even though they are essentially superior to the moral virtues,[47] as regards their mode of operation they are superior to all the infused virtues because the characteristic mode of the gifts is the divine or superhuman mode.

This divine mode of operation is completely alien to our human psychology. It is not something connatural to our manner of being and operation, it is entirely transcendent. For that reason, on producing an act of the gifts, the soul perceives that transcendent element as something completely foreign to itself, that is, as something which the soul itself has not produced by its own power and which the soul cannot retain any longer than is desired by the mysterious agent who produces it.[48] This is fundamentally the passive experience of the divine which we have been investigating.

The intensity of this experience will depend on the intensity with which the gift has been actuated. Because of this, the imperfect mystical acts given in the ascetical stage do not usually produce anything that can qualify as a truly mystical experience. The reason is that the gift has been actuated, but only imperfectly, with little intensity, because the imperfect disposition of the subject would not permit more. Of itself the gift has produced an experience of the divine, but it is so weak and imperfect that the soul scarcely notices it. If it is a question of one of the intellectual gifts, there will be a transitory act of infused contemplation, but in a very incipient grace which is almost imperceptible. St. John of the Cross explains this as follows:

> It is true, however, that when this condition first begins, the soul is hardly aware of this loving knowledge. The reason for this is twofold. First, this loving knowledge is apt at the beginning to be very subtle and delicate, so as to be almost imperceptible to the senses. Secondly, when the soul is used to the exercise of meditation, which is wholly perceptible, it is unaware and hardly conscious of this other new and imperceptible condition, which is purely spiritual; especially when, not understanding it, the soul does not allow itself to rest in it, but strives after the former, which is more readily perceptible. The result is that, however abundant the loving interior peace may be, the soul has no opportunity of experiencing and enjoying it. But the more ac-

[47]Cf. St. Thomas, *Summa,* I-II, q. 68, a. 8; a. 4, ad 3.

[48]It is necessary that the gifts operate if they are to be perceived; it is not sufficient to possess them simply as habits. Entitative realities are not perceived, but only dynamic realities. For that reason our soul is not aware of its own essence except through the acts of the intellect, nor is it aware of the habits which modify its faculties except through the acts of the habit. Cf. St. Thomas, *Summa,* I, q. 87, aa. 1-2.

customed the soul grows to this by allowing itself to rest, the more it will grow therein, and the more conscious it will become of that loving general knowledge of God in which it has greater enjoyment than in anything else, since this knowledge causes peace, rest, pleasure and effortless delight.[49]

THE MYSTICAL EXPERIENCE

Such is the nature of the mystical experience. At the beginning it is subtle and delicate and almost imperceptible because of the imperfect actuation of the gifts of the Holy Ghost; but the actuation is gradually intensified and becomes more frequent, until the activity of the gifts predominates in the life of the soul. Then the soul has entered into the full mystical state, whose essential characteristic is the predominance of the activity of the gifts in a divine mode over the simple exercise of the infused virtues in a human mode, that which was proper to the ascetical state.

In themselves, the gifts of the Holy Spirit tend to produce an experience of the divine by reason of their divine modality, which is alien to our human psychology. But there are exceptions, both on the part of the divine motion and on the part of the soul's disposition. During the passive purgations the divine motion of the gifts has as its purpose the purification of the soul from all its sensible attachments and even from spiritual delights which contemplation produces. It imposes a kind of motion which not only deprives the soul of an awareness of God filled with sweetness and delight, but gives the soul a contrary experience of absence and abandonment by God, which is of great purgative value. In these cases the gift is limited to its essential and primary effect, which is to dispose the soul for the superhuman exercise of the virtues, but it lacks its secondary and accidental effect, the experience of the divine. This is a logical and natural consequence of the purification which God intends to effect in the soul. The Holy Ghost is master of his gifts and he can do with them as he wills. Sometimes he actuates them in all their fulness, producing their double effect: the essential effect of the divine modality and the accidental effect of the awareness of God. At other times he exercises them only in their essential aspect and holds in suspense the accidental effects.

The night of the senses

If to this difference on the part of the divine movement we add the dispositions of the soul during the period of the passive purgation, it will be evident why the soul does not perceive the divine movement of the gifts during that period. As St. John of the Cross explains so well in the text that we have cited, when the first light of contemplation begins to dawn (in the night of the senses), the soul is not yet accustomed to that subtle, delicate and almost insensible light which is communicated to it. And since, on the other hand, the soul is incapacitated for the exercise of the discursive meditation to which it was accustomed, it is left apparently without the one or the other

[49]*The Ascent of Mount Carmel,* Bk. 2, Chap. 17, 7.

and in complete obscurity. It is limited to a simple loving gaze by which it perceives by gradual degrees the divine motion of the gifts, and at the completion of the night of the senses it enters upon a clear awareness of the divine.

The night of the spirit

Something similar occurs during the night of the spirit. God proposes to carry the purification of the soul to its ultimate consequences before admitting it to the transforming union or the spiritual marriage. To that end, he increases the power of the infused light to an intense degree. The soul, blinded by such light, can see nothing but the numerous miseries and imperfections with which it is filled, which it was incapable of perceiving before it had received that extraordinary light. It is, as St. Teresa says, like the water in a glass which seems very clear, but when the sun shines through it it is seen to be full of particles. The contrast between the sanctity and grandeur of God and the misery and weakness of the soul is so great that it seems to the soul that it will never be possible to unite light with darkness, sanctity with sin, the all with the nothing, and the Creator with the poor creature. This causes a frightful torture to the soul, and it is this which is the very substance of the night of the spirit.[50] The soul does not realize that it is the intensity of contemplative life which produces that state. It sees nothing more than ineffable majesty and grandeur on the one side, and misery and corruption on the other. It believes itself to be irreparably lost and separated from God. Nevertheless, it continues to practice the infused virtues, and especially the theological virtues, in a heroic degree and in a manner more divine than ever. The gifts are operating in the soul most intensely and producing their essential effect, that divine or superhuman modality with which the soul exercises the virtues; but because of the purification which is being suffered and because of the dispositions of the soul they do not produce their accidental and secondary effect.

COMPLEMENTARY QUESTIONS

From all that we have said, certain important conclusions can be drawn. We shall explain briefly the principal ones which are necessary for understanding the true nature of mysticism.

First Conclusion: The mystical act and the mystical state are not identical.

The mystical experience is produced by the actuation of the gifts of the Holy Spirit through their divine modality, which is completely alien to our

[50]Cf. St. John of the Cross, *The Dark Night*, Bk. 2, Chap. 5, 5.

human psychology. Consequently, there is a mystical act, more or less intense, as often as any gift of the Holy Ghost operates in the soul. The actuation of a gift in the divine manner, which is the only possible mode of operation for a gift, will give to the soul, if nothing prevents it, a passive experience of the divine which is more or less intense and constitutes, from a psychological point of view, the most frequent and ordinary phenomenon in mysticism. But it is evident that an isolated actuation of a gift of the Holy Spirit does not suffice to constitute the mystical state. A state is of itself something fixed, stable, permanent and habitual. It is incompatible with weak and transitory acts. There is no mystical state until the actuation of the gifts is so intense and frequent that this operation predominates over the simple exercise of the infused virtues in a human mode.

THE MYSTICAL STATE

It is evident that the expression "mystical state" must be understood correctly. Since the mystical state consists in the predominance of the rule of the gifts, that expression cannot be understood in an absolute manner, but only in a relative manner. It is not a question of a psychological state which is habitual in the proper sense of the word, but only of a predominant mode of operation. The mystical state, understood as a permanent and habitual mode of action without any kind of interruption, is never verified. The gifts of the Holy Spirit do not act continuously and uninterruptedly in any mystic; to be sure, they operate in the soul of the mystic in a manner that is increasingly intense and more frequent, but never in a permanent and uninterrupted manner.

The reason is evident: for the operation of the gifts a special motion of the Holy Ghost is required in each case, because he alone can actuate them directly and immediately; this motion corresponds to the movement of the actual graces which are of themselves transitory. Therefore, when theologians and mystics speak of the mystical state, they use the word "state" in a wide sense, meaning the habitual state of the simple predominance of the gifts. This means that ordinarily and habitually the acts of the gifts predominate over personal initiative which, with the help of grace, would put the infused virtues to exercise in a human manner. Understood in this sense, the expression is true and exact and has the advantage of conveying the idea of a soul that lives most of the time under the rule and movement of the gifts of the Holy Ghost.

Reducing this distinction to precise formulas, we would offer the following definitions: The *mystical act* is the simple actuation, more or less intense, of a gift of the Holy Spirit operating in a divine manner. The *mystical state* is the manifest predominance of the activity of the gifts, operating in a divine manner, over the simple exercise of the infused virtues, operating in a human manner.

Second Conclusion: There is a distinction between mysticism and infused contemplation.

Many authors speak of these two things as if treating of one and the same reality, but if we are to speak precisely, they are not only distinct but separable. There can be no infused contemplation without mysticism, since contemplation is the mystical act par excellence; but there can be mysticism without infused contemplation.

The reason for this apparent paradox is very simple. All theologians agree in stating that infused contemplation is produced by the intellectual gifts, especially the gifts of wisdom and understanding, and not by the affective gifts. This is common doctrine. Now one or another of the affective gifts, such as the gift of piety, could be actuated and thereby produce a mystical act in the soul without causing infused contemplation, which proceeds only from the intellectual gifts. And there is no contradiction in saying that these acts of the affective gifts could be multiplied and intensified to such a point that the soul would be introduced into the mystical state, without having experienced, at least not in a clear and evident manner, the habitual activity of contemplative prayer.[51] Such was the case, in our opinion, with St. Thérèse of Lisieux, who was a mystic because she was possessed completely by the Holy Ghost. The gift of piety was manifested in her to an extraordinary degree, but this gift is an affective gift and is incapable in itself of producing contemplation.

It is necessary to remark, however, that this is not usual in the lives of the saints. Ordinarily they did not enter the mystical state in a full and perfect degree without also receiving infused contemplation. The reason is that the gifts of the Holy Ghost are intimately connected with charity and they grow together with it proportionately like the fingers on the hand.[52] Consequently, although it is possible to have perfectly mystical acts which are not contemplative because of the actuation of an affective and not an intellectual gift, it is difficult to see how the soul could enter into the full mystical state without ever enjoying the activity of the intellectual gifts which produce infused contemplation. Even in those saints in whom the affective gifts predominated, infused contemplation was experienced from time to time. St. Thérèse herself confessed to her sister, Mother Agnes of Jesus, that she had frequently enjoyed the prayer of quiet (which is the second degree of infused contemplation according to St. Teresa) and that she experienced the flight of the spirit (which is a contemplative phenomenon, as explained by St. Teresa of Avila).[53]

---

[51]Cf. Jacques Maritain, "Une question sur la vie mystique et la contemplation," *La Vie Spirituelle,* March, 1923, pp. 636-50.

[52]Cf. *Summa,* I-II, q. 68, a. 5; q. 66, a. 2.

[53]Cf. St. Teresa, *Relation to Father Rodrigo Alvarez,* n. 4, n. 11; *Interior Castle,* Chap. 5; St. Thérèse of Lisieux, *Novissima verba,* July 11.

Third Conclusion: Asceticism and mysticism are so intermingled that there is never a purely ascetical state or a purely mystical state. Sometimes the ascetic proceeds mystically, and the mystic, ascetically. The ascetical state is that in which ascetical acts predominate; the mystical state is that in which mystical acts predominate.

This is a conclusion which follows from the doctrine as we have already explained it. The gifts of the Holy Spirit can and do act during the ascetical state and produce transitory mystical acts, although they may be weak and almost insensible because of the imperfect disposition of the soul.[54] On the other hand, mystical souls, even those who have arrived at the transforming union, sometimes need to proceed in the manner of ascetics because at a given moment they do not experience the supernatural influence of the Holy Ghost. St. Teresa speaks of this when she says that there is no state of prayer so lofty that it is not necessary to return to the beginning,[55] and when she says to her nuns that sometimes our Lord leaves to the natural order even those souls who have arrived at the sublime heights of the seventh mansions of the interior castle.[56]

This same doctrine is clearly stated by Father Arintero:

> What truly constitutes the mystical state is the predominance of the gifts of the Holy Ghost (and their consequences: the mature and ripe fruits of the beatitudes) over simple ordinary vivified faith with its corresponding works of hope and charity. The predominance of the latter over the former characterizes the ascetical state. But sometimes the good ascetic, moved by the Holy Spirit, can proceed mystically although he may not advert to it; and so also, on the other hand, the mystics, however elevated they may be, when the Holy Ghost withdraws from them for some time—although he leaves them rich in great affections and fruits which give their actions greater intensity and value—must proceed and do proceed after the manner of ascetics.
>
> Thus the soul that still proceeds by the most ordinary paths may sometimes produce truly mystical acts, just as a mystic on many occasions produces ascetical acts, and those acts increase until little by little, purified and illumined, they become habitual. When this happens, when the soul habitually produces acts of virtue and, denying itself, ordinarily permits itself to be moved without resistance by the touchings and breathings of the sanctifying Spirit who, as with a very delicate musical instrument, handles the soul as he wishes and draws from it divine melodies, then we can say that the soul is now in the full mystical state, although from time to time it will still have to return to the ascetical state.[57]

---

[54]Father Garrigou-Lagrange explains this concept very clearly in his *Christian Perfection and Contemplation,* 384 ff.

[55]Cf. *The Life,* Chap. 13, n. 15.

[56]Cf. *Interior Castle,* Seventh Mansions, Chap. 4, n. 1.

[57]*Questiones místicas* (Madrid: B.A.C., 1956), p. 663; F. Joret, O.P., *La contemplation mystique d'après Saint Thomas d'Aquin* (Paris: 1923), p. 103.

Fourth Conclusion: Mysticism is not an extraordinary grace similar to the graces gratis datae. *Christians may participate in it to some degree even in the early stages of the spiritual life.*

This consequence is nothing more than a corollary and confirmation of the former conclusion. If in the simple ascetic there are sometimes produced truly mystical acts and if the mystic must sometimes descend to ascetical activity, it follows that there is no definitive barrier between asceticism and mysticism. The passage from the one to the other is a normal and insensible one, since the mystic is distinguished from the ascetic only by the predominance of certain actions which already begin to occur, although rarely and with small intensity, in the very beginnings of the Christian life.

Father Arintero sets forth the proposition in this way:

> Since the gifts are infused in greater or less degree together with sanctifying grace, and since they grow with charity, all who live in charity can operate heroically and mystically through the gifts. And thus, even in a remiss state, in the very beginning of the spiritual life the mystical life begins and it embraces the whole development of the Christian life and the whole path of evangelical perfection, although its principal manifestations are reserved almost exclusively for the unitive way in which the soul possesses, as it were, the habit of heroism and of the divine and in which, exercising with perfection even the most difficult practice of virtue, the soul clearly operates in a superhuman manner.[58]

This doctrine gives the Christian life all of the grandeur and sublimity which we admire in the primitive Church, where the Christian spirit attained a maximum degree of splendor. In the first centuries of Christianity the supernatural, understood as synonymous with heroic or superhuman, was the normal atmosphere for the church of Christ. It was only later, when complications and divisions were introduced, that the ways of the Lord, simple in themselves, became confused. The epoch of the greatest confusion began in the seventh century and extended to the beginning of our own century, in which there was a reaction and a return to the traditional mystical doctrine. Today the truth has been so strongly established that there are few spiritual writers of any authority who would dare to present the mystical life as an abnormal and extraordinary phenomenon which is reserved for only a small group of the elite. The majority maintain that there is no impassable barrier between asceticism and mysticism. There are not two distinct paths which lead to Christian perfection; on the contrary, they are but two stages of the same path to perfection which all should travel until they reach sanctity.

---

[58]*Op. cit.*, p. 663.

3: MYSTICISM AND CHRISTIAN PERFECTION

One of the most controversial questions among the various schools of spirituality is the relationship between mysticism and Christian perfection. Theologians are divided into two principal opinions concerning this important question. The first opinion holds for the unity of way in the spiritual life, considering asceticism and mysticism as two phases of the same path which all souls ought to travel on the way to perfection. The ascetical phase serves as a basis and preparation for the mystical phase in which alone is found the full perfection of the Christian life.

The second opinion maintains a duality of ways—the one ascetical and the other mystical—and by either one the soul can arrive at Christian perfection, but in such wise that the ascetical way is the normal and common way according to the ordinary providence of God and is therefore the way which all souls should strive to follow. The mystical way is completely abnormal and extraordinary.

The exceptional importance of this question should be evident to all, not only as a theoretical question but in the practical order, since the solution to this problem in the speculative order will determine to a great extent the direction which should be given to souls in their progress toward sanctity.

THE PROBLEM

The first thing that we must do is clarify the state of the question, because not all authors understand the terms in the same way.

False notions

In the first place, some authors believe that the problem consists in determining whether or not there are various kinds of sanctity determined by the development of various kinds of sanctifying grace. But this is not the question in dispute. Sanctifying grace is one, both for those who affirm and for those who deny the unity of the spiritual life, because there is not nor can there be any other kind of participation in the divine nature which would be more perfect without ceasing to be so in an accidental manner. It is not a question, therefore, of determining whether there exists in the mystical way a sanctifying grace which is *specifically* distinct from the grace of the ascetical way. In this sense all theologians admit the unity of the spiritual life, since the grace is one, the faith is one, and the charity is one—and these constitute the spiritual life from beginning to end.

Neither is it a question of determining whether there exists in the mystical way, and in it alone, a call to perfection which is unknown in the ascetical way. Or to put the matter more clearly, it is not a question of trying to discover whether all souls, mystics or not, are called to Christian perfection. All the schools of spirituality would answer this question in the affirmative. What is disputed is whether this perfection falls exclusively under the dominion of the mystical way or whether it can be attained without leaving the boundaries of the ascetical way.

Finally, we are not attempting to verify the question *de facto*—whether they are many or few who actually reach the mystical stage—but only the question *de jure,* that is, whether the mystical state enters into the normal development of sanctifying grace or whether it is the effect of an extraordinary providence absolutely outside the common ways which are open to all Christians who possess grace.

The true question

Having isolated the false interpretations of the problem, let us now put the question in its true focus. All are called to Christian perfection. Perfection, or the development of grace and the virtues in the soul, is the terminus of the spiritual life. To reach this perfection, is it necessary that the soul experience mystical operations, or can the soul attain perfection without having experienced these things? In other words, are the ascetical and the mystical phases two parts of one and the same path which leads to the terminus of the spiritual life—the perfection of charity—or are there two different paths which lead to the same terminus?

As is evident, the question does not pertain to the beginning or to the end of the spiritual life. Neither in the one nor the other can there be any specific difference, since grace and charity cannot be otherwise than essentially one. The question refers to the means by which one can reach the terminus of this path: the perfection of charity. It is a question concerning the unity of the spiritual way rather than the unity of the spiritual life.

MYSTICISM AND PERFECTION

Keeping in mind the principles which we have established, it seems to us that the principal relations between Christian perfection and mysticism can be synthesized in the following conclusions:

First Conclusion: Mysticism enters into the normal development of sanctifying grace.

This conclusion should be evident in view of the doctrine already explained. There are three elements intermingled in this conclusion: grace, its normal development and mysticism. We have said that sanctifying grace is given to us in the form of a seed which by its very nature demands an increase and growth. This is so clear that it is admitted by all the different schools of Christian spirituality. If grace were infused in the soul already perfectly developed, the obligation to strive for perfection would be meaningless and absurd. We know also what mysticism is: the actuation of the gifts of the Holy Spirit in a divine mode and usually producing a passive experience of the divine. This point is also admitted by all theologians--with certain differences, to be sure, but these do not affect the substance of the matter. Those who deny the universal call to mysticism will suggest the possibility of a human mode in the operation of the gifts or some other subterfuge, but all admit substantially that mysticism is produced by the divine modality of the gifts. There is also perfect agreement among all schools concerning the meaning of the normal development of sanctifying grace. Whatever falls within the exigencies of grace evidently falls within its normal and ordinary development. And whatever is outside the exigencies of grace will be abnormal and extraordinary in its development. On this also all theologians are in agreement.

Actuation

Who can deny that the simple actuation of the gifts of the Holy Ghost falls within the normal exigencies of grace? Who would say that the simple actuation of a gift of the Holy Ghost is an abnormal and extraordinary phenomenon in the life of grace?

As a matter of fact, no one has ever dared to say such a thing. All the schools of Christian spirituality recognize that the simple actuation of a gift of the Holy Ghost cannot be classified among the extraordinary phenomena (as one would classify, for example, the graces *gratis datae*), but that it is something perfectly normal and ordinary in the life of grace.[1] And precisely because they are aware of the inevitable consequences which follow this evident fact, those who deny the universal call to mysticism are forced to say that the gifts of the Holy Spirit can operate in two different ways: the human mode, which

[1]How could it be otherwise when we recall that some participation in the gifts is necessary for salvation? (Cf. *Summa,* I-II, q. 68, a. 2.) Father Poulain, a decided adversary of the universal call to mysticism, admits that the actuation of the gifts in every soul in grace is perfectly normal and he quotes Suárez (*De gratia,* Bk. 6, c. 10, n. 4) and Billot (*De virtutibus infusis,* a. 63, 169-70), who teach that the gifts ought to operate and do operate throughout the Christian life (*The Graces of Interior Prayer,* p. 97). Therefore, theologians who deny the universal call to mysticism are forced to explain the intervention of the gifts in the ascetical life by their actuation in a human mode, and in this way they try to resolve the tremendous difficulty which threatens to destroy their fundamental thesis.

does not transcend the ascetical phase, and the divine mode, which is characteristic of and proper to the mystical phase. Consequently, they conclude that the actuation of the gifts of the Holy Ghost enters into the normal and ordinary development of grace, but that mysticism does not necessarily enter into this normal development, because the actuation of the gifts (according to their theory) can be explained by a human mode of operation which could occur in the ascetical phase.

This explanation would be incontestable if it were true. But in our opinion it is completely false. We have already demonstrated that the gifts of the Holy Ghost do not and cannot act in a human mode; this human manner of operation is absolutely incompatible with the very nature of the gifts. We have already seen that such a manner of operation, besides being useless and superfluous, is philosophically impossible, for it would destroy the very nature of the habits; and it is theologically absurd, because it would destroy the very nature of the gifts. Consequently, either the gifts do not operate, or they necessarily operate in a divine manner—and then we are in the domain of the mystical, because that actuation in a divine mode necessarily produces a mystical act (although we admit a variety in its intensity and its duration). In the ascetical state the gifts rarely operate, and when they do, it is only imperfectly and with little intensity, due to the imperfect disposition of the soul. But the superhuman mode of the gifts is surely present even in this case, although in a weak and latent manner, as Father Garrigou-Lagrange puts it.

The whole matter is reduced to the fact that the soul, with the aid of grace, disposes itself more and more for the more intense and more frequent actuation of the gifts. The gifts do not have to change specifically, and they do not need anything else to be added to their nature. It suffices merely that the latent and imperfect exercise of the gifts in the ascetical state be intensified and multiplied in order that the soul gradually enter into the full mystical state, whose essential characteristic consists in the predominance of the actuation of the gifts of the Holy Ghost in a divine manner over the simple exercise or predominance of the infused virtues in a human manner.

This explanation, which is demanded by the very nature of things, seems to us to be the only logical explanation. Until our adversaries can show us that the simple actuation of the gifts of the Holy Ghost is an extraordinary phenomenon in the life of grace (and we are certain that they will never be able to do that), we shall rest secure that our position is invulnerable.

Second Conclusion: Complete Christian perfection is found only in the mystical life.

This is another conclusion which follows from the theological principles which we have already established. Christian perfection consists in the full development of that sanctifying grace received at baptism as a seed. This development is verified by the increase of the infused virtues, both theological and moral, and especially that of charity, the virtue par excellence whose perfection coincides with the perfection of the Christian life.

But the infused virtues cannot attain their full perfection except under the influence of the gifts of the Holy Ghost, for without the gifts they cannot go beyond the human modality under the rule of reason to which they are restricted in the ascetical state. Only the divine modality of the gifts gives the infused virtues the atmosphere which they need for their perfection. It is this predominance of the activity of the gifts of the Spirit operating in a divine mode, however, which characterizes the mystical state.

We have already demonstrated the truth of these statements, and from them our conclusion follows with the logical force of a syllogism. The infused virtues cannot reach their full perfection without the influence of the gifts of the Holy Spirit operating on them in a divine manner. But this actuation of the gifts of the Holy Ghost in a divine manner constitutes the very essence of mysticism. Therefore, the infused virtues cannot attain their full perfection outside the mystical life. But if Christian perfection coincides with the perfection of the infused virtues, and especially that of charity, and if these virtues cannot attain their perfection except in the mystical life, it follows that Christian perfection is impossible outside the mystical life.

This conclusion, almost forgotten during the last three centuries of decadence in mystical theology, has once again received its proper place among the authors of modern spirituality. There are few theologians of any authority who insist on preserving the doctrines formerly held, and there are none who can offer a solid argument against this doctrine. Let us review the teaching of the three greatest lights in experimental mysticism: St. John of the Cross, St. Teresa of Avila and St. Francis de Sales, whose doctrines are in complete accord with the teachings of the Angelic Doctor.

St. John of the Cross

The teaching of St. John of the Cross, if studied in its totality, is orientated to mysticism as the normal and indispensable terminus for the attainment of Christian perfection. Of course, if one concentrates on an isolated text and abstracts from his whole system, it would be easy to defend any preconceived thesis; but it would not represent the authentic thought of St. John of the Cross. If a person reads his works without any preconceived notions, it will be evident that he teaches that one cannot attain Christian perfection except on the foundations of the passive purifications. The following two texts clearly indicate his thought:

> However assiduously the beginner practices the mortification in himself of all these actions and passions, he can never completely succeed—very far from it —until God works it in him passively by means of the purgation of the said night.[2]

[2] *The Dark Night,* Bk. 1, Chap. 7, n. 5.

> But neither from these imperfections nor from those others can the soul be perfectly purified until God brings it into the passive purgation of that dark night of which we shall presently speak. It is fitting for the soul, however, to contrive to labor, so far as it can, on its own account, in order that it may purge and perfect itself and thus may merit being taken by God into that divine care in which it becomes healed of all things that it was unable to cure itself. For however greatly the soul itself labors, it cannot actively purify itself so as to be prepared in the least degree for the divine union of perfection of love if God does not take its hand and purge it in that dark fire, in the way and manner that we have yet to describe.[3]

The thought of St. John of the Cross could not be expressed with more force concerning the necessity of the mystical purifications to attain perfection. He starts with a soul that labors seriously to purify itself of its imperfections; a soul that has reached the height of the ascetical way; a generous soul that does all it can and yet cannot, he says, be disposed for the perfect union of love until God himself prepares the soul by means of the mystical purifications. To attempt to avoid the difficulty by saying that St. John of the Cross is referring only to those who are to be purified by the mystical way is to distort the teaching of the mystical doctor. For him, Christian perfection is absolutely impossible outside the mystical state.[4]

St. Teresa of Avila

The teaching of St. Teresa of Avila is in conformity with that of St. John of the Cross. St. Teresa considered that anything that we ourselves might accomplish in the ascetical life would be nothing more than a "few little straws."[5] She not only teaches in many places that mysticism is the normal terminus of the Christian life and is not reserved for some few aristocrats of the spirit; but she expressly states that the reason she wrote her books is none other than to cause souls to covet so sublime a blessing.[6]

---

[3]*Ibid.,* Chap. 3, n. 3.

[4]It does not change this teaching to quote the famous text from *The Dark Night* (Bk. 1, Chap 9): "For not all those who walk of set purpose in the way of the spirit are brought by God to contemplation," in which the saint seems to deny the universal call to mysticism. This text is no proof whatever, because the interpretation which should be given to it is the one which St. John himself gives in *The Living Flame* (Stanza II, n. 27) when he states that the reason why there are so few contemplatives is due to the lack of generosity of souls and is not due to the will of God, who would wish that all should attain to this lofty state of the perfection of union with God. Note also that *The Living Flame* is posterior to *The Dark Night. The Dark Night* was completed in 1583 and *The Living Flame* was written between 1585 and 1587. Therefore, one must seek the definitive thought of St. John of the Cross in *The Living Flame.*

[5]*The Life,* Chap. 15, n. 7.

[6]Cf. *The Life,* Chap. 18, n. 8. In *The Way of Perfection* she clearly states: "Remember, the Lord invites us all; and since he is Truth itself, we cannot doubt him. If his invitation were not a general one, he would not have said: 'I will give you to drink.' He might have said: 'Come, all of you, for after all you will lose

As regards certain apparent contradictions in the writings of St. Teresa, she herself explains with all precision the true meaning of her words. The following passage is an example of her clarification:

> I seem to have been contradicting what I had previously said, since, in consoling those who had not reached the contemplative state, I told them that the Lord had different roads by which they might come to him, just as he also had many mansions. I now repeat this: his Majesty, being who he is and understanding our weakness, has provided for us. But he did not say: "Some must come by this way and others by that." His mercy is so great that he has forbidden none to strive to come and drink of this fountain of life.[7]

Note the importance of this passage for an understanding of the authentic teaching of St. Teresa. It is the saint herself who realizes perfectly that what she had just stated seemed to involve a contradiction of her previous teaching. Consequently, she attempts to clarify her thought by giving an authentic interpretation of her own words. Speaking with great care, she tells us that the Lord invites all of us to drink the clear and crystal waters of mystical contemplation. No defender of the universal call to mysticism could have expressed the doctrine with greater clarity. At the risk of an arbitrary denial of St. Teresa's obvious teaching, one cannot deny that she is decidedly of the opinion that all are called to mysticism.

As regards the teaching of St. Francis de Sales, one can study the beautiful commentary by Father Lamballe on the *Treatise on the Love of God,* where St. Francis states that "prayer is called meditation until it produces the honey of devotion; and after this it is changed into contemplation. . . . Meditation is the mother of love, but contemplation is her daughter. . . . Holy contemplation is the end and terminus to which all those exercises tend, and all of them are reducible to it."[8]

St. Francis de Sales

This sublime doctrine of St. Thomas Aquinas, St. John of the Cross, St. Teresa of Avila and St. Francis de Sales is also the teaching of St. Bonaventure, St. Catherine of Siena, Eckhart, Tauler, Suso, Ruysbroeck, Blosius, John of Avila and of all the mystical theologians previous to the seventeenth century, which begins the age of decadence. In modern times there has been a return to this traditional doctrine on the mystical life, and we can mention the following as examples: Marmion, Lehodey, Louismet, Stolz, Gardeil, Garrigou-Lagrange, Arintero, Joret, Philipon, Peralta, Bruno of Jesus and Mary, Gabriel of St. Mary Magdalen, de la Taille, Jaegher, Schrijvers, Cayré, Mercier, Saudreau and Maritain. In a word, most of the great names in modern Chris-

---

nothing by coming; and I will give drink to those whom I think fit for it.' But since he said that we were all to come, without making this condition, I feel sure that none will fail to receive this living water unless they cannot keep to the path" (Chap. 19, n. 15).

[7]*The Way of Perfection,* Chap. 20, n. 1.

[8]*Treatise on the Love of God,* Bk. 6, Chaps. 3 and 6.

tian spirituality have returned, after a period of three centuries, to the sublime concept of the mystical life as the normal culmination of the life of grace.

Third Conclusion: All are called, at least by a remote and sufficient call, to the mystical state.

To deny the universal call to the mystical life it would be necessary to deny also the universal call to perfection. If God does not wish all of us to be perfect, then it is evident that he does not wish all of us to be mystics. But if the call to perfection is absolutely universal—and this is so clear that all the schools admit it—it is necessary to say that the call to the mystical life is likewise universal.

Nevertheless, in spite of the fact that the question *de jure* is beyond all doubt, we do not think it inconvenient to make some practical restrictions. Here as elsewhere if one wants to remain in the area of truth and avoid all extremes, there is no other remedy but to make a distinction between the juridical order and the order of facts. The questions *de jure* hardly ever coincide completely with the questions *de facto,* especially in these matters in which our human limitations and weaknesses play such a great part.

We think that the most balanced and most realistic doctrine that has been offered today concerning the universal call to the mystical state is that of Father Garrigou-Lagrange. His magnificent chapter on the call to contemplation and the mystical life in *Christian Perfection and Contemplation* could be accepted as a point of convergence for all the schools of spirituality, and we strongly urge the reader to study this chapter with great care.[9] In practice, it seems, the true solution of the problem can be stated in the following propositions:

1) By a *remote and sufficient call,* by the very fact of being in the state of grace, all are called to the mystical life as the normal expression of sanctifying grace. As the child is called to maturity by the mere fact of being born, so as regards the mystical life, since grace is the seed of mysticism.

2) If the soul is faithful and places no obstacles to the plans of God, a moment will arrive in which that remote call is converted into a *proximate sufficient call* through the presence of the three signs stipulated by Tauler and St. John of the Cross.[10] The reason is that as habits the gifts of the Holy Ghost demand an operation which is more and more vital.

3) The proximate sufficient call becomes a *proximate efficacious call* if the soul, on receiving the first call, corresponds faithfully with it and

[9]Cf. Garrigou-Lagrange, *Christian Perfection and Contemplation,* Chap. 6, pp. 337 ff.

[10]*Divine Institutions,* Chap. 35; *The Dark Night,* Bk. 1, Chap. 9.

places no obstacle to the divine activity. The reason for this is that efficacious grace is always given to him who does not resist sufficient grace.

4) The greater or less degree of holiness which the soul will attain in the mystical life will depend on the degree of fidelity on the part of the soul and the free determination of God in view of the degree of sanctity to which that soul has been predestined. The degree of grace and glory is determined by God for each one by divine predestination. It should be noted that this doctrine is true, whether predestination is effected as the Thomists maintain, *ante praevisa merita,* or as the Molinist school teaches, *post praevisa merita.*

SOLUTION OF OBJECTIONS

FIRST *It is a universal law that every vital principle can reach its perfect development without going beyond its proper mode of being and operation. Therefore, if grace resides and works in the soul after the manner of the soul, that is, in a human and natural mode, it is evident that grace can attain its perfect development without going beyond that human mode. Whatever exceeds this mode of operation will be more or less fitting so far as it facilitates the development of grace, but it will never be absolutely necessary. As a proof of this argument, theologians sometimes quote the following words of St. Thomas: "Grace is in the soul as a form having complete existence in the soul; . . . but a complete form is in its subject according to the condition of the subject."*[11]

The text Let us first examine the text from St. Thomas, and then we shall proceed to the objection as stated. In the question of the *Summa* from which the quotation is taken, St. Thomas is asking whether a sacramental character can be blotted out from the soul. The objection which St. Thomas raises and answers can be summarized as follows: It seems that a character can be blotted out from the soul because the more perfect an accident is, the more firmly does it adhere to its subject. But grace is more perfect than a character, because a character is ordained to grace as to a further end. But grace is lost through sin and therefore much more can a character be lost.

The complete reply given by St. Thomas is as follows: Both grace and the character are in the soul, but in different ways. Grace is in the soul as a form having complete existence therein, whereas a character is in the soul as an instrumental power. Now a complete form is in its subject according to the condition of the subject, and since the soul, as long as it is a wayfarer, is changeable in respect of free will, it results that grace is in the soul in a changeable manner. But an instrumental power follows rather the condition

[11] *Summa,* III, q. 63, a. 5, ad 1.

of the principal agent; consequently, the character exists in the soul in an indelible manner, not from any perfection of its own, but from the perfection of Christ's priesthood, from which the character flows like an instrumental power.

The first question that should come to the mind of the reader is: what has all this to do with grace and the human mode of operation? It is surely strange that anyone should quote this text in order to prove something that is completely alien to the text itself. Whether or not grace is in the soul in a human mode is a question which we shall examine later, but it is as clear as the light of day that this text from St. Thomas does not have the slightest relation to the question.

St. Thomas is saying in this text that grace, as distinct from the character, is in the soul in an amissible manner, as is demanded by the intrinsic mutability of the soul itself wherein grace resides as in its proper subject. Grace is in the soul as a complete form in its own being; but this type of a form necessarily is subject to the characteristics of the subject in which it inheres, and for that reason grace is subject to the mutable condition of the human soul, which proceeds from the mutability of human free will. Consequently, grace can be lost and as a matter of fact is frequently lost. This is the only thing that St. Thomas says in the passage quoted. There is no reference whatever to the human mode or the superhuman mode.

We are not interested here in insisting on the thought of St. Thomas in the above text. As a matter of fact, we would prefer that the text quoted would have the meaning attributed to it, because that condition of grace wherein it must operate in a human mode, far from weakening our thesis, would fortify it.

The objection

But let us examine the objection itself. The fundamental statement of the objection refers to the universal law that any vital principle can reach its full perfection without going beyond its proper mode of being and of operation. We are in full agreement with this statement, and, if anything, we would complain that the statement itself has not been emphasized enough: it seems to us that any vital principle not only can but must reach its perfect development without going beyond its proper mode of being and of operation. How could it be otherwise, especially if the mode referred to is something specifically distinct? Could a plant grow and develop in the mode of an animal? Consequently, we not only admit the principle, but we would state it even more forcefully.

But what follows from this principle? According to the objection, the conclusion drawn is that grace is and works in the soul according to the mode of the soul, namely, in a natural and human mode, and that therefore it can reach its perfection without going beyond this human mode. We suspect that the objector must have suffered an involuntary distraction when he wrote those words. He certainly must know that grace does not work in the soul either in the human or in the divine mode, because grace does not operate at all; it is an entitative habit and is not ordained immediately to action. It is the infused virtues and the gifts of the Holy Ghost which operate, and they reside, not in the essence of the soul as does sanctifying grace, but in the soul's faculties. And those infused virtues and gifts of the Holy Spirit are really distinct from grace, although they are rooted in grace. The virtues and the gifts operate after the mode of the agent who governs them, that is to say, the virtues in a human mode under the rule of reason enlightened by faith, and the gifts in a divine mode under the direct and immediate movement of the Holy Ghost himself.

Accepting the basic principle concerning the perfection of a vital principle within its own mode of being and operation, the objector immediately concludes that grace should be developed through its operative powers in a human mode because it resides in the soul according to our human and connatural mode. Perhaps the reader has already seen the sophism which is hidden in this argument. The logician would perceive that the syllogism has four terms and that the true conclusion should be one which is diametrically opposed to the conclusion stated. The basic principle of the argument not only does not prove the thesis of the development of grace according to a human mode, but it becomes the foundation for proving the exact opposite: grace demands by its very nature a mode of development which is completely divine.

The mode of grace

What is the proper mode of sanctifying grace? Would any theologian dare to answer that it is a human mode? Have we not already seen in philosophy that operation follows being (*operari sequitur esse*)? And who would say that sanctifying grace is a human form? Has it not already been demonstrated as a truth of revelation that grace is a divine form which gives us nothing less than a physical and formal participation in the very nature of God himself? Does not St. Peter say that through grace we become participants in the very nature of God: *divinae consortes naturae?*[12] Now, if the being of grace is divine (and no one can deny this without a manifest error) and if operation follows being (and no one can deny this without denying a basic principle of philosophy), who would say that a divine form should develop in a human mode?

The objector confuses the operation which corresponds to grace itself with the operation which corresponds to the subject in whom grace resides. The operation which corresponds to the soul, or the subject wherein grace resides, is certainly an operation in a human mode because the soul itself is human and its operations must correspond to its mode of being (*operari sequitur esse*). But the operation demanded by sanctifying grace is an operation in a divine and superhuman mode, because the very essence of grace is divine and

[12] II Pet. 1:4. Cf. also St. Thomas, *In II Sent.*, dist. 26, q. 1, a. 4, ad 3; a. 5; a. 3.

the operations which flow from it must correspond to the being from which they proceed.

Consequently, the basic principle used in the objection is a valid one. But the principle does not assert that every vital principle can reach its full perfection without going beyond the mode which is proper to the subject in which it resides; it states, on the contrary, that it does so without going beyond its proper mode of being and operation. Now the proper mode of being of sanctifying grace is in no sense human, it is divine, as is expressly stated in divine revelation. And since it is a divine form, it demands for its perfect development, not the human mode of the soul, but the divine mode which corresponds to its own proper mode of being and operation. And precisely because in the ascetical phase grace can be developed—through the infused virtues which are its operative principles—only in that human modality which proceeds from the rule of reason, it needs the divine modality of the gifts of the Holy Ghost, which are perfectly adapted to the divine nature of grace, in order to reach its full perfection. Once more it is evident that the mystical state, far from being extraordinary or abnormal, is the normal atmosphere which grace demands by the very fact of its supernatural and divine nature. In a sense, it is the ascetical state which is abnormal and alien to the nature of sanctifying grace, and for that reason the ascetical state is only a provisional and imperfect state through which grace must pass in its development to the divine atmosphere of the gifts of the Holy Spirit where the soul is introduced into the full mystical state. There cannot be any doubt that mysticism is the normal atmosphere demanded by the very nature of grace and that Christian perfection is impossible outside of mysticism because the full development of grace would then be impossible.

SECOND

The second objection admits that mysticism consists in the actuation and predominance of the gifts of the Holy Ghost working in a divine manner, but it maintains that the gifts can also operate in a human mode and that this falls perfectly within the normal development of grace without going beyond the human modality which is proper to the ascetical state. Consequently, mysticism is not absolutely indispensable for Christian perfection.

This objection proceeds from the false supposition that the gifts of the Holy Ghost admit of a human mode of operation, which we have already seen is impossible.

THIRD

The third objection is based on a definition from the Council of Trent which states that the justified man can merit de condigno *the increase of grace, eternal life, the attainment of eternal life and an increase of glory.*[13] *Consequently, if mysticism were part of the ordinary and normal development of sanctifying*

[13]Cf. Sess. VI, Decree on Justification, can. 32; Denz. 842.

grace, one would have to conclude that it could be merited de condigno, *because that is the way in which the development and increase of grace are merited.*[14] *The majority of the mystics state emphatically that infused contemplation, which is one of the most characteristic acts of the mystical life, is gratuitous.*[15] *Therefore, mysticism, or at least infused contemplation, does not enter into the normal and ordinary development of sanctifying grace, unless we wish to place a contradiction between theology and the experience of the mystics.*

It is easy to solve this apparent contradiction between the data of the mystics and the teaching of theologians. The God of the mystics is also the God of the theologians, and if in our limited understanding of things there may appear to be a contradiction, the contradiction is only apparent.

The key to the solution of the problem is a simple distinction given by one of the greatest authorities in spiritual theology, Father Arintero. In one of his finest works, *Cuestiones Místicas,* he demonstrates that the gift of divine contemplation is the crown of justice and that it can be truly merited by a loving and persevering correspondence with grace.[16] From a theological point of view this article is the best that Father Arintero ever wrote. After explaining the terms of the problem, he establishes the simple distinction between *de jure* and *de facto.* As regards the question *de jure,* he demonstrates the possibility of meriting the mystical state *de condigno* by quoting texts from a vast number of mystical writers and speculative theologians. Anyone who reads this argument will certainly be convinced that, at least *de jure,* infused contemplation can be merited strictly or *de condigno.*[17]

It is quite another matter when we come to the question *de facto.* Father Arintero maintains that in practice the majority will not actually be given anything more than merit *de congruo.* The reason is that merit, as St. Thomas

---

[14]St. Thomas expressly states: "Whatever the motion of grace reaches to falls under condign merit. Now the motion of a mover extends not merely to the last terms of the movement, but to the whole progress of the movement. But the term of the movement of grace is eternal life; and progress in this movement is by the increase of charity or grace, according to Prov. 4:18: 'But the path of the just is like shining light, that grows in brilliance till perfect day,' which is the day of glory. And thus the increase of grace falls under condign merit" (*Summa,* I-II, q. 114, a. 8).

[15]Cf. St. Teresa, *Interior Castle,* Fourth Mansions, Chap. 2, n. 9.

[16]Cf. *Questiones Místicas,* II, art. 6.

[17]The same conclusion was reached by the eminent Thomist, Father Ramírez, O.P., in two articles which appeared in *La Vida Sobrenatural* (August and October, 1921), under the title: "El Mérito y la Vida Mística." Father Ramírez states his thesis as follows: From the theological principles of St. Thomas it can be clearly deduced that the gift of mystical contemplation falls under merit *de condigno* or, what is the same, it is an object of that merit.

teaches, implies only an essential ordination to a reward, but it does not always and necessarily imply the actual attainment of the reward, because obstacles can prevent this attainment. "Impetration implies the attainment of that which is asked; but merit does not imply the attainment, but an ordination to the attainment based on justice. Therefore, any obstacle which intervenes because of instability destroys the basis of the impetration because it destroys the attainment; but it does not destroy the ordination to the attainment and hence it does not destroy merit. Consequently, a man merits even if he does not persevere; but he does not impetrate unless he perseveres."[18]

This teaching throws great light on the solution of the question. There is no contradiction in the fact that we are able to merit *de jure* that which we do not attain *de facto* because of the obstacles which our misery and inconstancy have placed between the merit and the attainment of the corresponding reward. Just as an individual sometimes receives from God a mercy without meriting it, so also at other times he could very well have merited it but for one reason or another never have attained it.[19] As a matter of fact, the Christian who sins and is condemned after having lived in grace certainly merited eternal life by the works he performed in the state of grace, and nevertheless *de facto* he never attained eternal life because between the merit and the reward he placed the insuperable obstacle of final impenitence.[20]

Merit and grace

It can happen that he who has merited and attained an increase of grace by a merit *de condigno,* and has also by that fact merited an increase in the infused virtues and the gifts of the Holy Spirit as habits, may later on not be sufficiently faithful and generous to be disposed to receive from God the actual graces which would place those habits in operation and produce infused contemplation or any other mystical act. We must not forget that in the order of efficacious actual graces we do not have true merit *de condigno,* according to the common teaching of the theologians, but only the improper merit *de congruo* or the merit which is based on a certain fitness (based, as they say, *in jure amicabili, secundum leges amicitiae*). Man can and should dispose himself to receive these graces by not placing any obstacle to the divine action and by impetrating them with fervent, humble and persevering prayer. If he does this, he will infallibly obtain these graces, not because his efforts are equivalent to a true merit *de condigno,* but because of the divine promise which expressly states that a prayer which has all the necessary conditions

---

[18]St. Thomas, *In IV Sent.,* dist. 15, q. 4, a. 7, ad 4.

[19]As St. Thomas points out, "the impetration of prayer rests on mercy, whereas condign merit rests on justice. Therefore, a man may impetrate many things from the divine mercy in prayer which he does not merit in justice" (*Summa,* I-II, q. 114, a. 6, ad 2).

[20]Cf. Denz. 842.

will obtain whatever is fitting for our eternal salvation.[21] And that infused contemplation is most fitting in relation to eternal salvation cannot be doubted by anyone.

On the other hand, once the gifts of the Holy Ghost have attained a notable development as habits—and this is effected by merit *de condigno*—they demand operation, so to speak, unless we wish to admit that God increases them so that they will remain idle. Consequently, in practice, if the soul is faithful to grace and perseveres in prayer, God will infallibly actuate those habits and thereby produce the mystical activity which is perfectly normal within the ordinary development of sanctifying grace. In this way the mystical life is merited *de condigno* under one aspect (that of the development of the habit of the gifts) and it is attained by congruous merit but infallibly under another aspect (the act itself of contemplation or the actuation of any one of the gifts through an actual grace).

It is true that in practice our prayer will often lack the necessary condition for the infallible impetration of those actual graces, and then God will have to act out of pure mercy, so to speak, if he wishes to grant us the gift of infused contemplation in spite of our resistance and our infidelity to grace. God is not obliged to do this and as a matter of fact he may not do it, in order to punish our own faults or neglect; and yet sometimes, moved by his ineffable mercy, he sends us an efficacious actual grace which puts the gifts of the Holy Ghost in motion, thus causing in us—if it is a question of the intellectual gifts—the act of infused contemplation, not only in an entirely gratuitous manner, but even at times when the soul is most careless, as St. Teresa says. We should not forget the statement of St. Thomas to the effect that God in rewarding always goes beyond that which we merit.[22]

Contradictions resolved

This should explain the apparent contradiction, not only between the terminology of the mystics and that of the theologians, but even between the passages of one and the same mystical work. The Thomistic school has always quoted against the Carmelite school those passages of St. Teresa and St. John of the Cross in which they invite all souls to the heights of contemplation and to the mystical life. The Carmelite school opposes the Thomists by quoting other texts from St. Teresa and St. John of the Cross which seem to teach the contrary. Rather than attribute a true contradiction in the doctrine of either of these great mystics, it is necessary to say that the one passage states

---

[21]Cf. Matt. 7:7; 21:22; Mark 11:24; Luke 11:9; John 14:13, 16:23; Jas. 1:6. Prümmer says in this regard: "This proposition seems to be *de fide catholica* because of the evident testimony of Sacred Scripture" (*Manuale Theologiae Moralis,* II, n. 351).

[22]*In Matt.* 5: "The gifts of God always surpass our merits." *Summa,* I-II, q. 114, a. 6, ad 2: "A man may impetrate many things from the divine mercy in prayer which he does not merit in justice."

the question *de jure*—what ought to occur because of the proper and normal exigencies of grace—and the other refers to the question *de facto*—that which actually occurs in practice. St. John of the Cross has distinguished these two aspects in the following passage:

> And here it is fitting to note the reason why there are so few who arrive at such a lofty state of perfection of union with God. It should be known in this regard that it is not because God wishes that there be few of these elevated spirits, but rather he desires that all should be perfect, but the reason is that he finds few vessels to suffer such a lofty and elevated work.[23]

Father Garrigou-Lagrange has explained this whole question so well that we shall transcribe his exact words:

> It is true that we can merit condignly the increase of charity, of the virtues and of the gifts as *habitus,* and that in this life no limit can be placed on this augmentation. The Holy Ghost moves souls as a rule according to the degree of their infused *habitus,* of their habitual docility (provided there is no obstacle, venial sin or imperfection; in case there is, the meritorious act is weak, *remissus,* inferior to the degree of charity). Consequently, Thomists usually say that the just man who perseveres in fervor can merit *saltem de congruo* (at least in the broad sense of the word "merit") the grace of infused contemplation. Why do they say *saltem* (at least) *de congruo?* Because in the grace of infused contemplation there is something merited strictly or condignly, that is, a high degree of the gifts of understanding and wisdom considered as *habitus.* But in itself infused contemplation is not a habit, it is an act, and the mystical state is this act which lasts a certain time. But this act supposes an efficacious actual grace, and according to Thomists, we cannot strictly or condignly merit the efficacious help which keeps us in the state of grace. Why is this? Because the principle of merit does not fall under merit: that is why neither the first grace, nor the efficacious help which maintains us in the state of grace, nor the gift of final perseverance, though so necessary to salvation, can be merited condignly.
>
> Moreover, if a just man could strictly merit efficacious grace A, by it he would likewise merit efficacious grace B, and so on to the grace of final perseverance, which would thus be merited condignly. Whence it follows that many graces necessary to salvation cannot be the object of strict merit. It should not surprise us, then, that the actual efficacious grace of infused contemplation cannot be merited condignly, even though it is in the normal way of sanctity. It can be merited more than the grace of final perseverance, for it would be exaggeration to say that this last can be merited at least congruously. But in one sense the actual grace of infused contemplation is more gratuitous than that necessary to the obligatory exercise of the infused virtues, for we use infused virtues when we wish to do so. The same is not true of the gifts, although by our fidelity we can prepare ourselves to receive the inspiration of the Holy Ghost. Indeed, we ought to prepare ourselves for it; and if we do this generously, a day will come when the grace of contemplation will be given to us quite frequently. God ordinarily gives it to the perfect, provided there are no accidental obstacles; but he gives it either in aridity and night, or in light and consolation.[24]

[23]*The Living Flame,* Stanza II, n. 27.

[24]*Christian Perfection and Contemplation,* pp. 412-14.

In another place in the same work Father Garrigou-Lagrange completes his doctrine in the following manner:

> The grace of a happy death or of final perseverance cannot be merited condignly in the strict sense of the word, nor even strictly congruously. It is, however, necessary for salvation, and we ought certainly to desire it, to dispose ourselves for it, and to ask for it incessantly, because persevering prayer will obtain it for us. The same may be said for the grace of conversion or justification for a sinner. It cannot be merited, since it is the principle of merit; yet anyone in the state of mortal sin ought, with the actual grace offered him, to desire it and ask for it. These are profound mysteries of the efficacy of grace and of predestination. (Cf. I-II, q. 114, aa. 5, 9.)
>
> The grace of justification and that of final perseverance are necessary for salvation, but they cannot be merited condignly. The same is true of efficacious graces which keep us in the state of grace.
>
> The grace of infused contemplation is not gratuitous, since one can progressively merit condignly a very high degree of the gift of wisdom considered as a *habitus,* and since the Holy Ghost generally inspires souls according to the degree of their habitual docility.
>
> Moreover, we must add to merit the impetrative power of prayer. Since we ought to ask for the grace of a happy death, which we are unable to merit, a fervent soul may indeed, with as much confidence as humility, also ask for the grace of contemplation in order to live the mysteries of salvation more fully, to know its own wretchedness better, to humble itself on this account, and to be less indifferent to the glory of God and the salvation of souls. Reduced to common terms, this is what the soul requests when it recites the *Veni Creator* with sincerity. The grace of contemplation is thereby less gratuitous than graces *gratis datae,* such as the grace of a miracle or prophecy, which are in no way necessary to our personal sanctification. After all, the fact remains that the Holy Ghost breathes where he wills and when he wills; for we do not exercise at will the acts which proceed from the gifts of the Holy Ghost.[25]

Summary

We can summarize our doctrine on the question of the relationship between merit and the mystical life by stating the following conclusions:

1) The increase of grace and of the virtues and gifts of the Holy Spirit as habits can be merited *de condigno.*

2) By good works and fidelity to grace one can merit *de congruo* and by humble and persevering prayer one can impetrate infallibly (by reason of the divine promise) actual efficacious graces which will put the habit of the gifts into operation and thus normally produce the mystical phenomenon.

3) Due to human weakness and misery, it often happens in practice that a man does not do all that he should in order to merit actual graces by congruous merit, nor is his prayer accompanied by the conditions necessary to impetrate these graces infallibly, so that he lacks them by reason of his negligence or his lack of generosity.

[25]*Christian Perfection and Contemplation,* p. 354, footnote 18.

4) Where merit *de condigno* and merit *de congruo* are lacking, and also even the conditions necessary for the infallible impetration of actual graces through prayer, it may sometimes happen that God supplies the defect of his creature by granting him, out of pure mercy and in spite of the lack of the proper dispositions, those actual efficacious graces which produce the mystical phenomenon through the actuation of the gifts of the Holy Ghost. But God has no obligation to do this, and frequently he denies these things to souls that are voluntarily imperfect. This explains why *de facto* there are so few mystics in spite of the fact that *de jure* all souls are called to the mystical state. And this is the sense in which one must interpret the texts of the mystics when they say that God gives the grace of contemplation as he wills and when he wills, and sometimes even to souls that are negligent.

5) Consequently, *de jure* or by reason of the exigencies of grace, the mystical life is merited *de condigno* under one aspect (the development of the gifts as habits), and can be merited *de congruo* and obtained infallibly through prayer under another aspect (the actuation of the gifts which produces the mystical phenomenon under the impetus of an efficacious actual grace). In this sense, it can be said that the mystical life is infallibly available to all generous souls who place no obstacles to grace and properly dispose themselves for it. The fact that in practice there are so few mystics does not in any way compromise the normal order of the exigencies of grace *de jure*.

We believe that these conclusions can serve as a point of contact between the various mystical schools which appear to be antagonistic, such as the Thomists and the Carmelites, for the discrepancies are more apparent than real. The Thomistic school, accustomed to lofty theological speculation, forcefully states the exigencies of the juridical order and sees the mystical life contained virtually in the seed of grace. The Carmelite school, accustomed to follow the experimental mystics, emphasizes above all the remarkable scarcity of mystics and denies in the concrete order that which the Thomists affirm in the juridical order. We believe that both schools could come to agreement if they would state the meaning of the question with greater precision.

FOURTH

The fourth objection is given by Father Poulain in his work, The Graces of Interior Prayer:

> But if mystical contemplation is produced by the gifts of the Holy Ghost, the converse, namely, that every act produced by certain gifts is mystical is false. For that would be tantamount to saying that these gifts never operate in ordinary prayer. Now such a thesis has never been laid down. It is not in conformity with St. Thomas' teaching, which holds that the gifts are not reserved for difficult acts alone. And further, if this proposition were true, mystics would swarm upon our globe. For at confirmation and even at baptism every

Christian receives these gifts, and no one can hold that they continue in the state of pure habit without any actuation.[26]

It does not follow that if all Christians began to share imperfectly in mystical graces at the very beginning of the spiritual life, mystics would swarm all over the world. It would not occur to anyone to call a person a pianist who is just beginning to learn how to play the piano, although he plays it very often, but only when he is able to play with facility and by habit. In like manner, it is not correct to call the imperfect Christian a mystic, although the Holy Spirit may occasionally produce in him imperfect mystical acts, since the disposition of the soul is as yet too imperfect for anything else. The true mystic is not one who only occasionally performs a mystical act under the influence of the gifts of the Holy Ghost, but one who is habitually docile to the movement of the Holy Ghost and lets himself be led into the full mystical state.

This objection is absolutely without force because it contains an equivocation. It can be answered with a simple distinction: that imperfect mystical acts are to be found all over the world, we concede; that mystical souls are to be found all over the world, we deny. Mystical souls are few and are always rare because the mystical state requires heroic abnegation and a complete abandonment of self to the operation of the Holy Ghost without reservation. We should not forget that mystical souls are souls of heroic virtue; they are the souls of saints.

FIFTH *The last objection states that for the beatification and canonization of the servants of God, the Church never takes into account whether or not the individuals had infused contemplation or any other mystical phenomena, but only whether they habitually practiced the infused virtues in a heroic degree. This is stated by Pope Benedict XIV in his work,* De Beatificatione Servorum Dei et de Beatorum Canonizatione.[27]

This objection proves absolutely nothing. Even more, one could use it as a defense for the argument in favor of our thesis. For if the Church canonizes only those who have habitually practiced the infused virtues in a heroic degree, to which the virtues cannot reach without the influence of the gifts of the Holy Ghost operating in a divine manner, it follows that the Church canonizes only those who are mystics. It is not surprising that the process of canonization does not consider whether an individual had infused contemplation. Infused contemplation and the other mystical gifts which are related to the normal development of sanctifying grace (and not, we note, the graces *gratis*

[26]Cf. p. 97, 19 bis.

[27]This work was written by Prospero Lambertini before he became pope. The first edition, in five volumes, appeared in Bologna between 1734 and 1738; its author was elected pope in 1740.

datae, which are not necessary for perfection) are intimate graces which give the mystic an ineffable experience of the divine. And hence it follows that as such they can completely escape the examination of those who are testing the sanctity of a servant of God. They can be known only indirectly through their marvelous effects, which are the virtues practiced in a heroic degree under the modality of the gifts, and this it is which gives them that superhuman and heroic intensity. The cause of this phenomenon is purely internal, and therefore we must apply the principle of canon law: *de internis non judicat ecclesia.* The Church is concerned only with that which is externally evident and can be proved by testimony: the practice of the Christian virtues in a heroic degree. Once this has been proved, the Church merely awaits the manifestation of the divine will, which is the miracles effected through the intercession of the servant of God, in order to proceed to the beatification or canonization.

Consequently, this objection not only does not prove what it intends, but it favors the thesis which it was meant to attack. From the fact that the Church canonizes only those who have practiced the virtues in a heroic or superhuman degree, which cannot be effected without the actuation of the gifts of the Holy Ghost, it follows that the Church canonizes only those who are mystics.

4: MODELS OF PERFECTION

Configuration with Christ is the goal of our Christian life, since we thereby attain our own sanctification and at the same time give the greatest possible glory to God. In the present plan of divine providence we cannot perfectly sanctify ourselves nor give the greatest possible glory to God except through Christ and in Christ. For that reason it is of the greatest importance to have clear notions concerning the applications of Christology to the Christian life.

Until recently, relatively little emphasis was placed on the role of Christ in our sanctification, except for some of the outstanding classical works of spiritual doctrine, such as the writings of St. Bernard, St. Catherine of Siena and St. Teresa of Avila. This deficiency can be explained by recalling the exaggerated doctrines which were prevalent in France in the seventeenth century, with the result that the Church had to impose certain restrictions on the spiritual doctrines relative to the humanity of Christ. As a result, "devotion to Christ" was gradually relegated to a secondary place as one of the various means to sanctity, while in fact Christ is the cornerstone of our sanctification. We shall be saints only in the measure that we live the life of Christ, or rather, in the measure that Christ lives his life in us. The process of sanctification is a process of "Christification." The Christian must be converted into another Christ, and only when he can say in truth, "I live, now not I, but Christ liveth in me," can he be sure that he has reached the heights of perfection.

THE MYSTERY OF CHRIST

Christ's role in the life of his members is one of the predominant thoughts in the teaching of St. Paul. His entire apostolate consisted in revealing to the world the mystery of Christ (Col. 4:3), "to enlighten all men as to what is the dispensation of the mystery which has been hidden from eternity in God" (Eph. 3:9), in whom "dwells all the fulness of the Godhead bodily" (Col. 2:9), so that they "may be filled unto all the fulness of God" (Eph. 3:19). We can summarize the application of Christology to the Christian life by taking the words which Christ spoke of himself when he stated: "I am the way, and the truth, and the life" (John 14:6).

CHRIST THE WAY

Jesus Christ is the only way. No one can go to the Father except through him, for there has been given to us no other name under heaven by which we can be saved.[1] According to the divine plan of our predestination, the sanctity to which God calls us through grace and adoption consists in a participation in the divine life which was brought to the world by Christ. This is expressly stated in divine revelation: "As he chose us in him before the foundation of the world, that we should be holy and without blemish in his sight in love. He predestined us to be adopted through Jesus Christ as his sons, according to the purpose of his will, unto the praise of the glory of his grace, with which he has favored us in his beloved Son" (Eph. 1:4-6).

Christ has re-established the divine plan of our salvation, which had been destroyed by the sin of Adam. "In this has the love of God been shown in our case, that God has sent his only begotten Son into the world that we may live through him" (I John 4:9). Hence Christ is the only way by which we can go to the Father, and without him we can do absolutely nothing.[2] Therefore, the preoccupation of every Christian must be to live the life of Christ, to be incorporated in him, and to let the sap of the true Vine circulate through his veins. Christ is the Vine and we are the branches, and the life of the branch depends on its union with the vine which imparts to it the vivifying sap.[3]

St. Paul was unable to find any words in human language which could adequately express the incorporation of the Christian in the Vine. Everything about the Christian—his life, death and resurrection—must be intimately connected with Christ, and in order to express these profound truths, St. Paul had to invent expressions which had never before been used: "For if we have died with him (*conmortui*) (II Tim. 2:11), we were buried with him (*consepulti*) (Rom. 6:4), but God . . . raised us up together (*conresuscitati*) (Eph. 2:6), brought us to life together with Christ" (*convivificavit nos*) (*ibid.* 2:5), so that "we shall also live with him" (*et convivemus*) (II Tim. 2:11) and sit together in heaven in Christ Jesus (*et consedere*) (Eph. 2:6).

In view of the foregoing Pauline doctrine, we can heartily agree with the following observations of the saintly Dom Marmion:

> We must understand that we can only be saints according to the measure in which the life of Jesus Christ is in us: that is the only holiness God asks of

[1]Cf. Acts 4:12.
[2]Cf. John 15:5.
[3]Cf. John 15:1-6.

us; there is no other. We can only be holy in Jesus Christ, otherwise we cannot be so at all. There is not an atom of this holiness in creation; it proceeds from God by a supremely free act of his almighty will. . . . St. Paul returns more than once to the gratuitousness of the divine gift of adoption, and also to the eternity of the ineffable love which determined him to make us partakers of it, and to the wonderful means of realizing it through the grace of Jesus Christ.[4]

Christ is, therefore, the only way of going to the Father. He is the only possible form of sanctity according to the divine plan. Only through him, with him and in him can we attain the ideal intended by God in the creation, redemption and sanctification of the human race: the praise of his glory (Eph. 1:5-6). The Church reminds us of this daily in one of the most solemn moments of the Mass: *Per ipsum, et cum ipso et in ipso est tibi Deo Patri omnipotenti in unitate Spiritus Sancti omnis honor et gloria.* Only through his beloved Son will the Father accept our love and homage. For that reason the great saints, enlightened by God in a special manner to understand the mystery of Christ, wished to be dissolved and to be absorbed by Christ so that he could live their life in them. Sister Elizabeth of the Trinity, one of the souls who penetrated this mystery most profoundly, asked Christ:

I realize my weakness and beseech thee to clothe me with thyself, to identify my soul with all the movements of thine own. Immerse me in thyself, possess me wholly; substitute thyself for me, that my life may be but a radiance of thine own. Enter my soul as Adorer, as Restorer, as Savior! O Eternal Word, Utterance of my God! I long to pass my life in listening to thee, to become docile that I may learn all from thee. . . . O Consuming Fire! Spirit of Love! Descend within me and reproduce in me, as it were, an incarnation of the Word; that I may be to him another humanity wherein he renews his mystery. And thou, O Father, bend down toward thy poor little creature and overshadow her, beholding in her none other than thy beloved Son in whom thou has set all thy pleasure.[5]

How mistaken are they who consider devotion to Christ as merely another pious exercise! Our incorporation in Christ is the very basis of our sanctification and the very substance of our spiritual life. It is from this fundamental dogma that all other ascetical and mystical teachings spring. The souls that wish sincerely to sanctify themselves would do well, therefore, to ignore the disputes and arguments among the various schools of spirituality and dedicate themselves to living more and more profoundly the life of Christ. If they do this, they will surely reach the summit of sanctity, and there they will find all the saints without exception and will be able to repeat with them: "It is now no longer I that live, but Christ lives in me" (Gal. 2:20).

---

[4]Dom Columba Marmion, O.S.B., *Christ, the Life of the Soul* (St. Louis: Herder), pp. 39 f.

[5]Cf. M. M. Philipon, O.P., *The Spiritual Doctrine of Sister Elizabeth of the Trinity*, (Maryland: Newman, 1947), p. 54.

Christ is the Truth, the absolute and integral Truth. As the uncreated Wisdom of the Word, he communicated to his sacred humanity, and through it to us, all the treasures of wisdom and knowledge. This leads us to speak of the exemplary causality of Christ, which is exercised on us through his person, his works and his teaching.

CHRIST THE TRUTH

In his person

As regards his person, Dom Marmion has written the following sublime doctrine:

> The divine sonship of Christ is the type of our supernatural sonship; his condition, his "being" the Son of God is the exemplar of the state in which we must be established by sanctifying grace. Christ is the Son of God by nature and by right, in virtue of the union of the Eternal Word with human nature; we are so by adoption and grace, but we are so really and truly. Christ has, moreover, sanctifying grace; he possesses the fulness of it; from this fulness it flows into us more or less abundantly, but, in its substance, it is the same grace that both fills the created soul of Jesus and deifies us. St. Thomas says that our divine filiation is a resemblance of the eternal filiation: *quaedam similitudo filiationis aeternae.*
>
> Such is the primordial and supereminent manner in which Christ is first of all our example: in the Incarnation he is constituted, by right, the Son of God; we should become so by being partakers of the grace derived from him which, deifying the substance of our souls, constitutes us in the state of children of God. That is the first and *essential* characteristic of the likeness we must have to Christ Jesus; it is the condition of all our supernatural activity.[6]

Consequently, the entire Christian life and all sanctity, as Dom Marmion teaches, can be reduced to being by grace what Christ is by nature: a son of God.[7] This should be the basic preoccupation of every Christian: to contemplate Jesus and especially to form the attitude of a son before the heavenly Father who is also our Father, as Jesus himself has told us: "I ascend to my Father and your Father, to my God and your God" (John 20:17). "These realities," says Dom Marmion, "are precisely what constitute the essence of Christianity. We shall understand nothing of perfection and sanctity, and we shall not even know in what simple Christianity consists, as long as we are not convinced that fundamentally it consists in being sons of God and that this quality or state is given to us by sanctifying grace, through which we share in the eternal filiation of the Incarnate Word. All the teachings of Jesus Christ and the apostles are synthesized in this truth, and all the mysteries of Jesus tend to make it a reality in our souls."[8] There can be no doubt that this is the most important exemplary causality which Christ exercises upon us, although it is not the only one, for Christ is also our model in his works and in his virtues.

In his works

Jesus practiced what he taught and preached what he practiced; his life and doctrine form a harmonious unity from which there constantly issued glory

[6] *Op. cit.,* 50-51.
[7] Cf. *Christ in His Mysteries* (St. Louis: Herder, 1924), III, 6.
[8] *Ibid.*

to the Father. According to St. Thomas, the primary motive of the Incarnation was the redemption of the human race.[9] But in addition to this principal finality, the Incarnation also had other motives, and among them, doubtless, that of providing for us in Christ a most perfect model and exemplar of perfect virtue. And this was not without a special design of divine providence.

Speaking absolutely, the prototype and eminent exemplar of all perfection and sanctity is the Eternal Word. He is, if one may use the expression, the very ideal of God himself. The Father contemplates himself in the Word with infinite complacence and love, for the Word is the living, infinite, personal ideal with which the Father is well pleased through all eternity. Through the Word, the Father created the angels, men and the entire universe, as St. John teaches: "All things were made through him, and without him was made nothing that has been made" (John 1:3). The Word is also the ideal of angels and men and he would have been the ideal of all the possible beings which the Father could have created through all the centuries.

> Is it possible that we have the same ideal of life as God? Yes; and it is not given to us to choose a less elevated work. See, Christian soul, what is your dignity; see whether or not *noblesse oblige*. But this lofty ideal surpassed the powers of human reason and was too lofty even for faith itself. For that reason he came down: he became man, a child, a slave. He wished to know the weaknesses of our early years, our labors, our fatigues, as well as poverty, obscurity, silence, hunger, thirst, suffering and death. Of all our miseries there is only one which he did not experience and could not experience: sin, and certain moral disorders which derive from sin. Not being able to assume this weakness, he took upon himself its likeness and carried its punishment. Hence I need not rise to heaven to seek the thought of God in my regard; I need only, O my Jesus, contemplate thee. Thou art the perfect ideal in which I find my own.[10]

In his doctrine

Lastly, as the Eternal Word Jesus communicates his infinite wisdom to us by means of his sacred doctrine. The intellect of Christ is an abyss in which poor human reason, even when illumined by faith, is completely submerged. There are four classes of knowledge in Christ, completely distinct and yet in perfect harmony: *divine knowledge,* which he possesses as the Word of God; *beatific knowledge,* which is proper to the comprehensors and which Jesus possessed even here on earth; *infused knowledge,* which he received from God and in a degree which infinitely surpasses that of the angels; and *acquired knowledge,* which increased or was more and more manifested throughout his life.[11] Rightly did St. Paul speak of Christ as possessing all the treasures of wisdom and knowledge (Col. 2:3).

Christ did not wish to reserve all his treasures of knowledge for himself, but it pleased the Father that they should be communicated to his adopted

[9]Cf. *Summa,* III, q. 1, a. 3.
[10]Cf. Charles Sauvé, *Jésus Intime,* elev. 5, n. 5.
[11]Cf. St. Thomas, *Summa,* III, qq. 9-12.

sons in the measure and degree that is necessary. Christ himself said to the Father at the Last Supper: "The words that thou hast given me I have given to them. And they have received them, and have known of a truth that I came forth from thee, and they have believed that thou didst send me" (John 17:8).

And what sublime doctrine it is that Jesus has given us! Rightly did the ministers report to the Pharisees concerning the teaching of Christ: "Never has man spoken as this man" (John 7:46). The most beautiful compositions by human genius fade into nothingness when compared with a single statement from the Sermon on the Mount. All of Christ's doctrine, from the Sermon on the Mount to the poignant Seven Last Words, is a sublime summary of instruction for attaining sanctity. The soul that wishes to find the true way for going to God need only open the gospel of Jesus Christ and there drink divine knowledge at its source. As St. Thérèse of Lisieux declared: "I seldom find anything in books, except in the gospel. That book suffices for me."

CHRIST THE LIFE

In speaking of Christ as our life, we arrive at the most profound and the most beautiful aspect of the mystery of Christ. Christ is our life in three different manners: so far as he merited grace for us, which is the life of the soul (meritorious cause); so far as that supernatural life springs from him (efficient cause); and so far as he communicates that life to us (capital influence).

Meritorious cause

The merit of Christ in relation to us is intimately connected with his redemptive sacrifice. Let us review briefly the fundamental points concerning his infinite satisfaction, which merited for us and restored to us the supernatural life which had been lost through the sin of Adam.[12]

It was impossible for the human race to make condign satisfaction for the sin of Adam. If he had so desired, God could have freely forgiven the debt, but if he were to demand rigorous satisfaction, the impotence of the human race was absolute, due to the infinite distance between God and man. Only a God-man could bridge that infinite chasm and offer divine justice a complete satisfaction. Presupposing all this, the incarnation of the Word was absolutely necessary for the redemption of the human race.[13]

"And the word was made flesh and dwelt among us" (John 1:14). Since Christ united in himself the two natures—divine and human—in one divine person, all his actions had an infinite divine value. He could have redeemed millions of worlds by a mere smile or by his slightest action, but the redemption of the world actually was effected only through the sacrifice of the Cross. This is what the Father willed. Theologians have attempted to penetrate this

[12]Cf. St. Thomas, *Summa,* III, qq. 48-49; Marmion, *Christ, the Life of the Soul,* Chap. 3.

[13]Cf. St. Thomas, *Summa,* III, q. 1, a. 2, ad 2; I-II, q. 87, a. 4.

mystery of the crucifixion and death of Christ to redeem the world, but it will always remain a secret of the inscrutable designs of divine providence.[14]

Christ merited not only for himself but for us, with the merit of strict justice—*de condigno ex toto rigore justitiae,* as the theologians say. This justice has its foundation in the capital grace of Christ, in virtue of which he is constituted Head of the entire human race, and in the sovereign liberty of all his actions and the ineffable love with which he accepted his passion in order to save us.

The efficacy of his merits and satisfactions is strictly infinite and for that reason inexhaustible. That should arouse in us a boundless confidence in his love and mercy. In spite of our weaknesses, the merits of Christ have a superabundant efficacy to lead us to the heights of perfection. His merits are ours and they are at our disposition. In heaven he continues to intercede for us constantly (Heb. 7:25). Our weakness and poverty constitute a title to the divine mercy, and when we avail ourselves of this title we give great glory to the Father, because we thereby proclaim that Jesus is the only mediator whom it has pleased the Father to send to earth. For that reason, no man should become discouraged when he considers his own weakness and misery. The inexhaustible riches of Christ are at our disposition (Eph. 3:8).

Efficient cause

All the supernatural graces which man has received from the fall of Adam to the coming of Christ have been granted only in reference to Christ—*intuitu meritorum Christi.* And all the riches which men will receive until the end of time will spring forth from the heart of Christ. We do not have the *gratia Dei,* as did our first parents and the angels, but we have the *gratia Christi,* that is, the grace of God through Christ. This grace is given to us in many ways, but the source from which it flows is Christ, the sacred humanity united to the person of the Word. This is what is meant by the phrase: "Christ, the efficient cause of grace."

Jesus is the fountain of life. His sacred humanity is the instrument united to his divinity for the efficient production of the supernatural life.[15] Even more, the very humanity of Christ can also be a source of bodily life, for the gospel tells us that there went forth from Christ a power which cured the sick and raised the dead to life (Luke 6:19). But we are here interested primarily in Christ as the fountain and source of supernatural life.

In order to give us our natural life, God utilized our parents as instruments; to give us supernatural life, he utilizes the sacred humanity of Christ. Christ

---

[14]Cf. *ibid.,* III, q. 46, a. 3.

[15]The united or conjoined instrument is that which by its very nature is united to the principal cause which uses the instrument (the arm or hand is an instrument conjoined or united to the human body); the separated instrument is that which by its nature is separate from the principal cause which uses the instrument (as the brush in the hand of the painter).

has been constituted by the heavenly Father as Head, Pontiff, Mediator, Source and Dispenser of all graces, and particularly as Redeemer and in reference to his passion and death. St. Paul states that he "emptied himself, taking the nature of a slave and being made like unto men. And appearing in the form of man, and in habit found as man, he humbled himself, becoming obedient to death, even to death on a cross. Therefore, God also has exalted him and has bestowed upon him the name that is above every name, so that at the name of Jesus every knee should bend of those in heaven, on earth and under the earth, and every tongue should confess that the Lord Jesus Christ is in the glory of God the Father" (Phil. 2:7-11).

The gospel illustrates the manner in which Christ used his sacred humanity to confer supernatural life on souls. "Son," he said to the paralytic, "thy sins are forgiven thee." Immediately there was a reaction of surprise and scandal among the bystanders. "Who is this man who pretends to forgive sins? Only God can do this." But Jesus turns to them and gives them a convincing argument that he, as man, has the power to forgive sins. "Which is easier," he asks them, "to say thy sins are forgiven thee or to say arise, take up thy bed and walk? But that you may know that the Son of man has the power to forgive sins," and then he addresses the paralytic, "Arise, take up thy bed, and go into thy house."[16]

Christ used the expression "Son of man" deliberately. It is true that only God (or one who through the power of God is authorized to do so) can forgive sins. Therefore, he who would dare to forgive sins, not in the name of God but in his own name, and has in addition worked a stupendous miracle to testify to his power, must indeed have the personal power to forgive sins. Christ is the Son of God and the author of grace, and he alone has power to forgive sins by his own authority; but in so doing, he used his sacred humanity as an instrument in the production of supernatural life in souls. Hence he used the expression "Son of man" in order to signify that if he as man worked miracles, conferred grace and pardoned sins, it is because his sacred humanity is of itself vivifying. In other words, his humanity is an apt instrument for producing and causing grace by reason of its personal or hypostatic union with the divine Word.[17]

There is no difficulty in explaining the instrumental causality of the sacred humanity of Christ while he was yet on earth, but what is to be said of the

---

[16]Cf. Mark 2:1-12; Matt. 9:1-8; Luke 5:17-26.

[17]St. Thomas points out: "To give grace or the Holy Ghost authoritatively belongs to Christ as God, but to give it instrumentally belongs to him as man, since his humanity is the instrument of his divinity. And hence in virtue of his divinity his actions were salutary so far as they caused grace in us meritoriously and efficiently" (*Summa,* III, q. 8, a. 1, ad 1).

influence of his humanity after his ascension into heaven? Is the influence of his sacred humanity now only a moral causality or is it still physical?

Vital influence

Jesus is Head of the Mystical Body which is his Church. "And all things he made subject under his feet, and him he gave as head over all the Church, which indeed is his body, the completion of him who fills all with all" (Eph. 1:22-23).

St. Thomas asks whether Christ as man is Head of the Church and answers the question by establishing an analogy with the natural order.[18] In the human head, he states, we can consider three things: order, perfection and power. Order, because the head is the first part of man, beginning from the higher part; perfection, because in the head dwell all the senses, both interior and exterior, while in the other members there is only the sense of touch; power, because the power and movement of the other members, as well as the direction of their acts, is from the head, by reason of the sensitive and motive power which rules there.

Now all these characteristics are found in Christ spiritually, and therefore Christ is Head of the Church. He has the primacy of order because he is the firstborn among many brethren (Rom. 8:29) and has been constituted "above every Principality and Power and Virtue and Dominion—in short above every name that is named, not only in this world, but also in that which is to come" (Eph. 1:21), so that "in all things he may have the first place" (Col. 1:18). He has perfection above all others because in him is found the plenitude of all graces, according to St. John: "full of grace and of truth" (1:14). Lastly, he has the vital power over all the members of the Church because of his plenitude we have all received (John 1:16).

St. Paul summarizes these three characteristics in one statement when he writes to the Colossians: "He is the head of his body, the Church; he who is the beginning, the firstborn from the dead, that in all things he may have the first place. For it has pleased God the Father that in him all his fulness should dwell, and that through him he should reconcile to himself all things, whether on the earth or in the heavens, making peace through the blood of his cross" (1:18-20). And St. Thomas, in another place,[19] proves that Christ is Head of the Church by reason of his dignity, his government and his causality. But the formal reason for Christ's headship is the plenitude of his habitual grace, connoting the grace of union. Hence, according to St. Thomas, the personal grace by which the soul of Christ is sanctified is essentially the same as that by which he justifies others as Head of the Church; there is only a rational distinction between them.[20]

---

[18]Cf. *Summa,* III, q. 8, a. 1.
[19]Cf. *De veritate,* q. 29, a. 4.
[20]Cf. *Summa,* III, q. 8, a. 5.

How far does this capital grace of Christ extend? Who are affected by it and in what degree? According to St. Thomas, it extends to all the angels and to all men, except the damned, but in various manners and degrees. That Christ is Head of the angels is explicitly stated in the epistle of St. Paul to the Colossians (2:10). Christ is Head of this entire multitude because his sacred humanity, personally united to the Word, consequently shares in the graces and gifts of the Word much more perfectly than do the angels, and he also infuses in them many graces such as accidental glory, charisms, revelations of the mysteries of God, etc. Therefore, Christ is Head of the angels.[21]

Christ is also Head of men, but in different degrees.[22] He is Head of the blessed in a most perfect manner, because they are united with him definitely by confirmation in grace and glory; the same is true regarding the souls in purgatory as pertains to confirmation in grace. He is Head of all men in the state of grace, because they possess supernatural life and are united to Christ as living members through grace and charity. He is Head of Christians in the state of mortal sin, although less perfectly, since they are actually united to Christ through unformed faith and hope. Formal heretics and pagans are not actual but potential members of Christ, and those of this group who are predestined will one day pass from potential to actual members of Christ. The devils and the damned, on the other hand, are in no sense members of Christ, nor are the souls in limbo, for they are definitively separated from Christ and can never be united with him through sanctifying grace.

But how does Christ exercise his influence on those living members who are united to him in this life through grace and charity? He exercises it in many ways, but they can all be summarized under two headings: through the sacraments and through a contact by faith which is vivified by charity.

Sacramental influence. It is *de fide* that Christ is the author of the sacraments.[23] It must be so, because the sacraments are defined as sensible signs which signify and produce sanctifying grace, and only Christ, who is the unique source of grace, could institute them. And he instituted them precisely to communicate his own divine life to us through them. These sensible signs have the power of communicating grace by their own intrinsic power (*ex opere operato*), but only as instruments of Christ, that is, in virtue of the impulse which they receive from the humanity of Christ united to the Word. For that reason the unworthiness of the human minister who confers the sacrament (whether he be sinner or heretic) is no obstacle to its validity as long as he had the intention of doing what the Church does in the administration of the sacrament. Christ wished to place the communication of his divine grace

[21]Cf. *ibid.*, a. 4.
[22]Cf. *ibid.*, a. 3.
[23]Cf. Council of Trent, Sess. VII, can. 1; Denz. 844.

through the sacraments completely outside human weakness, with the result that we can have complete confidence in the efficacy of the sacraments as long as we ourselves do not place any obstacle to their sanctifying effects.

This last point needs special emphasis among modern Christians, for it is possible for us to place an insuperable obstacle to the sanctifying effects of a sacrament. No sacrament is valid if one does not interiorly consent to receive it.[24] The lack of repentance impedes the reception of grace in the sacrament of penance or in the baptism of an adult in the state of mortal sin; conscious mortal sin prevents the reception of grace in the five sacraments of the living and makes the action sacrilegious.[25]

But even if one possesses the necessary dispositions for the valid and fruitful reception of the sacraments, the measure of grace received in each case will depend not only on the excellence of the sacrament itself but on the perfection and fervor of one's dispositions. If the individual approaches the sacrament with a hunger and thirst to be united to God through grace, he will receive an abundance of grace. As the classical example of the fountain and the vessel illustrates, the amount of water received will depend, not only on the fountain, but also on the size of the vessel in which the water is received. From this follows the great importance of a proper preparation for the reception of the sacraments, and especially of the Eucharist, which brings us not only grace but the very fountain and source of grace. It is through the sacraments especially that Christ exercises his vital influence on us, and we should approach them with the desire of increasing our supernatural life and our union with God. They are the authentic channels of grace, and there is nothing else that can replace them. Some souls, not realizing these truths, prefer other pious practices and devotions which are infinitely less efficacious than the sacraments. It is an injury to Christ not to appreciate, or to regulate to a second place, these channels of grace which he instituted as a means of increasing our supernatural life.

Contact through faith. As regards our contact with Christ through a vivified faith, St. Paul uses a mysterious expression in one of his epistles. He says that Christ dwells in our hearts through faith (Eph. 3:17). What do these words mean? Is he referring to some kind of indwelling of Christ in our souls, similar to the indwelling of the Trinity? It would be a great error to think this. The humanity of Christ is physically present in us through Holy Communion, but this presence is so closely bound to the sacramental species that when they are substantially altered Christ's physical presence ceases entirely and there re-

[24]The Church supplies this consent for infants who receive baptism (and confirmation).

[25]We say "conscious" mortal sin, for it is the common teaching of theologians that a person in good faith (not conscious of mortal sin on his part) receives the sacrament validly and fruitfully, even though he is actually in mortal sin.

main in the soul only his divinity (together with the Father and the Holy Ghost) and the influence of his grace.

Nevertheless, it is a fact that Christ does in some way dwell in our hearts through faith. St. Thomas does not hesitate to interpret the words of St. Paul literally: "Christ dwells in us by faith (Eph. 3:17). Consequently, by faith Christ's power is united to us."[26] In other words, it is the power of Christ which dwells in us through faith, and as often as we turn to him through the contact of a faith vivified by charity, a sanctifying power emanates from Christ to our souls. The Christ of today is the same Christ of the gospel, and all who approach him through faith and love will share in the power that emanates from him to cure the sicknesses of body and soul (Luke 6:19). "How, then," asks Dom Marmion, "can we doubt that when we approach him, even outside the sacraments, with humility and confidence, divine power comes forth from him to enlighten, strengthen and help us? No one has ever approached Jesus Christ with faith without being touched by the beneficent rays that ever escape from this furnace of light and heat: *Virtus de illo exibat.*"[27]

Therefore, the soul that would sanctify itself should increase and intensify more and more this contact with Christ through an ardent faith vivified by charity. This exercise can be performed at any moment, many times a day, while the sacramental contact through Holy Communion can be had only once daily.

Physical influence. We can now return to our previous question concerning the nature of the vital influence which the humanity of Christ has on us. Is it a physical or only a moral influence? Theologians are divided on the answer. Some hold for a merely moral influence, but the Thomists energetically defend the physical influence of the humanity of Christ. This is simply an extension of their teaching on the physical causality of the sacraments in the production of grace. If the sacraments, which are separated instruments of Christ, produce grace physically, why would not the humanity of Christ, which is a conjoined instrument, do likewise?

The greatest difficulty which opposes this teaching is the fact that a physical action presupposes a physical contact between the agent and the patient. Such a contact was realized during the earthly life of Christ, as when he healed by a touch of his hand, but how can this physical contact be verified now that the humanity is triumphant in heaven?

The answer to the objection calls for various distinctions. In the first place, the objection supposes a type of physical causality on the part of the humanity of Christ which cannot be accepted, for it refers to a contact which is quantitative. But the humanity of Christ comprises both his body and his

---

[26]*Summa,* III, q. 62, a. 5, ad 2.

[27]Marmion, *Christ, the Life of the Soul,* p. 89.

soul, and the soul of Christ can operate through his will, as an instrument of the Word, even as regards supernatural effects which are physically distant from it. The human will of Christ was elevated to the production or immediate causality of supernatural works by his volitional power, and the rest of his humanity came under this command of the will.[28]

Moreover, if the humanity of Christ is not physically present in all places, the divine Word, to whom it is hypostatically united, is so present. And there is nothing inconvenient in the fact that the Word should use the instrumental power of his sacred humanity in the production of grace in our souls. For this, a *virtual* contact of the humanity of Christ would suffice, as St. Thomas explains in regard to the efficient causality of the resurrection of Christ on our resurrection.[29]

Again, one must attribute to the triumphant humanity of Christ all the prerogatives which it had here on earth, as long as they are not incompatible with the state of glory. But physical instrumental causality is perfectly compatible with the state of glory. Therefore, the humanity of Christ in glory possesses this physical instrumental causality. Otherwise, the sacred humanity would be less perfect in heaven than it was on earth.

Lastly, the whole plan of the Incarnation is more beautiful when seen in the light of this teaching. The physical action of Christ is not restricted to the Eucharist, but Christ's presence is felt in all places and through all the centuries. Christ continues to pass through the world, doing good and healing all (Acts 10:38).

OUR LIFE IN CHRIST

The quintessence of the Christian life can be summarized in the following statement: the glory of God as the ultimate end, our sanctification as the proximate end to which we should tend continually, and incorporation in Christ as the only possible way of attaining both ends. In a word, everything can be summarized in living the mystery of Christ with ever increasing intensity. With this thought in mind, there is a formula which admirably describes all that we ought to do in order to scale the heights of Christian perfection. It is used by the Church in the Mass and constitutes one of its most august rites. Immeditely before reciting the *Pater Noster,* the celebrant genuflects before the Blessed Sacrament which rests on the corporal, and then upon rising, he takes the Host in his hand and traces five crosses, three above the chalice and two in front of it, as he pronounces the sublime words: *Per ipsum, et cum ipso et in ipso est tibi Patri omnipotenti, in unitate Spiritus Sancti, omnis honor et gloria.*

---

[28]Cf. J. Solano, *Sacrae Theologiae Summa,* III, "De Verbo Incarnato" (Madrid: B.A.C.), n. 323.

[29]Cf. *Summa,* III, q. 56, a. 1, ad 3.

As is evident from the formula, the glory of the Trinity is the absolute end of the creation of the world and of the redemption and sanctification of the human race. But in the actual economy of divine providence, the glory of the Trinity is realized through Christ, with Christ and in Christ. Hence anything that man would use for giving glory to God apart from Christ would be completely inept for the purpose. Everything in the Christian life must be reduced to doing all things through Christ, with Christ and in Christ, under the impulse of the Holy Ghost, for the glory of the Father.

Per ipsum

Christ is the only Way, and no one can go to the Father except through him. Therefore, the principal preoccupation of the Christian who wishes to sanctify himself should be to incorporate himself in Christ until he does all things through Christ. Then he can offer all his works to the Father in and through Christ, and this will give great glory to the Father. For the Father has but one eternal obsession, so to speak, and it is his Word. Nothing else is of direct concern to the Father, and if he loves us it is because we love Christ and believe that he came from the Father. As Jesus himself has stated: "For the Father himself loves you because you have loved me, and have believed that I came forth from God" (John 16:27). This sublime mystery should convert our love of Christ into a kind of obsession. What else does the Church teach in the liturgy but this truth? Although the Church is the spouse of Christ, she does not dare to ask anything of the Father in her own name but always petitions *per Dominum nostrum Jesum Christum Filium tuum.*

Et cum ipso

It is not even enough to do all things *through* Christ, but the Christian should endeavor also to do all things *with* Christ. The divinity of Christ, the Word of God, is present in every soul in the state of grace. And the Word can always use the instrumental power of his sacred humanity, to which he is united hypostatically, to fill us with supernatural life. Christ, the man-God, is the source and fountain of grace, and the grace that sanctifies us is his capital grace, that is, the habitual grace which he possesses in its plenitude and which he as Head diffuses on his members.[30] Hence this notion of doing all things with Christ is not an illusion or a pious exaggeration; it is a theological fact. As long as we are in the state of grace, Christ is within us, physically in his divinity and virtually in his sacred humanity, and for that reason there is no repugnance in saying that we can do all things with him. And what great value our works have when they are presented to the Father as having been performed with Christ! But without this union, our works are worthless, as Christ has taught (John 15:5).

This notion, which is complementary to the preceding and preparatory for the following, appears constantly in the teaching of St. Paul. He who had been given an unequalled insight into the mystery of Christ was unable to

[30]Cf. St. Thomas, *Summa,* III, q. 8, a. 5.

describe adequately "the unfathomable riches of Christ" (Eph. 3:8) and the manner in which we have been given a share in them until we are filled with "all the fulness of God" (Eph. 3:19). All the efforts of the Christian should therefore be directed to an ever more intimate union with Christ, to the end that all his actions will be performed in unison with Christ. A single act performed by Jesus gives more glory to the Father than all the acts of all the angels and all the blessed, including the Blessed Virgin. But without Jesus, our acts are worthless, for they receive their eternal value from him alone.

Et in ipso

To perform one's actions through Christ and with Christ is something sublime, but to perform one's actions in him, identified with him, is still greater. The first two modalities are something extrinsic to us, but the third identifies us with Christ in a certain manner and makes our works his. In order to appreciate this truth, it is necessary to consider our incorporation in Christ as Head of the Mystical Body. By reason of this incorporation, the Christian forms a part of Christ. The total Christ of whom St. Augustine speaks is Christ plus ourselves. The Christian in grace forms one thing with Christ, and as a branch of the vine he lives the same life as Christ.

Once this truth is grasped, the expressions of St. Paul and the gospel take on a more profound meaning. Our sufferings fill up "what is lacking of the sufferings of Christ" (Col. 1:24); it is Christ who works in us and triumphs (Col. 1:29). When we are persecuted, he is persecuted (Acts 9:5); the slightest service done for us is accepted and rewarded as if it had been done for him (Matt. 10:42). The supreme desire of Christ is that we should be one with him (John 17:21), and to such a degree that we are perfect in unity in the bosom of the Father (John 17:23).

Consequently, there can be no doubt that Christ has incorporated us in himself and has made us his members. We are truly his body. We are not only Christ's, but we are Christ, as St. Augustine teaches: *Concorporans nos sibi, faciens nos membra sua ut in illo et nos Christus essemus. . . . Et omnes in illo et Christi et Christus sumus, quia quodammodo totus Christus, caput et corpus est.*[31] Hence the Christian should so live that all his works are performed through Christ, with Christ and in Christ, and he should be so identified with Christ that in looking upon the soul the Father sees his Son. This was the sublime desire of Sister Elizabeth of the Trinity: "Do not see in me anything but thy beloved Son, in whom thou hast placed all thy complacence." And in order to realize this sublime goal, she begged Christ to substitute himself for her, and she asked the Holy Ghost to effect in her a new incarnation of the Word.[32]

---

[31] *Enarrationes in Psalmas,* In Ps. XXVI, enarr. 2, n. 2; PL 36:200.

[32] Cf. Philipon, *The Spiritual Doctrine of Sister Elizabeth of the Trinity,* p. 54.

Est. The Church uses the indicative and not the subjunctive form of the verb, for it is not a question of desire or petition but of an accomplished fact. In these moments, when the Church is gathered around the altar to offer the body of the Lord who rests on it, God actually receives all honor and glory. The same thing is true of every action of a Christian which ascends to heaven through Christ, with Christ and in Christ. The slightest action thus acquires an infinite value and gives great glory to God. And this is another motivation for being intimately united with Christ.

Est

Tibi Deo Patri omnipotenti. Everything is directed to the Father. This was the constant and unique goal of every act performed by Christ. He sought always to do the Father's will (Matt. 26:39) and to give glory to his Father (John 17:1). The first words of Christ which are recorded in the gospel are: "Did you not know that I must be about my Father's business?" (Luke 2:49). The last words which he spoke from the cross were: "Father, into thy hands I commend my spirit" (Luke 23:46). Jesus lived and died, thinking of his Father. The Christian should strive to imitate Jesus in all things, and especially in this constant aspiration to the Father. St. Paul summarizes it beautifully when he says: "For all things are yours . . . and you are Christ's, and Christ is God's" (I Cor. 3:22-23).

Tibi Deo Patri Omnipotenti

In unitate Spiritus Sancti. The glory of God does not pertain exclusively to the Father; it is the glory of the divinity and hence of the entire Trinity. Consequently, the glory which the Father receives from Christ also pertains to the Holy Ghost, the ineffable bond of love and union in the adorable Trinity.

In unitate Spiritus Sancti

Omnis honor et gloria. All glory must ascend to the Trinity through, with and in Christ, for he is the way. And thus is the divine circular motion completed: Jesus as Head and as mediator brings grace and supernatural life to his members; they, in turn, give glory to God by returning the selfsame supernatural gifts to God through Christ.

Omnis honor et gloria

MARY AND OUR SANCTIFICATION

One of the outstanding authorities on the role of Mary in the Christian life has stated: "The more you look at Mary in your prayers, contemplations, actions and sufferings, if not in a clear and distinct manner, then at least with a general and imperceptible glance, the more perfectly will you find Jesus, who is always with Mary, great, powerful, active and incomprehensible, more than in heaven or in any other creature.[33]

[33]Cf. St. Louis Mary Grignion de Montfort, *True Devotion to the Blessed Virgin Mary,* Part II, Chap. 2, Fifth Motive, n. 4.

Mary is, in a word, the shortest and most secure path to Christ. God has wished that Mary should be so intimately associated with the divine plan of redemption and sanctification that they cannot be attained without her. Consequently, this is not merely a question of another devotion, but Mary has a basic and necessary role to play in the Christian life.

MARY'S ROLE

All the titles and glories of Mary stem from her divine maternity. She is immaculate, full of grace, co-redemptrix and mediatrix because she is the Mother of God. Her divine maternity places her on such an exalted level that St. Thomas did not hesitate to say that it bestowed upon her a certain infinite dignity.[34] And Cajetan says that Mary touches the boundaries of divinity.[35] There is no other creature that has as great an affinity with God.

Because of her divine maternity, Mary is an intimate part of the hypostatic union, and hence she enters into the incarnation of the Word and the redemption of the human race as an essential element. But the hypostatic union infinitely surpasses the order of grace and glory; therefore, the divine maternity surpasses the adoptive filiation through grace, because adoption establishes only a spiritual and mystical relationship, while the divine maternity establishes a relationship of nature and of blood with Jesus Christ, as well as one of affinity with the Blessed Trinity.[36] The divine maternity, which terminates in the uncreated person of the Word made flesh, surpasses, by reason of its end, the grace and glory of all the elect and the plenitude of grace and glory received by Mary herself. It surpassses all the graces *gratis datae* and the charisms, because these graces are less than sanctifying grace.[37] Because of this, Mary is intimately associated with the entire redemptive mission of Christ, and all that he merited for us in strict justice (*de condigno ex toto rigore justitiae*), she likewise merited for us, but in a different way.[38]

DEVOTION TO MARY

Mary's role in the sanctification of the Christian can be seen in the writings of St. Louis Grignion de Montfort, and we shall give a synthesis of his doctrine as found in *The Secret of Mary*. It is the will of God that we sanctify ourselves; to sanctify ourselves it is necessary to practice the virtues; to practice the virtues we need the grace of God; to find the grace of God it is necessary

---

[34]Cf. *Summa,* I, q. 25, a. 6, ad 4.

[35]Cf. *In II-II,* q. 103, a. 4, ad 2.

[36]Cf. E. Hugon, O.P., *Marie Pleine de Grâce,* p. 63.

[37]Cf. Reginald Garrigou-Lagrange, O.P., *The Mother of the Savior* (St. Louis: Herder, 1953), Part I, Chap. 1; St. Thomas, *Summa,* I-II, q. 111, a. 5.

[38]The type of merit which is found in Mary as co-redemptrix and mediatrix is disputed among the theologians. Some see only a merit of fittingness (*de congruo*); others defend a merit in strict justice but by a certain proportionality (*de condigno ex condignitate*).

to find Mary. Why is this so? The following reasons can be given: 1) because only Mary found grace before God, both for herself and for others; 2) because Mary gave life to the Author of grace and is therefore called mother of grace; 3) because in giving Mary his divine Son the Father gave Mary all graces; 4) because God has selected her as the dispenser of all graces and with this power she gives grace to whom she wishes, when she wishes and as she wishes; 5) because as in the natural order the child must have a father and a mother, so also in the supernatural order one must have God as his Father and Mary as his mother; 6) since Mary formed the Head of the predestined, so also she should form the members; 7) because Mary was and still remains the spouse of the Holy Ghost; 8) because as in the natural order the child receives its nourishment and strength from its mother, so also in the supernatural order we receive our spiritual nourishment and strength from Mary; 9) because he who finds Mary also finds Jesus, who is with her always.[39]

Having seen the reasons for Mary's sublime role in our sanctification, we again turn to St. Louis de Montfort to learn the characteristics of true devotion to the Blessed Virgin. First, our devotion to Mary should be *interior;* that is, it should come from the mind and heart. Secondly, it should be *tender;* that is, full of the confidence of a child in a loving mother. Thirdly, it should be *holy*; that is, it should lead souls to avoid sin and to imitate her virtues. Fourthly, it should be *constant*; that is, it should confirm the soul in good so that it will not abandon its spiritual practices. Fifthly, it should be *disinterested;* that is, it should inspire the soul to seek not itself but God alone.[40]

CONSECRATION TO MARY

A final word should be said about the holy slavery to Mary as proposed by St. Louis de Montfort as the basis of total abandonment to Mary. It consists in giving oneself entirely to Mary as her slave and to Jesus through Mary, and of doing all things with Mary, through Mary and in Mary. This act of perfect devotion to Mary implies a complete and total consecration to Mary, which results in a new state for the soul, and the effort to live in perfect conformity with this total giving of self to Mary. St. Louis explains this heroic act of consecration to Mary as follows:

> This devotion consists, then, in giving ourselves entirely to Our Lady, in order to belong entirely to Jesus through her. We must give her: 1) our body, with all its senses and its members; 2) our soul, with all its powers; 3) our exterior goods of fortune, whether present or to come; 4) our interior and spiritual goods, which are our merits and our virtues and our good works, past, present and future. In a word, we must give her all we have in the order of nature and in the order of grace, and all that may become ours in the future, in the orders of nature, grace and glory; and this we must do without the

[39]Cf. *The Secret of Mary* and especially *True Devotion to the Blessed Virgin Mary,* Part II, Chap. 2, Fifth Motive.

[40]Cf. *True Devotion to the Blessed Virgin Mary,* Part I, Chap. 3.

reserve of so much as one farthing, one hair or one least good action; and we must do it also for all eternity; and we must do it, further, without pretending to, or hoping for, any other recompense for our offering and service except the honor of belonging to Jesus Christ through Mary and in Mary—even though that sweet mistress were not, as she always is, the most generous and the most grateful of creatures.

Here we must note that there are two things in the good works we perform, namely, satisfaction and merit; in other words, their satisfactory or impetratory value and their meritorious value. The satisfactory or impetratory value of a good action is that action inasmuch as it satisfies for the pain due to sin, or obtains some new grace; the meritorious value, or the merit, is the good action inasmuch as it merits grace now and eternal glory hereafter. Now in this consecration of ourselves to Our Lady, we give her all the satisfactory, impetratory and meritorious value of our actions; in other words, the satisfactions and the merits of all our good works. We give her all our merits, graces and virtues—not to communicate them to others, for our merits, graces and virtues are, properly speaking, incommunicable, and it is only Jesus Christ who, in making himself our surety with his Father, is able to communicate his merits—but we give her them to keep them, augment them and embellish them for us. . . . Our satisfactions, however, we give her to communicate to whom she likes, and for the greatest glory of God.[41]

As is evident, this act of consecration and holy slavery to Mary is an excellent and even heroic act. For that reason it is not to be made lightly or too quickly, but only after mature deliberation and with the permission of a spiritual director. Although it is not a true vow, it would be irreverent to make the act and then live as if it had never been made. But those who, under the inspiration of the Holy Spirit and with the express authorization of their director, make this act of consecration to Mary can be sure that she will love them with a special love, will provide for their needs generously, will guide them along the path to holiness, will defend them against their enemies, and will intercede continuously for them so that they may receive the gift of final perseverance and attain eternal bliss.

[41]*Ibid.*, Part II, Chap. 1.

NEGATIVE ASPECT OF THE CHRISTIAN LIFE

1: STAGES OF THE CHRISTIAN LIFE

Having examined the end and the basic principles of the Christian life, we shall now consider its growth or practice. The manner of treating this part of the theology of Christian perfection varies with different authors. Some divide the material on the basis of the traditional three ways: purgative, illuminative and unitive, and then proceed to describe the principal characteristics manifested by souls as they pass through the various ways.[1] Those who defend the doctrine of two distinct paths to perfection consider those same three ways, first in the ascetical, and then in the mystical phase of the spiritual life.[2] Others describe the whole process of the spiritual life under the aspect of the practice of prayer.[3] Others, finally, abstract more or less from any chronological order in the treatment of the phenomena of the spiritual life and classify the material under the general principles of the means of sanctification.[4]

METHODS OF STUDY

All these methods, except the second, have their advantages and disadvantages. The principal advantage of using the three ways is that it is closer to the facts, but it has the serious disadvantage of isolating these three aspects of the spiritual life. In practice they do not fall into separate categories but intermingle to such an extent that at any moment or at any phase of the spiritual life one may find elements of purification, illumination and union. For that

---

[1]Cf. A. Saudreau, *The Degrees of the Spiritual Life* (London: Burns, Oates and Washbourne, 1907), and A. Tanquerey, S.S., *The Spiritual Life* (Westminster, Md.: Newman, 1948).

[2]Cf. Crisógono de Jesús Sacramentado, O.C.D., *Compendio de Ascética y Mística* (Avila: 1933). Francisco Naval, C.F.M., treats of the three ways only in regard to the ascetical and not the mystical phase (cf. *Curso de Teología Ascética y Mística*).

[3]Cf. J. G. Arintero, O.P., *Stages in Prayer* (St. Louis: Herder, 1957). However, Arintero treats of the three ways in his authoritative work, *The Mystical Evolution*.

[4]Cf. R. Garrigou-Lagrange, O.P., *Christian Perfection and Contemplation; The Three Ages of the Interior Life* (St. Louis: Herder, 1937, 1948); J. de Guibert, S.J., *The Theology of the Spiritual Life* (New York: Sheed and Ward, 1953); J. Schrijvers, C.Ss.R., *Les principes de la vie spirituelle* (Brussels: Ed. Universelle, 1935).

NEGATIVE ASPECT

reason, the authors who use this method are forced to repeat themselves time and again and to return constantly to material which they have already treated.

Those who develop the doctrine of the spiritual life on the basis of the grades of prayer will depend greatly on confirmation from experience. They will also perhaps recall the words of St. Pius X, in which he expressly declares that there is an intimate relation between the grades of prayer treated by St. Teresa and the growth of the spiritual life.[5] But it has this inconvenience, that it does not solve many problems which arise in regard to the Christian life in general.

Those who prefer to classify the material into homogeneous sections proceed with great clarity and avoid monotonous repetitions. However, they are then forced to study separately many things which in actual life are intimately related.

We do not think that there is any method which will have all the advantages and will avoid all the disadvantages. The spiritual life is very mysterious and complex. There is such a variety of manifestations when the divine combines with the individual psychology of a particular soul that it is practically impossible to reduce the whole matter to human categories. The Holy Spirit breathes where he will, and he leads souls in different ways to the heights of perfection. One could say that each soul follows a path that is proper to itself and never repeated in the case of any other soul.

Nevertheless, it is necessary to follow some method in order to proceed with order and the greatest possible clarity in these intricate questions. Therefore, recognizing its disadvantages, we intend to follow the method of dividing the material into homogeneous parts. Keeping in mind that the purpose of this work is pedagogical, we shall first give a brief summary of the growth of the spiritual life, and then we shall treat at length of the negative aspect and the positive aspect of this growth.

SPIRITUAL GROWTH

Each soul follows its own path to sanctity under the direction and impulse of the Holy Ghost; there are no two persons absolutely identical, either in body or in soul. The masters of the spiritual life have attempted to give various classifications by concentrating on the predominant dispositions of souls, a useful device to establish a point of reference for determining the state in which

[5]Cf. J. de Guibert, S.J., *Documenta Ecclesiastica Christianae Perfectionis Studium Spectantia* (Romae: Univ. Greg., 1931), n. 636.

a particular soul finds itself at a given time in the spiritual life. This knowledge is very important in practice, since the spiritual direction of a soul in the first stages of the spiritual life will be very different from that which is given to those who are advanced or already perfect.

The three principal classifications which have been proposed in the history of Christian spirituality are the classic division into the three ways (purgative, illuminative and unitive), that of the three degrees (beginners, proficient and perfect), and that of St. Teresa of Avila as outlined in her *Interior Castle.* We shall blend these three classifications in order to construct the following schema of the entire Christian life.[6]

THE OUTER COURT

The "outer court of the castle"[7] is the stage of the sinners who live habitually in the state of sin and are not interested in abandoning it. Perhaps the majority sin through ignorance or frailty, but there are also some who give themselves to sin because of a cold indifference or even because of an obstinate and diabolical malice. In some cases there is a complete absence of remorse and a deliberate rejection of all prayer or recourse to God. They consider mortal sin to be of little importance or something that is readily pardoned. For that reason, they imprudently place themselves in all kinds of occasions of sin, and they succumb to temptation with the greatest facility. They miss Mass on Sundays frequently and for the slightest reason; their annual confession, which is sometimes omitted, is made in a mechanical fashion, without any interior devotion and without a true desire to give up their sins definitively. They sometimes make use of vocal prayers, but without attention or true piety and usually to ask God for temporal things.

THE PURGATIVE WAY

When the soul begins to desire sincerely to live in a Christian manner, it enters the purgative way or the first degree of charity. Its basic dispositions are described by St. Thomas in the following words: "At first it is man's principal concern to avoid sin and resist the passions, which move him in opposition to charity. And this pertains to beginners, in whom charity must be nourished and augmented lest it be destroyed."[8]

The purgative way can be subdivided into the first three mansions described by St. Teresa of Avila. The *first mansions* are those of the *faithful* souls who struggle somewhat weakly against mortal sin but sincerely repent through

---

[6]We are indebted principally to St. Thomas Aquinas, St. Teresa of Avila, Saudreau and Dom Chautard.

[7]This allusion is to the famous text of St. Teresa: "Many souls remain in the outer court of the castle, . . . they are not interested in entering it and have no idea what there is in that wonderful place" (*Interior Castle,* First Mansions, n. 5).

[8]*Summa,* II-II, q. 24, a. 9.

NEGATIVE ASPECT

good confessions. Frequently, however, they voluntarily place themselves in the occasion of sin. They make no effort to avoid venial sin because they consider it to be of no importance. Their practices of piety are generally restricted to those which are commanded by the Church, and even here they sometimes fail. On rare occasions they may perform some pious work of supererogation. Their prayer is purely vocal and is accompanied by many distractions. Their petitions in prayer are usually in regard to temporal things and rarely pertain to the spiritual.

In the *second mansions* we find those *good* souls who valiantly struggle against mortal sin, although they find themselves in occasions which lead to their fall. When this happens, they repent sincerely and promptly go to confession. They still commit deliberate venial sins because their battle to overcome them is rather weak, their repentance is superficial, and they constantly fall back into the same venial sins. They frequent the sacraments, especially on the great feasts, the first Fridays, etc., and sometimes attend daily Mass, but with little preparation. They readily omit such devotions as the daily Rosary. Their prayer in general is still vocal, although at times they may attempt to make a meditation, which is often accompanied by voluntary distractions.

The *third mansions* of the purgative way comprise those *pious* souls who rarely commit mortal sin, and when they do their repentance is profound, they immediately confess their sin, and they take precautions to avoid a relapse. They sincerely combat venial sin and make use of the particular examen, although as yet it is not performed with fidelity and it produces little fruit. They usually attend Mass and receive Communion daily, but often it is with a certain spirit of routine. They confess their sins each week but with only a slight amendment of their defects. Such souls often say the rosary daily, make frequent visits to the Blessed Sacrament, and make the stations of the Cross regularly. They practice meditation daily but often do not make a good meditation because of their many distractions. They readily omit meditation, especially in times of dryness or numerous occupations which could have been avoided without failing in the duties of their state in life. Frequently they make affective prayer, which tends to become more and more simplified. The night of the senses usually begins here as a transition to the illuminative way.

THE ILLUMINATIVE WAY

When the soul has decided to enter upon a life of solid piety and to advance along the way of virtue, it has entered upon the illuminative way. This is what many spiritual authors call the second conversion. The principal concern of the soul at this point is to grow in the Christian life by increasing and strengthening its charity. We can divide the illuminative way into the following degrees or mansions.

The beginning of the illuminative way is found in those *fervent* souls who are in the *fourth mansions*. They never commit mortal sin. If they are suddenly surprised by unexpected temptation, their mortal sin is a doubtful one and is followed immediately by profound repentance, immediate confession and acts of penance. They exercise great care to avoid venial sin, and it is rarely fully deliberate when they commit a sin. They make use of the particular examen as a means of combatting all venial sin. Such souls, however, often avoid examining themselves concerning imperfections, lest they be obliged to combat them. They love abnegation and self-denial, but only to a certain point. Their daily Mass and Communion are accompanied by fervent preparation and thanksgiving. They are diligent in the weekly confession, they seek spiritual direction in order to make progress in virtue, and they have a tender devotion to Mary. They are faithful in prayer in spite of dryness or aridity in the night of the senses. They practice the prayer of simplicity, which is a transition to contemplative prayer, and in moments of particular intensity they enjoy the prayer of infused recollection and of quiet.

In the *fifth mansions* we find those souls that are *relatively perfect*. They never commit a deliberate venial sin, although sometimes they may fall by surprise or lack of advertence. Then they repent of their sin and make reparation. Any imperfections are immediately rejected and combatted with all their strength. There may be some deliberate imperfections, but they are quickly repented. There are frequent acts of abnegation and renunciation, and the particular examen is now aimed at seeking perfection in a definite virtue. Their practices of piety become more simple and less numerous but are practiced with greater love. Charity is beginning to have a more intense and a more actual influence on everything they do. They love solitude; they are more and more disinterested; they experience a great longing for God, a desire for heaven, a love of the cross, a disinterested zeal, and a great hunger for Communion. Their life of prayer is so habitual that it is as natural as breathing. They have reached the contemplative prayer of union, and frequently they undergo passive purifications and manifest certain phenomena that are concomitant with the mystical state.

THE UNITIVE WAY

When the life of prayer becomes, as it were, the very breathing of the soul, even amidst its occupations and duties of state, and when intimate union with God and the attainment of complete Christian perfection constitute the supreme ideal of its life, the soul has entered the unitive way. Its fundamental preoccupation is to be united with God and to enjoy him. The unitive way can be subdivided into two grades or mansions.

The first degree of the unitive way is that of the *heroic* souls who are in the *sixth mansions*. They never commit deliberate imperfections; at most they are only partially deliberate and are quickly rejected. They perform all their practices of piety with an exquisite fidelity, but they are concerned only with being united more intimately with God. Their disinterest in self has reached the point of forgetfulness of self. They have a great thirst for suffering and their penitential practices are severe. They would wish to offer themselves completely as a holocaust for the conversion of sinners. Frequently they offer themselves as victim souls. In their life of prayer, contemplation is practically habitual. They enjoy the prayer of union in a very high degree and it is frequently the prayer of ecstatic union. They undergo the passive purifications of the night of the spirit. The spiritual espousal occurs at this stage, as well as the concomitant mystical phenomena and sometimes graces *gratis datae.*

In the *seventh mansions* we find the *great saints,* in whom imperfections are scarcely apparent. Their practices of piety have been reduced to the simple exercise of love. As St. John of the Cross says: "Now loving is my only exercise." Their love has reached a point of incredible intensity, but it is still tranquil. They enjoy an unchanging peace and serenity; they manifest profound humility, unity of judgment and simplicity of intention. All that remains is the honor and glory of God. In their prayer life they enjoy what St. Teresa describes as a certain intellectual vision of the Blessed Trinity in the soul. They have reached the transforming union and mystical marriage, and sometimes confirmation in grace.

Such, in its general lines, is the path which souls usually travel in their journey to sanctity. It admits of an infinite variety of modification because no two souls are exactly alike, but the expert director who pays close attention to the general characteristics which we have described will be able to determine rather accurately the degree of the spiritual life which has been attained by a soul at any given time.

We shall now examine in detail the two basic aspects of the Christian life: the negative and the positive. Although in practice these two elements are usually intermingled and sometimes inseparable, for pedagogical reasons we shall treat first of the negative aspect in its entirety and then of the positive aspect.

2: THE STRUGGLE AGAINST SIN

Sin is the worst enemy of our sanctification and is in reality the only enemy, since everything else that impedes growth in holiness either comes from sin or is conducive to sin. Sin is a voluntary transgression against the law of God. It always presupposes three essential elements: forbidden matter, deliberation on the part of the intellect, and consent on the part of the will. If the matter is grave and the deliberation and consent are complete, one has committed a mortal sin; if the matter is light or if deliberation and consent are imperfect, the sin is venial. Within these two types of sin there is an infinity of degrees. The detailed study of sin pertains to moral theology; we shall discuss only those things which pertain to the struggle for sanctity and shall be concerned principally with the manner of combatting sin and voluntary imperfections.

MORTAL SIN

Unfortunately, there are countless men who live habitually in mortal sin. Absorbed almost entirely by preoccupations of this life, enmeshed in professional affairs, devoured by an insatiable thirst for pleasure and diversion, and overwhelmed with a religious ignorance which sometimes reaches incredible extremes, they never ask any questions concerning the life to come. Some, especially if they received some degree of Christian education during childhood and if they still preserve some remnant of faith, react in the face of approaching death and receive the last sacraments before appearing before God. But many others go down to the grave without any regrets save the fact that they must leave this world. These unfortunate people are what St. Teresa calls "paralyzed souls who, unless the Lord himself comes and commands them to rise, are like the man who had lain beside the pool for thirty years; they are unfortunate creatures and live in great peril."[1]

[1] *Interior Castle,* First Mansions, n. 8.

NEGATIVE ASPECT

They are actually in danger of eternal damnation. If death were to surprise them in this state they would be lost for all eternity. Habitual mortal sin has stained their souls to such an extent that there is, as St. Teresa says, "no darkness more black nor anything so obscure that this soul is not much more so."[2] St. Teresa also says that if sinners could understand what happens to a soul when it sins mortally, "it would not be possible for anyone to sin, even if he had to undertake the greatest efforts that can be imagined in order to avoid the occasions of sin."[3] Nevertheless, not all those who live habitually in the state of sin have contracted the same responsibility before God.

KINDS OF SINNERS

We can distinguish four classes of sins which serve as a basis for classifying sinners into as many categories.

Ignorance

We are not referring to a total and invincible ignorance, which would excuse entirely from sin, but to that ignorance which results from an anti-religious or completely indifferent education, or from an environment which is hostile or completely devoid of any religious influence. Those who live in such surroundings usually have some awareness of the malice of sin. They are perfectly conscious of the fact that certain actions which they commit with facility are not morally right. Perhaps from time to time they even feel a certain remorse. In any case, they are capable of committing deliberate mortal sin.

At the same time it is necessary to recognize that the responsibility of such persons before God is greatly lessened. If they have preserved a horror for that which seems unjust or sinful to them; if, in spite of external weaknesses, they have remained basically upright; if they have practiced even in a rudimentary fashion some devotion to the Blessed Virgin which they learned in childhood; if they have refrained from attacking religion and its ministers; and if especially at the hour of death they raise their heart to God, full of remorse and confident in his mercy, there is no doubt that they will be judged with special benignity at the divine tribunal. If Christ advises us that much more will be asked of him to whom much has been given (Luke 12:48), it is reasonable to think that little will be asked of him who has received little.

Souls such as these usually turn to God with comparative readiness if the opportunity presents itself. Since their careless life did not proceed from true malice, but from a profound ignorance, any situation that makes a strong impression on the soul and causes it to enter in upon itself will suffice to cause them to turn to God. The death of a member of the family, a sermon heard at a mission, the introduction to a religious environment, etc., ordinarily suffices to lead such souls to the right path. As a rule, such souls pass through their

---

[2]*Ibid.,* Second Mansions, n. 1.

[3]*Ibid.,* n. 2.

whole life lukewarm and ignorant, and the priest charged with their care should return time and again to the task of completing their formation lest they return to their former state.

Weakness

There are many persons who are sufficiently instructed in religion so that their sins cannot be attributed to the lack of a knowledge of their duties. And yet they do not sin through calculated malice. They are weak, lacking in will power, strongly inclined to sensual pleasure, intellectually dull, listless and cowardly. They lament their faults, they admire good people and would like to be one of them, but they lack the courage and energy to be so in reality. These dispositions do not excuse them from sin; on the contrary, they are more culpable than those who sin through ignorance, because they sin with a greater knowledge. But basically they are weak rather than evil. The person in charge of their spiritual welfare must be especially concerned with strengthening them in their good resolutions, leading them to the frequent reception of the sacraments, to reflection, avoidance of the occasions of sin, etc., in order to withdraw them from their sad situation and to orientate them toward the good.

Coldness, indifference

These people sin, knowing that they sin, not because they will the evil as such or as an offense against God, but because they do not wish to give up their pleasures, and it does not cause them any concern that their conduct is sinful in the sight of God. They sin coldly and with indifference, without remorse of conscience, silencing the faint voice of conscience in order to continue their life of sin without reproach.

The conversion of these persons is very difficult. Their constant infidelity to the inspirations of grace, their cold indifference to the postulates of reason and the most elementary morality, their systematic disdain for the advice which is given them by those who wish to help them—all this hardens their heart to such an extent that it would require a veritable miracle of grace for them to return to the right path. If death should overtake them in such a state, their eternal fate would be deplorable.

Perhaps the most efficacious means of leading them back to God would be to encourage them to practice certain spiritual exercises with a group of persons of the same profession or social condition as themselves. Although it may seem strange, it is not rare to find that this type of person will begin to practice some spiritual exercise in order to see what it is like, especially if it is proposed to them with a certain tenderness and affection. And it frequently happens that a great grace from God awaits them there. At times astounding conversions are effected, radical changes of life, and the beginning of a life of piety and fervor in persons who formerly lived completely forgetful of God. The priest who has the good fortune to be the instrument of such divine mercy should watch over the convert and by means of a wise and prudent direction try to assure the definitive and permanent return to God.

NEGATIVE ASPECT

Obstinacy, malice

This class of sinners is the most culpable and the most horrible. These people do not sin through ignorance, weakness or indifference, but through a refined malice and diabolical obstinacy. Their most common sin is blasphemy, which is pronounced strictly out of hatred for God. They may have begun as good Christians, but little by little they degenerated. Having yielded more and more to their evil passions, these passions gradually assumed gigantic proportions, until the moment came when their souls were definitively conquered. Then, in the arms of despair, came the inevitable consequence of defection and apostasy. The last barriers which kept them from falling over the precipice have been broken, and they are hurled, by a kind of vengeance against God and their own conscience, into every kind of crime and moral disorder. Fiercely they attack religion; they hate the good; they may enter into a non-Catholic sect and propagate its doctrines with zeal and ardor, until, finally driven to despair by the accusations of their own conscience, which speaks to them in spite of everything, they fall more and more deeply into sin. One of these unfortunate persons said on a certain occasion: "I do not believe in the existence of hell, but if there is a hell and if I go there, at least I shall have the satisfaction of never bowing down before God." Another such person, foreseeing that perhaps at the hour of death the grace of repentance would be offered to him, deliberately closed the door to any possibility of a return to God by saying to his friends and relatives: "If at the hour of death I ask for a priest to hear my confession, do not bring him, because I shall be delirious."

The conversion of one of these persons would require a miracle of grace greater than the resurrection of the dead in the natural order. It is useless to try to win these people by persuasion or advice. It will make no impression on them and may even produce contrary effects. The only method to be used with them is the strictly supernatural: prayer, fasting, tears, constant recourse to the Blessed Virgin. This requires a true miracle and only God can do it. And God will not always perform the miracle in spite of many prayers and supplications. It could almost be said that these unfortunate ones have exhausted the patience of God and are destined to be for all eternity the living testimony of inflexible and rigorous divine justice, because they have abused divine mercy.

HORROR OF SIN

Let us turn from these unfortunate souls whose conversion would require a miracle of grace and consider the great multitude of those who sin through weakness or ignorance. These are persons who have faith, practice some devotions at least superficially, and think now and then about their soul and eternity. But absorbed as they are in the affairs and preoccupations of the world, they live a life that is almost purely natural, rising and falling continuously and remaining at times in the state of mortal sin for a long period. Such are the majority of those Christians who observe the minimum obligations such as Sunday Mass, yearly confession, etc. The Christian life is only slightly developed in them, and they live a life that has no supernatural horizons. The senses predominate rather than faith and reason, and they are very much in danger of being lost.

What can be done to lead these poor souls to a Christian life which is more in harmony with the demands of baptism and their own eternal interests? Above all, it is necessary to inspire in them a great horror for mortal sin. To do this, there is nothing better, after prayer, than the consideration of the gravity of sin and its terrible consequences. St. Teresa of Avila says in this respect:

> While in a state like this, the soul will find profit in nothing; and hence, being as it is in mortal sin, none of the good works it may do will be of any avail to win it glory. . . . I know of a person to whom our Lord wished to show what a soul was like when it committed mortal sin. That person says that if people could understand this, she thinks they would find it impossible to sin at all and, rather than meet occasions of sin, would put themselves to the greatest trouble imaginable. . . . O souls redeemed by the blood of Jesus Christ! Learn to understand yourselves and take pity on yourselves. Surely, if you understand your own natures, it is impossible that you will not strive to remove the pitch which blackens the crystal. Remember, if your life were to end now, you would never enjoy that life again. O Jesus! How sad it is to see a soul deprived of it! What a state the poor rooms of the castle are in! How distracted are the senses which inhabit them! And the faculties, which are their governors and butlers and stewards—how blind they are and how ill-controlled! And yet, after all, what kind of fruit can one expect to be borne by a tree rooted in the devil?
>
> I once heard a spiritual man say that he was not so much astonished at the things done by a soul in mortal sin as at the things not done by it. May God, in his mercy, deliver us from such great evil, for there is nothing in the whole of our lives that so thoroughly deserves to be called evil as this, since it brings endless and eternal evils in its train.[4]

The evil of sin

The following is a brief schema of ideas which the director should strive to inculcate in the soul that he wishes to draw out of habitual mortal sin:

1) Mortal sin must be a most serious evil if God punishes it so terribly. Realizing that God is infinitely just and that he cannot punish anyone more than he deserves, and that he is at the same time infinitely merciful and therefore always punishes the guilty less than they deserve, we know certainly that as the result of mortal sin: a) the rebellious angels were changed into horrible demons for all eternity; b) our first parents were driven out of paradise and all humanity was subjected to every manner of sickness, desolation and death; c) God will maintain for all eternity the fire of hell as a punishment for those guilty ones who die in mortal sin (*de fide*); d) Christ, the dearly beloved Son of God, when he wished to satisfy for culpable man, had to suffer the terrible torments of the Passion and experience in himself, as the representative of sinful humanity,

---

[4] *Interior Castle*, First Mansions, Chap. 2.

NEGATIVE ASPECT

the indignation of divine justice, even to the point of exclaiming: "My God, my God, why has thou forsaken me?" (Matt. 27:46.)

2) Because of the injury against God's infinite majesty, sin possesses a malice which is in a certain sense infinite.[5]

3) Mortal sin instantly produces the following disastrous effects in the soul: a) the loss of sanctifying grace, the infused virtues and the gifts of the Holy Ghost; b) the loss of the indwelling of the Trinity in the soul; c) the loss of all merits acquired in one's past life; d) an ugly stain on the soul (*macula animae*), which leaves the soul dark and horrible; e) slavery to Satan, an increase of evil inclinations and remorse of conscience; f) the guilt of eternal punishment.

Mortal sin is, therefore, the death of the soul to the life of grace. If these ideas are well considered and if the soul humbly implores the help of God in prayer, it will gradually acquire a profound horror of mortal sin and eventually resolve to break with sin and even die rather than commit a mortal sin. But this decision of the will is not enough. The soul is still very weak and must be fortified by using the necessary means for acquiring the energy which it lacks. It must be advised to avoid all occasions of sin with the greatest care, to frequent the sacraments, to make a daily examination of conscience in order to prevent unexpected temptations, to have a tender devotion to Mary, to be always profitably occupied and thus combat sloth, the mother of all vices, and daily to ask of God the efficacious grace to avoid offending him.

VENIAL SIN

After mortal sin there is nothing that we should avoid more carefully than venial sin. Although it is much less serious than mortal sin, it is nevertheless a moral evil, and moral evil is the greatest of all evils. Before this type of evil all others of the physical order fade away as if they were nothing. Neither sickness nor death itself can be compared to the evil of sin. It is necessary therefore to have clear ideas about the nature, classes, malice and consequences of venial sin so that one can cultivate a horror of it and put into practice the means necessary to avoid it.

NATURE AND KINDS

This is one of the most difficult questions in all theology. For our purpose, however, it is sufficient to say that, as distinct from mortal sin, venial sin consists in a simple deviation and not a total aversion from the ultimate end. It is a sickness and not the death of the soul. The sinner who commits a mortal

[5]Cf. St. Thomas, *Summa,* III, q. 2, a. 2, ad 2.

sin is like the traveler who, intending to reach a certain point, turns his back on it and begins to travel in the opposite direction. But he who commits a venial sin merely departs from the straight path without abandoning his orientation toward the goal to which he is traveling.

It is possible to distinguish three classes of venial sins:

1) Those sins which *by their very nature* involve a disorder or deviation, although only a slight one, such as a small lie which does no damage to anyone.

2) Those sins which, although of themselves gravely forbidden, because of the *smallness of the matter involved,* constitute only a light disorder, as to steal a small amount of money.

3) Those sins which *lack complete deliberation or full consent of the will* in matters which would otherwise be serious sins, such as inadvertent or semi-deliberate impure thoughts.

Venial into mortal

The mere multiplication of venial sins does not of itself change the species of the sin. A thousand venial sins do not equal a single mortal sin. Nevertheless, a venial sin could become a mortal sin for any one of the following reasons:

a) Because of an erroneous conscience or a seriously doubtful conscience concerning the grave malice of a deliberate act. Thus he who erroneously believes that an action which is objectively only venially sinful is a mortal sin would commit a mortal sin if he performed that action. One would also commit a mortal sin in performing an action if he has serious doubts as to whether or not it is a mortal sin or only a venial sin, for one is obliged to solve such a doubt before performing the action.

b) By reason of an end which is gravely evil, as would occur if one performs an act which is a light sin for the purpose of causing another to commit a serious sin.

c) By reason of the proximate danger of falling into mortal sin if one commits a particular venial sin, as would be the case if one were to let himself become angry when he knows that he will very likely end by inflicting grave damage or injury on his neighbor.

d) By reason of the grave scandal which would be occasioned by the commission of a light sin, e.g., if a venial sin committed by a priest were to become the occasion of a serious sin on the part of a layman.

e) By formal contempt of a law which binds under light obligation. Contempt is called *formal* if it is directed against authority as such; it is called *material* if it is directed to some other element, such as a disdain for the thing forbidden because one thinks it is of little importance.

f) By the accumulation of material which may increase until it is grave matter.

MALICE OF VENIAL SIN

It is certain that there is a great difference between the malice of a mortal sin and that of a venial sin. The Church has condemned the following proposition of Baius: "There is no sin which is venial by its very nature, but every sin merits eternal punishment."[6] Nevertheless, venial sin does constitute a true offense against God, an effective disobedience of his law, and an act of ingratitude for his great benefits. On the one hand there is the will of God and his glory; on the other, our own desires and selfishness. In the case of venial sin, we in effect choose the latter. It is true that we should not prefer them if we knew that they would separate us radically from God (and in this we have the distinction between venial and mortal sin, because the latter consists in our turning away from God completely), but it is certain that the lack of respect toward God is of itself very great even in the case of venial sin. St. Teresa says in this regard:

> From any sin, however small, committed with full knowledge, may God deliver us, especially since we are sinning against so great a Sovereign and realize that he is watching us. That seems to me to be a sin of malice aforethought; it is as though one were to say: "Lord, although this displeases thee, I shall do it. I know that thou seest it and I know that thou wouldst not have me do it; but although I understand this, I would rather follow my own whim and desire than thy will." If we commit a sin in this way, however slight, it seems to me that our offense is not small but very, very great.[7]

Nevertheless, it is necessary to distinguish between venial sins committed out of weakness, surprise or lack of advertence and deliberation, and those which are committed coldly and with the complete awareness that one thereby displeases God. We can never completely avoid the former,[8] and God, who knows very well the clay of which we are made, readily forgives us these sins of weakness. The only thing that one can do about these faults is to try to diminish their number as far as possible and to avoid discouragement, which would be fatal for one who is striving for perfection and always presupposes a self-love which is more or less dissimulated. St. Francis de Sales says in this respect:

> Although it is reasonable to feel discouragement and to be sorry for having committed any faults, this discouragement should not be sour, angry, acrimonious or choleric; and this is the great defect of those who, seeing themselves angry, become impatient with their own impatience and become angry at their own anger. . . .
>
> Believe me, Philothea, that just as the sweet and cordial reproaches of a father make more of an impression on a son than his rage and anger, so also, if we reproach our heart when it commits some fault with sweet and peaceful reproaches, using more compassion than anger and arousing the heart to amend, we shall succeed in arousing a repentance which is much more profound and penetrating than that which could be aroused with resentment, anger and anxiety. . . . Therefore, when your heart falls, raise it sweetly, humbling

[6]Cf. Denz. 1020.

[7]*The Way of Perfection,* Chap. 41.

[8]This would require a special privilege from God, as was received by the Blessed Virgin, and was so defined by the Council of Trent. Cf. Sess. VI, Decree on Justification, can. 23; Denz. 833.

yourself greatly in the presence of God by the recognition of your misery, without being surprised at your fall; for what is so strange that sickness should be sick, that weakness should be weak, and that misery should be wretched. Nevertheless, detest with all your heart the offense which you have committed against God and, filled with courage and confidence in his mercy, begin again the practice of that virtue which you have abandoned.[9]

If one acts in this way, reacting promptly against those faults of weakness with a profound repentance full of meekness, humility and confidence in the mercy of God, they will leave scarcely any trace in the soul, and they will not constitute a serious obstacle in the path of our sanctification.

But when venial sins are committed coldly, with perfect deliberation and advertence, they constitute an insuperable obstacle to perfection. They make it impossible to proceed along the road to sanctity. Those sins sadden the Holy Ghost, as St. Paul says (Eph. 4:30), and they completely paralyze his sanctifying work in the soul. Father Lallemant says in this regard:

> One is astonished to see so many religious who, after having lived forty or fifty years in the state of grace, saying Mass every day and practicing all the holy exercises of the religious life, and, consequently, possessing all the gifts of the Holy Spirit in a very high degree—one is astonished, I say, to see that these religious give no recognition to the gifts of the Holy Ghost in their acts and in their conduct; to see that their life is completely natural; that, when they are corrected or when they are discouraged, they show their resentment; that they show so much concern for the praise, the esteem and the applause of the world; that they delight in it, and they love and seek its comfort and everything that will appeal to their self-love.
>
> There is no reason to be astonished. The venial sins which they commit continuously bind the gifts of the Holy Ghost, and it is no wonder that the effects of the gifts are not evident in them. It is true that these gifts grow together with charity habitually and in their physical being, but they do not grow actually and in the perfection which corresponds to the fervor of charity and increases merit in us, because venial sins, being opposed to the fervor of charity, impede the operation of the gifts of the Holy Ghost.
>
> If these religious would strive for purity of heart, the fervor of charity would increase in them more and more and the gifts of the Holy Ghost shine forth in their conduct; but this will never be very apparent in them, living as they do without recollection, without attention to their interior life, letting themselves be led and guided by their inclinations, and avoiding only the more grave sins while being careless about little things.[10]

THE EFFECTS OF VENIAL SIN

Venial sin has four effects in this life and certain effects in the life to come.[11] 1) It deprives us of many actual graces which God would otherwise have given us. This privation sometimes results in our falling into a temptation which we could have avoided by means of that actual grace of which we were deprived.

---

[9] *Introduction to the Devout Life,* Part III, Chap. 9.

[10] *The Spiritual Doctrine of Father Lallemant* (Westminster, Md.: Newman, 1955), Prin. 4, c. 3, a. 3.

[11] Cf. A. Tanquerey, S.S., *The Spiritual Life,* nn. 729-35.

NEGATIVE ASPECT

At other times it may result in the loss of a new advance in the spiritual life. It likewise results in a lessening of the degree of glory which we would have attained through resistance to that temptation or through the increase in grace. Only in the light of eternity—and then there is no remedy—shall we realize what we have lost as a result of deliberate venial sins.

2) It lessens the fervor of charity and one's generosity in the service of God. This fervor and generosity presuppose a sincere desire for perfection and a constant striving for it, which are totally incompatible with voluntary venial sin, because the latter implies a rejection of that lofty ideal and a deliberate halt in the struggle for greater holiness.

3) It increases the difficulties in the exercise of virtue. This is a result of the two previous effects. Deprived of many actual graces which are necessary to keep us on the path of the good and having lost a good part of its fervor and generosity in the service of God, the soul is gradually weakened and loses more and more of its spiritual energy. Virtue appears to be more difficult, the effort required for growing in holiness becomes more and more demanding, the experience of past failures for which we ourselves are responsible disheartens the soul, and while the world attracts the soul with its seductions and the devil intensifies his attacks, the soul ultimately abandons the path of perfection and perhaps gives itself without resistance to sin.

4) It predisposes for mortal sin. This is clearly testified in Scripture when it is stated that he who wastes the little he has is gradually stripped bare (Sirach 19:1). Experience confirms this proof. The soul seldom falls directly and immediately, however violent the attack of its enemies. Usually, the ultimate fall of a soul has been prepared little by little. The soul has gradually lost ground to the enemy, it has been losing its strength through voluntary imprudence in matters which it considered of little importance, it has been losing the divine inspirations, and little by little it has lowered its defenses until the moment arrives in which the enemy, in one furious assault, conquers the city.

5) The reason for the sufferings of purgatory is the punishment and purification of the soul. Every sin, in addition to the fault, carries with it the guilt of punishment which must be satisfied in this life or in the next. The punishment due to mortal sins already pardoned and that of venial sins, whether pardoned or not, not satisfied in this life is satisfied in purgatory. God cannot renounce his justice, and the soul must pay its debt completely before it can be admitted to beatific joy. And the pains which the soul will have to suffer in purgatory for those faults which on earth it considered light and of small importance surpass the greatest pains which one could suffer in this world. St. Thomas says this expressly when he teaches that there are two types of pain in purgatory: the one which consists in the delay in the reception of the beatific vision and the other which consists in the torment caused by a material fire.

And the smallest amount of either one surpasses the greatest suffering in this world.[12]

6) The increases of grace, of which the soul is deprived in this life because of venial sins, will have a repercussion in eternity. The soul in heaven will have a lesser glory than it could have attained had it been more faithful to grace in this life. For that reason, for all eternity it will be giving less glory to God than it could have. The degree of glory is in direct relation to the degree of grace attained in this life.

COMBATTING VENIAL SIN

It is above all necessary to conceive a great horror for venial sin. We shall never begin to make serious progress in our sanctification until we have done this. To this end, it will be of great help to consider often what we have said concerning its malice and consequences. We must return again and again to the battle against venial sin and never give it up even for an instant.

Actually, because of pauses and vacations in the life of fervor and of constant vigilance, one readily cultivates indolence and cowardice. It is necessary to be faithful to the examination of conscience, both general and particular; to increase one's spirit of sacrifice; to be faithful to the practice of prayer; to safeguard external and internal recollection to the extent that the duties of our state permit; and to remember the example of the saints, who would rather have died than commit a deliberate venial sin. When we have succeeded in cultivating this disposition in our soul in a permanent and habitual manner, when we are disposed with promptness and facility to practice any sacrifice necessary to avoid deliberate venial sin, we shall arrive at the second negative degree of piety, which consists in flight from venial sin. It is not an easy task. If in the first degree—the avoidance of mortal sin—such a great struggle was necessary, what can we say about the avoidance and flight from venial sin? But however difficult it may be, it is possible to approach that ideal by means of a constant struggle and humble prayer until one has reached the same status as that which was achieved by the saints.

IMPERFECTIONS

Although this matter is greatly disputed among theologians, we believe that moral imperfection is something distinct from venial sin. An act which is good in itself does not cease to be good even though it could have been better. Venial sin, on the other hand, is something intrinsically evil, however light an

[12]Cf. *Suppl.*, Quaestio de Purgatorio, a. 3.

NEGATIVE ASPECT

evil it may be. There is a great difference between the two. In theory the distinction between venial sin and imperfection seems very clear. In practice, nevertheless, the fully voluntary imperfection has harmful effects on the spiritual life and is of itself sufficient to impede the flight of the soul to sanctity. St. John of the Cross treats of this matter with great clarity when he distinguishes between venial sin and imperfection:

> But all the other voluntary desires, whether they be of mortal sin, which are the gravest, or of venial sin, which are less grave, or whether they be only of imperfections, which are the least grave of all, must be driven away every one, and the soul must be free from them all, howsoever slight they be, if it is to come to this complete union; and the reason is that the state of this divine union consists in the soul's total transformation, according to the will, in the will of God, so that there may be naught in the soul that is contrary to the will of God, but that, in all and through all, its movement may be that of the will of God alone. . . . For if this soul desired any imperfection that God wills not, there would not be made one will of God, since the soul would have a will for that which God has not.
>
> It is clear, then, that for the soul to come to unite itself perfectly with God through love and will, it must first be free from all desire of the will, howsoever slight. That is, it must not intentionally and knowingly consent with the will to imperfections, and it must have power and liberty to be able not so to consent intentionally. I say "knowingly," because, unintentionally and unknowingly, or without having the power to do otherwise, it may well fall into imperfections and venial sins, and into the natural desires whereof we have spoken; for of such sins as these which are not voluntary but surreptitious it is written that the just man shall fall seven times in the day and shall rise up again.
>
> But of the voluntary desires, which, though they be for very small things, are, as I have said, intentional venial sins, any one that is not conquered suffices to impede union. I mean, if this habit be not mortified; for sometimes certain acts of different desires have not as much power when the habits are mortified. Still, the soul will attain to the stage of not having even these, for they likewise proceed from a habit of imperfection. But some habits of voluntary imperfections, which are never completely conquered, prevent not only the attainment of divine union but also progress in perfection.
>
> These habitual imperfections are, for example, a common custom of much speaking, or some slight attachment which we never quite wish to conquer—such as that to a person, a garment, a book, a cell, a particular kind of food, tittle-tattle, fancies for tasting, knowing or hearing certain things, and such like. A single one of these imperfections, if the soul has become attached and habituated to it, is of as great harm to growth and progress in virtue as though one were to fall daily into a great number of other imperfections and casual venial sins which do not proceed from a habitual indulgence in some harmful attachment; these latter imperfections will not hinder the soul so much as will its attachment to something. For as long as it has this, there is no possibility that it will make progress in perfection, even though the imperfection be extremely slight. For it comes to the same thing whether a bird be held by a slender cord or by a stout one since, even if it be slender, the bird will be as well held as though it were stout, for so long as it breaks it not and flies not

away. It is true that the slender one is the easier to break; still, easy though it be, the bird will not fly away if it be not broken. And thus the soul that has attachment to anything, however much virtue it possesses, will not attain to the liberty of divine union.[13]

As can be seen, St. John of the Cross points out the basic reason why it is necessary to renounce absolutely all voluntary imperfections. At the same time, he emphatically distinguishes between voluntary imperfections and those which proceed from pure weakness or inadvertence. He does well to distinguish between an isolated act, though deliberately imperfect, and the deeply rooted habit of voluntary imperfection. It is the latter which impedes perfect union with God.

LACK OF PROGRESS

The magnificent doctrine of this great mystic finds confirmation in the Thomistic doctrine on the increase of habits. According to St. Thomas, charity and all the other infused habits increase only by a more intense act which flows from an actual grace itself more intense than the habit. Otherwise, a more intense act of any virtue would be impossible, because one cannot give what he does not have. It follows from this that prayer is of extreme importance in this regard, because the only way in which we can obtain actual grace is by impetration, since it does not fall under merit in the proper sense of the word. Now imperfection is by its very nature a remiss act or the voluntary negation of a more intense act. Consequently, it is impossible to proceed in perfection if one does not renounce habitual voluntary imperfections.

This is the reason why in practice so many potential saints are frustrated and why there are so few true saints. There are many souls who live habitually in the grace of God, who never commit mortal sins and even exert every effort to avoid venial sins. Nevertheless, they are paralyzed in the spiritual life, and they remain for many years in the same imperfections or even grow in imperfections. How can we explain this phenomenon? The answer is that they have not endeavored to root out their voluntary imperfections; they have not tried to break that slender cord which keeps them tied to the earth and prevents them from rising in flight to the heights. With what accents of pity and sadness St. John of the Cross laments this situation:

> It is sad to see certain souls in this plight; like rich vessels, they are laden with wealth and good works and spiritual exercises, and with the virtues and the favors that God grants them; and yet, because they have not the resolution to break with some whim or attachment or affection (which all come to the same thing), they never make progress or reach the port of perfection, though they would need to do no more than make one good flight and thus to snap that cord of desire right off, or to rid themselves of that sucking-fish of desire which clings to them.
>
> It is greatly to be lamented that, when God has granted them strength to break other and stouter cords—namely, affections for sins and vanities—they

[13]*The Ascent of Mount Carmel,* Bk. I, Chap. 11.

should fail to attain to such blessing because they have not shaken off some childish thing which God had bidden them conquer for love of him, and which is nothing more than a thread or a hair. And, what is worse, not only do they make no progress, but because of this attachment they fall back, lose that which they have gained, and retrace that part of the road along which they have traveled at the cost of so much time and labor;[14] for it is well known that, on this road, not to go forward is to turn back, and not to be gaining is to be losing. This our Lord desired to teach us when he said: "He that is not with me is against me; and he that gathereth not with me scattereth." He that takes not the trouble to repair the vessel, however slight be the crack in it, is likely to spill all the liquid that is within it. The Preacher taught us this clearly when he said: "He that contemneth small things shall fall by little and little." For, as he himself says, a great fire cometh from a single spark. And thus one imperfection is sufficient to lead to another; and these lead to yet more; wherefore you will hardly ever see a soul that is negligent in conquering one desire, and that has not many more arising from the same weakness and imperfection that this desire causes. In this way they are continually falling; we have seen many persons to whom God has been granting the favor of leading them a long way, into a state of great detachment and liberty, yet who, merely through beginning to indulge some slight attachment, under the pretext of doing good, or in the guise of conversation and friendship, often lose their spirituality and desire for God and holy solitude, fall from the joy and wholehearted devotion which they had in their spiritual exercises, and cease not until they have lost everything; and this because they broke not with that beginning of sensual desire and pleasure and kept not themselves in solitude for God.[15]

---

[14]These words need explanation. The merits which one gains before God are never diminished, no matter how many venial sins are committed. As long as there is no mortal sin to destroy completely the life of grace, the merits acquired remain integral before God, as does the habitual state or degree of the infused habits. St. Thomas expressly teaches this in regard to charity (*Summa,* II-II, q. 24, a. 10). The reason is that the conservation of a thing depends upon its cause. Now the cause of the acquired virtues is human acts; whence, if those human acts cease, the acquired virtues diminish and can ultimately disappear entirely. But this does not happen in regard to charity, because charity, as an infused virtue, has not been caused by human acts but by God alone. Whence it follows that even when the acts cease, charity is not diminished or corrupted. St. Thomas then explains how venial sin does not diminish the habit of charity nor, consequently, that of the other infused virtues, either effectively or as regards merit. Consequently, with even greater reason one would have to say that simple imperfections do not diminish the infused virtues.

Nevertheless, when rightly understood, the statement of St. John of the Cross is true. As he himself says later on in this same passage, a voluntary imperfection hardly ever occurs alone, but carries with it many others which weaken the forces of the soul (although the infused habits and acquired merits remain integral) and dispose it more and more to fall into venial sins and then into mortal sin, which completely destroys the supernatural life. St. Thomas also admits at the end of the article to which we have referred that venial sin (and we may also add voluntary imperfections) indirectly diminish charity by predisposing for its complete destruction through mortal sin.

[15]*Ibid,* nn. 4-5.

Perfect union

It is therefore absolutely necessary to wage an unceasing battle against our voluntary imperfections if we wish to arrive at perfect union with God. The soul must use all its efforts and all its energies to make them disappear. It must tend always toward the more perfect and try to do all things with the greatest possible intensity. Naturally, this greater intensity should not be considered as a physical or organic intensity, as if it were necessary to keep one's nervous system in a state of constant tension or to make an act of love of God accompanied by organic or psychic intensity. We are referring here simply to the perfection of one's motives which lead one to act: doing all things with the greatest possible purity of intention, with the greatest possible desire of glorifying God, with the ardent desire that God's action invade or dominate us completely, that the Holy Spirit take complete control of our soul and do with us as he wishes in time and in eternity, without taking any account of our own tastes or desires. It consists simply in an ever more perfect and docile abandonment to the will of God until we are led by him without the least resistance. And this will not occur before the total death of our human egoism and our full transformation in Christ, which will enable us to say with St. Paul: "It is now no longer I that live, but Christ lives in me" (Gal. 2:20).

It is evident that this profound transformation of our being and this complete death of our ego is an enterprise that surpasses human power, even assisted by ordinary grace. As long as man takes the initiative in his Christian life through the simple practice of the acquired virtues in a human mode, it is impossible to attain that profound purification of our innermost being. It is necessary that the Holy Ghost himself effect this transformation in its double aspect of the negative and the positive. St. John of the Cross expressly states this, and the obvious conclusion which follows is that sanctity is impossible outside the mystical life.[16]

---

[16]The following words of St. John of the Cross are proof of the necessity of mysticism for Christian perfection: "Let it suffice here to have described these imperfections, among the many to be found in the lives of those that are in this first state of beginners, so that it may be seen how greatly they need God to set them in the state of proficients. This he does by bringing them into the dark night whereof we now speak; wherein he weans them from the breasts of these sweetnesses and pleasures, gives them pure aridities and inward darkness, takes from them all these irrelevances and puerilities, and by very different means causes them to win the virtues. For, however assiduously the beginner practices the mortification in himself of all these actions and passions of his, he can never completely succeed—very far from it—until God shall work it in him passively by means of the purgation of the said night" (*The Dark Night*, Bk. I, Chap. 7).

3: THE STRUGGLE AGAINST THE DEVIL

The second enemy against whom we must struggle is the devil. Because of its great importance, we shall study this question in great detail, but presupposing the teaching of dogmatic theology concerning the existence of the devils, their nature and the reason for their enmity against us. We shall concentrate especially on the diabolical attacks upon souls, which can be divided into three basic types: temptation, obsession and possession.

TEMPTATION

According to St. Thomas, the proper office of the devil is to tempt.[1] Nevertheless, he immediately adds that not all temptations that a man suffers proceed from the devil. Some of them are the result of man's own concupiscence, as St. James says: "But everyone is tempted by being drawn away and enticed by his own passion" (Jas. 1:14). It is true, however, that many temptations do proceed from the devil as a result of his hatred of men and his pride against God. Divine revelation expressly states: "Put on the armor of God, that you may be able to stand against the wiles of the devil. For our wrestling is not against flesh and blood, but against the Principalities and the Powers, against the world-rulers of this darkness, against the spiritual forces of wickedness on high" (Eph. 6:11-12), and St. Peter compares the devil to a roaring lion who goes about, seeking someone to devour.[2]

There is no fixed rule or clear sign whereby one can distinguish whether a temptation proceeds from the devil or from some other cause. However, if the temptation is sudden, violent and tenacious; if there has been no proximate or remote cause which could have produced it; if it causes a profound disturbance in the soul or suggests the desire for marvelous and spectacular things,

[1]Cf. *Summa,* I, q. 114, a. 2.

[2]Cf. I Pet. 5:8.

incites one to lose confidence in superiors or not to reveal anything concerning it to one's spiritual director—in such circumstances one can surmise that this intervention was caused in some way by the devil.

God, as St. James teaches, never tempts anyone by inciting him to evil.[3] When Scripture speaks of the temptations from God, it uses the word in a wide sense to designate a simple experiment or test of a person, not in respect to God's knowledge (which is ignorant of nothing), but with respect to the knowledge and benefit of man himself. God permits us to be incited to evil by our spiritual enemies in order to give us an occasion for greater merit; he will never permit us to be tempted above our strength. "God is faithful," says St. Paul, "and will not permit you to be tempted beyond your strength, but with the temptation will also give you a way out that you may be able to bear it" (I Cor. 10:13). There are countless advantages to a temptation which has been conquered with the help and grace of God. Victory over temptation humiliates Satan, makes the glory of God shine forth, purifies our soul, fills us with humility, repentance and confidence in the divine assistance. It obliges us to be always vigilant and alert, to mistrust ourselves, to expect all things from God, to mortify our personal tastes. It arouses us to prayer, helps us grow in experience, and makes us circumspect and cautious in the struggle against our enemy. With good reason does St. James say: "Blessed is the man who endures temptation; for when he has been tried, he will receive the crown of life which God has promised to those who love him" (Jas. 1:12). But to obtain all these advantages, it is necessary to exercise oneself in the struggle in order to obtain victory with the help of God. To this end, it will be of great help to us to know the strategy of the devil and how to react against it.

STRATEGY OF THE TEMPTER

Perhaps in no other page of Scripture is the strategy of the devil as a tempter depicted so clearly as in the moving description of the temptation of Eve, which resulted in the ruin of all humanity. Let us examine the biblical account and draw from it some important conclusions.

Approach

The tempter is not always at our side. Some of the Fathers and theologians taught that, in addition to the guardian angel who is assigned by God to each person, there is also a devil assigned by Satan to tempt us to evil. But this supposition cannot be substantiated by any clear and indisputable text in Sacred Scripture. It seems more probable that the presence of the devil is not permanent and continual, but that he approaches only in times of temptation. This seems to be implied in certain biblical narratives, especially that concerning the temptations of Christ, because after the temptations Scripture expressly states: "And when the devil had tried every temptation, he departed from

[3] Cf. Jas. 1:13.

NEGATIVE ASPECT

him for a while" (Luke 4:13). But although the devil sometimes departs from us, it is certain that many other times he tempts us. And although on certain occasions the attack occurs suddenly and without warning, at other times the devil insinuates himself surreptitiously, not proposing the object of his temptation at once, but leading up to it by a conversation with the soul.

Thus he said to the woman: "Did God say, 'You shall not eat of any tree of the garden'?" (Gen. 3:1). As yet he is not tempting the woman, but the conversation is already in the area of the matter which he has in mind. His tactics are the same today as always. To persons particularly inclined to sensuality or to doubts against the faith, he will ask in general terms and without as yet inciting them to evil, concerning the problem of religion or of purity: "Is it true that God demands the blind consent of your intellect or the complete repression of all your natural appetites?"

Response

If the soul recognizes that the simple posing of the question represents a danger, it will refuse to converse with the tempter but will turn its thoughts and imagination to other matters. Then the temptation is thwarted in its very earliest moment, and an easy victory is won. The tempter withdraws in disgrace. But if the soul imprudently enters into conversation with the tempter, it is exposed to the great danger of succumbing.

This was Eve's mistake: "The woman answered the serpent, 'Of the fruit of all the trees in the garden we may eat; but "Of the fruit of the tree in the middle of the garden," God said, "you shall not eat, neither shall you touch it, lest you die"'" (Gen. 3:2-3).

The soul recognizes that God strictly forbids it to perform that action, to toy with that doubt, to arouse that desire, or to nourish that thought. The soul does not wish to disobey God, but it is wasting time in recalling that it ought not to do that. How much more simple it would be if it never had to recall its moral obligations at all but could destroy the temptation at the very start, without being bothered with weighing the reasons why it ought to do so.

Invitation

The soul has yielded ground to the enemy, and now the enemy gathers his forces to make a direct attack. "But the serpent said to the woman, 'No, you shall not die; for God knows that when you eat of it, your eyes will be opened and you will be like God, knowing good and evil'" (Gen. 3:4-5).

The devil presents an enchanting possibility. Behind the sin is hidden an ineffable happiness. He would not suggest to our soul that it will be as God, but he tells us that the soul will be happy if once more it abandons itself to sin. "In any case," the tempter adds, "God is infinitely merciful and will readily forgive you. Enjoy the forbidden fruit once again. No evil will come to you. Do you not remember your past experiences, how great was your enjoyment then and how easy it was to depart from sin by immediate repentance?"

If the soul listens to these diabolical insinuations, it is lost. There is still time to withdraw, because the will has not yet given its consent, but if the soul does not terminate this conversation, it is in the proximate danger of falling. Its forces are gradually being weakened, the graces of God are becoming less intense, and sin presents itself as more and more desirable and fascinating.

Vacillation

"Now the woman saw that the tree was good for food, pleasing to the eyes, and desirable for the knowledge it would give" (Gen. 3:6). The soul begins to vacillate and to be deeply disturbed. The soul does not wish to offend God, but the temptation is so alluring that a violent battle ensues and sometimes is prolonged for a long period of time. If the soul, in its supreme effort and under the influence of an actual grace (of which it is unworthy because of its imprudence), decides to remain faithful to its duty, it will be basically victorious; but its forces are disturbed, and it has venial sin on its conscience (a sin of negligence, semi-consent or vacillation in the face of evil). But only too often a soul which vacillates to this extent will take the fatal step to mortal sin.

Consent

"She took of its fruit and ate it, and also gave some to her husband and he ate" (Gen. 3:6). The soul has succumbed to the temptation. It has committed sin, and often, either because of scandal or complicity, it has caused others to sin.

Disillusion

How different the soul finds sin to be as compared with what the devil has suggested! As soon as the sin is completed, the soul experiences a great deception which casts it into misery and the darkest emptiness. "Then the eyes of both were opened, and they realized that they were naked; so they sewed fig-leaves together and made themselves coverings" (Gen. 3:7). The poor soul is now aware of the fact that it has lost everything. It stands completely naked before God, without sanctifying grace, without the infused virtues, without the gifts of the Holy Ghost, without the indwelling of the Trinity. It has lost all the merits that it has ever acquired during its whole life. There has been an instantaneous death of the supernatural life, and all that remains is bitter deception and the sneering laughter of the tempter.

Immediately the soul hears the terrible voice of conscience which reproaches it for the sin that has been committed. "When they heard the sound of the Lord God walking in the garden in the cool of the day, the man and his wife hid themselves from the Lord God among the trees of the garden. But the Lord God called the man and said to him: 'Where are you?'" (Gen. 3:8-9). This question, which the sinner's conscience also formulates, has no answer. The only thing the sinner can do is fall to his knees and ask pardon of God for his infidelity and learn from sad experience how in the future to resist the tempter from the very first moment, that is, from the first insinuation when victory is easy and triumph is assured under the loving gaze of God.

NEGATIVE ASPECT

CONDUCT OF THE SOUL

Before temptation

Let us now investigate what the soul ought to do before, during and after temptation. The fundamental strategy for preventing temptation was suggested by our Lord when he said to the disciples in Gethsemane: "Watch and pray, that you may not enter into temptation" (Matt. 26:41). This means that both vigilance and prayer are necessary even before temptations arise.

As regards vigilance, the devil never completely abdicates in his battle to win our soul. If sometimes he seems to leave us in peace and not tempt us, it is only to return to the attack when we least expect it. During the periods of calm we must be convinced that the battle will be resumed and perhaps with greater intensity than before. Therefore, it is necessary to keep an alert vigilance lest we be taken by surprise. This vigilance is manifested in the avoidance of all the occasions of sin, in trying to anticipate unexpected assaults, in the practice of self-control—especially of the sense of sight and of the imagination—in the particular examen, in the frequent renewal of one's firm resolution never to sin again, in avoiding sloth, the mother of vice. We are in the state of war with the devil, and we cannot abandon our post unless we wish to be overtaken during a moment of weakness or carelessness.

But vigilance alone is not enough. To remain in the state of grace and thereby to be victorious against all temptations requires an efficacious grace from God, obtainable only through prayer. The most careful vigilance and the most earnest efforts would be totally inefficacious without the help of God's grace. But with his grace victory is infallible. As we have said, efficacious grace does not fall under the merit of strict justice, and for that reason it is not owed to anyone, even to the greatest saints. But God has given us his word that he will infallibly grant us this grace if we ask for it with prayer that fulfills the necessary conditions. This should make it evident how important is the prayer of petition. With good reason does St. Alphonsus say in regard to the absolute necessity of efficacious grace that it can be obtained only through prayer: "He who prays, will be saved; and he who does not pray, will be condemned." This is the reason why Christ taught us to ask God in the Our Father: "And lead us not into temptation." It is also reasonable that in this preventative prayer we should invoke the Blessed Mother, who crushed the serpent's head with her virginal heel, and our guardian angel, who has as one of his principal duties to defend us against the assaults of the devil.

During temptation

During temptation the conduct of the soul can be summarized in one important word: resist. It does not suffice merely to remain passive in the face of temptation; positive resistance is necessary. This resistance can be either direct or indirect. Direct resistance is that which faces up to the temptation itself and conquers it by doing the precise opposite from that which is suggested. For example, to begin to speak well of a person when we are tempted to criticize him, to give a generous alms when our selfishness would prompt us to refuse, to prolong our prayer when the devil suggests that we shorten it or abandon it altogether. Direct resistance can be used against any kind of temptation, except those against faith or purity, as we shall see in a moment.

Indirect resistance does not attack the temptation but withdraws from it by distracting the mind to some other object which is completely distinct. This type of resistance is especially indicated in temptations against the faith or against purity, because in these cases a direct attack would very likely increase the intensity of the temptation itself. The best practice in these cases is a rapid and energetic but calm practice of a mental exercise which will absorb our internal faculties, especially the memory and imagination, and indirectly withdraw them from the object of the temptation. The important thing is to find some hobby or pastime or activity that is interesting enough to absorb one's attention for the moment.

Sometimes the temptation does not immediately disappear, and the devil may attack again and again with great tenacity. One should not become discouraged at this. The insistence of the devil is one of the best proofs that the soul has not succumbed to the temptation. The soul should resist his attacks as often as is necessary but always with great serenity and interior peace, being careful to avoid any kind of nervousness or disturbance. Every assault repulsed is a source of new merit before God and greater strength for the soul. Far from becoming weakened, the soul gains new energies. Seeing that he has lost, the devil will finally leave the soul in peace, especially when he sees that he has not been able to disturb the interior peace of the soul, which sometimes is the only reason he caused the temptations in the first place.

It is always advisable to manifest these things to one's spiritual director, especially if it is a question of very tenacious temptations or those which have occurred repeatedly. The Lord usually recompenses this act of humility and simplicity with new and powerful helps. For that reason we should have the courage to manifest our conscience frankly and honestly, above all when we feel inclined to remain silent about these matters. One should never forget the teaching of the masters of the spiritual life: "A temptation which is declared is already half conquered."

After temptation

When the temptation is over, one of three things has happened: the soul has been victorious, it has yielded to the temptation, or it remains in a state of doubt. If the soul has conquered and is certain of it, it has done so only with the help of God's grace. It should therefore give thanks and ask for a continuation of divine help on other occasions. This could be said very briefly and simply, as in the following short prayer: "Thanks be to thee, O God; I owe all to thee; continue to aid me in all dangerous occasions and have mercy on me."

If the soul has fallen and has no doubt about it, it should not become disheartened. It should remember the infinite mercy of God and the lesson of the prodigal son, and then cast itself in all humility and repentance into the arms of the Father, asking him for forgiveness and promising with his help never to sin again. If the fall has been serious, the soul should not be content with a simple act of contrition, but should approach the sacrament of confession and use this sad experience of sin to redouble its vigilance and to intensify its fervor in order not to sin again.

Doubts

If the soul remains in doubt as to whether or not it has given consent, it should not examine its conscience minutely and with scrupulosity, for this may possibly provoke the temptation anew and even increase the danger of falling. Sometimes it is better to let a certain period of time pass until the soul becomes more tranquil, and then examine one's conscience carefully as to whether or not sin has been committed. In any event, it is well to make an act of contrition and to make known to the confessor at the proper time the temptation that has been encountered, admitting one's guilt as it appears in the sight of God.

What should be done, however, in the case of those persons who receive Communion daily? May they continue to receive Communion until the day of their weekly confession, even if they are in doubt as to whether they have consented to a temptation?

It is impossible to give a categorical answer which will apply to all souls and to all possible circumstances. The confessor will have to make a judgment by taking into account the temperament and habitual dispositions of the penitent, and then apply the moral principle which governs the particular case. For example, if the habitual attitude of a soul is to die rather than to sin, and at the same time the soul has a tendency to scrupulosity, the confessor should advise the penitent to continue daily Communion, to ignore the doubts, and to make an act of contrition for any guilt that could have been incurred. If, on the other hand, it is a question of a soul which is accustomed to fall readily into mortal sin, of a lax conscience which is in no wise scrupulous, the presumption is against the soul, and it is probable that the soul has consented to the temptation. This soul should not be permitted to continue to receive Communion without sacramental absolution. In either case, the penitent should obey with all humility the advice of the confessor or spiritual director, without any contradiction or discussion.

DIABOLICAL OBSESSION

Simple temptation is the common manner in which Satan exercises his diabolical influence in the world. No one is exempt from temptation, not even the great saints. The soul experiences the attacks of the devil in all the phases of the Christian life. The manner may vary, the strategy may change, there may be greater or less intensity, but the fact of temptation remains throughout the whole of the spiritual life. Even our Lord consented to be tempted in order to teach us how to conquer the enemy.

But sometimes the devil is not content with simple temptation. At times, with God's permission, he focuses all his infernal power on advanced souls who are scarcely impressed by ordinary temptations. He does this by means of obsession and sometimes by corporal possession of his victim. The basic difference between these two forms of diabolical influence is that obsession is a diabolical action which is extrinsic to the person who suffers it, while possession signifies that the devil has actually entered the body of the victim and governs it from within, as one would drive a machine.

OBSESSION ITSELF

Its nature

Obsession occurs whenever the devil torments a person from without and in a manner that is so intense, sensible and unequivocal that there can be no doubt about his presence and his action. In simple temptation the diabolical action is not so evident; absolutely speaking, it could be due to other causes. But in true and authentic obsession, the presence and activity of Satan is so clear and unequivocal that neither the soul nor the director can have the least doubt of it. The soul is aware of its own vital activity and government of its bodily organs (something which disappears in cases of possession), but it is at the same time clearly aware of the external activity of Satan, who tries to exert incredible violence on the soul.

> Obsession is the attack of the enemy who attempts to enter into a citadel of which he is not yet the master. Possession, on the other hand, is the enemy already within the citadel and governing it despotically. The citadel in the first instance is the soul; in the second instance it is the body. There is, therefore, a notable difference between these two forms of diabolical influence. One is exterior and the other is interior. The latter is directed to the body, which the devil moves and agitates; the former is directed to the soul and has for its purpose to lead the soul to evil. Therefore, obsession is more to be feared than possession, because the enslavement of the body is infinitely less fearful than that of the soul.[4]

Kinds of obsession

Obsession can be either internal or external. The first affects the interior faculties, especially the imagination; the second affects the external senses in various manners and degrees. Rarely does it happen that there is only an external obsession, since the intention of the devil is to disturb the peace of the soul through the senses. Nevertheless, there are cases in the lives of the saints in which the most furious external obsessions were unable to destroy the peace of their soul.

Internal obsession is distinct from ordinary temptations only by reason of its violence and duration. Although it is difficult to determine exactly where simple temptation ends and true obsession begins, nevertheless, when the dis-

[4]M. J. Ribet, *La Mystique Divine,* III, Chap 9, n. 3.

turbance of the soul is so profound and the tendency to evil is so violent that the only possible explanation lies in some external force (even when there is nothing evident externally), it is certainly a case of diabolical obsession. This internal obsession can take many different forms. Sometimes it is manifested as a fixed idea which absorbs all the intellectual energies of the soul; at other times it is by means of such vivid images and representations that the subject feels that he is dealing with the most expressive realities; again, it may refer to one's duties and obligations, toward which one feels an almost insuperable repugnance, or it may be manifested by the inclination and vehement desire for something which one is obliged to avoid. This seizure of the interior almost always has repercussions in the emotional life, because of the intimate relation between the emotions and the cognitive faculties. The soul, even in spite of itself, finds itself filled with obsessive images which arouse doubt, resentment, anger, antipathy, hatred, despair or dangerous tenderness and an inclination to sensuality. The best remedy against such assaults is prayer, accompanied by true humility, self-disdain, confidence in God, the protection of Mary, the use of the sacramentals and obedience to one's director, from whom none of these things should be hidden.

External obsession is usually more spectacular, but in reality it is less dangerous than internal obsession, although the two normally occur together. External obsession can affect any of the external senses, and there are numerous examples of this in the lives of the saints. The eye is filled with diabolical apparitions. Sometimes they are very pleasant, as when Satan transforms himself into an angel of light to deceive the soul and fill it with sentiments of vanity, self-complacence, etc. By these and similar effects the soul will recognize the presence of the enemy, in addition to the other rules which we shall give when we speak of discernment of spirits. At other times Satan may appear in horrible and frightening forms in order to terrify the servants of God and to withdraw them from the practice of virtue, as one can discover in the lives of the Curé of Ars, St. Gemma Galgani and many others. Or the devil may present himself in a voluptuous form in order to lead souls to evil, as happened with St. Hilary, St. Anthony, St. Catherine of Siena, St. Rose of Lima and St. Alphonsus Rodríguez.

Other senses besides sight are likewise affected. The ear is tormented with frightful sounds and shouts (Curé of Ars), with blasphemy and obscenities (St. Margaret of Cortona), or with voluptuous songs and music to arouse sensuality (St. Rose of Lima). The sense of smell sometimes perceives the most pleasant odors or an unbearable stench. The sense of taste is affected in various ways. Sometimes the devil arouses feelings of gluttony by producing the sensation of the most delicious food or most exquisite liquors which the individual has never actually tasted. But usually he arouses a most bitter taste in the food that is taken, or he mixes repulsive objects with the food or objects which it would be dangerous or impossible to swallow or to digest. Finally, the sense of touch, which is diffused throughout the whole body, can be subjected in countless ways to the influence of the devil. Sometimes there are terrible blows upon the body, as occurred to St. Catherine of Siena, St. Teresa, St. Francis Xavier and St. Gemma Galgani. At other times there are sensations of voluptuous embraces or caresses, as St. Alphonsus Rodríguez relates of himself, or God may permit that his servant be tested by extreme experiences of sensuality, without any guilt on the part of the one who suffers these things.[5]

Causes of obsession

Obsession may be due to any one of the following causes:

1) The permission of God, who wishes thereby to test the virtue of a soul and to increase its merits. In this sense it is equivalent to a passive trial or a mystical night of the soul, and there is scarcely any saint from Job to the Curé of Ars who has not experienced this to some degree.

2) The envy and pride of the devil, who cannot bear the sight of a soul that is trying to sanctify itself and to glorify God to the best of its ability, thereby leading a great number of other souls to salvation or perfection.

3) Although more remotely, obsession may also be due to the natural predisposition of the person obsessed, which gives the devil an occasion to attack the individual at his weakest point. This reason is of no value in regard to external obsession, which has nothing to do with the temperament or natural predispositions of the obsessed, but it is valid for internal obsession, which finds a fertile soil in a melancholy temperament or in one which is inclined to scruples, anxiety or sadness. Nevertheless, however violent the obsession, it never deprives the subject of his liberty, and with the grace of God he can always overcome it and even derive benefit from it. It is only for this reason that God permits it.

ADVICE FOR THE DIRECTOR

One needs much discretion and perspicacity to distinguish true obsession from the various kinds of nervous illness and mental unbalance which are very similar to it. It would be foolish and even heretical to deny absolutely the reality of diabolical action in the world, especially since it is expressly mentioned in the sources of revelation and has been proved countless times by the experiences of many saints. In modern times there has been a tendency to exaggerate the purely natural causes of all phenomena, and with good reason one could lament that perhaps the most alarming victory of the devil is that he has succeeded in destroying the belief in his terrible power. There can be no doubt that many apparently diabolical phenomena are due to natural causes, and it is a fundamental principle advocated by the Church that one may not attribute to the supernatural or preternatural order anything that can probably be explained by purely natural causes.

[5]Cf. M. J. Ribet, *op. cit.*, n. 6.

NEGATIVE ASPECT

Rules of procedure

The director will proceed prudently if he observes the following rules:

1. Obsession usually occurs only in souls that are far advanced in virtue. As regards ordinary souls, and they are by far the majority of pious Christians, the devil is content to persecute them with simple temptations. Therefore, the director should first investigate the type of soul with which he is dealing, and in this way he will be able to conjecture as to the diabolical or purely natural origin of the apparent obsession.

2. The director should also investigate carefully whether he is dealing with a soul that is normal, balanced, of sound judgment and an enemy of any kind of exaggeration or sentimentality; or whether, on the contrary, he is dealing with a disquieted, unbalanced, weak spirit, with a history of hysteria, tormented by scruples, or depressed by reason of an inferiority complex. This rule is of exceptional importance, and very often it is the decisive rule for making a decision. Nevertheless, the director should avoid making a hasty judgment. Diabolical obsession could also occur in a person who is hysterical or unbalanced. It will be very difficult to differentiate between the manifestations of diabolical influence and those which follow from a nervous disorder, but it is possible to do so, and the director should not yield to the temptation of over-simplifying the matter by attributing everything to one cause or the other. He should give to the patient the moral counsels and rules which pertain to his office as a director of souls and then refer the individual to a trustworthy psychiatrist who can treat the other manifestations which proceed from a mental disorder.

3. The authentic manifestations of true diabolical obsession will be sufficiently clear if they are revealed by visible signs such as the moving of an object by an invisible hand, the marks of bruises or wounds which proceed from an invisible attack, etc. These effects cannot be attributed to any purely natural cause, and when the person who suffers them gives all the signs of equanimity, self-possession, sincerity and true virtue, the director can be certain that he is dealing with a case of obsession. We have already said that the devil does not usually obsess the ordinary soul; nevertheless, God sometimes permits diabolical obsession in these souls or even in hardened sinners, as a salutary expiation for their sins or to give them a vivid idea of the horrors of hell and the necessity of abandoning sin to be freed from the slavery of the devil. But ordinarily only souls of advanced virtue suffer the obsessive attacks of the devil.

4. Once it has been proved that one is dealing with a case of diabolical obsession, the director should proceed with the greatest possible patience and tenderness. The tormented soul needs the assistance and advice of someone to whom it can give its complete confidence and one who will in turn speak to the soul in the name of God.

The director's principal concern should be to encourage the soul and to raise its spirits. He will make the soul understand that all the attacks of hell are futile as long as the soul places all its confidence in God and does not lose its interior serenity. He will speak of the foolishness and imprudence of the devil, who will do nothing by these attacks except increase the merits of the soul. He will remind the soul that God is with it and will help it conquer: "If God is for us, who is against us?" (Rom. 8:31). Also, at the side of the suffering soul is Mary, our tender Mother, as well as the guardian angel, whose power is greater than that of the devil. He will advise the soul never to lose its tranquility, to hold the devil in utter disdain, to fortify himself with the sign of the cross and the other sacramentals, especially holy water, which has great efficacy against the attacks of the devil. Above all, he will warn the soul never to do anything that the devil suggests, even if it appears good and reasonable. He will demand a detailed account of everything that happens and will never permit the soul to conceal anything, however difficult and painful it may be to reveal it. Finally, he will try to make the soul understand that God frequently uses the devil as an instrument for purifying the soul and that the best way of co-operating with the divine plan is to abandon oneself entirely to God's holy will and to remain in a state of humble submission, ready to accept anything that God may decree and to ask only the grace of never yielding to the violence of the temptations but to be faithful until death.

5. In more serious and persistent cases, the director will use the exorcisms prescribed in the *Roman Ritual* or other formulas approved by the Church. But he will always do this in private and even without advising the penitent that he is going to exorcise him, especially if he fears that this knowledge would cause a great disturbance to the soul. For a solemn exorcism it is necessary to obtain express permission from the local ordinary and to use the prescribed precautions.[6]

DIABOLICAL POSSESSION

Much more impressive than obsession but less dangerous and less frequent is diabolical possession. The fundamental difference between the two, as we have already stated, consists in the fact that the first usually comprises a series of external attacks from the devil while the second is a true taking of possession of the body of the victim by Satan.

ITS EXISTENCE

The existence of diabolical possession is an indisputable fact that pertains to the deposit of faith. Various cases of authentic diabolical possession are described in the gospels, and it is one of the most impressive characteristics of

[6]Cf. *Codex Iuris Canonici,* can. 1151-52.

NEGATIVE ASPECT

the divine mission of Christ that he had power over the devils. Christ interrogated them with authority: "'What is your name?' And he said to him, 'My name is Legion, for we are many'" (Mark 5:9). He obliged them to leave their victim: "And Jesus rebuked him saying, 'Hold thy peace, and go out of the man'" (Mark 1:25). He forbade them to acknowledge his Messianic mission: "And he charged them strictly not to make him known" (Mark 3:12). He freed a great number of those who were possessed: "And they brought to him all the sick suffering from various diseases and torments, and those possessed . . . ; and he cured them" (Matt. 4:24). He conferred on his disciples the power to cast out devils: "Cure the sick, raise the dead, cleanse the lepers, cast out devils" (Matt. 10:8). And the disciples exercised this power frequently: "Lord, even the devils are subject to us in thy name" (Luke 10:17). St. Paul also exercised this power: "Paul being very much grieved, turned and said to the spirit, 'I order thee in the name of Jesus Christ to go out of her.' And it went out that very moment" (Acts 16:18).

In the long history of the Church countless cases of diabolical possession are recorded, as well as the intervention of the saints in liberating the victims. The Church has even instituted official rituals of exorcism which appear in the *Pontifical* and the *Roman Ritual*. For that reason one could not, without great temerity and probably not without heresy, deny the fact of diabolical possession. There is no inconvenience whatever in maintaining the metaphysical possibility of diabolical possession because it does not involve any contradiction; nor is there any physical difficulty because possession does not surpass the powers of the devil; nor is there any moral obstacle because God permits it either as a punishment for sin or for some greater good.

ITS NATURE

Diabolical possession is a phenomenon in which the devil invades the body of a living person and moves his faculties and organs as if he were manipulating a body of his own. The devil is introduced and truly resides within the body of the unfortunate victim, and he operates in it and treats it as his own property. Those who suffer this despotic invasion are said to be possessed.

Possession presupposes two essential elements: the presence of the devil in the body of the victim and his violent control of that body. There is, of course, no intrinsic information of the body in the way that the human soul is the substantial form of the human body, but only an entrance or a taking possession of the body of the victim by the devil. The government of the body by the devil is despotic, not as an intrinsic principle of its acts or movements, but by a violent external dominion. It could be compared to the function of a chauffeur driving an automobile and directing the energy of the motor as he pleases.[7]

[7]Cf. St. Thomas, *In II Sent.*, dist. 8, q. 1, a. 2, ad 1.

However it may be manifested, the presence of the devil is restricted exclusively to the body. The soul remains free, and even if the exercise of conscious life is suspended, the soul itself is never invaded. Only God has the privilege of penetrating into the essence of the soul, by his creative power and by establishing his dwelling there through the special union of grace.[8] Nevertheless, the primary purpose of the violence of the devil is to disturb the soul and to draw it to sin. But the soul always remains master of itself, and if it is faithful to the grace of God, it will find an inviolable sanctuary in its free will.[9]

Period of crisis

Two periods can be distinguished in diabolical possession: the period of crisis and the period of calm. The periods of crisis are manifested by the violent onslaught of evil, and its very violence prevents it from being continual or even very prolonged. It is the moment in which the devil openly reveals himself by acts, words, convulsions, seizures of anger or impiety, obscenity or blasphemy. In the majority of cases, the victims lose consciousness of what is happening to them during this seizure, as happens in the great crises of certain mental disorders. When they regain consciousness they have no recollection of what they have said or done, or rather, of what the devil has said or done in them. Sometimes they perceive something of the diabolical spirit at the beginning of the seizure when he begins to use their faculties or organs.

In certain cases, nevertheless, the spirit of the possessed remains free and conscious during the most serious crisis, and witnesses with astonishment and horror the despotic usurpation of its body by the devil. This is what happened to the saintly Father Surin who, after he exorcised the Ursulines of Loudun, was himself possessed and remained in this diabolical slavery for twelve years. In an interesting letter written to the Jesuit, Father D'Attichy, at Rennes, on May 3, 1635, Father Surin gives a moving description of his interior state. We shall quote a section of this letter because of the importance of the testimony.

> I cannot say what happens to me during this time nor how that spirit is united to my soul without depriving me of consciousness or of liberty. He is there as another I, and it then seems that I have two souls, one of which, deprived of the use of the bodily organs and remaining as it were at a distance, watches what the other one does. The two spirits struggle on the same field of battle, which is the body. The soul is, as it were, divided; open on the one hand to diabolical impressions, and abandoned on the other hand to its own movements and to those of God. In one and the same instant I experience a great peace under the approbation of God, and I do not in any way consent to the feeling of repulsion which moves me, on the other hand, to separate myself from God, to the great surprise of those who watch me. I am at the same time filled with happiness and overwhelmed with a sorrow which is expressed in complaints and groans, according to the caprice of the devils. I feel in myself the state of condemnation and I fear it.

[8]Cf. *ibid.*, dist. 8, q. 1, a. 5, ad 3.
[9]Cf. *loc. cit.*, ad 7.

NEGATIVE ASPECT

This strange soul which appears to be mine is transfixed with despair as with so many arrows, while the other soul, filled with confidence, disdains those impressions and curses with all its liberty him who causes them. I realize that the cries that come forth from my mouth proceed equally from those two souls, and it is impossible for me to say whether it is happiness or fury that causes them. The trembling which invades me when the Eucharist approaches me seems to come from the horror which its proximity arouses in me and from a respect filled with tenderness, although I cannot say which of these two sentiments predominates. If, at the instigation of one of those two souls, I wish to make the sign of the cross over my mouth, the other soul forcefully restrains my arm and makes me take the finger between my teeth and bite it in a kind of fury. During these seizures my consolation is prayer, and I have recourse to it while my body rolls around on the floor and the ministers of the Church speak to me as to a devil and pronounce curses over me.

I cannot tell you how happy I feel at being a devil of this kind, not because of any rebellion against God, but because of the punishment which reveals to me the state to which sin has reduced me. And while I apply to myself the maledictions which are pronounced, my soul can lose itself in its own nothingness. When the other possessed persons see me in this state, they must see how they triumph and can say, "Doctor, heal thyself; now ascend to the pulpit and it will be beautiful to hear you preach after you have rolled around on the ground." My state is such that there remain very few actions in which I am free. If I wish to speak, my tongue rebels; during the Mass I find myself constrained to stop suddenly; at table I cannot bring the food to my mouth. If I go to confession, I forget my sins; and I know that the devil is within me as in his house, coming and going as it pleases him. If I wake up, there he is waiting for me; if I pray, he distracts my thoughts as he wishes. When my heart is opened to God, he fills it with fury; if I wish to keep a vigil, I sleep; and he takes glory through the mouths of other possessed persons in the fact that he is my master, which I cannot actually deny.[10]

Period of calm

In the periods of calm there is nothing to manifest the presence of the devil in the body of the possessed. One would think that the devil had gone. Nevertheless, his presence is often manifested by some strange chronic illness which exceeds the categories of pathological disorders known to medical science and resists every form of therapeutic remedy.[11] Moreover, diabolical possession is not always continuous, and the devil may leave for a time and then return later to continue his possession. Not being bound by anything other than his own desire, it is understandable that the devil can come and go as he pleases, as long as he has God's permission to take possession of the person. That which is essential possession, according to Cardinal Bérulle, is the right which the evil spirit has to reside in a body and to actuate it in some way, whether the invasion be continuous or interrupted, violent or mod-

[10]Cf. M. J. Ribet, *op. cit.*, III, Chap. 10, n. 10.

[11]Cf. H. Thurston, S.J., *The Physical Phenomena of Mysticism* (Chicago: Regnery, 1952), Chap. XIII; Alois Weisinger, O.C.S.O., *Occult Phenomena* (Westminster, Md.: Newman, 1957), pp. 243 ff.

erate, involving only the privation of some action and the natural use of a faculty or some sensible torment.

It frequently happens that many devils possess one person. The gospel expressly states that Mary Magdalen was freed by Christ of seven devils (Mark 16:9), and that they were legion who had taken possession of the man of Gerasens and later entered into a herd of two thousand swine (Mark 5:9-13). These examples from the gospel have been multiplied during the course of history.

SIGNS OF POSSESSION

Lest we expose ourselves to the derision of the incredulous, it is necessary to be extremely cautious and prudent in making any pronouncements concerning the authenticity of a diabolical possession. There are countless nervous disorders which present external symptoms that are very similar to those of possession, and there are also some poor unbalanced souls or perverse spirits that have a remarkable facility for simulating the horrors of possession, to such an extent that they could deceive even the most circumspect observer. Fortunately, the Church has given us wise rules for discerning fraud and for making judgments that are certain. The first thing to be recognized is that authentic cases of possession are very rare, and it is much better and less inconvenient in practice to make a mistake on the side of incredulity than to be too anxious to admit diabolical possession, which could cause a great deal of ridicule. The extreme agitation of the victim, the blasphemies which he utters, the horror which he manifests for holy things—none of these are of themselves sufficient proof. These symptoms give nothing more than a conjecture of the possibility of diabolical possession, but they are never infallible signs because they could proceed from malice or from some natural cause.

In the chapter which deals with exorcism, the *Roman Ritual,* after recommending prudence and discretion before making a judgment, indicates certain signs which allow for a diagnosis to ascertain the authenticity of diabolical possession: to speak in a strange and unknown language, or to understand perfectly one who speaks in an unknown language; to perceive hidden or distant things; to manifest strength which is beyond one's age and condition. There are other similar symptoms, and the more numerous they are the greater proof they offer of a true diabolical possession. We shall explain a few of these signs in detail.

As regards the *speaking or understanding of unknown languages,* one must be cautious in evaluating this symptom. Experimental psychology has recorded surprising instances of pathological persons who suddenly began to speak in a language of which they had been completely ignorant but which they had once learned and forgotten at some time in their life, or which they had heard spoken by those who knew the language. This is what happened in the case of a servant girl of a Protestant minister who was able to recite passages in

Greek and Hebrew because she had heard the minister read them. If this symptom is to be a decisive proof of diabolical possession, it is necessary that one investigate and verify the absolute lack of any contact with that language and also the presence of other indubitable signs of possession, such as the spirit of blasphemy, the instinctive and unconscious horror of holy things, etc.

The *revelation of hidden or distant objects* without any ordinary explanation to explain this faculty has also been verified in the surprising phenomena of telepathy and "cumberlandism" (muscle reading), which have a natural explanation. On the other hand, future contingents and the secrets of hearts escape angelic knowledge, although angels could possibly have a conjectural knowledge of such matters.[12] One must also take into account the possibility of a purely fortuitous divination. Consequently, in order for this symptom to give true certitude, it must be very ample and varied and accompanied by the other signs of possession. Of itself, it does not give absolute certainty. The *Roman Ritual* speaks prudently when it demands a variety of symptoms for certitude.

The *manifestation of powers* that far surpass the nature of the subject is also equivocal. There are pathological states in which one's natural strength is doubled or tripled. At the same time, there are certain facts which are evidently preternatural: to fly through the air at a great height and for some distance as if one had wings; to remain suspended in the air for a long time without visible means of support; to walk on a ceiling with the head downward like a fly; to lift with great ease heavy weights which several men would not be able to move; etc. If any one of these manifestations is present together with other clear signs of possession, one may prudently decide that he is dealing with a case of diabolical action. We may say in passing that, as regards the horror of holy objects, such as holy water or the relics of the saints, if it is to be considered an evident sign of diabolical possession, it is absolutely necessary that this horror be truly instinctive and unconscious; that is, that the patient react in this way without knowing that he is subject to this type of reaction and that he does not have this experience when confronted with an object that is not holy or sacred.

Beginnings

As to the manner in which diabolical possession begins, it admits of great variety. Sometimes it is sudden and coincides with the cause that produces it, but usually a previous manifestation is given in the form of diabolical obsession. Before entering and taking up his dwelling, the devil usually acts upon the person from without, just as the enemy will besiege a citadel before he enters it. God permits these external manifestations to give a warning of the interior invasion of which they are the prelude and to arouse a more profound horror of this diabolical influence.

---

[12]St. Thomas, *In II Sent.*, dist. 8, q. 1, a. 5, ad 5.

Ordinarily, possession occurs only in sinners and precisely as a punishment for sin. There are exceptions, however, as in the case of Father Surin and Sister Mary of Jesus Crucified (an Arabian Carmelite who died in the odor of sanctity at Bethlehem in 1878 and whose cause for beatification has been inaugurated). In these cases the diabolical possession was used by God as a means of purification.

CAUSES OF POSSESSION

Possession is always regulated by divine permission. If the evil spirits could possess human beings at their own good pleasure, the whole human race would be their victims. But God constrains the devils, and they can exert their violence only in the measure and on the occasions which God permits. It is difficult in practice to specify the precise point of departure and the final purpose of a determined case of possession; in many instances it is a secret which God reserves to himself. Nevertheless, we can point out certain principal causes which are verified in cases of diabolical possession:

1) However strange it may seem, there have been instances in which possession occurred at the request of the victim. Sulpicius Severus recounts that a holy man who possessed a marvelous power over the devils was once tempted by vainglory, as a result of which he asked God to deliver him to the power of the devil and let him experience what had been suffered by the victims that he had cured. Immediately the devil took possession of him and caused him to suffer all the violence of diabolical possession for a period of five months. At the end of this time the man was liberated, not only from the power of the devil, but from every feeling of vanity.[13]

On other occasions the petition was made with good intentions, especially by pious women under the pretext of suffering for Christ. This petition is most imprudent, of course, nor does it avail to cite the example of some of the saints, who are more to be admired than imitated, for it presupposes a special inspiration from God it would be temerarious to presume.

At other times the petition has been directed to the devil himself, in order to establish a kind of pact or agreement with him in exchange for some temporal advantage. The unfortunate ones who dare to do this voluntarily give themselves to the devil, and as a just punishment from God it will be most difficult to liberate them. Such persons place themselves in great danger of eternal damnation.

2) The most frequent cause of possession is punishment for sin. God does not usually permit so great an evil except as a punishment and as a means to inspire a great hatred of sin. The punishment of diabolical possession seems to have a special efficacy in regard to certain sins. Thyrée, who is a specialist in this matter, points out the following sins

[13]Cf. *Contra Adimantum,* c. 17 (P.L. 20:196).

NEGATIVE ASPECT

as especially deserving of punishment by diabolical possession: infidelity and apostasy, the abuse of the Blessed Sacrament, blasphemy, pride, excesses of lust, envy and avarice, persecution of the servants of God, impiety of children toward their parents, violent anger, contempt of God and holy things, curses and pacts whereby one gives oneself to the devil.[14] In general, horrible crimes predispose to this terrifying slavery in which the body of a man becomes the dwelling place of the devil. History offers examples of this type of punishment which gives sinners a foretaste of hell.

3) Although it is not very frequent, there have been cases in the lives of the saints in which diabolical possession was permitted by God for the purification of a holy soul. The most notable case is that of Father Surin. When God abandons the body of one of his servants to the cruelty of the devil, it is to sanctify the soul which loves God and wishes to serve him with all its power. This terrifying trial has a marvelous efficacy for inspiring a horror of the devil, a fear of God's judgment, humility and the spirit of prayer. God sustains these faithful servants with his grace when they find themselves subjected to such violent attacks from the devil. This possession is also useful for one's neighbor. The sight of a creature who suffers the most atrocious attacks enables one to understand, on the one hand, the hatred and fury of the devil against man and, on the other hand, the merciful protection of God, as is evident in the case of Job.

Another lesson no less important can be learned from diabolical possession. The horrible fury of the devil in his attacks upon the bodies of those possessed is a prelude to condemnation and serves to remind us how worthy of compassion are the souls enslaved by sin and thereby placed in the vestibule of hell. As St. Augustine remarks, carnal men are more fearful of present evils than of future evils, and for that reason God wounds them at the present time in order to make them understand what will be the terrible punishments in eternity. Finally, possession serves to emphasize the divinity of Christ, the power of the Church and the merits of the saints. The devils tremble at the name of Jesus, at the exorcisms of his priests, and at the invocation of the great servants of God.

REMEDIES

Whatever will weaken the power of the devil over a person can be utilized as a general and remote remedy against diabolical possession. But more proximately and specifically the *Roman Ritual* specifies certain principal remedies which we can summarize as follows:

Sacramental confession. Since the usual purpose of diabolical possession is punishment for sin, it is necessary above all to remove the cause of possession by a humble and sincere confession. It will have a special efficacy if it is a

[14]Cf. *De Daemoniacis,* Pars II, c. 30, nn. 9-23.

general confession of one's whole life, because of the humiliation and renewal of soul which it presupposes.

Holy Communion. The *Roman Ritual* recommends frequent Communion under the direction and advice of a priest. One can readily see that the presence of Christ in the Eucharist will have a special efficacy for liberating the unfortunate victims from their slavery. Holy Communion, however, should not be given to a possessed person except in moments of calm, and one must also take great care to avoid any danger of irreverence or profanation, as the *Ritual* prescribes.

Fasting and prayer. A certain type of devil cannot be cast out except through fasting and prayer (Matt. 17:20). Humble and persevering prayer, accompanied by fasting and mortification, obtains from heaven the grace of a cure. This particular remedy should never be omitted, even when all the others are used.

The sacramentals. Objects blessed by the prayers of the Church have a special power against the devil. Holy water has particular efficacy, as has been verified on countless occasions. St. Teresa was most faithful in the use of holy water because she had witnessed its extraordinary power against the attack of the devil.[15]

The cross. The *Ritual* prescribes that the exorcist should have a crucifix in his hand or before his eyes. It has been verified many times that the devil will flee merely at the sight of a crucifix. The sign of the cross has always been used by Christians as a safeguard against the devil. And the Church, who uses the sign of the cross for most of the blessings which she confers, makes special use of it in the rite of exorcism. It frequently happened in the lives of the saints that they cured possessed persons simply by tracing over them the sign of the cross.

Relics of the saints. The *Roman Ritual* also recommends the use of relics in the rite of exorcism. Contact with these holy relics is like heaping coals of fire upon the demons. The most precious and venerated of all relics, and those which inspire the greatest horror in the demons, are the particles of the true Cross, because they remind the demons of the definitive victory which Christ won over them on Calvary.

The holy names of Jesus and Mary. The name of Jesus has a sovereign power to put the devil to flight. He himself promised in the gospel: "In my name they shall cast out devils" (Mark 16:17). The apostles used the Holy Name in this respect: "'I order thee in the name of Jesus Christ to go out of her.' And it went out that very moment" (Acts 16:18). The saints were accustomed to use their power over the devil by invoking the Holy Name and making the sign of the cross.

[15]Cf. *The Life,* Chap. 31; see also the formula for the blessing of water as given in the *Ritual.*

NEGATIVE ASPECT

The name of Mary is also terrifying to the devils. The examples of its salutary efficacy are innumerable and fully justify the practice of Christian piety which sees in the invocation of the name of Mary a powerful remedy against the attacks of the devil.

EXORCISMS

In addition to the means which we have described, and which any Christian can use as remedies against the power of the devil, the Church has also instituted other official means whose use is reserved to her ministers. These are the various exorcisms which we shall briefly describe.

In virtue of the power over the devil which the Church received from Christ, she instituted the order of exorcist, which is the third of the four minor orders. At the moment of conferring this order, the bishop hands the ordinand the book of exorcisms, saying these words: *Accipite et commendate memoriae et habete potestatem imponendi manus super energumenos sive baptizatas sive catechumenos.* From that moment, the ordinand has the power of casting out devils. However, since the use of this power presupposes much knowledge, virtue and discretion, the Church does not permit that it be used publicly and solemnly except by priests expressly designated by the bishop.[16] In private, any priest may use the rite of exorcism, but in this case the exorcism is not a sacramental properly speaking but simply a private prayer, and its efficacy is therefore much less.

Another possibility is the use of adjuration, which can be used in private even by the laity under the proper conditions. It has for its purpose to cast out the devil by invoking the name of God. It should be noted, however, that this adjuration is never to be used in a tone of supplication to the devil, which would presuppose a certain benevolence or submission to him, but it should be given in a tone of authority which presupposes a disdain and contempt for the devil.[17]

The *Roman Ritual* prescribes the procedure to be followed in solemn exorcism and gives prudent advice to the exorcist. But since this material is not of interest for the general public we shall not treat of it in detail. It is sufficient to remark that it is especially necessary to verify with certainty the reality of diabolical possession and then, once verified, to obtain the express permission of the bishop for the exorcism. In addition, the exorcist should prepare himself carefully by means of sacramental confession, fasting and prayer, and then perform the rite in a church or chapel (and only in exceptional circumstances in a private home), in the company of serious and pious witnesses (but only a few), and with sufficient assistants who will be able to control the patient in moments of crisis. The interrogations should be made with authority, but

[16]Cf. *Codex Juris Canonici,* can. 1151-3.

[17]Cf. St. Thomas, *Summa,* II-II, q. 90, a. 2.

they should be few in number, as is indicated in the *Roman Ritual.* The witnesses will observe silence and remain in prayer but should never interrogate the devil. The sessions should be repeated as often as is necessary until the devil is cast out. Once this has taken place and the liberation of the patient is verified, the exorcist should petition God to command the devil never again to enter the body which he has just left. He should give thanks to God and exhort the liberated patient to bless God and carefully to avoid sin lest he fall again under the domination of the devil.[18]

[18]It should be noted that it does not always happen that the victim is liberated from the devil by means of exorcism. Exorcism does not have the infallible efficacy of the sacraments, which work *ex opere operato.* It may happen that it is not within the plan of God that a soul be granted the grace of liberation. We should not forget that the saintly Father Surin remained for twelve years under the power of the devil. Nevertheless, St. Alphonsus teaches that exorcism always produces some salutary effect, at least to the extent that it weakens the power of the devil over the possessed.

4: THE STRUGGLE AGAINST THE WORLD AND THE FLESH

As it came from the hands of God, the world and all things in it were good. So we read in Genesis that at each new production of creatures in the six phases of creation, God looked upon what he had made and saw that it was good. But with the fall of our first parents and the tragedy of original sin, not only was the human race wounded in the sinful act of Adam and Eve, but the created universe has been marked with evil and thrown into disorder. As man's lower faculties and powers rebelled against the rule of reason enlightened by faith, so also the universe and all things in it, meant originally by God to be perfectly subject to man, are now difficult to control and at times are enemies of man and obstacles to his temporal and eternal welfare.

Nevertheless, it would not be exact to brand all created things as evil. In themselves they are good but can be used by man as instruments of spiritual destruction, depending on the use man makes of them or the great power for evil which is latent in them.

THE WORLD AS MAN'S ENEMY

The world as such is no obstacle to salvation and sanctity. Many Christians who were in the world and very much a part of the world have become great saints. The world can be an occasion for goodness or for evil, and therefore the only sense in which the world becomes the enemy of the Christian is when he becomes so attached to it that it prevents him from the perfect and total love of God. Therefore, for the person who is excessively attached to created things or for the individual who is too weak to resist the allurements of creatures, the world becomes a formidable enemy of holiness.

THE SPIRIT OF THE WORLD

When we speak of the world as an enemy of the Christian and an obstacle to his sanctification, we are referring not so much to the world itself as to the worldly or mundane spirit manifested by those who live in complete neglect of God and excessive attachment to created things. Thus it may happen that entire cities or nations are infected with a mundane spirit, living only for the pleasures and satisfactions which can be drawn from creature things. It is this *milieu* or environment which presents a great obstacle to the Christian who is in earnest about making progress in holiness through detachment and the positive practice of virtue.

The worldly spirit is generally manifested in four principal ways. The first and most deceptive is that of the false maxims which are directly opposed to the precepts of Christ. The world exalts pleasure, comfort, riches, fame, violence and might. It advises its followers to enjoy life while they can, to make the most of what the world has to offer, to find security and the maximum bodily comfort, to forget about tomorrow and give not a thought to a life hereafter. So far has this perversion of true values been carried that a common thief is considered to be efficient and adept in business, an agnostic or atheist is a man who thinks for himself, a person who rejects all authority and objective morality is one who values his personal freedom, and a woman of loose morals is considered sophisticated and mature.

The second manifestation of the mundane spirit is found in the ridicule and persecution of those who strive to live honestly and decently. The sensate person not only declares himself free of all moral restrictions and lives as he pleases, but he makes a mockery of any authority or law that would guide people along the path of self-control and obedience. Not wanting to observe the law himself, he cultivates a special hatred for those who honestly strive to lead good lives.

The third manifestation of a worldly spirit is found in the pleasures and diversions of those who observe no control in regard to their lower appetites. The excesses in the use of sex, drugs, alcoholic drinks and food are accepted as being in good taste socially. The theater, magazine and other media of entertainment know no restriction except the strong arm of the law or the startled indignation of the public. The abnormal becomes normal in the lives of these persons.

The fourth mark of a mundane spirit is the scandal and bad example which confront the earnest Christian at every turn. And it is not a question merely of malicious and irreligious persons who give scandal by their evil lives, but what is even worse, scandal is sometimes given by those who, because of their Christian belief or state in life, should be examples of virtue. With good reason could St. John complain that "the whole world is seated in wickedness" (I John 5:19). And Jesus himself warned: "Woe to the man through whom scandal does come!" (Matt. 18:7).

NEGATIVE ASPECT

REMEDIES AND RECOURSES

The most efficacious remedy against the pernicious influence of the world and worldly persons is to flee, but since the majority of Christians must live in the world and still pursue Christian perfection, it is necessary that they strive to acquire the mind and spirit of Christ, who also lived in the world but was opposed to its spirit. Of the various remedies for avoiding contamination by the world, we can emphasize the following:

1) *Avoid dangerous occasions.* "He who loves danger will perish in it." The world is filled with occasions of great danger to the spiritual life and to salvation. Whether it be a question of worldly possessions, mundane pleasures or creature attachments, the Christian must at any cost keep himself from all possible temptation. The occasions that are sinful for one may not be so for another, and for that reason it is difficult to make any universal laws in this matter. Nevertheless, there are some occasions which are so poisonous that they would be harmful to any Christian. As for the rest, each one must learn by experience where his weaknesses lie and then take the necessary steps by way of self-denial and self-control. And when in doubt, the honest Christian will base his practical judgment on whether or not the occasion in question would be dangerous for the average good Christian. If so, he also should avoid it. Still another rule of thumb is simply to ask oneself: "What would Jesus do?" It is likewise helpful to remember the admonition of St. Paul, to the effect that not all things that are lawful are prudent. In other words, there are times when the Christian will find it necessary to avoid occasions which in themselves are not evil or especially dangerous.

2) *To vivify one's faith.* St. John says: "This is the victory that overcomes the world: our faith" (I John 5:4). Faith is not only an intellectual assent to certain dogmas and mysteries; when it is perfected it gives us an attitude of mind or a way of judging things in a divine manner. It enables us to see things through the eyes of God, so to speak. A strong faith will enable the Christian to see God in all things and also to walk through great dangers unharmed, because he is able to rise above those things that are temptations for others. A strong faith will also enable the Christian to withstand the taunts and ridicule of worldly persons. In many works of art the martyred saint is surrounded by persecutors who wear a cynical smile or a leer on their faces. But the saint remains steadfast and tranquil amidst all manner of attack and suffering, because the eyes of his soul, through the light of faith, can peer into eternity and be focused on the divine.

3) *Meditation on the vanity of the world.* The world passes quickly, and life passes even more quickly. There is nothing stable and permanent in the world's judgments or friendships; there is nothing completely satisfying in its delights. Those who are applauded today are criticized to-

morrow; the evil prosper, for they have their reward in this world. But the Christian, who realizes that he has not here a lasting city but is a traveller to the eternal fatherland, knows that only God is changeless and only his justice and truth will remain forever. For that reason, only he who does the will of God "abides forever" (I John 2:17).

4) *Disregard for human respect.* To be concerned about "what they will say" is one of the attitudes which is most unworthy of a Christian. Jesus said explicitly that he would deny before his heavenly Father anyone who denies him before men (Matt. 10:33). It is therefore necessary for the Christian to take a firm stand in this matter and to follow the injunction of Christ to the letter: "He who is not with me is against me" (Matt. 12:30). And St. Paul warns that he is not a disciple of Christ who would be concerned about pleasing men (Gal. 1:10). One who desires to reach sanctity must be absolutely indifferent to what the world may think or say. His only concern must be to do the will of God, cost what it may. And it is best to make this decision from the very first, so that all may know at the outset where one stands. We have been warned by Christ that the world will hate and persecute us (John 15:18-20), but if the world sees that we stand firm in our decision to follow Christ and his laws, it will ultimately leave us in peace and consider the battle lost. The best way to conquer the world is not to yield a single pace, but to take an unswerving stand in renouncing its false maxims and its vanities.[1]

THE INSATIABLE DESIRE FOR PLEASURE

The world and the devil are our principal external enemies, but we bear within ourselves an internal enemy which is a thousand times more terrible: our own flesh. The world can be conquered with relative ease by disdaining its pomps and vanity; the devil cannot withstand the supernatural power of a little holy water; but our flesh has declared war against us without ceasing, and it is most difficult to withstand its terrible attacks.

Our flesh wages war against us in two distinct manners, and thus becomes the greatest enemy of our soul: by its instinctive horror of suffering and by its insatiable desire for pleasure. The first is perhaps the greatest of all obstacles to one's own sanctification, which necessarily presupposes the perfect renunciation of self and heroic abnegation; the second can compromise our

[1]See the beautiful meditations on this matter in Louis of Granada's *Summa of the Christian Life*, II, pp. 323 ff.

NEGATIVE ASPECT

eternal salvation. It is therefore most urgent to point out the manner in which to counteract and nullify those two dangerous tendencies.

We shall begin with the latter, which is of more necessary and universal application, since it is the proper and characteristic tendency of our sensuality, while the horror of suffering is nothing more than a logical consequence and the negative aspect of this desire. Victory over the desire for pleasure is necessary for all Christians in general, not only for those who are striving for sanctification. We flee from pain because we love pleasure, and the tendency to pleasure is what is known as concupiscence.

NATURE OF SENSUALITY

Following Aristotle, St. Thomas defines concupiscence as the appetite for pleasure. It resides properly in the sensitive appetite, but the soul also shares in it because the intimate union between soul and body causes a sensible good to be likewise a good of the whole composite.[2]

Pleasure, even sensible bodily pleasure, is not evil of itself. As the author of nature, God has placed pleasure in the exercise of certain natural operations, and especially those which pertain to the conservation of the individual and of the species. He does this in order to facilitate the use of those faculties and to stimulate man to their exercise. In the beginning the lower appetites were completely under the control of reason, but as a result of original sin, concupiscence, or the appetite for pleasure, often rises against the demands of reason and impels us to sin. No one has expressed with greater clarity and emphasis than has St. Paul this combat between the flesh and the spirit, this bloody and unceasing battle which all of us have to wage against ourselves in order to subject our bodily instincts to the control of reason illumined by faith.[3]

A difficulty arises in attempting to designate the boundary which separates honest pleasure from disordered and forbidden pleasure, and how to keep oneself always within the boundaries of the former. The difficulty becomes evident if one observes that the use of lawful pleasures frequently serves as an occasion or incentive to disordered and unlawful pleasures. For that reason, Christian mortification has always advocated that one deprive himself of many lawful things and of many honest pleasures, not to put sin where there is no sin, but as a defense of good, which is endangered if one imprudently approaches the borderline of evil.

The satisfactions granted to one sense awaken the appetite of other senses. The reason for this is that sense pleasure, which is localized in the external senses, is diffused throughout the entire body, and when one or another of these senses is stimulated, the whole organism vibrates. This is particularly true

[2]*Summa,* I-II, q. 3, a. 1.

[3]Cf. Rom. 7:14-25; II Cor. 12:7-10.

of the sense of touch, which is present in every part of the body and, since original sin, tends to animal pleasure with a violence and intensity which are much greater than in the other senses.

THE PRINCIPAL STRUGGLE

In spite of the variety of bodily instincts, the principal struggle revolves around those two tendencies which are necessary for the conservation of the individual and of the species: nutrition and generation. The other sensitive inclinations are almost always placed at the service of these two, in which concupiscence seeks only pleasure without any concern for the providential and moral purpose, the conservation of the individual and the species. Hence if reason does not intervene to keep these instinctive appetites within just limits, they can easily lead to the ruin of the individual and the species.

The following passage, taken from Bossuet, points out the two excesses which are the shame of man:

> The pleasure for food is captivating; instead of eating to live, they seem, as was said by an ancient writer and later by St. Augustine, to live only to eat. Even those who know how to regulate their desires and take food out of the necessity of nature, deceived by pleasure and seduced by gifts, go beyond the just limit they allow themselves to be conquered insensibly by their appetite, and they do not believe that they have ever satisfied their needs completely until the food and drink have satiated their taste. As St. Augustine says, concupiscence never knows where the need ends. There is here a sickness which the contagion of the flesh produces in the spirit; a sickness against which one should never cease to struggle nor to seek a remedy by means of sobriety and temperance, fasting and abstinence.
>
> And who would dare to think of those other excesses which are presented in a much more pernicious manner for that other pleasure of the senses? Who would dare to speak or think of them, since one cannot speak without shame nor think of them without danger, even to abominate them and to curse them? Who would dare to speak of that deep and shameful wound of nature, of that concupiscence which subjects the soul to the body with bonds so sweet and intimate, bonds so difficult to break, and causes such terrible disorder in the human race? Cursed be the earth, cursed be the earth, a thousand times cursed be the earth from which rises continually that heavy fog and those black vapors which ascend from these dark passions and hide heaven and its light from us and draw down the lightning and rays of divine justice against the corruption of the human race.[4]

These two types of shameful pleasures are intimately related. The pleasures of the table prepare for those of the flesh; gluttony is the threshold of lust. Sacred Scripture associates them frequently, and experience confirms daily the truth of the words of Scripture.[5] The root of this mutual and pernicious influence can be found in the physiological structure of man.

---

[4]Bossuet, *Traité de la concupiscence.*

[5]Prov. 20:1; Sirach 19:2; Eph. 5:18.

NEGATIVE ASPECT

It is incredible how much harm an unmortified appetite can cause in us, not only as regards perfection, which is absolutely impossible without mortification, but even as regards our eternal salvation. Such a subjection to the very slime of the earth is diametrically opposed to Christian perfection. The sensual man not only is not united with God, but he loses the taste for divine things, as St. Paul teaches, for his life is in the pleasures of the body.[6] A slave of his bodily members, he has abandoned the heights of the spirit to bury himself in the vileness of the flesh. If he preserves the light of the intellect and the use of reason, it is only for human things, and to satisfy his appetites and senses in a manner that is more and more refined and degenerate. The world of faith is closed to him, and he sees in it nothing but contradiction and impossibilities. There are many degrees in this blindness of the spirit, as there are in carnal slavery, but in almost every instance there is a mutual and inevitable proportion.

All that we have said regarding the evil effects of sensuality in general is particularly true of the degradation caused by impurity. It subverts the senses completely and takes the eyes of the soul away from heaven and the judgment of God.[7]

As Bourdaloue says:

> To wish that a carnal man have reasonable thoughts is to wish that the flesh become spiritual; and that is why the Apostle concludes that a man possessed by his passion, however intelligent he may appear in other matters, does not know and does not understand the things of God, because they have nothing to do with those things which constitute his unhappy patrimony. And so it is that men who are slaves of sensuality, when passion impels them, close their eyes to all human and divine considerations. Especially do they lose three fundamental types of knowledge: knowledge of themselves, knowledge of their sins, and knowledge of God.[8]

REMEDIES AGAINST SENSUALITY

The struggle against one's sensuality ends only with life itself; but it is especially violent at the beginning of the spiritual life, during the purgative way, and particularly if the individual has turned to God after a life of sin. Reason itself suggests certain remedies which are useful, but the most efficacious remedies proceed from faith and are strictly supernatural. The following are the principal remedies, both natural and supernatural:

1) *To mortify oneself in things that are lawful.* The first precaution which must be taken in the struggle against one's sensuality is that of never going to the limit in regard to satisfactions that are permitted. To say that we shall stop in time and that with the use of reason we shall recognize the necessary limitation before sin begins is both foolhardy and

[6] I Cor. 2:14.
[7] Cf. Dan. 13:9.
[8] Bourdaloue, *Serm. sur l'impureté.*

dangerous. Of all those who attempt this, scarcely one succeeds in preserving self-control. With good reason does Clement of Alexandria say that those who do everything that is permitted will very readily do that which is not permitted.[9]

On the other hand, what relationship can there be between perfection and a conduct that disregards advice and heeds nothing except strict commands? It is incredible how far one can go in the mortification of one's tastes and desires without injuring, but rather augmenting, the health of the body and the benefit of the soul. If we wish to keep ourselves far from sin and walk toward perfection in giant strides, it is necessary to restrict and reject a great number of satisfactions which would delight our eyes, our ears, our taste, our touch and our sense of smell. We shall return to this subject when we speak of the purification of the external senses.

2) *To cultivate a love of suffering and the Cross.* There is nothing which serves as a better safeguard against the attacks of sensuality than to suffer with calmness and equanimity of soul the pangs of sorrow and pain, and even to impose them upon oneself voluntarily. Such has always been the practice of the saints, who sometimes reached unbelievable extremes in the practice of Christian mortification. The reward for such privations is truly remarkable even here on earth. The moment arrives in which they can no longer suffer because they find their pleasure in suffering.

3) *To combat sloth.* The seed of sensuality finds fertile ground in a soul that is unoccupied and slothful. Sloth is the mother of all vices, as we read in Scripture, but in a special way it is fertile ground for sins of the flesh. He who wishes to preserve himself from the attacks of concupiscence must endeavor to keep himself occupied at all times in some useful and beneficial exercise. And of all occupations, those of an intellectual type are particularly apt for controlling sensuality. The reason is that the application of one faculty weakens the exercise of the other faculties, in addition to the fact that intellectual operations withdraw from the sensual passions the object on which they feed. It is a fact verified by daily experience that the sins of the flesh weaken the spirit, while temperance and chastity admirably predispose one for intellectual work.

4) *To flee dangerous occasions.* This is the most important and decisive of all the purely natural remedies. Even the most energetic will is disposed to succumb when subjected imprudently to an occasion of sin. St. Augustine wrote a dramatic page concerning this matter when writing to his friend, Alipius.[10] Sincere resolutions and unswerving determination are

[9]Cf. *Paedagogus,* Bk. II, Chap. I (P.G. 8: 399).

[10]Cf. *Confessions,* Bk. VI, Chap. 8.

NEGATIVE ASPECT

of no avail; everything is lost in the face of the terrifying fascination of an occasion of sin. The senses are aroused, the imagination is excited, passion is strongly stirred, self-control is lost, and the fatal fall takes place. It is especially necessary that one exercise scrupulous vigilance over the sense of vision, according to the axiom: "What the eyes do not see, the heart does not desire." Some temperaments are easily kept under control and are directed toward the good as long as the eyes do not see anything that would arouse concupiscence, but they readily fall before a suggestive image. Persons of this type must flee as from a pestilence anything that could make an impression on the sense of sight. Otherwise, a fall is almost certain to follow.

5) *To consider the dignity of the Christian.* Because of his rational nature man is a thousand times superior to the animal. Will he, then, let himself be carried away by the shameful sensuality which he shares in common with beasts, and disdain his human dignity? And a thousand times superior to man's human dignity in the natural order is his Christian dignity, which is strictly supernatural. Through grace man is elevated in a certain manner to the level of divinity. He has received a mysterious but real participation in the very nature of God, which makes him truly God's son by a kind of intrinsic adoption, not at all like human adoption, which is purely extrinsic. In the divine adoption through grace it can be said that the very blood of God courses through the veins of the Christian. As long as he remains in this state he is an heir of heaven by proper right (Rom. 8:17); his dignity is such that it surpasses immeasurably all creation, including the nature of the angels.[11] For that reason, St. Thomas states that the supernatural good of an individual soul, proceeding as it does from sanctifying grace, is of more value than the natural good of the entire universe.[12]

Is it possible, then, that a Christian who seriously believes these things would let himself be governed by his vile passions, that he would in one act cast away his divine grandeur and reduce himself to the level of a brute animal? St. Paul finds no other argument of greater force than this one to lead the early Christians from the disorders of the flesh: "Do you not know that your bodies are members of Christ? Shall I then take the members of Christ and make them members of a harlot? . . . Or do you not know that your members are the temple of the Holy Spirit, who is in you, whom you have from God, and that you are not your own? For you have been bought at a great price. Glorify God and bear him in your body" (I Cor. 6:15-20).

---

[11]This refers to the angelic nature as such, and not as endowed with sanctifying grace.

[12]*Summa,* I-II, q. 113, a. 9, ad 2.

6) *To consider the punishment of sin.* If the nobility of these sublime motives is too exquisite to make an impression on intellects that have been dulled by sin, it will be useful to offer other lesser motives. The first of these is the consideration of the punishment which awaits gluttony and lust in purgatory or in hell. Sacred Scripture offers abundant examples. The psalmist asks God to make the fear of his judgment penetrate into his flesh so that he will remain faithful to God's commandments (Ps. 118:120). St. Paul chastised his body and reduced it to subjection lest, having preached to others, he himself should be rejected (I Cor. 9:27). Against the passionate impulse of the flesh in pursuit of pleasure, there is nothing more opportune than the remembrance of the terrible torments which await the flesh in hell or the poor soul in a prolonged purgatory.

Even if a person rise from his sin and obtain forgiveness (and this for many is very uncertain), there still remains the debt of temporal punishment which must be paid either in this life with penance, or in the next life with the terrible pain of purgatory. In either case, the suffering which will have to be endured far exceeds the pleasure which the individual enjoyed in sinning. From this point of view alone the sinner should realize that it is a very poor risk.

7) *The remembrance of the passion of Christ.* Motives which are inspired by love and gratitude are much more noble than those which originate in fear. Jesus was nailed to the cross because of our sins. The sinner crucifies Christ anew and renews the cause of his death. The most basic gratitude toward the Redeemer ought to keep a man from sin. And even if it were true that our sin had nothing to do with the pain which Jesus suffered on Calvary, the consideration of the Savior crowned with thorns ought to make us ashamed of seeking our bodily delight, as St. Bernard reminds us.[13] St. Paul insists on this argument, and makes mortification of the flesh the decisive proof of truly belonging to Christ.[14] And St. Peter reminds use that, since Christ suffered in the flesh, it is necessary to break with sin.[15]

8) *Humble and persevering prayer.* Without the grace of God it is impossible to triumph completely over our concupiscence. This grace is infallibly promised to prayer that fulfills the required conditions, as is evident from the teaching of Sacred Scripture. The author of the Book of Wisdom acknowledges that he cannot remain continent without the help

---

[13]Cf. *Fifth Sermon on the Feast of All Saints,* n. 9 (P. L. 183: 480).
[14]Cf. Gal. 5:24.
[15]Cf. I Pet. 4:1.

NEGATIVE ASPECT

of God, which he implores with humility.[16] Sirach begs to be preserved from concupiscence and lustful desires.[17] St. Paul asks three times of the Lord that he free him from the thorn of the flesh, and the Lord answers that his grace is sufficient and that in his weakness he will arrive at the culmination of strength.[18] This is equivalent to saying that he should have recourse to prayer, the ordinary source of grace.

9) *Devotion to Mary.* Mary immaculate, the Queen of angels, is also the mediatrix of all graces and the refuge of sinners. A tender devotion to our heavenly Mother and an ardent appeal to her in the hour of danger is a guarantee of victory.

10) *Reception of the sacraments.* This is the most certain and efficacious remedy against all types of sin, but especially against the attacks of concupiscence. The sacrament of penance not only erases our past sins, but it gives us strength to protect ourselves from future sins. The soul that is enslaved by the vices of the flesh should approach this fountain of purification and should regulate the frequency of confession according to the strength it needs in order not to fall again. The practice of waiting until one has fallen and then to approach confession simply to rise again is a mistaken one, because in this way the individual will never completely uproot the vicious habit. Rather, the habit will become more deeply rooted by the repetition of acts.

It is necessary to anticipate possible falls and to approach the sacrament of penance when one notes that he is weakening and is losing strength. In this way he can regain his strength and thereby avoid the fall which threatened him. If it is necessary at the beginning to go to confession two or three times a week in order to achieve this result, one should not hesitate to do so. Even the greatest diligence is little enough when it is a question of freeing oneself from this type of slavery and of beginning to breathe the pure air of the glorious liberty of the sons of God. It will also prove helpful to have a definite confessor to whom one can reveal his soul completely and from whom he can receive the necessary advice. If one must give an account of his soul to a particular confessor, that very fact will bind the wings of his imagination and will act as a brake on the impetus of the passions.

Holy Communion has a supreme efficacy against the concupiscence of the flesh. In it we receive the Lamb of God, who takes away the sins of the world. He diffuses over us the graces of fortitude and resistance against the power of the passions. His most pure flesh is placed in contact with our sinful flesh to spiritualize and divinize it. It is not in vain that the Eucharist

[16]Cf. Wis. 8:21.
[17]Sirach 23:6.
[18]Cf. II Cor. 12:7-8.

has been called the Bread of Angels. The young especially need this divine remedy to counteract the ardor of their passions. Experience in the direction of souls shows clearly that there is nothing so powerful and efficacious for keeping a young person in temperance and chastity as frequent or daily Communion.

THE HORROR OF SUFFERING

This is the second aspect of the struggle against our own flesh. The insatiable desire for pleasure is a great obstacle to our eternal salvation; the horror of suffering, while not opposed so directly to salvation, is a great impediment to sanctification. The majority of souls who halt along the way to perfection do so because they have not dominated their horror for suffering. Only he who has determined to combat this tendency with an unswerving energy will arrive at the height of sanctity. This, says St. Teresa, is an absolutely indispensable condition for reaching perfection.[19] He who does not have the spirit for this can renounce sanctity, because he will never reach it.

THE NECESSITY OF SUFFERING

St. John of the Cross gives to the love of suffering an exceptional importance in the process of one's sanctification. Above all, it is necessary to have a clear idea about the necessity of suffering, both to make amends for sin and for the sanctification of the soul. We shall examine these two aspects separately.

Reparation for sin

It is a simple matter to prove this aspect of suffering. The balance of divine justice, which has been disturbed by original sin and was re-established by the blood of Christ, whose merits are applied in baptism, was again disturbed by actual sins. Actual or personal sin places the weight of pleasure on the scale of justice, for every sin carries with it some pleasure or satisfaction, and this is what the sinner seeks when he commits sin. It is therefore necessary from the very nature of things that the equilibrium of divine justice be re-established by the weight of sorrow which is placed on the other scale.

The principal reparation was effected by Christ's sorrowful passion and death, whose infinite value is applied to us by the sacraments; but the Christian, as a member of Christ, cannot separate himself from the divine Head. Something is lacking to the passion of Christ, as St. Paul dared to say (Col. 1:24), which must be contributed by the members of Christ co-operating in their own redemption. Sacramental absolution does not free us from all the guilt of punishment which is due to our sins, except in the case of a most intense

[19]Cf. St. Teresa, *The Way of Perfection,* Chap 21.

NEGATIVE ASPECT

sorrow, which is rarely given, and therefore it is necessary to pay back either in this life or in the next unto the last farthing (Matt. 5:26).

Sanctification of the soul

Sanctification consists in the ever more intense incorporation with Christ. It is truly a "Christification," for which every Christian ought to strive under pain of not reaching sanctity. When all is said and done, the saint is a faithful reproduction of Christ; he is another Christ.

Now the way to unite ourselves with Christ and to be transformed in him was traced for us by Christ himself. "If anyone wishes to come after me, let him deny himself, and take up his cross, and follow me" (Matt. 16:24). There is no other way; it is necessary to embrace suffering, to take up one's cross, and to follow Christ to the height of Calvary; not to see there how they crucified him, but to be crucified at his side. There is no sanctification without crucifixion with Christ. As a matter of fact, all the saints bleed. And St. John of the Cross was so convinced of this that he wrote the following strong words: "If at any time, my brother, anyone should persuade you, be he a prelate or not, of a doctrine that is wider and more pleasant, do not believe him, and do not accept the doctrine even if he were to confirm it with miracles, but rather penance and more penance and detachment from all things. And never, if you wish to possess Christ, seek him without the cross."[20]

EXCELLENCE OF SUFFERING

The excellence of Christian suffering is evident from a consideration of the great benefits which it brings to the soul. The saints are perfectly aware of this, and for that reason a thirst for suffering consumes them. If well considered, sorrow and suffering ought to be more attractive to the Christian than pleasure is to the pagan. The suffering passes, but that one has suffered well will never pass; it leaves its mark for all eternity. The following are the principal benefits which follow from Christian suffering:

Expiation of sins

We have already mentioned reparation. The guilt of punishment, which remains as a sad remembrance of the soul's sin once the sin has been pardoned, has to be repaid at the cost of suffering in this life or in the next. It is an extraordinary grace of God to enable us to repay our debt in this life, where we shall suffer much less than in purgatory, and shall at the same time greatly increase our supernatural merit and our degree of glory in heaven.

Subjection of the flesh

St. Paul spoke from his own experience when he wrote to the Corinthians: "I chastise my body and bring it into subjection" (I Cor. 9:27). The flesh tends to dominate the spirit. Only by means of severity and privations can one reverse the order and make the flesh serve the role of the slave and leave the soul at liberty. It is a fact proved many times in practice that the more comforts and pleasures one gives to the body, the more demanding the body becomes. St. Teresa warned her nuns of this because she was convinced of the

[20]Letter to Father John de Santa Ana.

great importance it had in the spiritual life.[21] When one subjects the body to a schedule of suffering and severe restrictions, he succeeds in reducing its demands to the minimum.[22] To arrive at a happy state, it is well worth the suffering to impose privation and voluntary penances upon oneself.

Detachment from things

There is nothing that makes us understand more clearly that the earth is a desert than the pains of suffering. Through the crystal of our tears the atmosphere of this world appears dark and gloomy. The soul raises its eyes to heaven, it sighs for the eternal fatherland, and it learns to disdain the things of this world, which are not only incapable of filling its infinite aspirations for perfect happiness, but it surrounds them with thorns.

Purification of the soul

As gold is cleansed and purified in the furnace, so the soul is made more beautiful and glorious by the harsh lime of suffering. Every sin, however insignificant it may appear, is a disorder and by that very fact is a deformity and ugliness of the soul, since the beauty of the soul consists in the splendor of order. Consequently, whatever by its nature tends to destroy sin or to erase its marks in the soul must, by that very fact, beautify the soul. For this reason does suffering purify and beautify our soul.

Attainment of God

God never ignores the tears and sighs of a heart that is afflicted with sorrow and suffering. Omnipotent and infinitely happy in himself, he cannot be overcome except by the weakness of one who suffers. He himself declares in Sacred Scripture that he does not know how to refuse those who come to him with tearful eyes.[23] Jesus worked the stupendous miracle of raising the dead to life because he was moved by the tears of a widow who mourned the death of her only son (Luke 7:11-17), of a father at the corpse of his daughter (Matt. 9:18-26), and of two sisters who were desolate at the death of their brother (John 11:1-44). And he proclaimed those blessed who weep and mourn because they shall be comforted (Matt. 5:5).

True apostles

One of the most tremendous marvels of the economy of divine grace is the intimate solidarity between all men through the Mystical Body of Christ. God accepts the suffering offered to him by a soul in grace for the salvation of another soul or for sinners in general. Bathing this suffering in the redeeming blood of Christ, the divine Head of that member who suffers, he places it in the scale of divine justice which has been disrupted by the sin of the unfortunate soul, and if the soul does not remain obstinate in its blindness, the grace of repentance and pardon will restore the equilibrium and give peace to the soul. It is impossible to measure the redemptive power of suffering offered to divine justice with a living faith and an ardent love through the wounds of Christ. When everything else fails, there is still recourse to suffering to obtain the salvation of a sinful soul. The saintly Curé of Ars said once to a

[21]Cf. *The Way of Perfection,* Chap. 11.
[22]*Ibid.,* Chap. 11.
[23]Cf. II Par. 34:27.

NEGATIVE ASPECT

priest who lamented the coldness of his parishioners and the sterility of his zeal: "Have you preached? Have you prayed? Have you fasted? Have you taken the discipline? Have you slept on boards? Until you have done these things, you have no right to complain."[24] The efficacy of suffering is of paramount value for reviving the soul that is dead through sin.

Assimilation to Jesus and Mary

This is the supreme excellence of Christian suffering. Souls illumined by God to understand the mystery of our incorporation in Christ have always felt a veritable passion for suffering. St. Paul considers it a very special grace to be able to suffer for Christ[25] in order to be configured with him in his sufferings and in his death.[26] He declares that he lives crucified with Christ[27] and that he does not wish to glory except in the Cross of Christ in which he lives crucified to the world.[28] And considering that the majority of men do not understand this sublime mystery of suffering, but flee from it as from a pestilence, he cannot help but weep with compassion for such blindness.[29]

And at the side of Jesus, the Redeemer, stands Mary, the co-redemptrix of the human race. Souls enamored of Mary feel a particular inclination to accompany her and to imitate her in her ineffable sorrow. Before the Queen of martyrs they feel ashamed that they have ever thought of their own comfort and pleausre. They know that, if they wish to be like Mary, they must embrace the Cross and do so with a true passion.[30]

IMAGING CHRIST

We should note the special sanctifying efficacy of suffering from this last point of view. Suffering configures us with Christ in a perfect manner; and sanctity does not consist in anything else but configuration with Christ. There is not, nor can there be, any way to sanctity which ignores or gives little importance to the crucifixion of self. With good reason does St. John of the Cross counsel that one should reject any doctrine that is broad and easy, even if it be substantiated by miracles. It is simply a question of repeating what St. Paul says to the Galatians: "If we or an angel from heaven should preach a gospel to you other than that which you have received, let him be anathema" (Gal. 1:8).

This is one of the principal reasons why there are so few saints. Many souls who strive for sanctity do not wish to enter upon the way of suffering. They would like to be saints, but with a sanctity that is comfortable and easy and would exempt them from the total renunciation of self to the point of crucifixion of self. And when God tests them with some painful affliction of spirit or

---

[24]Cf. Trochu, *Life of the Curé of Ars,* Chap. 15.
[25]Cf. Phil. 1:29.
[26]Cf. Phil. 3:10.
[27]Cf. Gal. 2:19.
[28]Cf. Gal. 6:14.
[29]Cf. Gal. 6:14.
[30]Cf. St. Louis Marie Grignion de Montfort, "Letter to the Friends of the Cross."

persecutions and calumny or any other cross which, if well carried, would lead them to the heights of sanctity, they draw back in cowardice and abandon the way of perfection. There is no other reason which explains the ruin of so many souls who seem to wish to become saints. Perhaps they have even reached the point where they asked God to send them some cross, but it is later proved very clearly that what they wanted was a cross of their own choosing and, when they did not find it, they considered that they had been deceived and gave up the road to perfection.

It is therefore necessary to decide once and for all to embrace suffering as God wishes to send it to us: sickness, persecution, calumny, humiliation, disappointment, etc.; whatever he wishes and in the manner which he wishes. The attitude of soul must be one of a perpetual *fiat,* a total abandonment to God without reserve, a complete subjection to God's loving providence so that he may do with the soul as he wishes, both in time and in eternity. But it is not easy to reach these heights. Frequently, the soul has to advance gradually from one step to another until ultimately it reaches a passionate love for the Cross.

DEGREES OF LOVE AND SUFFERING

The following are the principal degrees manifested by a soul in its progress toward a thirst for suffering:

1) *Never to omit any of our duties because of the suffering they cause us.* This is the initial grade or degree, and it is absolutely necessary for all for the preservation of the state of grace. One who neglects a serious obligation without any more reason than the inconvenience or slight difficulty involved commits a mortal sin and thereby loses grace.

But even in the matter of light obligation, the omission of which would not destroy our union with God through sanctifying grace, it is necessary to perform our duties in spite of our natural repugnance for them. There are countless deluded souls who neglect some duty of their state in life and nevertheless ask permission of their confessors to practice certain penances and mortifications of their own choosing.[31] The exact fulfillment of all our duties and obligations according to our state in life is the first degree which is absolutely indispensable for the crucifixion of self.

2) *Resignation to the crosses which God permits or sends to us.* The fulfillment of our duties and obligations in spite of the difficulties or inconvenience which they cause constitutes a meritorious grade or degree in the practice of the love of the Cross, but it is still more perfect to accept the crosses which God sends to us directly or permits to befall us. All these contradictions and trials which constitute the pattern of our daily life have a great value for sanctification if we know how to accept

[31]Cf. St. Teresa, *The Way of Perfection,* Chap. 10.

them with love and resignation as coming from the hands of God. Actually, these things are utilized by divine providence as instruments of our sanctification. God frequently uses persons around us in our daily life who, in good faith, or even motivated by less noble motives, afflict us in some way and thereby offer us an opportunity of performing some act which will be of great value in our progress to perfection. St. John of the Cross speaks of this to a religious in his famous *Cautions*:

> The first caution is that you should understand that you have come to the convent only in order that others may polish and exercise you. Thus . . . it is fitting that you should think that all are in the convent to test you, as they truly are; that some have to polish you by words, others by works, others by thoughts against you; and that in all these things you must be subject to them as the statue is to the artist who sculpts it, and the painting to the painter. And if you do not observe this, you will never know how to conquer your own sensuality and sentimentality, nor will you ever know how to conduct yourself well with the religious in the convent, nor will you ever attain holy peace, nor will you ever free yourself from your many evils and defects.[32]

3) *To practice voluntary mortification.* Resignation to the crosses which God sends us is a noteworthy degree of love of the Cross, but it presupposes a certain passivity on the part of the soul which receives them. More perfect yet is the soul who takes the initiative and, in spite of the repugnance which nature feels, advances in the love of suffering by voluntarily practicing Christian mortification in its various forms. It is not possible to give a universal rule for all souls in this regard. The degree and intensity of voluntary mortification will be determined in each case by the state and condition of the soul which is being sanctified. In the measure that the soul corresponds more and more with his inspiration, the Holy Ghost will be more and more demanding, but at the same time he will increase the strength of the soul so that it can accept and carry out these inspirations. It is the duty of the spiritual director to watch over the soul and never impose sacrifices which are beyond the strength of the soul. He should especially take care lest he limit the soul's desire for immolation and oblige it to be retarded, instead of letting it fly on the wings of the eagle. If he were to do this, he would contract a great responsibility, and he would not be free from the punishment of God, as St. John of the Cross warns.[33] There is no other way to reach sanctity than that traced for us by Christ along the way to Calvary.

4) *To prefer suffering to pleasure.* There is something still more perfect than the simple practice of voluntary mortification; it is to have such a great love of suffering that one would prefer it to pleasure. However contrary this may seem to our weak nature, the saints succeeded in reach-

---

[32]Cf. St. John of the Cross, *Cautions,* "First Caution against the Flesh."
[33]Cf. *The Living Flame of Love,* Chap. 3.

ing these heights. A moment arrives in which they felt an instinctive horror for anything that would satisfy their tastes and comfort. They were not content unless they were completely submerged in suffering. When everything went badly with them and the whole world persecuted and calumniated them, they rejoiced and gave thanks to God. If others applauded or praised them, they trembled as if God had permitted those things as a punishment for their sins. They hardly took any account of themselves at all, or of the heroism which such an attitude presupposes. They were so familiar with suffering that it seemed to them the most natural thing in the world to endure pain.

It is not impossible to reach these heights. Undoubtedly, they are the result of a general sanctification of the soul which is accustomed to live in a state of habitual heroism, but personal effort, aided by divine grace, can bring one closer and closer to this sublime ideal. St. John of the Cross has given us a marvelous rule for reaching this state. His words seem severe and are a torment to sensual ears, but it is only at this price that one can attain the treasure of sanctity:

> To endeavor always to incline oneself, not to that which is easier, but to that which is more difficult; not to that which is tasty, but to that which is more bitter; not to that which is more pleasing, but to that which is less pleasing; not to that which gives rest, but to that which demands effort; not to that which is a consolation, but to that which is a source of sorrow; not to that which is more, but to that which is less; not to the lofty and precious, but to the lowly and despicable; not to that which is to be something, but to that which is to be nothing; not to be seeking the best in temporal things, but the worst, and to desire to enter in all nakedness and emptiness and poverty through Christ in whatever there is in the world.[34]

5) *To offer oneself to God as a victim of expiation.* It would seem that it is impossible to go further in love of the Cross than to prefer sorrow to pleasure. Nevertheless, there is still another more perfect and more exquisite degree in the love of suffering: the act of offering oneself as a victim of expiation for the sins of the world. At the very outset, we must say with great insistence that this sublime act is completely above the ordinary way of grace. It would be a terrible presumption for a beginner or an imperfectly purified soul to place itself in this state. "To be called a victim is easy and it pleases self-love, but truly to be a victim demands a purity, a detachment from creatures, a heroism which is abandoned to all suffering, to all humiliation, to ineffable obscurity, that I would consider it either foolish or miraculous if one who is at the beginning of the spiritual life should attempt to do that which the divine Master did not do except by degrees."[35]

[34]Cf. *The Ascent of Mount Carmel,* Bk. I, Chap. 13.
[35]Cf. Plus, *Christ in Our Neighbors,* p. 50.

NEGATIVE ASPECT

The theological basis of offering oneself as a victim of expiation for the salvation of souls or for any other supernatural motive such as reparation for the glory of God, liberating the souls in purgatory, attracting the divine mercy to the Church, the priesthood, one's country, or a particular soul, etc., is the supernatural solidarity established by God among the members of the Mystical Body of Christ, whether actual or potential. Presupposing that solidarity in Christ which is common to all Christians, God selects certain holy souls, and particularly those who have offered themselves knowingly for this work, so that by their merits and sacrifices they may contribute to the application of the merits of the redemption by Christ. A typical example of this can be found in St. Catherine of Siena, whose most ardent desire was to give her life for the Church. "The only cause of my death," said the saint, "is my zeal for the Church of God, which devours and consumes me. Accept, O Lord, the sacrifice of my life for the Mystical Body of thy holy Church." She was also a victim soul for particular individuals, as is evident from the salvation of her own father, the promise that none of her family would be lost, etc. Other examples of victim souls are St. Thérèse of Lisieux, St. Gemma Galgani and Sister Elizabeth of the Trinity.

The souls offered as victims are for Christ like a new humanity which is added to him, as Sister Elizabeth of the Trinity referred to it. In these souls he can renew the whole mystery of redemption. The Lord is wont to accept this heroic offering, and he leads these victims to a terrifying martyrdom of body and soul. Only with the help of extraordinary graces can they support for any length of time the incredible sufferings and pains; they always terminate on the height of Calvary, totally transformed into Christ crucified. All of them at the height of martyrdom repeat the words which St. Thérèse pronounced on her bed of pain several hours before her death: "No, no, I do not repent of having abandoned myself to love."[36] Such souls have a perfect knowledge of the redemptive efficacy of their martyrdom. A multitude of souls which, without this heroic offering, would have been lost for all eternity will obtain pardon from God and eternal life. The ability to contribute in this way to the application of the redemptive merits of Christ is a source of ineffable joy to these victim souls. In heaven they will form one of the most beautiful crowns of glory.

In practice, the offering of oneself as a victim for souls should never be permitted except to souls of whom the Holy Ghost asks it with a persistent and irresistible motion of grace. It would be a ridiculous presumption for a beginner or for a soul that is not yet purified. It should be noted

[36] *History of a Soul,* Chap. 12.

that, rather than contributing to the sanctification of the individual (although it does add something), this particular act is ordained, rather, to the good of others. It means that the soul which would give itself in such a way for the salvation of its brethren in Christ must itself be very intimately united to him and must have traveled a great distance toward its own sanctification. It must be a soul that is well schooled in suffering and has a veritable thirst for suffering. Under these conditions the director could permit a soul to make this act of offering itself as a victim and thus, if God accepts it, be converted in its life into a faithful reproduction of the divine martyr of Calvary.

5: ACTIVE PURIFICATIONS

In order to arrive at the intimate union with God in which sanctity consists, it is not sufficient to win a victory against sin and its principal allies, the world, the flesh and the devil; it is likewise necessary to achieve an intense and profound purification of all the faculties and powers of soul and body. It is not required, nor is it even possible, that such a purification be entirely previous to the intimate union with God. In the long road which the soul must travel to achieve sanctity, the purifying process is inseparably united with its progressive illumination and the intensity of its union with God. There is an intimate relation between them; in the measure that the soul is more and more purified, its light and love likewise increase.

NECESSITY OF PURIFICATION

The explanation is simple. When a soul desirous of sanctifying itself begins the process of its spiritual life, it is already in possession of sanctifying grace, without which it could not even begin on the road to perfection. Together with grace, the soul has been enriched with the incomparable treasure of the infused virtues and the gifts of the Holy Ghost. The Trinity dwells in the soul as in a living temple, and the grace of adoption makes the soul an heir of heaven for all eternity.

But together with these grandeurs and marvels, the soul is filled with imperfection and defects. Since grace does not of itself exclude anything more than mortal sin, it leaves man with all the natural and acquired imperfections which he had at the moment of his justification. The soul remains subject to every kind of temptation, evil inclination, acquired evil habits, etc., and the practice of virtue becomes difficult and arduous. The infused virtues, which the soul has received with sanctifying grace, give the possibility of performing the corresponding acts, but they do not rid the soul of its acquired evil habits nor of the natural indispositions which the soul may have in regard to the practice of virtue. These acquired habits and natural dispositions are destroyed only by the repetition of acts of the contrary virtues, thus ridding the faculty of the contrary evil habit and disposing it to work in conformity with virtue. When the supernatural habit no longer finds any resistance or obstacle to its exercise by reason of a natural contrary habit, the virtuous act will be produced with facility and delight. Until that time, it cannot be produced with facility, in spite of the supernatural habit from which it flows, because it lacks the physical disposition required in the faculty.[1]

The reason for the resistance and rebellion of our nature against virtue must be sought in the dogma of original sin. Human nature, as it came from the creative hands of God, was perfect, a true masterpiece of divine wisdom, but original sin wounded it profoundly. St. Thomas explains this in the following words:

> In original justice, reason perfectly controlled the inferior powers of the soul, and reason itself was perfected by God, to whom it was subject. The original justice was destroyed by the sin of the first man. At the same time, all the powers of the soul remained destitute, in a certain manner, in their own order, in which they were naturally ordained to virtue. And this destitution is called *vulneratio naturae*. Now there are four faculties of the soul which can be subjects of virtue: reason, in which prudence resides; the will, in which justice resides; the irascible appetite, the subject of fortitude; and the concupiscible appetite, where temperance reigns. Therefore, so far as reason was deprived of its order to truth, we have the wound of ignorance (*vulnus ignorantiae*); so far as the will was deprived of its order to the good, we have malice (*vulnus malitiae*); so far as the irascible appetite was deprived of its order to the arduous and difficult, it acquired weakness (*vulnus infirmitatis*); and so far as the concupiscible appetite lost its order to delight moderated by reason, we acquired the wound of disorderly concupiscence (*vulnus concupiscentiae*). And so these four wounds are inflicted by original sin on all human nature.
>
> But as the inclination to the good of virtue diminishes in each one by actual sin, these wounds are also a consequence of the other sins; so far as by sin reason is dulled principally in the things it seeks to realize, the will is hardened toward the good, the difficulty in working well increases, and concupiscence is increased.[2]

We are not speaking, therefore, of mortal wounds or a substantial corruption of nature, as was taught by the Protestant doctrine condemned by the Church, but of a diminution of the natural inclination to good which human nature had in the state of original justice, and a considerable increase of obstacles to virtue.

From this follows the necessity of a profound purification of the soul and of the sensible faculties in which evil habits and vicious inclinations are rooted. One must be completely despoiled of all these traces of sin which impede or make difficult the perfect union with God in which sanctity consists. In this process of purification God reserves to himself the better part (passive purifications); but man, with the help of grace, must make an effort to cooperate with the divine action and achieve as much as he can (active purifications).

---

[1] Cf. St. Thomas, *Summa,* I-II, q. 65, a. 3, ad 2 and 3.
[2] *Ibid.,* q. 85, a. 3.

NEGATIVE ASPECT

We have already indicated the manner in which we shall treat these last two chapters which deal with the negative aspect of sanctification. First, we shall study the active purification of the faculties, or that which man can and ought to do, with the help of grace, in order to purify himself of his imperfections. In the next chapter we shall examine the part which God plays in this purifying process through the passive purification.

PRELIMINARY IDEAS

We shall recall, first of all, some simple notions of rational psychology which are necessary for an understanding of this question.

EXTERNAL SENSES

The organs of these faculties are located in various external parts of the body and directly perceive the material characteristics of external things. Whatever the metaphysical possibility of other corporeal senses distinct from those which we actually possess, it is certain that at the present time we admit only five external senses: sight, hearing, smell, taste and touch. By reason of their certitude, the principal external senses are sight and touch. Nothing appears so certain to us as what we have seen or touched, although illusions are possible. By reason of their necessity for physical life, the principal senses are touch and taste (therefore, they are not lacking even in the imperfect animals which lack the other senses). For the intellectual and social life, the principal senses are sight and hearing, because nothing so isolates us from society as blindness and deafness.

Sensation occurs through the immediate perception in the corresponding sense of the external qualities of those bodies which are proportioned to that sense (for example, color for the eye, odor for the sense of smell, etc.). The sensation is not received in the brain but in the corresponding end organ, such as the eyes or ears, etc. It is not something merely subjective but something real and objective, as experience demonstrates.

INTERNAL SENSES

These senses differ from the external senses by reason of the organ in which they reside and by reason of their proper objects. The internal senses are four in number, and they are distinct from one another: the common sense, the imagination, the estimative power and sensitive memory. All of these internal senses are localized in the brain, although science has not as yet agreed on the exact locality in the brain.

The *common sense* is the faculty which perceives as our own and unites into one all the phenomena which are experienced sensibly in the organs of the external senses. For example, when a bell rings, the ear hears only the sound, the sight perceives the color and shape of the bell, and the sense of touch is able to note the vibrations. The common sense unites all of these sensations which are so disparate and applies them to the one object, namely, the bell which has sounded. It is, therefore, the common root of the external senses, as St. Thomas refers to it.[3]

The *imagination* is the faculty which conserves, reproduces and composes or divides the images apprehended by the external senses. And thus it conserves the image of an object which the sensitive memory recognizes as already seen; it evokes or reproduces whenever it pleases; or it combines sensitive elements of different kinds to create an entirely new imaginary being, such as a mountain of gold. This last function is the reason why some psychologists speak of the creative faculty of the imagination, which can exercise itself either under control of the intellect or without it. The great artists usually have a strong creative imagination. When these creations are not controlled by the intellect and the will, they can produce extravagant results.

The *estimative power* is the faculty by which we apprehend sensible things as useful or harmful to ourselves. In virtue of this power the sheep knows instinctively that the wolf is its enemy. In animals, one speaks of a blind instinct which is purely natural and performs marvelous services for the conservation of the animal; in man, the estimative power is greatly influenced by the intellect, and this makes it more perfect and penetrating than it is in animals. For that reason, the human faculty is called the cogitative power or particular reason.[4]

The *sensitive memory* is the organic faculty of recognizing the past as past, or a sensation as previously received. Its functions are to conserve the record of a thing, to reproduce or evoke it by means of reminiscence when necessary, or to recognize a thing as past or already seen. It is distinguished from the imagination in this: the imagination conserves and reproduces images but it does not recognize them as past; this is proper to the sensitive memory. Moreover, the imagination can create, as we have said, and this is something that the memory is incapable of doing because it is limited simply to the recollection of the things of the past precisely as past.

PURIFICATION OF THE EXTERNAL SENSES

The active purification of the external senses has for its purpose to restrain their excesses and to subject them to the rule of reason illumined by faith. A

[3]*Ibid.*, I, q. 78, a. 4, ad 1 and 2.
[4]Cf. St. Thomas, *ibid.*, a. 4; q. 81, a. 3; q. 83, a. 1.

NEGATIVE ASPECT

disciplined human body is an excellent instrument for sanctification, but in the present state of fallen nature it is badly inclined and has an almost irresistible tendency to anything that can give pleasure to the senses. If it is not subjected, it becomes indomitable, and its demands become more and more excessive, until it constitutes an obstacle which is incompatible with the spiritual perfection of the soul. St. Paul speaks of the necessity of mortifying the body in order to be liberated from its tyranny and to assure one's own salvation: "I chastise my body and bring it in subjection, lest perhaps after preaching to others, I myself should be rejected" (I Cor. 9:27). In another place he says that "they who belong to Christ have crucified their flesh with its passions and desires" (Gal. 5:24). St. John of the Cross insists on the Pauline doctrine and gives a profound reason which is intimately connected with the divine union to which the soul travels:

> It is necessary to assume one truth, which is that the sense of the lower part of man, which is that whereof we are treating, is not and cannot be capable of knowing or comprehending God as God is. So that the eye cannot see him or anything that is like him; neither can the ear hear his voice or any sound that resembles it; neither can the sense of smell perceive a perfume so sweet as he; neither can the taste detect a savor so sublime and delectable; neither can the touch feel a movement so delicate and full of delight, nor aught like to it; neither can his form or any figure that represents him enter into the thought or imagination. Even as Isaias says: "Eye hath not seen him, nor hath ear heard him, neither hath it entered into the heart of man" (Is. 54:4).[5]

Hence in addition to the great inconvenience which follows when one does not have the corporal senses well mortified, it is evident that whatever those senses can convey to the soul is not God nor anything like him. Consequently, St. John of the Cross concludes with inflexible logic that "it would be, at the least, but vanity to set the rejoicing of the will upon pleasure caused by any of these apprehensions, and it would be hindering the power of the will from occupying itself with God and from setting its rejoicing upon him alone. This the soul cannot perfectly accomplish, except by purging itself and remaining in darkness as to rejoicing of this kind, as also with respect to other things."[6]

Nevertheless, it is necessary to understand this doctrine correctly in order not to draw erroneous conclusions. This doctrine does not mean to deprive the senses of their proper object but only to avoid placing one's joy and final repose in the sensible pleasure which these objects arouse without rising to God through them. Creatures are, in the words of St. John of the Cross, "mere crumbs or fragments which fall from the table of God."[7] And when one considers in them this vestige or trace of God, they not only cease to be an obstacle to the sanctification of the soul, but they can be converted into true means and instru-

[5]*The Ascent of Mount Carmel,* Bk. III, Chap. 24.
[6]*Loc. cit.*
[7]Cf. *ibid.,* Bk. I, Chap. 6.

ments for the divine union. The evil or the disorder lies in resting in creatures as if they were our ultimate end, prescinding from their relation to God. But when we enjoy their beauty, or the pleasure which they give, in order more easily to rise to God, we can and ought to use them as excellent aids for our own sanctification.

St. John of the Cross, who has been unjustly accused of being an implacable enemy of the senses and the faculties, explains this doctrine as follows:

> I said advisedly that, if the rejoicing of the will were to rest in any of these things, it would be vanity. But when it does not rest in them, but as soon as the will finds pleasure in that which it hears, sees and does, soars upward to rejoice in God, so that its pleasure acts as a motive and strengthens it to that end, this is very good. In such a case not only need the said motions not be shunned when they cause this devotion and prayer, but the soul may profit by them and indeed should so profit to the end that it may accomplish this holy exercise. For there are souls who are greatly moved by objects of sense to seek God.[8]

It is evident that the senses as such are not fixed, and do not rest in anything but sensible pleasure, without any further consideration for the higher things which escape the senses completely. Therefore, the soul must be vigilant and alert in order to rectify the intention and raise to God the pleasure which is experienced by the senses. St. John of the Cross tells us when these sensible pleasures are proper or not:

> But much circumspection must be observed here, and the resulting effects must be considered, for frequently many spiritual persons indulge the recreations of sense aforementioned under the pretext of offering prayer and devotion to God; and they do this in a way which must be described as recreation rather than prayer, and which gives more pleasure to themselves than to God. And although the intention that they have is toward God, the effect which they produce is that of recreation of sense, wherein they find weakness and imperfection rather than revival of the will and surrender thereof to God.
>
> I wish, therefore, to propose a test whereby it may be seen when these delights of the senses aforementioned are profitable and when they are not. And it is that whenever a person hears music and other things, and sees pleasant things, and is conscious of sweet perfumes, or tastes things that are delicious, or feels soft touches, if his thought and the affection of his will are at once centered upon God and if that thought of God gives him more pleasure than the movement of sense which causes it, and save for that he finds no pleasure in the said movement, this is a sign that he is receiving benefit therefrom and that this thing of sense is a help to his spirit. In this way such things may be used, for then such things of sense subserve the end for which God created and gave them, which is that he should be the better loved and known because of them. . . .
>
> But one that does not feel this liberty of spirit in these things and pleasures of sense, but whose will rests in these pleasures and feeds upon them, is greatly harmed by them and should withdraw himself from the use of them.

[8] *Ibid.,* Bk. III, Chap. 24.

NEGATIVE ASPECT

> For although his reason may desire to employ them in journeying to God, yet, inasmuch as his desire finds pleasure in them which is according to sense and their effect is ever dependent upon the pleasure which they give, he is certain to find hindrance in them rather than help, and harm rather than profit. And when he sees that the desire for such recreation reigns in him, he must mortify it; because the stronger it becomes, the more imperfection he will have and the greater will be his weakness.[9]

This magnificent doctrine needs no explanation or commentary. St. John is not attempting to annihilate the senses but to raise them to God through creatures. What must be avoided at any cost, under pain of compromising and making sanctification of the soul impossible, is final rest and complacency in creatures, seeking in them only the pleasure they can give to us. One must pass beyond them, while using them to rise to God, the supreme beauty and the greatest good, from whom creatures have received whatever goodness and beauty they possess.

Let us now consider the bodily senses one by one, in order to find out what needs to be rectified in them, and how they can be elevated and directed to God.

THE SENSE OF SIGHT

This is the most noble of all the external senses, but it is also the most dangerous because of the great seductive power it exercises upon the soul by means of its impressions. Let us examine the different classes of glances and the practical conduct which the soul should follow in each case.

1) *Glances that are seriously sinful.* Every voluntary glance toward a person or object which is a serious occasion of sin, especially if it is accompanied by an evil desire, is a grave sin. The gospel expressly states: "But I say to you that anyone who so much as looks with lust at a woman has already committed adultery with her in his heart" (Matt. 5:28). It is not necessary to mention that one must avoid this type of glance entirely. Without this first step, not only perfection but even eternal salvation is placed in great danger.

2) *Dangerous glances.* When, without an evil desire but also without sufficient reason, one fixes his glance on a person or any object which could lead him to sin, he commits an extremely dangerous imprudence. As a punishment for this imprudence the soul will often be deprived of the necessary efficacious grace for resisting temptation, and the individual will fall. There are various examples in Sacred Scripture of such falls (David, Solomon, Samson, etc.), and daily experience fully confirms the biblical statement: "Through woman's beauty many perish, for lust for it burns like fire" (Sirach 9:8). After the glance comes the arousal of the imagination, the irresistible desire and the shameful fall. Without control

[9] *Loc. cit.*

over the eyes it is impossible to stay on the road of virtue or even in the state of grace. The soul that aspires seriously to sanctification will flee from every dangerous occasion of this sort. One will keep a custody over the eyes, and, without going to ridiculous extremes, one will always be vigilant and alert lest he be taken by surprise.

3) *Curious glances.* These glances do not necessarily fall upon anything that is evil or even dangerous, but they have no other purpose than the simple joy of looking. Such glances are not in themselves reprehensible, and they may even help us to raise our minds to God. But when the soul gives itself to these things with an excessive attachment, or too frequently, they can become an obstacle to the life of prayer and recollection. A person who is constantly recreating certainly does not have recollection in prayer. He is before God with his body, but his heart is far removed from God. And if, contrary to all the merit of the soul, God would communicate some devout sentiment to the soul, this cannot remain, because, returning after his prayer to his free and uncontrolled glances, every holy affection vanishes. The spirit of the Lord is like certain liquors which evaporate if they are not tightly corked in the vessel that contains them. So also such a soul dissipates the spiritual fervor which God had imparted to it. In addition to living in an unhappy and distracted state, how is it possible that such a soul can give itself to the practice of mortification, charity, humility, penance and the other Christian virtues, when it has no thoughts or affections which could contribute to the religious life if the person lives in a cloister, or to the spiritual life if the person lives in the world?[10]

Mortification of sight is therefore necessary even in things which are lawful. Here, as in all else, it is necessary to proceed with serenity and equilibrium, without going to extravagant or ridiculous extremes. Certain episodes in the lives of the saints are more to be admired than imitated. Without going to these extremes, which God does not demand of all, it is certain that the mortification and custody of the eyes is a very important point in the spiritual life, not only in the negative aspect of protecting us from great evils, but also in the positive aspect of cultivating and increasing recollection and prayer which are absolutely indispensable to reach sanctity.[11]

HEARING AND SPEECH

Less noble than the sense of sight but more universal in its scope is the sense of hearing. Through this sense faith comes to us, as the Apostle says (Rom.

[10]Cf. J. B. Scaramelli, S.J., *Directorium Asceticum* (New York: Benziger), II, Tr. 1, a. 3, c. 2, n. 134.

[11]St. John of the Cross lists the following as evil effects caused by the lack of mortification of the sense of sight: vanity of spirit and distraction of the mind, unruly covetousness, immodesty, outward and inward unseemliness, impurity of thought, and envy (*The Ascent of Mount Carmel,* Bk. III, Chap. 25).

NEGATIVE ASPECT

10:17). It is therefore of great importance to subject this sense to the control of reason enlightened by faith. Moreover, St. James says: "If anyone does not offend in word, he is a perfect man" (3:2). Let us now consider the progressive purification of the sense of hearing and the use of speech.

1) *Evil conversations.* Simply to remain in the state of grace, it is necessary for the soul carefully to avoid any kind of sinful conversation. When one speaks or listens voluntarily and with satisfaction to things which gravely offend purity, charity, justice or any other Christian virtue, he commits a sin, and in some instances—as in the case of calumny—a sin which obliges one to restitution. It is impossible that a soul should give itself over to these shameful pastimes and still reach perfection. It places itself in great danger, and even compromises its eternal salvation. Lying, harsh words, useless discussions, murmuring, calumny, the violation of secrets, obscene or excessively free conversations, vulgar language, or envious or spiteful language, etc., must be definitively rejected by any soul that aspires to true sanctity, because without this, sanctity cannot be attained.

2) *Frivolous conversations.* There are conversations which, without constituting a grave sin by reason of their object or intention, are not justified either by necessity or profit to oneself or another. Under this heading fall all those idle words of which our Lord said we shall one day have to give an account (Matt. 12:36). To speak without usefulness to oneself or one's neighbor is to pervert the word or speech from the object which God in the plan of his divine providence has assigned to it. Instead of making it an instrument for good, one makes it serve futile things. One speaks to say nothing, and this is in itself a reprehensible act.

This doctrine has a particular application to those who are addicted to visiting and making social calls. There are countless ill effects which follow upon these frequent and interminable visits, apart from the loss of time and lack of recollection. We must see in this one of the principal reasons for the mediocrity of so many devout persons who, confessing with frequency, receiving Communion daily, and practicing a large number of pious exercises (sometimes too many), never seem to take a step forward on the road to sanctification. In many of these interminable conversations, one of two things usually happens: either the conversation turns to uncharitable criticism or it degenerates into a childish and useless prattle.

Souls that become bored when they are alone, that seek the company of others in order to give vent to their verbal incontinence, who refuse to repress this excess, who overwhelm their unfortunate victims with useless conversations, who are always the first to know new things and to spread news and to comment and criticize on everything can readily be dismissed from Christian perfection. They will never reach it, nor will they let others reach it.[12] The spiritual director must be very severe with these souls. Since one is treating here, not of faults of weakness, but of voluntary frivolity, after a few falls—and only a few, five or six—the director should refuse to continue a direction which would be completely useless.

3) *Useful conversations.* Anything that is perfectly honest in itself and harmful to no one and of benefit to one's neighbor or oneself is licit, and often advisable. This principle has a variety of applications and can be used to solve many cases. In recreation especially one will have to keep it in mind. To entertain one's neighbor with a joke in good taste could be an excellent act of charity, if one does so with the right intention. On the other hand, we should never allow ourselves, even under the pretext of cheering one who has been offended, to criticize our neighbor, to make a joke at the expense of another, to insinuate an evil suspicion, to arouse envy, or to foment rancor. Among persons who are dedicated to study, it is an excellent means for avoiding useless conversations if one introduces a discussion on some disputed point which will arouse the interest and attention of all, but one should carefully avoid passionate arguments or expressions of disrespect for those who hold the opposite opinion.

4) *Holy conversations.* These conversations have for their immediate purpose the spiritual welfare of oneself and one's neighbor. There is nothing so comforting or encouraging to a soul as a holy conversation with persons who are animated with a sincere desire of sanctifying themselves. The intellect is enlightened, the heart is inflamed, and the will easily makes holy resolutions. It is impossible to calculate the good that can be done with a discreet word and a timely counsel to a soul that is bothered with temptation or depressed with discouragement. With sweetness and discretion, without making oneself offensive with too much insistence, but after the fashion of a disciple rather than a master, the soul that aspires to perfection will try to encourage these holy conversations which bring so much good to souls and unite the heart more closely to God.

Positive mortification

It does not suffice to abstain from unfitting conversations nor to encourage holy conversations from time to time. It is also necessary to practice a positive mortification in hearing and speech. The principal methods of mortification are the following:

1) To abstain sometimes for the love of God from certain enjoyments in music or conversation. Certain innocent recreations can and should be permitted to souls that are as yet imperfect, while these same recreations

[12]"From joy in hearing useless things there may directly arise distraction of the imagination, gossiping, envy, rash judgments and vacillating thoughts; and from these arise many other pernicious evils" (*The Ascent of Mount Carmel,* Bk. III, Chap. 25).

NEGATIVE ASPECT

would perhaps be unfitting for souls that are more advanced in virtue. In all things, as St. Teresa warns, discretion is necessary.

2) By keeping a rigorous silence at certain periods in the day, for persons in the world, according to their own discretion, and for persons in religion, as their rule prescribes. Without the spirit of recollection and silence, the interior life and progress in virtue are impossible.

3) To renounce the desire for news and unnecessary curiosities, when one can do so without calling attention to the fact. If this cannot be done, to try to forget such things quickly and to remain in peace and solitude with God.

4) To keep in mind the following counsels of St. John of the Cross:

Restrain thy tongue and thy thoughts and keep thy affection habitually fixed upon God, and he will grant thy spirit divine fervor.

Feed not thy spirit on anything besides God. Cast away concern for all things and have peace and recollection in thy heart.

Be unwilling to admit into thy soul things that have in themselves no spiritual substance, lest they make thee lose the desire for devotion and recollection.

Endeavor that things be naught to thee and that thou be naught to things; forgetting all, dwell thou in thy recollection with the Spouse.

One word the Father spoke, which word was his Son, and this word he speaks ever in eternal silence, and in silence must it be heard by the soul.

He that seeks not the Cross of Christ seeks not the glory of Christ.

The faculties and senses must not be employed wholly upon things, but only so far as is unavoidable. With this exception, all must be left free for God.

If thou be detached from that which is without and dispossessed of that which is within, and without attachment to the things of God, neither will prosperity detain thee nor adversity hinder thee.

That which we most need in order to make progress is to be silent before this great God, with the desire and with the tongue, for the language that he best hears is that of silent love.[13]

This doctrine is severe, but it is worth the effort to put it into practice in the hope of attaining sanctity. Because they do not have the courage to do this, many souls remain halfway along the road to holiness, bound by the bonds which hold them to the earth. Sanctity presupposes an energetic and resolute determination of dying completely to self and to the world, cost what it may. And since there are so few souls that possess this type of courage, there have been, and always will be, few saints.

THE SENSE OF SMELL

This external sense is the least dangerous and the one which makes the fewest attacks upon our sanctification. Nevertheless, it is necessary to mortify it in two ways: a) in the tolerance of repulsive odors when charity demands it, as in visiting the poor or caring for the sick, without manifesting repugnance or

[13]St. John of the Cross, *Points of Love,* Peers translation, pp. 227-33, *passim.*

without complaining; b) by renouncing the excessive use of perfumes, which although they are not of themselves sinful, often indicate sensuality, and are indicative of an effeminate and worldly spirit. Persons consecrated to God, such as priests and religious, should be especially careful in this regard.[14]

THE SENSE OF TASTE

The sense of taste can constitute an obstacle to perfection by reason of its immoderate inclination to eat and drink. Lack of mortification in this sense is called gluttony. According to St. Thomas, gluttony is the disordered appetite for food and drink,[15] one of the vices opposed to the cardinal virtue of temperance. God placed in nourishment a pleasure which has for its purpose the guarantee of the nutritive function for the conservation of the life of the individual. In itself, to experience that pleasure does not imply any imperfection, and not to experience it would be a physiological deformity. But since original sin, the concupiscible appetite has been withdrawn from the control of reason and tends to exceed the limits of reason. Then this sensation becomes sinful, because the nature of man is rational and that which goes contrary to reason is evil for human nature and is contrary to the will of God.

Moderation of the sense of taste offers a special difficulty, since we cannot prescind entirely from it. On the one hand, it is necessary to nourish ourselves in order to preserve life; on the other hand, it is necessary to keep oneself within the limits of reason, without permitting the natural delight to become the primary purpose of eating.

According to St. Gregory and St. Thomas,[16] one can incur the vice of gluttony in the following ways: eating outside the proper time and without necessity; eating with too great an avidity; seeking exquisite fare; preparing food with excessive delicacy; eating too much in quantity.

Gluttony

According to St. Thomas gluttony can be either a venial or a mortal sin.[17] It is a mortal sin when one prefers the delight of eating and drinking to God and his precepts. In other words, when one would break a grave precept for the pleasure of eating or drinking, as when one breaks a fast or abstinence; when one causes serious injury to one's health; when one loses the use of reason as in the case of drunkenness; when it presupposes a serious waste of material goods; or when one gives grave scandal through gluttony. It will be a venial sin if, without going to any of the above mentioned extremes, one goes beyond the limits of prudence and reason. Ordinarily excess in food or

---

[14]"From joy in sweet perfumes there arise loathing of the poor, which is contrary to the teaching of Christ, dislike of serving others, unruliness of heart in humble things, and spiritual insensibility, at least to a degree proportionate with its desire for this joy" (*The Ascent of Mount Carmel,* Bk. III, Chap. 25).

[15]Cf. *Summa,* II-II, q. 148, a. 1.

[16]*Ibid.,* a. 4.

[17]*Ibid.,* a. 2.

NEGATIVE ASPECT

drink does not go beyond the limits of a venial sin, but the lack of mortification in regard to the sense of taste constitutes a great obstacle to one's sanctification.

As a capital sin, gluttony gives rise to many other vices and sins because the intellect, dulled and clouded by excessive food or drink, loses the control which it should have in the direction of our actions. St. Thomas, quoting St. Gregory, assigns the following as the daughters of gluttony: stupidity or dullness of intellect; excessive joy (especially because of drink), from which follow imprudent acts and unbecoming acts; excessive loquacity, in which there is usually sin, as Scripture states (Prov. 10:19); excess in words and in gestures, which proceeds from the lack of reason or weakness of intellect; lust, which is the most frequent evil effect of the vice of gluttony.[18] If we add to this that excess in eating and drinking destroys the organism, impoverishes the affections, degrades good sentiments, destroys the peace of the family, undermines society (especially with the plague of alcoholism), and incapacitates one for the practice of every kind of virtue, we shall have summarized the principal disastrous effects of this ugly vice which debases a man to the level of an animal.[19]

Counsels

The following counsels will be of great help if they are carried out with firmness and perseverance:

1) Not to eat or drink without first having rectified one's intention by directing it to the fulfillment of the will of God in the satisfaction of our bodily needs, and with a previous blessing of the meal. And never to omit thanksgiving after meals.

2) Carefully to avoid the defects which we have listed above.

3) To attempt gradually, over a period of time, to diminish the quantity of food until one reaches the amount which is necessary for the health of the organism. Many persons eat a great deal more than they really need.

4) To avoid singularity in the quality or quantity of food taken, especially if one lives in a community.

5) To mortify oneself positively in the use of food. This can be done in many ways without attracting attention: for example, by renouncing certain lawful satisfactions in food; by abstaining from some food that is particularly tasty or taking a smaller portion; by giving up wine or

[18] *Ibid.*, a. 6.

[19] "From joy in the savor of meat and drink, there arise directly such gluttony and drunkenness, wrath, discord and want of charity with one's neighbor and with the poor, as had that rich man who fared sumptuously every day, with Lazarus. Hence arise bodily disorders, infirmities and evil motions, because the incentives to luxury become greater. Directly, too, there arises great spiritual torpor, and the desire for spiritual things is corrupted, so that the soul can derive no enjoyment or satisfaction from them, nor can even speak of them. From this joy is likewise born distraction of the other senses and discontent with regard to many things" (*The Ascent of Mount Carmel,* Bk. III, Chap. 25).

liquors when one can do so prudently, or by reducing their use to a minimum. Generosity in self-renunciation and the increasing love of God will inspire the soul with many ingenious methods of practicing a mortification which is progressively more profound, without compromising bodily health.

THE SENSE OF TOUCH

This sense is the most material and, in a way, the most dangerous of all, because of its extension throughout the whole body and by reason of the vehemence of some of its manifestations. It requires severe mortification in order to avoid the sad consequences which follow upon an unmortified sense of touch.[20]

We shall not discuss the matters pertaining to lust, which is the most dangerous aspect of the sense of touch, since we have already spoken of the matter when treating of the battle against the flesh. Here we shall say only a few words concerning the manner of mortifying this sense directly.

There are two principal means of mortifying the sense of touch: 1) by depriving it of anything that may produce unlawful pleasure, and eventually by giving up even lawful pleasure, as one's circumstances permit or one's spiritual needs require; 2) by practicing positive mortification of the sense of touch by means of bodily penances. Mortification is necessary for all, and especially for beginners, until they succeed in dominating their passions by subjecting the flesh to the spirit. In addition to their reparatory aspect as regards past sins, bodily mortifications have two other lofty goals: the immolation of self in the imitation of Christ and a positive contribution to the Mystical Body by means of the apostolate of suffering. These two purposes pertain to the saints as much or more than to imperfect souls, for no one is excused from practicing bodily mortification in one form or another. St. Vincent de Paul says rightly: "He

[20]"From joy in the touch of soft things arise many more evil and more pernicious ones, which more quickly cause sense to overflow into spirit and quench all spiritual strength and vigor. Hence arises the abominable vice of effeminacy or the incentives thereto, according to the proportion of joy of this kind. Hence luxury increases, the mind becomes effeminate and timid, and the senses grow soft and delicate and are predisposed to sin and evil. Vain gladness and joy are infused into the heart; the tongue takes to itself license, and the eyes roam without restraint; and the remaining senses are blunted and deadened, according to the measure of this desire. The judgment is put to confusion, being nourished by spiritual folly and insipidness; moral cowardice and inconstancy increase; and, by the darkness of the soul and the weakness of the heart, fear is begotten even where there is no fear. At times again, this joy begets a spirit of confusion and insensibility with respect to conscience and spirit; wherefore the reason is greatly enfeebled, is affected in such a way that it can neither take nor give good counsel, remains incapable of moral and spiritual blessings, and becomes as useless as a broken vessel" (*The Ascent of Mount Carmel,* Bk. III, Chap. 25).

who has little regard for bodily mortification, under the pretext that interior mortifications are much more perfect, demonstrates very clearly that he is not mortified either interiorly or exteriorly."[21]

It is necessary to proceed prudently and slowly, increasing the exercises of penance as the powers of the soul increase and as the interior invitations of grace urge one on more and more. Especially at the beginning one should avoid any kind of severe corporal penance, until the will of God is made clearly manifest. One should not diminish the hours of sleep excessively or the quantity of food, for this could be prejudicial to one's health and leave the soul incapable of fulfilling the duties of state, which are more important than the voluntary practice of mortification. And the soul should take great care not to make an end or goal of that which is only a means, believing that sanctity consists in punishing the body severely.

In the lives of the saints there are many acts worthy of admiration, but it would be imprudent to imitate them. They received a particular inspiration and a special help from God, which is not always offered to all. If the Holy Ghost wishes to lead a soul by the way of extraordinary penances, he will inspire the soul to that effect and will give the strength necessary to carry it out. Meanwhile, the majority of souls should practice ordinary bodily mortification by accepting the little crosses of daily life with a spirit of faith and perseverance. This last point is very important. It is better to practice perseveringly, and without tiring, the little daily mortifications than to give oneself to occasional periods of great penance, alternated with other periods of relaxation.

PURIFICATION OF THE INTERNAL SENSES

There is nothing special to be said concerning the purification of the common sense and the estimative power. The former depends entirely on the external senses, whose impressions it gathers together and unifies. Whence the mortification of these senses will suffice at the same time to preserve the common sense from anything that is dangerous or useless. As regards the estimative power, if the imagination is kept under custody and the intellectual judgment exercises its proper function, any fault or defect of the estimative power will be prevented. On the other hand, the imagination and the sensitive memory need purification.

[21]Cf. Maynard, *Vertus et doctrine spirituelle de S. Vincent de Paul* (Paris: Tequi), c. 23.

THE IMAGINATION

The imagination is a very important faculty when one considers the intimate relationship between the soul and body. Every idea acquired by the natural operation of our faculties corresponds to a previous image which the imagination offered to the intellect. Without images, the intellect cannot know naturally. For that reason the use of sensible images is important for teaching abstract ideas and speculative principles, especially to the young and uneducated, who, without this sensible aid, would not be able to understand them. Our Lord continually made use of the imagination to place the great mysteries within the understanding of the simple and faithful people by means of his beautiful parables and allegories. The imagination also has a great influence over the sensitive appetite, which is moved with a great impetus toward its proper object when the imagination clothes it with special attractions.

Necessity of purification

Because of its great importance and influence, the imagination is one of the faculties which needs a most profound purification. When used in the service of the good, it can give incalculable assistance; but there is nothing which can cause greater difficulty on the way to sanctification than an imagination which has broken away from the control of reason enlightened by faith. Profoundly affected by original sin, it obeys only with difficulty the command of reason.

There are two principal obstacles which arise from an uncontrolled imagination: dissipation and temptation. Without profound recollection, an interior life and a life of prayer are impossible, and there is nothing which so impedes recollection as the inconstancy and dissipation of the imagination. As regards temptation, it is often attributed to the devil, when in reality it proceeds from one's uncontrolled imagination, which paints in vivid colors the pleasure sin will provide for the concupiscible appetite, or emphasizes the difficulty which the irascible appetite will have on the road to virtue, filling the soul with sadness and despair.

Means of purification

The principal means are the following:

1) *Custody of the external senses.* It is of great importance to keep a custody over the external senses, and especially the sense of sight, because through them enter the objects which the imagination retains, reproduces and re-assembles in a thousand ways, thus arousing the sensitive appetite, attracting the attention of the intellect, and encouraging the consent of the will. There is, therefore, no better way of avoiding all this than to deprive the imagination of such things by a custody of the external senses.

2) *Careful selection of reading matter.* It is necessary to avoid, not only reading matter that is evil or obviously dangerous, but that which is frivolous or vain, and fills the imagination with useless images. To this class of reading belong most of the modern novels, even those which would pass moral censorship, because the reading of such books (without sufficiently grave reason) does not befit persons who seriously intend to lead

NEGATIVE ASPECT

a life of recollection and prayer. A soul that is attached to the reading of such novels can hardly hope to sanctify itself.

3) *Avoidance of sloth.* The imagination is never quiet. If we do not keep it occupied with good and useful work, it will itself seek material on which to spend itself. And since it has a natural propensity to do anything that appeals to the lower appetite, it will readily place us in danger of temptation. The imagination should always be occupied with something that is good and useful, and when this is done, we shall have made a great step forward to peace of soul.

4) *To fill the imagination with good things.* It does not suffice to keep the imagination from harmful matter, or to avoid idleness, in order to keep the imagination under control; it is likewise necessary to provide holy and profitable material, so that the imagination will not only be withdrawn from evil but will be directed positively to the good. This is the reason for "composition of place" before one begins the practice of prayer. It consists in representing as vividly as possible the particular scene upon which one is about to meditate, thus offering food to the imagination so that it will not disturb the soul with its distractions. The reading of holy books in which edifying scenes are described can contribute a great deal to this positive formation of the imagination and can put it at the service of the intellect and the will as an excellent auxiliary.

5) *Attention to the duty of the moment.* The axiom of the ancients, *age quod agis,* is filled with profound meaning. The habit of attending to the duty of the moment has the double advantage of multiplying our intellectual powers and of disciplining the imagination by preventing it from being distracted to other objects.

6) *Ignoring distraction.* Frequently this is the only way of combatting certain vivid imaginations and the images produced, rather than trying to attack them directly. This is the advice of St. Teresa of Avila.[22] The will should be occupied in loving God even in the midst of many distractions, and the soul should be patient with the activity of the imagination until God transforms it profoundly by means of the passive purification. Meanwhile, it should take no account of it and should avoid what it must avoid and do what it must do, in spite of any contrary suggestions made by the uncontrolled imagination.

As regards Christian perfection, St. John of the Cross speaks at length to the effect that the imaginary apprehensions cannot be a means proportionate to the union with God because God is not contained in any imaginary species. He likewise speaks of the great harm that is done to the soul when it does not know how to rid itself of these imaginations or to remain detached from them

[22]Cf. St. Teresa, *The Life,* Chap. 17, n. 7.

when they are given in a supernatural way. One should read and meditate on this magnificent doctrine of St. John of the Cross.[23]

THE MEMORY

We shall treat of the purification of the memory in general, explaining the principles which can be applied both to the sensitive and the intellectual memory. The latter, according to St. Thomas, is not a faculty distinct from the intellect, but only a function of the intellect, having for its object the conservation and retention of intelligible species.[24] There is a great difference between the sensitive memory, which has for its object only the sensible, the particular and the concrete, and the intellectual memory, which deals with the suprasensible, the abstract and the universal; but the process of purification is exactly the same in each case. The means of purification affect both equally.

Necessity of purification

The memory is a very important faculty. It can give inestimable service to the intellect and can be its most powerful ally. Without it, our spirit would be like a sieve which is always empty, however much water is poured into it. For certain types of knowledge, such as languages, history, the physical and natural sciences, it is absolutely indispensable to possess an excellent memory.

Precisely because the memory stores up all kinds of knowledge, both good and evil, it is necessary to subject it to an energetic process of purification. Throughout life there is produced around us a series of acts which can be of no use whatever for the sanctification of the soul. Sometimes they are sad events regarding our own faults and sins; at other times they are certain spectacles or disedifying actions which we have witnessed; again, they may be useless information or news which leaves our spirit deeply disturbed; or they may be the unfortunate happenings of personal or family or social life: the disgraces, the forgetfulness, the ingratitude, the injury, etc., with which our poor human life is filled. None of these memories is profitable for the soul. They all tend in one way or another to destroy the soul's peace and tranquility, which are so necessary for a life of prayer and recollection. Let us, therefore, see what should be the practical conduct of the soul regarding the active purification of the memory.

Means of purification

The following are the principal means for the purification of the memory:

1) *To eliminate sinful memories.* This is the first step, and it is absolutely indispensable for all who aspire to eternal salvation. The remembrance of one's own sins or those of another, or the remembrance of spectacles or magazines that are immoral, has a strong power for suggesting to

[23]Cf. *The Ascent of Mount Carmel,* Bk. II, Chaps. 12, 16.

[24]Cf. *Summa,* I, q. 79, a. 7. The recognition of the species as past is not proper to the intellectual memory but only to the sensitive memory. Nevertheless, even the intellectual memory has a consciousness of the past, not by reason of its object, which always abstracts from the here and now, but by reason of its intellectual act, as St. Thomas says: *secundum quod intelligit se prius intellexisse.*

the soul these same things by way of a new temptation, and of causing it to fall again into sin, especially if a vivid imagination is associated with the recollection. The soul must reject immediately and energetically any remembrance of this kind, and be convinced that the simple approbation or voluntary enjoyment of those past sins is sufficient to make the individual guilty again of those sins, without committing them again externally.

b) *To combat useless memories.* There are many other things which, without being sinful in themselves, are nevertheless completely useless as far as recollection goes, and for that reason are harmful to the soul. Such, for example, are the sad happenings of our past life, family disgraces, humiliations, misfortunes of various kinds, or successful events which perhaps filled us with an excessive joy. The remembrance of the one or the other disturbs the peace and tranquility of the soul and is of no profit to anyone, because none of the sad or unfortunate events of life can be remedied by our present suffering, nor can any of the joys return. As long as the soul is occupied with these vain joys or sorrows, it will be incapacitated for giving itself completely to prayer and recollection.

c) *To forget past injuries.* This pertains to virtue and is indispensable for any soul that wishes to sanctify itself truly. In spite of the pardon which has been given, sometimes even beyond the call of strict justice, the remembrance of a past offense cannot help but disturb, at least momentarily, the peace of conscience, and present the guilty party in an unfavorable light. It is necessary to forget completely the disagreeable episode and even to give special attention to the one who voluntarily caused the injury.

We should try to forget completely and forever any offenses committed against us, realizing that those we have committed against God are much greater, and that he demands of us a complete pardon in order to give us his pardon without measure. The soul that nourishes rancor, however justifiable it may seem (and it never is in the eyes of God), can forget about reaching sanctity. And if it is a question of enmity which is manifested externally, the individual is also exposed to the grave danger of losing eternal salvation.

d) *To remember benefits received from God and our own ingratitude to God.* This pertains to the positive purgation of the memory, and offers a wonderful means for directing the memory to God. Who can doubt that the recollection of the immense benefits which we have received from God, of the infinite number of times that he has pardoned our faults, of the dangers from which he has preserved us, of the loving care which his providence has exercised over us and of those we love—that this memory is an excellent means of arousing our gratitude toward him and the desire of corresponding more faithfully with his graces? And if to this we add the recollection of our own misery and our own nothingness, of our disobedience and rebellion, of our constant ingratitude and resistance to grace, our soul will be filled with humility and confusion, and will experience the need of redoubling its vigilance and its efforts to be better in the future.

e) *To remember the motives for Christian hope.* This is one of the most efficacious means for directing our memory to God and for purifying it of contact with earthly things. St. John of the Cross makes the memory the seat of Christian hope, and although this is not exact, there is no doubt that one could find many points of contact between the two as regards purification of the memory. The remembrance of an eternity of happiness, which is the central object of Christian hope, is most apt for making us disdain the vain recollection of the things of earth and to raise our spirit to God. Here is the way in which this doctrine was explained by Father Garrigou-Lagrange:

> Proneness to forget God causes our memory to be as if immersed in time, whose relation to eternity, to the benefits and promises of God, it no longer sees. This defect inclines our memory to see all things horizontally on the line of time that flees, of which the present alone is real, between the past that is gone and the future that is not yet. Forgetfulness of God prevents us from seeing that the present moment is also on a vertical line, which attaches it to the single instant of immobile eternity, and that there is a divine manner of living the present moment in order that by merit it may enter into eternity. Whereas forgetfulness of God leaves us in this banal and horizontal view of things on the line of time which passes, the contemplation of God is like a vertical view of things which pass, and of their bond with God who does not pass. To be immersed in time is to forget the value of time, that is to say, its relation to eternity.
>
> By what virtue must this great defect of forgetfulness of God be cured? St. John of the Cross answers that the memory which forgets God must be healed by the hope of eternal beatitude, as the intellect must be purified by the progress of faith, and the will by the progress of charity.[25]

As regards perfection, the necessity of purifying the memory by ridding it of all earthly forms which could disturb our union with God follows the fundamental reason which was given for the purification of the other faculties: no creative form, whether sensible or intellectual, can serve as the proximate and proportionate medium for divine union. St. John of the Cross is inflexible in drawing conclusions from this principle in regard to the memory, in which he demands the forgetfulness of all the apprehensions received, naturally or supernaturally, in order to guide it solely by motives of Christian hope. One should read with great care the beautiful pages which St. John has written on this matter.[26]

[25] *The Three Ages of the Interior Life,* 1, p. 346.
[26] Cf. *The Ascent of Mount Carmel,* Bk. III, Chaps. 1-15.

PURIFICATION OF THE PASSIONS

Having examined the active purification of the external and internal senses, it is necessary to turn to a consideration of the purification of the sensitive appetite, in which the passions are located. We shall begin by recalling the general teaching of psychology.

PSYCHOLOGY OF THE PASSIONS

The sensitive appetite is that organic faculty through which we seek the good so far as it is material and is known through the senses. It is generically distinct from the rational appetite or the will, which seeks the good as apprehended by the intellect.[27] The sensitive appetite is ignorant of any good which is not purely sensual or pleasing to the senses. From this stems the battle against the rational appetite, which of itself seeks the rational good or the good of spirit. "For the flesh lusts against the spirit, and the spirit against the flesh, for these are opposed to each other" (Gal. 5:17).

The sensitive appetite, also called sensuality, is a power which is divided into two potencies, the two species of the sensitive appetite, namely, the concupiscible appetite and the irascible appetite. The former has as its object the delightful good which is easy to obtain; the latter has as its object the arduous good which is difficult to obtain. These two inclinations cannot be reduced to one unique principle, but they are two potencies which are really distinct from each other.[28]

The intellect and the will can influence the sensitive appetite; not, however, in the despotic manner in which they govern the hands or feet, which move without resistance to the command of the will, but only with a political government, as that of a chief over a subject who is able to resist the command of his superior. The different movements of the sensitive appetite to the good as known through the senses give rise to the passions. To regulate and purify the latter is equivalent to the regulation and purification of the sensitive appetite.

There are two principal ways in which the word passion is used. In its philosophical sense, the passions are movements or energies which we can use for good or for evil. In themselves, they are neither good nor evil; it depends upon the orientation which is given to them.[29] When placed at the service of the good, they can be of incalculable assistance, even to the point that one could say that it is morally impossible for a soul to arrive at great

[27]Cf. St. Thomas, *Summa,* I, q. 60, a. 2.

[28]Cf. *ibid.,* q. 81, a. 2.

[29]Cf. *ibid.,* I-II, q. 24.

sanctity without possessing a great energy or passion which is directed to God. But when placed at the service of evil, the passions are converted into a destructive force which is truly terrifying.

In popular language and in the works of many spiritual writers, the word passion is often used as synonymous with evil passion, which one must combat and dominate. We shall use the word in its philosophical sense to designate powers which of themselves are indifferent, but which one must channel along the way of the good; at the same time we will point out the deviations which may occur and the means of avoiding them.

Nature of the passions

The passions are movements of the sensitive appetite caused by the apprehension of the sensible good or evil, accompanied by a certain change, more or less intense, in the organism. Modern psychologists are accustomed to reserve the word passions to designate the more vehement and intense movements of the sensitive appetite, reserving the word emotion for those movements which are more gentle and ordinary. In any case, the passions always presuppose some knowledge, at least sensitive, of the good which is sought or the evil which is feared.

The movement of passion, properly speaking, can be very intense. From this there follows an organic change or disturbance which flows from the passions as a natural consequence. For example, anger inflames the countenance with indignation and places the nerves in a state of tension; fear causes one to grow pale; love enlarges the heart, and fear restricts the heart, etc. The intensity of the bodily change is not always uniform; it will depend in each case on the physiological constitution of the individual, the intensity of the movement of passion, and the greater or less dominion which the individual has over himself.

Number of the passions

St. John of the Cross, following Boëthius, lists four fundamental passions: joy, hope, sorrow and fear.[30] But the scholastic division is the classical one, and it lists eleven passions: six pertaining to the concupiscible appetite and five pertaining to the irascible appetite.

In the concupiscible appetite the good, which has a power of attraction, engenders three movements of passion. The simple awareness of good arouses love; if it is a question of a future good, it gives rise to desire; if it is a good already possessed and present, it produces joy. On the other hand, the apprehension of evil, which is of itself repulsive, produces hatred; if it is an impending evil, it causes a movement of flight or aversion; but if the evil has overtaken us, it causes sadness.

In the irascible appetite the absent good, if it is considered possible of attainment, engenders hope; but if it is impossible of attainment, it produces

[30]Cf. *De consolatione philosophiae,* Bk. I (M.L., 63: 657); cf. also *Summa,* I-II, q. 25, a. 4; St. John of the Cross, *The Ascent of Mount Carmel,* Bk. III, Chap. 16.

NEGATIVE ASPECT

despair. In like manner, the difficult evil which is absent, if it can be avoided, produces courage; but if the evil is unavoidable, it arouses fear. Lastly, the presence of a difficult evil produces anger in the irascible appetite and sadness in the concupiscible appetite, while the presence of a difficult good does not arouse any movement in the irascible appetite, but causes joy in the concupiscible appetite. For that reason, the irascible appetite has only five passions, while there are six passions in the concupiscible appetite. For greater clarity the passions can be enumerated according to the following schema:

In the concupiscible appetite:

The good simply apprehended—LOVE
The evil opposed to the good—HATRED
The future good—DESIRE
The impending evil—AVERSION OR FLIGHT
The present good—JOY
The present evil—SADNESS

In the irascible appetite:

The difficult good absent but possible of attainment—HOPE
The difficult good absent but impossible of attainment—DESPAIR
The difficult evil absent but superable—COURAGE
The difficult evil absent and insuperable—FEAR
The difficult evil actually present—ANGER

Bossuet observes that all the passions can be reduced to the passion of love, which is the fundamental passion and the root of all the others:

> We can say, if we observe what passes within ourselves, that our passions are all reducible to love, which enfolds and arouses all the others. Hatred for some object does not come except because of the love which is had for something else. I hate sickness because I love health. I do not have any aversion to anyone unless it is because he is an obstacle to me for the possession of that which I love. Desire is nothing more than a love which extends itself to a good which is not yet possessed, and joy is a love which is satisfied in the possession of the good. Aversion and sadness are a love which turns one away from an evil which would deprive him of his good. Courage is a love which undertakes, for the possession of the subject loved, that which is very difficult; and fear is a love which, under the threat of losing that which one seeks, is tormented by that danger. Hope is a love which has the confidence that it can possess the object loved; despair is a love which is desolate on seeing itself deprived of it forever, which causes a dejection from which one cannot rise. Anger is a love which is irritated on seeing that one wishes to deprive it of its good and rouses itself to defend that good. In a word, repress love, and there are no passions; arouse love, and all the other passions are born.[31]

[31]Bossuet, *Connaissance de Dieu et de soi-même,* Chap. 1.

The great importance of the passions can be deduced from their decisive influence in the physical, intellectual and moral life of man.

Importance of the passions

1) *In the physical life.* Without the previous stimulation of the appetite, we would take scarcely one step in our physical life, since the stimulation of the passions is what enables us to expend an extraordinary activity for good or for evil. Add to this the fact that certain passions have a powerful influence on bodily health, and could even be a cause of death, especially the passion of sadness, which, as St. Thomas says, is able to do more harm to the body than any of the other passions.[32]

2) *In the intellectual life.* It is impossible to overestimate the influence of the passions upon our ideals. The greater part of betrayals and apostasies have their most profound root in the disorder of one's passions. Father Bourget notes: "It is necessary to live as one thinks; otherwise, sooner or later, one ends by thinking as he lives."[33] How else can one explain the lamentable defections of so many brilliant men in the field of religion?

3) *In the moral life.* The passions increase or diminish the goodness or malice, merit or demerit of our actions.[34] They diminish human responsibility when a person seeks a good or evil more because of an impulsive passion than by the free choice of the will; they increase human responsibility when the will confirms the antecedent movement of passion and uses it in order to work with greater intensity.

TRAINING THE PASSIONS

It follows from the extraordinary importance of the passions that it is necessary to train them properly by withdrawing them from evil and placing them at the service of good. But is it possible to train the passions? Undoubtedly the answer must be in the affirmative. Since the passions are of themselves morally indifferent, their very nature demands direction and control. It is true that we do not have a despotic rule over our passions but only a political rule, but a prudent organization of all our psychological resources can result in a near-perfect control of our passions, even to the point that one has control over everything except what is called the first movements of passion, which do not affect morality.

Daily experience confirms these statements. All of us are aware of our responsibility for the movements of passion. When we let ourselves be carried away by a disordered impulse, we feel immediately the pangs of remorse. If, on the contrary, we have resisted this impulse, we experience a sense of satisfaction at a duty fulfilled. This is convincing proof of the fact that we are free agents as regards the impulse of the passions, and that their control

[32]Cf. *Summa*, I-II, q. 37, a. 4.
[33]*Le démonde midi*, II, 253.
[34]*Summa*, I-II, q. 24, a. 3.

NEGATIVE ASPECT

and government are in our hands. The history of conversions offers a new proof of the possibility of training the passions. Men who have lived for years under the domination of disorderly passions have been able to free themselves of this great force and to begin a life which is fully in harmony with the moral law. There is no doubt that there are grave difficulties and obstacles at the beginning, but gradually the individual can gain perfect control of himself.

Basic principles

But now let us consider the basic principles concerning the training of the passions.

1) *Every idea tends to produce its corresponding act.* This principle is particularly true if the idea or sentiment is accompanied by strong emotions and a vivid representation. From this principle one can deduce as a norm of conduct the necessity of formulating ideas which are in accordance with the actions which one hopes to realize, and carefully avoiding those ideas which refer to actions which one wishes to avoid. In this way one's acts are governed by one's ideas.

2) *Every act arouses the sentiment of which it is a normal expression.* The rule of conduct which follows from this principle is that in order to acquire the sentiment which is desired, or rather, to intensify the passion which we wish to arouse, it is necessary to work as if one already was experiencing it. In this way one's sentiments are controlled by means of one's acts.

3) *Passion augments and intensifies the psychological forces of the individual until it raises them to their greatest intensity and uses them to attain that which one seeks.* It follows from this that it is necessary to select a passion very carefully in order to obtain the most out of our psychological energy. In this way ideas and acts are governed by sentiment.

These are the basic principles concerning the control and government of the passions, but we shall now make more detailed applications as regards the rules of conduct in relation to good and evil.

THE STRUGGLE AGAINST THE PASSIONS

First it is necessary to be firmly convinced of the necessity of combatting disorderly passions because of the great disturbances which they cause in us.[35] The passions disturb our spirit, impede reflection, make it impossible to formulate a serene and balanced judgment, weaken the will, arouse the imagination, cause a change in the bodily organs, and threaten to destroy one's peace of spirit and tranquility of conscience.

The remedies to be applied for the control of one's passions will depend on the particular passion which must be dominated. One will struggle against the

---

[35]Cf. St. John of the Cross, *The Ascent of Mount Carmel,* Bk. I, Chaps. 6-13; Bk. III, Chaps. 16-45.

passions aroused by one's environment by means of distractions, journeys and a change of scenery; against those which proceed from the organism itself by means of a regular regime, work, custody of the senses and of the imagination; against those which have their origin in temperament or character by means of reflection and will power. From the psychological point of view, there can be no doubt that the best remedy against disorderly passions is the firm and decided will to conquer them. But a purely theoretical will or wishful thinking will not suffice; there must be an energetic and determined decision which is translated into action by use of the means necessary to obtain victory, and especially if it is a question of combatting a passion that has been deeply rooted through a long period of misuse.

Lines of action

The following are the fundamental lines of action to be followed in this battle against the passions.

1) *To struggle without ceasing against the causes of the passions.* Passions may be aroused by reason of temperament, external influences, intellectual and sensible abilities, proximate and remote occasions, etc. As regards the occasions which give rise to disorderly passions, it is a basic rule that they must be avoided. A will which has been weakened by a violent passion will readily succumb in a dangerous occasion. It must be imposed as an indispensable rule that one will flee from anything that could be an incentive to passion. Without this, a fall is almost certain to follow.

2) *To prevent energetically any new manifestation of the passion.* Every new act of a passion redoubles its strength. This is the secret of the failure of so many young people in their battle against impurity. When they feel themselves strongly tempted, they yield to the passion in order to remain in peace for a few days. This is a great mistake. Rather than quieting their passions, they do nothing more than increase the demands of passion and prolong indefinitely a struggle in which they can never win the victory. It is necessary to resist, even to the shedding of blood if necessary, as St. Paul says (Heb. 12:4). Only in this way can the force of passion be weakened until finally it leaves us in peace.

3) *To provide the passion with new objects.* As regards certain passions, one need only change the object of the passion in order to convert the whole activity into virtue. Sensual love can be transformed into supernatural and divine love. Ambition can become an excellent virtue when it is directed to the extension of the kingdom of God. The fear of dangers can be most useful in the flight from occasions of sin. Thus one can proceed to a positive orientation of the passions toward the good.

Orientation of the passions toward the good

We shall now point out, one by one, the principal objects toward which we should direct our passions.

1) As regards *love,* it should be directed in the natural order to one's family, good friendships, knowledge, art, one's country, etc. In the super-

NEGATIVE ASPECT

natural order it should be directed to God, to Christ, to Mary, to the angels and saints, to the Church and to the souls of our neighbors.

2) *Hatred* must be directed toward sin, the enemies of the soul and anything that could debase us or lead us to evil in the natural or supernatural order.

3) *Desire* must be transformed into lawful ambition; in the natural order, to be profitable for one's family and one's country, and in the supernatural order, to obtain perfection in sanctity.

4) *Flight* or *aversion* should be used in the avoidance of the occasions of sin and of anything that would comprise one's salvation or sanctity.

5) *Joy* should be experienced as a result of the perfect fulfillment of the will of God for us, of the triumph of good throughout the world, of the possession of sanctifying grace which makes one a child of God and a living member of Christ, etc.

6) *Sadness* will find its expression in the contemplation of the passion of Christ, the sorrows of Mary, the sufferings and persecution of the Church and her children, the triumph of evil in the world, etc.

7) *Hope* must feed upon the perspective of the eternal happiness which awaits us in the life to come, in trusting confidence in the assistance of God during our life, in the assurance of the protection of Mary, now and at the hour of our death, etc.

8) *Despair* must be transformed into a prudent distrust of ourselves, based on the knowledge of our sins and the weakness of our powers, but counterbalanced by a confidence in the love and mercy of God and the assistance of his divine grace.

9) *Courage* or *daring* must be converted into an intrepid and valiant spirit for confronting and conquering all the obstacles and difficulties which we meet in the fulfillment of our duties and in the work of our sanctification, remembering that "the kingdom of heaven has been enduring violent assault, and the violent have been seizing it by force" (Matt. 11:12).

10) *Fear* must focus itself on the possibility of sin, which is the only true evil which could befall us, and on the temporal or eternal loss of God which is the consequence of sin, but not to such an extent that one is led to discouragement, but as a stimulus to die rather than to sin.

11) *Anger* should be transformed into a holy indignation which will prove a strong defense against every kind of evil.

PRACTICAL COUNSEL FOR THE DIRECTOR

The director should carefully examine the passion or passions which predominate in the soul which is under his care. Once he has verified this, he should impose as matter for the examen, not the extinction of the passion (which would be a futile effort), but control and direction in the manner we have indicated. The director should aim principally at the reform and control of the dominant passion, attacking it primarily, but without neglecting the reform and control of the other passions. He should frequently demand an accounting of the soul's progress or falls in this matter, and he should not rest until he has succeeded in directing to God the whole passionate energy of the one directed. This is not an easy task, and without doubt the labor will last a lifetime, but it is a task of paramount importance. One of the most common reasons for so many frustrated saints is that they have not given the necessary attention to the control and use of the great energies of the passions. Without passion, indeed without great passion directed toward the good, it is practically impossible to become a saint.

ACTIVE PURIFICATION OF THE INTELLECT

With the active purification of the external and internal senses and of the sensitive appetite, one will have taken a great step toward Christian perfection. But it is necessary that the purification reach into the very depths of one's spirit to rectify the deviations of intellect and will. Then the passive purification will complete what a man cannot do by his own efforts with the assistance of ordinary grace.

INTELLECT AND WILL

According to traditional psychology, there are two spiritual faculties of the soul, the intellect and the will. Some authors, and especially the ancient mystical authors, considered the intellectual memory to be a third faculty of the soul, distinct from the other two, but in reality it is merely a function of the intellect which preserves intellectual species.[36] Only as an internal sense (the sensitive memory) is it an autonomous faculty distinct from the other internal senses and from the intellectual memory.[37] The purification of the intellectual memory follows a process which is analogous to the purification of the sensitive memory, of which we have already spoken. We shall, therefore, speak

[36]Among these authors is St. John of the Cross, who seems to follow John Bacon in making the intellectual memory the subject of theological hope (cf. *The Ascent of Mount Carmel,* Bk. III, Chap. 1). Nevertheless, Father Marcellus of the Child Jesus, O.C.D., maintains that the thought of St. John of the Cross fully coincides with Aristotelian-Thomistic psychology and that St. John of the Cross assigns the theological virtues to these three powers of the soul in order to expound with better order and greater clarity the detachment which must be effected in them. Cf. *El tomismo de San Juan de la Cruz* (Burgos: 1930), Chap. 11, p. 128; cf. also St. Thomas, *Summa,* I, q. 79, a. 7.

[37]St. Thomas, *Summa,* I, q. 78, a. 4; q. 79, a. 6.

NEGATIVE ASPECT

of the active purification of the two faculties of the soul which are really distinct: the intellect and the will.

NATURE OF THE INTELLECT

The intellect is the faculty of the soul by which we apprehend things in an immaterial way. Its proper effect is the idea which it abstracts from external objects by means of the phantasm of the imagination, which is illumined by the abstractive power of the intellect itself, called in psychology the agent intellect.[38] Intellectual knowledge is completely distinct and infinitely superior to the knowledge of the senses. Sensitive knowledge always refers to singular, concrete and determined objects, while the knowledge through ideas—the object of intellectual knowledge—is always universal, abstract and undetermined. We possess sensitive knowledge in common with the animals, but intellectual knowledge is proper and exclusive to intellectual beings (God, the angels and man).

When the intellect compares two ideas and affirms or denies something about them, it pronounces a *judgment*. If it compares two judgments in order to conclude a third judgment, it performs an act of *reasoning*. Explicit reasoning, in the form which we have just given, is called a syllogism.

Characteristics

It is well to note that our intellect functions in such a way that we can never have two thoughts at the same time. If we are occupied in some thought, it will be impossible for us at the same time to be conscious of another distinct thought. This phenomenon is the basis of the attention which is nothing other than the application of the mind to a subject. The custody of the senses, silence and tranquility of spirit are a great help to the fostering of attention and the preservation of attention over a long period of time. For that reason these things have great importance in practice.

The intellect is very delicate and subtle in discovering almost without effort a multitude of aspects surrounding an idea. It is profound in analyzing and dividing into its ultimate elements some concrete notion. It is solid if it is able to reason things out by logical deduction based upon a certain principle. It has foresight if, from past events or present events, it can deduce by means of an acute observation what will happen in the future.

Divisions

In spite of the simplicity of the intellect as a spiritual faculty, mystical theologians, in order to explain phenomena which otherwise would be difficult to understand, have established certain divisions or distinctions regarding the intellectual function of the soul.[39] The principal distinctions or divisions are the following:

1) What the mystical authors refer to as the mind (*mens*) is the most spiritual and elevated part of the soul which the disturbances of the physical world can never reach. Illumined by God, it always reflects his divine

[38]Cf. *ibid.*, qq. 84-88.

[39]Cf. *ibid.*, q. 79, aa. 8-12.

splendors and is far removed from the earth. In the midst of the most painful trials and darkness, this superior part of the spirit remains tranquil, as if it were already in eternity. It is also called by some authors "the supreme heaven" or "the light of understanding."

2) What the authors call reason is further subdivided into the superior reason and the inferior reason. The superior reason always obtains its conclusions from the principles of pure understanding, that is, without any influence of the passions. It is called "the middle heaven" and it always tends upward to that which is noble and elevated. The inferior part of the soul, on the other hand, judges by means of the experiences of the senses and under the influence of the passions, and for that reason it tends downward to that which is useful or delightful for the subject. It is "the lowest heaven" and is often closer to earth than it is to heaven.

PURIFICATION OF THE INTELLECT

This consists in the removal of the obstacles or evil inclinations which are the result of original sin and our own personal sin, which are opposed to perfect submission of the intellect to God. The principal obstacles are the following:

Useless thoughts

Useless thoughts. Our spirit is frequently occupied with a multitude of useless thoughts which cause us to waste time and divert our attention to that which is base or perishable, with the result that we pay no heed to those things which are of great interest and value to the soul in its sanctification. We should not forget that the intellect cannot be occupied at the same time with two distinct thoughts; one of the two will always be considered to the prejudice of the other. The majority of the distractions which we lament during prayer and the other exercises of piety proceed from the fact that we have previously wasted time in useless thought. The spirit cannot pass directly from one situation to another which is completely distinct. It needs time to react and adapt itself to the new occupation. For that reason it is necessary to combat useless thoughts with great energy and to reject anything that may dissipate the intellect by distracting it or withdrawing it from the great task of one's sanctification. It is necessary to renounce, as much as possible, the reading of useless books or indulging in frivolous conversations which fill our soul with useless thoughts. The reading of magazines and newspapers should also be curtailed. All of this is inconvenient, but it is precisely because they do not wish to suffer these deprivations that many who aspire to Christian perfection remain only halfway on the road to sanctity.

Ignorance

Ignorance. It is one thing to feed upon useless thoughts and it is something very different to welcome or encourage ignorance, lest one lose his tranquility. This would be a grave error and perhaps more harmful than useless thoughts. Not every kind of ignorance is voluntary and not every kind of ignorance is a sin. All Christians are not obliged to acquire a professional knowledge of theology, but certainly all are obliged to obtain that knowledge which, accord-

NEGATIVE ASPECT

ing to their ability and the obligation of their state in life, can contribute to their intellectual and moral perfection. A dislike or hatred of knowledge has always been a sign of an evil spirit and has been the origin of many heresies in the Church. Sacred Scripture reproves this attitude in no uncertain terms (Os. 4:6), and St. Paul frequently insists on the utility of knowledge for the service of God.[40]

Nevertheless, not all knowledge is useful or convenient for one's sanctification. St. Paul speaks of the knowledge which puffs up, in distinction to charity which edifies (I Cor. 8:1). In the acquisition of knowledge one can sin in two ways: 1) as regards the one who studies, by not following the impulse of the virtue of studiosity,[41] but studying out of curiosity, vanity or the mere pleasure which one experiences in study; 2) as regards that which is studied, when it is harmful to the soul or utterly useless.

It is especially necessary to combat ignorance in matters of religion and the spiritual life. It is certain that with the right intention we can and ought to study human sciences, and especially those which pertain to one's profession and duties of state, but above all we should apply ourselves to the science of our eternal salvation. It would be an absurdity to dedicate all our efforts to human science and neglect that supreme science which concerns our eternal destiny. Such is the sad spectacle of many persons who are eminent in literary culture, in art or science, but lack the most fundamental knowledge of religion. Others dedicate themselves weakly to the acquisition of sacred science but with an attitude that is opposed to study. They are interested only in the speculative knowledge of truth, but are not concerned with letting that knowledge affect their lives. Such souls are dying of spiritual anemia without even realizing that they have before their eyes a splendid table at which they can be nourished with holy doctrine. And even this is not so bad as those who neglect completely the practice of prayer to dedicate their time to the external works of the apostolate. Such persons should recall the teaching of St. John of the Cross, who says that a great deal more profit would be done for the Church, and it would be much more pleasing to God, if such souls would take half of that time spent in activity and devote it to prayer.[42] The soul should therefore dedicate itself to the study of truth, put aside the spirit of curiosity, and seek in this knowledge only the greater glory of God, the dissipation of its own ignorance, and the means of advancing along the way to sanctity.

Curiosity

Curiosity. In direct opposition to the virtue of studiosity is the vice of curiosity.[43] This is an immoderate desire to know that which does not pertain

[40]Cf. II Cor. 6:6, 8:7, 11:6; Phil. 1:9; Col. 1:19.
[41]Cf. St. Thomas, *Summa,* II-II, q. 166.
[42]Cf. *Spiritual Canticle,* Chap. 29, a. 3.
[43]Cf. St. Thomas, *Summa,* II-II, q. 167.

to us, or which could be harmful to us. Unfortunately, this sin is committed frequently, either in the acquisition of all types of useless knowledge or in the knowledge of those things which could only serve to give delight to the senses or arouse the senses. Under this heading belongs the unrestrained tendency to read every type of novel or book simply to pass the time or for recreation, as well as the insatiable desire for spectacles such as the theater or sports, which are sometimes truly dangerous or opposed to Christian morality. St. Thomas points out that the attendance at such things is vicious if it inclines a person to vice or lust or cruelty because of the things that are presented there.[44] It is impossible that persons who dedicate themselves to such things, especially if it happens with frequency, can keep their soul in the state of spiritual peace and tranquility which is necessary for attaining sanctity.

It is also an effect of the vice of curiosity to be constantly prying into the lives and sayings of others in order to find material for criticism and murmuring. St. John of the Cross severely condemns this vice, which is very common among devout persons. He advises souls that are accustomed to meddle in the lives of others that, if they do not correct this evil habit, they will never reach sanctity, but will fall back into a worse state:

> In order to observe the first of these—resignation—he must live in the monastery as if no other person lived there, and hence he should never meddle, either in word or in thought, with things that happen in the community, nor with those of individuals, nor should he take any note of anything concerning them, whether good or evil, nor of their personal qualities. And even if the world come to an end, he would neither remark upon them nor meddle with them, in order to preserve his tranquility of soul, remembering Lot's wife, who, because she turned her head at the cries and noise of those who were perishing, was turned into a hard stone. This the religious must observe very scrupulously, and he will thus free himself of many sins and imperfections, will preserve his tranquility and peace of soul, and will make great progress in the sight of God and men. Let great attention be paid to this, for it is of such great importance that many religious, by not observing it, have not only never profited by the other works of virtue and religion which they have performed, but have continually fallen away and have gone from bad to worse.[45]

However, it is not always forbidden to be concerned with the lives of others. Sometimes it is of obligation, especially for those who are charged by their office to correct their neighbor, as parents and lawful superiors. But this must always be done for a holy and lofty purpose, either to be edified by the good example of others and encouraged to improve one's own life, or for the spiritual good of one's neighbor by correcting his defects according to the order of charity and the duties of one's office,[46] but never merely to

[44]Cf. *ibid.*, a. 2, ad 2.

[45]St. John of the Cross, *Counsels to a Religious,* n. 2.

[46]Cf. St. Thomas, *Summa,* II-II, q. 53, a. 3.

NEGATIVE ASPECT

criticize or to murmur about one's neighbor without any reason or benefit to anyone.

Another type of curiosity, which is worse than the preceding, would be to wish to verify by means that are absolutely disproportionate (by divination, magic, spiritism, etc.) things that are hidden, such as the secrets of hearts or the future. If one should wish to verify some event by a supernatural means such as interrogating God, this would constitute the sin of tempting God, which is directly opposed to the virtue of religion.[47] St. John of the Cross insists strongly on the absolute necessity of renouncing every kind of knowledge which one could acquire by supernatural means (visions, revelations, prophecies, etc.), under pain of never arriving at the nudity of pure faith, which is the only means proportionate to the union of our intellect with God. Spiritual directors who, under any pretext, however reasonable it may seem, encourage souls to this type of desire fall into a great error for which they will have to give a strict account to God.[48]

Precipitation

Precipitation. Another great defect of the intellect is precipitation, one of the forms of the sin of imprudence.[49] St. Thomas points out why it is evil by setting up a comparison with the natural order. If we descend by leaps down the stairway, without touching each step, we act with precipitation. In like manner, in the spiritual order reason holds a superior place and the action or external work holds the lowest place. One must descend to a decision in orderly fashion by intermediate steps: memory of the past, knowledge of the present, sagacity in the consideration of possible eventualities, reason comparing one thing with another, and docility in accepting advice from others. If we omit or ignore these steps and immediately launch into a work or make a judgment without reflection, we shall have worked or acted with precipitation and imprudence.

There are other defects which are intimately connected with this, and which it is necessary to correct. *Inconsideration* judges without reflecting, without considering the state of the question, without taking account of the elements of judgment and thereby running the risk of false or incomplete judgments which give rise to a multitude of illusions and disappointments;[50] *inconstancy*, although it has its root in the will, finds its consummation in the intellect, which does not know how to follow the rules which have been given for working rightly, but lets itself be carried away by the caprice of passion.[51]

---

[47]Cf. *ibid.*, qq. 95, 96, 97.

[48]Cf. St. John of the Cross, *The Ascent of Mount Carmel,* Bk. I, Chap. 12; Bk. II, Chaps. 18-32.

[49]Cf. *ibid.*, q. 53, a. 3.

[50]Cf. *ibid.*, a. 4.

[51]Cf. *ibid.*, a. 5.

In order to combat these defects it is necessary to get into the habit of proceeding calmly and with reflection, avoiding lightness and precipitation in our judgments, and inconstancy and volubility in our manner of thinking, which denote a lack of firmness in our grasp of the principles and norms of action. We should never act without reflecting carefully and without weighing in the balance of discretion the pros and cons of all things in the eyes of God.

Attachment to one's own judgment

Attachment to one's own judgment. This is one of the forms of pride from which scarcely anyone is completely exempt. In its most acute form, it reaches the point of subjecting to one's own judgment the dogmas of faith and the decisions of lawful superiors. Even if it does not reach this extreme, it foments and preserves the spirit of division, not in the noble sense of serene exposition and a reasonable defense of some determined school or tendency which seems to possess the truth, but on the basis of mortifying the adversary by treating with disdain and irony those opinions which are contrary to our own.

There are few souls who love and serve truth above all, and whose judgments of the opinions of others are not influenced by the satisfaction of self-love and by the triumph of their own ideas, without any more reason than the fact that they are one's own ideas, or the teaching of the school to which one belongs. Such people forget that in those questions which God has left open and subject to the discussion of men, there is no philosophical or theological school that could claim that it possesses the entire truth to the exclusion of all other schools. Almost always there is to be found in the contrary opinion some part of the truth which has not been regarded sufficiently because of the prejudices with which it was examined. Intellectual sincerity, the love of truth, humility and charity urge that we listen with attention and impartiality to our opponents and that we readily grant whatever truth is to be found in their affirmations.

In private conduct it is also necessary frequently to renounce one's own judgment and to accept that of others. St. Thomas says that since prudence regards particular and concrete things to be realized, which are almost infinite in number, it is not possible for one man alone to examine all the aspects which must be taken into account in each one of these things in order to know what he should do or not do. For that reason, as regards prudence, we need to be informed and taught by others, and especially by those who are older and whose experience has taught them many things which escape the precipitous and unreflective knowledge of the young.[52]

POSITIVE PURIFICATION

Up to now we have examined the negative aspects of the purification of the intellect, or the defects which one must combat in order to destroy them completely. The positive aspect can be reduced to one point which is of

[52]Cf. *ibid.*, q. 49, a. 3, *corpus* and ad 2.

NEGATIVE ASPECT

capital importance to the Christian life: *the soul must let itself be led exclusively by the light of faith, which is the only proximate and proportionate means for the union of the intellect with God in this life.* No one has expounded this principle so forcefully as St. John of the Cross. He repeats it unceasingly in all of his works and he demonstrates it in a masterly fashion with all rigor and exactitude. The following are the fundamental points in his argumentation:

1) He begins by positing the infinite transcendence and incomprehensibility of God. The human intellect cannot comprehend the divine being:

> Before we treat of the proper and accommodated means for union with God, which is faith, it is fitting that we prove that no created thing nor imagined thing can serve the intellect as a proper medium for uniting itself with God, and that everything the intellect can attain rather serves as an impediment than a means.[53]

2) Every proximate means must have a proximate and proportionate relation with its end. Therefore, it is indispensable for the union of the intellect with God to find some proximate and proportionate means which is related to him:

> It is therefore necessary to know that, according to the rule of philosophy, all the means must be proportionate to the end, that is to say, that they must have some convenience and likeness to the end, so that it will be sufficient for them to attain the end which is desired. Whence it follows that for the intellect to be united with God in this life, as much as is possible, it must necessarily take that means which unites it with him and has a likeness to him.[54]

3) No corporeal or spiritual creature has any proximate likeness to the infinite being of God. Therefore, none of these things can serve the intellect as a proximate means for the divine union:

> Among all creatures, the highest or the lowest, there is none that comes near to God or bears any resemblance to his being. For although it is true, as theologians say, that all creatures have a certain relation to God and bear a divine impress (some more and others less, according to the greater or lesser excellence of their nature), yet there is no essential resemblance or connection between them and God; on the contrary, the distance between their being and his divine being is infinite. Hence it is impossible for the understanding to attain to God by means of creatures, whether these be celestial or earthly, because there is no proportion or resemblance between them.[55]

4) Since existing creatures cannot serve as a proximate means of the union of the intellect with God, how can creations of the phantasy or the imagination do so? They are even less able, because the concepts or images of the imagination have even less real entity than those which are known through the external senses:

---

[53]*The Ascent of Mount Carmel,* Bk. II, Chap. 8.
[54]*Loc. cit.*
[55]*Loc. cit.*

The reason for this is that the imagination cannot fashion or imagine anything whatever beyond that which it has experienced through the external senses, namely, that which it has seen with the eyes, heard with the ears, etc. At most it can only compose likenesses of those things which it has seen or heard or felt, which are of no more consequence than those which have been received by the aforementioned senses, nor are they even of as much consequence. For although a man imagines palaces of pearls and mountains of gold, because he has seen gold and pearls, all this is, in truth, less than the essence of a little gold or of a single pearl, although in the imagination it be greater in quantity and in beauty. And since, as has already been said, no created thing can bear any proportion to the being of God, it follows that nothing that is imagined in their likeness can serve as proximate means to union with him, but, as we say, quite the contrary.[56]

5) And passing beyond the world of reality and the world of imagination, will pure ideas serve as a means of union of our intellect with God? Neither can these serve, because all of them are restricted within the limits of an intelligible species which is abstracted from the data of the senses, and God cannot be restricted by any limits whatever:

Just so, all that the imagination can imagine and the intellect can receive and understand in this life is not, nor can it be, a proximate means of union with God. For if we speak of natural things, since the intellect can understand nothing but that which is contained within and comes under the category of forms and imaginings of things that are received through the bodily senses, which as we have said cannot serve as means, it can make no use of natural intelligence.[57]

6) There still remains the supernatural world. In this way, or through it, one of three things can come to the intellect: either the clear vision of God, or a clear awareness of him which is particular and distinct, or an obscure awareness which is general and indistinct. The first is not proper to this life but to the life to come, for it constitutes the beatific vision.[58] The second (visions, revelations, locutions and spiritual sentiments) cannot serve as a means or medium because "the wisdom of God, with which the intellect must be united, has no mode or manner and is not contained within any particular or distinct kind of intelligence because it is completely pure and simple."[59] There remains only the supernatural awareness of God which is obscure, general and indistinct, which is basically that which is given to us by faith. For that reason, only faith can serve as the proximate and proportionate means for the union of our intellect with God in this life:

From what has been said it is to be inferred that, in order that the intellect be prepared for this divine union, it must be pure and void of all that pertains

[56] *Ibid.*, Chap. 12.
[57] *Ibid.*, Chap. 8.
[58] *Loc. cit.*
[59] *Ibid.*, Chap. 16.

to sense, and detached and freed from all that can be clearly apprehended by the intellect, profoundly hushed and put to silence, and leaning upon faith, which alone is the proximate and proportionate means whereby the soul is united with God; for such is the likeness between itself and God that there is no other difference save that which exists between seeing God and believing in him. For even as God is infinite, so faith sets him before us as infinite; and as he is three and one, it sets him before us as three and one; and as God is darkness to our intellect, even so does faith likewise blind and dazzle our intellect. Thus by this means alone God manifests himself to the soul in divine light which surpasses all understanding. Therefore, the greater the faith of the soul, the more closely is it united with God.[60]

The value of faith

Therefore, the soul must travel in pure faith if it wishes to arrive at the perfect purification of the intellect and be intimately united with God. St. Thomas had already demonstrated that "the purification of the heart is an effect of faith."[61] The reason given by the Angelic Doctor is that the impurity of a thing consists in the fact that it is mixed with things that are more base than itself. Now it is evident that the rational creature is more worthy and has a greater dignity than all temporal and bodily creatures. It is, therefore, made impure if it is subjected to these things through love and purified of this impurity by the contrary motive, that is, when it tends to that which is above itself, which is God. And in this tendency to God, the first movement comes through faith. By the same token, the first principle of the purification of the heart is faith, which is consummated and perfected by supernatural charity.

It does not matter that faith is necessarily of things that are not seen (*de non visis*)[62] and that it is, therefore, essentially obscure and indistinct. It is precisely because of this fact that faith can give to us the only knowledge that is possible concerning the intimate life of God, because in this life it is not possible to have a clear and distinct knowledge of those things, due to the infinite transcendence of God, who cannot be expressed in any created, intelligible species. The clear knowledge of God pertains strictly to the beatific vision. In heaven we shall see God as he is (I John 3:2), without any created species but with our intellect directly united to the divine essence. Nevertheless, even in this world faith enables us to attain in some way the unfathomable mystery of the infinite life of God, although it be a dark and obscure knowledge. For that reason, the knowledge of faith is of itself immeasurably superior to all sensible and intellectual evidence which we could have of God in this life. In spite of this inevitable obscurity, faith illumines the soul and fills it with the splendors of heaven.

The entire preoccupation of the soul must, therefore, consist in making the light of faith inform one's whole life with greater intensity and in a

[60]*Ibid.,* Chap. 9.
[61]*Summa,* II-II, q. 7, a. 2.
[62]Cf. *ibid.,* q. 1, a. 4.

more perfect manner. It is necessary to contemplate all things through faith: one's life, the life of one's family and friends, the happy or unfortunate circumstances or events of life, etc. It is necessary to reach the point where one can, so to speak, lose the human vision of things and replace it with a certain divine instinct proceeding from the gifts of the Holy Ghost, with the clarity of faith, the only way in which one can see all things from the point of view of God. To contemplate all things in this manner is equivalent to contemplating them, in a certain way, as God himself contemplates them.[63]

PURIFICATION OF THE WILL

The will, also called the rational appetite, is the faculty by which we seek the good as known by the intellect. It is distinguished from the sensitive appetite, which instinctively seeks the good as known by the senses, ignoring the proper reason of goodness as such.[64] Even the animals possess a sensitive appetite, but the rational appetite is proper to intellectual beings.

PSYCHOLOGY OF THE WILL

The proper object of the will is the good proposed to it by the intellect, but in the appreciation or evaluation of the good error may creep in. The intellect can judge as a true good something which is only an apparent good, and the will, which is a blind faculty and always follows the apprehension of the intellect, will be impelled toward that object which is taken as if it were a true good.[65] This is the explanation of sin: the will seeks as a good that which in reality is evil. Every sin is consummated in the will by one's free choice, but it is rooted in an error of the intellect, which has taken as a real good that which was only good apparently (e.g., the pleasure attached to the sin). For that reason the blessed are intrinsically impeccable, because their intellect, completely occupied with the infinite truth which they contemplate, cannot fall into the slightest error; and their will, completely satiated with the infinite good which they enjoy, cannot enjoy anything apart from that good; hence sin is intrinsically impossible for the blessed.[66]

The will's acts

The proper act of the will is love, or the effective union of the will with a known good. All the movements or partial aspects of the human acts which take place in the will, such as simple volition, efficacious tendencies, consent,

[63]Cf. St. Thomas, *In Boetium, de Trinitate,* III, q. 1, ad 4.
[64]Cf. St. Thomas, *Summa,* I, q. 80, aa. 1-2.
[65]Cf. *ibid.,* I-II, q. 6, a. 1.
[66]Cf. *ibid.,* q. 5, a. 4; I, q. 94, a. 1.

NEGATIVE ASPECT

election of means, active use of the faculties and fruition, proceed from love or a consequence of love.

Love can be divided in many ways. The principal division for our purposes is the following: by reason of the object, love can be sensual or spiritual; by reason of the end, love can be natural or supernatural; by reason of the formal object or motive, love can be a love of concupiscence, of benevolence or of friendship. It is called a *love of concupiscence* when one desires the good so far as it is good for oneself (egotistic motive); it is a *love of benevolence* if one loves another precisely so far as the other is good and lovable (a most perfect and completely disinterested motive); it is a *love of friendship* if one loves his friend, not only because he is good in himself, but also because he on his part returns one's love (an intermediate love between the two). Thus the sensual man loves with a love of concupiscence the object which will give him pleasure; the blessed in heaven habitually love God with a love of benevolence, taking complacence in his infinite perfection and rejoicing that God is infinitely happy in himself;[67] and the blessed in heaven and the man sanctified by grace here on earth love God with a love of friendship under the impulse of the virtue of charity.[68]

Voluntary acts can be of two classes: elicited or imperated. They are called *elicited* if they proceed directly from the will, are emitted by the will itself, and are received under the will (e.g., to consent, to choose, to love, etc.); they are called *imperated* (commanded) acts when they are effected by some other faculty under the direction (command) of the intellect and the movement of the will (e.g., to study, to paint, to mortify oneself voluntarily, etc.). Command is essentially an act of the practical reason, because it places order in that which one must do, and only the reason can perceive order, but for the reason to move by imperating it needs the impulse of the will.[69]

NECESSITY OF PURIFICATION

As we have already seen, human nature and all its faculties were profoundly affected by original sin. The will became inclined to evil (*vulnus malitiae*).[70] Once the orientation to God had been destroyed, which previously was perfectly subjected to the control of reason, the absolute dominion of reason over the sensible faculties was also lost,[71] and it retained over them only a certain

[67]This most perfect love of God which is totally disinterested and prescinds from any advantage which could come to us is also possible in this life and has been practiced by all the saints, but it can happen only as a transitory act and not as a habitual state, for this would render the theological virtue of hope useless. The Church has condemned the contrary teaching, which was defended by Fénelon (cf. Denz. 1327).

[68]Cf. St. Thomas, *Summa,* II-II, q. 23, a. 1; cf. also *De Caritate.*

[69]Cf. *ibid.,* I-II, q. 17, a. 1.

[70]Cf. *ibid.,* q. 85, a. 3.

[71]Cf. *ibid.,* I, q. 95, a. 2.

moral power, a power of persuasion; in other words, a political power, not a despotic power.[72]

Two things necessary

Whence the necessity of a double effort involved in the rectification of the will: one required to subject the will wholly to God by means of a total submission and conformity to his divine will, the other to fortify the authority of the will with regard to the inferior faculties until it can subject them completely to itself. In other words, one must attempt to regain, at the cost of great effort and with the help of grace, that initial rectitude which the will enjoyed when it came forth from the creative hand of God. This is not an easy task, but it is one of the most important for the attaining of perfection.

We shall treat of this double aspect of the purification of the will, but for the time being we wish merely to insist on the necessity of the purification, first on the part of the will, in order to die to all external and internal things which could impede its flight toward God, through the perfect rejection of all created things, and then through death to one's own egoism by means of the perfect abnegation of self.

DETACHMENT FROM CREATURES

This is one of the conditions which is most important if one wishes to attain sanctity. St. John of the Cross reduces his whole mystical doctrine to this detachment from creatures, as the negative element, and to union with God through love as the positive element.[73] It is a fact that the soul is filled with God in the measure and to the degree that it empties itself of creatures.

The great mystic is inflexible in demanding total detachment of the soul which wishes to fly to God. Using the beautiful simile of the bird which is bound to earth with a thin cord which prevents the bird from flight,[74] he does not permit the slightest voluntary attachment to any earthly thing. His faithful disciple, Sister Elizabeth of the Trinity, wrote that any kind of desire whatever was sufficient to impede perfect union with God.[75]

The reason for the necessity of detachment from creatures for perfect union with God is given in a masterly fashion by St. John of the Cross. The following is a brief synthesis of his thought.[76]

> 1) God is all, the necessary and absolute being, most pure act without the shadow of potency, who exists of himself and possesses the absolute plenitude of being. Compared with him, creatures are nothing; they are contingent beings which have more of potency than of act.

---

[72]Cf. *ibid.,* I-II, q. 17, a. 7.

[73]Cf. *Poems,* n. 22.

[74]Cf. *The Ascent of Mount Carmel,* Bk. I, Chap. 1.

[75]Cf. Sister Elizabeth of the Trinity, *The Last Retreat,* Second Day.

[76]Cf. *The Ascent of Mount Carmel,* Bk. I, Chap. 8.

2) Two contraries cannot exist in the same subject because they mutually exclude each other. Therefore, light is incompatible with darkness and the All is incompatible with nothing.

3) If, then, creatures are nothing and darkness, and God is the All and light, it follows that the soul which wishes to be united with God must detach itself from creatures. Without this, union with God is impossible.

4) "And hence it is necessary that the way and ascent to God should consist in the ordinary care of mortifying the appetite; and the soul will more quickly arrive at a goal as it gives itself more energetically to this detachment. But until these appetites cease, the soul will not arrive at perfect union, although it may exercise many virtues, because it still does not perform those virtues with perfection, which consists in having the soul empty and naked and purified of every appetite."[77]

5) For that reason, one must weep at the ignorance of certain souls who burden themselves with extraordinary penances and many other exercises, and think that this or that will suffice for them to arrive at union with divine wisdom; such is not the case if they do not diligently endeavor to negate their appetite. If such persons would exert half the effort in mortifying their appetites, they would advance more in one month through this practice than they would in many years by means of the other exercises. Just as it is necessary that one labor over the earth if it is to bear fruit, and without labor it will bear nothing but weeds, so also mortification of the appetites is necessary if there is to be any fruit or profit in the soul. Without this, St. John dares to say that one will make no more progress than one would who would cast seed on untilled soil.[78] For that reason, the principal concern of spiritual masters should be to mortify every appetite in their disciples and to make them remain in emptiness as regards that which they desire.[79]

Negation according to St. John

St. John of the Cross develops these thoughts throughout all his writings, which teach both the negative element of detachment and the positive element of the love of God. Many persons have been frightened at the terrible negation mentioned in *The Ascent of Mount Carmel* and in *The Dark Night,* and as a result they have abandoned a system of spirituality they judge to be excessively rigorous and difficult. But apart from the fact that it is impossible to arrive at the summit of the mount except by means of the mortification of one's appetites and disordered affections (because, as St. John of the Cross points out, two contraries cannot exist in the same subject), it is necessary

[77]*Loc. cit.*

[78]Cf. *ibid.,* Chap. 8.

[79]Cf. *ibid.,* Chap. 12.

to complete the thought of the mystical doctor with the splendors of *The Spiritual Canticle* and *The Living Flame of Love,* which illumine with great clarity the dark nights described in the two preceding works.

Actually, the system of St. John of the Cross can be reduced to one important statement: God is all. His negations rest on affirmation, because they have as their object to detach the soul from the false appearances of creatures, which are nothing, in order to enable the soul, once purified and ennobled, to lose itself in the profundity of the All. He does not disdain creatures; he wishes only to withdraw the gaze from that which is imperfect and limited and enable the soul to see in creatures the traces and vestiges of the divine being. From the summit of that mountain the saint sings of the beauty of creation with lyrical accents that have never been surpassed by any other poet.

But in order to find them in God again, now purified and ennobled, it is necessary to leave the contemplation of creatures with carnal eyes and to detach oneself energetically from the bonds which hold the soul to the chains of earth. No one can arrive at the All except by the narrow path of the absolute negation of the nothing:

> In order to arrive at having pleasure in everything, desire to have pleasure in nothing.
> In order to arrive at possessing everything, desire to possess nothing.
> In order to arrive at being everything, desire to be nothing.
> In order to arrive at knowing everything, desire to know nothing.
> In order to arrive at that in which you have no pleasure, you must go by a way in which you have no pleasure.
> In order to arrive at that which you do not know, you must go by a way which you do not know.
> In order to arrive at that which you do not possess, you must go by a way that you do not possess.
> In order to arrive at that which you are not, you must go through that which you are not.
> When your mind dwells on anything, you are no longer casting yourself upon the All.
> In order to pass from the all to the All, you must deny yourself wholly in all.
> And when you come to possess it wholly, you must possess it without desiring anything.
> And if you will have anything in having all, you do not have your treasure purely in God.[80]

Orientation

St. John of the Cross does not intend to annihilate the natural tendencies of human nature by removing them from their object and leaving them suspended in nothing, but he wishes to orientate them to God, to make God the sole object of the tendency, thus reducing all of their forces to unity. It is true that this can never be attained perfectly until the soul has been

[80] *Ibid.,* Bk. I, Chap. 13.

NEGATIVE ASPECT

introduced by God himself into the obscurities of the passive nights,[81] but much can be done by one's own efforts and the help of grace. God does not usually complete the purification of the soul by means of the passive nights until the soul itself has done all that it can by using the ordinary means within its grasp. For that reason St. John of the Cross repeats with insistence that one must mortify the appetites which divide the forces of the soul to such an extent that it is spent entirely on the things of earth. When the soul shall have attained the emptiness from every creature, it will be filled with God.

PERFECT SELF-ABNEGATION

True detachment from all created things is very important and absolutely indispensable for arriving at Christian perfection.[82] But it would be of little avail to detach oneself from the bonds of external creatures if one's spirit had not likewise been detached from one's own ego, which constitutes the greatest of all the obstacles to one's free flight to God.

St. Thomas states that egoism or disordered self-love is the origin and root of all sin. He says this because every sin proceeds from the disordered appetite for some temporal good, but this would not be possible if we did not love ourselves in a disorderly fashion, for it is for ourselves that we seek the good in question. Whence it is manifest that disordered self-love is the cause of every sin.[83] From it proceed the three concupiscences of which St. John speaks (I John 2:16): the flesh, the eyes and pride of life, which are a compendium of all disorders.[84]

Disorders of self-love

Disordered self-love has constructed the city of the world against the city of God, as St. Augustine points out: "Two loves have erected two cities: self-love, carried to the extreme of disdain of God, has built the city of the world; the love of God, carried to the point of disdain for one's self, has constructed the city of God. The one glories in itself; the other glories in the Lord."[85]

---

[81]He expressly says this, and it is one of his strongest arguments to demonstrate that Christian perfection cannot be attained outside the mystical life, in which all those passive purifications occur (cf. *The Dark Night,* Bk. I, Chap. 7).

[82]Note that the essence of detachment lies in the affection of the will rather than the physical lack of created things. Simple material poverty is not a virtue, but only the love of poverty, which can be found even in those who materially possess many things. The same thing must be said of detachment in general. Material detachment is undoubtedly a great help, but the most important and necessary is the formal detachment of affection, which consists in a detachment of the will, regardless of whether or not one possesses created things (cf. *The Ascent of Mount Carmel,* Bk. I, Chap. 3).

[83]Cf. *Summa,* I-II, q. 77, a. 4.

[84]Cf. *ibid.,* a. 5.

[85]St. Augustine, *The City of God,* Bk. XIV, Chap. 28.

St. Augustine has pointed out in the last words of this quotation the most pernicious tendency of self-love. Precisely because it is the root of all sins, the manifestations of self-love are varied and almost infinite; but there is no result so harmful for one's own sanctification as that notion of glorifying oneself, for it constitutes one's ego as a center of gravity around which all other things must rotate. Some souls seek themselves in everything, even in holy things: in prayer, which they prolong when they find sweetness and consolation in it, but which they abandon when they experience desolation or aridity; in the reception of the sacraments, which they seek only for sensible consolation; in spiritual direction, which they consider a note of distinction and in which, therefore, they always seek the director who is most popular, or who will let them live in peace with their egoistic values and selfish aims; in the very desire for sanctification, which they do not subordinate to the greater glory of God and the good of souls, but which they direct to themselves as the best ornament of their souls here on earth and as the source of increased happiness and glory in heaven. We would never finish if we were to attempt to list the infinite manifestations of self-love and egoism.

The soul that aspires to perfect union with God must strive energetically against no other enemies as against its own self-love, which subtly penetrates even holy things. It must examine the true motive for its actions, continually rectify its intentions, and not place as its goal or the goal of all its activities and efforts anything other than the glory of God and the perfect fulfillment of his divine will. It must keep constantly in mind the decisive words of Christ himself, who makes perfect self-abnegation the indispensable condition for following him: "If anyone wishes to come after me, let him deny himself, take up his cross daily, and follow me" (Luke 9:23).

6: PASSIVE PURIFICATIONS

Up to this point we have been examining the active purifications which the soul can effect by its own efforts with the help of grace in order to purge itself of its defects. Now we shall consider the part which God reserves for himself in the purification of the soul: the passive purifications, which are divided into the night of the senses and the night of the spirit.

THEIR NECESSITY

This is one of the most important points in the theology of Christian perfection; its explanation will determine whether or not an individual has an accurate view of the theology of the supernatural life.

The thesis

In order to proceed with clarity and precison, we shall state and prove our thesis on the necessity of the passive purification in view of Christian perfection: *The full purification of the soul cannot be attained without passive purifications.*

St. John of the Cross

The thought of St. John of the Cross is most clear, and his words are so explicit and decisive that they do not leave the slightest doubt as to their meaning. In the first chapter of the first book of *The Dark Night,* St. John of the Cross treats of the imperfections of beginners. After having described these imperfections in the chapters which follow, he terminates with the following words:

> Let it suffice here to have described these imperfections, among the many to be found in the lives of those who are in this state of beginners, so that it may be seen how much they need God to set them in the state of proficients. This he does by leading them into the dark night of which we now speak, wherein he weans them from the breasts of these sweetnesses and pleasures, gives them pure aridities and interior darkness, takes from them all these unessentials and puerilities, and by a very different means causes them to gain the virtues. For however assiduously the beginner in mortification exercises himself in all these actions and passions, he can never completely succeed—far from it—until God shall effect it in him passively by means of the purgation of said night.[1]

[1]*The Dark Night,* Bk. I, Chap. 7.

The thought of St. John of the Cross as here stated leaves no doubt as to his teaching. Beginners cannot purify themselves entirely, however much they exert themselves in this activity. Even if they do all that is humanly possible, it is necessary that God effect the purification in them passively.[2]

But who are these beginners who need the passive purification in order to attain the complete purification of their souls? St. John of the Cross states this explicitly at the beginning of his work, *The Dark Night*:

> Souls begin to enter into this dark night when God takes them from the state of beginners, which is the state of those who meditate on the spiritual way, and begins to place them in the state of the advanced, which is that of the contemplative, so that by passing this way they may arrive at the state of the perfect, which is the state of divine union of the soul with God.[3]

For St. John of the Cross, those who practice meditation, which is the mental prayer proper to ascetics, are beginners in the spiritual life. In order to ascend to the category of the advanced or proficient, it is necessary that they pass through the first passive purification (the night of the senses) and begin contemplative prayer. And to reach the height of perfection, which is the divine union of the soul with God, it is necessary that they should have suffered the terrible passive purification which constitutes the night of the spirit.[4] To speak of perfection and sanctity without the soul's having endured any of the passive purifications is to depart radically from the doctrine of St. John of the Cross.

It cannot be said, as they have said who are defenders of the double way, that the necessity of passive purifications as taught by St. John of the Cross pertains only to those souls who are to attain perfection by the mystical way

---

[2]St. John of the Cross repeats this same doctrine in many other places. The following citation is perhaps even more expressive than those which we have already quoted: "But neither from these imperfections nor from those others can the soul be perfectly purified until God brings it into the passive purgation of that dark night, of which we shall soon speak. But the soul should labor, so far as it can, on its own account, so that it may purge and perfect itself, and thus merit being led by God into that divine care wherein it is healed of all things that it was itself unable to cure. For however greatly the soul labors by itself, it cannot actively purify itself so as to be prepared for the divine union of the perfection of love unless God takes its hand and purges it in that dark fire of love" (*The Dark Night*, Bk. I, Chap. 3).

[3]*The Dark Night,* Bk. I, Chap. 1.

[4]In speaking of the difference between the night of the senses and the night of the spirit, St. John says: "The night of sense is common and comes to many, and these are the beginners; the night of the spirit is the portion of very few, and these are the ones who are already practiced and proficient. . . . The first purgation or night is bitter and terrible to sense; the second bears no comparison with it, for it is horrible and terrifying for the spirit" (*The Dark Night,* Bk. I, Chap. 8). Later he explains in detail the necessity of the night of the spirit to reach the divine union (cf. Bk. II, Chaps. 1-3).

NEGATIVE ASPECT

and not to those who are to reach perfection by the ascetical way. This subterfuge is of no avail, since St. John of the Cross teaches that, however much the soul may exert itself, it cannot correct its imperfections unless God does this for the soul in a passive manner. The thought of St. John of the Cross is clear and his words are explicit. Therefore, one or the other conclusion must be accepted: either we must say that there is a perfection which is filled with imperfections (which is manifestly a contradiction), or there is no other perfection than that which results in the passive purification and is manifestly a mystical perfection.

Theological proof

In addition to the indisputable authority of St. John of the Cross, theological reason fully confirms his teaching. As a result of original sin, human nature is strongly inclined to evil. Egoism, which is imbedded in the very depths of our being, disturbs the clarity of our intellect and impedes the objective view of things, especially when self-love makes us see things through the perspective of its own evaluations.

Let us read what a contemporary theologian has written in this regard:

> There are countless vices and defects which beset our depraved nature. The majority of them escape the vision or consideration of beginners, and even of the advanced and the perfect. But if one considers the matter well, we scarcely perform a single work of those which seem good to us which is not filled with imperfection and sins by reason of our self-love and our attachment to earthly things. The result is that even souls that are already purified and apparently free from such defects are surprised when our Lord, with extraordinary light, reveals to them the multitude of their defects, which are comparable to the thousands of specks which the direct ray of the sun discloses in a glass of water, to use an expression of St. Teresa. By the same token, all the effort and labor of the soul in the active purgation of its vices is insufficient for perfecting the soul, because the soul neither recognizes all of the defects which are to be corrected nor does it reach down to the very depth and root of those defects.
>
> Consequently, it is necessary that there come from outside the soul an action that is more energetic and efficacious for removing from the depth of the soul all the dross and stain that are hidden there, and this is what we call the passive purgation. This does not represent nor does it signify a state of spiritual inertia or inactive suffering; it signifies merely that the purifying action is received in the soul without the soul itself causing it, although the soul must actively co-operate in this passive purgation. God in his adorable providence, wishing at any cost to have the soul for himself, lovingly sends to the soul new and efficacious means by which it is weaned away from creatures and self-love so that it can give itself entirely to his divine majesty. The greater the purity the Lord requires of the soul, and the less effort the soul had exerted in active purification, so usually the more painful and purgative are these means. Thus is fulfilled to the letter what St. Augustine and the Angelic Doctor teach in regard to sin, namely, that what was lacking by reason of action must be supplied by suffering or pain.[5]

[5]Naval, C.F.M., *Curso de ascética y mística,* n. 138. Cf. also St. Thomas, *Summa,* I-II, q. 87, aa. 1, 6.

PASSIVE PURIFICATIONS

The passive purifications are, therefore, necessary from the very nature of things. Naturally, not all souls will suffer them with the same rigor, because there are many degrees of impurity which have been contracted and there are many grades of perfection to which various souls are destined. But in every case, as Father Garrigou-Lagrange states, in order to conquer egoism, sensuality, natural impetuosity, self-love, the immoderate desire for sensible consolations, intellectual pride and whatever opposes the spirit of faith, and to arrive at a perfect love of God with all one's heart and all one's soul and all one's strength and all one's mind, and to remain firm, patient and persevering in charity, come what may, it is absolutely indispensable that there be a complete and total renewal of the soul through profound and painful passive purifications which cause the soul to progress in the mystical life, which is open to all souls as the normal development and expansion of sanctifying grace.[6]

Value of this teaching

This doctrine has the advantage of opening wide horizons to souls and of saving them from many dangers and illusions into which they could easily fall if they were obliged to remain, contrary to the attraction of grace, in that which has been called the ordinary way of sanctity. Some authors do not look with sympathy on the mystical way because they believe it to be filled with dangers and pitfalls, but in reality the contrary is true.[7] In the mystical state the souls are governed in a special manner by the Holy Spirit himself, operating through his precious gifts and divine motion. Illumined by the light of contemplation with the splendors of heaven, they discover much better their nothingness and their misery, at the same time that they see the snares of their enemies and their own sensuality. They are much more cautious, prudent and docile to their spiritual masters precisely because of the passive purifications to which they have been subjected before they entered or made progress in the mystical state.

---

[6]Reginald Garrigou-Lagrange, O.P., *Christian Perfection and Contemplation*, Chap. 3, art. 6.

[7]With good reason does St. Teresa exclaim, when speaking of the life of prayer: "Anyone who would tell you that this is a danger, consider him himself to be a danger, and flee from him; and do not forget that by chance it is necessary for you to receive this counsel. It would be a danger not to have humility and the other virtues; but to consider the way of prayer a dangerous way is something that God would never say. The devil seems to have invented these fears in order to cause some souls to fall who had been practicing prayer. And see the blindness of the world which does not consider the many thousands who have fallen into heresy and other evils without having prayer, but having many distractions; and in the multitude of these, if the devil, to better his business, has caused some souls to fall who practiced prayer, he has put such fear into others as regards the things of virtue. The souls that use this pretext for freeing themselves and protecting themselves are literally avoiding the good in order to free themselves from evil. I have never seen such an evil invention, and it seems certainly to come from the devil" (*The Way of Perfection*, Chap 21, nn. 7-8).

NEGATIVE ASPECT

There is, therefore, no doubt that the passive purifications, which according to the unanimous teaching of all the schools of spirituality are of a mystical order, are necessary and indispensable in one form or another for the full purification of the soul, and for arriving at complete Christian perfection.[8] Let us now see in particular the two principal manifestations of these passive purifications, which St. John of the Cross calls the night of the senses and the night of the spirit.

THE NIGHT OF THE SENSES

ITS NATURE

The night of the senses consists in a prolonged series of aridities, dryness and sensible obscurity produced in an imperfect subject by initial, infused contemplation.[9] Psychologically, it is characterized by that series of profound and persistent aridities which submerge the soul in a very painful state and severely test its perseverance in the desire for sanctification. It is so difficult to support this crisis of the senses that the great majority of souls draw back in fear and abandon the life of prayer.[10]

---

[8]Even Father Scaramelli recognizes this necessity. These are his own words: "Man cannot, however much he tries, succeed by means of his own efforts in reforming the disorders of his nature, corrupted by the sin of Adam, and frequently even more corrupted by himself through the sins and evil habits which he has contracted. Consequently, he cannot, with the ordinary powers of grace, properly dispose himself for the gift of infused contemplation. It is necessary that God place his omnipotent hand to the work, and by means of the purifications which the mystics call passive bring to completion the reform of man's natural disordered and corrupt state, and in this way make him apt for the divine communications" (*Directorium mysticum,* Tr. 5, Chap. 1, n. 10).

[9]We use the term "infused contemplation" for lack of a more accurate term. The passive purgation does not require that the individual have habitual contemplative prayer, for it may happen that the habitual activity of the gifts of a given soul is not contemplative but apostolic or active. The point at issue here is that the passive purgations always involve an illumination of the intellect, caused by the Holy Ghost operating through his gifts.

[10]The statement of Father Godínez, undoubtedly an exaggerated one, is well-known: "Of a thousand souls whom God calls to perfection, scarcely ten correspond with his grace; and of a hundred persons whom God calls to contemplation, ninety-five fail; and for that reason I say that many are called but very few are chosen" (*Práctica de la teología mística,* Bk. VII, Chap. 1). Without going this far, we can say that the failure of many souls who are called to perfection by God is due to their lack of spirit for suffering the painful passive purifications of the senses and of the spirit.

The cause of this night is the initial infused contemplation which is received by an imperfect subject who is not fully prepared for it. These two elements are absolutely necessary. There could be an active or ascetical purification without infused contemplation, but not a passive or mystical purification. And without the imperfect disposition of the soul, the contemplation would not cause torment, obscurity or aridity, but delight, light and ineffable sweetness. This requires a fuller explanation.

PASSIVE PURIFICATIONS

THE CAUSES

No one has explained with such precision and clarity as has St. John of the Cross the nature, necessity, causes and effects of the passive purifications. The first book of his *The Dark Night* is a complete treatise in which one can study the fundamental rules which regulate the night of the senses. We shall recall some of the fundamental points which indicate the direction of his thoughts.

Above all, it is necessary to note that St. John of the Cross includes under the word "senses," not only the external and internal senses, but also the sensitive appetite and the discursive intellect, so far as it uses the imagination to construct its discursus.[11]

St. John begins by describing the sweetness which beginners usually experience in the service of God, and he explains it by the beautiful metaphor of the mother who nurses her child:

> It must be known, then, that the soul, after it has been definitely converted to the service of God, is, as a rule, spiritually nurtured and caressed by God, even as is the tender child by its loving mother, who warms it with the heat of her bosom and nurtures it with sweet milk and soft and pleasant food, and carries it and caresses it in her arms; but as the child grows bigger, the mother gradually ceases caressing it, and, hiding her tender love, puts bitter aloes upon her sweet breast, sets down the child from her arms and makes it walk upon its feet, so that it may lose the habits of a child and betake itself to more important and substantial occupations.[12]

Beginners often make bad use of this sweet communication which they receive from God at the beginning of their spiritual life. They become strongly attached to the sensible consolations, and, without realizing it, the delight and sweetness which they find in the exercises and practices of devotion are the principal motive and cause for which they practice them. On feeling themselves so favored by God, their weak virtue makes them think that they are already saints, or not far from it. As a result, there springs up in them great imperfection as regards the seven capital sins, which St. John of the Cross describes with a very acute analysis, which one should read and meditate in the words of the saint himself.[13]

---

[11]*The Dark Night,* Bk. I, Chaps. 6 and 9.
[12]*Ibid.,* Bk. I, Chap. 1.
[13]*Ibid.,* Chaps. 2-7.

NEGATIVE ASPECT

A purification of such weakness and misery is necessary. And since those souls would not themselves ever begin such a purification, because they are to a great extent ignorant of their own imperfection and could never effect a complete purification by their own efforts, even if they did recognize their faults,[14] God intervenes with the first light of infused contemplation which, falling upon a subject so strongly attached to the sensible and dealing with a spiritual communication which is impressed immediately upon the intellect, necessarily produces obscurity of the senses, emptiness, negation and a kind of depression. The soul is then in the presence of the night of the senses. Let us turn again to the words of St. John of the Cross:

> Since, then, the conduct of these beginners upon the way of God is ignoble and has much to do with their love of self and their own inclinations, God desires to lead them farther. He seeks to bring them out of that ignoble kind of love to a higher degree of love for him, to free them from the ignoble exercises of sense and meditation (with which, as we have said, they seek God so unworthily and in so many ways that are unbefitting) and to lead them to a kind of spiritual exercise wherein they can commune with him more abundantly and are freed more completely from imperfections. For they have now had practice for some time in the way of virtue and have persevered in meditation and prayer, and because of the sweetness and pleasure they have therein found, they have lost their love of the things of the world and have gained some degree of spiritual strength in God. This has enabled them to some extent to refrain from creature desire, so that for God's sake they are now able to suffer a light burden and a little aridity without turning back to a time they found more pleasant. When they are going about these spiritual exercises with the greatest delight and pleasure, and when they believe that the sun of divine favor is shining most brightly upon them, God turns all this light of theirs into darkness and shuts against them the door and the source of the sweet spiritual water which they were tasting in God whenever and for as long as they desired. . . . And thus he leaves them so completely in the dark that they know not whither to go with their sensible imagination and meditation, for they cannot advance a step in meditation, as they were accustomed to do before, their inward senses being submerged in this night and left with such dryness that not only do they experience no pleasure and consolation in spiritual things and good exercises in which they were wont to find their delights and pleasures, but instead they find insipidity and bitterness in the things mentioned. For, as I have said, God now sees that they have grown a little and are becoming strong enough to lay aside their swaddling clothes and be taken from the gentle breast; so he sets them down from his arms and teaches them to walk on their own feet, which they feel to be very strange, for everything seems to be going wrong with them.[15]

Infused contemplation

St. John of the Cross expressly states that the cause of this emptiness and insipidity of the senses is infused contemplation, when he explains the signs by which the soul can know whether or not it has entered into the night of the senses:

[14] *Ibid.*, Chap. 7.

[15] *Ibid.*, Bk. I, Chap. 8.

The third sign whereby this purgation of sense may be recognized is that the soul can no longer meditate or reflect in the imaginative sphere of sense as it used to do, however much it may attempt to do so. For God now begins to communicate himself to it, no longer through sense, as he did before, by means of reflections which joined and sundered its knowledge, but by pure spirit, into which consecutive reflections cannot enter. But he communicates himself to it by an act of simple contemplation, to which neither the exterior nor the interior senses of the lower part of the soul can attain. From this time forward, therefore, imagination and fancy can find no support in any meditation and can gain no foothold by means of it.[16]

SIGNS OF THE DARK NIGHT

How can one discern the presence of the night of the senses and distinguish it from the dryness or aridity which may be caused by other reasons, such as dissipation of the soul, bodily indisposition, influence of the devil, etc.? The first author to speak of these things was the great German mystic, Tauler.[17] St. John of the Cross makes them even more precise.[18]

1) The first sign is that the soul finds delight or consolation neither in the things of God nor in any created thing. If the soul were to find consolation in the latter, it is evident that its distaste for the things of God would be due to a dissipation of the soul. The lukewarm find no consolation or delight in the things of God, but in the things of the world. But since this universal dryness or distaste could come from some indisposition of the body which causes one to lose one's taste for everything, it is necessary to add the second sign.

2) The second sign is that ordinarily the memory is fixed on God with great care, but the soul thinks that, rather than serving God, it is falling back, because of its lack of taste for the things of God. One can see that the distaste does not proceed from lukewarmness, because it is the nature of lukewarmness not to have any interior solicitude for the things of God. And if it comes from some bodily infirmity, everything becomes distasteful and there is not even any desire to serve God, but the desire remains in the dryness of the passive purification. The devil on his part does not arouse any desire to serve God. For that reason this second sign is one of the clearest and most unmistakable.

[16] *Ibid.*, Chap. 9. The first sign of the night of the senses is that the soul finds no pleasure or consolation in the things of God, although it also fails to find any satisfaction in created things. The second sign is that the memory is centered upon God with great solicitude, but the soul thinks it is falling back because it finds no sweetness in the things of God. Although St. John of the Cross says that during the night of the senses the soul can find no support in any meditation, he says later (Bk. I, Chap. 9) that this night of the senses is not usually continuous, so that sometimes the soul can meditate and at other times it cannot.

[17] Cf. Tauler, *Institutiones divinae,* Chap. 35.

[18] Cf. *The Dark Night,* Bk. I, Chap. 9; *The Ascent of Mount Carmel,* Bk. II, Chap. 13.

NEGATIVE ASPECT

3) The third sign is the inability to meditate or use reasoning by means of the imagination as one formerly did. The reason for this impotency is due to the initial infused contemplation, as St. John of the Cross states in the text which we have already cited.

When these three signs are all verified in a clear manner, the soul and the spiritual director can conclude that they are in the presence of the night of the senses and can act accordingly. But for greater certitude, we shall investigate the matter further in order to verify with certainty whether the dryness and the aridity which the soul experiences in this state are due to the night of the senses or to one of the other causes mentioned above.

If it is an effect of lukewarmness which has overtaken the soul, it can be known very easily, because this distaste for the things of God will be accompanied by a strong inclination for recreation and worldly diversion in which one finds his pleasure and well-being, together with a great dissipation of soul which sometimes takes little account of the danger of mortal sin, while the soul gives itself to venial sin without any resistance. The remedy for this is to repent sincerely for the evil done and to return again with new fervor to the road of the spiritual life.

If it is a question of mental infirmity or nervous unbalance, it is not difficult to distinguish it from the dryness and aridity of the night of the senses. The following text is significant:

> To distinguish neurasthenia from the passive purification, we should note that the most frequent symptoms in neurasthenics are the following: almost continual fatigue, even when they have not worked, accompanied by a feeling of prostration, of discouragement; habitual headaches. . . ; insomnia, to the extent that the neurasthenic wakes up more tired than when he went to bed; difficulty in exercising the intellectual faculties and in maintaining attention; impressionability (intense emotions for very slight causes), which leads the sufferer to believe that he has illnesses that he does not really have; excessive self-analysis even to minute details, and continual preoccupation not to become ill.
>
> Neurasthenics are, however, not imaginary invalids; the powerlessness they experience is real, and it would be very imprudent to urge them to disregard their fatigue and work to the limit of their strength. What they lack is not will but power.
>
> The causes of neurasthenia may be organic, like infections, endocrine or liver troubles, pre-paralysis; but often the causes are psychical: intellectual overloading, moral worries, painful emotions, which constitute too heavy a load for the nervous system. Even in these last cases, where the cause of the disease is mental, the illness itself affects the organism. For this reason neurasthenics must absolutely be made to rest; and they must be progressively led to perform easy tasks proportionate to their strength, and be encouraged.
>
> We should also note that psychoneuroses may be associated with a developed intellectual life and a lofty moral life. . . . But we see also that the passive night is distinguished from this state of nervous fatigue by the second sign (the soul ordinarily keeps the memory of God with solicitude and painful

anxiety for fear it may be falling back), and by the third sign (the quasi-impossibility to meditate, but the ability to keep a simple and loving gaze on God, the beginning of infused contemplation). The ardent desire for God and for perfection, which is manifested by these signs, distinguishes notably this passive purgation from neurasthenia, which may sometimes co-exist with it.[19]

If it is a question of diabolical temptation or disturbance, which God permits sometimes as a means of purifying a soul, it will be known from the fact that the aridity is accompanied by strong, sinful suggestions of an unusual tenacity, together with an instinctive horror of the soul toward such suggestions. The action of the evil one has for its object to disturb the peace and tranquility of the soul and to withdraw it from the practice of prayer. The soul will conquer the devil by insisting, in spite of all its sensible repugnance, on its exercises of piety, and by putting to use the other methods for conquering the devil which we have already indicated when we treated of diabolical obsession and temptation.

It should be remembered that sometimes it is possible that one or another of these other causes may coincide with the true night of the senses, and especially the second or third cause. In this case, a careful and penetrating analysis is required in order to discern what pertains to one or another cause and to combat it with the proper remedies. Sometimes also there will be joined to the night of the senses accessory or concomitant trials of various kinds. On the part of the devil there are terrible temptations against faith, hope and charity; strong suggestions against purity accompanied by abominable phantasms in the imagination; a spirit of blasphemy which is so violent and strong that at some times one is almost forced to pronounce the words, and this is a grave torment to the soul, as St. John of the Cross states; obscurities which fill the soul with a thousand scruples and perplexities, and other similar afflictions.[20] On the part of men there are often persecutions and ridicule, sometimes from the good, which is one of the greatest tribulations which one is forced to suffer, as St. Peter of Alcántara told St. Teresa of Avila,[21] or one's own superior or friends or spiritual director may torment the soul by judging its state to be one of lukewarmness or by not being able to discover the proper remedies to alleviate its condition. Lastly, there may be infirmities, misfortunes, the loss of one's good name or friends or possessions, etc. It would seem at times that heaven and earth have conspired against the poor soul which feels so discouraged, and that God is permitting all of these things in order to detach it completely from the things of earth and to remind it that it can do nothing without him and how much it needs his divine mercy and assistance.

---

[19]Reginald Garrigou-Lagrange, O.P., *The Three Ages of the Interior Life,* II, pp. 52-53.

[20]*The Dark Night,* Bk. I, Chap. 14.

[21]Cf. *The Life,* Chap. 30.

NEGATIVE ASPECT

Not all souls suffer the night of the senses to such a rigorous and severe degree. It depends on the grade of perfection to which God intends to elevate the soul, the greater or less number of imperfections from which the soul must be purified, the forces and energies of the soul itself, and its docility and patience in supporting this painful trial. In practice there are always degrees of more or less in these purifications; moreover, it must be admitted that God always gives his grace and strength in the measure that is needed by the soul.

NORMS OF CONDUCT

But when the three signs of the night of the senses are present in a clear manner, the soul is definitely passing through this passive purification. Therefore, we shall now point out the principal norms of conduct which the soul should observe during this state. The soul will work prudently if it attempts to follow these rules.

Submission

1) Complete and loving submission to the will of God, accepting with patience and resignation the painful trial for as long a time as God decrees. The soul should not consider this purgative state as something evil but see in it a means of fortifying itself and of making progress in the spiritual life. This is the advice given by St. John of the Cross:

> It is well for those who find themselves in this condition to take comfort, to persevere in patience, and to be in no wise afflicted. Let them trust in God, who does not abandon those that seek him with a simple and right heart and will not fail to give them what is needful for the road until he brings them into the clear and true light of love. This last he will give them by means of that other dark night, that of the spirit, if they merit his bringing them into it.[22]

Perseverance

2) Perseverance in prayer in spite of all difficulty, in imitation of Christ in the Garden of Gethsemane, who even in his agony prayed with greater intensity (Luke 22:43). Prayer in the midst of these terrible aridities is a veritable torment for the soul, and only by means of a violent force exerted upon oneself can the soul persevere in it; but it is necessary that the soul should do so, asking God for strength, if it does not wish to fall back and lose everything. This is the point at which the greater number of souls turn back. Tormented by those agonies of the dark night, they abandon the life of prayer when they were on the point of receiving the first rays of the rising sun which would have inundated their souls with the splendors of heaven and would have enabled them to make giant strides along the road to sanctity. But it is necessary that the soul know how to conduct itself in prayer, for it has now begun to enter upon a new type of prayer which is very different from its former prayer, and it would be a great imprudence to wish to maintain at any cost the former method of prayer.

[22]*The Dark Night,* Bk. I, Chap. 10.

Quietude

3) The soul should remain in peace and quiet, content simply with a loving gaze on God, without any particular consideration and without any desire for delight or sensation. The reason is that the soul is receiving in a pure spirit the light of infused contemplation, which has nothing to do with discursive methods of ascetical prayer or the meditation which was previously practiced. Whence, if the soul attempts to continue discursive meditation, it will be impossible to perceive the light of contemplation, nor will it attain the meditation it is striving for, because now is not the time for it.

For that reason quietude of soul is absolutely necessary, without any further exercise than that of a simple and loving awareness or turning to God without any particular consideration and without wishing to feel or perceive God by means of the sensible consolations which were formerly experienced in ascetical prayer, for these are incompatible with contemplation. As St. John of the Cross points out:

> And although further scruples may come to them—that they are wasting their time and that it would be well for them to do something else, because they can neither do nor think anything in prayer—let them suffer these scruples and remain in peace. . . . If such a soul should desire to make any effort of its own with its interior faculties, it will hinder and lose the blessings which . . . God is instilling into it and impressing upon it. . . . And thus, when the soul desires to remain in inner ease and peace, any operation or affection in which it may seek to indulge will distract it and disquiet it and make it conscious of aridity and emptiness of sense, for the more a soul endeavors to find support in affection and knowledge, the more will it feel the lack of these, which cannot be supplied to it upon that road.
>
> For these reasons such a soul should pay no heed if the operations of its faculties become lost to it; it should rather desire that this happen quickly. For by not hindering the operation of infused contemplation which God is bestowing upon it, it can receive this with more peaceful abundance and cause its spirit to be enkindled and burn with the love which this dark and secret contemplation brings with it and sets firmly in the soul. For contemplation is naught else than a secret, peaceful and loving infusion from God which, if it be permitted, enkindles the soul with the spirit of love.[23]

The soul should, therefore, not force itself to meditation. It should remain tranquil before God with a simple loving gaze, without thinking of anything in particular. And although it may seem to the soul that it is wasting time and going backward, it should remain in this state during the whole period that is devoted to prayer. The soul would actually be going back if it were at this time to return to the discursive use of its faculties. And yet the soul should remember that in the beginning it will not perceive any special attraction of the Holy Spirit to remain quiet and

[23]*Ibid.*, Bk. I, Chap. 23.

tranquil. In this case, as St. John of the Cross advises,[24] it ought to practice meditation in the usual manner, in order not to remain without the one or the other. But as soon as the soul encounters difficulty in the operations of the faculties and perceives a strong desire to remain in loving attention to God by means of a simple gaze and without any particular consideration, it should then let itself be led by this impulse of grace. The soul is then receiving infused contemplation, and to try at that time to continue its practice of meditation would be to lose everything.

Docility

4) Docility to a prudent and experienced director. At no other time is the advice of a prudent spiritual director so necessary as in this crisis. In the midst of its darkness and obscurity, the soul does not dare to seek a remedy for the evils which afflict it, and if, instead of a prudent director who will inspire the soul to remain tranquil and at peace, with that simple loving gaze of which we have spoken, the soul meets one who will tell it to go back, the pain and the agony will be increased to such an extent that the soul feels as if it would die.[25] The result of this mistaken direction will be a true setback in the spiritual life.

In this regard St. John of the Cross warns:

> These souls turn back at such a time if there is none who understands them; they abandon the road or lose courage or at the least they are hindered from going further by the great trouble which they take in advancing along the road of meditation and discursus. Thus they fatigue and overwork their nature, imagining that they are failing through negligence or sin, but the trouble that they are taking is quite useless, for God is now leading them by another road, which is that of contemplation and very different from the first; for the one is of meditation and discursus, and the other belongs neither to imagination nor to discursus.[26]

The soul should therefore understand that, if it wants to make progress in perfection, it must be careful into whose hands it places itself, because as the master is, so also shall be the disciple.[27] This is the greatest harm that could befall a soul, and yet it is so frequent that one will scarcely find a spiritual director who will not do this to the soul which God is beginning to lead into this type of contemplation.[28]

Let the soul remember that God does not abandon anyone, and certainly not the soul that sincerely desires to sanctify itself in order to give glory to God. If the soul does not have a spiritual director or does not have as excellent a one as would be desirable, God will supply in other ways as long as the soul

---

[24]Cf. *The Ascent of Mount Carmel,* Bk. II, Chap. 13; cf. also St. Teresa, *Interior Castle,* Fourth Mansions, Chap. 3.

[25]Cf. *The Ascent of Mount Carmel,* Prologue.

[26]*The Dark Night,* Bk. I, Chap. 10.

[27]Cf. *The Living Flame,* Chap. 3.

[28]*Ibid.*, Chap. 23.

remains humble and does not seek its own interests but seeks only the will of God in all things. What the soul should do when it perceives in itself the signs which we have given, is to remain tranquil and, with its loving gaze fixed on God, return to meditation without the slightest force or violence. God will take care of the rest.

EFFECTS OF THE DARK NIGHT

St. John of the Cross examines the great benefits which are produced in the soul by the night of the senses. The following is a summary of his teaching, taken from *The Dark Night,* Chapters 12 and 13.

1) Knowledge of one's self and one's misery on finding oneself so full of obscurity and weakness.
2) Greater respect and courtesy toward God than one had when one enjoyed sensible consolation.
3) More vivid light concerning the grandeur and excellence of God.
4) Profound humility upon seeing oneself so wretched.
5) Love of neighbor.
6) Submission and obedience.
7) Purification of avarice, lust and spiritual gluttony, and purification of anger, envy and sloth.
8) Recollection in God with a fear of falling back.
9) Exercise of the virtues.
10) Liberty of spirit in which one enjoys the fruits of the Holy Ghost.
11) Victory against the three enemies of the soul: the world, the flesh and the devil.

In the sight of the precious fruits which are obtained through the obscurities and agonies of the dark night of the senses, the soul considers itself blessed beyond measure and goes forth "to set out upon the road and the way of the spirit, which is that of progressives and proficients, and which, by another name, is called the way of illumination or infused contemplation, wherein God himself feeds and refreshes the soul, without meditation,"[29] having all of the lower appetites and the passions purified and held under subjection.

DURATION OF PURGATIONS

The duration of these painful trials of the night of the senses will vary in different cases. St. John of the Cross remarks that it depends upon the degree of love to which God wishes to raise the soul and the greater or less dross of imperfections from which the soul must be purified. God does not purify weak and flaccid souls with such intensity and profundity as he does the stronger, but there are alternate periods of light and obscurity so that weak souls will not become discouraged and fall back and seek the consolation of the world.[30]

[29] *The Dark Night,* Bk. I, Chap. 14.
[30] *Ibid.,* Chap. 14.

NEGATIVE ASPECT

These alternating periods of light and darkness are frequent in the spiritual life. Some souls pass through the night of senses without being able to know definitely and clearly when the night began and when it ended. As happens in the natural order, day and night alternate in such souls. The director must take into account this possibility so that he will not be deceived concerning the true state of the soul. But when God wishes to raise a soul to a very high degree of perfection, he is wont to subject it for a long time and with great intensity to these painful purifications of the senses. Cardinal Bona says that St. Francis of Assisi spent ten years in these purgations; St. Teresa, eighteen years; St. Clare of Montefalco, fifteen years; St. Catherine of Bologna, five years; St. Magdalen of Pazzi, five years at one time and then later sixteen years more.[31] These periods were, of course, interspersed with short intervals of sensible consolations in order to enable the soul to breathe a little and to regain its strength in order to follow through with the purification. Such is the working of God's ordinary providence, which is filled with sweetness and peace.

Is it lawful to ask God to shorten this painful trial? If it were done in a purely conditional manner and with perfect submission to the will of God ("Father, if it is possible, let this cup pass away from me; yet, not as I will, but as thou willest"), it would not be wrong to do so. But it is better to abandon oneself entirely to God and accept whatever he decrees and for as long a period as he desires. It should be remembered that the night of the senses is not an evil, but a painful trial from which the greatest goods follow. The best formula for any sorrowful or joyful situation in the spiritual life is that which was taught to us by Christ himself: "Thy will be done on earth as it is in heaven" (Matt. 6:10).

ROLE OF THESE PURIFICATIONS

Not all the authors of spiritual theology are in accord regarding the place or role of the night of the senses in the spiritual life. Some place it in the period of purgation, and this is the more common opinion (e.g., Philip of the Holy Trinity, Anthony of the Holy Ghost, Vallgornera). Others (e.g., Joseph of the Holy Ghost) maintain that it belongs to the illuminative way, and there are also some authors (Tanquerey, *The Spiritual Life,* nn. 1420 ff.) who place it in the unitive way.

It seems to us that according to the teachings of St. John of the Cross the night of the senses marks the transit between the purgative way and the illuminative way and that it therefore shares in something of these two states. When the soul enters into the night of the senses, it still belongs to the purgative way and it is still filled with imperfections and defects from which the night of the senses must purify it. But on leaving this night, purified by those imperfections and illumined by the splendors of infused contemplation, it

[31]Cf. A. Tanquerey, S.J., *The Spiritual Life,* n. 1434.

enters fully upon the illuminative way. The night of the senses marks the transit from one to the other, as St. John of the Cross teaches:

> Into this dark night souls begin to enter when God draws them forth from the state of beginners, which is the state of those that meditate on the spiritual road, and begins to set them in the state of progressives, which is that of those who are already contemplatives, to the end that, after passing through it, they may arrive at the state of the perfect, which is that of the divine union of the soul with God.[32]

The thought of St. John of the Cross is very clear in its reference to the three ways of the spiritual life. A little later, he clarifies his thoughts even more as regards the night of the senses, and his teaching is so explicit that he leaves no room for doubt:

> When this house of sensuality was now at rest, that is, was mortified, its passion being quenched and its desires put to rest and lulled to sleep by means of this blessed night of purgation of sense, the soul went forth, to set out upon the road and way of the spirit, which is that of progressives and proficients, and which, by another name, is called the way of illumination or of infused contemplation, wherein God himself feeds and refreshes the soul, without meditation or the soul's active help.[33]

Therefore, according to St. John of the Cross, the night of the senses marks the transition between the state of beginners and that of the advanced, from the purgative way to the illuminative way, from the ascetical state to the mystical state, from those who meditate in the spiritual life to those who begin to be enlightened by the splendors of infused contemplation. We shall now pass on to the second type of passive purification, namely, the terrible and fearful night of the spirit, to which only those souls attain who are to reach the most lofty heights of heroism and sanctity.

THE NIGHT OF THE SPIRIT

The night of the spirit is of less interest commonly, because only the most heroic souls who are to reach the heights of sanctity enter upon this night. Therefore, we shall restrict ourselves to certain brief indications.

ITS NATURE

The night of the spirit is constituted by a series of passive purgations which are extremely painful and have for their object the completion of the purification which was begun but not completed by the night of the senses. By means of the terrifying trials of this second night, the defects of the soul

[32] *The Dark Night,* Bk. I, Chap. 1.
[33] *Ibid.,* Bk. I, Chap. 14.

NEGATIVE ASPECT

are uprooted at their very source, something which could not be accomplished by the purification of the senses. St. John of the Cross says:

> The night which we have called that of sense may and should be called a kind of correction and restraint of desire rather than purgation. The reason is that all the imperfections and disorders of the sensual parts have their strength and root in the spirit, where all habits, both good and bad, are brought into subjection, and thus, until these are purged, the rebellions and depravities of sense cannot be purged thoroughly.[34]

ITS CAUSES

The causes of the night of the spirit are the same as those of the night of the senses, namely, infused contemplation and the imperfection of the soul, although in a higher degree of intensity as regards the contemplative light. The excess of this light torments and blinds the soul at the same time that it manifests to the soul its smallest and most insignificant imperfection.[35] The contrast between the ineffable grandeur of God as seen through the splendor of contemplation and the dross of imperfections and miseries which the soul discovers in itself makes the soul feel that an intimate union between such great light and such great darkness is impossible and that the soul is condemned to live eternally separated from God. This situation, which seems most evident and beyond remedy, submerges the soul into a state of anguish and torture which is so terrifying that it not only surpasses the torments of purgatory, in which the souls have the assurance of eternal salvation, but, except for the despair and hatred of God, it seems similar to the sufferings of the damned in hell.[36]

It is frightening to read the descriptions of this state as written by the souls who have passed through it.[37] Only through the particular assistance of God, who sustains and comforts the soul at the same time that he subjects it to such terrible trials, can the soul avoid falling into the most dark and deep despair.

---

[34]*Ibid.*, Bk. I, Chap. 3.

[35]St. Teresa uses very graphic comparisons in order to explain how this contemplative light, when it is very intense, discloses many things which escape the view of the soul at first glance. Cf. *The Life,* Chaps. 19, 20.

[36]St. John of the Cross says in this regard: "The soul feels itself to be so impure and miserable that it believes God to be against it and thinks that it has set itself against God. This causes the soul great grief and pain because it now believes that God has cast it away. . . . By means of this pure light, the soul now sees its impurity clearly, although darkly, and knows clearly that it is unworthy of God or of any creature, and what gives it most pain is that it thinks that it will never be worthy and that good things are all over for it." Cf. *The Dark Night,* Bk. II, Chaps. 6-8.

[37]Cf. A. Saudreau, *The Degrees of the Spiritual Life,* Bk. VI, Chap. 2, in which the author discusses the cases of St. Veronica of Juliani, St. Catherine of Genoa, St. Angela of Foligno, St. Teresa of Avila, St. Jane de Chantal and St. Paul of the Cross.

In order to explain the nature and effects of this terrible night of the spirit, St. John of the Cross uses the beautiful metaphor of wood which is cast into the fire:

EFFECTS OF THE NIGHT

> For the greater clearness of what has been said and what has yet to be said, it is well to observe at this point that this purgative and loving knowledge or divine light of which we here speak acts upon the soul it is purging and preparing for perfect union in the same way that fire acts upon a log of wood in order to transform it into itself. Material fire, acting upon wood, first of all begins to dry it, driving out its moisture and causing it to shed the water which is contained within it. Then it begins to make it black, dark and unsightly, and even to give forth a bad odor, and as it dries it little by little, it brings out and drives away all the dark and unsightly accidents which are contrary to the nature of fire. Finally, it begins to kindle it externally and give it heat, and at last transforms it into itself and makes it as beautiful as fire. In this respect, the wood has neither passivity nor activity of its own, save for its weight, which is greater, and its substance, which is denser, than that of fire. For it has in itself the properties and activities of fire. Thus it is dry and it dries; it is hot and it heats; it is bright and it gives brightness; and it is much less heavy than before. All these properties and effects are caused in it by the fire.[38]

St. John then applies this image to the purifying action of the night of the spirit and explains the admirable effects of sanctification which it produces in the soul that passes through this night. The soul comes forth from this trial resplendent and beautiful, completely transformed in God, and free forever from its weaknesses, imperfections and miseries. Having been completely purified of them by the terrible mystical purgatory which it has suffered, it scales the most lofty heights of sanctity, is confirmed in grace,[39] and awaits only death to break the bonds which still hold it in this world in order to penetrate, without any further purification,[40] the eternal splendors of the beatific vision.

ITS NECESSITY

Is the night of the spirit absolutely necessary in order to reach Christian perfection? In order to attain the relative perfection which corresponds to the souls that have passed through the fifth and are entering upon the first manifestations of the sixth mansions described by St. Teresa (contemplative prayer of quiet and of union), the dark night of the spirit is not necessary. God can supply and has, in fact, supplied for the purifications of the night

[38]*The Dark Night,* Bk. II, Chap. 10.

[39]This is the teaching of St. John of the Cross; cf. *Spiritual Canticle,* Chap. 22. He refers, of course, to a moral security and not to an absolute impeccability. St. Teresa of Avila was not so certain of this confirmation in grace, and she speaks of it with great caution, perhaps keeping in mind certain definitions of the Council of Trent (cf. Denz. 825, 826, 833) which she may have heard from one or another of her confessors (cf. *Interior Castle,* Seventh Mansions, Chaps. 2, 9, 4, 3).

[40]*The Dark Night,* Bk. II, Chap. 20: "These souls, who are few, do not enter into purgatory, because they have already been fully purged by love." Cf. also Chap. 6.

NEGATIVE ASPECT

of the spirit by means of other intermittent trials, alternating light with darkness, until he raises the soul to the degree of purity and perfection to which he has predestined them.[41] But in order to reach the seventh mansions and to scale the very heights of sanctity, the night of the spirit is indispensable. St. John of the Cross states this many times, and it must be so by the very nature of things. The soul cannot be united with God in the transforming union until it has been totally purified of all its weakness and misery. And this is the proper effect of the night of the spirit.

DURATION

It should be evident that there cannot be any fixed rule concerning the night of the spirit because circumstances are too variable. But these painful purifications usually last for a long period of time, sometimes for entire years, before the soul is admitted to the transforming union or the mystical marriage. From time to time, God is wont to lift his hand and let the soul breathe, but if it is a question of the true night of the spirit, these periods of relaxation are very brief. The soul immediately returns to the terrible pains and torture until the trial is finished by its entrance into the last classified degree of perfection, which is the deifying or transforming union.

ROLE IN THE SPIRITUAL LIFE

The passive purgations of the spirit, when they are intermittent, extend throughout the illuminative and the unitive way, but when it is a question of the true night of the spirit, they occur between the sixth and seventh mansions described by St. Teresa,[42] that is to say, when the soul is already far advanced in the unitive way and prior to its entrance into the transforming union for which the night is a preparation. Anyone who reads St. John of the Cross can see that, when he says that God places the soul in this terrible night to lead it to divine union,[43] he is not referring to the unitive way taken in its entirety, but only to the transforming union, which is the final union to which the soul attains. Otherwise, it would be necessary to exclude from the unitive way the marvelous phenomena of the ecstatic union, which do not appear in the transforming union, as St. John points out,[44] and which, nevertheless, evidently pertain to the unitive way according to the traditional teaching. We must in this respect disagree with Father Crisógono and Father Garrigou-Lagrange, who believe that the night of the spirit marks the transition from the illuminitive to the unitive way.[45]

---

[41]Cf. *ibid.*, Chap. 1.

[42]Cf.*Interior Castle,* Sixth Mansions, Chap. 1, where St. Teresa states that the night of the spirit occurs between the sixth and seventh mansions.

[43]Cf. *The Dark Night,* Bk. II, Chap. 1.

[44]*Loc. cit.*

[45]Cf. P. Crisógono, O.C.D., *Compendio de ascética y mística,* Part III, Chap. 2, a. 7; Garrigou-Lagrange, *The Three Ages of the Spiritual Life,* Part IV.

POSITIVE MEANS OF SPIRITUAL GROWTH

1: THE SACRAMENTS

Having examined the negative aspect of growth in perfection, we shall now consider the positive means of growth. Of the principal positive means, some (the sacraments) produce their effects *ex opere operato.* Other means work *ex opere operantis,* notably the practice of the infused virtues and the gifts of the Holy Ghost (which we shall discuss in the remaining chapters of this part) and the life of prayer (which we shall consider in Part V). Certain secondary means of advancement in the life of grace will furnish the subject matter of Part VI.

In this chapter we shall discuss the two sacraments which the faithful receive frequently: penance and the Eucharist. Three of the other five sacraments—baptism, confirmation and holy orders—cannot be received more than once by reason of the character which they impress upon the soul. The remaining two are ordinarily not received more than once, although absolutely speaking they could be received more frequently—extreme unction whenever one is in the danger of death and matrimony in succeeding marriages when the first marriage has been dissolved by the death of one of the spouses.

THE SACRAMENT OF PENANCE

We shall omit everything that pertains to the manner of obtaining pardon of grave sins, the ecclesiastical law which obliges Christians to the annual confession, and similar matters, the study of which pertains rather to moral theology. We shall concern ourselves simply with sacramental confession as a means of growing in perfection.

VALUE OF THE SACRAMENT

It would be a sad error to think that sacramental confession is ordained simply to the absolution of faults which have been committed or is merely a disposition for the better reception of the Eucharist. The sacrament of penance has in itself and independently of the other sacraments a great value and extraordinary efficacy as regards growth in the Christian life.

POSITIVE MEANS OF GROWTH

The sacraments increase grace if they find it already existing in the soul, and they do so by means of an efficacy which is infallible (*ex opere operato*). In this sense, as instruments of God applying the merits of Christ, the sacraments have a limitless power for sanctifying man. But in practice, the measure of this sanctifying effect will be in proportion to the disposition (*ex opere operantis*) with which one receives the sacraments; not because these dispositions are a co-cause in the production of grace (which proceeds exclusively from God), but because they act as a previous material disposition. Thus also the sun causes more heat in metal than in clay because the metal is a better conductor of heat.[1] For that reason the study of these dispositions is of great importance in spiritual theology because they admit of a great variety of degrees, and it is important that the soul be disposed as well as possible for the reception of the sacraments.

FRUITFUL DISPOSITIONS

The dispositions for receiving the sacraments with the greatest possible benefit may be either habitual or actual dispositions. The *habitual dispositions* may be summarized under the following three headings, which coincide with the exercise of the theological virtues:

Habitual propositions

1) *Spirit of faith.* The tribunal of penance is the tribunal of Christ. We must see Christ in the person of the confessor, since the latter takes the place of Christ and exercises the power which he has received from Christ (Jn. 20:22-23). The Pharisees were right when they said that only God can forgive sin (Lk. 5:21). Consequently, we must be prompt to accept the holy counsels of the confessor as if they came from Christ himself, and the confessor, on his part, should constantly remember the sublime dignity of his ministry and should exercise it with the fear and reverence which are demanded by his office as a legate of Christ.[2]

2) *Great confidence.* The tribunal of penance is the tribunal of mercy. For that reason, the confessor is not called a judge but a father. Whence the confessor should clothe himself, like Christ, in mercy, and the penitent should approach him with a heart filled with filial confidence.

3) *Love of God.* This love should be more and more intense, and this requires that even the slightest attachment to any kind of sin should be rejected and that we should arouse in our soul sentiments of true contrition for the sins that we have had the misfortune of committing.

Actual dispositions

As regards the *actual dispositions,* we should first of all approach the tribunal of penance in each instance as if it were to be the last confession of our life and as an immediate preparation for receiving Viaticum and for the judgment of God. It is therefore necessary to combat energetically the

[1] Cf. St. Thomas, *IV Sent.*, dist. 4, q. 2, a. 3, q. 2, ad 1.
[2] Cf. II Cor. 5:20.

spirit of routine, taking care not to confess one's sins merely out of the habit of doing so at certain definite intervals, but striving to effect in our souls, with the help of grace, a true conversion and renewal of our life. We shall examine the dispositions required in each of the various steps which are involved in making a good confession.

1) *Examination of conscience.* The examination of conscience should be made with the greatest sincerity and humility, with a serene and impartial spirit, without excusing our defects and without straining scrupulously to see faults where there are none. The time given to this examination will vary with the frequency of one's confessions, the need of the soul, and the degree of perfection of the soul at any given time. An excellent means of simplifying this task is to make a daily examination of conscience and to note especially those things which must be subjected to the confessor in the tribunal of penance. If one does this daily, it will take but a few moments to make a mental review before approaching confession. Moreover, this procedure has the advantage of keeping one's faults in mind during the week and of avoiding the anxiety that would be caused by forgetting to mention some sin at the time of confession.

But it is especially important that one should not lose himself in a multitude of unnecessary details. It is of much more importance to be able to discover the cause of distractions in prayer than to be able to recall the exact number of times that one was distracted. Some souls endeavor to do the impossible in seeking mathematical precision regarding the number of venial sins or imperfections, when it would be much more profitable for them to attack the causes of these sins directly rather than to spend so much time counting the external manifestations. This is to be understood, naturally, in regard to venial sins, because if it is a question of grave sins, it is necessary to confess the number exactly, or with the greatest possible precision.

2) *Sorrow for sin.* Sorrow or contrition is the fundamental disposition, together with the firm purpose of amendment, for obtaining the greatest possible benefit from the sacrament of penance. The lack of sorrow for sin would make the confession sacrilegious if it were done deliberately, or it would make the absolution invalid because of a lack of the proximate material needed for the sacrament, even if the sacrament were received in good faith.[3] Devout persons who generally or always confess light faults should be especially careful to cultivate true repentance for their

[3]St. Thomas teaches that the proximate matter in the sacrament of penance is not the sins of the penitent (which are the remote matter), but the acts by which the penitent rejects his sins (contrition, confession and satisfaction). The sacramental form falls directly upon the proximate matter and not upon the remote matter; and hence when the proximate matter is lacking, even indeliberately, there is no sacrament.

sins, however small, and to avoid any spirit of routine. Although there is no obligation to accuse oneself of venial sin in the confessional, it would be an irreverence and an abuse to accuse oneself of such things and not have sorrow for them or a purpose of amendment. That is why it is often suggested that one renew his sorrow and purpose of amendment for some serious sin from the past or for some present fault for which he is truly sorry and seriously intends not to commit again.

The intensity of repentance will be a measure of the grace which the soul will receive with the sacramental absolution. By means of an intense contrition or sorrow, the soul can obtain, not only total remission of all its faults and of the temporal punishment due to them in this life or in purgatory, but also a considerable increase in sanctifying grace, which will enable him to make giant strides along the road to perfection. It is important to keep in mind that the sinner, on regaining grace in the sacrament of penance (or outside penance by means of an act of perfect contrition with the intention to receive the sacrament), does not necessarily receive that grace in the same degree that he previously possessed it, but he will receive the same or more or less grace according to his actual disposition at the time.[4] It is, therefore, of the greatest importance to strive to have the most intense repentance and sorrow that is possible in order to regain one's former degree of grace or even a greater degree of grace than that which one possessed before his sin. This doctrine is also of value for the increase of grace even when the soul approaches the sacrament of penance in the state of grace. Consequently, there is nothing that the soul should strive for more energetically if it wishes to sanctify itself than this intensity of sorrow which is born of the love of God, of the consideration of his infinite goodness and mercy, of the love and sufferings of Christ, of the monstrous ingratitude of the sinner for such a good Father who has given us so many great benefits, etc. But being convinced that this grace of a perfect and intense contrition is a gift from God which can be petitioned only by prayer, the soul will profoundly humble itself before the divine majesty and implore this gift through the intercession of Mary, mediatrix of all graces.

3) *Firm purpose of amendment.* If the purpose of amendment is lacking, the confession is invalid, and one must therefore exercise great

[4]The following are the words of St. Thomas: "It may happen, therefore, that the intensity of the repentance of the penitent is sometimes proportionate to a greater grace than that from which he fell through sin, sometimes to an equal grace, and sometimes to a less grace. And therefore the penitent sometimes rises with a greater grace than that which he previously had, sometimes with an equal grace, and sometimes with less grace. And the same must be said of the virtues which depend upon and follow grace" (*Summa,* III, q. 89, a. 2).

diligence regarding this important point. One cannot be content merely with a general resolution not to sin again, because this is too unspecified to be efficacious. Without excluding the general purpose of amendment, we should likewise make a clear, concrete and energetic resolution to use all possible means to avoid all sin and to advance in the practice of a specific virtue. It is helpful to make this type of resolution at the end of the daily examination of conscience and to relate to the confessor in the following confession how faithful or remiss we were in this regard. It is unfortunate that confessions of devout persons are sometimes less beneficial because they disregard these fundamental points.

4) *Vocal confession.* St. Thomas examines and justifies the sixteen qualities which the ancient theologians listed for the perfect accusation of one's sins. They are: "The confession should be simple, humble, pure, faithful, frequent, clear, discreet, voluntary, without argument, integral, secret, sorrowful, prompt, strong, accusing and disposed to obey."[5] Not all of these conditions have the same importance, although none of them is useless. In the order of their sanctifying value, we can select the following:

a) *Profoundly humble.* The penitent should humbly recognize his weakness and begin to make reparation by voluntarily accepting his own abasement in the eyes of the confessor. In this respect, it is a great mistake for souls, when they commit a humiliating fault, to seek a confessor other than their ordinary confessor so that he will not suspect anything, or they will not lose anything in his eyes. How can they make progress toward perfection if they still preserve such deep-rooted self-love and are so far removed from true humility of heart?

How different it is with those who sincerely desire to sanctify themselves. Without offending the truth by voluntarily exaggerating the quality or number of their sins, they strive to accuse themselves in a manner that would be humiliating to themselves. Not only do they not "palliate them and make them appear less evil, and thus go to confession to excuse themselves rather than to accuse themselves,"[6] but they "are more anxious to speak of their faults and sins, or that these should be recognized rather than their virtues; and thus they incline to talk of their souls with those who account their actions and their spirituality of little value."[7]

---

[5]Cf. *Suppl.*, q. 9, a. 4.

[6]St. John of the Cross, *The Dark Night,* Bk. I, Chap 2. This entire magnificent chapter on the pride of beginners is well worth reading.

[7]Cf. *ibid.*, Chap. 2.

b) *Integral confession.* We do not refer here to the integrity of confession as regards the species and number of mortal sins (for this is absolutely indispensable under the pain of making a sacrilegious confession), but of the investigation of the causes and motives of sins, so that the confessor may apply the fitting remedy and thus prevent relapses. "It is not enough," says Father Garrigou-Lagrange, "to make a vague accusation that would tell the confessor nothing, as for example: 'I have had distractions in my prayer.' It is advisable to say: 'I have been especially distracted during such and such an exercise of piety through negligence, because I began it badly, without recollection, or because I did not sufficiently combat distractions springing from a petty rancor or from too sensible an affection or from study.' It is also fitting to recall resolutions taken and to tell whether we have failed more or less in keeping them. Thus routine and negligence will be avoided."[8]

c) *Sorrowful confession.* One should accuse himself in the confessional in words that make it evident that he has a sincere repentance, and he should strive more and more to arouse the interior sentiments of sorrow for all of his sins and weaknesses.

d) *Frequent confession.* In order that confession may be an exercise which has a great sanctifying value, it is necessary that it be frequent. Canon law urges bishops to make it an obligation for their clergy frequently to purify their consciences in the sacrament of penance (can. 125). And speaking of religious and seminarians, the law of the Church expressly states that they should go to confession at least once a week (cans. 595 and 1367). It does not matter that one has no new voluntary faults of which to accuse oneself; there will always be matter for confession from one's past life, and upon this one can again renew his sorrow and thereby justify a new absolution which will increase grace considerably. Some of the saints, such as St. Vincent Ferrer, St. Catherine of Siena, St. Ignatius Loyola, St. Francis Borgia, St. Charles Borromeo and St. Alphonsus, went to confession every day, not because of scrupulosity or anxiety of conscience, but because of their thirst for God and their realization that one of the most efficacious means for advancing in perfection is the humble and contrite reception of the sacrament of penance. The soul that aspires seriously to sanctify itself will never omit weekly confession.

5) *Sacramental satisfaction.* In addition to the vindicative purpose of restoring the proper order, sacramental satisfaction has a double value:

[8] *The Three Ages,* I, p. 400.

the remission of the temporal punishment due to sin (and this effect is produced *ex opere operato,* but according to the disposition of the penitent) and the medicinal value of preserving the soul from future sin and healing the wounds of sin by the application of opportune remedies. For that reason it is necessary to fulfill one's penance with the greatest possible fervor.

Keeping in mind the great benevolence which the Church manifests today as regards the reception of the sacrament of penance, those penitents who ask their confessor for a more severe penance are to be praised, because the satisfactory value of the works imposed as a penance in confession is much greater than if one were to undertake those same works by his own initiative, for they form a part of the sacrament and they receive their value from the power of the keys.[9]

EFFECTS OF CONFESSION

There is no doubt that confession made with the foregoing conditions is of great efficacy in the sanctification of the soul. The following are the effects of such a worthy confession:

1) The Blood of Christ has fallen upon the soul to purify and sanctify it. Therefore, the saints who received the most vivid light concerning the infinite value of the redeeming Blood of Jesus had a veritable hunger and thirst for receiving sacramental absolution.

2) Grace is increased in us *ex opere operato,* although in different degrees according to the disposition of the penitent. Of one hundred persons who have received absolution from the same faults, there may not be two who have received grace in the same degree. It will depend on the intensity of their repentance and the degree of humility with which they have approached the sacrament.

3) The soul is filled with peace and consolation, a psychological disposition indispensable for making progress on the road to perfection.

4) Greater lights are received concerning the ways of God. Thus after a worthy confession we understand more clearly the necessity of forgiving injuries, seeing how mercifully the Lord has pardoned us, or we understand with greater clarity the malice of venial sin, which is a stain which makes the soul ugly because it deprives it of some of its brilliance and beauty.

5) It increases considerably the powers of the soul by imparting the energy and the strength to conquer temptations and the fortitude to fulfill one's duties perfectly.

[9]These are the words of the Angelic Doctor: "Since satisfaction enjoined by the absolving priest is a part of penance, it is evident that the power of the keys operates in it, so that it is of more value for the expiation of sin than if one by his own initiative were to perform the same work" (*Quodlib.* III, a. 28).

PENANCE AND COMPUNCTION

The reception of the sacrament of penance has an extraordinary sanctifying efficacy, but it is a transitory act which cannot be repeated continuously. What should remain habitually in the soul is the *virtue* of penance and the spirit of compunction, which will preserve in the soul the fruits of the sacrament.[10] For the sake of brevity, we shall summarize the fundamental points which should be kept in mind in this matter.[11]

The virtue of penance

The virtue of penance is a supernatural habit by which we are sorry for past sins and have the intention of removing them from the soul.[12] Therefore, it implies the desire of expiating them. This virtue should be manifested by the acts which are proper to it, but in itself it is a habitual attitude of the soul which preserves in us the sorrow for having offended God and the desire of making reparation for our faults. This spirit of compunction is necessary for all those who have not lived in perfect innocence.

When it is profound and habitual, this sentiment of contrition gives great peace to the soul, keeps it in humility, is an excellent instrument of purification, helps the soul mortify its disorderly instincts, fortifies it against temptation, impels it to use all the means at its disposal to make reparation for its sins, and is a guarantee of perseverance on the way of perfection. Many souls experience an instinctive repugnance to anything that signifies penitence and renunciation. This instinctive movement, originating in the depths of the human spirit, which moves man naturally to flee from pain, is no obstacle to the possession and practice of the virtue of penance, which, as such, resides in the will and has nothing to do with the rebellion of the instinct.

The spirit of penance

The spirit of compunction was found in all the saints; all of them were aware that they were sinners in the eyes of God. And the Church herself has placed in her liturgy various formulas of contrition, especially in the Mass, in which such expressions are multiplied in an impressive manner. This is the spirit which animates the Church, the Spouse of Christ, as long as she performs this most sublime and most holy action in this world.

Penance makes us participants in the suffering and the merits of Christ. Union with Christ in our sufferings, besides being an indispensable condition for their value, is an ineffable source of consolation. The saints did not dare to live without the Cross.

Following the thought and the intention of the Church as manifested in the formula which accompanies sacramental absolution, we must refer, by an explicit intention, the act of the virtue of penance to the sacrament itself. This practice is of singular efficacy for the remission of our sins, for the

---

[10]Cf. St. Thomas, *Summa,* III, q. 84, aa. 8-9.

[11]We do not know of any better treatment of this important question than that by Dom Columba Marmion, *Christ the Life of the Soul,* Chap. 4, and *Christ the Ideal of the Monk,* Chap. 8.

[12]Cf. St. Thomas, *Summa,* III, q. 85, a. 1.

increase of grace and for the attainment of the reward which will be ours in eternal life.

The principal means for acquiring the spirit of penance and of compunction are: 1) prayer, since this is a gift from God; 2) meditation on the sufferings of Christ because of our sins and his infinite mercy in forgiving the repentant sinner; 3) the voluntary practice of mortification performed with the spirit of reparation in union with Christ.

THE EUCHARIST

Among all the exercises and practices of piety, there is none whose sanctifying efficacy can compare with the worthy reception of the Eucharist. Here we receive not only grace but the very source from whom grace comes. The Eucharist, in its twofold aspect of sacrament and sacrifice, should be the point of convergence for the entire Christian life. Everything should revolve around the Eucharist.

Sanctity consists in participating more and more fully and perfectly in the divine life which is communicated to us through grace. This grace springs from Christ as its unique source, in whom dwells the fulness of grace and divinity.

FOUNTAIN OF HOLINESS

Christ communicates grace to us through the sacraments and principally through the Eucharist, in which he gives us himself as the food of our soul. However, unlike material nourishment, it is not we who assimilate Christ to ourselves, but it is he who transforms us into himself. In the Eucharist the Christian can attain that maximum transformation in Christ in which sanctity consists.

Holy Communion, in giving us entirely to Christ, places at our disposition all the treasures of sanctity, of wisdom and of knowledge which are contained in him. With Communion the soul receives an infinite treasure which becomes the property of the soul.

Together with the Word Incarnate, with his body, soul and divinity, there is given to us in the Eucharist the other two Persons of the Blessed Trinity, the Father and the Holy Ghost, by reason of the ineffable mystery of circuminsession which makes them inseparable. Never as perfectly as after receiving Communion is the Christian converted into the temple and tabernacle of the divinity. By reason of this divine and ineffable contact with the Blessed Trinity, the soul (and by redundance from the soul, the body also) is made more sacred than the tabernacle or a ciborium, and even more sacred than the sacramental species themselves which contain Christ but without receiving from him any sanctifying influence.

The eucharistic union associates us in a mysterious but real manner with the infinite life of the Blessed Trinity. In the soul which has just received Communion, the Father engenders his only-begotten Son, and from both proceeds that current of love and veritable torrent of fire which is the Holy Spirit. The Christian, after Communion, should be rapt in an ecstasy of adoration and love and should let himself be born through the Father to the Son and through the Son to the Father in the unity of the Holy Ghost. There should be a simple movement of flaming love and intimate adoration which could be translated in this simple formula: "Glory be to the Father and to the Son and to the Holy Ghost."

These notions are fundamental and they will suffice, if meditated upon, to give us the tone and the norm of our Christian life, which should be essentially eucharistic. But now let us speak of the preparation and thanksgiving which are of capital importance for obtaining from the Eucharist its maximum sanctifying power.

PREPARATION

It is necessary here to distinguish a twofold preparation: remote and proximate. St. Pius X, by his decree, *Sacra Tridentina Synodus,* of December 20, 1905, settled once and for all the historical controversy concerning the *remote dispositions* required for the reception of Holy Communion. The Pope determined that, in order to receive frequent or even daily Communion, the following conditions alone were required: a) the state of grace; b) the right intention (that is, that one should not receive Communion for reasons of vanity or out of routine, but only to please God); c) freedom from venial sins so far as possible, although this is not absolutely necessary, since Communion will help to conquer them. A diligent preparation and devout thanksgiving are highly recommended, and one should follow the advice of a confessor. One who fulfills these conditions should not be deprived of frequent or daily Communion.[13]

It is evident that persons who wish seriously to advance in Christian perfection must endeavor to intensify these conditions as much as possible. One's remote preparation should consist in living a life that is worthy of one who has received Communion in the morning and intends to receive Com-

[13]In order to remedy the abuses which may originate from frequent and daily Communion in schools, seminaries, religious communities, etc., where there is a danger that one may approach the Communion rail unworthily because of a fear of attracting the attention of one's companions or superiors, the Sacred Congregation of the Sacraments, on December 8, 1938, issued a prudent instruction reserved to ordinaries and major religious superiors, which was not published in the *Acta Apostolicae Sedis*. One can see the text and a commentary in any standard manual of Canon Law.

munion again the following day. He must reject any attachment to venial sin, especially to deliberate venial sin, and avoid a lukewarm and imperfect manner of acting; this presupposes self-abnegation and a tendency to the practice of more perfect acts in view of given circumstances.

Proximate dispositions

There are four principal *proximate dispositions* which the fervent soul should try to arouse, asking God for them with a humble and persevering insistance.

1) *A living faith.* Christ always demanded this as an indispensable condition before granting any grace, even the grace of a miracle. The Eucharist is the *mysterium fidei* because in it natural reason and the senses can perceive nothing of Christ. St. Thomas recalls that on the Cross only the divinity was hidden, but on the altar the holy humanity of Christ likewise is veiled to our gaze. This mystery demands of us a living faith filled with adoration.

But not only in this sense of a vital assent to the eucharistic mystery is faith absolutely indispensable; it is also indispensable in relation to the vivifying power of contact with Christ. We must consider in our souls the leprosy of sin and repeat with the leper of the gospel: "Lord, if thou wilt, thou canst make me clean" (Matt. 8:2), or as the blind man of Jericho, who was less unfortunate with his privation of physical vision than we are with our blindness of soul: "Lord, that I may see" (Mk. 10:51).

2) *Profound humility.* Christ washed the feet of his apostles before he instituted the Eucharist, in order to give them an example (Jn. 13:15). If the Blessed Virgin was prepared to receive the Word of God in her virginal womb with that profound humility which caused her to exclaim: "Behold the handmaid of the Lord" (Lk. 1:38), what ought we to do in a similar situation? It does not matter that we have repented perfectly of our sins and that we find ourselves in the state of grace. The fault was pardoned, perhaps the guilt of punishment was also remitted (if we have done sufficient penance), but the historical fact of having committed that sin will never disappear. We should never forget, whatever be the grade of sanctity which we actually possess, that we have been ransomed from hell and that we are former children of the devil. The Christian who has had the misfortune to commit a single mortal sin in his life ought always to be overwhelmed with humility. At least on approaching Communion we should repeat three times with profound sentiments of humility and a sincere repentance the sublime words of the centurion: "Lord, I am not worthy."

3) *Unbounded confidence.* It is necessary that the remembrance of our sins should lead us to humility but never to despair, which would be a disguised form of pride. Christ is the great pardoner who has

embraced with infinite tenderness all the sinners who approach him in search of pardon. The conditions for this pardon have not changed; they are the same as in the gospel. We should approach him with humility and reverence and also with great confidence in his goodness and mercy. He is the Father, the Good Shepherd, the Healer, the Divine Friend, who wishes to hold us close to his Sacred Heart which throbs with love for us. Confidence conquers him and he cannot resist it, for it overwhelms his heart.

4) *Hunger and thirst for Communion.* This is the disposition which most directly affects the sanctifying efficacy of Holy Communion. The hunger and thirst for receiving the sacramental Christ, which proceeds from love and is almost identified with love, enlarges the capacity of the soul and disposes it to receive sacramental grace from the Eucharist in great measure. The amount of water which is taken at a fountain depends in each case on the size of the vessel in which the water is received. If we strive to beg ardently of the Lord for this hunger and thirst, and if we ourselves strive to arouse it with all possible means, we shall very soon be saints. St. Catherine of Siena, St. Teresa of Avila and many other saints had such a hunger and thirst for Communion that they would rather have been exposed to the greatest sufferings and dangers rather than endure a single day in which their souls were not sustained by this divine nourishment. We should see in these dispositions, not only an effect, but also one of the most efficacious causes of their exalted sanctity. The Eucharist received with such ardent desire increased the grace in their souls to an incalculable degree, causing them to advance in giant strides along the road to perfection.

Each one of our Communions should be more fervent than the preceding one, increasing our hunger and thirst for the Eucharist. For each new Communion increases in us our sanctifying grace and disposes us, as a result, to receive the Lord on the following day with a love that is not only equal but much greater than our love of the preceding day. Here, as throughout the spiritual life, the soul should advance with an accelerated movement in much the same way as a stone falls with greater rapidity as it approaches closer to the earth.[14]

THANKSGIVING

As regards the grace which will increase in us in this sacrament *ex opere operato,* preparation for Communion is more important than thanksgiving after

[14]St. Thomas states: "The natural movement (e.g., that of a stone falling to earth) is more accelerated as it approaches its terminus. The contrary happens in the case of violent movement (e.g., a stone thrown upward into the air). Now grace inclines after the fashion of the natural movement; therefore, those who are in grace ought to grow the more as they approach their terminus" (*In Epist. ad Heb.,* 1:25).

Communion, because the grace is in relation to the actual disposition of the soul which receives Communion.[15]

In any case, thanksgiving after Communion is likewise very important. As St. Teresa said to her nuns: "Do not lose so good an opportunity of negotiating as the hour after receiving Communion."[16] Christ is present in us and he desires nothing so much as to fill us with blessings. The best way of giving thanks is to identify oneself through love with Christ himself and to offer him to the Father with all his infinite riches as a sweet oblation for the four purposes of sacrifice: adoration, reparation, petition and thanksgiving.

Avoidance of routine

It is necessary to avoid at any cost a routine spirit, for this renders sterile the greater part of thanksgiving after Communion. There are many devout souls who make a thanksgiving which is composed of certain formulas or prayers read from a book, and they are not satisfied until they have recited them mechanically. There is no intimate contact with Christ, no cordial conversation with him, no fusion of hearts, no humble petition for the graces which we need today and which may perhaps be completely different from the graces we needed yesterday or shall need tomorrow. "I do not know what to say to the Lord," is the answer of some who abandon their prayer books and attempt to give themselves over to loving conversation with Christ. For that reason they do not even try to leave their routine formality. If they loved Christ truly and if they would try to carry on with him a conversation of friendship, they would very soon experience a repugnance for those formulas which they had only read out of a prayerbook and which have been written by others. The voice of Christ, sweet and tender, would resound in their souls and show them the way to heaven and establish in them that peace which "surpasses all understanding" (Phil. 4:7).

Another excellent means of giving thanks is to reproduce in one's mind some of the scenes of the gospel, imagining that we ourselves are present before Christ who is truly present within us in the Eucharist. Then we could present our petitions as they were presented by others when Christ was on earth: "Lord, behold, he whom thou lovest is sick" (Jn. 11:3); "Lord

[15]Some theologians maintain that the sacrament can produce new increases of grace *ex opere operato* throughout the whole time that the sacramental species remain incorrupt in the person who has received Communion if new dispositions are found on the part of the recipient. But this theory is very improbable. It is much more theological to say that the effect *ex opere operato* is produced only once by the sacrament, at the very moment of receiving Communion. (Cf. St. Thomas, *Summa,* III, q. 80, a. 8, ad 6.) It is true, however, that there can be new increases of grace *ex opere operantis* (by intensifying one's dispositions), but this has nothing to do with the proper effect of the sacrament *ex opere operato.* Indeed, grace can be produced independently of the sacrament by any act of virtue which is more intense than the habit which one actually possesses.

[16]Cf. *The Way of Perfection,* Chap. 34, n. 10.

if thou wilt, thou canst make me clean" (Matt. 8:2); "Rabboni, that I may see" (Mk. 10:51); "Lord, give me this water" (Jn. 4:15); "Lord, increase our faith" (Lk. 17:5); "I do believe; help my unbelief" (Mk. 9:23); "Lord, teach us to pray" (Lk. 11:1); "Lord, show us the Father and it is enough for us" (Jn. 14:8); "Lord, to whom shall we go? Thou hast words of everlasting life" (Jn. 6:68). How our Lord would rejoice at seeing the simplicity, the faith and the humility of such souls, who approach him with the same confidence and love as those recorded in the gospel. How could it be possible that he would not answer our prayers, if he is the same now as then and if we are so wretched, and even more so, than many who are described in the gospel? There is nothing that so moves his divine heart as a soul that thirsts for God and humbles itself by recognizing its wounds and miseries and implores a remedy for them.

Duration of thanksgiving

It is a kind of irreverence to the divine guest to be too prompt to terminate the visit which he has condescended to make to us. With persons of the world who are deserving of all respect we would never act in this manner, but we would wait for them to bring the visit to a close. Jesus prolongs his visit within us for as long as the sacramental species remain substantially unchanged, and although one cannot give a fixed rule in this regard, since it depends on the physical condition of each person, we could say that the sacramental species normally remain in a person for a half hour. We should, therefore, try to remain during all this time at the feet of the Savior, listening to his divine teaching and receiving his sanctifying influence. Only by reason of unusual circumstances, such as an urgent duty or necessity, should we cut short our thanksgiving, and even then we should ask the Lord to supply with his goodness and mercy the time which we were not able to give.[17]

SPIRITUAL COMMUNION

A great help or complement to sacramental Communion and a means of prolonging its influence is the practice which is called spiritual communion. It consists essentially in a fervent desire to receive the Eucharist and in giving God a loving embrace as if he had truly entered our hearts. This pious practice, blessed and encouraged by the Church, has a sanctifying efficacy and can be repeated frequently throughout the day. We can never sufficiently praise this excellent devotion, but even in this matter one must avoid carefully anything that is routine or mechanical, because this would diminish the merit of the act.

---

[17]St. Philip Neri on one occasion commanded two altar boys to accompany such a person with lighted candles when he left immediately after receiving Communion. If, because of some exceptional circumstance, we are obliged to interrupt our thanksgiving, we should at least try to preserve a spirit of recollection and prayer in the midst of inevitable duties.

VISITING THE BLESSED SACRAMENT

Another excellent practice which should not be omitted is that of visiting Christ in the tabernacle. It consists in passing a short time at the feet of the Master present in the Eucharist; we should do so several times a day if possible. A most opportune time is toward the close of day. At this twilight hour everything in nature invites us to recollection and silence, and these are excellent conditions for hearing the voice of the Lord in the depths of the soul. The best method for making a visit to the Blessed Sacrament is to open one's heart by means of a fervent conversation with Christ. It is not necessary to be educated or to be eloquent, but simply to love the Lord a great deal and to have confidence and a childlike simplicity toward him. Books may be of help to certain individuals,[18] but books can never take the place of the spontaneity of a soul which opens its heart to the outpourings of love which emanate from the sacramental Christ.

THE SACRIFICE OF THE MASS

The Mass is substantially the same sacrifice as that of the Cross, and has all of its infinite value: the same victim, the same oblation, the same priest. There is only an accidental difference: the manner in which the sacrifice is realized (a bloody sacrifice on the Cross, an unbloody sacrifice on the altar). This is the teaching of the Church in the Council of Trent.[19] As a true sacrifice, the Mass realizes the four purposes of sacrifice: adoration, reparation, petition and thanksgiving.[20] Its value is infinite, but its effects, so far as they depend on us, are applied to us only in the measure of our internal dispositions.

THE END AND EFFECTS OF THE MASS

As a reproduction of the redeeming sacrifice, the Mass has the same purposes and produces the same effects as the sacrifice of the Cross. They are also the same as those of a sacrifice in general, the supreme act of religion, but they are incomparably more sublime.

1) *Adoration.* The sacrifice of the Mass renders to God an adoration which is absolutely worthy of him and is infinite in the strictest sense. This effect it always produces infallibly, *ex opere operato,* even if the Mass were celebrated by a priest in the state of mortal sin. The reason is that the value of adoration depends on the infinite dignity of the principal priest who offers the sacrifice (Christ) and the value of the victim offered (Christ).

We should recall the great longing of the saints to give glory to God.

[18]The books of St. Alphonsus Liguori are especially suitable.
[19]Sess. XXII, Chap. 2; Denz. 940.
[20]*Ibid.,* Chap. 1; Denz. 948.

With the Mass we give to God all the honor which is due to him in recognition of his sovereign grandeur and supreme dominion, and this is done in the most perfect way possible, in an infinite degree. One Mass gives more glory to God than do all the angels and saints in heaven, including the Blessed Virgin Mary, the Mother of God.

In return for this incomparable glory, God inclines lovingly to his creatures. From this proceeds the sanctifying value of the Mass. And to think that many Christians, even devout Christians, have not yet become aware of this, but prefer their routine practices of devotion to an incorporation and participation in this sublime sacrifice which constitutes the principal act of religion and of Catholic worship!

2) *Reparation.* After adoration, there is no other debt which is more pressing than that of making reparation for the offenses which we have committed against the Creator. In this sense also the value of the Mass is absolutely incomparable, because by means of it we offer to the Father the infinite reparation of Christ with all its redeeming efficacy.

The world is flooded with sin each day, and we may well ask why God does not punish us. The reason is that each day, indeed each hour, the Son of God, immolated on the altar, appeases the wrath of his Father and withholds the arm which is prepared to punish. Yet this reparatory effect is not applied to us in all of its infinite fulness, but in a limited and finite degree, according to our dispositions. Nevertheless, it is well to keep in mind the following points:

a) We receive *ex opere operato,* unless we place an obstacle to it, the actual grace which is necessary for repentance for our sins.[21] Consequently, there is nothing more efficacious for obtaining from God the conversion of a sinner than to offer the Holy Sacrifice of the Mass for this intention, asking God at the same time to rid the heart of the sinner of the obstacles for infallibly obtaining that grace.

b) The Mass remits always and infallibly, as long as there is no obstacle, at least part of the temporal punishment which is due to sin in this world or in the world to come. Hence the Mass is likewise of great profit for the souls in purgatory. The degree and measure of this remission, however, will depend on our dispositions.[22]

---

[21]Note that we speak of actual grace and not habitual grace, which is the fruit of repentance and sacramental absolution. Cf. the Council of Trent, Sess. XXII, Chap. 2; Denz. 940.

[22]That is, so far as pertains to the punishment for one's own sins. As regards the remission of punishment for the souls in purgatory, it is more probable that the *ex opere operato* effects depend simply and solely on the will of God, although *ex opere operantis* the Mass will be of greater benefit because of the devotion

No suffrage is of such efficacious value to the souls in purgatory as the sacrifice of the Mass, and no sacramental penance of greater value could be imposed by confessors on their penitents than that of having a Mass offered to God.

3) *Petition.* "Our indigence is immense; we constantly need light, fortitude, consolation. We shall find all this in the Mass. There is, in effect, he who said: 'I am the Light of the world, I am the Way, I am the Truth, I am the Life. Come to me, those who suffer, and I will refresh you. If anyone comes to me, I will not reject him.' "[23]

Christ is offered to the Father in the Mass in order to obtain for us, through the infinite merit of his oblation, all the graces of divine life which we need. There he is "always living to make intercession for us" (Heb. 7:25), strengthening our supplications and petitions by his infinite merits. Therefore, the impetratory value of the Mass is incomparable. Of itself, *ex opere operato,* infallibly and immediately, it moves God to grant to men all the graces they need, without exception, although the effective distribution of those graces will be measured by the degree of our dispositions and can even be frustrated completely because of a voluntary obstacle which we may place to it.[24]

When incorporated with the Mass, our prayer not only enters into the river of liturgical prayer, which gives it a dignity and efficacy *ex opere operantis ecclesiae,* but it blends it with the infinite prayer of Christ, and in attention to him God will grant us whatever we need. Consequently, there is no novena or triduum which can compare to the impetratory efficacy of one Mass.

What a disorientation frequently exists among the faithful as regards the objective value of things! That which we cannot obtain by means of the Holy Mass cannot be obtained in any other way. It is very well and good to make use of other practices and exercises which are approved by the Church, and it is beyond doubt that God does grant many graces through them, but let us put each thing in its proper place. The Mass is above everything.

4) *Thanksgiving.* The immense benefits of the natural and supernatural order which we have received from God cause us to contract with him an infinite debt of gratitude. An entire eternity would not suffice to pay this debt if we were not able to make use of other means

---

of the one who says the Mass and the one who has it offered. Cf. the Council of Trent, *loc. cit.;* St. Thomas, *Summa,* III, q. 79, a. 5; *Suppl.,* q. 71, a. 9, ad 3 and 5.

[23]Dom Columba Marmion, *Christ the Life of the Soul,* Chap. 7.

[24]Cf. R. Garrigou-Lagrange, O.P., *The Three Ages,* II, Chap. 31.

which we are able to offer him on our account. But there is at our disposition a wonderful means of completely liquidating our debt: the sacrifice of the Mass. Through it we offer to the Father a eucharistic sacrifice or a thanksgiving which is more than our debt because it is infinite. It is Christ himself who is immolated for us, and in our place he gives thanks to God for his immense benefits. At the same time, the Mass is a fountain of new graces because it pleases God to reward those who do good. The eucharistic effect or thanksgiving is produced by the Holy Mass of itself always and infallibly *ex opere operato* and independently of our dispositions.

Such are, in brief, the infinite riches contained in the Mass. For that reason the saints, illumined by God, always held the Mass in the highest esteem. It was the center of their life, the fountain of their spirituality, the resplendent sun around which all of their activities revolved. But in order to obtain the maximum sanctifying benefits from the celebration of or attendance at Mass, it is necessary to insist on the necessary dispositions on the part of the one who celebrates or the one who attends.

DISPOSITIONS FOR MASS

Someone has said that in order to celebrate or attend one Mass worthily, three eternities would be required: one to prepare oneself, another to celebrate or attend the Mass, and a third to give thanks. Without going to this extreme, we can say that it is certain that every preparation will be too little as regards the diligence and fervor which are fitting for the Mass. The principal dispositions are of two kinds: external and internal.

1) *External dispositions.* For the priest, these dispositions will consist in the perfect fulfillment and observance of the rubrics and ceremonies which the Church requires. For the faithful they will consist in respect, silence and attention in assisting at Mass.

2) *Internal dispositions.* The best possible disposition is to identify oneself with Christ who is immolated on the altar, to offer him to the Father and to offer oneself in him, with him and through him. This is the hour of asking that we be converted into bread in order to be consumed by our brothers through the complete giving of ourself in charity. We ask for an intimate union with Mary at the foot of the Cross, with St. John, the beloved disciple, with the priest who celebrates the Mass and is another Christ here on earth; a union with all the Masses which are being celebrated in the whole world. We should never ask anything of God without adding, as an infinite price of the grace which we desire: "Lord, by the adorable blood of Jesus, who at this moment is being elevated in the chalice by some priest somewhere in the world." There is no doubt that the Mass celebrated or attended with these dispositions is an instrument of sanctification of the first order.

MEANS OF SPIRITUAL GROWTH

After the sacraments, which are the primary fountain of our Christian life for augmenting grace *ex opere operato,* it is necessary to examine the fundamental means for the development of this life *ex opere operantis.* These means are, principally, the ever more intense practice of the infused virtues, perfected by the actuation of the gifts of the Holy Spirit (an actuation which, although it does not depend on us, we can nevertheless anticipate by disposing ourselves so that the Spirit may move us), and the progressive increase of the life of prayer. These are the great means which we shall now examine as extensively as is possible. We have already considered the general theory and doctrine of the infused virtues and the gifts of the Holy Ghost. Now we shall consider the method of practicing the virtues with greater intensity and perfection and what is necessary to dispose ourselves to the actuation of the gifts of the Holy Ghost. We shall insist especially on the seven principal virtues, theological and cardinal, but without omitting certain indications which pertain to their derived and annexed virtues. We shall likewise add to each virtue a consideration of the gift of the Holy Spirit which corresponds to that virtue, as St. Thomas does in his *Summa Theologiae.*

2: THE VIRTUE OF FAITH

The theological virtues are the most important virtues of the Christian life because they are the basis and foundation of all the other virtues. Their function is to unite us intimately to God as infinite truth, as supreme beatitude and as the greatest good. They are the only virtues which are immediately related to God; all the others refer directly to things that are distinct from God. Here lies the supreme excellence of the theological virtues.

THE NATURE OF FAITH

DEFINITION Faith, the first of the theological virtues, is a virtue infused by God in the intellect by which we firmly assent to divinely revealed truths on the authority of God who reveals them. In these words are contained all the essential elements which should enter into a good definition: the proximate genus (theological infused virtue); the specific difference (intellectual assent, as distinct from hope and charity, by which the will loves with a love of concupiscence or a love of friendship); the material object and the formal *quod* object (God supernaturally known as the first truth and all the truths revealed as related to God); the formal *quo* object (by the authority of God, who can neither deceive nor be deceived).

The nature of faith In revealing to us his intimate life and the great mysteries of grace and glory, God enables us to see things from his point of view, as he himself sees them. The assent to the truths of faith is of itself most firm and certain because it is based on the authority of God revealing. The revealed truths remain for us obscure and non-evident, however, and hence the will must intervene, under the motion of grace, to impose upon the intellect that firm assent—not by reason of intrinsic evidence, which is lacking to us concerning those truths, but simply by reason of the infallible authority of God, who can neither deceive nor be deceived. In this sense the act of faith is free, supernatural and meritorious.

THE VIRTUE OF FAITH

Faith is incompatible with intellectual or sensible vision. Of itself it is of those things which are not seen.[1] Therefore, faith disappears in heaven and is replaced by the face-to-face vision. Nevertheless, faith is the first of the Christian virtues so far as it is the positive foundation of all the others,[2] although charity is more excellent than faith and all the other infused virtues, inasmuch as it bespeaks a relation to God in a more perfect manner and is the form of all other virtues.[3] Without charity, no virtue can be perfect.[4]

The Council of Trent states that faith is the beginning, the foundation and the root of justification, and without faith it is impossible to please God and to be numbered among his sons.[5] It is the beginning because it establishes the first contact between ourselves and God, the Author of the supernatural order. The first thing is to believe in God. It is the foundation, inasmuch as all the other virtues, including charity, presuppose faith, and are established upon it as an edifice on its foundation. Without faith it is impossible to hope or to love. It is the root, because in it, when informed by charity, all the other virtues live. When informed by charity, faith produces, among other things, two great effects in the soul: the filial fear of God which helps the soul keep itself from sin, and the purification of the heart which raises it to the heights and cleanses it of its affection for earthly things.[6]

THE FORMS OF FAITH

It is important to have clear ideas concerning the distinct forms of faith which are distinguished in theology. Faith can be considered, in the first place, by reason of the subjects who believe (subjective faith) or by reason of the object believed (objective faith). Subjective faith admits of the following subdivisions:

1) *Divine faith,* by which we believe whatever has been revealed by God; *Catholic faith,* by which we believe whatever the Church proposes to us as divinely revealed.

2) *Habitual faith,* a supernatural habit infused by God at baptism or at the justification of the unbeliever; *actual faith,* the supernatural act which proceeds from the infused habit (i.e., the supernatural act by which we believe here and now that God is one and three).

3) *Formed or living faith,* which is united with charity when the soul is in the state of grace and is perfected by charity as the extrinsic form

[1] Cf. St. Thomas, *Summa,* II-II, q. 1, a. 4. It follows from this that private visions and revelations, especially if they are not clear and distinct, may be more of an obstacle than a help to pure faith, as St. John of the Cross explains in his *The Ascent of Mount Carmel,* Books II and III.

[2] Cf. *ibid.,* q. 4, a. 7.

[3] Cf. *ibid.,* q. 23, aa. 6-8.

[4] Cf. *ibid.,* a. 7.

[5] Sess. VI, Decree on Justification, Chap. 8, Denz. 801.

[6] Cf. St. Thomas, *Summa,* II-II, q. 7.

of all the virtues; *unformed or dead faith,* which is separated from charity in the soul of the believer who is in the state of mortal sin.

4) *Explicit faith,* by which a person believes a particular mystery concretely as revealed by God; *implicit faith,* by which a person believes everything revealed by God, although he may be ignorant of many details.

5) *Internal faith,* which remains in the interior of our soul; *external faith,* which is manifested externally by words or signs.

Objective faith, on the other hand, can be subdivided in the following way:

1) *Catholic faith,* which is constituted by the revealed truths proposed by God to all men for obtaining eternal life (or everything contained in Sacred Scripture and tradition explicitly or implicitly); *private faith,* which is constituted by the truths which God manifests at times in a supernatural manner to some particular person (e.g., to St. Margaret Mary). The first type obliges all men; the second type obliges only the person who has received it directly from God.

2) *Defined faith,* which pertains to those truths which the Church proposes explicitly to the belief of the faithful under pain of sin of heresy and of excommunication (e.g., the dogma of the Immaculate Conception); *definable faith,* which refers to those truths which as yet have not been defined by the Church as dogmas of faith but which can be defined because they are explicitly contained in the deposit of divine revelation (all the Catholic dogmas before their official definition).

3) *Necessary faith, with a necessity of means,* that which pertains to those truths whose ignorance, even inculpable ignorance, prevents the salvation of the soul;[7] *necessary faith, with a necessity of precept,* which refers to all those truths which the Church proposes for the belief of the faithful but whose inculpable ignorance does not compromise one's eternal salvation (and this pertains to each and every one of the Catholic dogmas).

SINS AGAINST FAITH

According to St. Thomas Aquinas (*Summa,* II-II, qq. 10-15), the sins opposed to the virtue of faith are: *infidelity or paganism,* which, when it is voluntary, is the greatest of all sins except for the direct hatred of God; *heresy,* which

[7]What these truths are concretely is a disputed question among theologians. All theologians agree, since the contrary doctrine is condemned by the Church (Decree of the Holy Office, March 4, 1679; Denz. 1172) that the minimum required is faith in the existence of God as rewarder of the good and punisher of the evil. Some theologians also require the knowledge, however imperfect and rudimentary, of the mystery of the Blessed Trinity and of Christ the Redeemer. St. Thomas seems to say this latter (cf. *Summa,* II-II, q. 2, aa. 7-8), but he does not exact of unbelievers an explicit faith in divine providence but only an implicit faith.

denies some revealed doctrine in particular, or voluntarily doubts it; *apostasy*, which is the complete abandonment of the Christian faith received at baptism; *blasphemy*, especially that against the Holy Ghost; and *blindness of heart* and *dullness of the senses*, which are opposed to the gift of understanding and proceed especially from sins of the flesh. The detailed study of these sins pertains to moral theology.

INCREASE IN FAITH

Both objectively and subjectively faith can grow and develop in our souls until it reaches an extraordinary degree. The saint reaches the point at which he lives his faith, as St. Paul says: "The just man lives by faith" (Rom. 1:17). But it is necessary to understand this doctrine correctly. No one has explained it better than St. Thomas, and we quote his words at some length, adding in parentheses the points which clarify the doctrine for those who are not well-versed in theology:

> The quantity of a habit can be considered in two ways: by reason of the object and by reason of its participation in the subject. (In the present instance, this would mean objective faith and subjective faith.) Now the object of faith (the revealed truths, objective faith) can be considered in two ways: according to its formal reason or motive (the authority of God revealing) or according to the things which are materially proposed for belief (all the truths of faith). The formal object of faith (the authority of God) is one and simple, namely, first truth. Whence, from this point of view, faith is not diversified in believers, but it is specifically one in all (one either accepts the authority of God or he does not; there is no middle course for anyone). But the things which are materially proposed for our belief are many (all the truths of faith), and they can be known more or less explicitly (the theologian knows many more and more clearly than the simple believer). Accordingly, one man can know and believe explicitly more truths than another person, and thus one can have a greater faith according to the greater explication of that faith.
>
> But if faith is considered according to its participation in the subject (subjective faith), it can also have two modes, because active faith proceeds from the intellect (the intellect assents to revealed truths) and from the will (which, moved by God and man's liberty, imposes this assent on the intellect). In this sense faith can be greater in one than in another; by reason of the intellect because of the greater certitude and firmness (in its assent), and by reason of the will because of the greater promptness, devotion or confidence (by which the will commands the intellect to its assent).[8]

There is nothing to add substantially to the foregoing doctrine, but it is fitting to point out the manner in which souls can intensify their faith in their Christian life.

Beginners

As happens with incipient charity,[9] the principal concern of beginners as regards their faith is to nourish and foment it so that it will not be lost or corrupted. In order to do this, certain things are required:

[8] *Summa*, II-II, q. 5, a. 4.
[9] Cf. St. Thomas, *ibid.*, q. 24, a. 9.

POSITIVE MEANS OF GROWTH

1) They must be convinced that faith is a completely gratuitous gift of God and no one can merit it.[10] Consequently, they will ask the Lord in fervent prayer that he always conserve in their souls that divine light which shows them the way to heaven in the midst of the darkness of our ignorance. Their favorite ejaculation, repeated fervently throughout the day, will be that of the gospel: "I do believe, help my unbelief" (Mk. 9:23).

2) They will reject energetically, with the help of divine grace, anything that could be a danger to their faith: diabolical suggestions by way of doubts and temptations against the faith (which they will combat indirectly by distracting themselves or thinking of something else, but never directly by confronting the temptation or disputing with it or by searching for reasons, because this would rather increase the disturbance of soul and the violence of the attack of the enemy); dangerous reading or imprudent reading, in which there is manifested a worldly or anti-Christian viewpoint concerning faith or religion in general; intellectual pride, the most radical and insuperable obstacle by which the incredulous opposes the mercy of God, who would otherwise grant the gift of faith, and an easy way to lose the faith in the case of those who already possess it, as we read in Scripture: "God resists the proud, but gives grace to the humble" (I Pet. 5:5).

3) They will attempt to extend and increase their knowledge of the truths of faith by studying Catholic doctrine to the best of their ability, thus augmenting their religious culture and extending their knowledge to a greater number of revealed truths. This constitutes the extensive increase of objective faith.

4) As regards the increase of subjective faith, they will endeavor to augment it by the frequent and devout recitation of acts of faith and the practice of the rules for thinking with the Church as given by St. Ignatius Loyola in his *Spiritual Exercises.* They will repeat with fervor the supplication of the apostles to the divine Master: "Increase our faith" (Lk. 17:5).

Advanced souls

These souls will be preoccupied with the increase of this fundamental virtue until their whole life is informed by an authentic spirit of faith which will place them on a strictly supernatural plane from which they can see and judge all things. "He who is just lives by faith" (Rom. 1:17). In order to do this, the following things are necessary:

1) They must see God through the light of faith, without taking any account of self-love or selfish views. God is always the same, infinitely good

[10]Cf. Eph. 2:8: "For by grace you have been saved through faith; and that not from yourselves, for it is the gift of God; not as the outcome of works, lest anyone boast."

and merciful, and his nature does not change, regardless of the consolations or dryness which we may experience in prayer, in praise from others, in persecution, in adversity or prosperity.

2) They must strive to make their evaluation of things coincide perfectly with the teachings of faith in spite of anything that the world may say or think. Consequently, they must be convinced that poverty, meekness, tears of repentance, hunger and thirst for perfection, mercy, cleanness of heart, peace and the suffering of persecution (Matt. 5:3-10) are of more value toward eternal life than all the world's riches, violence, arguments, vengeance, pleasures of the flesh or the dominion of the whole world. They must see in Christian suffering an authentic blessing from God, although the world does not understand these things. They must be convinced that it is a greater evil to commit a deliberate venial sin than to lose one's health or life itself; that the supernatural good of a single individual is of much greater worth than the whole world; that the most insignificant or minimum participation in sanctifying grace is of greater value than the universe;[11] that a long life is much less important than a holy life; and that they should not renounce their life of mortification and penance even if their austerities were to shorten their days on earth. In a word, they must see and judge all things from the point of view of God and renounce absolutely all worldly criteria and any points of view which are simply and purely human. Only by faith do we definitely conquer the world. "This is the victory that overcomes the world, our faith" (I Jn. 5:4).

3) This spirit of faith intensely lived will be for them a source of consolation in the suffering of this life and even in bodily infirmity, in bitterness and trials of soul, in the ingratitude or hatred of men, in the sorrowful loss of one's relatives and friends. It will make them see that suffering passes, but that the reward for having suffered well will never pass; that things are as God sees them and not as we would like to judge them by our mundane criterion; that those who have preceded us with the sign of faith await us in a better life (*vita mutatur, non tollitur*); and that after the sufferings and difficulties of this night have passed, there await us the external splendors of the city of the blessed. What great strength and fortitude are caused in the soul by these divine lights of faith for enduring suffering and even embracing it with joy, knowing that the passing tribulations of this life prepare us for the sublime and incomparable glory of eternity! It is not strange, then, that the apostles, and after them all the martyrs, inflamed by the light of faith, walked steadfastly and tranquilly to their death, joyful at being able to suffer these extremes for the name of Jesus (Acts 5:41).

[11]Cf. St. Thomas, *Summa,* I-II, q. 113, a. 9, ad 2.

POSITIVE MEANS OF GROWTH

Perfect souls, illumined by the gifts of understanding and knowledge, cause faith to reach its greatest intensity, and in their lives it shines forth resplendently as a prelude to the beatific vision and the light of glory.

THE GIFT OF UNDERSTANDING

DEFINITION

The gift of understanding can be defined as a supernatural habit, infused in the soul with sanctifying grace, by which the human intellect, under the illuminating action of the Holy Ghost, is made apt for a penetrating intuition of the speculative and practical revealed truths, and even for natural truths, so far as they are related to the supernatural end.

NATURE OF THE GIFT

All the gifts of the Holy Spirit, as supernatural habits, spring from sanctifying grace. Therefore, all souls in grace possess the gifts of the Holy Ghost, and the gifts grow together with grace.[12] The gift of understanding resides in the speculative intellect, which it perfects (the intellect having been informed previously by the virtue of faith) in order to receive in a connatural way the motion of the Holy Ghost, who puts the gift into operation.

Only the Holy Ghost can put the gifts into operation. Without his divine motion they remain idle, since man is absolutely incapable of actuating them, even with the assistance of grace. The gifts are direct and immediate instruments of the Holy Ghost, and from this the divine modality of the acts of the gifts follows. All that man can do with the aid of grace is to dispose himself for the divine movement, removing obstacles, remaining faithful to grace, imploring humbly the sanctifying actuation of the gifts, and seconding freely and meritoriously the movement of the Holy Spirit when the gifts actually operate.

Its objects

The formal object of the gift of understanding is a penetrating intuition, and it points out the specific difference between the gift and the virtue of faith. The virtue of faith gives to the created intellect a knowledge of supernatural truths in an imperfect manner (*modo humano*), which is proper to, and characteristic of, the infused virtues; the gift of understanding makes the intellect apt for the profound and intuitive penetration (*modo superhumano*) of those same revealed truths.[13] Simply speaking, this is infused contemplation, which consists in a simple and profound intuition of truth (*simplex intuitus*

[12]Cf. *ibid.*, II-II, q. 8, a. 4; I-II, q. 68, a. 6.

[13]Cf. *ibid.*, q. 8, a. 6, ad 2.

veritatis).[14] The gift of understanding is distinguished in turn from the other intellectual gifts (wisdom, knowledge and counsel), inasmuch as its proper function is the profound penetration of the truths of faith by way of a simple apprehension, without making any judgment concerning them. It pertains to the other intellectual gifts to make a right judgment concerning them. This judgment, so far as it relates to divine things, pertains to the gift of wisdom; so far as it relates to created things, to the gift of knowledge; and so far as it pertains to the application of these truths to particular actions, to the gift of counsel.[15]

The material object of the gift of understanding comprises speculative and practical revealed truths, and even natural truths so far as they are related to the supernatural end. It embraces everything that pertains to God, Christ, man and all creatures, as regards their origin and end, in such wise that its material object extends primarily to the truths of faith and secondarily to all other things which have some relation to the supernatural end.[16]

NECESSITY OF THE GIFT

However much the virtue of faith is used in the human and discursive manner, it can never attain its full perfection and development; for this the influence of the gift of understanding is indispensable. The reason is simple. Human knowledge is of itself discursive, by composition and division, by analysis and synthesis, and not by the simple intuition of truth. The infused virtues are not exempt from this general condition of human knowledge, since they function under the rule of reason and in a human mode. But since the primary object of faith is the first and supreme truth as it manifests itself (*veritas prima in dicendo*),[17] which is most simple, the discursive complex mode of knowing it cannot be more inadequate and imperfect. Faith is of itself an intuitive and not a discursive habit; therefore, the truths of faith cannot be comprehended in all their perfection except by the intuitive and penetrating vision which is obtained by the gift of understanding—in other words, when faith has been completely liberated from all the discursive elements and converted into a contemplative faith. Then one has reached

[14]Cf. *ibid.*, q. 180, a. 3, ad 1.
[15]Cf. *ibid.*, q. 8, a. 6.
[16]Cf. *ibid.*, a. 3.
[17]As first truth, God can be considered in a threefold manner: *in essendo, in cognoscendo* and *in dicendo*. He is called first truth *in essendo* when we refer to the Deity itself as distinct from false gods; *in cognoscendo* when we refer to the infinite wisdom of God who cannot be deceived; *in dicendo* when we refer to the supreme veracity of God who cannot deceive us. In the first sense (*in essendo*) we have the formal *quod* object of faith; in the second and third senses, that is, the authority of God revealing, which proceeds from his wisdom (*in cognoscendo*) and his veracity (*in dicendo*), we have the formal *quo* object, which is properly the specifying object of faith.

the pure faith which is repeatedly recommended by St. John of the Cross as the only means proportionate for the union of our intellect with God.[18]

ITS EFFECTS The gift of understanding produces admirable effects in the soul, and all of them perfect the virtue of faith to the degree which was attained in the saints. It reveals truths with such clarity that, without sounding the mystery entirely, it gives an unshakable security concerning the truth of our faith. This is seen in the experimental order in those mystical souls in whom the gift of understanding has developed to an eminent degree. They were disposed to believe the contrary of what they saw with their own eyes rather than to doubt in the slightest any of the truths of faith.

This gift is most useful for theologians, and St. Thomas Aquinas possessed it to an extraordinary degree. It enables the theologian to penetrate into the depths of revealed truth and to deduce, by means of theological discursus, the conclusions which are implicit in these truths. The Angelic Doctor points out six different manners in which the gift of understanding enables us to penetrate into the truths of faith.[19]

1) *It enables us to see the substance of things which are hidden under their accidental manifestations.* In virtue of this divine instinct, the mystics perceived the divine reality which is hidden under the eucharistic veils. From this follows their obsession with the Eucharist, an obsession which becomes in them a veritable martyrdom of hunger and thirst. In their visits to the tabernacle they do not pray or meditate, but merely contemplate the divine prisoner of love with a simple and penetrating gaze which fills their soul with great peace and tenderness. "I look at him and he looks at me," as the old man said to the Curé of Ars.

2) *It discloses the hidden meaning of Sacred Scripture.* This is what the Lord effected in regard to the disciples at Emmaus when "he opened their intellect so that they could understand the Scriptures" (Lk. 24:45). All the mystics have experienced this phenomenon. Without any discursus or study or any human assistance, the Holy Spirit suddenly disclosed to them with a most vivid intensity the profound meaning of some statement in Scripture which immersed them in a deluge of light. There, in

[18]"By pure faith is meant the adherence of the intellect to revealed truth, an adherence which is based solely on the authority of God revealing. It excludes all discursus. From the moment that reason enters into play, pure faith disappears, because it is mixed with an element which is alien to its nature. Reasoning can precede or follow faith, but it cannot accompany it without denaturalizing it. The more there is of discursus, the less there is of adherence to the truth by the authority of God and, consequently, the less there is of pure faith" (Father Crisógono, *Compéndio de ascética y mística,* II, c. 2.

[19]Cf. *Summa,* II-II, q. 8, a. 1.

this profound understanding of some scriptural passage, many of the saints found the theme of their whole spiritual life: "The favors of the Lord I will sing forever" of St. Teresa (Ps. 88:1); "let whoever is simple turn in here" of St. Thérèse of Lisieux (Prov. 9:4); "the praise of glory" of Sister Elizabeth of the Trinity (Eph. 1:6). For that reason also these great mystics are not at all moved by books written by men. They reach a point in which they find satisfaction only in the inspired words which come from Scripture, and especially in those which come from the lips of Christ himself.[20]

3) *It reveals to us the mysterious significance of symbols and figures.* Thus St. Paul saw Christ in the rock which gushed forth with living water to appease the thirst of the Israelites in the desert: "And the rock was Christ" (I Cor. 10:4). St. John of the Cross reveals to us, with a startling mystical intuition, the moral, anagogical and parabolic meaning of many of the symbols and figures of the Old Testament which reached their full realization in the New Testament or in the life of grace.

4) *It reveals spiritual realities to us under sensible appearances.* The liturgy of the Church is filled with sublime symbolism which for the most part escapes the notice of superficial souls. But the saints experienced a great veneration and respect for the slightest ceremony of the Church.[21] The gift of understanding enabled them to see the sublime realities which were hidden beneath those symbols and sensible signs.

5) *It enables us to contemplate the effects which are contained in causes.* "There is another aspect of the gift of understanding which is particularly noticeable in contemplative theologians. After the hard labor of human science, everything is suddenly illuminated under an impulse of the spirit. A new world appears in a principle or in a universal cause: Christ the Priest, the one Mediator between heaven and earth; or the mystery of the Blessed Virgin as the co-redemptrix, spiritually carrying in her bosom all the members of the Mystical Body; or the mystery of the identification of the innumerable attributes of God in his sovereign simplicity and the conciliation of the unity of essence with the trinity of persons in one deity, which infinitely surpasses the most secret investigation of all creation. Many other truths there are which the gift of understanding is able to plumb without effort and with great taste in the beatifying joy of an eternal life begun on earth in the very light of God."[22]

---

[20]Cf. St. Thérèse of Lisieux, *Novissima Verba.*

[21]Cf. St. Teresa, *The Life,* Chap. 33.

[22]M. M. Philipon, O.P., *The Spiritual Doctrine of Sister Elizabeth of the Trinity,* Chap. 8.

6) *It makes us see causes through their effects:*

In an inverse sense, the gift of understanding reveals God and his all-powerful causality in his effects without resorting to the lengthy discursive processes of human thought under its own power, but through a simple, comparative gaze and by an intuition after the manner of God himself. In the most imperceptible signs, in the slightest events of his life, the soul that is attentive to the Holy Spirit discovers in one glance the whole plan of divine providence. Without any dialectic reasoning concerning causes, the simple view of the effects of the justice or mercy of God makes the soul comprehend the whole mystery of divine predestination, the excessive love (Eph. 2:4) with which God pursues the soul to unite it to the beatifying Trinity. Through all things, God leads to God.[23]

Intensity of faith

Such are the principal effects which the actuation of the gift of understanding produces in the soul. One can see that, perfected by this gift, the virtue of faith reaches an astounding intensity. The veils of mystery are never parted in this life, but the unfathomable depths are penetrated by the soul with a gaze that is so clear that it approaches an intuitive vision. St. Thomas, a model of serenity and reserve in all his statements, writes the following words: "In this very life, when the eye of the spirit is purified by the gift of understanding, one can in a certain way see God."[24] On reaching these heights, the influence of faith is extended to all the movements of the soul, all its acts are illuminated, and it sees all things through the prism of faith. These souls seem to lose human instinct and to be guided entirely by the divine instinct. Their manner of being, of thinking, of speaking or reacting to the events of their own lives or to the lives of others is disconcerting to the world, which is incapable of understanding these souls. One could say that they suffer an intellectual stoicism in order to see all things just the opposite from the way in which the world sees them. But the truth of the matter is that the distorted vision is that of the world. These souls have had the blessed good fortune that the Holy Ghost, through the gift of understanding, has given to them the *sensus Christi* which makes them see all things in the light of faith. "He who is just, lives by faith" (Rom. 1:17).

THE BEATITUDE AND THE FRUITS

The sixth beatitude pertains to the gift of understanding: "Blessed are the clean of heart, for they shall see God" (Matt. 5:8). In this beatitude, as in the others, two things are indicated: first, something by way of disposition and merit (purity of heart); secondly, something by way of reward (to see God); the gift of understanding is applicable to both. There are two types of purity: purity of heart, by which all sins and disorderly affections are

---

[23] *Loc. cit.*

[24] Cf. *Summa,* II-II, q. 69, a. 2, ad 3.

rejected, which is effected by the virtues and the gifts which pertain to the appetitive part; and purity of mind, by which all phantasms and errors against faith are rejected, and this is proper to the gift of understanding. And as regards the vision of God there is also a double aspect: the perfect vision of God, by which one sees the very essence of God, and this is proper to heaven; and the imperfect vision of God, which is proper to the gift of understanding, by which, although we do not see what God is in himself, we see what he is not and know him the more perfectly in this life as we understand better that he exceeds everything that our human intellects could imagine.[25]

As regards the fruits of the Holy Ghost, which are exquisite acts proceeding from the gifts, the fruits which pertain to the gift of understanding are faith (or the certitude of faith) and joy (spiritual joy), which pertains to the will.[26]

VICES AGAINST THE GIFT

St. Thomas dedicates an entire question to the study of these vices.[27] They are two in number: spiritual blindness and dullness of the spiritual sense. The first is the complete privation of vision (blindness); the second is a notable weakening of vision (myopia). Both of them proceed from carnal sins (gluttony and lust), in the sense that there is nothing that is such an impediment to the flight of the intellect—even naturally speaking—as the vehement attachment to corporal things which are contrary to it. For that reason, lust produces spiritual blindness, which excludes almost completely the knowledge of spiritual goods, and gluttony produces dullness of the spiritual sense, for it weakens man as regards this knowledge.[28]

> This blindness of mind is that which is suffered by all lukewarm souls; for they possess the gift of understanding, but their mind is engulfed with the things of this world. They are lacking in interior recollection and the spirit of prayer; they are constantly pouring themselves out through the channels of the senses, without any attentive or constant consideration of divine truths. Hence they never arrive at discovering the exalted clarity which is hidden in their obscurity. For that reason we see that very frequently they are easily deceived and mistaken when they speak of spiritual things, of the delicacy and fine points of divine love, of the first stages of the mystical life, of the heights of sanctity, and that sometimes they engage themselves in external works which are covered with the veil of human evaluations, and they consider as exaggerations or eccentricities the delicacies which the Holy Spirit of God asks of souls.
>
> These are the souls who wish "to go by the cowpath," as one says vulgarly. They are attached to earth, and for that reason the Holy Ghost cannot raise

---

[25]Cf. St. Thomas, *ibid.*, q. 8, a. 7.

[26]Cf. *ibid.*, a. 8.

[27]Cf. *ibid.*, q. 15.

[28]Cf. *ibid.*, a. 3.

them into the air with his divine motion and breathing. They are busy making sandpiles by which they think they can reach heaven. They suffer that spiritual blindness which prevents them from seeing the infinite holiness of God, the marvels which grace works in souls, the heroism of abnegation which he asks of souls to correspond to his immense love, the foolishness of love by which the soul is led to the folly of the Cross. Such lukewarm souls think nothing of venial sins and perceive only those sins which are more serious; as a result, they ignore what is commonly called imperfections. They are blind because they never take into their hands the torch that would give light in this dark space, and many times in their presumption they attempt to guide others who are blind.

He who suffers such a blindness or shortsightedness in his interior vision, which prevents him from penetrating the things of faith, cannot be free of fault because of his negligence and carelessness or because of the tedium which he experiences in regard to spiritual things, since he loves more those things which appeal to the senses.[29]

MEANS OF PROGRESS

The actuation of the gifts depends entirely on the Holy Spirit, but the soul can do much to dispose itself, with the help of grace, for that divine actuation.[30] These are the principal means of disposing oneself:

1) *The practice of a vital faith with the help of ordinary grace.* The infused virtues are perfected by the ever more intense practice of their proper acts. And although it is true that unless they go beyond the human mode of operation they can never reach their perfection, it is nevertheless an excellent disposition so that the Holy Spirit will perfect the virtues with his gifts if the soul does all that it can by the exercise of the infused virtues. It is a fact that, according to his ordinary providence, God gives his graces to those that are best disposed.[31]

2) *Perfect purity of soul and body.* As we have already seen, the sixth beatitude, which pertains to the clean of heart, corresponds to the gift of understanding. Only through perfect cleanness of soul and body is one made capable of seeing God: in this life, by the profound illumination of the gift of understanding in the obscurity of faith; in the next life, through the clear vision of glory. Impurity is incompatible with either one.

3) *Interior recollection.* The Holy Ghost is the friend of recollection and solitude. Only there does he speak in silence to souls. "I shall lead

[29]P. I. Menéndez-Reigada, O.P., *Los dones del Espíritu Santo y la perfección cristiana,* Chap. 9.

[30]Cf. St. Teresa, *Interior Castle,* Fifth Mansions, Chap. 2.

[31]St. Teresa of Avila speaks of this point in many places in her works. Cf. *The Way of Perfection,* Chap. 18; *Interior Castle,* Third Mansions, Chap. 1; Seventh Mansions, Chap. 2.

her to the desert and I shall speak to her heart" (Os. 2:14). The soul that is a friend of dissipation and worldliness will never perceive the word of God in its interior. It is necessary to empty oneself of all created things, to retire to the cell of one's own heart in order to live there with the divine guest until the soul succeeds gradually in never losing the sense of God's presence even in the midst of the most absorbing occupation. When the soul has done all that it can to be recollected and detached from the world, the Holy Spirit will do the rest.

4) *Fidelity to grace.* The soul must be always attentive and careful not to deny the Holy Ghost any sacrifice that he may ask. "Oh, that today you would hear his voice: Harden not your hearts" (Ps. 94:8). Not only must the soul avoid every voluntary thought, however small, which would sadden the Holy Ghost—according to the mysterious expression of St. Paul: "And do not grieve the Holy Spirit of God" (Eph. 4:30) —but it must positively second all his divine movements until it can say with Christ: "I do always the things that are pleasing to him" (Jn. 8:29). It does not matter if sometimes the sacrifices which he asks of us seem to be beyond our strength. With God's grace, all things are possible. "I can do all things in him who strengthens me" (Phil. 4:13). And there is always left to us the recourse to prayer, to ask the Lord in advance that which he wishes us to give to him: "Give me what you ask and ask what you wish."[32] In any case, in order to avoid anxiety in the matter of positive fidelity to grace, we should always rely on the rule and counsel of a wise and experienced spiritual director.

5) *To invoke the Holy Ghost.* We cannot practice any of these methods without the help and prevenient grace of the Holy Ghost. For that reason we must invoke him frequently and with the greatest possible fervor, remembering the promise of Jesus to send the Holy Spirit to us (Jn. 14:16-17). The Sequence of Pentecost (*Veni Sancte Spiritus*), the hymn for Tierce (*Veni Creator Spiritus*), and the liturgical prayer for the feast of Pentecost (*Deus, qui corda fidelium*) should be, after the Our Father, the favorite prayers of interior souls. We should repeat them often until we attain that *recta sapere* which the Holy Spirit can give us. And in imitation of the apostles when they retired to the Cenacle to await the coming of the Paraclete, we should associate our supplications with those of the Immaculate Heart of Mary (Acts 1:14), the most faithful Virgin and the heavenly Spouse of the Holy Ghost. The divine Spirit will be communicated to us in the measure of our fidelity to grace and this fidelity must be obtained through Mary, the universal mediatrix of all graces.

[32]Cf. St. Augustine, *Confessions,* Bk. X, Chap. 29.

THE GIFT OF KNOWLEDGE

Some authors assign to the gift of knowledge the function of perfecting the virtue of hope, but St. Thomas assigns it to the virtue of faith, while to hope he assigns the virtue of fear of the Lord.[33] We shall follow the teaching of the Angelic Doctor on this matter because it seems to us to be based on the very nature of things.

DEFINITION The gift of knowledge is a supernatural habit, infused with grace, through which the human intellect, under the illuminating action of the Holy Ghost, judges rightly concerning created things as ordained to the supernatural end.

Nature of the gift It is not a question of human or philosophical knowledge, which gives certain and evident knowledge of things deduced by natural reason from their principles or proximate causes, nor is it a question of theological knowledge, which deduces from revealed truths the virtualities contained therein by making use of natural reasoning. It is a question of a certain supernatural knowledge which proceeds from a special illumination by the Holy Ghost, who reveals to us and enables us to appreciate rightly the connection between created things and the supernatural ultimate end. More briefly, it is the correct estimation of the present temporal life in relation to eternal life. It is an infused habit, supernatural, inseparable from grace, which is distinguished essentially from the acquired habits of knowledge and of theology. As a habit it resides in the intellect, as does the virtue of faith which it perfects. It is primarily speculative and secondarily practical.[34]

Its objects The Holy Spirit is the agent who puts the supernatural habit of this gift into action. In virtue of that divine motion, which is very different from the motion of ordinary grace which actuates the virtues, the human intellect apprehends and judges created things by a certain divine instinct, by a certain connaturality, which the just soul possesses potentially through the theological virtues as regards anything that pertains to God. Under the action of this gift the individual does not proceed by laborious reasoning but judges rightly concerning all created things by a superior impulse and by a higher light than that of simple reason illumined by faith. This is the formal reason which distinguishes the gift of knowledge from the gift of understanding. The latter, as we have seen, has as its object to seize and to penetrate revealed truths by a profound supernatural intuition, but without forming

[33]Cf. *Summa,* II-II, q. 9 and q. 19.
[34]Cf. St. Thomas, *ibid.,* q. 9, a. 3.

any judgments concerning them (*simplex intuitus veritatis*). The gift of knowledge, on the other hand, under the special movement of the Holy Ghost, *judges* rightly concerning created things in relation to the supernatural end. In this it is likewise distinguished from the gift of wisdom, whose function it is to judge divine things and not created things.[35]

"Wisdom and knowledge have something in common, both of them giving knowledge of God and of creatures. But when God is known through creatures and when we are elevated from a knowledge of secondary causes to a knowledge of the first and universal cause, it is an act of the gift of knowledge. When human things are known through the taste one has of God and when one judges created things through the knowledge one has of the First Being, it is an act of the gift of wisdom."[36]

The material object of the gift of knowledge is the relation of created things to the supernatural end. It understands created things inasmuch as they have some relation to the supernatural end, and since creatures can be related to the end either by tending toward that end or by attempting to depart from that end, the gift of knowledge gives the just man a correct judgment in both respects.[37] Even more, the gift of knowledge extends also to the divine things which are contemplated in creatures, proceeding from God to manifest his glory,[38] according to the expression of St. Paul: "His invisible attributes are clearly seen—his everlasting power also and divinity—being understood through the things that are made" (Rom. 1:20).

"This right judging of creatures is the knowledge or science of the saints, and it is based on that spiritual taste and affection of charity which does not rest only in God, but passes also to creatures through God, ordaining them to him and forming a judgment of them according to their properties; that is, through the inferior and created causes. This distinguishes the gift of knowledge from the gift of wisdom, which springs from the Supreme Cause and is united to it through charity."[39]

NECESSITY OF THE GIFT

The gift of knowledge is absolutely necessary if the virtue of faith is to reach its full expansion and development in yet another aspect, which is distinct from that which we have seen in relation to the gift of understanding. It is not sufficient to apprehend the revealed truth even with that profound and intuitive penetration which comes from the gift of understanding; it is necessary also that we have a supernatural instinct for discovering and judging

[35]Cf. *ibid.*, q. 8, a. 6.

[36]Louis Lallemant, S.J., *Spiritual Doctrine*, Principle IV, Chap. 4, a. 3; cf. St. Thomas, *Summa*, II-II, q. 9, a. 2, ad 3.

[37]Cf. St. Thomas, *ibid.*, a. 4.

[38]Cf. *ibid.*, a. 2, ad 3.

[39]John of St. Thomas, *In I-II*, Dist. 18, a. 4.

rightly concerning the relation of those divine truths with the natural and sensible world which surrounds us. Without this supernatural instinct, faith itself would be in danger, because attracted and seduced by the allurement of created things; being ignorant of the method or manner of relating them with the supernatural order, we could easily fall into error, and, at least in the practical order, we could lose the light of faith. Daily experience confirms this all too well to make it necessary to insist upon it.

The gift of knowledge performs invaluable services for the virtue of faith, especially in the practical order. Through this gift, under the movement and illumination of the Holy Ghost, and through a certain affinity or connaturality with spiritual things, we are able to judge rightly, according to the principles of faith, concerning the use of creatures, their value, their utility or danger as regards eternal life. Consequently, he who works under the influence of the gift of knowledge can be said truly to have received the knowledge of the saints.

EFFECTS OF KNOWLEDGE

The effects of this gift are admirable and all of them have a great sanctifying value. The following are the principal effects:

1) *It teaches us how to judge rightly concerning created things in relation to God.* This is proper to the gift of knowledge:

> Under its impulse, a double movement is produced in the soul: the experience of the emptiness of the creature, of its nothingness; and also, through the vision of creation, the discovery of the vestige of God. The gift of knowledge drew tears from St. Dominic when he thought of the miserable lot of poor sinners, while the spectacle of nature inspired in St. Francis of Assisi his famous *Canticle to the Sun*. The two sentiments appear in the well-known passage of the spiritual canticle of St. John of the Cross, in which the saint describes the consolation and the torment of the mystical soul in the view of creation, when the things of the universe reveal to the soul a trace of its Beloved, while he remains invisible until the soul, transformed in him, finds him in the beatific vision.[40]

The first aspect caused St. Ignatius Loyola to exclaim, when contemplating the spectacle of a starry night: "O how vile the earth appears to me when I contemplate heaven!"; the second aspect caused St. John of the Cross to fall to his knees before the beauty of a little fountain, of a mountain, of a landscape, of the setting sun. The nothingness of created things, when contemplated through the gift of knowledge, made St. Paul esteem all things as base and wish all the more to gain Christ (Phil. 3:8); the beauty of God reflected in the beauty and fragrance of the flowers obliged St. Paul of the Cross to speak to them in transports of love:

---

[40]M. M. Philipon, O.P. *Spiritual Doctrine of Sister Elizabeth of the Trinity*, Chap. 8.

"Be silent, little flowers, be silent." And this same sentiment is what gave St. Francis of Assisi that sublime sense of the universal brotherhood of all things that come forth from the hand of God. It was likewise the gift of knowledge which gave St. Teresa of Avila that extraordinary facility for explaining the things of God by making use of comparisons and examples taken from created things. The same can be said of the outstanding ascetical writer, Louis of Granada.

2) *It guides us with certitude concerning that which we must believe or not believe.* The soul in whom the gift of knowledge operates intensely instinctively possesses the sense of faith (*sensus fidei*). Without having studied theology or without having had any education, such souls are aware whether or not a devotion, a doctrine, a counsel or any kind of maxim is in accord with faith or is opposed to faith. They experience this with an irresistible power and with an unflinching assurance. It is admirable how St. Teresa of Avila, in spite of her humility and her complete submission to her confessor, could never accept the erroneous doctrine which held that in certain states of prayer it was necessary to prescind from the consideration of the adorable humanity of Christ.[41]

3) *It enables us to see promptly and with certitude the state of our soul.* Everything is clear to the penetrating introspection of the gift of knowledge: "our interior acts, the secret movements of our heart, its qualities, its goodness, its malice, its principles, its motives, its goals and intentions, its effects and consequences, its merits and demerits."[42] Rightly did St. Teresa say that "in a place where the sun enters, there is no hidden dust."[43]

4) *It inspires us concerning the safest method of conduct with our neighbor as regards eternal life.* In this sense the gift of knowledge in its practical aspect influences the virtue of prudence, whose perfection is directly under the gift of counsel, according to the teaching of St. Thomas.

By this gift a preacher knows what he ought to say to his hearers and what he ought to urge upon them. A director knows the state of the souls he has under his guidance, their spiritual needs, the remedies for their faults, the obstacles they put in the way of their perfection, the shortest and the surest road by which to conduct them safely; how he must console or mortify them, what God is working in them, and what they ought to do on their part in order to co-operate with God and fulfill his designs. A superior knows in what way he ought to govern his inferiors.

---

[41]Cf. *Interior Castle,* Sixth Mansions, Chap. 7; *The Life,* Chaps. 22, 23, 24.

[42]Louis Lallemant, S.J., *Spiritual Doctrine,* Principle IV, Chap. 4, a. 3.

[43]*The Life,* Chap. 19.

5) *It detaches us from the things of earth.* This is, in reality, nothing more than a consequence of that right judgment of things which constitutes the proper characteristic of the gift of knowledge. Before God, all creatures are as if they were not.[44] For that reason it is necessary to rise above created things in order to rest in God alone. But only the gift of knowledge gives to the saints that profound vision concerning the necessity of the absolute detachment which we admire, for example, in St. John of the Cross. For a soul illuminated by the gift of knowledge, creation is an open book, for the soul discovers without effort the nothingness of creatures and the all of the Creator. "The soul passes by creatures without seeing them in order not to be detained in anything but Christ. . . . The whole of all creation, is it worth even a glance from him who has experienced God, if only once?"[45]

6) *It teaches us how to use created things in a holy way.* This sentiment, which is complementary to the former, is another consequence of the right judgment of created things proper to the gift of knowledge. It is certain that created things are nothing when compared with God, and yet they are crumbs which fall from the table of God, and they speak to us of him and lead us to him if we know how to use them rightly. This is what is effected by the gift of knowledge. There are countless examples of this in the lives of the saints. The contemplation of created things raised their souls to God because they could see the vestige or trace of God in creation. Sometimes the most insignificant detail, which would pass unnoticed by an ordinary person, made a strong impression on these holy souls and led them to God.

7) *It fills us with repentance and sorrow for our past errors.* This is an inevitable consequence of a right judgment concerning created things. In the resplendent light of the gift of knowledge, the souls discover the nothingness of creatures, their fragility, their vanity, their short duration, their inability to make us truly happy, the harm which attachment to them can cause to the soul. And then, on recalling other periods of life in which perhaps they were subject to such vanity and misery, holy souls feel deep within their hearts a most profound repentance which is manifested externally by intense acts of contrition and self-disdain. The pathetic accents of the *Miserere* spontaneously spring to their lips as a psychological necessity to alleviate the weight of sorrow that overwhelms them. For that reason, the beatitude which corresponds to the gift of knowledge is the beatitude of those who weep.[46]

---

[44]Cf. St. John of the Cross, *The Ascent of Mount Carmel,* Bk. I, Chap. 4.
[45]M. M. Philipon, O.P., *loc. cit.*
[46]Cf. St. Thomas, *Summa,* II-II, q. 9, a. 4, ad 1.

Such are the principal effects of the gift of knowledge. Through it, far from seeing creatures as obstacles to union with God, the soul uses them as instruments to be united to God more easily. Perfected by the gifts of understanding and knowledge, the virtue of faith reaches its greatest intensity and makes the soul experience the divine brilliance of the eternal vision.

THE BEATITUDE AND FRUITS

To the gift of knowledge corresponds the third beatitude: "Blessed are they who mourn, for they shall be comforted" (Matt. 5:5). This is true both as regards the merit and the reward. As regards the merit (tears), because the gift of knowledge, since it implies a right judgment and estimation of creatures in relation to eternal life, impels the just man to weep for his past errors as regards the use of creatures. In regard to the reward (consolation), because through the light of the gift of knowledge created things are rightly judged and ordained to the divine good, and from this spiritual consolation follows, which begins in this life and will reach its plenitude in the life to come.[47]

As regards the fruits of the Holy Ghost, the same ones correspond to the gift of knowledge as to the gifts of understanding and wisdom, since all three have as their object the true as related to the supernatural ultimate end. By the same token, there is produced in the intellect that special certitude concerning supernatural truths which is called faith (*fides*), and in the will, by redundance, a certain taste, delight and fruition which is called spiritual joy (*gaudium*).[48]

VICES OPPOSED TO THE GIFT

In the prologue to the question on the sins opposed to the gift of understanding, St. Thomas refers to ignorance as a vice opposed to the gift of knowledge.[49] The gift of knowledge is indispensable for avoiding or rejecting completely, as by a certain divine instinct, the multitude of errors which in the matter of faith and morals are constantly threatening us by reason of our ignorance and mental weakness. Not only among uneducated persons but even among professional theologians, in spite of the sincerity of their faith and efforts of their studies, there is rampant a multitude of opinions and differing views in dogma and moral, and necessarily they must all be false except one, because truth itself is one. Who, then, will give us a sound and certain criterion so that we shall not deviate from the truth in any of these complicated questions? In the personal and subjective order, this is something which surpasses human power, even the power of theologians. Only the Holy Spirit, by the gift of knowledge, can give us that certitude by means of a divine instinct. And so it is that many persons who are uneducated and unlettered

[47]Cf. St. Thomas, *loc. cit.*

[48]Cf. *ibid.*, q. 8, a. 8.

[49]*Ibid.*, q. 15.

have astounded the greatest theologians by the security and depth with which they penetrate the truths of faith and the facility and clarity with which they resolve, as if by instinct, the most intricate problems of moral theology. On the other hand, how many illusions have those persons suffered in the ways of the Lord who have not been illumined by the gift of knowledge? All false mystics are so because of ignorance, which is contrary to this gift of knowledge.

Ignorance

This ignorance may be culpable and may constitute a true vice because it can sometimes be voluntary. And it may be voluntary because an individual occupies himself in vain or curious things, or in human sciences without the proper moderation, so that he is excessively absorbed by them and gives no time or study to the most important science of his own salvation and sanctification, or because of vain presumption by which he trusts too much in his own knowledge and thus places an obstacle to the judgments which he should form under the light of the Holy Ghost. This abuse of knowledge is the principal reason why there are many more mystics among simple and uneducated persons than among the wise and the intellectual. As long as souls do not renounce their voluntary blindness and intellectual pride, there is no likelihood that the gifts of the Holy Spirit will ever be actuated in their souls. Christ himself warned us in the gospel: "I praise thee, Father, Lord of heaven and earth, that thou didst hide these things from the wise and the prudent, and didst reveal them to little ones" (Matt. 11:25). Consequently, the ignorance contrary to the gift of knowledge, which is often found in those who are considered to be very wise and intelligent, is usually indirectly voluntary and culpable and therefore constitutes a true vice against the gift of knowledge.

MEANS OF PROGRESS

In addition to the recollection, fidelity to grace and invocation of the Holy Spirit which are the common means for fomenting the gifts of the Holy Ghost in general, we can point out certain special means which pertain particularly to the gift of knowledge.

1) *To consider the vanity of created things.* We can never attain, however much we try by means of our poor consideration, to the penetrating intuition of the gift of knowledge concerning the vanity of created things. And yet there is no doubt that we can achieve something by meditating seriously on this point by means of the discursive methods which are at our disposal. God does not ask of us more than we are able to give him at a given time, and he who does what he can, will never be refused the divine assistance for further progress.[50]

---

[50]It would prove very helpful in this regard to read certain spiritual works which treat of this matter. Louis of Granada has written marvelous pages on this point throughout his works. Cf. *Summa of the Christian Life.*

2) *To accustom oneself to refer all created things to God.* This is another psychological method for attaining gradually to the point of view in which the gift of knowledge definitely places us. We should never rest in creatures but should pass through them to God. Are not created beauties a pallid reflection of the divine beauty? We should endeavor to discover in all things the vestige or trace of God and thus prepare the way for the action of the Holy Spirit in us.

3) *To oppose energetically the spirit of the world.* The world has the sad privilege of seeing all things precisely contrary to what they really are from a supernatural point of view. The world is not concerned with anything but enjoying created things, putting all its happiness in them, and turning its back upon God. For that reason there is no other attitude which is more contrary to the spirit of the gift of knowledge, which makes us disdain created things or use them only in relation to God or as a means to God. We should avoid the false maxims of life which are completely opposed to the spirit of God. We should renounce the spectacles and diversions which are saturated or greatly influenced by the poisonous atmosphere of the world. We should always be alert lest we are taken by surprise by the artful enemy, who is constantly striving to turn our gaze away from the great panorama of the supernatural world.

4) *To see the hand of providence in the government of the world and in all the events of our life, whether prosperous or adverse.* It costs a great deal to acquire this point of view, and it will never be acquired completely until the gift of knowledge operates in us as well as the gift of wisdom. Nevertheless, we must endeavor to do as much as we can in this respect. It is a dogma of faith that God cares for us with a loving providence. He is our Father, and he knows much better than we what things are good for us. He governs us with an infinite love, although many times we cannot discover the secret design in that which he disposes or permits to happen to us or to our family or to the world.

5) *To be preoccupied greatly with purity of heart.* This concern and preoccupation will attract the blessing of God, and he will not neglect to give us the gifts which we need to attain perfect purity of heart, if we are faithful to his grace. There is a very close relationship between the custody of the heart and the exact fulfillment of all our obligations. "I have more discernment than the elders because I observe thy precepts" (Ps. 118:100).

3: THE VIRTUE OF HOPE

DEFINITION Hope is a theological virtue infused by God into the will, by which we trust with complete certitude in the attainment of eternal life and the means necessary for reaching it, assisted by the omnipotent help of God. The primary material object of hope is eternal beatitude; the secondary material object consists in all the means which lead to it. The formal *quod* object is God himself, as the objective beatitude of man, connoting formal beatitude or the beatific vision. The formal motive of hope (formal *quo* object) is the assisting omnipotence of God, connoting divine mercy and God's fidelity to his promises.

HOPE ITSELF

ITS NATURE Hope resides in the will, because its proper object is a movement of the rational appetite toward the good, which is the object of the will.[1] Charity and faith are more perfect than hope.[2] Absolutely speaking, faith and hope can exist without charity (unformed faith and hope), but no infused virtue can exist in the soul without faith.[3]

As St. Thomas points out, hope tends to its object with absolute certitude,[4] a truth which requires some explaining. As the Church teaches, without a special revelation we cannot be certain that *de facto* we shall attain our eternal salvation,[5] although we can and ought to have absolute certitude that with the assistance of the omnipotent help of God (the formal motive

---

[1]Cf. St. Thomas, *Summa,* II-II, q. 18, a. 1.

[2]*Ibid.,* q. 17, aa. 7-8.

[3]Cf. *ibid.,* I-II, q. 65, aa. 4-5.

[4]*Ibid.,* II-II, q. 18, a. 4; cf. the Council of Trent, Sess. VI, Decree on Justification, Chap. 13; Denz. 806.

[5]The Council of Trent, *ibid.,* Chap. 12; Denz. 805.

of hope) there can be no insuperable obstacle to our salvation. Hope treats, then, of a certitude of inclination and of motive, but not of a previous infallible knowledge nor of any event or exercise that cannot be frustrated.[6] The goods of this world fall under the secondary object of hope, but only to the extent that they can be useful to us for salvation. For that reason, St. Thomas says that, apart from the salvation of our soul, we ought not ask God for any other good unless it is in some way related to our salvation.[7]

Theological hope is impossible in infidels and formal heretics, for no infused virtue can exist without faith. Sinners who have not despaired may possess unformed hope, but this virtue is properly found in the just on earth and in the souls in purgatory. Those who are in hell do not have hope because they have nothing to hope for; the blessed in heaven do not have this virtue because they are already enjoying the infinite good for which they had hoped. For the same reason, Christ did not have hope, since he was at once a blessed (or comprehensor) and a wayfarer.[8]

The act of hope

The act of hope, even of unformed hope, is of itself good and virtuous (as opposed to the teaching of Calvin, Baius and the Jansenists, who stated that any act of virtue performed out of the hope of an eternal reward was selfish and immoral). This is expressly stated in Sacred Scripture and can be demonstrated theologically, since eternal life is the supernatural ultimate end of man.[9] Therefore, to work with one's gaze fixed on this end is not only good and virtuous but necessary. The contrary doctrine has been condemned by the Church in a decree of the Holy Office (December 7, 1690; Denz. 1303) condemning the errors of Jansenism.

By the same token, in this life there is no state of perfection which habitually excludes the motives of hope. The opposite view is an error of the Quietists and semi-Quietists, also condemned by the Church in various decrees (Denz. 1227, 1232, 1327 ff.). The error of the Jansenists and the Quietists consisted in the affirmation that to work out of hope is immoral and imperfect and gives evidence that the individual desires God as a good for himself, thus subordinating God to his own personal happiness. But such is not the case. As Cajetan explains (*In II-II*, q. 17, a. 5, n. 6): "It is one thing to desire this thing for me, and it is another thing to desire it because of me." We desire God for ourselves, not because of ourselves but because of himself. God continues to be the end or goal of the act of hope, not ourselves. On the other hand, when we desire some inferior thing, such as a created good, we desire it for ourselves and because of ourselves (*nobis et propter nos*).

---

[6]Cf. S. Ramírez, O.P., *De certitudine spei christianae* (Salamanca: 1938).
[7]*Summa*, II-II, q. 17, a. 2, ad 2.
[8]Cf. St. Thomas, *ibid.*, q. 18, aa. 2-3.
[9]Cf. Ps. 118:112; Matt. 6:33; Col. 3:1; Heb. 11:26.

SINS AGAINST HOPE

St. Thomas explains that two vices are opposed to hope: one by defect, *despair,* which considers eternal salvation impossible and proceeds principally from spiritual sloth and lust; and the other by excess, *presumption.* Presumption takes two principal forms: that which considers eternal beatitude as attainable by one's own efforts without the aid of grace (heretical presumption), and that which expects to be saved without repentance for sin or to obtain glory without any merit (a sin against the Holy Ghost). Presumption may be caused by vainglory and pride.[10]

THE INCREASE OF HOPE

Like any other virtue, hope can increase more and more. Let us consider the principal phases of its development in the various stages in the spiritual life.

In beginners

Above all, beginners will avoid falling into one of the two extremes contrary to hope: presumption and despair. To avoid the first, they should consider that without the grace of God we can do absolutely nothing in the supernatural order. "Without me, you can do nothing" (Jn. 15:5). Without God's help one could not have a single good thought or even pronounce worthily the name of Jesus (I Cor. 12:3). They should keep in mind that God is infinitely good and merciful, but that he is also infinitely just and no one can laugh at him (Gal. 6:7). He is disposed to save us, but on the condition that we voluntarily co-operate with his grace (I Cor. 15:10) and that we work out our salvation in fear and trembling (Phil. 2:12).

Against despair and discouragement the beginner will remember that the mercy of God is untiring in pardoning the repentant sinner; that the violence of our enemies can never overcome the omnipotent help of God; and that, if it is certain that of ourselves we can do nothing, it is likewise certain that with God's grace we can do all things (Phil. 4:13). It is necessary, then, to rise courageously from one's falls and renew the journey with greater effort and zeal, taking occasion from the fault itself to redouble one's vigilance and effort. "All things work for the good with those who love God" (Rom. 8:28); and St. Augustine dares to add, "even sins," so far as they are an occasion of making the soul more vigilant and cautious.

Beginners should also endeavor to raise their gaze to heaven, and this for several reasons:

1) *In order to disdain the things of earth.* Everything here below is shadow and vanity and deceit. No created thing can fill completely the heart of man, in whom God has placed an infinite capacity. And even in the event that such things could satisfy man completely, this would be a transitory and fleeting happiness, as is life itself on this earth. Pleasures, wealth, honors, the applause of men—all these things pass and vanish like

[10] Cf. St. Thomas, *ibid.,* qq. 20-21.

smoke. St. Francis Borgia was right when he said: "I shall no longer serve a master who can die to me." When all is said and done, "What does it profit a man, if he gain the whole world, but suffer the loss of his own soul?" (Matt. 16:26).

2) *To be consoled in the midst of their labors and sufferings.* The earth is a valley of tears and miseries. Suffering accompanies us inevitably from the cradle to the grave, and no one escapes this inexorable law. But Christian hope reminds us that all the sufferings of this life are as nothing in comparison with the glory which is to be manifested in us (Rom. 8:13), and that if we bear them in a holy manner, these momentary and light tribulations prepare us for the eternal weight of a sublime and incomparable glory (II Cor. 4:17). What a consolation this is for the soul that suffers tribulation if it is able to contemplate heaven through its tears!

3) *To be encouraged to be good.* The practice of virtue is arduous indeed. It is necessary to be detached from everything, to renounce one's own tastes and caprices, and to turn back the continuous attacks from the world, the devil and the flesh. Especially at the beginning of the spiritual life this constant battle is most difficult. But what great encouragement the soul can experience in raising its eyes to heaven! It is well worth while to struggle for a short time during the brief years of this life in order to obtain the possession for all eternity of the fatherland. Later, when the soul begins to advance along the paths of union with God, the motives of disinterested love will prevail over those of the soul's own happiness, but these desires for perfect happiness will never be completely abandoned. Even the greatest saints experienced a kind of nostalgia for heaven, and this is one of the most powerful stimuli for advancing without discouragement along the way of heroism and sanctity.

Advanced souls

In the measure that the soul progresses along the path of perfection, it will strive to cultivate the virtue of hope by intensifying as much as possible its confidence in God and in his divine assistance. To this end, the following practices are necessary:

1) *Never to be preoccupied with anxious solicitude for tomorrow.* We are submerged in the divine and loving providence of our own good God. Nothing will be lacking to us if we trust in him and if we hope for all things from him. As regards the temporal order, we have the words of Christ himself: "Look at the birds of the air. . . . Consider how the lilies of the field grow. . . . How much more you, O you of little faith" (Matt. 6:25-34). In the order of grace, the same Christ tells us: "I come that they may have life, and have it more abundantly" (Jn. 10:10). And St. Paul remarks: "This grace has abounded beyond measure in us." (Eph. 1:7-8).

2) *To simplify their prayer as much as possible.* "But in praying, do not multiply words . . . , for your Father knows what you need before you ask him." (Matt. 6:7-13). The formula of the Our Father, which came from the lips of the divine Master, will be their favorite prayer, together with those other prayers from the gospel which are so brief and filled with confidence in the goodness and mercy of God: "Lord, he whom thou lovest is sick"; "if thou wilt, thou canst make me clean"; "Lord, that I may see"; "teach us to pray"; "increase our faith"; "show us the Father and this will suffice." What simplicity and sublimity in the Gospel, but how much complication and confusion in us when we pray! The soul must endeavor to attain that ingenuous confidence which is simple and which draws miracles from Christ.

3) *To advance in detachment from all earthly things.* Of what value are all created goods when compared with a smile from God? "Since the time that I have known Jesus Christ, no created thing has seemed to me sufficiently beautiful to be desired" (Père Lacordaire). Before the thought of the sovereign beauty of God, whose contemplation will make us intoxicated with happiness in eternal life, the soul will readily renounce all earthly things, and reach the point of conquering the threefold concupiscence to which so many souls are subject on earth and which prevents them from flying to heaven. (I Jn. 2:16).

4) *To advance with great confidence along the path of union with God.* Nothing will be able to detain the soul if it wishes to proceed at any cost. God, who calls the soul to a life of intimate union with himself, extends his divine hand with the absolute guarantee of his omnipotence, mercy and fidelity to his promises. The world, the devil and the flesh will declare war against the soul, but "those who trust in the Lord will renew their strength, and they will have wings like the eagles, and they will fly speedily without tiring, and they will run without becoming weary" (Is. 40:31). With good reason did St. John of the Cross say that hope "is that which especially makes the soul pleasing to the beloved, and that by it the soul will attain all that it desires."[11] The soul that continues courageously in spite of all contradictions and obstacles and with all confidence in God will undoubtedly arrive at the height of perfection.

The perfect

The following are the principal characteristics of the operation of the virtue of hope in perfect souls:

1) *Universal confidence in God.* Nothing is able to discourage a servant of God when he enters upon an enterprise which pertains to the divine glory. One would say that contradictions and obstacles, far

[11]*The Dark Night,* Bk. II, Chap. 21.

from diminishing the virtue of hope, intensify and augment it; such a soul's confidence in God will sometimes reach the point of audacity. One need only recall the obstacles which St. Teresa of Avila had to overcome in the reform of the Carmelites, and the most firm assurance of success with which she began that work, far beyond all human power, trusting only in God. As St. Paul said of Abraham, these holy souls hope "against hope" (Rom. 4:18). They are disposed at any moment to repeat the heroic phrase of Job: "Slay me though he might, I will wait for him." (Job 13:15). This heroic confidence glorifies God greatly and is of the greatest merit for the soul.

2) *Indestructable peace and serenity.* This is a natural consequence of their universal confidence in God. Nothing is capable of disturbing the tranquility of their spirit. Ridicule, persecution, calumny, injury, sickness, misfortune—everything falls upon their soul like water on marble, without leaving the slightest trace or alteration in the serenity of their spirit. The saintly Curé of Ars received an unexpected slap, and he merely smiled and said: "Friend, the other cheek will be envious." St. Louis Bertrand inadvertently drank a poisoned drink and remained completely tranquil when he discovered it. St. Charles Borromeo remained unmoved and continued to recite the rosary when a gun was discharged and a bullet passed by his cheek. St. Hyacinth of Poland did not defend himself when he was a victim of a terrible calumny but trusted in God to clarify the mystery. What peace, what serenity, what confidence in God these heroic examples of the saints presuppose! One would say that their souls had lost contact with the things of this world and were as "immovable and tranquil as if they were already in eternity" (Sister Elizabeth of the Trinity).

3) *The desire to die in order to reach the fatherland.* This is one of the clearest signs of the perfection of hope. Nature experiences an instinctive horror of death. No one wishes to die; only when grace has taken complete possession of the soul can one desire death in order to live the true life hereafter. Then the soul gives expression to the "I die because I do not die" of St. Augustine, which was repeated later by St. Teresa and St. John of the Cross and constitutes one of the most ardent desires of all the saints. The soul which continues to be attached to the life of this earth and looks with horror on the death which approaches shows by that fact that its vision of the reality of things and its Christian hope are as yet very imperfect. All the saints desire to die in order to go to heaven.

4) *Heaven begun on earth.* The saints desire to die to go to heaven, but in reality their life in heaven has already begun on earth. What do the things of this world matter to them? The servants of God live on earth

only in their bodies, but their soul and their yearning are fixed in heaven. It is simply another way of stating the phrase: "But our conversation is in heaven" (Phil. 3:20).

THE GIFT OF FEAR

The sublime dispositions of the saints which we have just recorded are an obvious effect of the superhuman actuation of the gifts of the Holy Ghost. The virtues, if left to themselves, would never arrive at such heights. The rule of reason, even when illumined by faith, is too imperfect to perceive these exquisite actions. According to St. Thomas, the gift which pertains to the perfection of the virtue of hope is fear of the Lord.

ITS NATURE

The gift of fear is a supernatural habit by which the just soul, under the instinct of the Holy Ghost, acquires a special docility for subjecting itself completely to the divine will out of reverence for the excellency and majesty of God, who is capable of inflicting punishment on us. In order to understand this doctrine it is necessary, first of all, to discuss a problem which can be formulated in the following question: "Should God be feared?" The answer is that God in himself, as supreme and infinite goodness, cannot be an object of fear, he is an object of love. But so far as he is able to inflict evil upon us in punishment for our sins, he can and ought to be feared. In answering this question, St. Thomas harmonizes fear and hope, which at first glance seem to be incompatible, by saying that in God there is justice and mercy, the first of which arouses fear in us, the second, hope. And thus, for different reasons, God is the object of fear and of hope.[12]

Kinds of fear

It is necessary to examine the nature of this fear, however, because there are many types of fear and not all of them are gifts of the Holy Ghost. Some of them are not even virtues. Fear can be divided into mundane fear, servile fear, filial fear and initial fear. Mundane fear is that which would not hesitate to offend God in order to avoid some temporal evil. Thus one would apostatize from the faith in order to avoid the torments and sufferings of persecution. This fear is always evil, because it places its end and goal in this world and turns its back completely upon God. It flees temporal suffering and falls into sin before God.

Servile fear is that which serves God and fulfills his divine will because of the evils which would fall upon us if we did not do so (temporal punishment

[12] *Summa*, II-II, q. 19, a. 1 and ad 2.

or the eternal punishment of hell). This fear, although imperfect, is substantially good; when all is said and done, it enables us to avoid sin and it is directed to God as to its end, not considering the pain or punishment as the only evil, because if that were so, the fear itself would be evil and sinful. It flees from sin to avoid punishment.[13]

Filial fear (also called reverential or chaste fear) is that which serves God and fulfills his divine will, fleeing from sin only because it is an offense against God and for fear of being separated from him. It is called filial fear because it is proper for sons to fear the loss and separation of their father. This fear, as is evident, is good and perfect. It flees from sin without taking any account of punishment.

Initial fear is that which occupies an intermediate place between the last two types of fear. It flees from sin principally as an offense against God, but there is mixed with this flight a certain fear of punishment. This fear is better than servile fear, but it is not as perfect as filial fear.

The gift of fear

The question now arises: which of these fears is the gift of the Holy Ghost? Evidently the gift of fear is not mundane or servile fear. Mundane fear is sinful because it fears more the loss of the world than the loss of God, whom it would abandon for the world. And servile fear, although not evil of itself, could be found even in a sinner by means of an actual grace which would move him to the sorrow of attrition because of the fear of punishment. This fear is a grace from God which moves one to repentance, but as yet it is not connected to charity and therefore could not be related to the gift of the Holy Ghost.

---

[13]The right understanding of the morality of servile fear offers some difficulty. One should keep in mind that the fear of punishment can influence a person in three manners as regards the performance of a good work or the avoidance of sin. 1) As the only cause, as if one were to say, "I would commit sin if there were no hell." In this sense it is called servilely servile fear and is evil and sinful because, although *de facto* the individual materially avoids the sin, he formally commits a sin because of the affection which he has admitted. It does not matter to him that sin is an offense against God; what keeps him from doing evil is simply the pain or punishment; therefore he would sin were it not for the fear of punishment. 2) As a remote cause added to the proximate and principal cause; e.g., as when one would say that he does not wish to sin because it is an offense against God and, moreover, it would redound to his own misfortune. This type of fear is good and virtuous and is called initial fear. 3) As the proximate cause, although without excluding the higher reason; e.g., if one were to say that he does not wish to commit a certain sin because it would lead him to hell and, moreover, would be an offense against God. This is what is called simply servile fear. It is imperfect, but it is basically virtuous because, although more remotely, it nevertheless does reject sin as an offense against God. There is no inconvenience in having an inferior proximate end related and subordinated to a higher remote end; the two things are not incompatible.

According to St. Thomas, only filial or chaste fear is the gift of fear, for it is based on charity or reverence of God as Father, and it fears to be separated from him. But as initial fear does not differ substantially from filial fear, that also is a part of the gift of fear, although only in its incipient and imperfect manifestations. In the measure that charity increases, initial fear is gradually purified, so that it loses the servile aspect which still fears punishment and gradually considers sin simply as an offense against God.

In Sacred Scripture we are told that the fear of the Lord is the beginning of wisdom (Ps. 110:10). But this must be understood, not as regards the essence of speculative wisdom, whose first principles are the articles of faith, but as regards practical wisdom, whose first effect is to subject souls to the law of God. This is done imperfectly by servile fear and perfectly by filial fear. The gift of fear, like all the other gifts, will remain in heaven, not as servile fear, which is not a gift of the Holy Ghost, nor as initial fear, since there will be no possibility of punishment in heaven, but only as filial fear. And only in its reverential aspect before the majesty of God will the gift of fear remain, not in its aspect of a fear of offending God, for this also is completely impossible because of the intrinsic impeccability of the blessed in heaven.

THE NECESSITY OF FEAR

The necessity of the gifts in general is based on the imperfection with which the infused virtues operate, even when subjected to the rule of human reason illumined by faith. There are three principal virtues which need to be strengthened by the divine rule or government of the gift of fear: hope, temperance and humility.

Hope

A man feels a natural inclination to love himself excessively, to presume that he is something, that he is able to do much in the pursuit of eternal beatitude. Such is the sin of presumption, the contrary to the virtue of hope, which can be uprooted only by the gift of fear. For fear gives us that supernatural awareness of our absolute impotence before God and, as a consequence, inclines us to rely only on the omnipotent help of God, the formal motive of hope. Without the gift of fear, the virtue of hope would never be completely perfect in us.[14]

Temperance

St. Thomas states that the gift of fear looks principally at God, whom we must avoid offending, and in this sense it pertains to the virtue of hope, as we have already indicated. But secondarily fear can also look at any other thing which would be able to help man avoid offending God. In this sense the gift of fear helps to correct the disorderly tendency by which a man experiences a strong attraction to carnal delight, by repressing or controlling

[14]Cf. St. Thomas, *Summa,* II-II, q. 19, a. 9, ad 1 and 2; q. 141, a. 1, ad 3.

it through fear of the Lord and thus aiding and strengthening the virtue of temperance.[15]

Humility

A man especially loves his own grandeur, and he loves to be considered greater than he really is. This is the result of pride; humility reduces this self-magnification, so that a man will not pretend to be more than he is. The gift of fear acts in this matter by submerging the soul in the abyss of its own nothingness before God and in the depths of its own misery before the divine justice and majesty. And thus, when the soul is permeated with this gift, when it sees that it is nothing when compared to God, and that it has nothing of itself but misery and sin, it does not seek its own glory apart from God nor does it judge itself to be worthy of anything but disdain and punishment. Only in this way does humility reach its perfection. Such was the humility we see in the saints, who had a complete disdain for themselves.[16]

In addition to these three fundamental virtues, the gift of fear also exercises its influence in regard to other virtues; there is no moral virtue which does not receive the influence of some gift. Thus the gift of fear acts upon the virtue of chastity, by elevating it to the most exquisite delicacy; on the virtue of meekness, by totally repressing disordered anger; on the virtue of modesty, by suppressing any disorderly internal or external bodily movements. Moreover, it combats the passions which, together with vainglory, are the daughters of pride: criticism, presumption, hypocrisy, pertinacity, discord, insolence and disobedience.[17]

EFFECTS OF THE GIFT

The effects of the gift of fear are of greatest value in the sanctification of souls. The following are the principal effects of this gift:

1) *A lively sentiment of the grandeur and majesty of God, which arouses in the soul a profound adoration filled with reverence and humility.* This is the most characteristic effect of the gift of fear, and it follows from its definition. The soul that is acted upon by this gift feels itself transported by an irresistible force before the grandeur and majesty of God, which makes even the angels tremble (*tremunt potestates*). Before this infinite majesty the soul feels as if it is nothing or less than nothing. It is overwhelmed with a sentiment which is so strong and penetrating as regards reverence, submission and subjection that it would like, if it could, to suffer a thousand deaths for God. Humility reaches its full perfection here. The soul feels great desires to suffer and to be disdained for God (St. John of the Cross). It never occurs

[15]Cf. *ibid.*, q. 141, a. 1, ad 3.
[16]Cf. *ibid.*, q. 19, a. 9, ad 4.
[17]Cf. *ibid.*, q. 132, a. 5.

to the soul to have the slightest thought of vanity or presumption. It sees its own misery so clearly that, when others praise it, it seems that they are ridiculing it (Curé of Ars). This respect and reverence for the majesty of God is also manifested in all the things which have any relationship to God. The church or oratory, the priest, sacred vessels, the images of the saints—all are regarded with the greatest respect and veneration. The gift of piety produces similar effects, but from another point of view, as we shall see later. This aspect of the gift of fear will continue forever in heaven.[18] There it will not be possible, given the impeccability of the blessed, to have any fear of offending God, but the gift will remain for all eternity to express reverence and subjection before the infinite grandeur and majesty of God.

2) *A great horror of sin and a lively sorrow for ever having committed sin.* Once its faith is illumined by the splendor of the gifts of understanding and knowledge and once its hope has been subjected to the action of the gift of fear, which brings the soul directly to the divine majesty, the soul understands as never before the almost infinite malice which is contained in any offense against God, however insignificant it may appear. The Holy Ghost, who wishes to purify the soul for the divine union, subjects it to the action of the gift of fear so that it understands the rigor with which divine justice, offended by sin, must punish in the next life if penance is not done in this life. The poor soul experiences a mortal anguish which reaches its greatest intensity in the terrifying night of the spirit. It seems to the soul that it is condemned and has nothing else to hope for. In reality, it is then that the virtue of hope reaches an incredible degree of heroism, because the soul has now reached the point of hoping against hope and gives the sublime cry of Job: "Slay me though he might, I will wait for him" (Job 13:15).

The horror which these souls experience before sin is so great that St. Louis Gonzaga fell at the feet of his confessor to accuse himself of two light venial sins. St. Alphonsus Liguori experienced a similar phenomenon on hearing a person blaspheme. St. Teresa of Jesus writes that there could be no death more terrible for her than to think that she had offended God (*The Life,* Chap. 34). The repentance of such souls for the slightest fault is most profound. From it proceeds the anxious desire to make reparation, a thirst for self-immolation, an irresistible tendency to crucify oneself in a thousand ways. This is a natural consequence of the gift of fear.

3) *An extreme vigilance to avoid the slightest occasion of offending God.* This is a logical consequence of the previous effect. These souls

[18]Cf. *ibid.,* q. 19, a. 11.

fear nothing so much as the slightest offense against God. They have seen clearly, in the contemplative light of the gifts, that in reality there is only one evil in the world and that the others do not deserve to be called evil. How far these souls are from voluntarily placing themselves in the occasion of sin! No person is as apprehensive as they are to flee with the greatest rapidity and promptness from any possibility or danger of offending God. Their extreme vigilance and constant attention cause them to live, under the special movement of the Holy Ghost, with a purity of conscience that is so great that at times it seems impossible to receive sacramental absolution because of a lack of matter and they must be satisfied with confessing some sin from their past life and thus renewing their sorrow and their repentance.

4) *Perfect detachment from all created things.* We have already seen that the gift of knowledge produces this effect in the soul, but from another point of view. The gifts are mutually interrelated among themselves and with charity, and for that reason they mutually influence each other.[19] This is perfectly understandable. The soul which has become aware of the grandeur and majesty of God must necessarily consider all created things as base and useless. Honors, wealth, power, dignity—all are considered as less than straw and unworthy of a moment of attention. We need but recall the effect produced in St. Teresa of Avila when a friend of hers showed her some precious jewelry; the saint could not understand how people could have such a great esteem for such things (*The Life,* Chap. 38). Keeping this in mind, we can see why St. Thomas links the gift of fear with the first beatitude, poverty of spirit.

THE BEATITUDES AND FRUITS OF FEAR

Two beatitudes are connected with the gift of fear: "Blessed are the poor in spirit, for theirs is the kingdom of heaven" (Matt. 5:3) and "blessed are they who mourn, for they shall be comforted" (Matt. 5:5). The first corresponds directly to the gift of fear because, in virtue of the filial reverence which it causes us to experience before God, it impels us not to seek our own grandeur nor to exalt ourselves (pride) nor to become attached to external goods (honors and wealth). All of this pertains to poverty of spirit, whether as the annihilation of the proud and puffed-up spirit of which St. Augustine speaks, or as the detachment from all temporal things of which St. Ambrose and St. Jerome speak.[20]

Indirectly the gift of fear is also related to the beatitude which pertains to those who weep and mourn.[21] The reason for this is that from the knowledge

[19]Cf. *ibid.,* I-II, q. 68, a. 5.
[20]Cf. *ibid.,* II-II, q. 19, a. 12.
[21]Cf. *ibid.,* ad 2.

of the divine excellence and of our own littleness and misery follows the disdain of all earthly things and a renunciation of all carnal delights, accompanied by weeping and mourning for one's past sins. Whence it is evident that the gift of fear moderates all the passions, whether of the irascible appetite or of the concupiscible appetite. The reverential fear of the divine majesty offended by sin restrains the impetus of the irascible passion and moderates the power and impulses of the concupiscible passions. For that reason this is a gift of indescribable value, although in the list of the gifts it occupies the last place.

As regards the fruits of the Holy Ghost, the following pertain to the gift of fear: modesty, which is a consequence of the reverence of man for the divine majesty; and continence and chastity, which follow upon the moderation of the concupiscible passions as a proper effect of the gift of fear.[22]

VICES OPPOSED TO FEAR

The principal vice opposed to the gift of fear is pride, as St. Gregory states,[23] but in a much more profound manner than to the virtue of humility. The gift of fear is fixed especially on the eminence and majesty of God, before whom man, by an instinct from the Holy Ghost, is aware of his own nothingness and vileness. Humility likewise is fixed on the grandeur of God, in contrast to the nothingness of man, but in the light of reason illumined by faith and in a human and imperfect modality.[24] Whence it is evident that the gift of fear excludes pride in a more lofty manner than does the virtue of humility. Fear excludes even the root and beginning of pride, as St. Thomas states.[25] Therefore, pride is opposed to the gift of fear in a more profound and radical manner than it is to the virtue of humility.

Indirectly the vice of presumption is also opposed to the gift of fear because it injures the divine justice by trusting inordinately in the divine mercy. In this sense St. Thomas says that presumption is opposed to the gift of fear so far as it disdains something divine.[26]

MEANS OF PROGRESS

In addition to the general means for attracting to oneself the merciful glance of the Holy Spirit—recollection, purity of heart, fidelity to grace, frequent invocation of the Holy Ghost, etc.—there are other methods which are more closely connected with the gift of fear.

1) *To meditate frequently on the infinite grandeur and majesty of God.* We can never by our own poor discursive methods acquire con-

[22]Cf. *ibid.,* ad 4.
[23]*Moralia,* Bk. I, Chap. 32; cf. St. Thomas, *Summa,* I-II, q. 68, a. 6, ad 2.
[24]Cf. St. Thomas, *Summa,* II-II, q. 161, aa. 1-2.
[25]*Ibid.,* q. 19, a. 9, ad 4; q. 161, a. 2, ad 3.
[26]*Ibid.,* q. 130, a. 2, ad 1; cf. q. 21, a. 3.

templative knowledge, which is given to the soul by the gifts of the Holy Ghost. But we can do something by reflecting on the power and majesty of God, who made all things out of nothing (Gen. 1:1), who calls all the stars in the heavens by their names (Bar. 3:33-36), who is more admirable and imposing than the turbulent sea (Ps. 92:4), who will come upon the clouds of heaven with great power and majesty to judge the living and the dead (Lk. 21:27), and before whom all the principalities and powers will tremble for all eternity.

2) *To accustom oneself to converse with God with filial confidence, filled with reverence and respect.* We should never forget that God is our Father, but that he is also a God of terrible grandeur and majesty. Sometimes pious souls forget the latter and allow themselves to be excessively familiar with God and even to give expression to irreverent audacity. It is certainly incredible to see the extent to which the Lord gives expression of his familiarity with souls that are pleasing to him, but it is necessary that he take the initiative and not the soul. Meanwhile the soul should remain in an attitude of reverence and submission, which is very far from being prejudicial to the sweet and intimate confidence of adopted children.

3) *To meditate frequently on the infinite malice of sin and to arouse a great horror for sin.* In itself, love is much more powerful and efficacious than fear as a motive for avoiding sin. Nevertheless, the consideration of fear is a great help in keeping souls from sin. The recollection of the terrible punishment which God has prepared for those who definitively reject his law would be sufficient to make us flee from sin if we would meditate on it. It is a fearful thing, as St. Paul says (Heb. 10:31), to fall into the hands of an offended God. We should think frequently of the evil of sin, especially in times of temptation. It is necessary to arouse such a deep horror of sin that we would be disposed to lose all things and even life itself rather than commit sin. To this end, it will be of great help if we avoid all dangerous occasions which may lead us to sin, practice the daily examination of conscience with fidelity (in order to avoid sin and to weep for those which we have committed), and to consider Jesus crucified as the victim of propitiation for our crimes and sins.

4) *To be meek and humble in dealing with our neighbor.* He who has a clear concept of what God is in his infinite majesty and realizes that God has mercifully pardoned him thousands of times, how can he dare to exact with haughtiness and disdain that which is owed to him by his neighbor (Matt. 18:23-35)? We must pardon injuries, and we must treat all our neighbors with exquisite delicacy, profound humility and meekness. We should consider them to be better than we are, at least in the sense that probably they have not resisted grace as much as we

have or they would not have done what they have done if they had received the gifts which God has given us. He who has committed any mortal sin in his life can never humiliate himself sufficiently; there is no place so low that it is not too high for him who, having sinned mortally, at one time deserved a place in hell.

5) *To beg frequently of the Holy Spirit a reverential fear of God.* When all is said and done, every perfect disposition is a gift of God and it can be attained only by humility and persevering prayer. Scripture is filled with sublime formulas by which we can petition holy fear: "Fulfill for your servant your promise to those who fear you" (Ps. 118:38); etc. Such sentiments should spring frequently from our hearts and our lips, once we are convinced that the fear of the Lord is the beginning of wisdom (Sirach 1:16) and that it is necessary to work out our salvation in fear and trembling (Phil. 2:12), as the Holy Spirit himself warns us through the psalmist: "Serve the Lord with fear, and rejoice before him." (Ps. 2:11).

4: THE VIRTUE OF CHARITY

We have already treated of the intimate relations between Christian perfection and charity. Now it is necessary to treat of certain other aspects of this virtue which is the most excellent of all virtues.

CHARITY IN ITSELF

St. Thomas begins his treatise on charity by stating that it is friendship between God and man. Like every friendship, it necessarily implies a mutual benevolence which is based on the communication of good. For that reason charity necessarily presupposes sanctifying grace, which makes us children of God and heirs of glory.

ITS NATURE

Man, who by nature is nothing more than a servant of the Creator, becomes, through grace and charity, the son and friend of God. And if our servitude ennobles us so greatly, since to serve God is to reign, how much more are we elevated by the charity of God which "is poured forth in our hearts by the Holy Spirit who has been given to us" (Rom. 5:5). Such is the incomprehensible dignity of the Christian.

Definition

Charity is a created reality, a supernatural habit infused by God into the soul. It can be defined as a theological virtue infused by God into the will, by which we love God for himself above all things, and ourselves and our neighbor for God. The material object of charity is primarily God, secondarily ourselves and all rational creatures which have arrived or can arrive at eternal beatitude, and even, to a certain extent, all creatures so far as they are related to the glory of God. The formal *quod* object of charity is God himself as supreme goodness in himself and as our ultimate end. The formal motive (*ratio sub qua, objectum formale quo*) of charity is the uncreated goodness of God considered in itself so far as it embraces the divine essence, all the divine attributes and the three divine Persons.

As an infused habit, charity resides in the will, since it involves a movement of love toward the supreme good, and love and the good constitute the act and the proper object of the will. It is a supernatural habit which God infuses in the degree which pleases him, without taking into account the natural qualities or dispositions of the one who receives charity.

Charity as a virtue is specifically one, for although its material object embraces various elements (God, ourselves and our neighbors), the motive of love or its formal specifying reason is the divine goodness. From this it follows that, when we love ourselves or our neighbor for any motive other than the goodness of God, we do not make an act of charity, but an act of natural human love, whether selfish love or benevolent love. There are countless acts which seem to flow from charity but are far from being acts of charity. Purely human love as such is of no value in the supernatural order.

Excellence of charity

Charity is the most excellent of all virtues, not only because of its own intrinsic goodness as the virtue which most intimately unites us with God, but because without it no other virtue can be perfect, since it is the form of all the infused virtues. We have already explained in what sense charity is the form of all the virtues. Its intrinsic excellence derives from the fact that it is the virtue which unites us most intimately with God, since it rests in him as he is in himself by reason of his divine goodness. The only virtues which could challenge charity for this primacy are the other two theological virtues of faith and hope, but charity far surpasses these virtues. Faith, which is an intellectual knowledge, limits God by trying to bring his divine greatness into the limited capacity of our intellect, while through charity the will goes out from itself and rests in God in all his infinite grandeur. Moreover, the knowledge of faith is obscure, while charity loves God as he is in himself. As regards hope, it is a desire for the divine goodness, the true possession of which is granted us through charity, imperfectly in this life and perfectly in the life to come. The excellence and superiority of charity over the other two theological virtues, and by consequence over all the other virtues, is a dogma of faith which is contained in the deposit of revelation. "So there abide," says St. Paul, "faith, hope and charity, these three; but the greatest of these is charity" (I Cor. 13:13).

The act of charity

By the proper act of charity, the will goes forth from itself to rest in God as he is in himself. This profound doctrine gives us the key to the solution of the much debated question concerning the superiority of the intellect or the will. There is no doubt that the will in itself is inferior to the intellect, for the will is a blind faculty and cannot produce its acts if the intellect does not place the desirable object before the will. The intellect precedes and guides the will, which could not love anything without the intellect, since it is impossible to love what one does not know. But the operation of the intellect is completely distinct from that of the will. The intellect draws things to itself or absorbs them, so to speak, into its own intellectual mold. Consequently, when it knows inferior beings such as material things it ennobles them and dignifies them by raising them to the intellectual order; but when it knows superior beings such as God or the angels or supernatural truths, it limits or debases them by obliging them to assume an inferior intellectual mold.

The exact opposite is true of the will. By reason of its proper act, which is to love, the will goes forth from itself to rest in the beloved object as it is in itself. Consequently, if the will loves objects that are inferior to itself, such as the things of earth, it is degraded to an inferior level; but if it loves superior beings, such as God or the angels, it is ennobled and elevated to the level of those superior beings in which it rests through love. For that reason St. Augustine could say: "If you love the earth, you are earthly; but if you love God, what must be said except that you are God?"[1]

It must be concluded, therefore, that although the intellect is in itself and in its natural power more perfect than the will, nevertheless, in this life, by the very nature of the operation, it is more perfect to love God than to know him. A theologian may know a great deal about God, but in a manner that is cold and purely intellectual, while a humble and simple soul who knows almost nothing about theology may love God intensely, and this is much better.

Another practical consequence of great importance follows from this sublime doctrine. The only way to avoid debasing ourselves by the love of inferior created things is to love them in God, through God and for God; in other words, for the formal motive of charity. It follows from this that charity is a magic wand which changes to gold whatever it touches, even those things that are inferior to us but are ordained through charity to the love and glory of God.

THE INCREASE OF CHARITY

Charity can increase in this life because it is a movement toward God, our ultimate end, and as long as we are wayfarers in this life it is possible to approach more and more closely to the goal. This greater proximity is effected precisely through the increase of charity. Moreover, charity does not admit of any term or limit in this life; it can grow indefinitely. This does not mean, however, that charity cannot reach a relative perfection here on earth, as we have already explained.

[1] *In Epist. Joan.*, tr. 2, n. 14.

POSITIVE MEANS OF GROWTH

Like all the other habits, charity increases, not by the addition of one form to another form, but by a greater radication of the virtue in the subject.[2] It cannot increase by addition because such an increase is not possible in qualitative but only in quantitative things, and habits are classified as qualities. For anything to be united by addition to another, it is necessary that it be really distinct from that other, as when a new quantity of sand is added to a quantity that already exists; in this case, rather than speaking of a union, we should speak of an addition, because, in the example given, the sand is not intrinsically united to the other sand but is placed alongside it. But this is impossible in regard to qualities—whiteness cannot be added to whiteness nor can charity be added to charity, as one would add a quantitative object to another. Qualitative habits increase only by a more profound radication in their subject. Thus the will participates more and more in charity so far as it is more penetrated by charity.

More intense acts

Like the other virtues, charity is not increased by any act whatever, but only by an act that is more intense than the habit as actually possessed here and now.[3] This is an inevitable consequence of the foregoing. If charity were increased by addition, any act of charity, however weak and remiss, would increase charity quantitatively, and thus if an individual possessing one hundred degrees of habitual charity were to perform an act of the love of God of three degrees, this would be added to the one hundred degrees to raise the total to one hundred and three degrees. In this way, simply by the multiplication of many remiss acts, the thermometer of habitual charity would rise to a surprising degree and even surpass the charity of many of the saints. It is evident that such an explanation of the increase of charity leads only to absurdity.

The true nature of the increase of charity is far different. As a qualitative form, it can increase only by a more profound radication in the subject, and this is impossible without a more intense act. The thermometer cannot register a higher degree of heat if the temperature of the air does not likewise rise in degree. This is exactly what happens in regard to the increase of charity and the other virtues.

Practical consequences

We now have an important practical conclusion. If we live in slothfulness and tepidity, we can paralyze our Christian life completely, even if we live habitually in the grace of God and perform a large number of good but

[2]"The increase of charity denotes a change from less having to more having, so that it is not necessary that something be there which was not there before, but that something be more there which previously was less there. This is what God does when he increases charity: he makes it have a greater hold upon the soul, and the likeness of the Holy Spirit is thereby more participated by the soul" (St. Thomas, *Summa,* II-II, q. 24, a. 5).

[3]Cf. St. Thomas, *ibid.*, a. 6.

remiss works. The essential degree of charity, and consequently of grace and the other infused virtues (since all of them grow together with grace and charity), will be paralyzed in spite of the number of our good works.[4] This consequence, which is an inevitable corollary of the principles which we have just explained, is amply verified in daily experience. A large number of good souls live habitually in the grace of God, without committing any serious faults and performing an infinite number of good works and acts of sacrifice, but they are far from being saints. If they encounter any contradiction or difficulty, they become angry; if they are lacking anything, their laments are raised to heaven; if their superiors command something which does not please them, they murmur and complain; if anyone criticizes or humiliates them, they become enemies of those persons. All this shows clearly that such individuals are still very far from Christian perfection. But how can one explain this phenomenon after these persons have performed so many good works for so many years in the Christian life or in the religious or priestly life? The theological explanation is simple: they have performed a great many good works, it is true; but they have performed them in a lukewarm manner and not in such a way that each new act is more fervent. Rather, each succeeding act is more remiss and more imperfect. The result of all this is that the thermometer of their charity and the degree of grace and the other virtues have been stopped completely. They are as lukewarm and imperfect as if they were at the very beginning of their conversion or their religious life.

Remiss acts

But one may ask: "Then are all those good works which were remiss and imperfect of no avail whatever? Are remiss acts, inferior to one's habitual degree of charity, completely useless and sterile?"

To this we reply that the remiss acts are not completely useless and sterile. They serve a two-fold purpose, one in this life and the other in glory. In this life they prevent the dispositions of soul from becoming completely cold, which would put these people in the proximate occasion of committing a grave sin and thus destroying their Christian life completely. It is certain that he who does not perform an act that is more intense than the virtuous habit which he possesses will never increase the virtuous habit, but neither will he lose the habit completely. As St. Thomas teaches,[5] the grade of charity attained will never diminish of itself, even if a person lives for many years in tepidity and performs acts that are remiss or less intense. But if a mortal sin is committed, the virtue of charity is completely destroyed in the soul. The thermometer registers zero. The reason why charity cannot diminish is that the degree of intensity, once acquired, carries with it the title to an eternal reward, and the soul never loses this even though for the rest of its

[4]However, an increase in grace and charity *ex opere operato* is possible by means of the sacraments.

[5]Cf. *ibid.*, a. 10.

life it does not increase the essential degree of charity. The right or title remains before God, and God never turns back. Charity and the title to it could be lost by mortal sin, but as long as there is no serious sin committed, the merits acquired before God will have their corresponding reward in eternal life. Therefore, something is achieved by these remiss acts, because they at least help to preserve the soul in the state of grace. They likewise preserve in an essential degree all the merits already gained, although the individual may never increase the essential degree of his charity.

In the life to come, remiss acts do not remain without their proper reward, although it is certain that, however numerous, they do not increase the degree of essential glory, which corresponds exactly to the *habitual* degree of one's grace and charity at the time of death. In addition to the essential reward in heaven, however, there are many different accidental rewards. Each remiss act, since it was good and meritorious for having been performed in a state of grace and under the influence of charity, will receive its corresponding accidental reward in heaven. As Báñez says, the increase of essential glory pertains to the more intense acts of charity; the increase of accidental glory pertains to remiss acts of charity. We should realize, however, what a great loss is caused as a result of slothfulness or lukewarness in the exercise of the virtue of charity.

Objections and answers

We shall now examine some of the objections which may be raised against this doctrine.

Objection 1. If this doctrine is true, the saint would be in a worse condition than a lukewarm Christian. For the saint, whose degree of charity is already intense, would have to make an immense effort in order to arrive at a still higher degree, while the lukewarm, who may have only a minimum degree of charity, would find it easy to perform a more intense act.

Answer. It is actually easier for the saint to perform a more intense act than it is for the lukewarm. The increase of grace and charity is accompanied by an increase in the capacity and power of the soul. Even in the purely physical order, a little child may not be able to lift a weight of ten pounds, but an older boy could easily lift a weight of thirty pounds. And although in the natural order there is a limit which cannot be surpassed, due to the limitation of human strength, this is not true as regards the increase of grace, which also causes an increase in the powers of the soul, whose obediential potency is absolutely without limit. Therefore, the saints perform more intense acts of charity with great facility.

Objection 2. Let us suppose that a saint makes an act of love of God which is fifty degrees in intensity and therefore greatly inferior to the degree of his habitual charity. Meanwhile, a lukewarm soul performs an act of twenty-five degrees, which is greatly superior to his habitual charity. The latter receives for his act an essential increase of grace and glory, while the saint receives nothing for his act of charity. Therefore, the condition of the saint is worse than that of the lukewarm Christian.

Answer. The saint who performs an act of fifty degrees performs an act which is remiss in relation to that which he could have done, due to his higher degree of habitual charity. For that reason, it is fitting that he should receive no reward, at least no essential reward, and this is a kind of punishment for his remiss act. On the other hand, the imperfect soul who performs a more intense act deserves an essential increase because of the fervor with which he performs the act. We should not forget that the master in the gospel demanded five talents from the servant who had received five and only two from him who had received only two (Matt. 25:14-23). The remiss act of a saint is not entirely useless, however, because he will receive the corresponding accidental reward in heaven.

Objection 3. The Council of Trent has defined that the just man, by reason of his good works, merits an increase of grace and glory (Denz. 842). It says nothing about the remiss or less intense acts. Therefore, it is not necessary that an act of charity be more intense in order to merit an increase of grace and glory.

Answer: Three centuries before the Church made that definition, a difficulty was presented and a solution was given by St. Thomas Aquinas. "It must be said that every act of charity merits eternal life, but not that it should be given immediately, but in due time. In like manner, every act of charity merits an increase in charity, but only when the soul is disposed for this increase" (i.e., when the act is more intense). The just man merits by means of his remiss good works, but the reward is not given at once. Indeed, it could happen that he would die in mortal sin and would lose the reward of eternal life in spite of having merited it previously by his good works. Similarly, every act of charity, even a less intense act, merits an increase of grace and charity, but the increase is not given until the person produces the physical disposition which is indispensable for it, namely, the more intense act of charity. And if this act is not produced, the remiss act will still have an accidental reward, but it will in no way increase the essential reward of the soul in heaven, as we have explained previously.[6]

Objection 4. De facto, it is of faith that the sacraments increase grace *ex opere operato* without any need for a dispositive act which is more intense.

---

[6]We are not convinced of the theory which is held even by some Thomists that the soul upon entering heaven will make a most intense act of charity, and this will be the immediate physical disposition for receiving the increase which was merited on earth by all of one's remiss acts. Apart from the fact that this is a completely gratuitous statement, the doctrine of Báñez, which demands the physical disposition in this life, is much more logical.

All that is required is that the recipient place no obstacle, as the Council of Trent teaches (Denz. 849). Therefore, the same can happen as regards the increase of charity outside the sacraments.

Answer. There is no comparison here. The sacraments produce or increase grace by their own intrinsic power (*ex opere operato*), something which does not happen in the increase of the virtues by way of merit, which is produced only by the power of the one who performs those acts with the help of grace (*ex opere operantis*). The two cases are different. Therefore, in the sacraments no other disposition is required but the purely negative one of not placing any obstacle, which presupposes simply the state of grace for the sacraments of the living and supernatural attrition for the sacraments of the dead. But in the increase of grace by way of extra-sacramental merit, the physical and more intense disposition is required if the increase is actually to be effective.

One should keep in mind, moreover, that even in the reception of the sacraments the degree of grace conferred will vary according to the disposition of the one who receives the sacraments. Of two persons who receive Communion, it is possible that the first will receive ten degrees of grace and the other will receive one hundred. The reason is that the *ex opere operato* effect of the sacrament is joined with *ex opere operantis* dispositions of the one who receives the sacrament. The minimum *ex opere operato* effect which the sacrament confers of itself will be produced equally in all as long as there is no obstacle to the reception of the grace. This is the case with infants at baptism; they all receive *ex opere operato* the same degree of grace which the sacrament brings with it.[7] But the greater or less degree of grace received by adults *ex opere operantis* depends on the disposition of those who receive the sacrament.[8]

Objection 5. How can a more intense act proceed from a habit which is less intense? How can an effect be greater than its cause?

Answer: A more intense act cannot proceed from a less intense habit unless there is a previous impulse or movement of an actual grace which is likewise more intense. Without the actual prevenient grace, man can do absolutely nothing in the supernatural order, and without the more intense grace, the more intense act is likewise impossible. That actual grace which is more intense cannot be merited, for this would be a contradiction; but it can be infallibly impetrated, although under a gratuitous title, through prayer which fulfills the necessary conditions.

---

[7]Cf. *ibid.*, III, q. 69, a. 8.

[8]Cf. the Council of Trent, Sess. VI, Decree on Justification, Chap. 7 (Denz. 799). The Council, speaking of justification, states that each one receives it in the measure and degree which the Holy Ghost desires and according to his proper dispositions. The same thing must be said of the sacraments.

Conclusions

Having explained the principles and resolved the objections, we shall now draw certain conclusions of great practical importance.

1) *One more intense act of charity is of greater value than countless remiss or lukewarm acts.*

The intense acts will increase our habitual degree of charity, but remiss acts are absolutely incapable of doing this. Therefore, a simple prayer recited with ardent devotion is of much greater value than an entire Rosary recited in a distracted manner or out of routine. For that reason, it is wise not to impose too many prayers or particular devotions on individuals. What is important is devotion and not devotions.[9]

2) *A perfect just man is more pleasing to God than many imperfect and lukewarm men.*

If an ardent act of charity is of greater value before God than a thousand imperfect acts, then the just man who continuously performs such acts is much more pleasing to God than those who perform many imperfect acts. This can be proved from a consideration of God's own love. God's love for his creatures is not only affective but effective; that is to say, it produces in others the good which God desires for them (cf. St. Thomas, *Summa,* I, q. 20). One must therefore conclude that God loves the perfect more because he bestows upon them those more intense actual graces, which are many times more valuable than less perfect graces.

3) *The conversion of one sinner to lofty perfection is more pleasing to God and of greater glory to God than the conversion of many sinners to a lukewarm and imperfect life.*

This follows as a conclusion from the principles already stated.

4) *The preacher or spiritual director is more pleasing to God and gives greater glory to God if he converts a single sinner and leads him to Christian perfection than the one who converts many sinners but leaves them imperfect and lukewarm.*[10]

This is another logical conclusion from the principles already enunciated, and it ought to serve as a source of great consolation and inspiration for directors of souls who lack the eloquence necessary for preaching. In the silence of the confessional they may do much more for the glory of God and much more good for souls than the greatest preachers.

---

[9]Cf. St. Thomas, *Summa,* II-II, q. 83, a. 14, where he asks whether prayer should be lengthy and answers that it should last as long as is useful for arousing fervor or devotion, no more and no less. Hence one must take care to avoid prayers that are too lengthy, but at the same time take care not to fall into lukewarmness or negligence which may easily become a pretext for shortening one's prayers.

[10]However, one should not draw the false conclusion that the conversion of sinners is not an important work.

THE OBJECTS OF CHARITY

Charity does not refer to God alone, but also to one's neighbors. The love of God causes us to love whatever pertains to God or whatever reflects his goodness, and it is evident that one's neighbor is a good of God and shares, or can share, in eternal happiness. For that reason the love of charity with which we love our neighbor is exactly the same charity with which we love God. There are not two charities but only one, since the formal motive of loving one's neighbor is the goodness of God reflected in him. Hence, when we love our neighbor for any other motive distinct from God, we do not love him with the love of charity.

We should also love the very habit of charity as such, as a good which we wish for ourselves and for others. To desire a supernatural good for one's neighbor is true love and true friendship.

Irrational creatures can also be loved in charity, not with the love of friendship, which requires a rational nature and the communication of goods, but insofar as they are goods which we can utilize for the glory of God and the service of our neighbor. St. Thomas does not hesitate to add: "And thus God himself loves them likewise in charity." From this point of view, one can readily understand the apparent foolishness of St. Francis of Assisi in addressing lower creatures as his brothers and sisters.

Love of self

We should also love ourselves with the love of charity. Although we cannot love ourselves as friends, since friendship requires another individual, we are a good of God, capable of receiving his grace and sharing his love. In this sense we can and ought to love ourselves. If, in our desire to provide pleasure for ourselves, we compromise with the law of God even in regard to little things, we are actually performing an act of hatred for ourselves. The reason is that we are doing ourselves harm and we are inflicting evil upon ourselves, and this is contrary to charity. We love ourselves truly only when we love ourselves in God, for God and through God.

Love of one's body

By the same token, we must love in charity our own body, inasmuch as it is a work of God and is called to share in the enjoyment of eternal happiness. But since it is inclined to sin and is often the stimulus to evil and an obstacle to our salvation, we must, under these aspects, not love our body but desire to depart from it, and say with St. Paul: "Who will deliver me from the body of this death?" (Rom. 7:24) and "desiring to depart and to be with Christ" (Phil. 1:23). Christian mortification, which has as its object the control of the evil tendencies of the body, is not an act of hatred against oneself but a true and authentic love. "Pardon me, my poor body," said St. Francis of Assisi, "but you know that I treat you so badly in this world because I love you much and I wish you to be eternally happy." And St. Peter of Alcántara, who, by the severe penance to which he subjected his body, was nothing but skin and bones, appeared to St. Teresa and said to her joyfully: "O blessed penance which has given to me such great glory."

This is what it means to love one's own body in charity. On the other hand, the disgrace of sin, which gives to the body every kind of sinful taste and pleasure, is preparing it for a terrible judgment in the world to come. And then one will see that what has often appeared here on earth to be a love for one's own body was actually a true hatred of the body.

Love of sinners

Sinners *as such* are not worthy of our love since they are enemies of God and they voluntarily place obstacles to their eternal happiness. But *as men* they are images of God and capable of eternal blessings, and in this sense we can and ought to love them. "Whence, as regards sin, which makes such a person an enemy of God, every sinner is deserving of hatred, even if it be a matter of one's father or mother or relatives, as we are told in the gospel (Lk. 14:26). We must, therefore, hate in sinners what they have as sinners, and we must love what they have as men, still capable (through repentance) of eternal happiness. And this is to love them truly for God with the love of charity."[11] This doctrine has particular application when parents are unlawfully opposed to the religious or priestly vocations of their children, thereby committing a grave offense. It is necessary to break with them in such a case because one must obey God rather than men.

Sinners naturally love themselves so far as they desire their own preservation, but in reality they fall into error in believing that the best thing in them is their sensitive nature, to which they give every kind of pleasure. If to this we add that they are walking in danger of great loss in the supernatural order, it will be clear that sinners, far from loving themselves truly, are their own worst enemies. Cardinal Cajetan makes the following commentary on this particular article of the *Summa Theologiae* (II-II, q. 25, a. 7):

> Engrave deeply on your heart the conclusions of this article and the manner in which the evil, as such, do not love themselves, and the signs of true love which are found only in the good, namely: 1) to love the interior man or to live according to one's rational nature; 2) to wish for oneself the good of virtue; 3) to work in this sense; 4) to preserve oneself joyfully in interior recollection; 5) to keep oneself in perfect harmony by a total orientation to unity and the good. One can examine himself carefully by these signs in order to see whether or not he is his own enemy, and one should meditate frequently and even daily on these points.

Love of enemies

It is also necessary to love one's enemy, or those who wish us evil, or have done some injury to us, or treat us uncharitably. It is not required that we love them precisely as enemies, for this would be to love what is evil, but to love them so far as they are human beings, with that general love which we owe to all men. And when our enemy is in need of our particular love by reason of some spiritual or corporal danger, we have the obligation of attending to him in particular as if he were not our enemy. Apart from these cases of necessity, we are not obliged to give our enemy any special

[11]Cf. St. Thomas, *Summa.*, II-II, q. 25.

signs of love because we are not obliged to love each and every human being with a particular love, since that would be impossible. It is required simply that we do not refuse our enemies the ordinary signs of affection which we owe to all our neighbors, such as a polite greeting and ordinary courtesy.

However, the saints went further than this. They loved God and each thing related to God so much that this immense love made them overlook any evil will which they discovered in their neighbors. Even more, some of the saints felt a particular attraction and love for those persons who persecuted and calumniated them, as is evident in the life of St. Teresa of Avila. This heroic love is not of obligation to all men, but the soul that wishes to sanctify itself should tend to this love with all its power, in order to be a perfect child of him "who makes his sun to rise on the good and the evil, and sends rain on the just and the unjust" (Matt. 5:45).

By the same token, it is an obligation for all, under pain of mortal sin, not to refuse to our enemies the benefits or signs of affection which are given to all neighbors in common; e.g., not to exclude them from our general prayers, etc. But it is not necessary for salvation to make them participants of the special benefits and signs of love which are not given to all men in general but only to one's friends or relatives. It would be a grave sin to exclude one's enemy from common prayer or alms or ordinary polite association; but special signs of friendship are not required except in those circumstances where scandal would be given by refusing them, or when this would be the only means of converting the enemy from his hatred, or if the enemy himself has begged pardon and has given special signs of repentance and affection. Not to respond in these cases would be a sign of true hatred. It is evident, however, that the perfection of charity demands much more than this. The perfect man not only takes care that he is not overcome by evil, but he also aspires to overcome evil by good (Rom. 12:21), so that he not only avoids hatred but tries to draw forth the love of his enemy by showering benefits on him.

Love of others

It is necessary to love the angels, the blessed and the souls in purgatory with a true love of charity, because this type of love is based on the communication of eternal happiness which is common to them and to us. The love of the angels and of the blessed is in itself a sign of exquisite charity, and it is a great act of charity to have a love for the souls in purgatory and to manifest it by suffrages for those suffering souls.

It is not lawful to love the devils or the condemned with the love of charity. Although by nature they are creatures of God (in which respect they reflect the divine justice), they are, nevertheless, obstinate in evil and incapable of eternal beatitude, which is the basis for the love of charity. To love them would be equivalent to hating God or rejecting his infinite justice. In order to understand something of the terrible catastrophe which is involved in eternal damnation, one should consider that those doomed souls have lost for all eternity the right to be loved. As obstinate enemies of God, they must be hated for all eternity by the same hatred with which one rejects sin.

Summary

To summarize, the general list of beings or objects to which charity extends is as follows: first, God, who is the fountain of all happiness; then our own soul, which participates directly in the infinite happiness; thirdly, our neighbors, both men and angels, who are companions of our happiness; and last of all, our bodies, upon which redounds the glory of the soul, and even irrational things so far as they can be related to the love and the glory of God. Charity is the virtue *par excellence* which embraces heaven and earth.

THE ORDER OF CHARITY

Charity must observe some kind of order, because it extends to many different things which participate in eternal happiness in varying degrees. In the first place, one must love God absolutely and above all things because he is infinitely lovable in himself and is the first principle of eternal happiness, which consists essentially in the eternal possession of God. For that reason we ought to love God more than we love ourselves, since we merely share in the happiness which is found in God in all its plenitude, inasmuch as he is the first principle from which all other things are derived.

Love of God

We must love God with all our strength and in all possible ways in which he can be loved. Thus *by the love of conformity* we fulfill the divine precepts conscientiously and accept all the trials and difficulties which God may send, not only with a spirit of resignation, but with gratitude and joy, however difficult and painful they may be, asking God for the grace to be faithful at every moment. *By the love of benevolence* we would desire, if possible, to give to God some new good or some new happiness which he does not yet possess; and since this is impossible, because God is absolute and infinite good, we endeavor to increase his external glory by laboring for the salvation and sanctification of souls, thus extending his kingdom of love in all hearts. As St. Thomas says, zeal proceeds from the intensity of love.[12] *The love of friendship,* which is based on that of benevolence, adds to it mutual correspondence and communication of good. Finally, *by the love of complacency,* which is a pure love without any admixture of self-interest, we rest in the infinite perfections of God, rejoicing in them because they make him infinitely happy and blessed, and we take no account of the advantages and blessings which are reflected in us because of God's goodness. This pure love can never be habitual in this life,[13] because we cannot and we ought not prescind from hope and the desire for our own happiness, which we shall find in God. But it is possible to experience this pure love as an isolated and transitory act, as was experienced by the saints.

---

[12] Cf. *ibid.,* I-II, q. 28, a. 4.

[13] So Pope Innocent XII declared in a brief of March 12, 1699; cf. Denz. 1327.

Love of self

Secondly, we ought to love the spiritual good of our own soul more than that of our neighbor. The reason is that our soul participates directly in blessedness, while that of our neighbor is only a companion in the participation of that infinite good. "The proof of this is that man ought not suffer the injury of committing a sin, which would be contrary to the participation of blessedness, even to free his neighbor from sin."[14] Consequently, a man should not tell a deliberate lie and thereby offend God, even if by that means he could convert many sinners, free many souls from purgatory, or save a soul from hell. And if, in view of these great advantages, a man should decide to commit a small sin, he would do a great injury to God because he would consider rather the good of creatures than the honor of God whom he offends. We must always serve God rather than men.

Love of neighbor

For the same reason, it is necessary to love the spiritual good of one's neighbor more than one's own body. The soul of our neighbor shares directly with us in eternal glory, but our body shares only indirectly and by redundance in the glory of the soul. Hence, when the eternal salvation of one's neighbor requires it, we are obliged in charity and under serious sin to go to the aid of our neighbor, even at the risk of our own life. His eternal life is of greater value than our own bodily life. The applications of this principle are numerous. Thus a voluntary abortion, even to save the life of the mother, is a grave sin because it sacrifices the eternal life of the child, who dies without baptism, in order to save the temporal life of the mother. The same thing is true in regard to the spiritual help that must be given to those who are suffering from contagious diseases.

Moreover, among our various neighbors there is a certain hierarchy of charity which we ought to observe, because not all participate equally in the divine goodness. Thus, objectively speaking, one should wish greater blessings to those who are better, to those who are more holy, to those who are closer to God, although we may have a more intense subjective love for those who are closer to us by reason of blood and, as a result, may desire that they more than anyone else should reach sanctity. But under equal conditions, one must always love more those who are closer to him by blood, and then his fellow citizens and those who are bound to him by other ties. Among our relatives, the objective order gives first place to one's parents because they are the principles of our life, and to them, after God, we owe our very being. Again, the father is more deserving of love than the mother, because he is the active principle of generation, which is more excellent than the passive principle; but this does not prevent us from having a more intense subjective love for our mother, spouse or child.

---

[14]Cf. St. Thomas, *Summa,* I-II, q. 26, a. 4.

Charity in heaven

The order of charity here on earth will remain substantially the same in heaven, but in heaven God will be our all in all (I Cor. 15:28). For that reason the order of charity will be taken exclusively in relation to God and not in relation to ourselves. Hence we shall have a more intense subjective and objective love for those who are closer to God, in other words, for those who are most holy. We shall not necessarily love more intensely those who are closer to us, such as our relatives and friends, although we shall love these latter under a double title, namely, their nearness to God and what they mean to us.

LOVE, THE ACT OF CHARITY

It is more proper to charity to love than to be loved. As friendship, it necessarily presupposes both these activities, but the first is an act proper to oneself and the second is an act proper to one's friends. As an act of charity, love presupposes benevolence or well-wishing for one's friends, but it also includes affective union. For that reason benevolence is the basis of friendship.

Loving God

God is infinitely lovable in himself and charity loves him as such, without subordinating him to any other end. But there is something else which should also dispose us to advance in the love of God, namely, the benefits we have received from him or which we hope to receive, as well as the punishments which we strive to avoid. It is possible to love God immediately even in this life because, unlike the intellect which draws things to itself, the will goes out in love, in order to rest immediately in the object which is loved. God cannot be loved by creatures as much as he deserves to be loved, for this would necessitate an infinite love, but we can and ought to love God completely, that is, love him for all that he is and for everything that pertains to him in any way, and love him with all our being—at least habitually—by ordaining all things to him. Objectively there can be no measure or limit to the love of God because in himself he is infinitely lovable, but there can and must be some limit on our part, not as regards the internal limits of charity (since the more intense it is, the better), but as regards the external manifestations of charity, which cannot be continuous, although they can and ought to be habitual and under the virtual influence of God. Thus it is necessary for us to sleep or to be absorbed in other occupations which necessarily suspend the actual exercise of love.

Friends and enemies

As regards the love of one's friends and the love of one's enemies, which of the two is better and more meritorious? To answer this question, it is necessary to make a distinction. If one's enemy is loved simply and solely for God and if one loves one's friend for God and for some other reason, then the love of one's enemy is better because it has God as its exclusive cause. But if one loves both his friends and his enemies only for God, that love would be more perfect and meritorious which is practiced with greater intensity, and this ordinarily would be the love of one's enemy, since a greater force and impetus of the love of God is required in this case. But if one loves for God both his friends and enemies and loves them both with equal intensity of love, it is more perfect and meritorious to love one's friends because the object of love is better and closer to ourselves. In like manner, if one considers separately the love of God and the love of neighbor, there is no doubt whatever that the love of God is better. But if one unites them, then the love of neighbor for God is better than the love of God alone, because the first includes both loves and the second embraces God alone. And that love of God is most perfect which extends also to one's neighbor, because we have received from God the commandment that he who loves God also loves his neighbor (I Jn. 4:21).

THE EFFECTS OF CHARITY

The effects of charity are internal and external. The internal effects are three in number:

Internal

1) *Spiritual joy,* which can exist at the same time with sorrow because we do not yet enjoy the perfect possession of God as we shall in the beatific vision.

2) *Peace,* which is the tranquility of order, and results from the harmony of our desires and appetites through charity.

3) *Mercy,* which is both a special virtue and a fruit of charity (although distinct from it), and inclines us to have compassion on the miseries of our neighbors, considering them in a certain way as our own, insofar as whatever causes sorrow to our brother likewise causes sorrow to us. This is the virtue *par excellence* of all the virtues that refer to our neighbor. God himself manifests mercy in an extreme degree by having compassion on us.

External

The external effects of charity are also three in number:

1) *Beneficence,* which consists in doing good to others as an external sign of our internal benevolence. It is related to justice if it is a question of what we owe to our neighbor; it is related to mercy when we assist him in his necessities; and sometimes it is connected with some other virtue.

2) *Almsgiving,* which is an act of charity which binds all, but in different degrees, and can be exercised through the spiritual or corporal works of mercy, although the former are greater than the latter.

3) *Fraternal correction,* which is an excellent remedy for the sins of our neighbor. It requires a great deal of prudence, however, in order to select the proper moment and the apt means for making this correction. It belongs not only to superiors with regard to their subjects, but even to subjects themselves, as long as prudence is observed and there is some hope of amendment. Unless these conditions are present, we should not correct our neighbor. But this prohibition does not always apply to superiors, for they have an obligation by reason of their office to correct and even to punish those who do wrong or are a threat to the common good.

There are many sins opposed to the virtue of charity, but the detailed study of them belongs to moral theology. Here only a summary treatment of these defects can be attempted.

SINS OPPOSED TO CHARITY

To love

Hatred is the first sin against charity. If it pertains to God, it is a most grave sin and indeed the greatest that man could commit. If it is directed to one's neighbor, it is also a serious sin and designates an internal disorder, even though it is not the one that is most harmful to one's neighbor. The worst is that which proceeds from envy.

To joy

Spiritual sloth, which is opposed to the joy of the divine good which proceeds from charity, is a capital sin; it usually proceeds from the sensate taste of men who find no pleasure in God and find divine things to be distasteful. The vices which flow from spiritual sloth are malice, rancor, pusillanimity, despair, indolence as regards commands, flightiness of mind and distractions by unlawful things.

Envy is opposed to spiritual joy occasioned by the good of one's neighbor. It is an ugly sin which saddens the soul because of the good seen in another, not because that particular good threatens us, but because it is seen as something that diminishes our own glory and excellence. Of itself, it is a mortal sin against charity, which commands us to rejoice in the good of our neighbor. But the first indeliberate movements of sensibility or envy regarding insignificant things could be a venial sin. From envy, as a capital vice, proceed hatred, murmuring, defamation, delight at the adversities of one's neighbor and sorrow at another's prosperity.

To peace

Discord, which is opposed to peace and concord, signifies a dissension of wills in those things that pertain to the good of God or the good of one's neighbor.

Contention is opposed to peace by means of words, either by argument, complaint or disagreement. It is a sin if it is done in a spirit of contradiction, if it is harmful to one's neighbor or to the truth, or if one defends himself by means of harsh words and in an unseemly manner.

Schism, war, strife and *sedition* are opposed to the peace of charity by means of deeds. Schism signifies a departure from the unity of faith and the sowing of division in religious matters. War between nations and peoples, when it is unjust, is a grave sin against charity by reason of the countless injuries and upheavals it causes. Strife, which is a kind of particular war, almost always proceeds from anger; in itself it is a great fault in him who provokes such a situation without the lawful mandate of public authority. It has its maximum manifestation in dueling, which is punished by the Church by the penalty of excommunication. It is also expressed by sedition, which consists in forming bands or parties within a nation with the object of conspiring against legitimate authority or promoting tumults or rebellions against lawful authority.

To beneficence

Scandal, which is also opposed to justice, is frequently a grave sin against charity because it is diametrically opposed to beneficence. Scandal consists in saying or doing anything which could be an occasion of sin for one's neighbor.

THE GIFT OF WISDOM

DEFINITION

The gift of wisdom is a supernatural habit, inseparable from charity, by which we judge rightly concerning God and divine things through their ultimate and highest causes under a special instinct and movement of the Holy Ghost, who makes us taste these things by a certain connaturality and sympathy. We shall explain the definition in order to gain a clear idea of it.

NATURE OF THIS GIFT

Like all the gifts of the Holy Ghost, wisdom is a supernatural habit, but it is precisely that gift which perfects charity by giving it the divine modality it lacks as long as charity is subject to the rule of human reason, even illumined by faith. By reason of its connection with charity, all the souls in the state of grace possess the gift of wisdom as a habit, and it is incompatible with mortal sin. The same is true of all the other gifts.

The judgment of wisdom

It is proper to the gift of understanding to have a penetrating and profound intuition of the truths of faith in the order of simple apprehension, without making any judgment concerning them. Such a judgment is made by the other intellectual gifts, but in different ways: concerning divine things, by the gift of wisdom; concerning created things, by the gift of knowledge; concerning the application to our concrete acts, by the gift of counsel.[15] So far as it presupposes a judgment, the gift of wisdom resides in the intellect as in its proper subject, but since it is a judgment by a kind of connaturality with divine things, it necessarily presupposes charity. Hence the gift of wisdom *causaliter* has its root in charity, which resides in the will.[16] The consequence is that this is not a purely speculative wisdom but a practical wisdom. To be sure it belongs to the gift of wisdom, in the first place, to contemplate the divine, which is like the vision of first principles; but in the second place, it pertains to wisdom to direct human acts according to divine things.

[15]Cf. *ibid.,* II-II, q. 8, a. 6.

[16]Cf. *ibid.,* q. 45, a. 2.

The objects of wisdom

Whereas other gifts perceive, judge or act on things distinct from God, the gift of wisdom is primarily concerned with God himself, giving us a savory and experimental knowledge of him which fills the soul with indescribable sweetness. By reason of this ineffable experience of God, the soul judges all things else so far as they pertain to God, and does so in their highest and supreme reasons, that is, through divine reasons. As St. Thomas explains, he who knows and tastes the highest cause *par excellence,* which is God, is disposed to judge all things by their proper divine reason.

Thus though the gift of wisdom pertains properly to divine things, there is no reason why its judgment cannot also extend to created things and discover in them their ultimate causes, which connect them in some manner to God. This is like a vision from eternity which embraces all creation in one scrutinizing glance, relating all things to God. Even created things are contemplated by wisdom in a divine manner.

It is evident from this that the primary object (formal *quod* object) of the gift of wisdom embraces the formal *quod* object and the material object of faith, because faith looks primarily to God and secondarily to revealed truths. But it is differentiated from faith by reason of its formal *quo* object, since faith is limited to believing, while the gift of wisdom experiences and tastes that which faith believes. In like manner, the primary object or the formal *quod* object of the gift of wisdom embraces the formal *quod* object and the material object of theology, which considers God and all revealed truths with their conclusions. But they are differentiated inasmuch as theology takes revealed truths as first principles and, by reasoning, deduces conclusions from them, while the gift of wisdom contemplates the same principles by the illumination of the Holy Spirit and does not properly deduce the theological conclusions, but perceives them by a kind of intuition or by a special supernatural illumination. Finally, the secondary or material object of the gift of wisdom can be extended to all the conclusions of the other sciences which are contemplated in that same divine light which shows their relation to the supernatural ultimate end.

Knowledge through causes

The philosophers defined wisdom as certain and evident knowledge of things through their ultimate causes. He who contemplates a thing without knowing its causes has only a superficial knowledge of that thing. He who contemplates a thing and knows its proximate or immediate causes has *scientific* knowledge. He who can reduce his knowledge to the ultimate principles of the natural being possesses *philosophic* wisdom, that purely natural wisdom which is called metaphysics. He who, guided by the light of faith, scrutinizes with his natural reason the revealed data of revelation in order to draw from them their intrinsic virtualities and to deduce new conclusions possesses *theological* wisdom, the highest type of natural wisdom which is possible in this life, but based radically on the supernatural order.

But he who, presupposing faith and sanctifying grace, judges divine things and human things through their ultimate causes by a kind of divine instinct possesses *supernatural* wisdom, and this is the gift of wisdom. Beyond this, there is no higher type of wisdom in this life. It is surpassed only by the beatific vision and the uncreated wisdom of God.

From this, it is evident that the knowledge which the gift of wisdom gives to the soul is incomparably superior to all human sciences, even theology, which already possesses something supernatural.[17] For that reason a simple and uneducated soul who lacks the theological knowledge acquired by study may sometimes possess, through the gift of wisdom, a profound knowledge of divine things, which causes amazement even to eminent theologians.

Breath of the Spirit

The special instinct and movement of the Holy Ghost is characteristic of all the gifts of the Holy Ghost; this attains its highest perfection, however, in the gift of wisdom, by reason of the loftiness of its object, which is God himself and divine things. Man does not proceed laboriously and by means of rational discursus when he acts under the influence of the gifts, but in a rapid and intuitive manner by a special instinct which proceeds from the Holy Ghost. It is useless to ask why such a person acts in this or that way, or says this or that thing, because even he himself does not always know; it is the Holy Spirit who operates in him. He has experienced something with great clarity and a certitude which far surpasses all human discursus or reason.

The sympathy of wisdom

A certain connaturality and sympathy is another note that is typical of the gifts of the Holy Ghost which reaches its highest perfection in the gift of wisdom. Of itself, wisdom is a savory and experimental knowledge of God and of divine things. The souls that experience these things understand very well the meaning of the words of the psalm: "Taste and see how good the Lord is" (Ps. 33:9). They experience a divine delight which sometimes causes them to fall into ecstasy and brings to them something of the ineffable joy of eternal beatitude.

It is remarkable how precisely and profoundly St. Thomas explains this note, which is characteristic of the gift of wisdom:

> As we have said, wisdom implies a certain rectitude of judgment according to divine reason. Now the rectitude of judgment can take place in two ways: according to the perfect use of reason, or by a certain connaturality for the things which are to be judged. And so we see that through the discursus of reason one judges rightly concerning the things which pertain

[17]The habit of theology is entitatively natural because it proceeds from the natural discursus of reason after an examination of the data of faith, extracting its intrinsic virtualities or theological conclusions. But radically it can be called supernatural in the sense that it departs from the principles of faith and receives the illuminating influence of faith throughout the whole theological discursus. (Cf. St. Thomas, *Summa,* I, q. 1, a. 6, ad 3.

to chastity if he has studied moral science, but there is a certain connaturality with these things in judging rightly of chastity in the person who habitually practices chastity. In like manner, to judge rightly concerning divine things through the discursus of reason pertains to wisdom insofar as it is an intellectual virtue; but to judge rightly concerning those divine things by a certain connaturality for them pertains to wisdom insofar as it is a gift of the Holy Ghost.[18]

NECESSITY OF WISDOM

The gift of wisdom is absolutely necessary if charity is to develop to its full perfection and plenitude. Precisely because charity is the most excellent of all the virtues and the most perfect and divine, it demands by its very nature the divine regulation of the gift of wisdom. Left to itself, or to the control of man in the ascetical state, it would have to be regulated by human reason according to the human mode. Charity is a divine virtue and has wings for soaring to heaven, but it is obliged to move along the earth because it is under the control of human reason and because, in a certain sense, it is necessary to compromise in accordance with prudence, due to its weak condition. Only when it begins to receive the full influence of the gift of wisdom is there given to charity the divine atmosphere and modality which it needs as the most perfect of all the theological virtues. Then charity begins to breathe and to expand in its proper element. As an inevitable consequence, it begins to grow and to increase rapidly, carrying the soul with it as if in flight, soaring to the regions of the mystical life and to the very summit of perfection, which it never could have done if it had remained under the control of human reason in the purely ascetical state.

Conclusions

From this sublime doctrine follow two inevitable conclusions which are of great importance in the theology of Christian perfection. The first is that the mystical state is not something abnormal and extraordinary in the full development of the Christian life, but it is the normal atmosphere which grace, as a divine form, demands, so that it can develop in all its virtualities through the operative principles of the infused virtues, and especially through the theological virtues, which are substantially divine. Therefore, the mystical state ought to be something normal in the Christian life, and it is, as a matter of fact, normal in every perfect Christian.

The second conclusion is that an actuation of the gifts of the Holy Spirit in the human mode, besides being impossible and absurd, would be utterly useless for the perfecting of the infused virtues, and especially of the theological virtues. Since the latter are superior to the gifts of the Holy Ghost by reason of their nature, the only perfection which they could receive from the gifts is that of the divine mode, which is exclusive and proper to the gifts, because the theological virtues, under the rule of human reason, would remain forever in a purely human mode of operation.

---

[18]Cf. *Summa,* II-II, q. 45, a. 2.

By reason of its elevation and grandeur and by reason of the sublimity of the virtue which it perfects, the effects which wisdom produces in the soul are truly remarkable. The following are the more characteristic effects of this gift:

THE EFFECTS OF WISDOM

Divine sense

1) *It gives to the saints a divine sense by which they judge all things.* This is the most impressive of all the effects of the gift of wisdom so far as they are manifested externally. One would say that the saints have completely lost the human instinct or the human manner of judgment and that it has been replaced by a certain divine instinct by which they judge all things. They see everything from God's point of view, whether the little, commonplace episodes of daily life, or the great events of life. In all things they see the hand of God. They never attach their attention to immediate secondary causes but pass them by, to arrive immediately at the Supreme Cause who governs and rules them from above.

The saints would have to do great violence to themselves in order to descend to the point of view which judges from a purely human and rational standard. An insult or any other injury that is done to them causes them to turn immediately to God, who is the one that wishes or permits that they be exercised in patience and thus increase their glory. They do not dwell for an instant on the secondary cause, which is the evil or malice of men, but they rise immediately to God and judge all things from the divine heights. They do not consider something disgraceful in the way that men of the world do, but they consider as disgraceful only that which God would consider such, namely, sin, lukewarmness, infidelity to grace, etc. They do not understand how the world can consider as treasures those little baubles which sparkle and glitter, because they see clearly that there is no true treasure but God and the things that lead to God. As St. Aloysius Gonzaga used to say: "Of what avail is this to me for eternity?"

The gift of wisdom shone most brilliantly in St. Thomas Aquinas. He possessed a remarkable supernatural instinct in discovering in all things the divine aspect by which they were related to God. There is no other way of explaining his divine instinct and insight except that the gift of wisdom operated in him in an eminent degree. In modern times, another admirable example of the operation of the gift of wisdom is Sister Elizabeth of the Trinity. According to Father Philipon, who studied her case profoundly, the gift of wisdom was the outstanding characteristic of the doctrine and life of this saintly Carmelite nun of Dijon. She was perfectly aware of her sublime vocation and even succeeded in contemplating the Trinity, so that she experienced the distinct Persons of the Trinity present in her soul. The greatest trials and sufferings were unable to disturb for a moment her ineffable peace of soul. No matter what misfortunes befell her, she remained as unmoved and tranquil as if her soul were already in eternity.

Living the faith

2) *It makes saints live the mysteries of faith in an entirely divine manner.* As Father Philipon says: "The gift of wisdom is the royal gift which enables one to enter most profoundly in the participation of the deiform mode of divine science. It is impossible to be elevated any higher outside of the beatific vision." Introduced by charity into the intimacy of the divine Persons and the very heart of the Trinity, the divinized soul, under the impulse of the Spirit of love, contemplates all things from this center. God is present to the soul in all of his divine attributes and in all of his great mysteries. In the measure in which it is possible for a simple creature, the gaze of the soul tends to become identified with the vision which God has of himself and of the entire universe. It is a godlike type of contemplation experienced in the light of the Deity, and in it the soul experiences ineffable sweetness.

In order to understand this, it is necessary to recall that God cannot see anything except in himself and in his causality. He does not know creatures directly in themselves nor in the movement of contingent and temporal causes which regulate their activity. He contemplates all things in his Word and in an eternal mode, according to the decrees of his providence and in the light of his own essence and glory. The soul which becomes a participant in this divine mode of knowledge by means of the gift of wisdom penetrates into the unsounded depths of the divinity, and it contemplates all things through the divine. One would say that St. Paul was thinking of such souls when he wrote: "The Spirit searches all things, even the deep things of God" (I Cor. 2:10).

Union with the Trinity

3) *It makes them live in union with the three divine Persons through an ineffable participation in their trinitarian life.* As Father Philipon writes:

> While the gift of knowledge acts by an ascending movement, raising the soul from creatures to God, and the gift of understanding penetrates all God's mysteries from without and within by a simple loving gaze, the gift of wisdom may be said never to leave the very heart of the Trinity. It looks at everything from that indivisible center. Thus made godlike, the soul can see things only from their highest and most divine motives. The whole movement of the universe, down to its tiniest atoms, thus lies beneath its gaze in the all-pure light of the Trinity and of the divine attributes, and it beholds them in order, according to the rhythm with which these things proceed from God. Creation, redemption, hypostatic order—it sees all, even evil, ordained to the greater glory of the Trinity.
>
> Finally it looks aloft, rising above justice, mercy, prudence and all the divine attributes. Then it suddenly discovers all these uncreated perfections in their eternal Source: in the Godhead of the Father, Son and Holy Spirit which infinitely surpasses all our narrow human concepts and leaves God incomprehensible and ineffable even to the gaze of the blessed, and even to the beatified

gaze of Christ. It beholds that God, who is supereminent in his simplicity, is simultaneously Unity in Trinity, indivisible Essence and fellowship of three living Persons, really distinct according to an order of procession which does not affect their consubstantial equality. Human eye could never have discovered such a mystery, nor could human ear have caught such harmonies, and the human heart could never have suspected such beatitude had not the Godhead stooped to us by grace in Christ, in order that we might enter into the unfathomable depths of God under the guidance of his own Spirit.[19]

The soul that has reached these heights never departs from God. If the duties of one's state should so demand, it gives itself externally to all types of work, even the most absorbing work, with an unbelievable activity; but in the most profound center of the soul, as St. John of the Cross used to say, it experiences and perceives the divine company of the Three, and does not abandon them for an instant. In such souls Martha and Mary have been joined in an ineffable manner, so that the prodigious activity of Martha in no way compromises the peace and tranquility of Mary, who remains day and night in silent contemplation at the feet of the divine Master. For such a soul, life on earth is the beginning of eternal beatitude.

Heroic charity

4) *It raises the virtue of charity to heroism.* This is precisely the purpose of the gift of wisdom. Freed from human bondage and receiving in full the divine atmosphere which the gift gives, the fire of charity reaches tremendous proportions. It is incredible what the love of God can do in souls that are under the operations of the gift of wisdom. Its most impressive effect is the complete and total death of self. Such souls love God with a pure love only for his infinite goodness and without the mixture of any human motives or self-interest. True, they do not renounce their hope for heaven; they desire it more than ever, but they desire it primarily because there they shall be able to love God with even greater intensity and without any interruption. If it were possible to glorify God more in hell than in heaven, they would without hesitation prefer the eternal torments.[20] It is the definitive triumph of grace and the total death of one's own self. Then one begins to fulfill the first commandment of the law of God in all the fulness which is compatible with the state of misery and weakness on earth.

As regards one's neighbor, charity also reaches a sublime perfection through the gift of wisdom. Accustomed to see God in all things, even in the most minute details of daily life, the saints see him in a very

[19] M. M. Philipon, O.P., *The Spiritual Doctrine of Sister Elizabeth of the Trinity,* p. 183.

[20] This sentiment has been expressed by many saints. We mention only St Thérèse of Lisieux, who states that she would gladly consent to be cast into the abyss of hell, in that place of torment and blasphemy, so that there also he could be loved for all eternity.

special manner in their neighbor. They love their neighbor with a profound tenderness which is completely supernatural and divine. They serve their neighbor with heroic abnegation, which is at the same time filled with naturalness and simplicity. Seeing Christ in the poor, in those who suffer, in the heart of all their brothers, they hasten to aid their brethren with a soul that is filled with love. They are happy to deprive themselves of even the necessities of life in order to give them to their neighbor, whose interest they place and prefer before their own, as they would put the interests of Christ before their own. Personal egoism in relation to neighbor is completely dead. Sometimes the love of charity which inflames their heart is so great that it is manifested externally in the divine foolishness which is so disconcerting to human prudence. St. Francis of Assisi embraced a tree as a creature of God, and desired to embrace all creation because it came from the hands of God.

Perfection of all virtues

5) *It gives to all the virtues their ultimate perfection and makes them truly divine.* This is an inevitable consequence of the previous effect. Perfected by the gift of wisdom, charity extends the divine influence to all the other virtues, because charity is the form of all the other virtues. The whole pattern and organism of the Christian life experiences the divine influence of the gifts of the Holy Ghost, that perfect plenitude which is seen in the virtues of the saints and is sought in vain in souls which are less advanced. By reason of the influence of the gift of wisdom through charity, all the Christian virtues are cultivated, and they acquire a godlike modality which admits of countless shades and manifestations, according to the personal character and particular type of life of the saints. But in any case they are all so sublime that one could not say which of them is most exquisite. Having died definitively to self, being perfect in every type of virtue, the soul has arrived at the summit of the mount of sanctity, where it reads that sublime inscription written by St. John of the Cross: "Here on this mountain dwell only the honor and glory of God."

BEATITUDES AND FRUITS

Following the teaching of St. Augustine, St. Thomas states that the seventh beatitude corresponds to the gift of wisdom: "Blessed are the peacemakers, for they shall be called the children of God" (Matt. 5:9). He proves the fittingness of this application from two points of view: as regards the reward and as regards the merit. As regards the merit ("blessed are the peacemakers"), because peace is nothing other than the tranquility of order, and to establish order pertains precisely to wisdom. As regards the reward ("they shall be called the children of God"), because we are adopted children of God by reason of our participation and likeness with his only-begotten Son, who is Eternal Wisdom.[21]

[21]Cf. *Summa,* II-II, q. 45, a. 6.

POSITIVE MEANS OF GROWTH

As regards the fruits of the Holy Ghost, the following three pertain especially to the gift of wisdom: charity, spiritual joy and peace.[22]

VICES OPPOSED TO WISDOM

To the gift of wisdom is opposed the vice of *spiritual dullness.* It consists in a certain defect of judgment and lack of spiritual sense, which prevents one from discerning or judging the things of God through that connaturality by taste or contact with God which comes from the gift of wisdom. Worse yet is the vice of *fatuity,* which prevents a person from judging in any way of divine things. Dullness is opposed to the gift of wisdom by privation; fatuity is opposed to it by negation.[23] When this dullness is voluntary because a man is submerged in earthly things, it is a true sin, according to the teaching of St. Paul, who says that the animal man does not comprehend the things that are of God.[24] And since there is nothing that so engrosses a man with earthly things as the vice of lust, it is primarily from lust that spiritual dullness proceeds, although the vice of anger also contributes to it so far as its violent movements impede right judgment.[25]

MEANS OF PROGRESS

Apart from the general means such as recollection, a life of prayer, fidelity to grace and humility, one can dispose himself for the actuation of the gift of wisdom by using the following means, which are within the workings of ordinary grace:

1) *To see and evaluate all things from God's point of view.* How many souls, even among those who are consecrated to God, fall into the habit of judging things from a purely natural and human point of view! If things do not go their way, they accuse others of all sorts of imperfections and even malice; but when things proceed according to their personal good pleasure, they attribute everything to God. Actually, they are willing to do God's will whenever it happens to coincide with their own interests. The truly spiritual man accepts all things, whether pleasant or painful, with a spirit of equanimity, and if things are painful or even unjust, he can still see the spiritual value of such experiences, if only as means of purification and penance. Even the smallest works are seen in the light of supernatural value and merit and while he is conscious of the defects of others, he is even more aware of his own imperfections.

2) *To combat the wisdom of the world, which is foolishness in the eyes of God.* St. Paul speaks frequently in this manner, but the greater part of men rely on this world's wisdom. Yet Christ constantly warns us in his teaching that we should expect to be a contradiction and a paradox

[22]Cf. *ibid.,* I-II, q. 70, a. 3; II-II, q. 28, aa. 1 and 4; q. 29, a. 4, ad 1.
[23]Cf. *ibid.,* I-II, q. 70, a. 3; II-II, q. 28, aa. 1 and 4; q. 29, a. 4, ad 1; q. 46.
[24]Cf. I Cor. 2:14.
[25]Cf. St. Thomas, *Summa,* II-II, q. 46, a. 3.

to the world. This does not mean that the world as such is evil, but it does mean that those who live and act for worldly goals and according to worldly standards will inevitably have to jettison the standards of God. The lives of the saints are replete with instances in which the gift of wisdom caused them to perform actions which were foolish in the eyes of the worldly men but were divine and prudent from a supernatural point of view.[26]

3) *Not to be attached to things of this world, however good and useful.* Everything in its proper place. Even the most holy and most beneficial created goods can become a source of temptation and sin if a man is too attached to them. As soon as anything outside of God himself becomes a goal or end in itself rather than a means to God, the soul is diverted from its proper orientation to God. This applies not only to the obvious dangers, such as wealth and pleasure and ambition, but to the study of theology, the liturgy, devotion to particular saints, penitential practices—even the use of the means to sanctity itself. All of these, if exaggerated or sought after with a selfish spirit, can become obstacles to union with God and the operation of the gift of wisdom which flows from that union.

4) *Not to be attached to spiritual consolations.* It is God's way to lead a soul to him by conferring spiritual consolations, but the time comes when these consolations are removed and the soul is tested, purified and made strong in love. One must strive diligently to cultivate a true devotion, which implies a resolute will to serve God at any cost. Man naturally is drawn to those things which give pleasure, whether spiritual or sensual; hence all the more reason for detachment and self-denial. The common error is to love the gift rather than the giver, and for that reason God withdraws consolations when the soul is ready to pass on to another phase of its spiritual development. To love and serve God in darkness and privation is by far a greater proof of one's fidelity than to love him in periods of delight and consolation.

---

[26]Cf. L. Lallemant, S.J., *Spiritual Doctrine,* IV, Chap. 4, a. 1.

5: THE VIRTUE OF PRUDENCE

Once the various faculties of the soul are rectified in regard to the supernatural order through the theological virtues, it is necessary to rectify them in regard to the means for attaining that end. This is the role of the moral virtues, of which there are two classes: the acquired natural virtues and the infused supernatural virtues. As we have already mentioned, it is impossible to enumerate all the moral virtues, since there can be a virtue wherever there can be a morally good habit regarding a given area of human activity, and human activities are indefinite. However, theologians generally group a large number of virtues around the basic or cardinal virtues, which serve as hinges for all the other moral virtues. We shall limit ourselves to a discussion of the cardinal virtues and a brief exposition of some of the more important virtues which are connected in one way or another with these cardinal virtues. To do more would carry us too far into the domain of moral theology.

PRUDENCE IN ITSELF

DEFINITION The first of the four cardinal virtues and the most important as a fulcrum for all the other moral virtues is the virtue of prudence. Natural or *acquired* prudence is defined as right reason applied to actions. As an *infused* moral virtue, it is a special virtue infused by God into the practical intellect for the right government of one's actions in view of the supernatural end.

ITS NATURE Prudence is a special virtue, distinct from the others. Whether acquired or infused, it resides in the practical intellect, because it is concerned with particular concrete human actions. But infused and acquired prudence are distinguished by reason of their origin, by reason of their extension, and by reason of their formal motive. By reason of origin, acquired prudence is attained through the repetition of acts; infused prudence is given by God with sanctifying grace. By reason of extension or application, acquired prudence governs the natural order, while infused prudence governs the supernatural order. By reason of the formal motive, acquired prudence operates according to simple synderesis (the first law of natural morality: "Do good and avoid evil") and the natural appetite for the moral good, while infused prudence operates under reason enlightened by faith and informed with charity.[1] Hence, whereas natural acquired prudence is concerned with the particular action in view of man's natural happiness and perfection, infused prudence will operate in view of man's supernatural goal of sanctity and salvation.

IMPORTANCE OF PRUDENCE

Prudence is the most perfect and the most necessary of all the moral virtues because its function is precisely to point out and command the just mean or measure in regard to any and all human actions. It enables a man to judge accurately what is the morally good thing to do under particular circumstances. In a certain sense, even the theological virtues come under the domain of prudence—not that they must observe a given mean, but by reason of the subject in which they inhere and the mode of their operation. In other words, there are occasions and circumstances in which supernatural prudence must dictate the proper operations of faith, hope and charity. Indeed, it can be said that, without prudence, no other virtue can be practiced with perfection.

The importance of the virtue of prudence is especially evident in certain aspects of human life. First, to help the individual avoid sin, pointing out through experience the causes and occasions of sin as well as the opportune remedies. Secondly, for the increase and growth of virtue, judging in each instance what should be done or avoided in view of one's sanctification. It is sometimes difficult to judge in a given instance which of two virtues is to be practiced; for example, justice or mercy, recollection or apostolic zeal, fortitude or meekness. Thirdly, prudence assists greatly in the works of the apostolate, whether in the pulpit, the confessional, the works of mercy or the classroom.

VICES OPPOSED TO PRUDENCE

Of the vices opposed to prudence, some are manifestly contrary to prudence and others have the false appearance of prudence. The vices contrary to prudence are *imprudence* and *negligence.* Imprudence may be manifested in three ways: a) by *precipitation,* when one acts without due deliberation but out of passion or caprice; b) by *inconsideration,* when one spurns making a judgment or pays no heed to those elements necessary for making a right judgment; and c) by *inconstancy,* when one readily abandons, for insufficient reasons, the right judgments made under prudence. One of the primary causes of these defects of prudence is lust, although they may also spring from envy and anger.

[1]Cf. St. Thomas, *Summa,* II-II, q. 47.

POSITIVE MEANS OF GROWTH

Negligence occurs when one lacks the solicitude required for efficaciously commanding the action which ought to be performed or is deficient in performing the action in the proper manner. It differs from inconstancy in the sense that the inconstant person fails to carry out the act commanded by prudence, whereas the negligent person fails even to command the action.

Of the vices which have the false appearance of prudence there are five: a) *carnal prudence,* which consists in the ability to find ways and means of satisfying self-love and the disordered passions; b) *craftiness,* which is the ability to obtain an end, whether good or evil in itself, by false, simulated or only apparently good means; it is sinful even if the end be good, for the end does not justify the use of evil means; c) *guile,* which is craftiness practiced principally by words; d) *fraud,* which is craftiness practiced by actions; e) *excessive solicitude* for temporal goods or future events, which designates an excessive concern about temporal goods or a lack of confidence in divine providence. Most of the foregoing vices proceed from an avaricious spirit.

METHODS OF PROGRESS

The practice of a given virtue will differ in the various stages of the spiritual life, and according to the age and circumstances of a given person. This is especially evident in regard to the virtue of prudence, which is usually lacking in the very young, due to their lack of experience and the predominance of emotions over reason in their lives. Consequently, it is of practical help to point out certain basic practices by which an individual can cultivate prudence according to his needs and circumstances.

Beginners, whose principal concern will be to remain in the state of grace and not turn back, will seek principally to avoid the sins opposed to prudence. They will always reflect before acting, especially before more important decisions, never postponing decisions until the last minute or being unduly influenced in their decisions by passion or selfish caprice. They will do their utmost to envisage the good or evil effects of an action and the circumstances surrounding a given act. They will endeavor to remain firm in their good resolutions and not be influenced by inconstancy or negligence. They will take special precautions against carnal prudence, which often uses subtle pretexts and rationalization to excuse them from their obligations or to induce them to yield to the demands of the passions. They will proceed always with utmost simplicity, avoiding any duplicity or any semblance of deceit or craftiness. They will live for the day and give full attention to the duty of the moment, without being too much concerned about the morrow, having a firm trust in divine providence.

So much for the negative aspect. It is likewise necessary to have a positive orientation if one is to perfect the virtue of prudence. Hence it is a salutary practice to refer all things to the ultimate end and to make sure that in every act and in the use of all created goods one refers all to God. Likewise it is of great help to keep constantly in mind the basic question: what does this profit me toward eternal salvation?

Advanced souls

Advanced souls, who will be even more solicitous in perfecting the virtue of prudence, will gain great assistance from raising the level of their daily actions even higher, to the domain of the glory of God, seeking that first and always. More immediately concerned with personal sanctification than with salvation, they will begin to apply that higher rule of prudence which states that, even of those things that are lawful, not all are prudent in view of sanctity and the glory of God. Consequently, they will practice a more intense mortification and self-denial and will strive to be ever more docile and attentive to the movements of grace and the impulses and inspirations of the Holy Ghost. In the actual performance of their daily actions they will keep in mind the important question: what would Jesus do?

The perfect. Those who are perfect in charity will practice the virtue of prudence under the impulse of the gift of counsel, of which we shall soon speak.

THE PARTS OF PRUDENCE

As we have already explained, there are three aspects to be considered in any cardinal virtue: the integral parts, the subjective parts and the potential parts. The integral parts are those elements which are required for the perfection of a given virtue; the subjective parts are the species into which the virtue is divided; and the potential parts are the annexed or related virtues which for one reason or another are connected with the virtue in question.

INTEGRAL PARTS OF PRUDENCE

Eight integral parts are required for the perfection of the virtue of prudence, five of which pertain to the intellectual aspect and three to the practical aspect. Each and every part will not necessarily function in every instance of the exercise of the virtue, but all must be possessed so that they will function when particular circumstances require. The eight parts are:

1) *Memory of the past,* so that one may learn from experience what is to be done or avoided in particular circumstances.

2) *Understanding of the present,* so that one may judge whether a given action is lawful or unlawful, morally good or evil, fitting or unfitting.

POSITIVE MEANS OF GROWTH

3) *Docility,* so that those who lack experience may accept the counsel and advice of those who have experience.

4) *Sagacity,* so that one may act rightly in urgent cases when time or circumstances do not permit delay.

5) *Reasoning power,* so that when time permits, one may act after the required consideration and reflexion.

6) *Foresight,* so that one may judge the immediate means in view of the end or goal which is sought.

7) *Circumspection,* so that one may take into consideration the special circumstances which surround a given act, as to persons, places, etc.

8) *Precaution,* so that one will take into consideration the possible obstacles from without, or one's own weakness or incapacity in view of a given action.

SUBJECTIVE PARTS

Prudence is divided into basic species: *personal* prudence and *social* prudence. The names indicate the basis of the distinction. Personal prudence has to do with one's government of oneself; social prudence is concerned with the government of others and the common good. We have already enumerated the integral parts which pertain to personal prudence. Social prudence, however, admits of many other kinds according to the type of society or group under consideration: regnative prudence, military prudence, domestic prudence, political prudence, etc. These types can be studied in a manual of moral theology.

POTENTIAL PARTS

The potential parts of prudence are three in number, and they are concerned with those matters which are secondary or which lead to perfect prudence. *Good counsel* differs from prudence in the sense that the latter commands and decides, whereas good counsel, as its name designates, merely advises what are the most apt means in view of a given end. *Common sense* is also dispositive to the virtue of prudence, because it enables the individual to make the proper judgment according to common laws. *Perspicacity,* which is intimately related to equity, enables an individual to make a judgment in those cases in which the law is not known, or its application fails because of certain circumstances, so that one must base a judgment on higher and more general principles.

THE GIFT OF COUNSEL

DEFINITION

Counsel is the gift which perfects the operation of the virtue of prudence. It is a supernatural habit by which the soul, under the inspiration and motivation of the Holy Ghost, judges rightly in particular events what ought to be done in view of its supernatural ultimate end.

ITS NATURE AND NECESSITY

Counsel is a true habit, although infused by God and operative under the Holy Spirit as the principal mover, thus resulting in a mode of action that is completely divine. While the virtue of prudence operates according to the dictates of reason enlightened by faith, the gift of counsel operates under the impulse of the Holy Ghost. Thus it often commands actions for which human reason would never be able to give an explanation, nor would human reason alone, even with the light of faith, be able of itself to come to such practical and particular judgments.

It is therefore evident that the gift of counsel is necessary in those cases in which an immediate judgment is required but there is neither the ability nor the opportunity to make the decision under the virtue of prudence, which works always in a human mode. For example, it is at times most difficult to know how to equate suavity with firmness, how to reconcile the necessity of guarding a secret with the obligation to speak the truth, the interior life with the apostolate, an affectionate love with perfect chastity. It is even more difficult for persons charged with government and administration—in religion, in the family, in civil and economic life—to be able at every instance to do that which is prudent. In many instances, the prudent action will have to be the result of the operation of the gift of counsel.

ITS EFFECTS

When the gift of counsel operates in souls, it produces marvelous effects, of which the principal ones are the following:

1) *It preserves one from the danger of a false conscience.*

2) *It provides the solution to many difficult and unexpected situations and problems.* If a soul is habitually faithful to grace and intent on doing all for the glory of God, the gift of counsel will frequently come into play when human reason, either alone or enlightened by faith, would be incapable of making the proper judgment. The solution may not be one which prudence would suggest or which reason would approve, but since it comes from the Holy Spirit working through the gift, it is always the right solution.

3) *It inspires superiors with the most apt means for governing others.* Prudence is not restricted to one's personal actions but is the primary virtue required for the government of others. Great indeed is the need for a delicate sense of judgment in the many difficult problems which are presented in the direction and government of others. Hence the gift of counsel is often necessary for the decisions and commands to be made by the religious superior, the spiritual director and even the parents of a family.

4) *It increases one's docility to legitimate superiors.* Strange as it may seem, the gift of counsel has as one of its most wonderful effects the

POSITIVE MEANS OF GROWTH

beautiful practice of docility. God has determined that men should be governed by superiors in all the various phases of life, and the Holy Ghost, through the gift of counsel, inspires this subjection to lawful superiors. This spirit of docility, as we shall see, is one of the surest signs that a given revelation or vision is from God, for any mystical experience which inspires disobedience or rebellion cannot be from God.

BEATITUDE AND FRUITS

St. Augustine assigns to the gift of counsel the fifth beatitude: blessed are the merciful. St. Thomas, however, maintains that this beatitude is related to counsel only in the sense that counsel pertains to things useful and proportionate to the end, and mercy is most proportionate to the end. In an executive or elicited sense, however, mercy belongs properly to the gift of piety.

Again, there is no fruit which corresponds directly to the gift of counsel because counsel pertains to practical knowledge, which has no other fruit than the operation which it directs and in which it terminates. Nevertheless, since this gift is related to the works of mercy, one could say that it is related in a sense to the fruits of goodness and benignity.

OPPOSED VICES

St. Thomas assigns special vices in opposition to the speculative gifts of wisdom, understanding and science, but he assigns no special vices opposed to the practical gifts. Consequently, any vices opposed to the virtue of prudence will likewise be opposed to the gift of counsel: *precipitation* in acting on one's own human judgment when one should wait for the Holy Spirit; *tenacity* in holding to one's own judgment and depending on one's own efforts instead of deferring to the Holy Ghost; and *procrastination* when one should act immediately under the impulse of the gift but delays and loses the occasion for acting at all.

MEANS OF GROWTH

Apart from the general means for disposing oneself for the operation of the gifts of the Holy Ghost, there are special predispositions necessary for the actuation of the gift of counsel:

1) *To cultivate a profound humility,* in order to recognize one's own weakness and ignorance, and thus have recourse to the Holy Ghost for light and guidance.

2) *To proceed always with reflexion and without haste,* realizing that in some circumstances all possible human diligence is insufficient and that the Holy Spirit alone can perform the operation in us, although we must do what we can and not tempt God by waiting for divine and supernatural methods when our own strength under ordinary grace suffices.

3) *To listen in silence to the voice of God,* avoiding the noise and tumult of the world as much as possible.

4) *To practice perfect docility and obedience to those whom God has placed over us in the Church,* for there is nothing that so prevents the Holy Ghost from operating in us as does an independent and insubordinate spirit.

6: THE VIRTUE OF JUSTICE AND ITS PARTS

Our study of this important moral virtue will consider, not only the cardinal virtue itself, but its chief allied virtues (religion, piety and the gift of piety, observance, obedience). A word will also be said about some of the less important related virtues to complete our investigation of the wide and varied area of human activity which should be regulated by this hinge on which man's moral life turns.

JUSTICE IN ITSELF

DEFINITION The word justice is frequently used in Scripture as synonymous with sanctity, but as a special virtue it is a supernatural habit which inclines the will constantly and perpetually to render to each one that which is due strictly.[1]

ITS NATURE AND NECESSITY We say that justice is a constant and perpetual disposition of the will because a habit requires more than an occasional act of virtue. This virtue, moreover, perfects the will and not the intellect, for it pertains to the practical order of regulating one's relations with one's neighbors. Further, it pertains to those things which are due to another in the strict sense, unlike the virtues of charity, affability and gratitude, which are based on a certain fittingness and not on a strict obligation. Hence for justice there must always be present the three characteristics: reference to another, strict obligation and exact adequation (neither more nor less than what is owed).

After prudence, justice is the most excellent of all the moral virtues, although it is inferior to the theological virtues and even to the annexed virtue of religion. Its importance in both personal and social life is evident. It puts things in their right order and thus prepares the way for true peace, which St. Augus-

[1]Cf. St. Thomas, *Summa,* II-II, q. 58.

tine defines as the tranquility of order, and Scripture defines as the work of justice.[2]

THE PARTS OF JUSTICE

Integral parts

In every kind of justice two things are required in order that one may be called just in the full significance of the word: to refrain from evil toward one's neighbor and society, and to do the required good for one's neighbor and society. These two aspects are, therefore, the *integral parts* without which perfect justice is impossible. While it is important to stress the one aspect by stating that no one ever has any right to do wrong to his neighbor, it is likewise important to insist that justice demands that one render to his neighbor that which is due.

The close connection between the integral parts of justice and the first law of morality (do good; avoid evil) makes it evident that justice is essential for even natural human perfection. It is likewise required as the foundation for the perfection of charity, since it would be a strange paradox for an individual to attempt to operate according to the higher standard of charity when he ignores the demands of justice.

Moreover, it is important to realize that justice is not a purely negative virtue, not merely a matter of refraining from evil toward one's neighbor or from violating his rights. It requires, on the one hand, a rejection of such evil and, on the other hand, the faithful fulfillment of those obligations to which we are bound by various kinds of laws. And while it is generally true that it would be more serious to do evil than to omit doing the good to which we are obliged, in certain cases the sin of omission against justice is more serious by far than a sin of commission.

Subjective parts

The virtue of justice admits of three species: legal justice, distributive justice and commutative justice. *Legal justice* is the virtue which inclines the members of a society to render to that society what is due in view of the common good or goal of the society. It is called legal because it is based upon, and determined by, the laws of the society in question, which laws bind in conscience if they are just. And since the common good of society takes precedence over the particular good of any member of society, justice sometimes requires that the individual relinquish his personal goods in view of the well-being of the society as a whole.

Distributive justice is the virtue which inclines the person in charge of the distribution of goods or favors in a society to bestow these things proportionately to the dignity, merits or needs of each one. Although the titles of justice may vary with the goods or the persons involved, distributive justice works

[2]Strictly speaking, peace flows directly and immediately from charity, which is the bond of union, but it proceeds indirectly from justice, which removes the obstacles to peace. Cf. St. Thomas, *Summa,* II-II, q. 29, a. 3, ad 3.

POSITIVE MEANS OF GROWTH

on the principle of rendering to each what is his due. Thus the distribution of goods should be according to the needs of each person, and the bestowal of favors or offices should be according to the merits or abilities of each one. And although one may think that justice is measurable in mathematical equality, when it is a question of distributive justice it is rather a question of proportion, with the result that strict equality of distribution would often be an injustice rather than justice.

Commutative justice is justice in the fullest sense of the word, since it has to do with the rights and duties of individual persons among themselves. It coincides almost exactly with the definition of justice itself: the constant and perpetual will of one individual person to render to another individual what is due in strict equality. Hence its transgression always involves the obligation to make restitution. It is violated by a great number of sins, such as homicide, calumny, injury, theft, damage and many others which are enumerated and explained in moral theology.[3]

Potential parts

The potential parts of justice are those related virtues which are connected with justice by reason of one or another of its elements, namely, something owed to another by a strict obligation and in some measure of equality. On the other hand, these annexed virtues lack something of the perfect concept of justice, and for that reason they do not have the full force of justice.

They are divided into two groups: those which fail through defect of the equality to be observed between what is given and what is received, and those which are not based on a title of a strict right on the part of the other party. To the first group belong *religion,* which controls the cult due to God, *piety,* which regulates the duties to one's parents, and *observance, dulia* and *obedience,* which are concerned with one's obligations to superiors. The second group is comprised of *gratitude* for benefits received, *vindication* or just punishment of the guilty, *truth, affability* and *liberality* in one's social contacts, and *equity,* which enables one to depart from the letter of the law in order to preserve its spirit. We shall discuss these virtues in particular, but first we shall indicate the principal means to be used for the growth and perfection of the virtue of justice in general.

MEANS OF PROGRESS

Negative means

Among the negative means of fostering the virtue of justice, we may mention the following:

1) *To avoid even the slightest injustice.* It is extremely easy to form a false conscience in the matter of justice, saying that one or another

[3]Social justice and international justice are not different species of justice but are either modifications of one of the three already mentioned or a mixture of several of those mentioned.

moral law has no importance, which opens the way to the commission of habitual venial sins. Granted that there may be smallness of matter in many instances, the evils to be sedulously avoided are the cultivation of a disdain for little things because they are little, and losing sight of the frequency of small injustices which pave the way for a more serious fall.

2) *To avoid contracting debts without necessity and to pay one's debts promptly.* This is an excellent ascetical practice, namely, to learn to do without things which of themselves are not necessities. And when necessary debts have been contracted, the most important duty is to pay those debts owed in justice before contracting new ones.

3) *To treat the possessions of others as carefully as one's own.* Whether it be a question of things rented for use or shared in the family or religious community, it is common to find a lack of regard for the possessions of others. It is often the sign of selfishness if a person assumes the attitude that what is not his, need not be cared for.

4) *To be extremely careful not to injure the good name of one's neighbor.* One's good name is of much greater value than created goods, and yet it is often the least respected. How frequently one hears the saying that a certain fault of another is common knowledge and therefore there is no need to refrain from discussing it. Even worse is the frequency of rash judgment, ridicule, contumely, defamation, etc. One must always speak the truth when he speaks, but this does not mean that one always has the right to reveal the faults of others. Both in private conversation and in the modern newspapers and magazines many sins are committed against justice in this matter.

5) *To avoid any kind of acceptance of persons,* which means favoring them without sufficient reason or denying them their lawful rights. This is a sin against distributive justice; it is committed not only in civil society but even in some ecclesiastical and religious communities. The basic rule which should determine the distribution of offices and honors and the application of punishments should be simply to give to each individual what his merits or faults require in justice. As regards the distribution or assignment of offices, the objective consideration should usually be conclusive, namely, what does the given position or office require, and which person has the capacity and talents to fulfill the task? One of the surest safeguards of peace and harmony in any community or society is distributive justice on the part of the authorities or superiors.

Positive means

The positive means for growing in justice can be determined under the headings of the three species of justice:

1) *Commutative justice.* To give to each his own is a basic rule for the observance of commutative justice. Nothing is small in the eyes of

God, and everything good can be an occasion for growth in grace and holiness. One of the severest blows we can deliver to our own self-love is to maintain a delicate sense of justice toward each of our fellow men. This is not an area of like or dislike, of taste or feeling, but simply of doing what we are supposed to do, regardless of any other consideration.

2) *Distributive justice.* No superior is anything more than an administrator or steward in the eyes of God. Even more, he is the servant of those he governs. The common good of a society or community must be preserved at all costs, and this common good is not necessarily the selfish good of the majority; it is the good or goal for which the society exists as such. Consequently, the superior will always judge in favor of the society as a whole, and in the distribution of goods or offices he will seek the individual who will best contribute to that same common good of the society.

3) *Legal justice.* In a certain sense, the members of a society are the servants and stewards of that society. Every society has its common good or goal protected by the laws which will lead to the accomplishment of that goal. In this sense, therefore, all the members of a society are bound in legal justice to comply with the laws which further the common good. Any movement of separatism or rebellion is destructive of the society as such. Thus the citizen of a state, the member of the Church, the children in a family, and the religious in a religious institute must constantly keep in mind their obligations to the society to which they belong. They should be conscientious in fulfilling the laws of the society as perfectly as possible, unless special circumstances honestly allow for a dispensation or exemption.

ALLIED VIRTUES

While it is the proper domain of moral theology to discuss and examine the various virtues in particular, there are certain virtues annexed to justice which are so essential to growth in Christian perfection that they demand special treatment in any manual of the theology of Christian perfection. For that reason, we single out those virtues under justice which have a special importance for all those who are striving for the perfection of the Christian life and suggest that the reader refer to manuals of moral theology for a study of the remaining annexed virtues.

THE VIRTUE OF RELIGION

DEFINITION

The virtue of religion may be defined as a moral virtue which inclines man to give to God the worship that is due him as the first principle of all things. It is the most important of all the virtues derived from justice, and in perfection it surpasses all the other moral virtues, including justice itself. This is by reason of the excellence of its object, which is the worship of God, and in this sense it closely approaches the theological virtues.[4] The material object of the virtue of religion comprises the internal and external acts by which we give worship to God; its formal object or motive is the supreme excellence of God as the first principle of all that exists.

ACTS OF RELIGION

Religion has various acts, both internal and external. The internal acts are devotion and prayer; the external acts are adoration, sacrifice, offerings, tithes, vows, oaths, adjuration and praise.[5]

Devotion

Devotion consists in a promptness of will for giving oneself to the things that pertain to the service of God. Hence they are called devout who in some way devote themselves to God and remain completely subject to him. The essential note and characteristic of devotion is promptness of will, ever disposed to give itself to the things that pertain to God's service. The truly devout are always available for the service of God.

But how, then, is the virtue of religion distinguished in this respect from the virtue of charity? If one seeks loving union with God, it is an act of charity; if one intends the worship or service of God, it is the act of devotion which proceeds from the virtue of religion, but under the imperation of charity.[6] Charity causes devotion because love makes us more prompt for the service of the one we love, and devotion increases charity because friendship is preserved and increased by our services for our friend.

St. Thomas remarks that, as an act of religion, devotion always is directed to God and not to his creatures. Hence devotion to the saints should not terminate in the saints themselves, but it should pass through them to God. We venerate in the saints that which they have of God, that is to say, we venerate God in them.[7] It is evident from this how mistaken those persons are who attach their devotion, not only to a particular saint as an end in itself, but even to some particular image of a saint, without which they would have no devotion whatever. Priests and other persons who are entrusted with directing the piety of the faithful should never let these things occur under the pretext that the persons involved are ignorant, or that otherwise they would have no religion at all. It is necessary to instruct the faithful and to correct abuses.

---

[4]Although some writers have attempted to classify religion among the theological virtues, it cannot be done, because this virtue does not have God himself as its proper object, but the worship of God. Cf. St. Thomas, *Summa,* II-II, q. 81, a. 5.

[5]Cf. St. Thomas, *Summa,* II-II, q. 84.

[6]Cf. *ibid.,* q. 82, a. 2, ad 1.

[7]Cf. *loc. cit.,* ad 3.

The principal extrinsic cause of devotion is God, who calls those whom he wishes and inflames in their hearts the fire of devotion. But the intrinsic cause so far as it pertains to us is meditation on the divine goodness and the benefits received from God, together with the consideration of our misery, which excludes presumption and impels us to subject ourselves completely to God. The most proper effect of devotion is to fill the soul with spiritual joy, even if it may sometimes cause sadness in respect to God.[8]

Prayer

Prayer is the second interior act of the virtue of religion. Unlike devotion, which is localized in the will, prayer pertains properly to the intellect. By reason of its extraordinary importance in the spiritual life, we shall dedicate an entire section to this matter.

Adoration

Adoration is an external act of the virtue of religion by which we express the honor and reverence which is due to the divine excellence.[9] Although of itself adoration prescinds from the presence of the body, for even angels adore God, in us, composed as we are of matter and spirit, it is usually manifested bodily. Exterior adoration is an expression and an overflow of interior adoration, which is primary, and serves at the same time to arouse and preserve interior adoration. And because God is in all places, we can adore God both internally and externally in all places, although the most proper place is in his temple, because he resides there in a special manner. Moreover, the very atmosphere of a church or chapel helps to withdraw us from the noise and distractions of the world, while many holy objects contained there serve to arouse devotion, and the presence of other worshipers likewise nourishes the spirit of adoration.

Sacrifice

Sacrifice is the principal act of the external and public worship of God; it consists in the external offering of a sensible thing, together with a real change or destruction of the thing, effected by the priest in honor of God, as a testimony of his supreme dominion and our complete submission to him.[10] Under the New Testament there is no other sacrifice than the sacrifice of the Mass, which is the unbloody renewal of the sacrifice of Calvary. The Mass gives infinite glory to God and has superabundant value for drawing upon men all the graces which they need. We have already considered the sacrifice of the Mass in a previous discussion.

Offerings

Oblations signify the spontaneous offering of something for divine worship and for the veneration of God.[11] There are two classes of oblations: one, by

---

[8]Cf. *ibid.*, a. 4. See also the interesting objections and replies given by St. Thomas in the third article of the same question.

[9]Cf. *ibid.*, q. 84.

[10]Cf. *ibid.*, q. 85.

[11]Cf. *ibid.*, qq. 86-87.

which something is offered for the honor of God, whether for his worship or for the sustaining of his ministers or the poor (e.g., the first fruits offered in ancient times, and modern collections for charitable causes); the other, that which is offered to the priest for his own use (e.g., tithes in ancient days, and the stipends offered in modern times for the celebration of Mass and other religious services). The Church has the power to designate the amount of these offerings, but in many cases it is left to the custom which is prevalent in a given nation or diocese.

Vows

A vow is a free and deliberate promise made to God concerning some good which is possible and better than its contrary.[12] When made under the proper conditions, it is an excellent act of religion, which increases the merit of one's good works by directing them to the worship and honor of God. By the same token, the voluntary transgression of a vow is a sin against religion, and if it pertains to a matter which is already forbidden by precept, it constitutes a second sin and must be declared as such in confession. If the vows which are broken pertain to a person publicly consecrated to God, the sin committed against religion is a sacrilege. Such is not the case, however, with the breaking of a private vow of chastity, although it would surely be a grave sin against the virtue of religion—of infidelity to God—and would have to be declared explicitly in confession. A detailed study of the vows pertains to the field of moral theology.

Oaths

An oath is the invocation of the name of God in witness to the truth, and it cannot be taken except with truth, judgment and justice.[13] Under these conditions it is an act of the virtue of religion. An oath may be assertory or promissory, depending on whether it is used to testify to some truth or to give assurance of the fulfillment of some promise. The validity, liceity, obligation, dispensation, etc., of a promissory oath coincide almost exactly with that of a vow.

Adjuration

Adjuration is an act of religion which consists in the invocation of the name of God or of some sacred thing to oblige another to perform or to cease performing some action.[14] When performed with due respect and under the necessary conditions (truth, justice and judgment) it is licit and honest. The Church uses it principally in exorcisms against the devil.

The name of God

The invocation of God's holy name consists primarily in the external praise of the name of God in public or private worship as a manifestation of internal fervor.[15] It is useful and fitting to accompany the invocation of the holy name of

---

[12]Cf. *ibid.*, q. 88.
[13]Cf. canon 1316; St. Thomas, *ibid.*, q. 89.
[14]Cf. *ibid.*, q. 90.
[15]Cf. *ibid.*, q. 91.

God with singing so that the souls of the weak may more readily be aroused to devotion.[16]

Opposed to this act of religion by which one invokes the name of God is the use of God's name in vain. The name of God is holy and should never be pronounced without due reverence and certainly never in vain or without cause. For that reason it is stated in Sirach: "Let not your mouth form the habit of swearing, or becoming too familiar with the Holy Name. Just as a slave that is constantly under scrutiny will not be without welts, so one who swears continually by the Holy Name will not remain free from sin."[17]

SINS OPPOSED TO RELIGION

The principal sins opposed to the virtue of religion by way of excess can be classified under superstition, and those opposed by way of defect under various other names.

Superstition is a vice by which one offers to God a type of worship that is unworthy of him, or renders to creatures that which belongs to God alone. The following are types of superstition: 1) unfitting worship of God by means of false or superfluous objects; 2) idolatry, which consists in giving to a creature the worship that is due to God; 3) divination, which consists in attempting to discover future events by means that are disproportionate or unsuitable; 4) vain observance, which consists in trusting in certain circumstances which are totally disproportionate or fortuitous (such as Friday the 13th) to conjecture about beneficial or adverse events, and governing one's own life or the lives of another by these conjectures.

The following vices are opposed to the virtue of religion by defect: 1) *tempting God,* which consists in asking or demanding, without respect for the divine majesty, the intervention of God in certain events, as if to put his omnipotence to the test, or to expect God's direct intervention in circumstances which are unworthy of him. We tempt God whenever we expect his assistance without having done our part in those things which we can and ought to do. 2) *Perjury,* which consists in calling God as a witness to a falsehood; this is always a serious sin, even when the matter in which one perjures himself is only a small lie or the refusal to fulfill what has been promised under oath. 3) *Sacrilege,* which consists in the violation or profane treatment of something that is sacred, whether it be a person, place or some object. 4) *Simony,* which is the deliberate intention of buying or selling something that is intrinsically spiritual, such as the sacraments, or some material object which is inseparably united to something spiritual, such as a consecrated chalice.[18]

---

[16]Cf. *ibid.*, q. 91, a. 2.

[17]Sirach 23:9-11.

[18]Cf. St. Thomas, *Summa,* II-II, qq. 92-100.

THE VIRTUE OF PIETY

The word piety can be used in various senses: 1) as a synonym for devotion, a religious spirit, the attention to things that pertain to the worship of God (thus we speak of pious or devout persons); 2) as signifying compassion or mercy, and thus we may say: "O Lord, have pity (piety) on us"; 3) to designate a special virtue derived from justice, the virtue of piety which we treat here; 4) as referring to one of the seven gifts of the Holy Ghost: the gift of piety.

DEFINITION

As a special virtue derived from justice, piety is defined as a supernatural habit which inclines us to render to our parents, our country and to all those connected with them the reverence and services which are due to them.[19] The material object of this virtue consists in all the acts of honor, reverence, service and material or spiritual aid which are given to one's parents and relatives and country. The formal *quo* object or motive of these acts is that one's parents and country are the secondary principle of one's being and government. To God, as the first principle, is owed the special worship which is given him by the virtue of religion.[20] To one's parents and country, as secondary principles, is owed the special reverence of the virtue of piety. This same reverence is owed likewise to one's blood relatives so far as they proceed from the same common family tree.[21]

Its nature

Accordingly, the virtue of piety has three different subjects to whom the debts of piety are owed: 1) one's parents, to whom this virtue refers primarily, because after God they are the principles of one's being, education and government; 2) one's country, because that also is, in a certain sense, a principle of our being, education and government insofar as it furnishes our parents—and through them, us—with a multitude of things that are necessary or helpful; 3) one's blood relatives, because, although they are not the principle of our being and government, nevertheless our parents are in some way represented in them, since all proceed from the same family tree. By extension one can also consider as relatives those who form part of the same spiritual family, for example, the members of a religious order, who call the founder their father.

[19]Cf. *ibid.*, q. 101, a. 3.

[20]This is true if we consider God simply as our Creator, the First Principle of everything that exists, but since he has raised us through grace to the status of his adopted children, God is also our true Father, and in this sense we owe him certain debts out of piety. Cf. St. Thomas, *loc. cit.*, ad 2.

[21]Cf. *ibid.*, a. 1.

POSITIVE MEANS OF GROWTH

From what has been said, it should be evident that the virtue of piety is distinct from other virtues which resemble it, for example, charity toward one's neighbor and legal justice. Piety is distinguished from fraternal charity inasmuch as piety is based on the intimate union which results from the same family tree, while charity is based on the bonds which unite the whole human race with God. Again, piety for one's country is distinguished from legal justice, in the sense that the latter is related to one's country by considering the good of the country as a common good for all the citizens, while piety considers one's country as a secondary principle of one's own being. And since our country always preserves this second aspect in relation to us, one must conclude that, even if a man lives far from his country and has become a citizen of another country, he is nevertheless obliged to preserve piety toward the country of his birth. He may not, however, be obligated to the duties which proceed from legal justice, because he has ceased to be subject to the government of his native land.

Since piety is a special virtue, it follows that the sins committed against this virtue are special sins which must be declared explicitly in confession. For example, to strike or mistreat one's father or mother is a special sin against piety and more serious than to strike a stranger. The same thing is to be said regarding the sins committed against one's country or against one's relatives.

SINS AGAINST PIETY

Sins against family piety may be by way of excess or by way of defect. By excess, one sins by having an *excessive love for one's parents,* with the result that he would neglect duties which are more binding than the duties he owes to his parents. For example, it would be a sin by excess of piety to renounce one's religious or priestly vocation for the sole motive of not displeasing one's family. The sin by defect of piety is called *impiety,* the neglect to fulfill one's obligations of reverence, honor or economic or spiritual aid when he could and ought to fulfill them. Piety toward one's country becomes a sin of excess in the case of exaggerated nationalism, which disdains the rights of other nations. By defect, one sins against piety to one's country by becoming a citizen of the world or a man without a country.

GROWTH IN PIETY

In order to grow in the virtue of piety, it is well for children frequently to recall the many benefits which they have received from their parents and usually are unable to repay. They should endeavor to manifest to their parents ever greater affection, respect and veneration, even if to do so means that they must overcome their own melancholy temperament, or try to forget some injustice which they may have suffered at the hands of a parent. Parents are always parents, and there is never any reason sufficient to lessen the esteem and respect which they deserve as parents.

The same respect, affection and veneration should be shown to all of our relatives, and especially to those who are closest to us and live under the same roof. There is nothing that contributes so much to one's own happiness and well-being, and to the edification of others, as the picture of a Christian family intimately united in the Lord. By the same token, there is nothing that gives greater scandal to others and contributes so much to domestic unhappiness as constant family arguments and discord.

Moreover, it is necessary to cultivate a love for one's country. This can be greatly fostered by studying its history and trying to serve it in any way we can, even, if necessary, to give our life for our country. But we must at the same time avoid all envy or disdain of other countries.

THE GIFT OF PIETY

DEFINITION

The gift of piety is defined as a supernatural habit infused with sanctifying grace, which arouses in the will, through the motion of the Holy Ghost, a filial love for God considered as Father, and a sentiment of universal brotherhood for all men as our brothers and as sons of the same heavenly Father.[22]

ITS NATURE

As a supernatural habit, the gift of piety is classified within the proximate genus which is common to all the gifts of the Holy Ghost. In saying that it is infused together with sanctifying grace, we signify that all the just possess the gifts of the Holy Spirit as habits and that they are inseparable from sanctifying grace. The virtue of piety is an affective gift, and therefore it is radicated in the will in union with the other infused virtues also localized in the will. The expression, "by the movement of the Holy Ghost," signifies what is proper and characteristic in the gifts, as distinct from the acquired virtues, which are governed exclusively by the light of natural reason, and the infused virtues, which are governed by reason under the light of faith.

God as Father

That which is formal and proper in the gift of piety and distinguishes it from the virtue of religion, acquired or infused, which venerates God as Creator or as the First Principle of everything that exists, is that it considers God as a Father who has engendered us in the supernatural life by giving us, with sanctifying grace, a physical and formal participation in his divine nature. In this sense, God is truly our Father, and the worship which we give to

[22]St. Thomas treats of the gift of piety at the end of his tract on justice, but due to its special relationship with the virtue of the same name we prefer to discuss it here.

him as Father through the gift of piety is more noble and more excellent even than that which we give him by the virtue of religion.[23] The principal secondary effect of the gift of piety is the sentiment of universal brotherhood with all men. St. Thomas expressly states that, just as through the virtue of piety a man offers worship and veneration not only to his own father but also to all his blood relatives so far as they are related to the father, so also the gift of piety is not restricted to the worship and veneration of God, but extends to all men so far as they are related to God.[24]

THE NECESSITY OF THE GIFT

The gift of piety is absolutely necessary in order to perfect to a heroic degree the matter which falls under the virtue of justice and the other virtues related to justice, especially those of religion and piety. What a great difference there is, for example, in practising the worship of God only under the impulse of the virtue of religion, which presents God to us as Creator and sovereign Lord, from practising the same worship under the movement of the gift of piety, which enables us to see God as a most loving Father! The service and the worship of God are then fulfilled without effort and with exquisite perfection. And as regards one's association with other men, how much more exquisite is the affection which we show to our neighbor when we realize that he is our brother and a child of the same heavenly Father.

Even as regards material things, the gift of piety can change one's outlook completely. For those who are governed by the gift of piety, the world and all creation are considered as the house of the Father, and everything in the universe becomes a testimony of his infinite goodness. Such persons are able to discover the religious meaning which is hidden in all things, as is evident in the life of St. Francis of Assisi and Venerable Louis of Granada. Then the Christian virtues acquire a sublime perfection which would be impossible to achieve without the influence of the gift of piety, because without the gifts of the Holy Ghost no infused virtue can reach its perfect development and expansion.

EFFECTS OF PIETY

The effects which the actuation of the gift of piety produces in the soul are truly marvelous. The following are the principal effects:

Filial love

1) *It places in the soul a truly filial tenderness toward our heavenly Father.* This is the primary and fundamental effect of the gift of piety. The soul understands perfectly and experiences with ineffable sweetness the words of St. Paul: "Now you have not received a spirit of bondage so as to be again in fear, but you have received a spirit of adoption of sons, by virtue of which we cry: 'Abba! Father!' The Spirit himself gives testimony to our spirit that we are sons of God" (Rom. 8:15-16).

[23]Cf. St. Thomas, *Summa,* II-II, q. 121, a. 1, ad 2.
[24]Cf. *loc. cit.,* ad 3.

St. Thérèse, in whom the gift of piety was manifested to a sublime degree, could not think of these words without weeping out of love. We read in her biography that, when a novice entered her cell on one occasion, she was amazed at the heavenly expression on the face of the saint. Sister Thérèse was very busy with her sewing, and yet she seemed at the same time to be absorbed in profound contemplation. When the novice asked her what she was thinking about, the saint replied: "I am meditating on the Our Father. It is so sweet and consoling to call so good a God by the name of Father." And as the saint was speaking, her eyes filled with tears.

Dom Columba Marmion, the saintly abbot of Maredsous, also possessed to a high degree this awareness of our adoptive filiation. For him God was above all our Father. The monastery was the house of the Father and all its members formed God's family. The same thing must be said of the whole world and of all men. Dom Marmion insists repeatedly on the necessity of cultivating this spirit of adoption which should be the Christian's basic attitude toward God. He himself mentally prayed for this spirit of adoption at the inclination for the *Gloria Patri* at the end of each psalm in the Office.

> We should never forget that the whole Christian life as well as all sanctity is reduced to being through grace what Jesus is by nature: Son of God. This is the sublimity of our religion. The source of all the excellencies of Jesus, of the value of all his states, of the fruitfulness of all his mysteries, lies in his divine generation and in his quality as Son of God. Therefore, the most lofty saint in heaven will be he who in this world was the best son of God, he who best made fructify the grace of his supernatural adoption in Jesus Christ.[25]

Adoration

2) *It enables us to adore the ineffable mystery of the divine paternity within the Trinity.* In its most sublime manifestations the gift of piety makes us penetrate the mystery of the intimate life of God by giving us a most vivid awareness, filled with respect and adoration, of the divine paternity of the Father in relation to the Word. It is now no longer a question merely of his spiritual fatherhood of us through grace, but of his divine paternity which is eternally fruitful in the bosom of the Trinity. The soul rejoices with ineffable sweetness in this profound mystery of the eternal generation of the Word which constitutes, so to speak, the happiness of the Father, who is well pleased in his divine Son. In view of this eternal and ever actual generation within the Trinity, the soul is impelled to be silent and to love, without any other language than that of adoration and tears. It loves to repeat in the depth of its soul the sublime words of the *Gloria*: "We give thee thanks because of thy great glory." It is an adoration of God for his own sake and without

[25]Dom Columba Marmion, O.S.B., *Christ in His Mysteries,* Chap. III, n. 6.

any consideration of the benefits which the soul has received from him. This sentiment was especially manifested in the life of Sister Elizabeth of the Trinity.[26]

Abandonment

3) *It arouses in the soul a filial abandonment to the heavenly Father.* Intimately penetrated with the sentiment of its adoptive divine filiation, the soul abandons itself calmly and confidently to the heavenly Father. It is not preoccupied with any care, and nothing is capable of disturbing its unalterable peace, even for an instant. The soul asks nothing and rejects nothing. It is not concerned about health or sickness, a long life or a short life, consolations or aridity, persecution or praise, activity or idleness. It is completely submissive to the will of God, and seeks only to glorify God with all its powers, desiring that all men should realize their adoptive divine filiation and live as true sons of God. There is nothing rigid or complicated in their spiritual life or practices of piety which could paralyze the impulses of the heart. These souls run to God as a child runs to its Father.

Love of neighbor

4) *It causes us to see in our neighbor a son of God and a brother in Jesus Christ.* This is a natural consequence of our adoptive filiation through grace. If God is our Father, we are all sons of God and brothers in Christ, either actually or potentially. But those souls in whom the gift of piety operates are able to perceive and live this sublime truth. They love all men with a great tenderness because they see them as most dear brothers in Christ, and they would like to shower upon them every kind of grace and blessing. This is the sentiment that St. Paul experienced when he wrote: "So then, my brethren, beloved and longed for, my joy and my crown, stand fast thus in the Lord, beloved" (Phil. 4:1). Filled with similar sentiments, the soul under the impulse of the gift of piety dedicates itself to the works of mercy for the unfortunate and looks upon them as true brothers, serving them in order to please the Father of all. Whatever sacrifices are demanded by this service to their neighbors seems little or nothing to them. They see in each of their brethren Christ, their brother, and they do for their neighbor what they would do for Christ. And whatever works they perform, even those that require superhuman heroism, seem so natural and easy to them that they would be greatly surprised if anyone should consider them to be heroic. In their amazement, they would perhaps reply: "But he is my brother!" All their activities and works in the service of their neighbor are performed with the thought of the common Father of all, and the works themselves are considered as something that is owed to one's brothers in the family of

---

[26]Cf. M. M. Philipon, O.P., *Spiritual Doctrine of Sister Elizabeth of the Trinity,* Chap. 8, n. 4.

God. As a result, their works become sublime acts of religion. Even the love which they have for the members of their own family is deeply penetrated with this lofty vision, in which they see all men as sons of God and brothers in Christ. It is this same piety which caused St. Paul to be afflicted with the afflicted, to weep with those who wept, and to bear the weaknesses and miseries of his neighbor for the purpose of saving all.[27]

Love of others

5) *It moves us to love all those persons and things which are related to the Fatherhood of God and the Christian brotherhood.* The gift of piety perfects and intensifies the soul's filial love for the Blessed Virgin, whom it considers as a tender Mother in whom it has the confidence that any child has in its mother. The soul loves the angels and the saints, whom it considers as brothers who are now enjoying the continual presence of God in heaven; it has a tender affection for the souls in purgatory, whom it assists by frequent suffrages; a tender regard for the Pope as the vicar of Christ on earth, visible head of the Church and father of all Christians. It looks upon all lawful superiors as fathers and endeavors to obey them with filial joy. In regard to its country, it would wish to see the spirit of Christ manifested in its laws and customs. It has a deep veneration for Sacred Scripture, and reads the revealed word of God as if it were a letter sent from heaven by the heavenly Father. It has a respect for all holy things, and especially those articles which are used as instruments in the service and the worship of God.

BEATITUDES AND FRUITS

According to St. Thomas, there are three beatitudes which flow from the gift of piety: "Blessed are the meek," because meekness removes the impediments to the exercise of the gift of piety; "blessed are they who hunger and thirst after justice," because the gift of piety perfects the works of justice; "blessed are the merciful," because piety is exercised in the works of mercy.

The fruits of the Holy Spirit of goodness and benignity should be attributed directly to the gift of piety, and the fruit of meekness should be attributed indirectly, inasmuch as it removes the impediments to the acts of piety.[28]

OPPOSED VICES

The vices opposed to this gift can be grouped under the generic name of impiety, because, as it belongs to the gift of piety to offer to God with filial affection whatever pertains to him as our Father, anything that in one form or another involves a deliberate infraction of this duty deserves to be called impious. On the other hand, as St. Thomas states so beautifully, "piety as

[27]Cf. I Cor. 9:19-22.
[28]Cf. *Summa,* II-II, q. 121, a. 2.

a gift consists in a certain superhuman benevolence toward all," considering others as sons of God and our brothers in Christ.[29] In this sense St. Gregory the Great names hardness of heart as the fundamental vice opposed to the gift of piety when he states that the Holy Ghost with his gifts bestows piety against hardness.[30]

Hardness of heart

Father Lallemant has written the following profound observations concerning the vice of hardness of heart:

> The vice that is opposed to the gift of piety is hardness of heart, which springs out of an ill-regulated love of ourselves; for this love makes us naturally sensible only to our own interests, so that nothing affects us except in reference to ourselves. We behold the offenses committed against God without tears, and the miseries of our neighbor without compassion; we are unwilling to inconvenience ourselves to oblige others; we cannot put up with their faults; we inveigh against them on the slightest ground and harbor in our hearts feelings of bitterness and resentment, hatred and antipathy against them.
>
> On the other hand, the more charity or love of God a soul possesses, the more sensitive it is to the interests of God and those of its neighbor.
>
> This hardness is worst in the great ones of the world, in rich misers and voluptuaries, and in those who never soften their hearts by exercises of piety and familiarity with spiritual things. It is also often found among men of learning who do not join devotion to knowledge and who, to disguise this fault from themselves, call it strength of mind. But the truly learned have been the most pious, such as St. Thomas, St. Bonaventure, St. Bernard and, of the Society, Laynez, Suárez, Bellarmine and Lessius.
>
> A soul which cannot weep for its sins, at least with tears of the heart, is full either of impiety or of impurity, one or the other, as is generally the case with those whose heart is hardened.
>
> It is a great misfortune when natural and acquired talents are more esteemed in religion than piety. You will sometimes see religious, and perhaps superiors, who will loudly declare that they attach much more value to a practical active mind than to all those petty devotions which, they say, are all very well for women but are unbecoming in a strong mind, meaning by strength of mind that hardness of heart which is so opposed to the spirit of piety. They ought to bear in mind that devotion is an act of religion, or a fruit of religion and of charity, and consequently that it is to be preferred to all the moral virtues, since religion follows immediately in order of dignity the theological virtues.[31]

MEANS OF PROGRESS

In addition to the general means for disposing oneself for the activity of the gifts of the Holy Ghost, such as recollection, prayer, fidelity to grace, etc., the following practices are more immediately related to the gift of piety.

---

[29]*In III Sent.*, dist. 9, q. 1, a. 1, q. 1, ad 4.

[30]*Moralia,* II, Chap. 49; cf. also St. Thomas, *Summa,* I-II, q. 68, a. 2, ad 3; a. 6, ad 2; II-II, q. 159, a. 2, ad 1.

[31]*Spiritual Doctrine,* IV, Chap. 4, a. 5.

Adopted sons

1) *To cultivate the spirit of adopted sons of God.* There are few truths which have been repeated as often in the gospel as the truth that God is our Father. In the Sermon on the Mount Christ repeated this truth fourteen times. Indeed, this basic doctrine concerning our adopted sonship is so predominant in the New Testament that some writers have seen it as the basic and essential theme of all Christian teaching. We could never insist too much on the necessity of cultivating the spirit of filial trust and abandonment to our heavenly Father. God is our Creator and will be our Judge at the moment of death, but he is always and above all our Father.

The gift of fear arouses in us a respectful reverence for God, and this is in no way incompatible with the tenderness and filial confidence inspired in us by the gift of piety. Although a full awareness of one's condition as a child of God and the experience of tender sweetness which flows from this realization can come to the soul only through the activity of this gift of piety, we can nevertheless do much to experience this sweetness if, with the help of grace, we dispose ourselves to remain always before God as a child before its loving parent. We should constantly beg for the spirit of adoption, and we should endeavor to do all things for the love of God in order to please our heavenly Father.

Universal brotherhood

2) *To cultivate the spirit of universal brotherhood toward all men.* This is, as we have seen, the principal secondary effect of the gift of piety. Even before it is practiced in all its plenitude by the actuation of the gift, we can prepare ourselves for it with the help of ordinary grace. We should strive ever to increase the capacity of our love so that we may embrace the whole world with the arms of love. We are all sons of God and brothers of Christ. With what persuasive insistence St. Paul repeated this truth to the early Christians: "For you are all the children of God by faith in Christ Jesus. For all you who have been baptized into Christ have put on Christ. There is neither Jew nor Greek; there is neither slave nor freeman; there is neither male nor female. For you are all one in Christ Jesus" (Gal. 3:26-28). If we would do as much as we could to treat our neighbors as true brothers in God, we would undoubtedly attract to ourselves his merciful glance, which is delighted in nothing so much as in seeing us intimately united in his divine Son. Christ himself desired that the world should know that we are his disciples by the love which we have for each other.

The house of God

3) *To consider all things, even material things, as pertaining to the house of God.* What a profoundly religious sense is discovered in all things by those souls that are ruled by the gift of piety! St. Francis of Assisi is one of the outstanding examples of those souls who saw and judged all things in this visible world as belonging in some way

to the heavenly Father. The same spirit of the gift of piety was manifested in this way in St. Paul of the Cross, St. Thérèse of Lisieux and the Venerable Louis of Granada.

Although many souls do not attain the exquisite delicacy of the spirit of piety as manifested in these great souls, how differently they could evaluate created things if they would strive to discover the religious meaning which is hidden deep within them. The created universe is truly the house of the Father, and all things in it belong to him. If one could live in this world with this religious sense and appreciation of created things, it would be a great help in avoiding sinful attachments to created goods, and the goods themselves as vestiges of God could lead the soul to greater union with God. One's whole life could thus be elevated to a loftier plane.

Spirit of abandonment

4) *To cultivate the spirit of complete abandonment to God.* We will not attain this spirit perfectly until the gift of piety is intensely actuated in us, but we should try to do what we can to cultivate total abandonment to God. To this end, we should be fully convinced that, since God is our Father, it is impossible that any evil could befall us unless he permits it. For that reason, we should strive to remain indifferent in regard to the shortness or the length of our life, consolation or dryness in our spiritual life, and the many other questions that could cause us concern or anxiety. Our basic attitude as Christians should be that of complete filial abandonment to the divine will of our heavenly Father. Since we know for certain that he loves us as a father and that he cares for us even as regards our daily needs, it should not be too difficult for us to do the best we can in our daily life and to leave in his hands those things which are beyond our power or which are hidden as yet in the unknown future.

THE VIRTUE OF OBSERVANCE

DEFINITION

This virtue, which is another potential part of justice, has for its object the regulation of the relationships of inferiors to superiors other than God, parents or the rulers in civil society; the regulation of these latter relationships pertains to the virtues of religion and piety respectively. Observance may be defined as that virtue by which we give due reverence and honor to those who possess some kind of special dignity.[32] Any person possessing a

[32]Cf. St. Thomas, *Summa,* II-II, q. 102.

true dignity is deserving, by that very fact, of our respect and veneration. Thus the servant should respect his master, the soldier should respect his officers, the young should have reverence for the old, the student should respect his teacher, etc.

The habitual attitude of reverence and respect toward those who surpass us by reason of some excellence or dignity proceeds basically from the virtue of observance. Persons who have positions of dignity deserve honor by reason of their excellence, and they deserve obedience from their subjects or inferiors by reason of the office which they hold over others. For this reason, honor is due to any excellent person, but obedience is due only to those who have some kind of jurisdiction over us. Hence the virtue of observance is divided into two parts: *honor* and *obedience*.[33]

HONOR

As its name in Greek indicates, the word *dulia* (honor) in a strict sense consists in the honor and reverence which a servant owes to his master. In a wider sense, it signifies the honor which is due to any person who possesses some special dignity. And in the sense in which the word is commonly used by the Church, it signifies the honor and veneration due to the saints who now enjoy eternal happiness in heaven. By reason of her excellence above all the saints, the honor given to the Blessed Virgin is called *hyperdulia,* while the honor given to St. Joseph is sometimes called *protodulia,* signifying that the honor given to Mary is something more than simple *dulia,* and that St. Joseph is ranked as the first among all those who receive the simple veneration of *dulia.*

In its philosophical meaning, the honor of *dulia* always presupposes some superiority or excellence in the person who is honored. It is not necessary, however, that he be more excellent than the one who honors him, as long as he possesses some superiority over others (as when a general honors a captain as superior to a simple soldier), or even possesses some excellence in particular which is not possessed by the individual who honors him (as when the ruler of a nation honors a professor or scientist). The honor or worship which is due to God (*latria*) may be merely interior, because God knows perfectly the movements of the human heart and mind. But the honor owed to human superiors must be manifested by some external sign or action, because they are to be honored not only before God but also before men.

OBEDIENCE

Obedience is a moral virtue which makes one's will prompt to carry out the commands of a superior.[34] The word "commands" signifies, not only a precept which would oblige an individual in conscience, but also the simple

[33]Cf. *ibid.*, qq. 103-104.
[34]Cf. *ibid.*, q. 104, a. 2.

will of the superior as manifested externally, either explicitly or tacitly. The obedience will be the more perfect as the individual is more prompt to execute the will of the superior even before an express command is given. Moreover, one should not think that only religious are bound to practice obedience. All subjects of all legitimate superiors are obliged to obey authority, whether that authority be one's parents, the civil officials, the pastor in a parish, the teacher in a classroom, a military officer, one's employer, etc.

Its basis

The basis of obedience is the authority of the superior, received directly or indirectly from God. Actually, it is God whom one obeys in the person of the lawful superior because, as St. Paul says,[35] all power comes from God. For that reason St. Paul adds that he who resists authority resists God. If one externally performs the act which has been commanded by a superior, but does so with internal rebellion, the obedience is purely material and is not a virtue in the strict sense of the word. Nevertheless, even material obedience suffices to avoid breaking the vow of obedience in case the subject is bound by vow. But when one obeys both internally and externally precisely because something has been commanded by a superior, the obedience is then called formal obedience and is an excellent act of virtue.

It follows from this that there are many acts which seem to be acts of obedience but actually are not so in the sight of God. Whenever a person performs the external act which has been commanded, but at the same time complains or criticizes or rebels, the action has lost its essence as an act of the virtue of obedience. The same thing is true if one obeys *exclusively* out of an attachment or affection for the superior as a particular person, or because the command seems reasonable to us or suits our particular taste and liking, etc. In all of these cases the formal motive of obedience—the authority of the superior as representing God—is lacking, and for that reason, as the Angelic Doctor points out, there is no act of the supernatural virtue of obedience.[36] St. Thomas teaches that not even martyrdom would have any value if it were not directed to the fulfillment of the divine will.[37]

The excellence of obedience

As a virtue, obedience is inferior to the theological virtues. By reason of its object it is also inferior to some of the moral virtues (e.g., religion). But by reason of that which is sacrificed or offered to God, it is the most excellent of all the moral virtues, because through the other virtues one sacrifices external goods (poverty), corporal goods (virginity), or certain goods of the soul which are inferior to the human will, which is sacrificed in the virtue of obedience. For this reason St. Thomas does not hesitate to affirm that the religious life, primarily because of the vow of obedience, is a true holocaust offered to God.[38]

[35]Cf. Rom. 13:1.
[36]*Summa,* II-II, q. 104, a. 2, ad 3.
[37]Cf. *ibid.,* a. 3.
[38]Cf. *ibid.,* q. 186, aa. 7-8.

Grades of obedience

The classical division of the grades or degrees of obedience is as follows: a) mere external execution; b) internal submission of the will; c) submission of the internal judgment. St. Ignatius Loyola explains these grades in an inspiring letter to the fathers and brothers of the Society in Portugal.[39] The following outline gives the basic points of doctrine contained in the letter.

1) St. Ignatius desires that obedience should be the characteristic virtue of the Society because of the blessings produced by this virtue, because it is highly praised in Sacred Scripture, and because it is the compendium of all the other virtues. He states as the fundamental principle of obedience that one should see Christ in the superior, without thinking of the goodness or evil of the superior as an individual person.

2) Listing the grades of obedience, he states that the first is obedience of execution, which is of little value; the second grade is obedience of the will, which possesses the intrinsic value of the sacrifice of obedience, so that it is of great merit and it perfects man's free will; the third degree is obedience of the intellect. As regards obedience of the intellect, St. Ignatius states that it is *possible* because the will can control the intellect; it is *just* because it is reasonable to control one's judgment and to conform one's will to God's; it is *necessary* for the attainment of perfect subordination, for safeguarding oneself against the illusions of self-love, for preserving one's tranquility in obedience, and for preserving union with God; and it is *perfect* obedience, because in this grade of obedience a man immolates that which is most excellent, which implies a marvelous victory over self.

3) Then the saint lists the general and particular means for achieving the third grade of obedience. The general means are humility and meekness. The particular means are to see God in one's superiors, to seek reasons in favor of the command that is given, and to accept the command blindly, that is, without any further inquiry, but with a docility similar to that which one should have in regard to matters of faith. This does not mean, however, that it would be opposed to the perfection of obedience if one were to state reasons to the superior for desisting from that which has been commanded, as long as due conditions are observed. However, if a subject should make such a representation to his superior, he should do so with complete indifference and with full freedom.

4) In his final observation, St. Ignatius remarks that obedience also extends to those who have some charge or office under lawful authority. And he says that the prosperity of religious institutes depends on obedience, because of the principle of subordination which applies to

[39]The letter was written at Rome on March 16, 1553, and it can be seen in its entirety in *Obras Completas de San Ignacio de Loyola,* pp. 833-843 (Madrid: B.A.C., 1952).

religious institutes. In his final exhortation he refers to the example of Christ in regard to obedience and the great reward that is earned through obedience.

QUALITIES OF OBEDIENCE

The fundamental quality which comprises all the others is that obedience should be supernatural, that is, inspired by supernatural motives. Only then is obedience a truly Christian virtue. Obedience inspired by any purely human motive, however right and lawful in itself, cannot be supernatural. But in order that the supernatural quality of obedience may be augmented and preserved, we shall enumerate some of the more important characteristics of Christian obedience. We do not mean to imply that this list is exhaustive, but if one keeps in mind the fundamental quality which we have just mentioned, all the other characteristics of obedience will spring forth spontaneously.

1) A spirit of faith, by which the subject obeys and reveres his superior as another Christ, and looks upon the commands of the superior as coming from God himself.

2) The firm conviction that by obeying lawful commands of superiors we are fulfilling the will of God, and that, although a superior may make a mistake in commanding, the subject never makes a mistake in obeying lawful commands.

3) Obedience out of love of God and acceptance of difficult or distasteful commands in a spirit of sacrifice.

4) Promptness in fulfilling the commands that are given, realizing that we should not make Christ wait for our obedience but that we should be prompt to do his will.

5) A true devotion by which we give complete submission of our will to the superior as the representative of God.

6) Spontaneity and joy in obedience, and even the attempt to anticipate the desires of the superior, manifesting by our instant and joyful acceptance of commands that obedience makes us happy.

7) Humility and simplicity, so that we can perform the act of obedience as if it were the most natural thing in the world, without giving any attention to the heroism involved in our self-immolation.

8) Magnanimity, which gives virility to our obedience and provides us with the energy of heroes and the fortitude of martyrs.

9) Universality, so that at all times and to any superior whatever, we obey all commands without exception.

10) Perseverance, so that in times of joy or sorrow, in health or in sickness, regardless of any personal condition or taste, we would obey, realizing that obedience gives power and that the obedient man shall speak of victory.

BLESSINGS OF OBEDIENCE

The blessings of obedience are very great, both for the intellect and the will, as well as for the heart. Obedience gives to the intellect a certitude that one knows and does the will of God. It gives the assurance of divine assistance, because God has promised that he would be with those who are obedient to his will. Obedience also gives certitude to the outcome of one's actions, because, as St. Paul says, "For those who love God all things work together unto good" (Rom. 8:28).

Obedience is also the source of true liberty for the will, because there is nothing that so enslaves a man as attachment to his own will. It is likewise the source of fortitude; to obey to the point of heroism one needs great valor. And it is the guarantee of one's perseverance in good. As regards the heart, obedience gives peace and tranquility, which can come only from doing the will of God. It preserves right order in the life of the individual and in the community, because the best assurance of order is found in the subjection of inferiors to superiors. It is, finally, one of the greatest safeguards against scrupulosity; for that reason, one of the first demands that the spiritual director must make of a scrupulous penitent is that he give complete obedience to all commands.

FALSE OBEDIENCE

Without reaching the excess of formal disobedience, there are many actions which constitute a falsification or deformation of the virtue of obedience. The following are some of the principal manifestations:

1) *Routine or mechanical obedience*—the purely external act of obedience, without any internal spirit. One acts like a machine or a robot, and may perform the external act with the greatest precision and perfection, but he lacks the proper attention and awareness of the supernatural motive for his obedience, or he may even lack the supernatural motive entirely.

2) *Legal obedience*—the obedience of the person who is constantly referring to a law or rule, in order to know how far his obedience extends, or to check lest the superior exceeds his authority in commanding. Such persons are pharisaical, and very often lack the generosity of spirit which should prompt them to obey out of love.

3) *Critical obedience*—the obedience of those who recognize the superior's authority and obey him, but constantly find fault with the superior for being unsympathetic, too rigorous, too impulsive, lacking in tact, etc. Such persons obey the superior and at the same time criticize him for his personal defects, thus predisposing themselves to lose respect for the authority of the superior, and even to disobey him.

4) *Paralyzed obedience*—one does not have the occasion to practice formal obedience because the superior does not dare to give commands, or is too lax or indifferent in the discharge of his duties. This defect on the part of the superiors is more frequently noticed in communities of

men than in communities of women, and it is likewise true in family life in many instances. However, it is not always due to incompetent superiors. There are some subjects who do not obey because, for one reason or another, they find reasons to excuse themselves from carrying out commands that are given, or they obtain all permissions by bending the will of the superior to their own.

5) *Pseudo-mystical obedience*—the individual who disobeys the superior under the pretext of obeying the Holy Ghost. This is pure illusion because the general norm of obedience is that we are bound to obey the lawful commands of legitimate superiors.

6) *Camouflaged disobedience*—the art of inducing the superior, by means of excuses and objections, to withdraw his commands or to modify them.

7) *Paradoxical obedience*—the pretense of giving obedience to a superior while one does his own will, or even imposes his will upon the superior. This defect is frequently noted in those communities in which the superior has special friends in the community, or is afraid to govern as he ought.

8) *Pharisaical obedience*—an obedience in which one performs the act commanded but does not submit his will. This is a combination of cowardice and hypocrisy.

9) *The spirit of opposition*—the existence of groups or parties within a community which are opposed to the superior and are usually waging a constant war against the superior. This is a diabolical spirit, which sows the seeds of discord and division in the community.

10) *Egoistic obedience*—inspired by the desire to win the sympathy and affection of the superior and to obtain from him the duties or commands which are in accordance with one's own tastes and desires.

11) *The spirit of murmuring*—the obedience of him who accepts unwillingly the commands of his superiors and murmurs interiorly or sometimes complains to others about the superior or the task assigned.

12) *Half-hearted obedience*—the imperfect or careless execution of orders. This is sometimes malicious, as in the case of those who do not wish to obey and therefore deliberately perform their tasks badly so that the superior will change the assignment.

13) *Slothful obedience*—the neglect to fulfill commands without sufficient reason. Such persons must be commanded repeatedly before they perform the task, and when they finally do it, it is often done badly because they had no desire to do it in the first place.

Such are the principal falsifications and defects in the practice of the virtue of obedience. With good reason did Christ say to St. Catherine of Siena: "My dear daughter, how numerous they are who live in the practice of obedience, but how few they are who obey perfectly."[40] But those who obey perfectly offer to God a sacrifice of praise which rises to heaven with the odor of sweetness because of the perfect immolation of their self-love.

ALLIED VIRTUES

GRATITUDE

The virtue of gratitude, which is a potential part of justice, has for its object to recompense in some way a benefactor for some benefit that has been received. The benefactor, in giving us a free gift to which we had no strict right, merits our gratitude, and in every noble heart the need to demonstrate this gratitude spontaneously springs forth when the occasion offers. On the other hand, the sin of ingratitude is a vile and ugly sin. Both gratitude and its opposite vice admit of various degrees, as St. Thomas states in the following summary:

> [Gratitude] has various degrees which correspond in their order to the thing required for gratitude. The first is to recognize the favor received, the second is to express one's appreciation and thanks, and the third is to repay the favor at a suitable place and time according to one's means. And since the last in the order of generation is first in the order of destruction, it follows that the first degree of ingratitude is to fail to repay a favor, the second is to decline to notice and acknowledge that one has received a favor, and the third and supreme degree is to fail to recognize the reception of a favor, whether by forgetting it or in any other way. Moreover, since an affirmation implies the opposite negation, it follows that it belongs to the first degree of ingratitude to return evil for good, to the second degree to find fault with a favor received, and to the third degree to esteem kindness as though it were unkindness.[41]

In another article, St. Thomas asks whether the innocent man has a greater obligation to give thanks to God than the penitent. He answers by saying that, as regards the greatness of the benefit received, the innocent man has the greater obligation, but that by reason of the gratitude for the gift the penitent has the greater obligation, because instead of receiving the punishment which he merited, he has received pardon.[42]

VENGEANCE

This is a difficult virtue to explain because it is easily confused with the sin against charity. It has for its object the punishment of the evil-doer for the sins he has committed. St. Thomas explains its nature with precision in the following words:

---

[40]Cf. St. Catherine of Siena, *Dialogue,* Chap. 162.
[41]*Summa,* II-II, q. 107, a. 2.
[42]*Ibid.,* q. 106, a. 2.

Vengeance consists in the infliction of punishment on one who has sinned. Accordingly, in the matter of vengeance we must consider the mind of the avenger. If his intention is directed primarily to the evil of the person on whom he takes vengeance and remains there, then his vengeance is completely unlawful, because to take pleasure in another's evil belongs to hatred, which is contrary to the charity by which we should love all men. Nor does it suffice for him to excuse himself by saying that he intends the evil to one who has unjustly inflicted evil on him. For a man is not excused for hating one who hates him—a man may not sin against another merely because the latter has already sinned against him, since this is to be overcome by evil, which was forbidden by the Apostle, who says: "Be not overcome by evil, but overcome evil with good" (Rom. 12:21).

If, however, the avenger's intention is directed primarily to some good which will be obtained by means of the punishment of the person who has sinned (for example, the amendment of the sinner, or at least his restraint so as not to disturb others; preservation of justice and honoring of God), then vengeance may be lawful, as long as other due circumstances are observed.[43]

In practice, it is seldom fitting that an individual should exercise this virtue or request that punishment be inflicted. The reason is that very often, under the pretext of justice and equity, there is hidden an excessive self-love and sometimes a true hatred of one's neighbor. For that reason, this virtue has been called a "little virtue," and it is always advised that persons should pardon injuries received from their neighbor rather than seek vengeance, unless the love of God, of one's neighbor or of the common good requires that reparation be done for the injury or crime.

The two vices opposed to this virtue are *cruelty,* by excess of vengeance, and *indulgence,* by a defect in the spirit of punishing offenders.

VERACITY

The virtue of veracity inclines one always to speak the truth and to manifest externally what he is internally.[44] This virtue is closely related to simplicity, which rectifies one's intention and preserves him against duplicity; it is also related to fidelity, which inclines the will to fulfill what has been promised.[45]

We are not always obliged to speak the truth, but we are always obliged not to lie. When charity, justice or some other virtue requires that we should not reveal the truth, it will then be necessary to find some way of not revealing it (silence, mental reservation, etc.), but it is never lawful directly and positively to tell a lie. Nor does a great good which would result from a lie make the telling of the lie licit.

Sins against veracity

There are various kinds of sins opposed to veracity. *Lying* consists in manifesting externally in words the contrary of that which is in one's mind. It is divided into jocose lies, officious lies and pernicious lies, according as one

[43]*Ibid.,* q. 108, a. 1.
[44]Cf. *ibid.,* q. 109, a. 1; a. 3, ad 3.
[45]Cf. *ibid.,* a. 2, ad 4; q. 111, a. 3, ad 2; q. 110, a. 3, ad 5.

intends to amuse others, to obtain some benefit for himself or another, or to do harm to another. The first two types of lies are not usually more serious than venial sins, but the third type of lie is by its very nature a mortal sin, although it may in a particular instance be only a venial sin.[46]

Simulation and *hypocrisy* consist in lying, not in words, but in one's external action (simulation) or in pretending to be that which one is not (hypocrisy). *Boasting* is a sin by which one attributes to himself qualities that he does not possess, or in raising himself above his station. *Irony* or *false humility* consists in denying that one possesses certain qualities or talents which in reality he does possess. However, we should not accuse the saints of this sin when in their humility they deny qualities of virtue to themselves. The lie consists in speaking contrary to that which one knows. The saints, illumined by God's grace to see their weaknesses and imperfections, or comparing themselves with the divine sanctity of God, could not help feeling and confessing that they were nothing better than unworthy sinners, filled with defects.

AFFABILITY

Affability is the social virtue *par excellence,* and one of the most exquisite manifestations of the true Christian spirit. It is defined as a virtue by which our words and external actions are directed to the preservation of friendly and agreeable association with our fellow men. Although it may seem at first glance that this virtue is nothing more than the external sign of friendship, there is this great difference between them: true friendship proceeds from love, and among Christians it should be a natural result of fraternal charity; affability, on the other hand, is a kind of friendliness which consists in words or deeds in our relation with others, requiring us to conduct ourselves in a friendly and sociable manner with all our neighbors, whether they be intimate friends or strangers.[47]

There are numerous acts or manifestations of the virtue of affability, and all of them arouse sympathy and friendliness in our neighbors. Benignity, politeness, simple praise, indulgence, sincere gratitude, hospitality, patience, meekness, refinement in words and deeds, etc., exert a kind of attraction which it is difficult to resist. This precious virtue is of extreme importance, not only in one's association with friends, neighbors and strangers, but in a special way within the circle of one's own family, where it is often most neglected.

Flattery and quarreling

The two vices opposed to the virtue of affability are *flattery* and *quarreling.* *Flattery* sins against affability by excess. The flatterer fears to displease others and therefore resorts frequently to insincerity in word or deed. It also happens that flattery is sometimes used as a means to obtain one's own end, and

[46]Cf. *ibid.,* q. 110, a. 4.

[47]Cf. *ibid.,* q. 114, a. 1, ad 1 and 2. St. Thomas also points out that the virtue of affability does not require us to manifest signs of friendliness toward sinners if this action can be interpreted as an approval of the sins of another.

when used for this purpose the flatterer often resorts to lying and dissimulation. *Quarreling* is the result of a lack of affability, and consists in the contradiction of another by means of speech. This does not mean that one may never disagree with another, for that would be contrary to veracity, but we are speaking here of that defect of affability by which an individual becomes disagreeable and quarrelsome. It is a vice to contradict others or to quarrel with them when fraternal charity demands that we live in peace and concord. Sometimes, indeed, prudence dictates that we should suffer in silence rather than speak out against another, even when justice would permit this.

LIBERALITY

Liberality is a virtue which moderates one's love of external things, especially of riches, and inclines one readily to use one's goods for the benefit of others. It differs from mercy and beneficence, for one is moved to mercy by compassion and to beneficence by love, but one is prompted to liberality by the lack of attachment to external goods. As a result, the liberal man readily gives of his possessions, not only to friends, but to strangers. Liberality is likewise distinguished from magnificence in the sense that the latter refers to great works which involve the expenditure of large sums of money, while liberality refers to more modest sums. The liberal man realizes that it suffices to have relatively few possessions, and therefore he is quite willing to give to others.

Opposed vices

The two vices opposed to liberality are *avarice* and *prodigality*. *Avarice* is the result of an excessive attachment to wealth, and since it is opposed to the right order of reason, it is a sin. Avarice is both a special sin against the virtue of liberality and a capital sin. As a capital sin it is the cause of many other sins in the lives of those who are excessively attached to wealth: treachery, fraud, lying, perjury, violence, theft. These are only a few of the sins that are born of avarice.[48]

By way of excess, one sins against liberality by *prodigality*. The prodigal man violates the rule of reason by giving away or spending money when he should retain it or use it for other purposes. Prudence requires that one observe a reasonable economy and provide for the future. The prodigal man lives only for the moment and has no solicitude for tomorrow.

EQUITY

This virtue inclines us, in special circumstances, to depart from the letter of the law in order the better to observe its spirit. The very weakness of a law lies in the fact that it looks to the preservation of the common good in a general way and cannot apply to every particular case. Legislators usually look to what commonly happens when they are framing laws, and yet they realize that there can be and usually will be exceptions.[49] What is of great importance

[48]Cf. *ibid.*, q. 118, aa. 7-8.
[49]Cf. *ibid.*, q. 120, a. 1.

in this matter of the application and interpretation of laws is the preservation of the spirit of the law by understanding the motive for which the law was written. Whether it be a matter of an interpretation of law given by one in authority or the application of a law by a particular person to particular circumstances, it is of extreme importance that one should know the mind of the legislator in framing a given law.

A good rule of thumb would consist in asking what the lawmaker would say or command in given circumstances which make the observance of the law onerous, or when there is a conflict of several laws. The virtuous man will desire to do that which is in accordance with right reason and for the common good. He will understand that no law obliges when circumstances make the observance of the law impossible. When there is doubt concerning the obligation under the law, or the manner in which the law is to be fulfilled, his desire to obey will help him to interpret the mind of the legislator, and thus arrive at an understanding of the true spirit of the law. It is of special importance for superiors of all kinds to understand and to cultivate the virtue of equity.

Severity

The vice opposed to equity is *severity*. Christ frequently condemned the Pharisees for this vice, and as a result of their example the word pharisee has come to signify the legalistic and purely literal observance of law. Laws are directed to the preservation of right order and the pursuit of the common good of the society which they govern. But law is not an end in itself; it is merely a necessary means for the insurance and protection of the pursuit of the common good. If it is impossible to frame laws that cover every possible contingency, then it is imprudent to insist on the observance of the law in every particular circumstance. It is the spirit of the law and the motive in the mind of the lawgiver that give life and guidance; the letter of the law, applied imprudently, defeats the very purpose of law.

7: THE VIRTUE OF FORTITUDE

The word "fortitude" can be understood in two principal senses. The first sense signifies in general a certain firmness of spirit and vigor of character, general conditions which must accompany all virtues if they are to be truly such. In the second sense it designates a special virtue, bearing the same name, which we shall here study in itself, in its parts and with its accompanying gift of the Holy Ghost.

FORTITUDE IN ITSELF

DEFINITION As a special supernatural virtue, fortitude is infused with sanctifying grace to strengthen the irascible appetite and the will so that they will not abandon the pursuit of the arduous or difficult good, even when faced with grave danger to bodily health and life. This virtue has as its proper subject the irascible appetite, because it is especially concerned with the control of fear and daring. However, it is necessary to mention the will because this faculty must intervene if fortitude is to be a true virtue, although the will itself is not the proper faculty in which fortitude resides. As regards the movements of fear and daring, fortitude has for its object to prevent unreasonable fear in the face of an evil that threatens, and to restrain the individual from unreasonably attacking an impending evil. Since the greatest natural evil is the loss of one's life, the virtue of fortitude is principally concerned with the fear of death.

ACTS OF FORTITUDE The two acts by which fortitude manifests itself in the external order are to attack and to endure. Since man's life on earth is a constant warfare, there will be occasions in which the individual is called upon to defend the good by means of attack, and there will be times in which the individual cannot attack but must resist by not yielding. Of the two acts of fortitude, the principal and most difficult act is to resist or to endure. Contrary to common opinion, it is more painful and more heroic to resist an enemy or to suffer an evil than to attack. Psychologically it is easier to attack an evil, especially when the passion of anger has been aroused. But to suffer sickness or persecution or death with a tranquil and sturdy spirit requires the fortitude of a hero. For that reason the Greek drama portrayed the hero of the tragedy as a man who knew how to accept death courageously, and Christians have always considered the martyrs as the outstanding examples of Christian fortitude.[1]

Fortitude is especially manifested in sudden and unexpected events. It is evident that one who spontaneously reacts with courage in the face of an unexpected danger or evil has greater fortitude than he who so reacts only after deliberation.

THE NECESSITY OF FORTITUDE

Fortitude is an important and excellent virtue, although it is not the greatest of the moral virtues. The good of reason—the object of every virtue—pertains essentially to prudence, effectively to justice, and only defensively (in the sense of removing obstacles) to fortitude and temperance. But of the last two virtues, fortitude is the more excellent because, in the pursuit of the good, it is more difficult to overcome the dangers of death than the delights of the sense of touch. Consequently, in the order of their perfection, the cardinal virtues are listed in the following sequence: prudence, justice, fortitude and temperance.

In its double activity of attacking and resisting evil, fortitude plays an important role in the spiritual life. There are countless obstacles and difficulties to be overcome along the road which leads to perfection. To succeed in reaching the goal, one must resolutely begin the journey to perfection, he must not be surprised at the presence of the enemy, he must have courage to attack and conquer when prudence dictates, and he must have the constancy and perseverance to carry on without ever surrendering to the enemy. And even when one has made great progress in the spiritual life and has achieved a moral victory over the enemy, fortitude will still be necessary in order to endure the passive purgations which are sent by God to test and strengthen and purify the spirit.

OPPOSED VICES

Three vices are opposed to the virtue of fortitude. By defect of the virtue one falls into the vice of *cowardice* and refuses to suffer the necessary hardships which accompany the pursuit of the good or the dangers of death. By excess one falls into the vices of *fearlessness* or *recklessness*. As a vice, fearlessness is a kind of insensitivity or indifference to fear, which prevents an individual from prudently fearing and avoiding the dangers which he ought to avoid.

[1]Cf. St. Thomas, *Summa,* II-II, q. 123, a. 6.

Recklessness causes the individual to disdain the prudent judgment or right reason and to go forth to attack an evil which he cannot overcome. In both cases there is involved a lack of prudence.[2]

THE PARTS OF FORTITUDE

The virtue of fortitude has no subjective parts or species, because it deals with a very particular matter which cannot be further subdivided. There are, however, integral and potential parts of fortitude. They refer to the same virtues materially but are differentiated by the fact that the integral parts of fortitude refer to the dangers of death and the potential parts or annexed virtues refer to lesser dangers.[3] The virtues in question are magnanimity, magnificence, patience, longsuffering, perseverance and constancy.

MAGNANIMITY

Magnanimity is a virtue which inclines one to perform some great act which is worthy of honor. This virtue always looks to actions which are great and splendid. It is therefore incompatible with mediocrity, and in this sense it is the crown of all the other virtues.

Its nature

The virtue of magnanimity presupposes a noble and lofty soul. It is often described as greatness of soul or nobility of character. The magnanimous person is a superior type of person. He is never envious, nor a rival of others, nor does he feel humiliated or embarrassed by the good of others. He is calm and leisurely in his action; he does not give himself to many activities, but only to those which are of greater importance. He is truthful, sincere, somewhat reserved in speech, and a loyal friend. He never lies, but he speaks his mind without being concerned about the opinion of others. He is open and frank, and never imprudent or hypocritical. He is objective in his friendships, and yet does not close his eyes to the defects of his friends. He is never excessive in his admiration of other people, nor attached to anything. He looks primarily to virtue and to that which is noble. The petty affections or disagreements that cause so many difficulties in social life mean nothing to him. If he has been injured by others, he quickly forgets and forgives. He is not overjoyed at the praise and applause of others, nor is he saddened at the criticism he may receive from others. He does not complain about the things that he lacks, but he learns to do without. This virtue is very rare, because it presupposes a high degree of perfection in the other virtues.

---

[2]Cf. *ibid.*, qq. 126-127.

[3]Cf. *ibid.*, q. 128.

Vices opposed to magnanimity

There are four vices opposed to magnanimity, three by excess and one by defect. The following vices are the result of excessive magnanimity: *presumption,* which inclines an individual to attempt actions or projects that are beyond his strength or ability; *ambition,* which impels one to seek honors which are not due to his state or merit; *vainglory,* which seeks fame and popularity without sufficient reason, or without directing them to their true end, which is the glory of God and the good of one's neighbor. As a capital sin vainglory is the cause of many other sins, especially disobedience, boastfulness, hypocrisy, contention, obstinacy, discord and love of novelties.

The vice which results from a deficiency of magnanimity is that of *pusillanimity.* This vice is characterized by an unreasonable lack of confidenec in oneself, or by a false humility which prevents the individual from using all the talents which he has received from God. It is contrary to the natural law, which obliges all beings to develop and perfect themselves by using all the talents and energies which God has given them.

MAGNIFICENCE

Magnificence is a virtue which inclines one to undertake splendid and difficult projects without being disheartened by the magnitude of the work or the great expenses which are connected with it. It differs from magnanimity in the sense that the latter tends to that which is great in any virtue or material, while magnificence pertains only to those great works in which something is to be constructed in a material sense, such as the foundation or construction of hospitals, universities, churches, etc. In other words, while magnanimity is concerned with doing, magnificence is concerned with making or producing. In a sense, magnificence is a virtue which should characterize the wealthy, who could scarcely find any better use for their riches than to devote them to the worship of God or the corporal works of mercy for their neighbor.

Vices opposed to magnificence

The two vices opposed to magnificence are *meanness* and *wastefulness.* In the first case, the individual intends some magnificent work, but he holds back on the expenditure of money because he is unwilling to spend that which the work requires. He fails to observe the proportion which reason demands between the expenditure and the work.[4] Wastefulness, on the other hand, involves the expenditure of money far in excess of that which the work requires. It is a vice because it neglects to observe the due proportion which reason requires between the work and the expenditure, spending a great deal of money when the work could have been done with much less.

PATIENCE

Patience enables one to bear physical and moral sufferings without sadness of spirit or dejection of heart. It is one of the most necessary virtues in the Christian life, because the trials and sufferings which all men must in-

[4]Cf. *ibid.,* q. 135, a. 1.

evitably suffer in this life require the assistance of some virtue to keep them strong and firm lest they yield to discouragement and sorrow. Many souls lose the merit of their trials and sufferings because they fail to exercise the virtue of patience. Indeed, they suffer even more than they would have suffered because of their lack of conformity to the will of God.

Motives for patience

The principal motives for the practice of Christian patience are the following:

1) Conformity with the loving will of God, who knows better than we the things that are good for us and therefore sometimes sends us suffering and tribulation.

2) The recollection of the suffering of Jesus and Mary, incomparable models of patience, and the sincere desire to imitate them.

3) The necessity of making reparation for our sins by the voluntary and virtuous acceptance of suffering in atonement for the unlawful satisfactions and pleasures which we have enjoyed in our sins.

4) The necessity of co-operating with Christ in the application of the fruits of redemption, bearing our sufferings in union with his in order to make up what is wanting to his passion.[5]

5) The prospect of an eternity of happiness which awaits us if we know how to suffer in patience. The suffering passes, but the fruit of having sanctified our suffering will never pass.

Degrees of perfection

As with the virtue of humility, so also with patience we distinguish various grades or degrees which give some indication of the perfection of the virtue in individual Christians. The following constitute five fundamental degrees of patience:

1) Resignation without complaint or impatience to the crosses which God sends us or permits to come to us.

2) Peace and serenity in the face of affliction, without any of the sadness or melancholy which sometimes accompany mere resignation.

3) Sweet acceptance of one's cross for the love of God.

4) Complete and total joy, which leads one to give thanks to God for being associated with him in the mystery of the Cross.

5) The folly of the Cross, which prefers suffering to pleasure and places all one's delight in external or internal suffering by which one is configured with Christ. As St. Teresa used to say: "To suffer or to die."[6]

---

[5]Cf. Col. 1:24.

[6]Two distinct miraculous experiences in the lives of St. Thomas Aquinas and St. John of the Cross serve to illustrate the different approaches of each saint to the spiritual life. Each of them had heard a question from the lips of the crucified Christ: "What reward do you ask?" St. Thomas answered: "Nothing but thyself, O Lord." St. John replied: "To suffer and to be despised for thee."

Vices opposed to patience

Two vices are opposed to the virtue of patience. By way of defect, *impatience* manifests itself externally by anger, complaints and murmuring, and internally by a feeling of antipathy to any trial or suffering, and an excessive inclination to defend oneself or to protect oneself against all discomfort. By way of excess, *insensibility* or hardness of heart is manifested in those who remain stoically unmoved and insensible in the face of suffering, whether it be their own or that of another. Some individuals, because of their temperament, have a strong natural predisposition to impatience; others become impatient as the result of the lack of some other virtue, such as fraternal charity, obedience, prudence, temperance, humility, etc.

As regards the vice of insensibility, it should be noted that a purely stoical attitude toward suffering is not of itself a virtue, and that it is no defect of patience if a person is sensitive to pain. The ability to suffer is not of itself virtuous; what makes suffering a virtue is the manner in which one accepts the suffering and the motive for which he suffers.

LONGANIMITY

According to St. Thomas, longanimity is a virtue which animates a man to strive for some good which is a long way off.[7] It has to do with the attainment of some goal which involves a great deal of time. St. Thomas explains the connection of longanimity with the virtue of patience on two grounds:

> First, because patience, like fortitude, suffers certain evils for the sake of good, and if the good is awaited for only a short time, endurance is easier; but if the good be delayed for a long time, it is more difficult. Secondly, because the delay in attaining the good we desire is of a nature to cause sorrow. . . . Accordingly, longanimity and constancy are both contained under patience, so far as both the delay of the expected good (longanimity) and the effort which a man expends in persistently accomplishing a good work (constancy) may be considered under the one aspect of grievous evil.[8]

PERSEVERANCE

The virtue of perseverance inclines one to persist in the practice of the good in spite of the difficulties involved in this continued practice. To remain unmoved and resolute in the practice of virtue from day to day requires a fortitude of spirit which is provided by this virtue. All the virtues need the help of perseverance, because without it no virtue could be preserved and practiced over a long period of time, nor would any virtue ultimately attain its perfection. Although every virtue is by definition a habit of operation which is difficult to remove and is, therefore, of itself a persistent and stable quality, the special difficulty which arises from a lifelong fidelity in the practice of any given virtue requires the special virtue of perseverance. Thus we see how one virtue comes to the aid of another.

---

[7]Cf. *Summa,* II-II, q. 136, a. 5.

[8]*Loc. cit.*

However, the virtue of perseverance, even when perfected, requires a special assistance of grace which theologians call the grace of perseverance.[9]

Grace of perseverance

St. Thomas briefly summarizes the difference between this virtue and the grace required for its exercise:

> Perseverance has a double meaning. First, it denotes the habit of perseverance which is a virtue. And as a virtue, it requires the gift of habitual grace as do the other infused virtues. Secondly, it may be understood as signifying the act of perseverance which endures until death, and in this sense it requires not only habitual grace but also the gratuitous help of God, which sustains man in good until the end of life.[10]

The reason for the necessity of a special grace from God to insure man's final perseverance is that sanctifying or habitual grace does not change man's free will, in the sense that grace alone is a guarantee that the just man will never sin. However just and however perfect a man may be, he is always able to sin, and for that reason he needs, over and above the infused virtue of perseverance, the special grace of final perseverance which the Council of Trent calls "that great gift."[11]

CONSTANCY

Constancy is closely related to the virtue of perseverance, but is distinguished from the latter by reason of a special difficulty to be overcome. The essential note of perseverance is that it gives firmness and strength of soul in the face of the difficulty which is connected with the prolongation of a virtuous life; constancy strengthens the soul against the difficulties that proceed from any other external obstacle, such as the influence of bad example or special temptations from without. "Perseverance," says St. Thomas, "takes precedence over constancy as a part of fortitude, because the difficulty involved in the continuation of an action is more intrinsic to the act of virtue than that which arises from external obstacles."[12]

Vices opposed to constancy

The vices opposed to perseverance and constancy are *inconstancy* (which St. Thomas calls effeminacy or softness) and *pertinacity*. Inconstancy causes a man to give up the practice of virtue as soon as difficulties and obstacles are encountered. There is, therefore, a certain softness and instability or fickleness to be found in inconstant persons. The tendency to desist from the pursuit of a good which is difficult to attain, as is the faithful practice of a virtue, is especially manifested in effeminate persons, because they are

---

[9]This doctrine has been proclaimed by the Church in the Council of Trent: "If any one say that he who is justified can, without the special assistance of God, either persevere in the justice received or with that assistance cannot persevere, let him be anathema" (Sess. VI, canon 22 on Justification; Denz. 832).

[10]Cf. *Summa,* II-II, q. 137, a. 4.

[11]Cf. Council of Trent, Sess. VI, canon 1 on Justification; Denz. 826.

[12]Cf. *Summa.,* II-II, q. 137, a. 3.

especially attracted to pleasures, and as soon as pleasures are lacking in any given activity, their first impulse is to abandon that activity.[13]

The vice of pertinacity is opposed by excess to the virtue of perseverance, and is defined as an obstinacy in the refusal to yield or to cease some effort when right reason requires it. As a vice, it is often found in those persons who are self-opinionated and headstrong, but its origin is usually vainglory.[14] Quite frequently the reason why an individual persists in his own opinion, or refuses to abandon some effort or work when reason demands, is because he wishes to make a show of his talents and abilities. In this sense the pertinacious man takes a certain pleasure in persisting unreasonably against difficulties and opposition.

MEANS OF GROWTH

The principal means of growth in the virtue of fortitude and in those virtues related to it are the following:

1) *Constantly to beg it of God,* for although it is true that this is a general means which applies to all the virtues, since every supernatural gift comes from God (Jas. 1:17), when it is a question of the virtue of fortitude we need the special assistance of God, due to the laxity and weakness of our human nature, wounded by sin. Without the help of God, we can do nothing (John 15:5), but with his help we can do all things (Phil. 4:13). For that reason Scripture repeatedly insists on the necessity of asking help from God, who is our strength: "You are my rock and my fortress" (Ps. 30:4). "The God of Israel . . . gives power and strength to his people" (Ps. 67:36).

2) *To foresee the difficulties which we shall encounter on the path of virtue.* St. Thomas recommends this practice to all Christians, and especially to those who have not yet acquired the habit of working with fortitude.[15] In this way one gradually overcomes his fear, and when

[13]Cf. *ibid.*, q. 138, a. 1. St. Thomas, in referring to the causes of effeminacy, makes some interesting observations which could provide new insights to psychiatrists in the treatment of certain types of neuroses and psychoses. Thus he states: "Effeminacy is caused in two ways. In one way, by custom, for when a man is accustomed to enjoy pleasures, it is more difficult for him to endure the lack of them. In another way, by natural disposition, because his mind is less persevering because of the frailty of his temperament. This is the way in which women are compared to men, . . . and therefore those who react in a womanish manner are said to be soft or effeminate" (*ibid.*, ad 1). However, in his commentary on this particular article, Cajetan remarks that one should always take into account the question of temperament and habit, because that which would be a vice of inconstancy or effeminacy for one person would not necessarily be so for another, just as that which would be excessive drink for one person could be moderate drink for another.

[14]Cf. St. Thomas, *ibid.*, a. 2.

[15]Cf. *Summa,* II-II, q. 123, a. 9.

difficulties actually arise, he will overcome them much more easily because he has anticipated them.

3) *To accept with a generous spirit the little annoyances of daily life.* Every vocation in life is accompanied with its own particular crosses and difficulties, even if it be merely a matter of the monotony of one's daily activities. If we do not learn to accept the inevitable inconveniences and small trials of daily life, such as cold and heat, pain and discomfort, small illnesses and aches, contradictions and ingratitude, we shall never make any progress in cultivating the Christian virtue of fortitude.

4) *To meditate frequently on the passion and death of Christ.* There is nothing which so animates and comforts delicate souls as the contemplation of the heroism of Christ. He was a man of sorrows and was acquainted with infirmities (Is. 53:3), and he left us an example of suffering so that we would follow in his footsteps.[16] We shall never have to suffer in our sinful bodies any pains comparable to those which he voluntarily suffered out of love for us. However great our sufferings of soul or body, we can raise our eyes to the crucifix, and Christ will give us the fortitude to bear them without bitterness and without complaining. It is likewise helpful to remember the ineffable sorrows of Mary, of whom it is said: "Come, all you who pass by the way, look and see whether there is any suffering like my suffering" (Lam. 1:12).

5) *To intensify our love of God.* Love is as strong as death (Cant. 8:6), and it does not yield to any obstacle in the pursuit of pleasing the beloved. That is what gave St. Paul the superhuman fortitude by which he overcame tribulation, anguish, persecution, hunger, danger and the sword. "But in all these things we overcome because of him who has loved us" (Rom. 8:37). When one truly loves God, there are no longer any difficulties in serving him, and one's very weakness becomes the basis for hoping in him. "Gladly therefore I will glory in my infirmities, that the strength of Christ may dwell in me. . . . For when I am weak, then I am strong" (II Cor. 12:9-10).

THE GIFT OF FORTITUDE

DEFINITION The gift of fortitude is a supernatural habit which strengthens the soul for the practice, under the movement of the Holy Ghost, of every type of virtue, with invincible confidence of overcoming any dangers or difficulties that may arise.

[16]Cf. I Pet. 2:21.

ITS NATURE

Like the other gifts and infused virtues, the gift of fortitude is a supernatural habit. Its precise function is to elevate the powers of the soul to a divine plane. The operations of this gift, as of the other gifts, is always under the inspiration of the Holy Ghost, in such wise that the soul does not reason or discourse, but acts by a kind of instinctive interior impulse which proceeds directly from the Holy Ghost. And although the virtue of fortitude has the same name as the gift by which it is perfected, the gift extends to all the heroic actions of the other virtues, because this heroism demands an extraordinary fortitude which is beyond the power of the virtue alone.[17] Therefore, the gift of fortitude, since it extends to the acts of various virtues, requires in its turn to be directed by the gift of counsel.[18] One of the clearest marks of distinction between the virtue of fortitude and the gift of fortitude is the confidence which one experiences in being able to overcome great dangers and difficulty. It is true that the virtue of fortitude gives strength to the soul for overcoming obstacles, but it is the gift alone which imparts the confidence of success.[19]

NECESSITY OF THE GIFT

The gift of fortitude is absolutely necessary for the perfection of the infused virtues, especially the virtue of fortitude, and sometimes it is required for perseverance in the state of grace. As to the perfection of the other virtues by the gift of fortitude, we should recall that a virtue is called perfect when its act springs from the soul with energy, promptness and perseverance. The continued perfection in any virtue is manifestly supernatural, and it can be explained

[17]St. Thomas expressly teaches this in his earlier work, *III Sent.,* d. 34, q. 3, a. 1, q. 2, sol.

[18]Cf. St. Thomas, *Summa,* II-II, q. 139, a. 1, ad 3. "This gift," says Father Lallemant, "is a habitual disposition which the Holy Ghost communicates to the soul and the body, both to do and to endure extraordinary things; to undertake the most arduous actions; to expose oneself to the most formidable dangers; to undergo the most toilsome labors; to endure the most grievous pain, and that with constancy and heroism" (*Spiritual Doctrine,* IV, Chap. 4, a. 6).

[19]Cf. St. Thomas, *Summa,* II-II, q. 139, a. 1, ad 1. "Natural or acquired fortitude," says John of St. Thomas, "strengthens the soul for undertaking the greatest labors and for exposing oneself to the greatest dangers—as is evident in the lives of many pagan heroes—but not without a certain fear or anxiety which proceeds from the clear perception of the weakness of one's own powers, which are the only ones utilized by the acquired virtue. Infused fortitude relies on the divine help, which of itself is omnipotent and invincible, but it operates in a human mode, that is, according to the light of reason illumined by faith, which does not rid the soul completely of all fear. The gift of fortitude, on the other hand, enables the soul to undertake the greatest work and expose itself to the greatest dangers with great confidence and security, because the Holy Spirit himself moves the soul, not through the dictates of simple prudence, but through the lofty direction of the gift of counsel, that is, through reasons that are entirely divine" (*In I-II,* dist. 18, a. 6).

only by the supernatural mode of operation of the gift of fortitude. Thus the perfection of any of the virtues will at some time or other require the operation of the gift of fortitude.

As regards the perfection of the virtue of fortitude, St. Thomas explains that, although the virtue of fortitude strengthens the soul against every kind of difficulty and danger, it cannot extend to all possible situations as long as it operates in the purely human mode of reason enlightened by faith. It is necessary that the gift of fortitude remove from the virtue of fortitude all fear and indecision, so that it can be subjected directly to the divine mode of action which is imparted by the Holy Ghost.[20]

As regards the necessity of the gift of fortitude for perseverance in the state of grace, there are occasions in the lives of most Christians when they are confronted, suddenly and inexorably, with the decision either to practice heroic virtue in a given instance or to commit a mortal sin. If the virtue of fortitude in a given Christian is not sufficiently perfect, it will be necessary that the gift of fortitude come into play so that the individual will have the supernatural strength to perform the act of heroic virtue. Moreover, by the very fact that some of these violent temptations are sudden and unexpected, while the operation of the virtues of prudence and fortitude is usually slow and discursive, one will need the prompt intervention of the gifts of counsel and fortitude. It is precisely on this point that St. Thomas bases his teaching on the necessity of the gifts of the Holy Spirit for eternal salvation.[21]

EFFECTS OF FORTITUDE

Of the remarkable effects which the gift of fortitude produces in the soul, the following are the principal ones:

Vigor in practicing virtue

1) *It gives the soul a relentless vigor in the practice of virtue.* This is an inevitable result of the supernatural mode by which the virtue of fortitude operates when under the influence of the gift of fortitude. At such times the soul does not feel any weakness or lack of confidence in the practice of virtue. It may suffer from the obstacles and dangers which it encounters, but it proceeds against them with supernatural energy in spite of all difficulties. That is the reason why St. Teresa placed great emphasis on the necessary disposition of soul for the practice of perfect fortitude:

> I say that it is very important, indeed, all important, that they should have a great and most resolute determination not to stop until they have reached [perfection], come what may, happen what will, however great the labor, however much others may murmur against them, whether they reach perfection or whether they die on the way or have no heart for the labors involved or even if the world itself should be dissolved.[22]

[20] *Loc. cit.*
[21] Cf. *ibid.*, I-II, q. 68, a. 2.
[22] *The Way of Perfection,* Chap. 21, n. 2.

The effects of the gift of fortitude in respect to the vigor which it bestows are both interior and exterior. Internally there is a vast area of a generosity and sacrifice which frequently reaches the point of heroism. There are incessant struggles against the temptations of the devil and self-love. Externally there are magnificent victories against error and vice; sometimes the body itself, sharing in the effect of a truly divine fortitude, abandons itself with ardor to the practice of the most heroic mortification, or suffers without flinching the most cruel agonies and pains. The gift of fortitude is, therefore, the true principle and source of great things which are undertaken or suffered for the love of God.

Overcoming lukewarmness

2) *It completely overcomes all lukewarmness in the service of God.* This is a natural consequence of the superhuman energy which is imparted to the soul by the gift of fortitude. Lukewarmness is like a tuberculosis of the soul which retards many persons on the way to perfection. It is due almost always to a lack of vigor and fortitude in the practice of virtue. Lukewarm souls consider that it is too much of an effort to have to conquer themselves in so many things and to maintain their spirit from one day to another in the monotonous fulfillment of the details of their daily obligations. The majority of such souls give in to weariness and renounce the battle, with the result that henceforth they live a purely mechanical life of routine, if indeed they do not turn their back completely on the life of virtue and abandon the pursuit of perfection. Only the gift of fortitude, which strengthens the power of the soul in a supernatural way, is an efficacious remedy against lukewarmness in the service of God.

Makes the soul intrepid, valiant

3) *It makes the soul intrepid and valiant in every type of danger or against every kind of enemy.* This is another of the great effects of the gift of fortitude and is particularly marked in the lives of the saints. The apostles themselves, gentle and meek by nature, and even cowards when abandoned by their Master on the eve of Good Friday, presented themselves once more to the world on Pentecost Sunday with a superhuman fortitude and courage. They were then afraid of no one, for they realized that it was necessary to obey God rather than man.[23] They confessed the teachings of Christ and sealed their apostolate with their own blood. All of this was the supernatural effect of the gift of fortitude, which the apostles received in all its plenitude on the first feast of Pentecost. In addition to the apostles, we have countless examples of saints who have been raised up by God throughout the centuries to give testimony to his doctrine of love, to combat the enemies of his Church, and in many instances to lay down their lives for Christ. From the earliest days of the Church and the ages of persecution to our own century, there have been men and women and even children who have manifested in their lives

[23]Cf. Acts 5:29.

the power and the valor that are imparted to holy souls by the gift of fortitude.

Suffering with patience and joy

4) *It enables souls to suffer extreme pain with patience and joy.* Although resignation is a praiseworthy virtue, it is nevertheless imperfect, and the saints do not manifest it in their lives once they have reached the perfection of virtue. We mean by this that, in a strict sense, the saints did not resign themselves to suffering; rather, they sought it voluntarily. Sometimes this "folly of the Cross" was manifested in extraordinary and terrifying acts of penance, as in the case of Mary Magdalen, Henry Suso, Peter of Alcántara, etc. At other times it found expression in the heroic patience with which holy souls endured the greatest conceivable sickness and pain, their faces radiant with joy, as in the case of St. Thérèse of Lisieux, who said that she had reached a point in which she could no longer suffer because all suffering had become sweet to her. This is the language of heroism which proceeds directly from the intense operation in the soul of the gift of fortitude.

The quality of heroism

5) *It gives the soul the quality of heroism in great things and in small things.* No greater fortitude is required to suffer the martyr's death at one stroke than to endure without failing the prolonged martyrdom of the heroic practice of virtue and the fulfillment of one's daily duties to the smallest detail. This principle is valid for every state of life, and it is a point which should be preached more frequently to the faithful. Given the weakness and instability of human nature, it is evident that for most people the most difficult test of fortitude consists in faithful perseverance in the performance of even the smallest duties of one's state in life.

Applying this doctrine to the religious life, Father Philipon makes the following observations:

> The religious life is a real martyrdom. The souls of saints find in it an abundant harvest of crucifying sacrifices, the merit of which may equal and even surpass martyrdom by blood. If religious never neglect a single opportunity for mortifying human nature and surrender without reserve to the demands of love, God can reveal to every soul, in the setting of its vocation, the road to Calvary which will lead it, without a single deviation, to perfect conformity with his crucified Son. The absolutely faithful observance of a religious rule approved by the Church would suffice to lead souls to the highest peaks of holiness. For that reason, Pope John XXII said: "Give me a Friar Preacher who keeps his rule and his constitution, and I will canonize him without any further miracle." As much might be said of the legislation of Carmel and of every other form of religious life.
>
> The perfect fulfillment of humble duty calls for the daily exercise of the gift of fortitude. It is not the extraordinary things they do which make the saints, but the divine manner in which they do them. This "heroism of little things," of which Saint Thérèse of the Child Jesus is perhaps the most striking example in the Church, was realized in a new way in the Carmelite of Dijon.

Extraordinary mortifications were always forbidden her, but she supplied for them by heroic fidelity to the smallest observance of her order, and she knew how to find in the Carmelite rule "the form of her sanctity" and the secret of "giving her blood, drop by drop, for the Church" until she was completely spent.

The fact is that, contrary to what is commonly believed, the gift of fortitude consists less in courageously undertaking great works for God than in patiently bearing life's trials, meeting them with a smile. This strength of soul bursts out gloriously in the saints in the hour of martyrdom and in the life of Jesus at the moment of his death on the Cross. Joan of Arc is greater bound to the stake than triumphantly entering Orleans at the head of her army.[24]

BEATITUDE AND FRUITS

Following the teaching of St. Augustine, St. Thomas attributes the fourth beatitude to the gift of fortitude: "Blessed are they who hunger and thirst for justice, for they shall be satisfied" (Matt. 5:6). Fortitude is concerned with arduous and difficult things, and the desire to sanctify oneself, not in any manner whatever but with a veritable hunger and thirst, is extremely arduous and difficult.[25] Thus we see that souls who are completely dominated by the gift of fortitude have an insatiable desire to do and to suffer great things for God. Even in this world they begin to receive their reward in the increase of the virtues and the intense spiritual joy with which God sometimes floods their soul.

The fruits which correspond to the gift of fortitude are patience and longanimity. The first, to endure suffering and evil with heroism; the second, in order not to fall away from the prolonged and continual practice of the good.[26]

OPPOSED VICES

According to St. Gregory, the vices opposed to the gift of fortitude are *inordinate fear* or *timidity,* often accompanied by a certain natural *sloth* which proceeds from the love of one's own ease and comfort, and prevents one from undertaking great things for the glory of God and impels one to avoid all suffering and difficulty. Father Lallemant makes the following observations on the vice of timidity:

A thousand apprehensions hinder us at every moment and prevent us from advancing in the way of God or from doing a vast amount of good which we could do if we followed the inspiration of the gift of counsel and possessed the courage which proceeds from the gift of fortitude. But there is too much in us of human views and everything frightens us. We fear lest a task which obedience imposes on us will not succeed, and this fear makes us refuse it. We are apprehensive of ruining our health, and this apprehension makes

---

[24]*The Spiritual Doctrine of Sister Elizabeth of the Trinity,* Chap. 8, n. 3.
[25]Cf. St. Thomas, *Summa,* II-II, q. 139, a. 2.
[26]*Loc. cit.,* ad 3.

us limit ourselves to some easy task, without the possibility of zeal or obedience impelling us to attempt anything more. We are afraid of inconveniencing ourselves, and this makes us shrink from corporal penances or leads us to spare ourselves too much in the practice of mortification. It is impossible to say how many omissions we are guilty of because of fear. There are few who do for God and their neighbor all that they could do. We ought to imitate the saints in fearing nothing but sin, like St. John Chrysostom; in braving danger, like St. Francis Xavier; in desiring insults and persecution, like St. Ignatius.[27]

MEANS OF PROGRESS

In addition to the general means for the increase and strengthening of the gifts (prayer, recollection, fidelity to grace, etc.), the following are more immediately concerned with strengthening the gift of fortitude:

Duties

1) *To accustom ourselves to the exact fulfillment of our duties in spite of any repugnance.* There are some heroic acts which surpass our powers at any given moment, but there can be no doubt that, with the assistance of the ordinary grace which God denies to no one, we can all do much more than we actually do. We shall never arrive at the heroism of the saints until the gift of fortitude operates intensely in us, but this operation is not likely to be effected in us by the Holy Spirit as a reward for our spiritual sloth and voluntary lukewarmness. But to him who does the best that he can, the assistance of God will never be lacking. On the other hand, no one can complain at not receiving the help of God through the operation of the gift of fortitude if he has not done all that he can. We must pray as if it all depended upon God, but we must strive as if it all depended upon ourselves.

Crosses

2) *Not to ask God to remove our cross but only that he give us the strength to carry it.* The gift of fortitude is given to holy souls so that they will be able to bear the great crosses and tribulations through which they must inevitably pass in order to arrive at the height of sanctity. If, on experiencing any kind of suffering, or on feeling the weight of a cross which God sends to us, we begin to complain and to ask God to take it from us, why should we then be surprised if the gifts of the Holy Spirit and especially the gift of fortitude do not operate in us? If, on being tested in little things, God finds that we are weak, how can his purifying action proceed in us? We should never complain about crosses, but we should ask the Lord that he give us the strength to bear them. Then we should remain tranquil and remember that God will never be outdone in generosity.

Mortification

3) *To practice voluntary mortification with all fidelity.* There is nothing which so strengthens an individual against the cold than to accustom himself to live outdoors. The person who freely embraces suffering no

[27] *Spiritual Doctrine*, IV, Chap. 4, a. 6.

longer fears it and may eventually deliberately seek it with a kind of spiritual joy. This does not mean that one must scourge the body with the discipline or practice the terrifying acts of penance that we read about in the lives of some of the saints. This sort of mortification is not for every soul. But there are in every life countless details and innumerable sufferings that can be accepted and eventually embraced as a means of penance and mortification. To observe silence when one feels an inclination to talk without necessity, not to complain about the inclemency of the weather or the quality of one's food or the hardships of one's vocation, to make a determined effort to preserve recollection and attention in prayer, to observe basic Christian politeness and fraternal charity toward those who by temperament are disagreeable or unsympathetic to us, to accept with humility and patience the contradictions or accusations which befall us without any fault on our part—these and many other daily crosses can be accepted in the spirit of true Christian fortitude and can be the coin by which we purchase, so to speak, an increase in grace and holiness of life. It is, indeed, a paradox to see certain Christians embrace truly difficult voluntary penances when as yet they are unable to bear the little crosses of daily life. Nor is it necessary that one be especially strong to be able to carry these small crosses. In fact, St. Teresa of Avila used to rejoice at finding herself so weak, because then she could place all her confidence in God.

The Eucharist

4) *To seek in the Eucharist strength for our souls.* The Eucharist is the food of our souls, and, like any food, one of its properties or characteristics is to strengthen the one who eats it. St. John Chrysostom used to say that we should rise from the Sacred Banquet with the strength of a lion to cast ourselves into the battle against every kind of attack. While the sacrament of the Eucharist produces its effects *ex opere operato,* nevertheless it is a great help if we, at the moment of receiving the Eucharist, not only recall that it is the food and nourishment of our soul, but explicitly petition of our eucharistic Lord the strength and fortitude we need for the faithful performance of the duties of our state in life and perseverance in our efforts to grow in sanctity.

8: THE VIRTUE OF TEMPERANCE

The word temperance can be employed to signify either the moderation which reason imposes on every human act or passion, in which case it is not a special virtue but a general condition which should characterize all the moral virtues,[1] or a special virtue among the moral virtues. Our study of this cardinal virtue will embrace temperance itself, its integral, subjective and potential parts, and the gift of fear connected with it.

TEMPERANCE IN ITSELF

DEFINITION As a moral virtue, temperance is a supernatural habit which moderates the inclination to sense pleasures, especially those which refer to touch and taste, and keeps them within the limits of reason illumined by faith.

ITS NATURE We refer to temperance as a supernatural habit in order to distinguish it from the natural or acquired virtue of temperance. The proper function of temperance is to refrain or control the movements of the concupiscible appetite in which it resides, as distinct from the virtue of fortitude, which controls the irascible appetite.[2] Although temperance should moderate all of the sense pleasures to which the concupiscible appetite is drawn, it refers in a special way to the pleasures of taste and touch, because they provide the most intense sense delectation and are, therefore, most apt to draw the appetite beyond the rule of reason. That is why the special virtue of temperance is required, and we may say that temperance is concerned principally with the pleasures of the sense of touch and secondarily with the pleasures enjoyed through the other senses.[3]

---

[1]Cf. St. Thomas, *Summa,* II-II, q. 141, a. 2

[2]Cf. *ibid.,* aa. 2 and 3.

[3]Cf. *ibid.,* a. 5.

Natural or acquired temperance is regulated simply by the light of natural reason, and therefore contains or restricts the functions of the concupiscible appetite within rational or purely human limits;[4] supernatural or infused temperance extends much further because it adds to simple reason the light of faith, which imposes superior and more delicate demands.[5]

ITS NECESSITY

The virtue of temperance is one of the most important and most necessary virtues in the spiritual life of the individual. The reason is that one must moderate the two strongest and most vehement instincts of human nature within the limits imposed by reason and faith. One could easily be led to excess without some virtue to moderate these strong demands of the body. Divine providence has united a special delight with those natural operations which are necessary for the conservation of the individual and the species. This is the reason for man's strong inclination to the pleasures of taste and the sex function, which have a noble purpose intended by God as the Author of nature. But precisely because of this strong impulse which proceeds from human nature itself, these sense delights can easily make demands beyond the limits that are reasonable and just, namely, the necessities required for the conservation of the life of the individual and of the species in the manner and circumstances determined by God. And since it is so easy for an individual to go beyond the limits of reason and enter the area of the illicit and sinful, it is necessary that the individual possess the infused virtue of temperance, which will moderate and restrain those natural appetites.

It is important to recognize, however, that the instincts, the functions and the pleasures which are involved in the preservation of the individual or the species are good in themselves and have a noble purpose. Consequently, it is not a question of annihilating or completely suppressing these basic human instincts, but of regulating their use according to the rule of reason, the light of faith, and one's particular vocation and circumstances of life. Thus the infused virtue of temperance enables the individual to use these functions and enjoy their concomitant pleasures for an honest and supernatural end. Nevertheless, since pleasure of any kind has a strong attraction and easily leads one beyond reasonable and just limits, temperance will incline one to a mortification which extends even to some things that are lawful in themselves. In this way the individual has greater security and assurance of preserving himself from sin, of keeping himself under perfect control, and of governing the life of the passions.

OPPOSED VICES

There are two vices opposed to temperance as a general virtue. By way of excess, *intemperance* surpasses the limits of reason and faith in the enjoyment

[4]Cf. *ibid.*, a. 6.
[5]Cf. *ibid.*, I-II, q. 63, a. 4; q. 142, a. 1.

of pleasures of taste or touch, and although this is not the worst of all sins, it is the basest because it reduces a man to the level of an animal.[6] By defect, *insensibility* causes an individual to avoid even those pleasures which are necessary for the conservation of the life of the individual or of the species as required by the right order of reason. Such necessary functions and pleasures can lawfully be renounced only for some honest end, such as the recovery of one's health, the strengthening of one's bodily powers, etc., or for some higher motive, such as the good of virtue or the good of one's neighbor in particular circumstances. In other words, it is always necessary to have a justifying reason for deliberately relinquishing or refraining from the natural function related to the preservation of the individual or the species, because these functions are implanted in us by God, and as such they are intended for a good and noble purpose. Indeed, even in the matter of embracing a life of celibacy or of practicing severe mortification in the use of food, one must always bear in mind that the natural vocation of the human being is to marriage and that the first law of nature is self-preservation. Consequently, any renunciation of the use of these basic human instincts must be founded on a justifying cause.

INTEGRAL AND SUBJECTIVE PARTS

INTEGRAL PARTS

As we have already explained, the integral parts of a virtue are those elements which integrate the virtue or facilitate its exercise. Although they do not constitute the essence of the virtue, they are necessary conditions for the virtue. There are two integral parts assigned to the virtue of temperance: a sense of shame and a sense of honor.

Sense of shame

The *sense of shame* is not a virtue in the strict sense of the word, but a certain praiseworthy passion or feeling which causes us to fear the disgrace and confusion or embarrassment which follow upon a base action. It is a passion because it is accompanied by a change in the body, such as blushing, and it is praiseworthy because the fear, regulated by reason, arouses a horror of anything that is base and degrading.[7] It should be noted that we are more ashamed of being embarrassed before wise and virtuous persons—by reason of the rectitude of their judgment and the worth of their esteem—than before those who have little education or judgment or virtue (thus one does not have a feeling of shame in front of animals or very small children). Above all, we have a feeling of shame and a fear of embarrassment before our own friends

[6]Cf. *ibid.*, II-II, q. 142, aa. 2 and 3.

[7]Cf. *ibid.*, q. 144, a. 2.

and members of our own family, who know us better and with whom we have to live.

St. Thomas remarks that the sense of shame is the exclusive patrimony of the young who are moderately virtuous. Those who are evil and habituated to sin do not have a sense of shame; they are so shameless that they would even boast of their sins. Those who are old or very virtuous do not have a strong sense of shame because they consider that any base or disgraceful actions are far removed from them or easy to avoid. Nevertheless, the virtuous are so disposed that they would be ashamed if they were ever to commit a disgraceful action.[8]

Sense of honor

The *sense of honor* signifies a certain love or appreciation for the spiritual beauty and dignity connected with the practice of temperance. It is properly connected with the virtue of temperance because this virtue possesses a certain degree of spiritual beauty, and since the beautiful is opposed to the base and ugly, a sense of honor will pertain in a special way to that virtue which inclines us to avoid base and ugly actions. The importance of cultivating a sense of honor can hardly be overemphasized, since sense pleasures readily lead to excess and to disgraceful and base actions. One should not, however, lose sight of the positive beauty of temperance and the fact that the sense of honor and the sense of shame would cease to be virtuous if they were understood to forbid the lawful and reasonable use of the sex instinct. Their purpose as elements or parts of the virtue of temperance is to moderate the enjoyment of lawful sense pleasures and thus enable the individual to enjoy them in a manner which is in keeping with his dignity as a human being and as a child of God. It is natural for a man to take pleasure in that which is becoming to him. Therefore, anything comely is naturally pleasing to man.[9]

SPECIES OF TEMPERANCE

Since the virtue of temperance has for its purpose the moderation of the inclination to the pleasures which proceed from taste and touch, its subjective parts or species can be divided into two groups: those which refer to the sense of taste (abstinence and sobriety) and those which refer to the sense of touch (chastity, purity and virginity).

Abstinence

Abstinence is a virtue which inclines one to the moderate use of bodily nourishment according to the dictates of reason enlightened by faith.[10] As an infused supernatural virtue, abstinence is very different from the acquired virtue of the same name. The latter is governed by the light of natural reason alone, and uses nourishment in the degree and measure which the needs or health of the body require. But the infused virtue of abstinence likewise

[8] *Ibid.*, a. 4.
[9] Cf. *ibid.*, q. 145, a. 3.
[10] Cf. *ibid.*, q. 146.

takes into account one's needs in the supernatural order (for example, to abstain on certain days according to the law of the Church).

The act proper to the virtue of abstinence is fasting,[11] whose obligatory exercise is regulated by the laws of the Church. In addition to the general ecclesiastical laws, there are also other particular laws which bind certain individuals or groups (for example, the constitutions of a religious institute); or one may practice fasting out of devotion, or as a means of atonement, usually following the advice of a spiritual director, or at least according to the dictates of prudence.

The vice opposed to abstinence is gluttony,[12] which we have already discussed.

Sobriety

Sobriety in a general sense signifies moderation or temperance in any matter, but in the strict sense it is a special virtue which has for its object the moderation of the use of intoxicating drinks in accordance with reason enlightened by faith.[13] The use of non-intoxicating drinks is regulated by the virtue of abstinence; its excess constitutes gluttony. Intoxicating drinks are the object of a special virtue because of the rapidity with which they may cause the loss of self-control and the ease with which one can form the habit of drinking to excess. When moderated by the virtue of sobriety, however, the use of intoxicating beverages is not only lawful but may be an act of virtue in given circumstances. The use of intoxicating drinks is not evil in itself, as some have tried to maintain, but it may become evil by reason of some special circumstance.

The vice opposed to sobriety is *drunkenness,* which involves a deliberate excess in the use of intoxicating drink leading to the loss of reason.[14]

Chastity

Chastity is a moral virtue which moderates the desire for venereal pleasures according to the necessities of life as judged by right reason illumined by faith.[15] The use and enjoyment of the sexual function in accordance with the married state is both lawful and virtuous, but even those persons for whom this action is lawful have an obligation to observe conjugal chastity. For all others who are not married there is a strict prohibition against the use and enjoyment of the sexual powers, because this function has as its purpose the procreation of the human race, and this is something that is restricted to the married state.

Purity moderates the external acts which of their nature lead to, and prepare for, sexual union. While chastity is concerned with the sexual act itself, purity is directed to chastity, not as a distinct virtue, but as pertaining to

[11]Cf. *ibid.,* q. 147.
[12]Cf. *ibid.,* q. 148.
[13]Cf. *ibid.,* q. 149.
[14]Cf. *ibid.,* q. 150.
[15]Cf. *ibid.,* q. 151.

certain circumstances related to chastity.[16] Purity, like all the parts of temperance, must be judged according to the rights and duties of one's state in life according to the dictates of right reason illumined by faith. In other words, the practice of purity for married persons will be different from the purity that is required of the unmarried.

The vice opposed to chastity is *lust*; it signifies an inordinate desire for venereal pleasure. The various kinds of lust are divided into general classifications by the theologian: internal acts of lust (thoughts or desires), incompleted external acts of lust (impure kisses or embraces which do not terminate in the completion of sexual gratification), and completed external acts of lust (when the individual terminates the sexual action and has gratification either in a natural or an unnatural way). Further explanation of the various sins of lust can be found in any standard manual of moral theology.

Virginity

Virginity is a special virtue, distinct from and more perfect than chastity, and it consists in the resolute will to preserve one's integrity of body by abstaining perpetually from all voluntary venereal pleasure.[17] In order to be a true virtue, virginity must be ratified by a vow, and in this it differs from perfect chastity, which is found in those who have never experienced deliberate venereal satisfaction but have made no vow to preserve perfect chastity throughout their life.[18] Perfect virginity voluntarily preserved for a supernatural motive is not only lawful but as such it is more excellent than matrimony.[19] This is exemplified in the lives of Jesus and Mary, who are models of sanctity. It would be a mistake, however, to conclude from the superiority of the state of virginity to the superiority of individuals who have vowed virginity,[20] because spiritual excellence is measured in terms of charity.

POTENTIAL PARTS OF TEMPERANCE

In addition to the species which comprise the subjective parts of temperance, there are numerous other virtues which are related in some way to the virtue of temperance as potential parts of the virtue. They are generally enumerated

[16]Cf. *ibid.*, q. 151, a. 4.
[17]Cf. *ibid.*, q. 152.
[18]Cf. *ibid.*, a. 3, ad 4. In his commentary on the *Sentences* (IV *Sent.*, d. 33, q. 33, a. 2, ad 4) St. Thomas taught that a vow was not essential for receiving the aureole of virginity in heaven; this is also the teaching of several outstanding Thomists such as Soto, Sylvius, Billuart and others.
[19]Cf. I Cor. 8:34; Council of Trent, Sess. XXIV, canon 10 (Denz. 980); Pope Pius XII, encyclical *Sacra Virginitas*, March 25, 1954.
[20]Cf. St. Thomas, *Summa*, II-II, q. 154, a. 4, ad 2.

as continence, meekness, clemency and modesty in general, which embraces the virtues of humility, studiousness, modesty of action, eutrapelia and modesty of dress.

CONTINENCE

Continence is a virtue which strengthens the will in order to resist the disordered vehemence of the passions.[21] It is a virtue which resides in the will, but as a virtue it is imperfect, for it does not lead immediately to the realization of any work which is positively good and perfect but is content to prevent evil by a disposition of the will which restrains the impetus of passion. The perfect virtue of chastity controls the passions in such a way that they do not produce any vehement movements contrary to reason;[22] continence, on the other hand, resists the inclination of passion only when it arises, and thus a continent person may be subject to violent attacks of passion. The proper material of the virtue of continence is the pleasures of the sense of touch, especially those connected with sex, although in a more general and less proper sense continence can also refer to other matters.[23] The vice opposed to continence is *incontinence,* which is not a habit in the strict sense but merely the lack of continence in the rational appetite, which would restrain the vehement movement of passion. St. Thomas remarks that the will of an intemperate man is inclined to sin by reason of its own choice, which is the result of a habit acquired through custom, but the will of the incontinent man is inclined to sin because of the surge of vehement passion which he could have resisted.[24] Hence the importance of resisting the first impulses of disorderly passions.

MEEKNESS

Meekness is a special virtue which has as its object the moderation of anger in accordance with right reason.[25] Although it is listed as a potential part of the virtue of temperance, meekness resides in the irascible appetite because it is concerned with restraining anger. As a passion, anger in itself is neither good nor evil, and therefore there is such a thing as just anger. The virtue of meekness is, therefore, not a purely negative habit; its purpose is to enable an individual to use anger according to the rule of right reason.

Moreover, it would be a caricature of virtue to confuse meekness with timidity or cowardice. The meek man does not lose the virtue when he gives expression to just anger, any more than Jesus ceased to be meek when in anger he drove the merchants from the temple. Indeed, if one were to fail to utilize anger on those occasions which demand it, he could be guilty

---

[21]Cf. *ibid.*, q. 155.
[22]Cf. *ibid.*, a. 1.
[23]Cf. *ibid.*, a. 2, ad 1 and 4.
[24]Cf. *ibid.*, q. 156, a. 3.
[25]Cf. *ibid.*, q. 157.

of a sin against justice or charity, virtues more excellent than meekness. But since it is easy to be mistaken in judging the just motives of anger, one must always be vigilant lest he be overtaken by a sudden movement of passion which would carry him beyond the limits of justice and charity. In case of doubt it is always better to incline to the side of meekness than to the danger of excessive rigor.

The vice opposed to meekness is *anger,* not considered as an irascible passion, but as an inordinate desire for revenge, which involves the intellect and the will. The vice of anger is a form of intemperance because it designates a lack of self-restraint and moderation of the irascible appetite. Indeed, anger may reach the point of an insane rage in which an individual has lost all self-control.

CLEMENCY

Clemency is a virtue which inclines a person in authority to mitigate a punishment for a fault so far as right reason allows.[26] It proceeds from a certain sweetness or gentleness of soul which causes one to abhor anything that would cause sorrow or pain to another. Clemency does not refer to a complete and total pardon but to a mitigation of the punishment. It should not be exercised for unworthy motives, such as respect of persons or the desire to be liked, but it should be motivated by an indulgence and kindness which will not compromise the demands of justice.

Opposed to clemency there are three vices: *cruelty,* which is hardness of heart in the infliction of penalties to the point of exceeding the demands of justice; *savagery* or *brutality,* which signifies a pleasure in inflicting punishment on others; and *excessive leniency,* which pardons or mitigates punishment when justice demands that they be imposed on guilty parties.

MODESTY

Modesty is a virtue derived from temperance which inclines the individual to conduct himself in his internal and external movements and in his dress in accordance with the just limits of his state in life and position in society.[27] In other words, just as the virtue of temperance moderates the desire for the pleasures of the sense of touch, as meekness moderates anger, and as clemency moderates the desire for revenge, so modesty moderates other less difficult movements, which yet require the control of virtue.

These secondary movements are as follows: 1) the tendency of the soul toward one's own excellence, moderated by the virtue of *humility;* 2) the desire for knowledge, regulated by the virtue of *studiousness;* 3) bodily movements and actions, which in serious matters are moderated by the virtue of

[26]Cf. *loc. cit.*

[27]Cf. *ibid.,* q. 160.

modesty of action, and by *eutrapelia* in games and diversions; 4) movements relative to dress and external appearance, which are regulated by *modesty of dress.*

HUMILITY Humility is one of the most fundamental virtues in the spiritual life, and for that reason we shall discuss it in greater detail.

Its nature

It is a virtue derived from temperance which inclines an individual to restrain the inordinate desire for his own excellence, giving him a true evaluation of his smallness and misery before God.[28] Humility derives from temperance by way of the virtue of modesty, because its proper function is to moderate the appetite for one's own greatness, and all moderation belongs to the virtue of temperance. Nevertheless, humility resides in the irascible appetite, unlike temperance itself which resides in the concupiscible, because it refers to a difficult good. There is no contradiction between the virtue of humility and the virtue of magnanimity, which impels one to great things, because both, as virtues, function according to the rule of right reason, but from different points of view.[29] Based as it is on self-knowledge, true humility enables an individual to see himself as he is in the eyes of God, not exaggerating his good qualities and not denying the gifts that he has received from God. This virtue, therefore, primarily implies the subjection of man to God, and for that reason St. Augustine attributes the gift of fear to the perfection of the virtue of humility.[30]

How is it possible for a person who has received great gifts from God to recognize these gifts and at the same time be aware of his littleness and misery before God? St. Thomas answers this question by pointing out that we may consider two things in man, namely, that which he has of God and that which he has of himself. Whatever pertains to defect and imperfection is of man; whatever pertains to man's goodness and perfection is from God. And since humility properly regards man's subjection to God, every man, in regard to that which he has of himself, ought to subject himself, not only to God, but to his neighbor, as regards that which his neighbor has from God. But humility does not require that a man subject himself to his neighbor as regards that which he himself has from God, for those who have a share in the gifts of God know that they have it, and therefore they may, without prejudice to humility, set the gifts they have received from God above those that others seem to have received from him. Likewise, humility does not require that a man subject what he has of himself to that which his

[28]Cf. *ibid.,* q. 161.

[29]Cf. *ibid.,* a. 1, ad 2; a. 4, ad 3.

[30]Cf. *ibid.,* a. 2, ad 3; cf. also a. 1, ad 4 and 5.

neighbor has of himself; otherwise each man would have to consider himself a greater sinner than anyone else.[31]

The foundation of humility

It is, therefore, the comparison with the infinite perfections of God which constitutes the ultimate basis and foundation of humility. For that reason this virtue is closely related to the theological virtues and possesses a certain aspect of worship and veneration of God, which also relates it to the virtue of religion.[32] In the light of this basic principle, one can understand the apparently exaggerated humility of the saints and the incomparable humility of Christ. As they grew in perfection, the saints received from God ever increasing knowledge of his infinite perfections, and as a result of that knowledge they perceived with ever greater clarity the infinite abyss between the grandeur of God and their own littleness and weakness. This resulted in a humility so profound that they would have cast themselves gladly at the feet of the most lowly and despicable person in the world. For that reason also, Mary, the greatest of all God's creatures, was also the most humble.

While Christ could not consider himself as vile or imperfect in an absolute sense (for he was aware of his excellency and impeccability, the result of the hypostatic union, and that he was, therefore, deserving of all honor and reverence), he likewise recognized that his humanity was from God. And he knew that if, *per impossibile,* his humanity were to be abandoned by the divinity, it would fall into the ignorance and inclination to sin which is proper to our weak human nature. For that reason he was truly humble as man, and was profoundly subjected to the divinity, referring all things and all honors to the divinity.

Humility is therefore based on two principal things: truth and justice. The truth gives us a knowledge of ourselves, with the recognition that whatever good we have we have received from God. Justice demands of us that we give God all honor and glory (I Tim. 1:17). The truth requires that we recognize and admire the natural and supernatural gifts which God has bestowed on us, but justice demands that we glorify the giver of those gifts.

The excellence of humility

Humility is not the greatest of all the virtues. It is surpassed by the theological virtues, the intellectual virtues and by justice, especially by legal justice.[33] But in a certain sense humility is the fundamental virtue in the spiritual life, i.e., in a negative sense or, as the theologians says, *ut removens prohibens.* It is humility which removes the obstacles to the reception of grace, since

[31]Cf. *ibid.,* a. 3.

[32]For an inspiring explanation of the religious character of the virtue of humility, see Dom Columba Marmion, O.S.B., *Christ, the Ideal of the Monk,* Chap. 11.

[33]Cf. St. Thomas, *ibid.,* q. 161, a. 5.

Scripture expressly states that God resists the proud and gives his grace to the humble.[34] In this sense humility and faith are the two basic virtues, inasmuch as they constitute the foundation of the entire supernatural structure, for humility removes the obstacles and faith establishes our first contact with God.[35]

From what has been said, it is evident that without humility it is impossible to take a single step in the spiritual life. God is supreme truth, and he cannot tolerate that anyone should voluntarily depart from that truth. But to walk in truth it is absolutely necessary that one be humble, because humility is based on self-knowledge. The more lofty the edifice which we desire to construct in the spiritual life by the grace of God, the more deep and profound must be the foundations of humility upon which that edifice is built.[36]

Degrees of humility

Various classifications of the degrees of humility have been proposed by saints and spiritual writers. We shall enumerate the most important ones, and it will be observed that, although they may differ in particular details, they all coincide as regards the basic element. A familiarity with the various degrees of humility is of great help in examining oneself in regard to the principal internal and external manifestations of this virtue.

According to St. Benedict, there are twelve degrees of humility, listed in the following manner: 1) fear of God and recognition of his precepts; 2) not to desire to follow one's own will; 3) to subject oneself by obedience to a superior; 4) patiently to embrace through obedience difficult and painful things; 5) to recognize and confess one's own defects; 6) to believe and admit that one is unworthy and useless; 7) to believe and admit that one is the most vile and wretched of all; 8) to subject oneself in all things to the common life and to avoid singularity; 9) not to speak without being addressed; 10) to speak in few words and in a humble tone of voice; 11) not to be easily disposed to laughter; 12) to keep one's eyes cast downward.[37]

St. Anselm enumerates seven degrees of humility: 1) to acknowledge oneself as worthy of disdain; 2) to grieve at one's unworthiness because of one's defect; 3) to confess one's unworthiness; 4) to convince others of one's unworthiness; 5) to bear patiently that others say of us that we are unworthy; 6) to allow oneself to be treated with contempt; 7) to rejoice in being treated with contempt.[38]

---

[34]Cf. Jas. 4:6.

[35]Cf. St. Thomas, *loc. cit.*, ad 2.

[36]Cf. St. Teresa of Avila, *Interior Castle*, Sixth Mansions, Chaps. 4 and 10; *The Life*, Chaps. 12 and 22; *The Way of Perfection*, Chap. 4.

[37]For a commentary on these degrees of humility, see St. Thomas, *Summa*, II-II, q. 161, a. 6, and Dom Columba Marmion, *Christ, The Ideal of The Monk*, Chap. 11.

[38]Cf. St. Thomas, *ibid.*, ad 3.

St. Bernard simplifies the degrees of humility by reducing them to three basic grades: 1) sufficient humility, that is, to subject oneself to superiors and not to prefer oneself to one's equal; 2) abundant humility, that is, to subject oneself to one's equals and not to prefer oneself to one's inferiors; 3) superabundant humility, that is, to subject oneself to one's inferiors.

The three degrees of humility described by St. Ignatius Loyola are not restricted to the virtue of humility alone, but refer to the self-abnegation which is required in the Christian life, as is evident from the context of his writings. The following are the three degrees described by St. Ignatius: 1) *necessary* humility (the humility necessary for salvation), namely, that one humble himself as much as possible, so that in all things he obeys the law of God, and in such wise that, although he could become the lord of all created things in this world, he would never do anything that would involve the commission of a mortal sin; 2) *perfect* humility, that is, when one does not care to have riches rather than poverty, honor rather than dishonor, a long life rather than a short life, as long as one can serve God so faithfully that he would not commit a deliberate venial sin for all the world; 3) *most perfect* humility, that is, when, in imitation of Christ, one prefers to be poor with Christ, to suffer opprobrium with Christ, and to be considered a fool with Christ, rather than to be wealthy or honored or considered wise by the world.[39]

Pride

The vice opposed to humility is *pride,* which is the inordinate desire for one's own excellence.[40] In itself it is a grave sin, although it admits of smallness of matter and can be a venial sin by reason of the imperfection of the act as such. In some of its manifestations, such as pride against God, it is a most grave sin and the greatest sin after direct hatred of God. Pride is not a capital sin but rather the queen and mother of all vices and sins, because it is the root and principle of all sin.[41] It was the sin of the fallen angels and the sin of our first parents.[42] Although it may be manifested in various ways, St. Thomas, following the teaching of St. Gregory, points out four principal manifestations of pride: 1) to think that one's gifts and talents are from oneself; 2) to believe that the gifts of God are due strictly and solely to one's own merits; 3) to boast of possessing that which one does not

---

[39]The Venerable Olier, founder of the Sulpicians, also describes three degrees of humility which are to be found in fervent and devout souls: 1) to accept one's weakness and misery; 2) to desire to be considered as wretched and lowly; 3) to desire to be treated with contempt and to suffer humiliations at the hands of others.

[40]Cf. *ibid.,* q. 162.

[41]Cf. *ibid.,* q. 162, aa. 7, 8.

[42]Cf. *ibid.,* I, q. 63, a. 2; II-II, q. 163, a. 1.

have; 4) to despise others and wish to appear the exclusive possessor of that which one has.[43]

STUDIOUSNESS

Studiousness is a virtue which moderates the inclination or desire for knowledge according to the dictates of right reason. Man has a natural desire for knowledge, a noble and a lawful desire. This natural inclination can be misdirected toward that which is unlawful or sinful, however. Or it can be exercised to excess, so that one neglects other duties which are serious or indispensable. Or it can be used less than one ought, with the result that one lacks the necessary knowledge for the fulfillment of the duties of his state in life. In order to regulate this and to direct the natural inclinations for knowledge according to the rules of reason and of faith, one needs the special virtue of studiousness.

Opposed vices

There are two vices opposed to studiousness. By excess, the vice of *curiosity* signifies an inordinate desire for knowledge, and it can refer either to intellectual knowledge or sensitive cognition. As regards intellectual knowledge, the vice of curiosity may arise by reason of an evil motive for obtaining the knowledge, by reason of an excessive attachment to knowledge as such, by reason of sinful means used for acquiring knowledge, by reason of not referring the knowledge in some way to God, or by attempting to know that which is above our powers and capacities. As regards sensitive cognition, the vice of curiosity is often referred to as "concupiscence of the eyes"; it is manifested in two ways: by not orientating sensitive knowledge to something useful, or by directing it to some evil end. These basic principles have a variety of applications in regard to lectures, conversations, theatrical spectacles and many other events of this type.

By defect, the vice of *sloth* or *negligence* in the acquisition of knowledge is a sin against studiousness; it is the deliberate omission of learning those things which one has an obligation to know according to his state and condition of life.

BODILY MODESTY

Modesty is a virtue by which one observes proper decorum in his gestures and bodily movements, in his posture, and in the matter of dress. In the matter of modesty it is necessary to attend especially to two considerations: the dignity of the individual person and those who are in the company of that person. Bodily modesty has great importance both for the individual and for society. Ordinarily, a person is judged by externals, and for that reason any inordinate movement, staring, indiscreet glances or any other uncontrolled movements are generally interpreted as signs of an inordinate and unruly interior. With good reason does St. Augustine recommend in

[43]Cf. *ibid.*, II-II, q. 162, a. 4.

his Rule that individuals should be especially careful to observe external modesty of deportment lest they scandalize others. And we read in Sacred Scripture: "One can tell a man by his appearance; a wise man is known as such when first met. A man's attire, his hearty laughter and his gait, proclaim him for what he is" (Sirach 19:25-26).[44] The vices opposed to modesty of deportment are *affectations* and *rusticity* or *rudeness.*

As regards modesty of dress, St. Thomas states that any sin that arises in this matter is due to something immoderate on the part of the person in view of particular circumstances.[45] This immoderation may be due to a lack of conformity to the customs of the persons with whom one lives, or to an excessive attachment and concern in regard to clothing and personal adornment. It may become inordinate because of vanity, sensuality or excessive interest in one's apparel. It may also happen that one could sin against modesty of clothing by being deficient in a concern for one's personal attire, for example, if one were to be unreasonably negligent in dressing according to his state in life, or were to seek to attract attention by his lack of concern in his manner of dressing.[46]

RECREATION

Eutrapelia is a virtue which regulates man's recreation, games and diversions according to the rule of reason.[47] It pertains to external modesty, of which it is a modality. In discussing this virtue, St. Thomas begins by insisting upon the necessity of spiritual and bodily refreshments and relaxations in order to restore the energies and powers that have been exhausted by labor. He points out, however, that three defects in recreation must be avoided: to recreate by means of harmful or sinful things, to lose all sense of propriety or seriousness in the midst of recreation, or to do anything that would be inordinate in regard to persons, place, time or other circumstances.

The vices opposed to the virtue of eutrapelia are *excessive and inordinate recreation,* either by reason of the length of time spent in recreation or the types of diversion, and *excessive austerity,* with the result that an individual would not desire to recreate nor permit others to recreate.

---

[44]Cf. *ibid.,* q. 168, a. 1.

[45]Cf. *ibid.,* q. 169, a. 1.

[46]By reason of its special importance and danger, St. Thomas also discusses the adornment of women and the use of cosmetics, perfume, jewelry and such things. His basic principle for the use of these is that a married woman could lawfully use them in order to please her husband, but if any woman uses them out of simple vanity or for sinful motives, their use would become sinful according to the purpose for which they are used. St. Thomas is prudent enough, however, to take into consideration the customs of particular countries in which such things may be used as a normal practice without sin. Cf. *ibid.,* a. 2.

[47]Cf. *ibid.,* q. 168, aa. 2-4.

THE GIFT OF FEAR

To conclude our discussion of the virtue of temperance, we ask which of the gifts of the Holy Ghost corresponds to the virtue of temperance. We have already seen that the gift of fear of the Lord corresponds primarily to the virtue of hope and secondarily to the virtue of temperance. St. Thomas explains this by saying that the gift of fear corresponds to the virtue of temperance by withholding a man from the pleasures of the flesh. The principal object of the gift of fear is God, whom it avoids offending, and in this way fear corresponds to the virtue of hope. But as a secondary object, fear enables a man to avoid those things which are most seductive, and in this respect it perfects the virtue of temperance.[48]

According to this doctrine, the gift of fear pertains to the theological virtue of hope insofar as it moves the individual to avoid sin out of reverence for God and his infinite grandeur, and it pertains to the cardinal virtue of temperance inasmuch as, in consequence of the great respect for the divine majesty which the gift inspires, it prevents one from falling into those sins to which man is principally inclined, such as those whose object is carnal pleasure.

Certainly the virtue of temperance itself, with its entire cortege of related virtues, has the same ultimate purpose in view. But since it must operate through simple natural reason illumined by faith, it can never achieve this end with the full efficacy and perfection of the gift. This is precisely what the Holy Spirit, by means of the gift of fear, accomplishes: with his divine and omnipotent motion he comes to man's aid so that he can perfectly control the pleasures of the senses and their incentives to sinning. In fine, this is but the application to a particular case of the general doctrine of the necessity of the gifts for the perfection of the infused virtues and, in consequence, for the perfection of the Christian life itself.

[48]Cf. *ibid.*, q. 141, a. 1, ad 3.

THE LIFE OF PRAYER

THE LIFE OF PRAYER

1: THE PRACTICE OF PRAYER

Prayer has been defined in various ways, but basically all the definitions agree in emphasizing that prayer is an elevation of the mind to God in order to converse with him. Theologically, prayer is an act of the virtue of religion, a virtue related to justice; in the higher degrees of prayer, however, as the soul is more and more permeated by the virtue of charity, prayer becomes the language of love. Psychologically, prayer is an operation of the intellect—the practical intellect—under the impetus of the will.[1]

As conversation with God, prayer will admit of as many types or species as there are different needs or sentiments which the human heart can express. Thus both vocal and mental prayer can be used to ask God to satisfy our needs, to forgive us our sins, to bless those we love, etc., or they can be expressions of our gratitude to God, our love of God, our sorrow for having offended him or our reverence and adoration. The classical division of prayer, however, summarizes all prayer under the headings of petition, thanksgiving, contrition and adoration. The first in excellence is prayer of adoration, but usually the first in practice is petition. Consequently, we shall first consider the nature of the prayer of petition and the various questions that are related to it, before treating the other kinds of prayer.

In succeeding chapters we will discuss the grades of prayer, contemplative prayer and the prayer of union.

---

[1]In treating of prayer in the *Summa,* St. Thomas emphasizes prayer as petition (II-II, q. 83) because, as an act of the virtue of religion, prayer in its most proper sense is prayer of petition. Louis of Granada has enlarged upon a question raised by St. Thomas concerning the relation between meditation and contemplation and devotion (II-II, q. 82, a. 3) and has given us an inspiring treatise on the practice of prayer in this wider context (cf. *Summa of the Christian Life* [St. Louis: Herder, 1955], II, pp. 286-326).

PRAYER OF PETITION

Governed as he is by his instincts and body needs, an infant is concerned almost exclusively with those things which relate to self preservation—nourishment, sleep, warmth, etc. This concern for self extends all through the childhood years, with the result that the child's concept of its parents is that of providers and protectors. And as the child begins to speak, a large portion of the language addressed to its parents takes the form of petition for its needs.

Something similar occurs in the evolution of man's religion, whether personal or social. Whether impelled by fear or some other motive, primitive man has almost always approached God by way of petition, expressed in word or action. Even when a man's religion has become purified and perfected, his deep awareness of personal weakness and insufficiency finds its expression in the petitions which he addresses to God. There is no need, therefore, to justify the use of the prayer of petition, for it springs naturally from our recognition of the omnipotence of God and our own great need.

USEFULNESS OF PETITION

Following the teaching of St. Thomas, the first question to be asked concerning prayer of petition is in regard to its fittingness and utility.[2] God knows our needs better than we do; therefore, it seems unnecessary to give voice to our petitions. Moreover, God knows from all eternity what he will grant us and what he will not grant us; therefore, since we cannot change the immutable will of God, it is useless to pray.

In answer to these difficulties, St. Thomas replies, first, that we need to pray to God, not to make known to him our needs, but that we may be reminded of the necessity of having recourse to God; secondly, that our motive in praying is not to change the divine will in our regard but, by our prayers, to obtain what God has decreed.[3] Scripture explicitly commands us to pray always;[4] the theological reason is that divine providence decrees what effects are to take place, by what causes, and in what order. Human actions, and among them prayer, are causes of certain effects under God's dispensation, and hence when men achieve something by their prayers, they are receiving what God has decreed they shall receive through their prayers.[5]

The causality of prayer

The prayer of petition is not, therefore, an extrinsic cause which moves or determines the will of God, for this is impossible. It is a cause only in the sense that God has related some things to others in such a way that, if certain

[2]Cf. *Summa,* II-II, q. 83, a. 2.
[3]Cf. *loc. cit.,* ad 1 and 3.
[4]Cf. Lk. 18:1.
[5]Cf. St. Thomas, *loc. cit.*

causes are placed, certain effects will follow. Moreover, prayer is a conditional cause, as if God were to decree: "If you ask for such and such a benefit, it will be granted you; but if you do not ask, you will not receive it." It follows from this that it is an error to believe that if we persevere in prayer, come what may, we shall always obtain that which we seek. Some things will be granted to us whether we pray for them or not, because God has decreed that they shall be granted to us absolutely; some things will never be granted to us, no matter how earnestly and how long we pray for them; still others will be granted to us only if we pray, because God has decreed that they will be given only on the condition that we ask for them.

OBJECTS OF PRAYER

The next question concerns the things for which one should pray. Although the very notion of petition of any kind is that the petitioner desires something for himself, our petitions to God should always be made with the condition that what we ask is according to his will. And there are certain things which by their very nature are in accordance with, or contrary to, the divine will. Thus one can in an absolute sense petition God for any of those things which pertain to God's glory, eternal salvation and growth in grace and virtue, for then we conform our wills to God's will.[6] But it would never be lawful to ask God for anything that would work to one's spiritual detriment, for this would be asking God to go against his own divine will.

But what of temporal goods? Is it commendable and lawful to ask God for such things as the necessities of life, good health, a long life, etc.? The principle used by St. Augustine was that it is lawful to pray for anything that it is lawful to desire.[7] Man's need for temporal goods is based on the natural law of self-preservation, his rights and duties as a member of society, and the requirements of his particular profession or vocation. All things being equal, it matters not whether a man possess many worldly goods or only the minimum; what matters greatly is the manner in which he uses them and the degree of his attachment to them. Therefore, as long as a man uses temporal goods virtuously and subordinates them to his true ultimate end, it is lawful to possess them and to petition for them from God. But since so many persons are excessively attached to temporal goods or are led into occasions of sin through the possession of them, one can readily surmise why prayers for such things often go unanswered. We do not know what things are for our good, and for that reason we should always pray for temporal goods under the condition that such things be in accordance with God's will and for our own spiritual benefit.

THE NECESSITY OF PETITION

If used in the proper way, the prayer of petition is of great spiritual benefit. It is in itself an excellent act of the virtue of religion, it exercises us in the virtue of humility, and it increases our confidence in God. The man who prays

[6]Cf. *ibid.*, a. 5.
[7]Cf. *ibid.*, a. 6.

enters into the workings of divine providence by placing the secondary conditional cause from which certain effects will follow, according to the divine decrees. Lastly, a man on his knees before God is thereby raised to a greater dignity, for the proper use of prayer will conform man's will to God's.

But prayer is not only fitting and useful; it is absolutely necessary in the economy of divine providence. In order to understand this, it is necesary to review the various types of necessity. The *necessity of precept* is that which follows upon the mandate of a superior and not from the very nature of things, and therefore it is revocable (e.g., the Friday abstinence imposed by the Church). The *necessity of means* is that which follows from the very nature of things and of itself admits of no exceptions (e.g., nourishment for the preservation of life). When we speak of human acts, we make a further division of necessity of means: *necessity of means by ordinary law* (*ex institutione*), which is a general disposition imposed by God but could admit of an exception (e.g., the necessity of sacramental baptism for salvation could be supplanted by an act of perfect contrition with the implicit desire for baptism), and *necessity of means ex natura rei,* which admits of no possible exception for anyone under any circumstances (e.g., the necessity of sanctifying grace for salvation).

Necessity of precept

Applying these distinctions to the practice of prayer, we say that prayer is necessary both by necessity of precept and by necessity of means *ex institutione divina.* As to the first, prayer is necessary by divine, natural and ecclesiastical precept. Scripture repeatedly commands that we pray: "Watch and pray" (Matt. 26:41); "they must always pray and not lose heart" (Lk. 18:1); "ask, and it shall be given you" (Matt. 7:7); "pray without ceasing" (I Thess. 5:17); "be assiduous in prayer" (Col. 4:2). Natural precept obliges man to pray because he is so weak and lacks many things which only God can supply. The ecclesiastical law prescribes certain prayers on certain occasions, such as during the administration of the sacraments, during times of great peril, the canonical recitation of the Office, etc.

Theologians commonly designate certain times in which one is bound *per se* to pray and other times when one is bound *per accidens.* Thus one is gravely obliged to pray upon reaching the age of reason, when the child has an obligation to turn to God as his last end; in danger of death, in order to obtain the grace of a Christian death and final perseverance; and frequently during life, although there is much dispute as to details. If a person fulfills his religious obligations by attendance at Mass on days of obligation and says some prayers daily, however, he can be at ease in his conscience as regards this precept.[8]

---

[8]Parents, teachers and the clergy should beware of imposing detailed obligations where none are specified by law. The law does not determine exactly the frequency of prayer and, therefore, while it is commendable and prudent to say certain prayers

The precept to pray will oblige *per accidens* in the following circumstances: a) when prayer is necessary for the fulfillment of some other precept (e.g., the fulfillment of the sacramental penance); b) when one encounters a severe temptation which cannot be overcome except through prayer;[9] c) in times of great public peril or calamity. There may be many other circumstances in which a given individual will be obliged *per accidens* to resort to prayer, but each person would have to decide in his own case. We would only mention that in one's striving for perfection and growth in virtue it may not occur to the individual to ask God in prayer for the graces and increase in virtue that he needs, or for the special helps necessary for the performance of one's duties of state in life. In this regard it is a good practice to work as if it all depended on oneself and to pray as if it all depended on God.

Necessity of means

As regards the necessity of means *ex institutione divina,* it is common and certain theological doctrine that prayer is necessary by necessity of means for the salvation of adults. There are many testimonies from the Fathers to substantiate this doctrine, but perhaps the most conclusive is that of St. Augustine, which was quoted by the Council of Trent: "For God does not command impossibilities, but by commanding admonishes you both to do what you can do and to pray for what you cannot do, and assists you that you may be able."[10] Final perseverance, which is a completely gratuitous gift of God, is not ordinarily received without humble and persevering prayer. St. Alphonsus Liguori was so convinced of this that he wrote: "He who prays will be saved; he who does not pray will be condemned." This statement must, of course, be accepted with due reservation, for while it is the ordinary law of grace that one will not be saved without prayer, God could give his graces to those who have not prayed for them. But God will not refuse grace to him who prays for it with the proper dispositions, for it is the divine will that all men be saved. In this sense spiritual writers have listed the faithful practice of prayer as a sign of predestination and the lack of prayer as a negative sign of reprobation.

---

at specified times, such as before and after meals and in the morning and at night, the law itself makes no mention of such prayers as binding under pain of sin. Nevertheless, it is a praiseworthy practice for Christians to set aside certain times for prayer each day.

[9]This is not to be understood as a universal principle, however, for there are certain types of temptation which would be strengthened rather than overcome if the individual were to attempt to pray at such a time; for example, temptations against faith and purity. Temptations that arise in the intellect or imagination may gain a stronger hold on those faculties if one tries to pray them away, for the very act of prayer causes the individual to turn his full attention to the temptation and to concentrate on it.

[10]Cf. St. Augustine, *De natura et gratia,* cap. 43, n. 50; Council of Trent, Sess. VI, Decree on Justification, Chap. 11 (Denz. 804).

PRAYER TO THE SAINTS

Having defined prayer as conversation with God and identified it as an act of the virtue of religion, which has the worship of God as its proper object, it would seem unnecessary to ask whether it is lawful to pray to anyone but God. But the practice of the Church and the objections of certain religious groups make it necessary to clarify the practice of praying to the saints. St. Thomas gives the answer as clearly and succinctly as one could wish:

> Prayer is offered to a person in two ways: first, to be fulfilled by him, and secondly, to be obtained through him. In the first way we offer prayer to God alone, since all our prayers ought to be directed to the acquisition of grace and glory, which God alone gives, according to Ps. 83:12: "Grace and glory he [the Lord] bestows." But in the second way we pray to the saints, whether angels or men, not that God may know our petitions through them, but that our prayers may be effective through their prayers and merits.[11]

The Council of Trent solemnly defended the practice of praying to the saints to intercede for us, and of venerating their relics and images.[12] The principal theological bases for the practice are the goodness of God, who deigns to associate the saints in the obtaining and distribution of graces, the doctrine of the communion of saints, and the perfect charity and abundant merits of the blessed, who know our needs and desire to assist us to attain glory.[13]

Prayer to the souls in purgatory

What is to be said of the practice of praying to the souls in purgatory and the possibility of their interceding for us? The Church has made no definite statement on this matter, and therefore it is an open question among theologians. St. Thomas taught that the souls in purgatory are not in a position to pray for us, but rather that we should pray for them.[14] Many theologians, however, and among them some Thomists, defend the practice of praying to the souls in purgatory. Their primary argument is based on the doctrine of the communion of saints, for it is unlikely that those who are in purgatory and assured of ultimate glory would be entirely ignorant of the needs of souls on earth, especially of those they have loved in this life. Also, although we cannot know for certain the amount of suffrage and relief that is granted the souls in purgatory by our prayers and good works, it is probable that the souls realize that their relief is due to someone here on earth, and they would logically be moved to gratitude toward their benefactors.

---

[11]*Summa,* II-II, q. 83, a. 4.

[12]Cf. Sess. XXII, Chap. 3 and canon 5 (Denz. 941 and 952) Sess. XXV, *De invocatione, veneratione et reliquiis Sanctorum et sacris imaginibus* (Denz. 984).

[13]Cf. St. Thomas, *ibid.,* a 11; *Suppl.,* q. 72.

[14]The reasons for the position of St. Thomas are: a) the souls in purgatory do not yet enjoy the beatific vision wherein they would be able to know our needs, and b) although they are superior to us by reason of their impeccability, they are inferior to us by reason of the pains which they suffer (*Summa,* II-II, q. 83, a. 4, ad 3; a. 11, ad 3).

FOR WHOM TO PRAY

The last question we shall discuss in regard to the prayer of petition is whether we should pray for ourselves alone or for others as well. We can state as a general principle that we can and ought to pray not only for ourselves but for any person who is capable of attaining eternal glory. The doctrines of the communion of saints and the Mystical Body make this possible, and Christian charity makes it an obligation. As St. James says: "Pray for one another, that you may be saved" (Jas. 5:16).

We can summarize this doctrine in the following statements:

1) We should pray for all those whom we are obliged to love, namely, all those who are capable of eternal salvation, including sinners, heretics, the excommunicated, our own enemies, etc. It suffices to pray for these latter in general, however, as long as we do not positively exclude anyone.

2) Ordinarily we are not obliged to pray in particular for our enemies, although this would be a mark of greater perfection.[15] Nevertheless, there may be occasions in which we are obliged to pray for a particular enemy; e.g., when he is in grave spiritual need, when he asks pardon, or to avoid scandal by refusing to pray for an individual. Jesus expressly commands: "Love your enemies, do good to those who hate you, and pray for those who persecute and calumniate you" (Matt. 5:44).

3) We ought to pray for the souls in purgatory at least out of charity, sometimes out of piety (members of our own family) or out of justice (if some souls are in purgatory through our bad example or evil influence).

4) It is possible for us to pray for the increase of the accidental glory of the blessed in heaven, though we can do nothing to increase their essential glory, which is immutable for all eternity.

5) It would be useless and unlawful to pray for the condemned, but since we cannot know for certain who are condemned, we may pray for any of the deceased on the condition that if they are in need of our prayers and can benefit from our suffrages, we offer them for that purpose.

DIFFICULTIES IN PRAYER

Before proceeding to a consideration of other kinds of prayer, we shall discuss the two main sources of difficulty in the practice of prayer: distractions and dryness. It goes without saying that these difficulties are not restricted to the prayer of petition nor to any particular type of prayer; consequently, what is said here should be applied to all of the grades of prayer which we shall discuss shortly.

[15]Cf. St. Thomas, *Summa,* II-II, q. 83, a. 8.

DISTRACTIONS IN PRAYER

Since prayer is an operation of the practical intellect under the impetus of the will, by its very nature it requires attention, as does any other intellectual operation. St. Gregory says that God does not hear the prayer of those who pay no attention to their prayer. But there are various degrees of attention, and not every type of prayer requires the same degree of attention; indeed, in the higher grades of prayer it would seem that the individual pays no attention at all to the act of prayer as such. With beginners in the practice of prayer, on the other hand, there may be a great deal of attention, but the prayer is as yet very imperfect.

Attention

In order to understand this apparent paradox it is necessary to consider the kinds of attention which can be used in prayer and the psychology of habit formation. Since prayer is conversation with God, it involves the use of words, whether one read or speak or merely think them. In the act of praying, one may focus his attention on any one of three elements: the words themselves (e.g., to pronounce them correctly or use them rightly), the meaning of the words and content of the prayer as a whole, or the one to whom the prayer is addressed and the purpose of the prayer. In vocal prayer it is essential that one be attentive to the words which are spoken; in meditation one must give attention to the meaning of the words; but in any kind of prayer the most important element is to fix the mind on God by the third kind of attention.[16]

Like any other human activity, the practice of prayer can become habitual, and therefore it falls under the laws of habit formation. Habits are acquired by the repetition of acts, and as a habit becomes more deeply rooted and perfected, the acts which flow from it are more facile, more pleasant and require less actual attention. For that reason habits are said to be "second nature." In the practice of prayer a beginner will have to give scrupulous attention to all the details and mechanics of prayer so that he will learn to do things correctly from the start. Thus a child learning the Rosary will carefully pronounce each word of the vocal prayers, and the beginner in meditation will follow some method. But as one becomes more facile in the practice of prayer, the focal point of attention changes from words and methods and other mechanical details to the content of the prayer and the purpose of the prayer. Attention is still present—as indeed it must be for all prayer—but it is a different and more excellent type of attention. At this stage one recites the Rosary with practically no awareness of the words or their meaning but with attention to a given mystery, or one's attention in mental prayer has shifted from methods and devices to the content and purpose of the meditation. At this point the soul is liberated, so to speak, so that it can soar to the higher grades

---

[16]Cf. St. Thomas, *ibid.*, a. 13.

of prayer in which the mind is fixed on God so strongly that it forgets all other things.[17]

But however much one endeavors to keep his attention fixed on one thing, he cannot do so for an extended period of time. Even in the act of concentration the human mind wavers, if only for a second. Fixed attention becomes all the more difficult as the object of one's concentration is more lofty or the time spent in concentration is longer.[18] There is, of course, a great discrepancy in the powers of concentration and attention of various individuals, due to temperament and training, but the human mind is also limited by the inherent weaknesses of man's psychosomatic structure.

Nature of distractions

Our concern with distractions in prayer is not from the viewpoint of their effect on the merit of prayer, but their effect on the practice of prayer as such.[19] Whether voluntary or involuntary, a distraction consists in any alien thought or imagination which prevents the mind from attending to that which it is doing. If the distraction affects the external senses or internal senses only, the mind can still give attention to what it is doing, but with difficulty. If the distraction consists in an alien thought in the mind itself, attention is completely destroyed, or rather, it is shifted to another object. Divided attention or the complete lack of attention in the performance of actions which involve manual operations or bodily movements (e.g., walking, dancing, eating) does not necessarily affect the perfection of the operation,[20] but when it is a question of the operation of the higher faculties, some degree of attention is absolutely necessary. Distractions in prayer, therefore, will always render it less perfect or will nullify it completely.

Causes of distractions

We have stated that distractions in prayer may be voluntary or involuntary. In either case they are obstacles to prayer, and they must be reduced and ultimately eliminated if one is to make progress in this spiritual exercise. To achieve this it is necessary to examine the following causes from which distractions spring:

---

[17]Cf. *loc. cit.*

[18]See *Summa,* II-II, q. 83, a. 14, where St. Thomas states that prayer should continue as long as fervor is aroused and that it should end when weariness sets in, whether it be a question of private prayer or public prayer. St. Augustine seems to commend the practice of many short, fervent prayers, and warns against forcing attention in prayer.

[19]If one has the proper intention at the beginning of prayer and then suffers involuntary distractions, the merit of the prayer is not destroyed nor is its impetratory value lost, but one does thereby lose some or all of the spiritual refreshment of prayer (cf. St. Thomas, *ibid.*, a. 13).

[20]This applies also to the acquired virtues, so far as their external acts are concerned. One may perform the external act of a virtue perfectly and yet lack the interior dispositions which make it a truly virtuous act.

1) *Constitutional factors*: nervous or sanguine temperament; vivid and unstable imagination; weak powers of concentration; vehement and uncontrolled passions; sensate nature.[21]

2) *Physical or mental illness*: brain disorders; glandular malfunction; physical exhaustion; mental fatigue; neurotic traits; psychotic predispositions.[22]

3) *Character defects*: any acquired habits which are inimical to the practice of prayer (lack of recollection; dissipation; lukewarmness; vain curiosity; slothfulness; lust; gluttony; pride).

4) *Improper spiritual direction*: if the spiritual director imposes his own preconceived ideas upon the individual without understanding the needs of the soul, the capacity of the soul, and the movements of grace in the soul (e.g., to force a soul to practice meditation when God moves the soul to a higher degree of prayer).

5) *The devil*: with God's permission the devil sometimes acts directly on the external and internal senses, or indirectly distracts from prayer by working through any of the other causes enumerated.

6) *Unsuitable circumstances*: uncomfortable posture; improper time; external noises; lack of proximate preparation; excessive heat or cold; etc.

Remedies

There is no infallible method for ridding oneself of all distractions in prayer because, as we have seen, it is the nature of the human mind to waver in its attention. Nevertheless, this does not excuse us from doing the best we can to pray with full attention and to forestall possible distractions to the best of our ability. To this end, one should approach prayer with a recollected spirit, putting aside all concerns and interests and entering into prayer with the simple and pure motive of addressing God. In particular, one should prevent external distractions by selecting the proper time and place and a reasonably comfortable posture for prayer. When this is not possible, one should make every effort to withdraw oneself mentally from one's surroundings and to enter into the cell of the heart to speak with God. Even more important, one should rid oneself of internal sources of distraction by putting aside all thoughts of one's duties, anxieties, interests, etc., except so far as they may be the subject matter of one's prayer. In a word, it is necessary to give full attention

[21]Since temperament and other constitutional factors are radically fixed and subject only to secondary modification, some persons may never succeed in totally eliminating distractions from their prayer life. They will do the best they can and trust that God will forgive their frailty (cf. St. Thomas, *ibid.*, a. 13, ad 3). These factors should be considered in the selection of candidates for the contemplative religious life.

[22]In certain types of physical or mental illness the patient will be unable to concentrate on anything at all, unless it be himself and his suffering. In such cases the most that can be expected in the practice of prayer will be occasional aspirations and short vocal prayers.

to the duty of the moment, which in this instance is the practice of prayer. As a remote preparation for prayer the following points are of special importance: a spirit of silence and recollection, avoidance of vain curiosity, custody of the senses, spiritual reading practiced faithfully, and the practice of mortification.

DRYNESS IN PRAYER

Aridity or dryness in the practice of prayer consists in a certain inability to produce the necessary intellectual and affective acts, or in an actual distaste for prayer. It is usually encountered in the practice of mental prayer, and it reaches its most painful state in the higher stages of mystical prayer when it seems that God has abandoned the soul completely.

Causes of dryness

Dryness in prayer may be caused by the individual, by God or by the devil, but those who actually experience dryness should first suspect that they themselves are the cause. Among the internal and involuntary causes of dryness we may list the following: bad health, bodily fatigue, excessive activity or absorbing duties, vehement and prolonged temptations which exhaust one's powers, improper training in the practice of prayer, methods of prayer unsuited to the individual, etc. Sometimes, however, dryness is the natural result of one's own imperfections: lukewarmness in the service of God, infidelity to grace, habitual venial sin, habits of sensuality, vain curiosity, instability and superficiality, excessive activism, etc.

At other times dryness may be sent by God as a purification or a test. After a soul has become somewhat adept in the practice of prayer, God usually deliberately withdraws all sensible consolation so that the soul will be purified of any excessive attachment to such consolation, will be humbled at seeing how little it can do without God's help, and will thus be disposed for the next grade of prayer. Throughout one's advancement in the life of prayer this alternation between dryness and consolation is usually perceptible at regular intervals, and especially when God is preparing the soul for some new advance or some greater grace. If the dryness is prolonged over a long period, in spite of the soul's fidelity to grace and earnest efforts, one may suspect that the soul is entering upon the night of the senses or some other passive purification.

If, however, there is every indication that the dryness is caused by the devil, the soul should strive to be faithful in the practice of prayer, even if this means that it must return from a higher grade of prayer to the simple recitation of vocal prayers. The important thing is that the soul do the best it can and under no pretext give up the practice of prayer, for that is precisely the goal which the devil seeks to achieve.

Remedies for dryness

But since one should always suspect that dryness in prayer is due to his own weakness and imperfection, the best remedy is to correct any defects in the practice of prayer, and especially lukewarmness and negligence in the service of God. If the causes of the dryness are beyond one's control, the best thing to do is to resign oneself to the trial for as long a time as God wills, to realize that sensible devotion and consolation are not essential to the true love of God, to humble oneself with a sense of one's unworthiness, and to persevere in prayer at any cost. The periods of involuntary dryness can be periods of great merit and purification, especially if one unites himself with the suffering Christ in the Garden of Gethsemane.

FURTHER PITFALLS

Other pitfalls which should be avoided in the practice of prayer are the following:

1) Purely mechanical recitation of vocal prayers and lifeless routine in the practice of mental prayer.

2) Excessive personal effort, as if one were able to do all by sheer force, or undue passivity and inertia, as if one should leave all to God alone.

3) Discouragement at not perceiving the consolations which one expected, or rash optimism that one is farther advanced in prayer than one really is.

4) Attachment to sensible consolation, which causes in the soul a certain spiritual gluttony which impels one to seek the consolations of God rather than the God of consolations.

5) Persistence in the use of a particular method, as if that were the only possible method, or premature abandonment of a method.

2: GRADES OF PRAYER

We are indebted to St. Teresa of Avila for the clearest and best classification of the grades of prayer which has ever been compiled. Being a contemplative by vocation, it is natural that this great saint should have traced the path to sanctity according to the grades of prayer. Her concept that the intensity of one's life of prayer coincides with the intensity of one's charity is based on solid theology and was confirmed by St. Pius X in a letter to the Carmelites, in which he stated that the grades of prayer taught by St. Teresa represent so many grades of elevation and ascent toward Christian perfection.[1] These grades of prayer are: 1) vocal prayer; 2) meditation; 3) affective prayer; 4) prayer of simplicity; 5) infused recollection; 6) prayer of quiet; 7) prayer of union; 8) prayer of ecstatic union; 9) prayer of transforming union. In this chapter we will discuss the first four grades of prayer, which belong to the predominantly ascetical stage of the spiritual life. Contemplation, infused recollection and the prayer of quiet will be treated in the chapter immediately following and the various prayers of union in a final chapter on prayer.

VOCAL PRAYER

The first thing to be noted is that, although we classify the grades of prayer under the headings of ascetical and mystical, there may be mystical prayer in the early stages of the spiritual life and there may be a return to ascetical activity on the part of the souls who are well advanced in mystical ways. Hence it is important to keep in mind that what is meant by ascetical and mystical signifies that which is predominant and not that which is exclusive.

[1]Letter of March 7, 1914, cited by J. de Guibert, S.J., *Documenta ecclesiastica christianae perfectionis studium spectantia,* n. 636.

NECESSITY OF VOCAL PRAYER

Little remains to be said concerning vocal prayer, since much of what we have already written concerning the prayer of petition applies to this first grade of prayer. By vocal prayer we mean any form of prayer which is expressed in words, whether written or spoken. This kind of prayer is practically the only form used in public or liturgical prayer, but it is also much used by private individuals. In speaking of the use of vocal prayer, St. Thomas states that the public prayers recited by the ministers of the Church, in which the faithful are expected to participate, should always be vocal.[2] He then gives three reasons why vocal prayer is also suitable for private individuals: 1) to arouse interior devotion; 2) to give homage to God with our body as well as our mind and heart; 3) to give vent, by way of overflow, to the spiritual sentiments that flood the soul in prayer.

In view of the foregoing reasons, we should observe that our consideration of vocal prayer as the first grade in the practice of prayer is not restricted to prayer of petition (although petition would surely be included); what we would wish to emphasize rather is the use of vocal prayer as a means of arousing one's devotion or of expressing one's deep love for God. In this sense, it is readily seen how vocal prayer leads naturally to the second grade of prayer, which is meditation. Moreover, the use of vocal prayer, understood in this way, depends upon, and is subordinate to, mental prayer. In this wider context of vocal prayer we include both public liturgical prayer and individual private prayer as the expression by the Church and individuals of their worship, love, thanksgiving, contrition and all the other sentiments which spring up in the human heart in reference to God.[3]

CONDITIONS FOR VOCAL PRAYER

The two requirements for vocal prayer are attention and piety. What we have already said concerning the attention required for prayer of petition has application here also; we would merely add that attention may be actual or virtual.[4] Actual attention is present when the person who prays has complete awareness of what he is doing here and now; virtual attention is that which is had at the beginning of prayer and extends throughout the prayer without being retracted, although there may be involuntary distractions. St. Teresa says in this regard:

---

[2]Cf. *Summa,* II-II, q. 83, a. 12.

[3]All things being equal, public and liturgical prayer is much more profitable and gives greater glory to God than does private prayer. Nevertheless, honor is in the one honoring, and therefore those who are most fervent in love are capable of the most perfect prayer. The liturgical prayers of the Church have a special efficacy, however, by reason of the intervention of the Church as spouse of Christ.

[4]Although some authors speak of habitual attention, which perdures while persons practiced in prayer are asleep or occupied in some other task, we consider it an excessive extension and an abuse of the word.

As far as I am able to understand, the door of entry into this castle is prayer and meditation; I do not say mental prayer rather than vocal prayer, for to be prayer at all it must be made with consideration. For that prayer which does not attend to the one it is addressing and what it asks and who it is that asks and of whom it asks, such I do not call prayer at all, however much one may move the lips. For although it is true that sometimes it will be true prayer even if one does not take heed of these things, it is more truly prayer on those occasions when one does. But if one is accustomed to speak to the majesty of God as he would speak to his servant, without taking care whether he speaks badly but says whatever comes to his lips because he has learned it through doing it repeatedly, I do not consider such an activity prayer, and God grant that no Christian should have this habit.[5]

GRADES OF PRAYER

The second requirement—piety—is complementary to that of attention. It goes without saying that we do not mean by piety the sensible consolation or sentimentality which sometimes accompanies prayer. By attention we apply our intellect to the practice of prayer; by piety we direct our will to God. Piety, therefore, involves several virtues: charity, vitalized faith, confidence, humility, devotion, reverence and perseverance.[6] Piety is so important for vocal prayer that it would be better by far to recite one Our Father piously and devoutly than to say many prayers in a routine and mechanical fashion, unless it is a question of prayers which must be recited by reason of some obligation. Piety should also be the measure for the duration of one's personal vocal prayers, for it is futile to attempt to pray well when one is fatigued. By the same token, public prayers should also be arranged in such a way that they arouse the devotion of the faithful and do not cause them tedium. "But in praying, do not multiply words as the Gentiles do; for they think by saying a great deal they will be heard. So do not be like them; for your Father knows what you need before you ask him" (Matt. 6:7-8).

FORMULAS OF PRAYER

As regards the formulas to be used in vocal prayer, it is not possible to give any fixed rule or detailed directions. Perhaps the best principle to follow is that given for the selection of books for one's spiritual reading, namely, to use that which is beneficial. The words by which we express ourselves in vocal prayer will vary with our needs and our spiritual sentiments. Moreover, some persons find it very difficult to express themselves, and therefore they make use of the prayers composed by others. Objectively, the best prayers are usually those which have been composed by the Church and the saints and inserted in the liturgy. There is no better vocal prayer than the Our Father, which was taught us by Christ himself, and the prayers which have been culled from the pages of Scripture: the *Ave Maria, Gloria,* psalms, etc. Unfortunately, their

[5]*Interior Castle,* First Mansions, Bk. I, Chap. 7; St. Thomas teaches the same doctrine in more technical language in *Summa,* II-II, q. 83, a. 13.

[6]Cf. St. Thomas, *ibid.,* a. 14.

constant repetition easily causes us to recite them in a purely mechanical fashion, oblivious of the sentiments which they contain.

The necessity of fervent recitation of vocal prayer cannot be emphasized too much, because vocal prayer is one type of prayer that can never be omitted completely, even when one arrives at the height of sanctity. The time comes in the practice of mental prayer when the inferior grades yield to the superior grades as one progresses in union with God, but this never occurs with vocal prayer. It is always beneficial, either to arouse devotion or to give expression to the intensity and fervor of one's love of God. Any attacks on the practice of vocal prayer must, therefore, be interpreted as the sign of an evil spirit, and this spirit has been manifested by many deluded souls and false mystics in the history of spirituality.

MEDITATION

DEFINITION

Discursive meditation can be defined as a reasoned application of the mind to some supernatural truth in order to penetrate its meaning, love it and carry it into practice with the assistance of grace. The distinguishing note of meditation is that it is a reasoned or discursive type of prayer, and therefore attention is absolutely indispensable. As soon as one ceases to reason or discurse, he ceases to meditate. He may have given way to distraction, deliberately turned his mind to something else, passed on to affective prayer or contemplation, but without discursus there is no meditation.

NATURE OF MEDITATION

How, then, is meditation distinguished from simple study or speculation on a supernatural truth? Unlike the latter activities, meditation is a form of prayer, and it is such by reason of its purpose or finality. Actually, meditation has a double finality, one intellectual and the other affective and practical. The intellectual purpose is to arrive at firm convictions concerning some supernatural truth; hence the importance of the intellect in meditation. But one could acquire firm convictions by speculative study, and therefore this cannot be the principal finality of meditation nor that which makes meditation true prayer. The most important element in meditation is the act of love aroused in the will on the presentation of some supernatural truth by the intellect. If one were to spend the entire period of meditation on speculative discursus, he would not have prayed but speculated. As St. Teresa points out, meditation consists not so much in thinking a great deal but in loving a great deal.[7] When the will bursts forth with acts of love, an intimate and profound

[7]Cf. *Interior Castle,* Fourth Mansions, Bk. I, Chap. 7.

contact is established between the soul and God, and then it is that the soul can truly be said to be praying. Far from being the goal of meditation, discursus is merely a kind of disposition and necessary preparation for the arousal of love.

Resolution

But neither is a meditation complete when the individual has been aroused to love the supernatural truth on which he has speculated; there is yet a final step for the completion and perfection of meditation—the practical resolution. Any meditation that is properly made should terminate in a practical resolution for the future. Love cannot be idle; by its very nature it urges one to action. When the meditation has passed through the steps of discursus and acts of love, therefore, charity itself impels one to put love into action. Failure to make efficacious resolutions is the reason why many souls who practice daily meditation get little or no practical benefit from this exercise of prayer. They insist too much on that which is merely a preparation for prayer properly speaking. They pass the time in simple spiritual reading or study or in distractions of one sort or another, but there does not come forth from their hearts a single act of love, nor do they make any practical concrete resolutions.

Subjects of meditation

One final element of the definition of meditation requires explanation: that of the subject matter. We have stated that meditation is the reasoned discursus on some supernatural truth, meaning any truth related to God and the spiritual life. By reason of the subject matter, some authors have made a further division of meditation into imaginative meditation, dogmatic meditation, liturgical meditation, moral meditation, etc. Whether or not such classifications are warranted, it is true that one can meditate on a variety of subjects; e.g., some scene or mystery from the life of Christ, the life and virtues of Mary or the saints, some particular virtue to be acquired or vice to be uprooted, a truth from dogmatic theology, such as the attributes of God or the indwelling of the Trinity, the prayers and actions of the sacraments, the Mass and the liturgy, etc.

The basic guiding principle as regards subject matter is to select that which is needed at a particular time and will be beneficial according to one's capacities. Consequently, it is important to insist upon prudence in the selection of the material for meditation. Not all subject matters are suited for all souls, not even for a given soul in varying circumstances. In general, young people or beginners in the practice of meditation will do well to utilize what has been called imaginative meditation (scenes from the life of Christ, Mary and the saints), liturgical meditations or moral meditations (which help one to uproot vices, avoid sin and cultivate virtue).

METHODS OF MEDITATION

As regards the various methods of meditation, two extremes are to be avoided: excessive rigidity and instability. At the beginning of the practice of prayer it is generally necessary to adhere to some method or other, because as yet the soul does not know how to proceed in the life of prayer. In these early stages it is of great importance that the soul not only follow a method but that it select the most beneficial method, for the needs of souls are not identical. As the soul progresses in the practice of prayer, however, and is more at ease in conversing with God, the method becomes less and less important and eventually may even become an obstacle to further progress. Methods of prayer are like crutches to a man with an injured leg; he needs crutches as long as he cannot walk alone, but he should put away the crutches as soon as he has regained the use of his limb; otherwise the crutches will prevent him from walking on his own two feet. It should also be noted that, since the individual is not usually the best judge of his own needs, a prudent and wise spiritual director is of great help in leading the soul from one grade of prayer to another, as long as he himself is not slavishly addicted to one method exclusively.

Although ancient writers such as Cassian and St. Bernard spoke about methods of prayer, it was not until the sixteenth century that spiritual writers began to offer detailed methods of discursive prayer. Since that time, methods of prayer have been compiled or adapted by such writers as Louis of Granada, O.P., St. Peter Alcántara, O.F.M., Jerome Gracián, O.C.D., St. Ignatius Loyola, St. Francis de Sales, St. Alphonsus Liguori, St. John Baptist de la Salle and Cardinal Bérulle. We shall content ourselves with offering the outlines of the most popular methods of prayer and leave the others to the personal research of the reader.[8]

Method of St. Ignatius Loyola:[9]

Preparation	acts of faith and reverence in the presence of God
	general preparatory prayer to ask the grace of making a good meditation
	composition of place (exercise of the imagination)
	petition for the special grace sought in the meditation
Body of the meditation	exercise of the memory to recall the material to be meditated upon
	exercise of the intellect by reflection and consideration of the material of the meditation and practical applications and conclusions to be drawn from it
	exercise of the will by arousing devout feelings and affections and by making practical, particular resolutions
Conclusion	colloquy or conversation with God
	vocal prayer, such as Our Father, Hail Mary, etc.

[8]For detailed explanations, cf. *Methods of Mental Prayer* by Cardinal Lercaro.

[9]St. Ignatius composed at least six methods of meditation, as can be seen in his *Spiritual Exercises.*

Method of St. Francis de Sales:

Before meditation: preparation of material; use of books recommended

Immediate preparation
- exercise of the presence of God
- invocation to God
- representation of the mystery or composition of place

Body of meditation
- considerations (exercise of the intellect)
- exercise of the will (affections, colloquy, resolutions)

Conclusion
- act of thanksgiving
- act of offering
- act of petition

After meditation
- spiritual reflections
- recollection
- return to duties of one's state
- immediate execution of resolutions

Method of St. Alphonsus Liguori:

Preparation
- acts of faith and adoration
- acts of humility and contrition
- petition for light

Body of meditation
- meditation or reflection (from a book)
- affections of faith, adoration and love
- renunciation, oblation, resignation, conformity to God's will
- prayer of petition
- practical resolutions

Conclusion
- thanksgiving
- purpose to carry out resolutions
- request for God's help to be faithful
- petition for one's neighbors, souls in purgatory, etc.

After meditation
- spiritual reflections
- put resolutions into practice
- preserve recollection

Method of Saint Sulpice:

Remote preparation: life of recollection and solid piety

Proximate preparation	select meditation material the night previous go to sleep thinking of the material make meditation as soon as possible after rising
Immediate preparation	place oneself in the presence of God acts of humility and contrition invocation of Holy Ghost: *Veni Sancte Spiritus*
First point of meditation (adoration)	consider words or actions of Jesus or some saint render homage and veneration, thanksgiving, etc.
Second point of meditation (communion)	convince oneself of necessity of practicing virtue in question sorrow for the past, confusion for the present and desire for the future petition God for virtue in question
Third point of meditation (co-operation)	form a particular resolution renew resolution of particular examen
Conclusion	thanksgiving to God ask pardon for faults committed petition blessings on one's resolutions and whole life spiritual reflection for the rest of the day place all in Mary's hands: *Sub tuum praesidium*

Carmelite Method:[10]

Introduction	preparation reading
Meditation	imaginative representation of material reflection or meditation properly so called affective colloquy or conversation with God
Conclusion	thanksgiving oblation petition

[10]Cf. also *Conversation with Christ* by Peter-Thomas Rohrbach, O.C.D. See note 8.

As is evident from the outlines given above, all meditation can be reduced ultimately to a basic framework which contains all the essential parts or very soul of meditation: consideration of some supernatural truth, application of that truth to one's life and personal needs, and the resolution to do something about it. These three steps, we believe, are absolutely essential for true meditation; the other details may be used or not according to the needs of individual souls.

PRACTICE OF MEDITATION

Before leaving the consideration of the second grade of prayer, we shall discuss briefly a few details which are related to the practice of meditation.

Time for meditation

The first is a question of the proper time for meditation. It is better by far to select the most opportune time of the day and then to endeavor to observe that same time each day. Regularity in prayer is of extreme importance, for it is very easy for a person to alter the schedule, then change the time for any pretext whatever, and ultimately abandon the practice of prayer. As regards the most opportune time, it should be noted that not all times are equally satisfactory. As a general rule it is more difficult to meditate after a heavy meal, immediately after recreation, or when the mind is distracted or fatigued by many occupations. Most writers on the spiritual life state that the best times for meditation are early in the morning, the late afternoon before the evening meal, or late at night when one has finished all the duties and occupations of the day. But even this cannot be given as a hard and fast rule, and perhaps the best norm to be followed is to meditate when one's mind is most alert and one can be recollected.[11]

Duration of meditation

The duration of meditation cannot be the same for all individuals or for all states of life. It should, as far as possible, be adjusted to the needs of each. Religious, however, are usually obliged by their constitutions to devote a definite period of time to mental prayer. Although it is possible to find a variety of opinions concerning the length of time to be spent in meditation, it is reasonable to state that, if the time spent in meditation is too brief, most of the period is used in getting ready to pray and not in actual prayer; but if the time is too long, devotion is stifled and the period assigned for prayer becomes a period of penance.[12]

---

[11]The time for meditation presents a problem in many religious communities devoted to the active life, and it would seem to be more prudent to allow local superiors to set the time for meditation according to the need and circumstances of the community rather than attempt to follow a universal rule throughout the entire religious institute.

[12]St. Alphonsus Liguori maintains that beginners should not spend more than a half hour at meditation, but the time should gradually be increased as they advance in the practice of prayer. St. Francis de Sales and St. Ignatius Loyola stipulate one hour as the normal length of time for meditation.

St. Thomas Aquinas teaches that prayer should last as long as the soul is in a state of fervor and devotion, and that it should terminate when it can no longer be prolonged without tedium and continual distractions.[13] One must take care, however, not to yield to negligence and sloth under the pretext of not being able to pray without distraction or fatigue. Whatever the length of time given to meditation, it should never be considered as a spiritual exercise which is isolated and unconnected with the rest of the spiritual life. Its influence should be felt throughout the whole day, and in this way, as St. Thomas suggests, prayer should be constant and uninterrupted.[14] The practice of meditation will be greatly assisted by the assiduous use of fervent ejaculatory prayers which will preserve the fire of devotion throughout the day. The important thing is that one lead a life of prayer; without it, one can hope to gain little benefit from the particular times set aside for meditation.

Place and posture

We have already spoken of the place and posture for prayer when we treated of vocal prayer, but something further needs to be said concerning meditation. The church is the most fitting place for meditation, because of the sanctity of the place, the presence of Christ in the Eucharist, and the solitude and recollection which are usually found there. Meditation can be made in any place, however, in which a person can be recollected and can concentrate on the material of the meditation. Here again it is a question of particular dispositions, and the best rule of conduct is that which is based on one's personal experience.

In regard to the posture during meditation, it is of great importance because of the necessity of recollection and attention in discursive prayer. The posture should be humble and respectful, but it need not be any particular posture. Some persons may find it most effective to meditate while kneeling, but for others the discomfort may prove a cause of distraction. But whether kneeling, seated or standing, two extremes should be avoided: excessive comfort and excessive mortification. If one is too comfortable, he will find it difficult to keep his mind on the material of meditation or may even fall asleep; if one's posture is too uncomfortable, it will be a cause of distraction and will soon kill devotion.

CONCLUSION

From what has been stated, it should be evident that the practice of meditation is a great spiritual help. A great number of persons who live habitually in the state of sin continue in that state simply because they never reflect seriously upon the state of their souls. Some of them do not have malicious hearts nor do they hate the things of God or their own salvation; they have simply given themselves entirely to purely natural activities and have for-

[13]Cf. *Summa,* II-II, q. 83, a. 14.
[14]Cf. *loc cit.*

gotten those things that are of importance to their soul. As a result, they have been easily overwhelmed by the impetus of their disordered passions and have passed year after year in the state of sin. One of the greatest proofs that their sad condition is due not so much to malice as to the lack of reflection and introspection is the fact that when they return to the practice of their religion, or attend a retreat or mission, they usually experience a strong impression which leads them to a complete conversion of life.

With good reason does St. Alphonsus Liguori maintain that the practice of mental prayer is incompatible with the state of sin. It is, therefore, a great help for salvation to cultivate the practice of daily meditation.

Sanctification, self-knowledge, profound humility, recollection, mortification and many other things which are necessary for the attainment of perfection are morally impossible to a person who does not practice meditation. A person who aspires to sanctity by giving himself completely to the active life while neglecting the life of prayer may just as well forget about Christian perfection. Experience proves that there is absolutely nothing that can supply for the life of prayer, not even the daily reception of the Eucharist. There are many persons who receive Communion every day, yet their spiritual life is mediocre and lukewarm. The reason is none other than the lack of mental prayer, either because they omit it entirely or they practice it in a mechanical and routine fashion. We repeat that without prayer it is impossible to attain Christian perfection, no matter what our state of life or the occupation to which we dedicate ourselves. The spiritual director must insist constantly on the faithful practice of mental prayer.

AFFECTIVE PRAYER

Although St. Teresa of Avila does not use this expression in any of her writings, she does refer to this grade of prayer,[15] and it has been accepted by all the schools of spirituality. One of the first writers to use the name affective prayer was Alvarez de Paz, following the Jesuit, Antonio Cordeses.[16]

ITS NATURE

Affective prayer may be defined as a type of prayer in which the operations of the will predominate over discursus of the intellect. We do not believe that there is any specific difference between affective prayer and meditation, as there is between meditation and contemplation. It is merely a simplified

[15]Cf. *The Life,* Chap. 13.
[16]Cf. Alvarez de Paz, *De inquisitione pacis.*

meditation in which the heart predominates; nothing more. For this reason the transition from meditation to affective prayer is usually gradual and more or less easy, depending on the temperament of the individual, the effort that is made, the education received, and the method used. Some persons are by nature so affectionate and responsive that they very easily rise from intellectual discursus to the movement of the will. Sometimes the slightest reflection is sufficient to arouse their affection. Others, on the contrary, are so cold and rigid by nature that their prayer is almost entirely discursive and they seldom give expression to affections of the will. Such individuals need more time and more practice to arrive at the practice of affective prayer. It should be noted that the method of St. Ignatius is not as conducive to affective prayer as is the simpler method used by the Carmelites and the Franciscans.

When should one expect to make the transition from discursive meditation to affective prayer? Two extremes must be avoided: to leave meditation too quickly or too late. In practice, however, these extremes can easily be avoided if one takes care to simplify discursive meditation gradually, without trying to force oneself. One should never use violence in order to arouse the affections of the will, but should give oneself to these movements if one feels the attraction of grace to do so. It is almost certain that any person who practices daily meditation will from time to time experience the inclination to yield to affections of the will which have been stimulated by some particular point in the meditation. When this occurs, one should give himself gently to the movements of love, and as these moments become more and more frequent, the individual makes the transition from discursive meditation to affective prayer.

PRACTICE OF AFFECTIVE PRAYER

Discursive meditation is a requisite for the practice of affective prayer and should normally lead to this type of prayer. It would be impossible to have a prayer which is exclusively affective, because the will is a blind faculty which needs direction and enlightenment before it can love and desire the good. For that reason discursive meditation and spiritual reading play an important part in the practice of affective prayer, since they supply the material which will stimulate the activity of the will. Hence one must be careful not to terminate discursive meditation before the affections have been stimulated. This would be a waste of time and could also be the source of illusion. Neither should one force the affections; when they do not come forth spontaneously, or when they have run their course, one should return to discursive prayer and not try to prolong the affection by his own efforts.

Neither should the individual be anxious to pass from one affection to another. Rather, he should attempt gradually to simplify the movements of the will. It is important that the operations of the will be reduced to unity and that the affections be intense rather than numerous. The practice of affective prayer is best guaranteed by the use of discursive meditation, in which one considers the material point by point and pauses at any given moment in which the affections of the will have been stimulated. Gently and without any effort, one should yield to this affection until it has run its course, and then return to the next point in the meditation. This is likewise a commendable method to be followed in spiritual reading or in the use of a manual of prayer. As soon as some thought has stimulated and aroused a movement of the will, one should stop reading and allow the will to perform its operation.

THE VALUE OF AFFECTIVE PRAYER

If properly used, affective prayer confers many benefits on the soul. Psychologically, it provides a delightful respite from the dry labor of discursive meditation. It also prevents the individual from becoming excessively introspective or relying too greatly upon his own efforts, as could happen easily if one were to devote himself exclusively to discursive meditation and never allow the will to break forth in acts of love. Spiritually, since affective prayer is essentially an operation of the will, it is effective in deepening the union of the soul with God by acts of love. And since all of the infused virtues are increased with the increase of charity, affective prayer is a powerful means for growth in virtue. It is likewise a great stimulus for the practice of the Christian virtues because of the sweetness and consolation which it gives. It is, lastly, an excellent disposition and preparation for the prayer of simplicity and eventually for infused contemplation.

POSSIBLE DANGERS

But certain dangers and abuses must be avoided in the practice of affective prayer. First of all, one should never use force in order to produce the affections and movements of the will. Since these affections are acts of the will and the will as such is not subject to force and violence, it is of no avail to clench one's fist, to distort one's face, and to groan or sigh in an effort to produce an intense act of the love of God. The act of love must be aroused spontaneously, and this is best effected by supernaturalizing one's motives and striving in all things simply and solely to give glory to God out of pure love.

Another possible danger in the practice of affective prayer lies in the fact that it often fills the heart with sensible consolation. Those who are easily stimulated to movements of affection may erroneously judge themselves to be more advanced in perfection than they really are, because they feel at times as if they are going into ecstasy. Unfortunately, many of these persons see no contradiction in the fact that in their daily life they are constantly falling into imperfections and venial sins. True progress in the spiritual life consists in the ever more perfect practice of the Christian virtues and not in the sweetness which one experiences in prayer. Moreover, persons who place great value on sensible consolations are in danger of practicing prayer solely for the delight which it gives them. This is the spiritual gluttony which St. John of the Cross criticizes with severity.[17]

Lastly, there is the danger that persons who have tasted the delight and consolation of affective prayer may fall into a sterile slothfulness which will prevent them from returning to the discursive meditation which they had formerly practiced. It is a serious mistake to think that once the soul has enjoyed habitual affective prayer it need never return to the practice of meditation. St. Teresa warns her nuns that sometimes it is necessary to return to the lower grades of prayer after having been introduced to mystical contemplation.[18]

FRUITS OF THIS PRAYER

There is an infallible rule for judging the value of any kind of prayer: examine the fruits which it produces. This is the supreme norm for the discernment of spirit, as given by Christ himself.[19] The value of affective prayer cannot be measured by the intensity or the frequency of the sensible consolations which are experienced; it must be evaluated by the increasing perfection in the life of the individual. This means that the fruits of affective prayer should be a more intense practice of the Christian virtues, an increasing purity of intention, the practice of abnegation and detachment, an increase in charity, and the faithful and exact fulfillment of the duties of one's state in life. Affective prayer, in spite of the consolations which it gives, is not the goal or terminus of the life of prayer; it is only a step along the way to the perfection of prayer in the mystical state.

PRAYER OF SIMPLICITY

It seems that Bossuet was the first author to use this expression,[20] but this type of prayer was recognized by St. Teresa, who called it the prayer of acquired recollection, to distinguish it from infused recollection, which for her was the first grade of mystical contemplation.[21] Other authors call this type of prayer the prayer of simple gaze, of the presence of God, or of the simple vision of faith.

---

[17]Cf. *The Dark Night of the Soul,* Bk. I, Chap. 6.

[18]Cf. *Interior Castle,* Seventh Mansions, Chap. 4.

[19]Cf. Matt. 7:16.

[20]Cf. P. Pourrat, S.S., *Christian Spirituality* (Westminster, Md.: Newman, 1953-55), IV, 129.

[21]Cf. *The Way of Perfection,* Chaps. 28-29; *Interior Castle,* Fourth Mansions, Chap. 3.

In the seventeenth century some writers began to call this prayer acquired contemplation. St. John of the Cross and St. Teresa of Avila never used that expression, and while we do not see any inconvenience in admitting the type of prayer designated by that term (it is simply the prayer of acquired recollection according to St. Teresa or the prayer of simplicity according to Bossuet), we prefer to restrict the word contemplation to the mystical grades of prayer.

ITS NATURE

The prayer of simplicity was defined by Bossuet as a simple loving gaze upon some divine object, whether on God himself or one of his perfections, or on Christ or on one of his mysteries, or on some other Christian truth.[22] It is a form of ascetical prayer which is extremely simplified. The discursus formerly used in meditation has been transformed into a simple intellectual gaze; the affections which were experienced in affective prayer have been unified into a simple loving attention to God. The prayer is ascetical, meaning that the soul is able to attain to this type of prayer by its own efforts with the help of ordinary grace, but frequently one begins to experience the beginnings of infused prayer.

The prayer of simplicity is thus the transition point between ascetical and mystical prayer. It is, as it were, the final disposition before the Holy Ghost begins to operate in the soul by means of his gifts. For that reason, one frequently perceives a blending of acquired and infused elements in the practice of the prayer of simplicity. If the soul is faithful, the infused elements will gradually be increased until they dominate the practice of prayer entirely. Thus, without any violence and almost insensibly, the soul proceeds gently and gradually from the ascetical practice of prayer to mystical contemplation, and this is another proof of the unity of the spiritual life and of the fact that there is only one road to perfection.

PRACTICE OF THIS PRAYER

Because of its simplicity, there is no particular method for this type of prayer. It is simply a question of gazing and loving. It is useful, however, to keep in mind certain counsels. Before one actually enters upon the prayer of simplicity, great care must be taken not to try to hasten the entrance into this type of prayer. As long as one is able to meditate and to obtain benefit from meditation, he should continue practicing that type of prayer. Otherwise he would be in danger of falling into that spiritual sloth which St. Teresa classified as foolishness.[23]

The contrary extreme should likewise be avoided, namely, not to continue with the practice of meditation or even of affective prayer if one perceives

[22]Cf. Bossuet, *Manière courte et facile pour faire l'oraison en foi et de simple présence de Dieu.*

[23]Cf. *Interior Castle,* Fourth Mansions, Chap. 3.

clearly that the soul wishes to remain before God in a loving attention without any particular discursus or affective movement. St. John of the Cross severely criticizes those spiritual directors who try to keep souls restricted to the practice of discursive meditation when they have advanced far enough to enter the prayer of simplicity.[24]

During prayer

For the practice of the prayer of simplicity it is fitting that the soul dispose itself by means of some material, as was done in the use of simple meditation, but it should abandon it immediately if the attraction of grace so inclines. Nothing is lost if a person prepares himself for the prayer of simplicity by reading from a spiritual book or a manual of prayers, even if one is later moved by grace to turn the loving gaze of the soul to something else; but it would be a waste of time if one were merely to sit in idleness and wait for some material to come to mind spontaneously. The preparation that is made for the practice of the prayer of simplicity, however, should be very brief and should not be concerned with many details. The essence of the prayer of simplicity requires that the powers of the soul be intimately united in this loving gaze, and this requires in turn that the object of attention should be simple and unified.

During the practice of the prayer of simplicity the soul should strive to preserve the loving attention which is fixed on God, but without doing violence to itself. It must avoid distractions and empty sloth, but if it exerts too much effort it will destroy the simplicity of the prayer. Psychologically it is difficult for a person to remain attentive over a long period of time, and therefore one should not expect, at least not in the beginning, to be able to practice the prayer of simplicity for long periods of time. As soon as the loving attention begins to waver, one should turn to the use of affective prayer or simple meditation. All must be done gently and without violence. Nor should the soul be upset if periods of dryness occur. The prayer of simplicity is not always a sweet and consoling type of prayer. Since it represents the transition from ascetical to mystical prayer, the soul may begin to experience the aridity of the night of the senses.

FRUITS OF THIS PRAYER

The fruit of the prayer of simplicity should be manifested in a general improvement and progress in the Christian life in general. One's entire life and conduct should therefore benefit from the practice of this prayer. And since grace tends more and more to simplify our conduct until it is reduced to unity in love, we should foster this tendency by avoiding every kind of affectation and multiplicity in our relations with God and our neighbor. This simplification of life should characterize those who have entered upon the prayer of simplicity. It should be especially manifested in a deep and con-

[24]Cf. *The Living Flame of Love,* Chap. 3.

tinuous recollection in God. Even when occupied with the ordinary duties of daily life, the soul should be interiorly gazing upon God and loving him. The presence of God should be especially felt during liturgical prayer and in the recitation of vocal prayer. The examination of conscience should be so simplified that a rapid glance reveals the faults and imperfections of the day. All external works should be performed with the spirit of prayer and with the ardent desire of giving glory to God, and even the most common-place tasks should be penetrated with the spirit of faith and love.

All of the advantages of affective prayer over simple meditation should be found as well in the prayer of simplicity, but noticeably increased. As affective prayer is an excellent preparation for the prayer of simplicity, so the latter is a disposition for infused contemplation. With much less effort than before, the soul achieves magnificent results in the practice of prayer. So it is seen that each new grade of prayer represents a new advance in the Christian life.

3: CONTEMPLATIVE PRAYER

The prayer of simplicity marks the passage from ascetical prayer to mystical prayer. Strictly speaking, it is not possible to make a complete separation between the ascetical and the mystical grades of prayer as manifested in any particular soul, because the ascetical and the mystical aspects of the Christian life are so blended that persons in the ascetical state are capable of receiving certain mystical influences through the operations of the gifts of the Holy Ghost, and mystics may sometimes operate in a purely ascetical fashion when the gifts are not actually operating. The only thing that is certain is that in the ascetical state there will be a predominance of ascetical actions and in the mystical state the operations of the gifts of the Holy Ghost will be predominant. Consequently, it is not surprising that the operations of the gifts of the Holy Spirit should begin to predominate while the soul is in the highest grade of the ascetical life, namely, the practice of the prayer of simplicity.

The general name given to mystical prayer is that of infused contemplation, which admits of various grades or degrees. Before discussing the various grades, however, it is necessary to examine the nature of contemplation and the dispositions necessary to attain it.

CONTEMPLATION

The word contemplation signifies a type of knowledge which is accompanied by pleasure, and the object of the knowledge is usually of such a type that it arouses admiration and captivates the soul. Since contemplation is by its essence an operation of the cognitive powers, any one of the faculties of knowledge, whether vision, imagination or the intellect, is capable of performing a contemplative act more or less perfectly. Consequently, there is such a thing as a purely natural and acquired contemplation in the sensible, imaginative or intellectual order.

ITS NATURE

But contemplation is a distinctive type of knowledge. It is an experimental knowledge in the sense that it calls into play the affective powers of the individual, and these may be, like contemplation itself, on the purely sensible or on the spiritual plane. Contemplation is, therefore, an operation in which one experiences the happy blending of the cognitive and the affective powers in an activity which is at once intuitive and delightful. The knowledge involved is not speculative and discursive but experimental and intuitive; the movement of love is not toward the possession of the object of contemplation but one of surrender to the object that is loved. Perhaps the best example of natural contemplation is to be found in the aesthetic experience of the beautiful.

Supernatural contemplation

Supernatural or infused contemplation has been defined by various formulas throughout the centuries, but the essential note which all of the definitions have in common is that supernatural contemplation is an experimental knowledge of God. It goes without saying that our knowledge of God admits of various types. For example, by means of a sensible contemplation, one can gaze upon the created universe as a symbol or trace of God; one can picture in the imagination various scenes from the life of Christ; or one can consider theological truths and the mysteries of religion on a purely intellectual plane. For the supernatural contemplation of God, however, it is necessary that one possess supernatural faculties or powers, because an effect cannot be greater than its cause. When we speak of supernatural and infused contemplation, therefore, we must necessarily restrict the word to signify a type of contemplation which involves the operations of the supernatural faculties which flow from sanctifying grace.[1] What these supernatural faculties are can best be seen by stating them in the following series of conclusions:

1) *Infused contemplation is not a* gratia gratis data. There are several reasons for this statement: a) infused contemplation is substantially (*quoad substantiam*) supernatural and the *gratiae gratis datae* are only modally (*quoad modum*) supernatural; b) contemplation is ordained to the spiritual

[1]This statement is opposed to the doctrine of certain mystics, such as Eckhart, Ruysbroeck, Tauler, etc., who taught that the highest peak of contemplation consisted in the absolute quiet of the faculties. For them, the height of contemplation consisted in some kind of substantial contact or union between God and the substance of the soul. The human soul is not immediately operative, however, but operates through the faculties. Moreover, contemplation is meritorious, but it could not be so if it did not consist in the operation of the faculties. The only way in which the expressions of these mystics can be justified is to understand that the lofty contemplation of which they speak is so smooth and facile an operation that it gives the impression that there is no activity of the faculties. There is in fact an activity of the highest degree, although it is not experienced as such by the contemplatives.

good of him who receives it and the *gratiae gratis datae* are ordained to the good of others; c) infused contemplation is formally sanctifying and the *gratiae gratis datae* are not.

2) *Infused contemplation necessarily requires sanctifying grace.* Infused contemplation is never given without the operation of the gifts of the Holy Ghost, and these are inseparable from grace and charity. Moreover, contemplation is one of the effects of an intense love of God, which presupposes sanctifying grace, and at the same time it increases charity. Finally, contemplation would otherwise be a *gratia gratis data* and not formally sanctifying.

3) *In addition to sanctifying grace, contemplation requires the impulse of actual grace and charity.* The reason for this is that contemplation is a supernatural act, and therefore it requires a previous supernatural divine movement of actual grace.

4) *The ordinary actual grace which moves the infused virtue does not suffice for the contemplative act; contemplation further requires the actual grace which moves the habit of the gift of the Holy Ghost.* If the first part of this statement were not true, every act of an infused virtue of the intellectual order would be contemplative. The reason for the second part of the statement is that infused contemplation proceeds from the gifts of the Holy Ghost.

5) *In addition to habitual and actual grace, contemplation requires the habits of the infused virtues and the gifts of the Holy Ghost.* Sanctifying grace, which is to the spiritual life what the soul is to man's natural life, is not immediately operative, but it works through the faculties of the supernatural life, which are the infused virtues and the gifts of the Holy Ghost. Without these supernatural habits, actual grace would produce a supernatural act in a violent manner, whereas contemplation is an activity filled with sweetness and facility.

6) *No infused virtue or gift of the Holy Spirit of the affective order could be the immediate, formal and eliciting principle of the act of contemplation, although it may be an antecedent disposition or a consequent effect.* Contemplation is an elicited act of the intellect, and therefore the faculties from which it proceeds immediately are not faculties of the affective order. But the infused virtues of the affective order are necessary as dispositions or a preparation for contemplation, because it is impossible to have contemplation without the control of the passions. Consequently, the affective moral virtues remotely prepare for the contemplative act by rectifying the lower appetites, and the affective gifts of the Holy Spirit produce a purification of the senses and the passions. The affective theological virtues of hope and charity have a direct and immediate influence on the act of contemplation by elevating man to an intimate union with God, and the gifts of fear and wisdom which correspond to these affective theological virtues produce the passive

purification of the will, which is a most excellent proximate disposition for contemplation.[2]

7) *The immediate eliciting principle of contemplation is faith informed by charity and strengthened and perfected by the intellectual gifts of the Holy Ghost. Informed faith provides the substance of the act of contemplation, and the intellectual gifts of wisdom, knowledge and understanding provide the supernatural mode of operation.* Since the faculty in which contemplation takes place is the intellect, the habit by which contemplation is produced must also be intellectual. Moreover, this habit will necessarily be a virtue or gift which perfects the speculative intellect, because contemplation is an act of the speculative intellect. In addition to habitual grace, actual grace and the act of charity, therefore, contemplation requires the operation of the virtue of faith and the gifts of wisdom, understanding and knowledge.

Role of faith and the gifts

One and the same action, however, cannot proceed in exactly the same way from habits which are specifically distinct. Faith provides the substance of the act of contemplation by formally establishing contact with God as First Truth, but without giving any vision of the truth. Faith is of things that are not seen, and therefore its manner of knowledge is obscure. Faith provides the material for contemplation, but the intellectual gifts of the Holy Ghost are, as it were, the form. The virtue of charity plays its part in contemplation, not by establishing the formal contact with God, but as a proximate disposition which applies the object to the subject. Through charity the object of faith is made present to the subject in a connatural manner. It is, therefore, a dispositive element in contemplation, although it is indispensable that faith be informed by charity.

The intellectual gifts of the Holy Ghost provide the supernatural mode by which contemplation becomes an experimental knowledge and acquires a certain stability. The gifts depend on the operation of faith, and therefore the virtue of faith must operate in every contemplative act. As regards the intellectual gifts in particular, the gift of understanding provides the formal mystical knowledge by making the object present as something known.[3] The gift of wisdom conforms man with God by a certain adoptive filiation;[4] it perfects the virtue of faith by giving a knowledge of God which is not discursive but intuitive and experimental; and it perfects the virtue of charity by giving a savory experience of God and supernatural mysteries. The gift of knowledge refers to the secondary object of contemplation, namely, created things by which man is raised to a knowledge of God.

---

[2]This does not mean that no individual could enjoy infused contemplation without having suffered the passive purification, for we have already stated that it is possible for a person in the ascetical state to perform mystical acts.

[3]Cf. St. Thomas, *Summa,* I-II, q. 9, a. 2, ad 3; a. 3; II-II, q. 8, a. 7; q. 45, a. 6.

[4]Cf. *ibid.,* I-II, q. 9, a. 3, ad 1; II-II, q. 45, a. 6.

DISTINCTIVE NOTES

Having considered the nature of contemplation from a theological point of view, we shall now describe the psychological and experimental characteristics by which the spiritual director can recognize infused contemplation and distinguish it from other manifestations of the spiritual life.

Experimental knowledge

1) *An experience of the presence of God.* Father Poulain and other authors of mystical theology place great emphasis on this characteristic and consider it the essential note of infused contemplation. "The real point of difference from the recollection of ordinary prayer is this: in the mystical state God is not satisfied merely to help us think of him and to remind us of his presence, but he gives an experimental, intellectual knowledge of his presence. In a word, he makes us feel that we truly enter into communication with him."[5] Following the same doctrine, Father de Grandmaison states that the mystics are the witnesses of the loving presence of God in us.[6] We would not deny that this characteristic is the most frequent and ordinary one in the mystical experience, but we would not consider it as an essential note of mystical experience in general, because the soul may lack the experience of the presence of God when it is undergoing the passive purification of the soul.

Invasion of the soul

2) *The invasion of the soul by the supernatural.* This is another of the most frequent characteristics of infused contemplation, although it is often lacking during the periods of passive purgation. When it is produced, the soul feels in an unmistakable and ineffable manner that it is invaded and permeated with something which it cannot describe with precision, but which the soul feels clearly is something supernatural. It is, in fact, an effect of the operation of the gifts of the Holy Ghost, which inundate the soul with supernatural life. As a result, the mystics who have attempted to describe this particular experience have spoken in terms that may seem exaggerated—for example, to be immersed in the supernatural, to be fused with the divine, or to be overwhelmed in a deluge of the supernatural. Some mystical theologians would describe this experience as a divine or interior touch, but the mystics themselves seem to favor those expressions which pertain to submersion in water.

Not produced by one's own efforts

3) *Impossibility of producing the mystical experience by one's own efforts.* This characteristic is never lacking in any of the grades of mystical prayer. The soul is fully aware of the fact that the ineffable experience which it is enjoying has not been produced by its own efforts and that it will not last a second longer than is desired by the mysterious agent who causes it. The soul is a passive subject of a sublime experience which it could not produce of itself.[7] The reason for this is that contemplation is produced through the

---

[5]A. Poulain, S. J., *The Graces of Interior Prayer* (St. Louis: Herder, 1928), Chap. 5, n. 3.

[6]L. de Grandmaison, S.J., *Religion personelle* (Paris: 1927), 178.

[7]St. Teresa, *The Life,* Chap. 17, n. 1; Chap. 15, n. 1.

operation of the gifts of the Holy Ghost, and the individual soul is unable by his own efforts to activate the gifts, since they are not instruments under his control, as are the virtues, but are directly under the control of the Holy Ghost. They operate when he desires and only as long as he desires.

Consequently, one cannot contemplate mystically whenever he wishes, but he can and ought to dispose himself for receiving the influence of the Holy Ghost. It may happen that a soul receives mystical contemplation unexpectedly and without any positive preparation; at other times it does not receive mystical contemplation, however much the soul may dispose itself. Once the divine motion of the Holy Spirit has been put into operation, the soul cannot do anything by its own power to intensify the activity; rather, its efforts will prove an obstacle to the divine activity.

Neither can the soul determine by its own effort the degree or grade of mystical union and mystical prayer. This depends entirely on God, who does not always follow the classification or order of mystical degrees which have been pointed out by the mystics themselves. God works in the soul according to his own good pleasure. Sometimes the mystical experience begins, is intensified, and then gradually diminishes until it disappears entirely, and this is what happens most frequently. But at other times the mystical experience may appear and disappear suddenly, without the soul being able to do anything to stimulate it or to terminate it. Consequently, it would be most imprudent for a spiritual director to command a soul to discontinue its mystical prayer in order to return to ordinary prayer.[8]

More passive than active

4) *In contemplation the soul is more passive than active.* This is a consequence of all that we have already stated. The soul cannot contemplate whenever it wishes, but only when the Holy Spirit desires and in the measure and degree that he desires. It is true that under the action of the gifts, the soul reacts in a vital manner and co-operates with all its efforts in the divine movement, but it is an activity that is received, so to speak, as an immediate effect of operating grace. This is the famous *patiens divina* of pseudo-Dionysius which has been experienced by all the mystics. St. Thomas says that the spiritual man is not inclined to perform a work as moved principally by his own will but as moved by the instinct of the Holy Ghost.[9] He also states that in the operations of the gifts of the Holy Ghost the human soul does not act as mover, but rather as the thing moved.[10]

[8]Father Poulain points out that a person who is commanded by the spiritual director to leave mystical prayer and return to the ordinary way of prayer should show his good will by trying to obey, even if it is impossible for the soul to fulfill the command (cf. *The Graces of Interior Prayer,* Chap. 7, n. 6). In practice, the individual would be well advised to change spiritual directors.

[9]*In Epist. ad Rom.,* 8:14.

[10]*Summa,* II-II, q. 52, a. 2, ad 1.

Knowledge obscure and confused

5) *The experimental knowledge of God enjoyed during the mystical experience is not clear and distinct but obscure and confused.* St. John of the Cross explains this characteristic of infused contemplation in his *The Ascent of Mount Carmel.* The theological reason for this confused and obscure knowledge is that the contemplative light of the gifts of the Holy Spirit is cast upon the substantial act of faith to illumine it extrinsically and subjectively, but not intrinsically and objectively, since faith is of things not seen and the supernatural mysteries remain mysteries however much they may be illumined in this life. Only the light of glory (*lumen gloriae*) will break the seals of the mystery and give us a clear and distinct contemplation of God and his mysteries, and this will be nothing other than the beatific vision. In this life, however, as long as we live by faith, the contemplative vision must necessarily be obscure and confused.

Nevertheless, it is possible that certain extraordinary phenomena which are clear and distinct may occur during the mystical experience. There are certain *gratiae gratis datae,* such as visions and revelations, which present new infused species and are the result of a special divine action which is gratuitous and extraordinary. But these extraordinary phenomena have nothing to do with the normal activity of infused contemplation, which does not necessitate the infusion of new species into the intellect.[11]

Security of soul

6) *Infused contemplation gives full security and assurance to the soul that it is under the action of God.* According to the testimony of mystics, as long as the contemplative activity continues, the soul cannot have the slightest doubt that God is acting upon it. Once the prayer is finished, the soul may doubt the experience, but during the mystical prayer it is impossible for the soul to have any doubts. It is true that this assurance admits of different degrees, just as there are different degrees of mystical prayer.[12] The reason for this assurance and confidence is that the soul is fully aware that the divine experience is not the result of its own efforts. The Holy Ghost, who causes the experience through the operation of his gifts, gives the soul a certitude so firm that, as long as the soul is enjoying the experience, it would sooner doubt its own existence than the divine reality which it is experiencing. As St. Paul says: "The Spirit himself gives testimony to our spirit that we are sons of God" (Rom. 8:16).

[11]It is of utmost importance that the spiritual director remember this characteristic of mystical contemplation. When the soul describes an experience in which it feels some great impulse toward God but is unable to know what it is or how to describe it, an experienced director will immediately suspect that the soul in question has been given true mystical experience. An inexperienced and imprudent director may judge the soul to be a dreamer or the victim of illusion and try to force it to return to the ordinary and ascetical forms of prayer.

[12]Cf. St. Teresa, *Interior Castle,* Fifth Mansions, Chap. 1.

7) *Infused contemplation gives the soul moral certitude that it is in the state of grace.* This is a natural consequence of the previous characteristics, but it is necessary to understand it properly in order to avoid erroneous notions. It is of faith and so defined by the Council of Trent that, without a special revelation from God, no one can be certain that he belongs to the number of the predestined, that he will not sin again, that he will be converted again after sin, or that he will receive the gift of final perseverance.[13] Neither can one know with certainty whether he is in the state of grace.[14]

Moral certitude

The question arises, therefore, whether the certitude of one's state of grace which flows from contemplation is equivalent to a divine revelation. We believe that those who enjoy mystical union without any special revelation concerning their state of grace have a moral certitude of being in that state, and this certitude is far superior to that possessed by an ordinary Christian who judges from his dispositions. Mystical union presupposes an act of love which would be sufficient to place a person in the state of grace if he did not already possess sanctifying grace. For that reason the proof that one is in the mystical union is likewise solid proof that he is in the state of grace. Moreover, mystical contemplation is produced by the operation of certain gifts of the Holy Spirit, and these gifts necessarily presuppose the state of grace. This should be a great consolation for those souls who are assaulted by doubts concerning their mystical experiences. But we repeat that this certitude is not absolute and infallible, because this, according to the Council of Trent, is never given in this life except by a special divine revelation. Yet it is a moral certitude which is nevertheless of much greater value and assurance than the signs which are given for determining whether the ordinary Christian is in the state of grace.[15]

Ineffable experience

8) *The mystical experience is ineffable.* The mystics are unable to express clearly what they experience in their mystical activities. It is only by means of examples, comparisons and metaphors or circumlocution that they are able to give some notion of what transpires during these operations. Unless a person has had the same experience, it is likely that the descriptions given by mystics will seem to be exaggerated or even untruthful. The reason for this is that the supernatural activity of the gifts transcends the discursive power of human reason. These mystical experiences are intuitive, and as such they can be experienced but they cannot be expressed in human language.

Various forms

9) *Contemplation admits of various forms.* Mystical contemplation sometimes consists primarily in an illumination of the intellect (*cherubic* contemplation), and sometimes it is predominantly an inflammation of the will

[13]Cf. Sess. VI, Decree on Justification, Chap. 5 (Denz. 805) and canons 15, 16 and 23 (Denz. 825, 826 and 833).

[14]Cf. *ibid.*, Chap. 9 (Denz. 802) and canon 13 (Denz. 823).

[15]Cf. St. Thomas, *Summa,* I-II, q. 112, a. 5.

(*seraphic* contemplation). Usually it is sweet and delightful, but it can also be painful and purifying. As a rule, it leaves the soul peaceful and quiet, so that the soul desires no other happiness; at other times it may inflame the soul with a devouring thirst to possess the infinite good in a more profound manner. There are two factors which account for the variety of types of contemplation: the subjective dispositions and capacities of the soul, and the infinite variety of ways in which God may act in the soul.

Variations and fluctuations

10) *The mystical union admits of variations and fluctuations.* St. Teresa states that the mystical union may last for a long time, or it may sometimes be of short duration, according to the desires of God who communicates this experience.[16] Sometimes the mystical experience is so brief that it seems to be nothing more than a divine touch, and as a rule it does not remain in the same degree of intensity for a long time. During the period of intensification the soul yearns for the ineffable crisis which is to come, but as soon as that point is reached, it seems to the soul that the experience immediately begins to diminish. Then it is that the soul is tempted to cry out in the words of St. John of the Cross:

O living flame of love
That dost tenderly wound
My soul in its deepest center,
Since you no longer afflict me,
Finish all now, if you wish;
Break the thread of this sweet encounter.[17]

Bodily reactions

11) *Mystical contemplation frequently causes reactions in the body.* Sometimes the intense spiritual delight experienced by the soul causes startling phenomena in the sensitive order.[18] St. John of the Cross teaches, however, that this occurs only in beginners in the mystical life and that they should ignore these reactions and continue the practice of prayer. When contemplation is very intense, the organism may be changed visibly. The eyes become clouded and dull; respiration is weak and intermittent, with an occasional deep breathing as if trying to absorb the necessary quantity of air; the limbs are partly paralyzed; the heat of the body decreases, especially in the extremities. All of these phenomena have been manifested time and again in mystical souls, and St. Teresa speaks of them in her works.[19]

The reason for the phenomena which accompany infused contemplation is that the human organism can react in only a certain number of ways, and when the spirit is absorbed in an intense activity, the body necessarily participates in this activity. On the other hand, if an individual gives himself completely and energetically to corporal things, the faculties of the soul are

[16]Cf. *Interior Castle,* Sixth Mansions, Chap. 2, n. 4.
[17]*The Living Flame of Love,* Stanza I.
[18]Cf. St. John of the Cross, *The Dark Night,* Chap. 1.
[19]Cf. *The Life,* Chaps. 18-20.

weakened as regards spiritual things. For that reason St. Paul warns that the carnal man cannot understand spiritual things (I Cor. 2:14).

Suspension of faculties

12) *Mystical contemplation often produces a suspension or binding of the faculties.* Mystical contemplation may be so intense that it results in an ecstatic trance. When this occurs, it is inevitable that there should be a suspension of the sense faculties. Even if the contemplative activity does not produce this effect, however, it is frequently difficult and even impossible for the mystic to give attention to any other prayers or activities because of its absorption in God. The mystical state or activity usually tends to exclude everything that is alien to it, especially the operations that proceed from the industry and effort of the subject. If it is a question of the recitation of certain vocal prayers or the reading of a pious book, the practical advice to be followed during mystical activity is simply to submit to the action of God within the soul and to let oneself be carried by the divine impulses. Only in the case of prayers or external works that are of obligation should the individual make every effort to fulfill his duties.[20]

Impulse to virtue

13) *Infused contemplation causes a great impulse for the practice of virtue.* This is one of the surest signs of true contemplation. The soul that does not leave its prayer with a great impulse toward solid virtue can be sure that it has not enjoyed truly contemplative prayer. One of the marvelous facts of mystical experience is that a contemplative soul sometimes finds that it instantaneously possesses a certain virtue which it has not been able to perfect over a long period of time in spite of its efforts.

Yet it is necessary to avoid exaggeration in this matter. In the early stages of contemplative prayer, the transformation is not so profound that the soul is freed from its defects. For that reason the spiritual director would be greatly mistaken if he were to judge a contemplative soul to be deluded if, after having experienced mystical contemplation, it should still be subject to certain defects. Frequently such defects are caused more by one's temperament or character than by one's deliberate will. Mystical contemplation greatly aids the sanctification of a soul, but it does not instantaneously or necessarily produce a saint.[21]

DEGREES OF MYSTICAL PRAYER

Having explained the nature and characteristics of mystical contemplation, we pass now to the consideration of the principal degrees or grades of mystical prayer. We shall follow the terminology of St. Teresa of Avila, because most of the writers on this subject have taken her as their guide

[20]There are abundant examples in the lives of the saints which verify the suspension of the faculties during mystical contemplation.

[21]The excellence of the contemplative life and the relationship between the active life and the contemplative life have been treated in a masterly fashion by St. Thomas Aquinas in the *Summa,* II-II, qq. 179-182.

and authority. It is interesting to note that in the soul's progress through the ascetical phase of the spiritual life the purgation and perfection of the various faculties have proceeded from the inferior to the superior powers, and this has likewise been the path which was followed by the soul in its progress through the ascetical grades of prayer. Now, however, in the mystical grades of prayer, in which God is the primary mover through the operation of the gifts of the Holy Ghost, the divine activity begins with the highest faculty and progresses through the inferior faculties until the entire person is transformed in God.

In this chapter we will consider infused recollection and the prayer of quiet. In the chapter which follows, the prayer of union, the prayer of ecstatic union and the prayer of transforming union will be studied.

INFUSED RECOLLECTION

Infused recollection is a type of mystical contemplation which is especially characterized by the union of the intellect with God, who captivates this faculty by the operation of the gifts of understanding, knowledge and counsel, so that the intellect penetrates the ineffable divine marvels.

ITS NATURE

St. Teresa of Avila describes this prayer in the following passages:

> In my opinion, the first prayer which I experienced as supernatural, by which I mean that which cannot be acquired by our own industry or diligence however much we strive (although one can certainly dispose himself for it and certainly ought to do so), is an interior recollection which is experienced in the soul. In that state the soul seems to have other senses somewhat like the external senses in the present state, and it seems desirous of withdrawing from exterior affairs. Hence [this type of prayer] sometimes carries the external senses away with it, because it wants to close the eyes and not let the soul hear or see or understand anything but that with which the soul is then occupied, namely, to be able to converse with God alone. No sense or faculty is lost; each one is operative, but it is so in order to be occupied with God.[22]
>
> It is called recollection because in it the soul gathers together all its faculties and enters within itself with its God, and its divine Master comes more quickly than in any other way to give it the prayer of quiet. . . . Those who can thus enclose themselves in this little heaven of the soul wherein he dwells who made heaven and earth, and are able to accustom themselves not to look at anything or to remain in any place in which these external senses would be distracted, may be sure that they are traveling along an

[22]*Spiritual Relations,* V.

excellent way and that they will not fail ultimately to drink the water of the fountain because they will travel far in a short time. . . . If their recollection is genuine, it is clearly perceived, because it performs some kind of operation (I do not know how to explain this, but he who has experienced it will understand). It seems to the soul that it has abandoned a game, for that is how it now sees the things of the world. . . . The senses are withdrawn from external things, which have been rejected to such an extent that, without knowing how, the eyes are closed to them and the spiritual sight of the soul is awakened. . . . The soul seems to fortify itself and strengthen itself at the expense of the body, which it leaves alone and in a weakened condition.[23]

Do not think that it is by means of an acquired understanding, striving to think of God within oneself, nor by means of the imagination, trying to picture him within oneself. This is good and it is an excellent type of meditation, because it is based upon the truth that God dwells within us; but I am not speaking of this, for anyone can do this (with God's help, of course). What I am talking about is something quite different, and sometimes, even before they have begun to think about God, these people are already in the castle and I do not know how they entered it or how they heard the call of their Shepherd. Surely it was not with their ears, because there is nothing to be heard externally; but there is felt in a noticeable manner a sweet recollection to the interior, as anyone will understand who experiences these things. . . . [This type of recollection] is not subject to our will but occurs only when God wishes to grant this mercy. I believe that when his Majesty grants it, it is to persons who are already abandoning the things of the world.[24]

CONCOMITANT PHENOMENA

Infused recollection is usually characterized by certain phenomena which are antecedent, concomitant or consequent to the practice of this grade of prayer. According to Father Arintero, the principal phenomena are the following:

1) A lively sense of the supernatural and infused presence of God, which usually precedes infused recollection. St. Teresa speaks of this explicitly.[25]

2) A delightful admiration which fills the soul with joy and gladness as it discovers in God so many marvels of love, goodness and beauty.

3) A certain suspension or spiritual silence in which the soul remains astonished, absorbed and annihilated, so to speak, before the majesty of God, accompanied by a sense of profound humility and deep respect.

4) A most vivid light and illumination concerning God and the divine mysteries, with the result that the soul instantaneously receives an illumination and knowledge that it could never have gained over a period of many years of meditation and study.[26]

---

[23]*The Way of Perfection,* Chap. 28.
[24]*Interior Castle,* Fourth Mansions, Chap. 3.
[25]Cf. *Spiritual Relations,* V; *The Life,* Chap. 10.
[26]Cf. J. G. Arintero, O.P., *Stages in Prayer* (St. Louis: Herder, 1957), Chap. 8.

The spiritual director should take great care to guide the soul which begins to receive these first lights of contemplative prayer, and he must be especially careful lest he place any obstacle to their advance in prayer. The following are the principal counsels which he should give to the soul in this particular grade of prayer:

PRACTICAL CONDUCT

1) *Not to cease discursive meditation until one clearly perceives the invitation to a higher grade of prayer.* In the practice of prayer, as in the exercises of the spiritual life in general, the individual should always be prepared to do as much as he can with the assistance of ordinary grace. It would be a source of great harm if an individual were to attempt to enter upon a mystical grade of prayer when the Lord has not yet called that person to such a high degree of prayer. St. Teresa warned that, as long as the soul is not sure that God is drawing it to a mystical grade of prayer, it should not attempt to remain passive and inactive, because that would produce nothing but aridity and the individual would soon grow restless because of its inactivity.[27]

2) *Immediately to terminate all discursive prayer as soon as one feels the impulse of grace toward infused recollection.* This is a consequence of the foregoing counsel. It would be foolish to anticipate mystical prayer, but it would be tantamount to obstructing the action of God in the soul if one were to attempt to proceed by his own efforts when grace impels one to the recollection and quasi-passivity of contemplation. The teaching of St. Teresa on this particular point should be read with great attention.[28] The spiritual director will usually have to exert great effort to convince the soul that it should immediately abandon itself to the action of God as soon as this is felt. Some souls become disobedient and stubborn at this point of their development. Accustomed as they are to certain vocal prayers and discursive meditations, it seems to them that it would be a waste of time to put themselves in a passive state, and they may feel scruples about neglecting their customary private devotions. They do not realize that it is of much more value for a soul to experience even the slightest touch of the Holy Spirit than to practice all manner of spiritual exercises under their own initiative.

3) *To give themselves completely to the interior life.* Souls that receive these first mystical communications can usually suspect that God has predestined them for great things in the spiritual life. If they do not resist God, they can arrive at the summit of perfection. Fully convinced of the necessity of a conscientious correspondence with grace, they must definitively break with all the attachments which still keep them bound to earth, and must give themselves completely and with all their strength to the practice of virtue.

[27]Cf. *Interior Castle,* Fourth Mansions, Chap. 3.

[28]*Loc. cit.*

The director must especially insist upon the practice of habitual recollection, interior and exterior silence, the mortification of the senses, the absolute detachment from earthly things, profound humility and, above all, an ardent love of God which will inform and vivify everything that they do. They must therefore give themselves fully to the practice of prayer and remain attentive to the voice of God, which will call them frequently to the sweet and holy repose of contemplation. Nevertheless, they must take great care not to use violence on themselves, because God will come in his own time, and until he does they should try to do all things gently and without violence under the assistance of ordinary grace.

THE PRAYER OF QUIET

The prayer of quiet is a type of mystical contemplation in which the soul experiences an intimate awareness of God's presence which captivates the will and fills the soul and body with ineffable sweetness and delight. The fundamental difference between the prayer of quiet and that of infused recollection, apart from the greater intensity of contemplative light and the more intense consolations, is that infused recollection is an invitation from God for the soul to recede further into its interior, but the prayer of quiet begins to give the soul an actual possession and joyful fruition of the sovereign Good.

ITS NATURE

Infused recollection principally affects the intellect, which is withdrawn from the other faculties, but the prayer of quiet especially affects the will. Although the intellect and the memory are now tranquil, they still remain free to realize what is occurring, but the will is completely captivated and absorbed in God. For that reason, the prayer of quiet, as its name indicates, tends to contemplative silence and repose. Since the other faculties remain free, however, they can be occupied with the work of the active life, and they do so frequently with great intensity. The will does not then lose its sweet quietude, but the activities of Martha and Mary begin to merge in a beautiful manner, as St. Teresa points out.[29] Yet the perfect blending of the active and contemplative life will not be achieved until the soul has reached the state of perfect union with God.

Description of St. Teresa

St. Teresa describes the prayer of quiet in the following way:

> From this recollection there sometimes proceeds an interior quiet and peace which are full of happiness, because the soul is in such a state that

[29]Cf. *The Way of Perfection,* Chap. 31, n. 5.

it does not seem to lack anything, and even speaking (I refer to vocal prayer and meditation) wearies it; it wishes to do nothing but love. This state may last for some time and even for long periods of time.[30]

What I call consolations from God, which I have elsewhere called the prayer of quiet, is something very different, as those of you will understand who have experienced them by the mercy of God. In order to understand it better, let us imagine that we are looking at two fountains with two basins which are filled with water. . . . These two basins are filled with water in different ways: the water in one comes from a distance by means of conduits and mechanical means; the other basin has been placed at the very source of the water and is gradually filled, without any noise. If the flow of water is abundant, as in the case of which we are speaking, once the basin is filled the water overflows the basin in a great deluge. No mechanical means are necessary, nor does one need to construct any conduits because the water is constantly flowing.

As applied to the practice of prayer, the difference is that the water which is carried by conduits is, in my opinion, similar to the results which I have already said are gained by the practice of meditation, which we obtain by means of thoughts, making use of creatures in our meditation and tiring the intellect. And since, finally, it is produced by our own efforts, it makes a noise when it produces a certain fulness of consolation in the soul.

To the other fountain the water comes directly from its source, which is God, and when his Majesty wishes. When he is pleased to grant some supernatural favor, he produces it with the greatest peace and quiet and sweetness of our interior. I do not know whence it comes or how; nor are that contentment and delight experienced as those of earth are experienced in the heart, at least not in the beginning. But later the basin is completely filled, and the water begins to overflow through all the interior mansions and faculties until it reaches the body. That is why I have said that it begins with God and ends in ourselves.[31]

Peace of soul

This is something supernatural, and we cannot acquire it by our own efforts, because it is a state in which the soul is put at peace, or better yet, a state in which the Lord gives peace to the soul by his presence, as he did to the just Simeon, because all the faculties are at rest. The soul understands, in a manner far different from understanding with the help of the external senses, that it is now closely united with God and that with a little more it would become one thing with him through union. This is not because the soul sees him with the eyes of the body or of the spirit. Neither did the just Simeon see anything more in the glorious poor little Infant. Considering that he was wrapped in swaddling clothes and accompanied by a few people, one would judge that he was merely the son of poor people rather than the Son of the heavenly Father; but the Child himself revealed himself to Simeon.

In like manner does the soul in this state of prayer understand, although not with such clarity, because as yet it does not understand how it knows him, but it sees that it is in the kingdom (or at least that the King is near

[30] *Spiritual Relations,* V.

[31] *Interior Castle,* Fourth Mansions, Chap. 2.

who will grant the kingdom), and the soul itself is overwhelmed with such reverence that it does not even dare to ask for anything. It is, as it were, paralyzed interiorly and exteriorly, so that the exterior man (I shall say the body so that you will better understand me) does not care to be distracted, but, like one who has almost reached the end of the journey, it rests so that it may more easily resume its journey with redoubled strength.

A great delight is experienced in the body and a great satisfaction in the soul. It is so content to find itself at the fountain that it is filled without even drinking from the fountain. It seems to the soul that there is nothing left for it to desire. The faculties are at rest and do not wish to be disturbed because anything would seem to prevent the soul from loving. The faculties are not lost completely, however, because the two faculties that are still free are able to realize with whom they are united. The will is held captive here, and if it is able to suffer any pain in this condition it is from the realization that it must return to its liberty. The intellect does not wish to understand anything but the one thing, and the memory does not wish to be occupied with anything else; both of these faculties see that only this one thing is necessary and that anything else will disturb them. They do not wish the body to become active, because then it seems to them that they would lose that peace, and therefore they do not dare to stir. It gives them pain to speak, and sometimes it would take them a whole hour to recite the Our Father. . . . They do not seem to be in this world at all. They do not wish to see or hear anything but their God. Nothing disturbs them and it seems that nothing could ever do so. In a word, as long as they experience this satisfaction and delight within themselves, they are so overwhelmed and absorbed that they do not think of anything else to desire, but they would gladly repeat with St. Peter: "If thou wilt, let us set up three tents here."[32]

EFFECTS OF THIS PRAYER

The sanctifying effects produced in the soul by the prayer of quiet are enumerated by St. Teresa in the fourth mansions of her *Interior Castle*: 1) great liberty of spirit; 2) filial fear of God and great care not to offend him; 3) profound confidence in God; 4) love of mortification and suffering; 5) deep humility; 6) disdain for worldly pleasures; and 7) growth in all the virtues.

CONCOMITANT PHENOMENA

The concomitant phenomena which usually accompany the prayer of quiet are two in number: *sleep of the faculties* and *inebriation of love.* In her autobiography St. Teresa listed the sleep of the faculties as a distinct grade of mystical prayer which is superior to the prayer of quiet, but in her later works she changed her opinion and considered the sleep of the faculties as an effect of the prayer of quiet in its highest degree of intensity.[33]

---

[32]*The Way of Perfection,* Chap. 31.

[33]Cf. *The Life,* Chap. 16; *The Foundations,* Chap. 6; *Spiritual Relations,* V; *Interior Castle,* Fourth Mansions. Since the *Interior Castle* is the most mature work of St. Teresa, we consider that it contains her definitive teaching.

Sleep of the faculties

According to St. Teresa, the sleep of the faculties is a phenomenon in which the faculties are not completely captivated, and yet they do not understand how they work. The sweetness and delight which they experience is beyond anything which they have known previously. The soul seems to be unable to advance or to turn back; it wishes only to enjoy this great delight. It is as if the soul were almost completely dead to the things of this world and were enjoying God alone. It is a heavenly foolishness in which the soul learns true wisdom.[34]

In this phenomenon both the intellect and the will are united with God, although as yet the memory and the imagination remain free. The lower powers may still function in regard to their proper objects, but the soul is not aware of anything but its absorption in God.[35]

Inebriation of love

Sometimes the intense delight produced by the sleep of the faculties causes a kind of divine inebriation, which is manifested externally in a kind of foolishness of love. Sometimes there are cries of love, or even bodily movements such as leaps of joy or the singing of spiritual hymns. The love of God is so intense that it cannot be contained, but must burst forth into external acts.[36]

PRACTICAL CONDUCT

The general rule of conduct for the soul in any of the states of contemplative prayer is to co-operate completely with the working of grace and to cultivate an increasingly profound humility. As regards the prayer of quiet in particular, the following rules should be carefully followed:

1) *Never to attempt to force oneself into this grade of prayer.* It would indeed be futile, because mystical prayer cannot be attained by one's own efforts.

2) *To co-operate with the divine movement as soon as it is experienced.* One should not delay for a single instant under any pretext, but should follow the divine movement with all docility and humility.

3) *Not to disturb the quiet of the will by attending to the activities of the lower faculties.* The memory and the imagination, since they are still free for their own operations, could easily become a distraction in the prayer of quiet, but St. Teresa advises that the soul should pay no attention to these operations, but should ignore them until such time as God will bind them and captivate them.[37]

4) *Scrupulously to avoid any occasion of offending God.* St. Teresa warns that the devil frequently provides temptations and occasions of sin to souls who are in this degree of prayer, and she emphasizes the great damage that is done even by little acts of infidelity to grace.[38]

---

[34]Cf. *The Life,* Chap. 16.
[35]Cf. *ibid.,* Chap. 17.
[36]Cf. *ibid.,* Chap. 16.
[37]Cf. *ibid.,* Chap. 17; *Interior Castle,* Fourth Mansions, Chap. 1.
[38]Cf. *Interior Castle,* Fourth Mansions, Chap. 3.

5) *Never to abandon the practice of prayer in spite of any difficulty or obstacle.* St. Teresa places great stress on this particular rule, and she repeats it again and again throughout her writings. She states that, if a soul in this grade of prayer should fall into sin through weakness or malice, it can always recapture the good which it had lost, but if it does not return to the practice of prayer, it will go from bad to worse.[39]

Sleep of the faculties

As regards the sleep of the faculties, St. Teresa warns that the soul should not abandon itself excessively to this weakness and languor, because there is the possibility of mental unbalance. She states that some persons have such a weak constitution that as soon as they experience any spiritual joy or consolation they are overwhelmed by physical weakness which they mistakenly think is a true spiritual sleep. The more they abandon themselves to this experience, the weaker they become physically, with the result that they think that they are in a state of rapture. Actually, all they are doing is wasting their time and ruining their health. She makes it very clear that when there is a truly spiritual sleep of the faculties, there is no weakness or languor in the soul; rather, the soul is filled with a great joy. Moreover, the experience does not last for a long time, although the soul may quickly return to this sleep of the faculties. Nor is there any exterior sensation or rapture when this experience is truly from God. St. Teresa advises that persons of a weak constitution should sleep and eat well until they have regained their physical strength, and if their constitution still remains weak, they can take this as a sign that God is not calling them to the mystical degrees of prayer.[40]

Inebriation of love

In regard to the inebriation of love, one should take great care not to confuse this effect of the prayer of quiet with a purely natural effervescence and sentimentality, which are often found in enthusiastic and impressionable individuals. And even if it is a question of a true phenomenon, the soul should not willingly let itself be carried away by this experience, but should strive to control and moderate it. Above all, one should not take this phenomenon as a sign that it is far advanced in the spiritual life, but should humble itself before God and never seek to practice prayer in order to obtain consolations from God. The spiritual director should always insist on the necessity of the practice of virtue, and he should attach little importance to these phenomena, especially if he perceives that the soul is itself attaching great importance to them, or is beginning to manifest a certain degree of vanity. As a matter of fact, when these phenomena are truly from God, the soul is usually submerged in true humility. Thus humility is the great touchstone for distinguishing true gold from dross.

[39]Cf. *The Life,* Chap. 15.

[40]Cf. *Interior Castle,* Fourth Mansions, Chap. 3.

4: THE HIGHEST GRADES OF PRAYER

As previously mentioned, at this point we shall consider the three highest types of prayer, all of which are called prayers of union to signify the close relationship between the soul and God in the highest reaches of the mystical life. The first of these highest degrees is the prayer of union; the second, the prayer of ecstatic union; the third, the prayer of transforming union.

THE PRAYER OF UNION

The prayer of union is that grade of infused contemplation in which all the internal faculties are captivated and occupied with God.[1] In the prayer of quiet only the will was captivated; in the sleep of the faculties the intellect was also captivated, although the memory and the imagination remained free and sometimes warred against the intellect. In the prayer of union *all* of the interior faculties, including the memory and the imagination, are captivated. Only the external bodily senses are now free, but they too will be captivated in the following grade of prayer (ecstatic union), and it is only in this respect that the seventh and eighth degrees of prayer are differentiated.[2]

[1]There is no uniformity among authors in designating this degree of prayer. St. Teresa uses the expression "prayer of union"; others call it the "prayer of simple union"; still others use the expression "prayer of full union." None of the expressions is completely exact, but we prefer to use the expression of St. Teresa, although it should not be interpreted to mean that there was no union between the soul and God in the previous grades of mystical prayer. The second expression seems to refer most aptly to the prayer of quiet, in which there is a simple union with God; the third expression seems to pertain to the eighth grade of prayer (ecstatic union), in which all the faculties, both interior and exterior, enjoy full union with God.

[2]As can be seen, progress in mystical prayer proceeds from the highest faculties to the lowest, and in such a way that in the ultimate stages the whole person, body and soul, is transformed through grace and charity.

The intensity of the mystical experience caused by the prayer of union is indescribable. It is superior beyond compare to that of the preceding grade, to the point that the body itself comes under the influence of the working of God in the soul. Without being entirely captivated, the external senses become almost helpless and inoperative. The soul experiences divine reality with such intensity that it could easily fall into ecstasy. At the beginning, this sublime absorption of the faculties in God lasts but a short time (a half hour at most), but as the intensity increases, it may be prolonged for several hours.

ITS NATURE

Description of St. Teresa

The following excerpts from the writings of St. Teresa will serve as an admirable description of the prayer of union.

> Do not think that it is something dreamed, as in the previous state; I say dreamed because the soul seems to be drowsy and is neither asleep nor awake. But in this state the soul is asleep, and fully asleep, to the things of the world and to self because, as a matter of fact, the soul remains without consciousness during that little time while the condition lasts, and it could not think even if it desired to do so. Consequently, there is no necessity for the soul to suspend its thought by the use of any method. And if it loves, it does not understand how or what it loves nor what it would desire. In fact, it is like one who has completely died to the world in order to live more fully in God. It is, as it were, a delightful death, a snatching of the soul from all the activities it can perform while in the body. It is a delightful death because, although the soul seems truly to have been separated from the body, to such an extent that I do not even know if there remains in it enough life to be able to breathe, it does so in order to be united with God. . . .
>
> The intellect would like to occupy itself completely with understanding something of that which it feels, but since it does not have the strength to do so, it is overwhelmed to such an extent that, if the control of the intellect is not completely lost, it cannot move hand or foot, as we previously stated of a person who has fallen into such a swoon that he appears to be dead. . . . As long as the soul remains in this state, it can neither see nor hear nor understand. The period is always short, and it seems to the soul to be even shorter than it really is. God impresses himself upon the interior of the soul in such a way that, when the soul is restored to full awareness, it cannot possibly doubt that God has been in it and that it has been in God.[3]

Occupation with God

> The faculties possess the power to occupy themselves completely with God; not one of them ventures to be occupied with anything else, nor can we cause any of them to operate except by trying very diligently to fix our attention on something else, and even then I do not think that we should succeed entirely. Many words are spoken during this state in praise of God, but they are disordered unless the Lord himself put order into them. At any rate, the intellect avails nothing here. The soul would like to shout out praises because it cannot contain itself; it is in a state of delectable disquiet.[4]

---

[3]Cf. *Interior Castle,* Fifth Mansions, Chap. 1. In the following chapter St. Teresa explains the prayer of union by her famous comparison with the silkworm, its cocoon and the butterfly.

[4]Cf. *The Life,* Chap. 16.

Union with God

It seems to me that this kind of prayer is very definitely a union of the entire soul with God, although it seems that his Majesty desires to give permission to the faculties to understand and enjoy the great things that he is effecting there. It sometimes happens, and indeed very often, that when the will is in union, the soul understands that the will is captive and enjoying fruition and that the will alone is experiencing much quiet, while the intellect and the memory are so free that they can attend to other matters and be engaged in works of charity. This, although it may seem to be the same, is actually different from the prayer of quiet of which I have already spoken, partly because, in that prayer, the soul would not wish to be occupied in anything else, or to be active, since it is enjoying the holy repose of Mary; but in this prayer it can also be Martha, so that it is, as it were, occupied in both the active and the contemplative life, performing works of charity and the duties of its state, and reading, although souls in this state are not masters of themselves and they realize that the better part of the soul is occupied elsewhere. It is as if we were speaking to one person while another person is speaking to us, with the result that we cannot be fully attentive to the one or the other.[5]

SIGNS OF THIS PRAYER

The essential characteristics of the prayer of union and the signs by which it can be recognized and distinguished from other grades of prayer are the following:

1) *Absence of distractions.* The reason for this is that the memory and imagination, which are the faculties which usually cause distraction, are now fixed on God and held captive. There may be a return to lower grades of prayer from time to time, and then distractions may again disturb the soul, but during the prayer of union distractions are psychologically impossible.[6]

2) *Certitude of being intimately united with God.* The soul cannot doubt that it experiences God during the prayer of union. On leaving the lower grades of prayer, the soul may experience certain doubts or fears that it was not truly united with God, or that it was deceived by the devil, but in the prayer of union the certitude of experiencing God is so absolute that St. Teresa maintains that, if the soul does not experience this certitude, it did not have the true prayer of union.[7] The devil cannot falsify this type of prayer, and St. Teresa believes that the devil does not even know of the existence of this secret and intimate prayer.

3) *Absence of weariness and tedium.* The soul absorbed in God never wearies of its union with the Beloved. It is overwhelmed with ineffable delight, and however long the prayer of union may last, the soul never experiences

---

[5]Cf. *ibid.*, Chap. 17.

[6]Cf. St. Teresa, *ibid.*, Chaps. 17-18.

[7]Cf. *Interior Castle,* Fifth Mansions, Chap. 1.

any fatigue. For that reason, St. Teresa says that this grade of prayer can never do any harm to the soul, no matter how long it may last.[8]

EFFECTS OF THIS PRAYER

St. Teresa lists the principal effects of the prayer of union in a remarkable chapter of her *Interior Castle*.[9] The soul is so anxious to praise God that it would gladly die a thousand deaths for his sake. It has an intense longing to suffer great trials and experiences vehement desires for penance and solitude. It wishes that all souls would know God, and it is greatly saddened when it sees that God is offended. The soul is dissatisfied with everything that it sees on earth, since God has given it wings so that it can fly to him. And whatever it does for God seems very little by comparison with what it desires to do. Its weakness has been turned into strength, and it is no longer bound by any ties of relationship or friendship or worldly possessions. It is grieved at having to be concerned with the things of earth, lest these things should cause it to sin against God. Everything wearies it because it can find no true rest in any created thing.

CONCOMITANT PHENOMENA

The prayer of union is usually accompanied by certain concomitant phenomena which are distinct from the *gratiae gratis datae*. Although these phenomena are not produced at any definite moment and are transitory graces which God grants according to his good pleasure, they are nevertheless usually manifested when the soul reaches this degree of prayer. There are four principal concomitant phenomena: *mystical touches, flights of the spirit, fiery darts of love* and *wounds of love*. St. John of the Cross and St. Teresa of Avila give admirable descriptions of these phenomena,[10] but we shall limit ourselves to a brief description.

Mystical touches

The mystical touches are a kind of instantaneous supernatural impression which give the soul a sensation of having been touched by God himself. This divine contact imparts to the soul an ineffable delight which defies description. The soul sometimes utters a cry or falls into ecstasy. The touches themselves admit of varying degrees of intensity; the most sublime are those which the German mystics and St. John of the Cross describe as "substantial touches." This expression is used in order to designate that the soul senses these sublime mystical touches as if they had been experienced in the very center or apex of the soul, although in reality they are experienced in the spiritual faculties of intellect and will. St. John of the Cross warns souls that they should not attempt to experience these mystical touches by their own efforts but

[8]Cf. *The Life,* Chap. 18.

[9]Cf. *Interior Castle,* Fifth Mansions, Chap. 2.

[10]Cf. St. John of the Cross, *The Ascent of Mount Carmel,* Bk. II, Chap. 32; *The Dark Night,* Bk. II, Chap. 23; *The Living Flame of Love,* Chap. 2; *Spiritual Canticle,* Stanzas 1, 7; St. Teresa of Avila, *The Life,* Chap. 29; *Spiritual Relations,* V.

should remain humble and resigned before God and passively receive whatever he deigns to send them.[11]

Flights of the spirit

Flights of the spirit, as the name indicates, are strong and unexpected impulses of love of God which leave the soul with a consuming thirst for God. The soul feels that it could never satiate its thirst for love, even if all creation were permeated with divine love. Sometimes the mere mention of God causes the soul to react with such a violent impetus that the body is overwhelmed by an ecstatic trance. A remarkable note in regard to these violent impulses is that they never cause any physical or mental harm to the individual, although any similar impulse in the purely natural order could be seriously harmful. St. Teresa wisely cautions individuals to make a careful distinction between those impulses of love which flow from sentimentality or temperament or some other natural cause, and which must therefore be controlled by reason, and the truly mystical touches which are passively received by the soul from God himself.[12]

Fiery darts of love

According to St. John of the Cross, the fiery darts of love are certain hidden touches of love which, like a fiery arrow, burn and pierce the soul and leave it completely cauterized with the fire of love.[13] St. Teresa describes this phenomenon as a wounding of the soul, as if an arrow had pierced the soul. It causes the soul great affliction, and at the same time it is very delectable. The wound is not a physical one, but it is deep within the soul and seems to spring from the soul's inmost depths. It arouses profound desires for God and a kind of hatred of the body, which seems at that time to be an obstacle to the soul's fruition of God.[14]

Wounds of love

The wounds of love are similar to the preceding phenomenon, but they are more profound and more lasting.[15] St. John of the Cross remarks that the fiery darts of love are usually caused by the knowledge of God which the soul receives through created things, while the wounds of love are caused by the knowledge of the works of the Incarnation and the mysteries of faith. The effects of these wounds are similar to the effects of the fiery darts, but they are much more profound. The soul lovingly complains to God at not being able to leave this life and to enjoy the intimate union with him in heaven. One of the best commentaries on this phenomenon is to be found in the *Spiritual Canticle,* Stanzas 9-11.

---

[11]Cf. *The Ascent of Mount Carmel,* Bk. II, Chap. 32.

[12]Cf. *The Life,* Chap. 29.

[13]Cf. *Spiritual Canticle,* Stanza 1.

[14]Cf. *Spiritual Relations,* V.

[15]For the distinction between these two phenomena, cf. St. John of the Cross, *Spiritual Canticle,* Stanza 7; *The Living Flame of Love,* Chap. 2.

THE PRAYER OF ECSTATIC UNION

The prayer of ecstatic union, also designated as the conforming union, often terminates in the spiritual espousal. It adds to the former degree of prayer, in which the faculties of the soul and the internal senses were intimately united with God, the suspension of the external senses. The intensity of the mystical union is so great that the body cannot withstand it and falls into ecstasy. As regards its external aspect, ecstasy is nothing more than a bodily weakness which disappears at the height of the transforming union, when the body is able to withstand the profound divine communications.

THE NATURE OF ECSTASY

As an external phenomenon, ecstasy consists in a gentle and progressive swooning which terminates in the complete alienation of the senses. Although the ecstatic person does not see or hear or feel anything, it is evident that the individual is neither dead nor asleep. Usually the expression on the face of the individual is radiant, as if the person has been transported to another world. If the ecstasy is perfect and complete, it is useless to call the person, to shake him, or to use any of the means by which one is normally restored to awareness. The ecstatic will not return to consciousness unless commanded to do so by a person in authority, and in this case it is sufficient that the superior give the command mentally.

There are three possible causes for the state of trance: supernatural, preternatural or diabolical, and purely natural.[16] Supernatural ecstasy presupposes two elements: the elevation of the soul to God and its detachment from the sensible world. It is a sublime absorption of the soul in God which causes the complete suspension of the operations of the external senses. It admits of two distinct forms: *prophetic ecstasy* and *mystical ecstasy*.

Prophetic ecstasy

Prophetic illumination is frequently accompanied by alienation of the external and internal senses, so that these faculties will not disturb or obstruct the supernatural action of God by their own images. It is a *gratia gratis data,* and for that reason it does not necessarily presuppose sanctifying grace in the soul. In an absolute sense it could be received by a sinner. This type of ecstasy has as its purpose the illumination of the intellect; it does not affect the will, and it does not have of itself any sanctifying power. For that reason prophetic ecstasy does not enter into the normal development of grace, nor can it be classified as one of the degrees of contemplative prayer.

Mystical ecstasy

Mystical ecstasy, on the other hand, is a concomitant phenomenon of supernatural contemplation, characterized by an intimate union of the soul with

[16]Cf. St. Thomas, *Summa,* II-II, q. 175, a. 1.

God and accompanied by alienation of the senses. As a concomitant phenomenon, it enters into the normal development of mystical contemplation and has a sanctifying power. The essential note of mystical ecstasy is the intimate union of the soul with God, or the *elevatio mentis,* as the ancients called it; the secondary aspect or consequence is the alienation of the senses. All of these elements are essential for true mystical ecstasy. Without the intimate union of the soul with God, the suspension of the senses would be nothing more than a type of sleep; without the suspension of the senses, there would be mystical prayer, but not ecstatic prayer; without infused contemplation properly speaking, the ecstasy would be prophetic ecstasy, natural ecstasy or diabolical ecstasy, but not mystical ecstasy.

CAUSES OF MYSTICAL ECSTASY

The efficient cause of mystical ecstasy is the Holy Ghost, working through his gifts. Ecstasy is appropriated to the Holy Spirit because it is an operation of love which sanctifies the soul, and the Holy Spirit is the Spirit of love. Operating through the gifts of wisdom and understanding, he uses the latter to illuminate faith and the former to arouse charity, until a most vehement love is aroused in the soul, causing the alienation of the senses.

The formal cause of ecstasy is infused contemplation in a very intense degree, although not the maximum degree. A less intense form of contemplation would not cause the suspension of the faculties of the soul nor of the bodily senses. Yet it need not be contemplation in the maximum degree of intensity, because the highest degrees of infused contemplation do not produce any ecstasy.

As regards the material cause, the imperfection or natural weakness of the subject who receives the infused contemplation may be called a quasi-material cause. When the individual is accustomed to the divine illumination and is strengthened sufficiently to withstand it, however, as will occur in the highest degrees of the mystical life, all ecstasy will disappear. This natural weakness of the subject does not refer exclusively to the body but also refers to the psychological order. The soul not yet accustomed to the intensity of light and love which are communicated, experiences an alienation of the senses. The reason for this is that, although the ecstasy occurs primarily in the faculties of the soul, it is communicated by natural redundance to the faculties of the body.

The final cause or purpose of the ecstasy is the sanctification of the soul that receives it. We have already stated that mystical ecstasy is not a *gratia gratis data* but a concomitant and sanctifying phenomenon of the mystical life.[17]

---

[17]Cf. St. Teresa, *Interior Castle,* Sixth Mansions, Chaps. 4 and 6, in which she explains the marvelous effects which ecstasy produces in the soul.

St. Thomas distinguishes three grades of ecstasy. In the first, the external senses are suspended, but not the internal senses. In the second, the internal senses are also suspended, and the soul perceives by intelligible species which are independent of the phantasms of the imagination. In the third, there is a direct contemplation of the divine essence.[18]

FORMS OF ECSTASY

The principal forms of ecstasy are the gentle and delightful ecstasy, and the violent and painful ecstasy. In the first, it seems that the soul is no longer in the body, and the body itself has the experience of losing its natural warmth. Nevertheless, this is accompanied by great sweetness and delight.[19] This form of ecstasy is in no way harmful to health; rather, it frequently improves the health of the individual.[20]

In its violent and painful form, the bodily suffering is so intense that the individual can hardly bear it. It seems sometimes as if the entire body has been dislocated.[21] St. John of the Cross states that this type of ecstasy may cause weakness and harm to the stomach, and that it seems as if all the bones have dried up and that the body has lost all of its strength. It sometimes happens that the body becomes completely cold and appears as if dead.[22] The sweet and delightful form of ecstasy is called ecstasy simply, and the painful form is called seizure, flight of the spirit or rapture.[23]

EFFECTS OF ECSTASY

Ecstasy usually produces noticeable effects on the body and soul of the ecstatic. The principal bodily effects are insensibility, facial expression and agility or levitation. When the ecstasy is total, the organic insensibility is complete. Blows and wounds and burning are ineffective in bringing the individual back to natural consciousness. The ecstatic has no sensation of any material thing, and there is no awareness through vision of any objects in the vicinity, as can be proved by passing some object, even a bright light, in front of the opened eyes of the ecstatic. Nevertheless, there have been mystics who spoke of their contemplative vision during the state of

---

[18]Cf. *Summa,* II-II, q. 175, a. 3, ad 1.

[19]Cf. St. Teresa, *The Life,* Chap. 20.

[20]Cf. St. Teresa, *ibid.,* Chaps. 10, 11, 20 and 21.

[21]Cf. St. Teresa, *ibid.,* Chaps. 12 and 20.

[22]Cf. *The Dark Night,* Bk. II, Chaps. 1 and 2; *Spiritual Canticle,* Stanzas 13 and 14.

[23]Cf. St. Teresa, *Interior Castle,* Sixth Mansions, Chap. 5. St. Teresa states that it is possible for the soul to gain merit during ecstasy. The reason given in *The Life* is that the time spent in ecstasy is not wasted. Another and more profound reason is that the soul does not lose its freedom during ecstasy, because only the beatific vision suffices to attract the soul by necessity. Consequently, although it would be very difficult for a soul to return to complete self-control when in ecstasy, nevertheless the soul is perfectly submissive to the divine action, and this suffices for merit.

ecstasy, or have even moved around during the ecstasy, as in the cases of St. Catherine of Siena and St. Magdalen of Pazzi. But these are exceptional cases; ordinarily a person in ecstasy is insensible and completely immovable.

We have already noted that during an ecstasy the natural heat of the body gradually diminishes, especially in the hands and feet. The vital functions seem to be interrupted: there is no evident sign of respiration, of circulation of the blood, or any movement of the lips. The vital functions gradually return to normal as the individual returns to consciousness. The sweet and gentle ecstasy is never harmful to bodily health, but often restores or improves it; after the violent ecstasy, on the other hand, the body sometimes remains exhausted and painful over a period of days.

Effects on the soul

As regards the effects of ecstasy on the soul of the individual, the proper and characteristic effect is to communicate a supernatural energy which leads the soul to heroism in the practice of virtue. It is a fact that true ecstasy proceeds from love, and at the same time arouses in the soul a love that is yet more ardent and more intense. It is the "ecstasy of works," of which St. Francis de Sales speaks,[24] and it always accompanies and is the clearest sign of the true "ecstasy of love." St. Teresa has written some beautiful passages on the remarkable effects which divine ecstasy produces in the soul.[25]

Spiritual espousal

The spiritual espousal, which is the promise of God to lead the soul to the transforming union or spiritual marriage, usually occurs during one of these ineffable ecstasies. St. Teresa believes that a rapture is indispensable at this point, lest the individual die before the splendor of the divine Majesty.[26] On receiving this divine promise of the spiritual espousal, the soul experiences such a profound joy that it falls into a death-like trance. St. John of the Cross teaches that at this point the soul no longer experiences the vehement longings and complaints of love but enters upon a state of peace and delight wherein it enjoys the full sweetness of love.[27] If the soul remains faithful, it will certainly arrive at the summit of the mountain of love because, as St. Teresa says, there is no closed door between the sixth and the seventh mansions.[28]

FALSIFICATION OF ECSTASY

Before terminating our consideration of ecstatic prayer, it will be helpful to discuss briefly the falsifications of mystical ecstasy. These are generally classified as natural ecstasy and diabolical ecstasy.

There is no doubt that a type of ecstasy can occur in the purely natural order, and may even possess all or most of the characteristics of true super-

[24]Cf. St. Francis de Sales, *Treatise on the Love of God,* Bk. VII, Chap. 6.
[25]Cf. *The Life,* Chap. 20; *Interior Castle,* Sixth Mansions, Chaps. 4-6.
[26]Cf. *Interior Castle,* Sixth Mansions, Chap. 4.
[27]Cf. *Spiritual Canticle,* notation for Stanza 14.
[28]Cf. *Interior Castle,* Sixth Mansions, Chap. 4.

natural ecstasy. The effects and characteristic qualities of each are so evident, however, that the two types of ecstasy can be readily distinguished by those who have sufficient knowledge of these matters. Natural ecstasy may be classified as follows: *fainting, somnambulism, hypnotic trance* and *hysteria.*

Swooning

It is relatively easy to distinguish the natural faint or swoon from mystical ecstasy. The former is usually of short duration; the patient can be brought back to consciousness by slapping the face or hands, dashing cold water on the face, the use of smelling salts, etc. None of these things have any effect on mystical ecstasy. Moreover, in the faint or swoon there is a complete loss of consciousness, so that all the mental faculties are suspended, while in mystical ecstasy there is usually an intensification in the activity and tension of the higher faculties in regard to the supernatural object. Further, the mystic has a clear recollection of everything that occurred during the ecstasy, whereas there is no recollection whatever of a natural faint or swoon.

Somnambulism

The cerebral automatism which characterizes somnambulism has characteristics which are completely contrary to those of mystical ecstasy. The somnambulist moves about and may even perform manual tasks; the mystical ecstatic is usually immobile and absorbed in profound contemplation.[29] The face of the somnambulist is usually flabby and expressionless, and if the eyes are open, they do not seem to be focused on anything in particular; the face of the mystic is usually radiant and transfigured.

Hypnosis

Hypnosis also presents certain external manifestations which are similar to those of ecstasy, but the differences are so profound that it is relatively easy to make a diagnosis. The hypnotised person awakens as soon as the hypnotist gives the signal or command; the ecstatic can be brought back to consciousness only by a lawful superior. In hypnosis, the will is almost entirely suspended, the conscience is dulled, and there is no recollection of what took place during the hypnotic trance. The mystic distinctly remembers what occurred during ecstasy, the intellect and will are consciously fixed upon some supernatural object, and the conscience is not affected. In the catalepsy or rigidity which is sometimes effected by hypnosis, the patient appears as one dead, for there is no psychic activity, the muscles are rigid, and the face is expressionless; in the immobility of mystical ecstasy, the face remains animated, the psychic functions are not impaired, and the appearance of death is primarily a matter of the immobility of the mystic.

Hysteria

Hysteria is a type of neurosis to which many rationalistic and materialistic philosophers have reduced true mystical ecstasy. Hysteria profoundly disturbs the organic functions of the body, and rather than resembling true ecstasy, it bears the marks of diabolical possession. The crisis of the hysteria is

---

[29]We have already referred to the fact that there have been mystics who moved about in the state of ecstasy, but that this is a very rare phenomenon.

violent, there is a propensity to illusions and fantasies, the hysteric is greatly agitated and nervous, sometimes vain, blustery and extremely impressionable. Sometimes there is insensibility to touch in certain areas of the body. In true mystical ecstasy there are none of the terrible convulsive movements of the hysteric, no incongruous or indecent postures, no inarticulate cries. Rather, the mystical ecstasy is always tranquil, decorous and edifying.

Diabolical ecstasy

Diabolical ecstasy is much easier to distinguish from mystical ecstasy than is natural ecstasy. It is a special form of diabolical obsession. It should be noted at the outset that the human intellect and will are beyond the direct reach of the influence of the devil, but he can control the activity of the internal and external senses. In mystical ecstasy, all the effects and fruits are holy, supernatural and divine. In diabolical ecstasy a person may continue to live in sin, be subject to vain caprices, enjoy the ecstatic seizure at will, contort the face and body in a repulsive manner, speak an incoherent language during the seizure, have no recollection after the seizure is ended, seek to call public attention to the ecstatic trance, remain disturbed and upset after the seizure, and often be incited to evil actions.[30]

THE PRAYER OF TRANSFORMING UNION

The last grade of prayer classified by the mystics is the transforming union or the mystical marriage. It constitutes the seventh mansions of the *Interior Castle* of St. Teresa, and is also designated as the consummate union or deification of the soul. It is the highest degree of perfection that one can attain in this life and the prelude and immediate preparation for the beatific life of glory.

ITS NATURE

According to St. John of the Cross, this grade of prayer is a total transformation of the soul in the Beloved, in which God and the soul give themselves completely to each other with a certain consummation of divine love, so that the soul is made divine, so to speak, and participates in God as much as is possible in this life.[31] According to this definition there are three essential elements in the mystical marriage: total transformation in God, mutual surrender, and the permanent union of love.

Transformation in the Beloved. As iron which is cast into the furnace becomes completely transformed by fire without ceasing to be iron, so the

[30]Cf. Pope Benedict XIV, *De servorum Dei beatificatione,* Lib. III, cap. 49.
[31]Cf. St. John of the Cross, *Spiritual Canticle,* Stanza 22.

soul which is plunged into the furnace of divine love is transformed into God without losing its condition as a creature.

> The soul becomes brilliant and transformed in God, and God communicates to the soul his supernatural being to such an extent that the soul appears to be God and to have all that God has. Such a union is effected when God grants to the soul this supernatural mercy, as a result of which all the things of God and the soul are one in a participated transformation. The soul seems to be more God than soul and is truly God by participation, although it is true that its being, so distinct by nature, is possessed by the soul as something distinct from the being of God as it was formerly, even though transformed, just as the window is distinct from the ray of the sun which illumines it.[32]

On reaching this sublime height, the soul acquires certain divine characteristics, so that it can say that it has become God by participation. It is the complete transformation in the Beloved which had been so ardently desired in the previous grades of prayer. It should be obvious, however, that this transformation could not possibly be understood in an ontological sense, but must refer to a transformation of the superior faculties as regards their mode of operation. As Father Poulain explains, baptism and sanctifying grace bestow on the soul a participation in the divine nature, but in a static and unconscious state. In the transforming union, however, the soul is conscious of the communication of the divine life. God is not now merely the object of the supernatural operations of the intellect and the will, but is the co-principle of the soul's operation. The transforming union is the prelude to the experimental knowledge of the beatific vision.[33]

Mutual surrender. The mutual surrender or submission between God and the soul is a natural consequence of the transformation of the soul in God. As between two spouses there is a perfect communication of goods, so between God and the soul which has been admitted to spiritual marriage. This indissoluble surrender constitutes the essence of spiritual matrimony, as the mutual surrender and acceptance of a man and woman constitutes the essence of the sacrament of matrimony. No one should be scandalized that the mystics have used this comparison, because the Holy Spirit made use of it in the Canticle of Canticles. Christ also used it in the gospel to express the gifts of grace and glory.[34] St. Paul likewise refers to this symbol on frequent occasions.[35] Following the example of Scripture, Christian tradition has made use of this symbol throughout the ages in order to signify the intimacy of the union of the soul with God at the height of sanctity.

[32]Cf. *The Ascent of Mount Carmel,* Bk. II, Chap. 5. Cf. also *The Dark Night,* Bk. II, Chap. 10, in which St. John of the Cross compares the process of the soul's sanctification to the action of fire on a log.

[33]Cf. A. Poulain, S.J., *op. cit.,* Chap. 19.

[34]Cf. Matt. 22:3; 25:10; Lk. 12:36.

[35]Cf. II Cor. 11:2; Eph. 5:23-32.

Sometimes, as in the case of St. Catherine of Siena and St. Teresa of Avila, there was a vision of Christ and the bestowal of a ring. This in itself, however, constitutes an extraordinary phenomenon and is not essential to the transforming union and mystical marriage.

Permanent union of love. St. Teresa of Avila stresses that there is a great difference between the mystical marriage and all the degrees of prayer which preceded it, especially because the mystical marriage carries with it an awareness of the permanency of this mutual love between the soul and God.[36] Although there may be brief interruptions, it can be said that the soul enjoys a constant companionship of love. At times the soul seems to fulfill literally the beautiful expression of the Canticle of Canticles (5:2): "I was sleeping, but my heart kept vigil."[37]

CONFIRMATION IN GRACE

Since we speak of the permanent union of love in the mystical marriage, the question naturally arises as to whether this is equivalent to confirmation in grace. St. John of the Cross states that this is so, for he says that it is his belief that the state of the transforming union never falters and that the soul is confirmed in grace, and that this is the highest state which a soul can attain in this life.[38] But St. Teresa holds the contrary opinion. She states repeatedly that as long as the soul remains in this world it must walk with great caution, lest it offend God.[39] Nevertheless, we believe that, if it is rightly understood, the opinion of St. John of the Cross can be followed. It is not a question of intrinsic impeccability, because that is stated by the Church to be an impossibility in this life.[40] It is rather a question of the special assistance of God which prevents the soul from sinning mortally, and it should be noted that this special assistance refers only to mortal sins, because it would be impossible, without a special privilege similar to that given to the Blessed Virgin, to avoid all venial sins.[41] In the light of these principles it is necessary to interpret the expressions of the mystics as referring only to the special help granted by God to avoid all future mortal sins, with moral certitude of salvation.

---

[36]Cf. *Interior Castle,* Seventh Mansions, Chaps. 1, 2.

[37]Cf. also St. Teresa of Avila, *The Life,* Chap. 29.

[38]Cf. *Spiritual Canticle,* Stanza 22.

[39]Cf. St. Teresa of Avila, *Interior Castle,* Seventh Mansions, Chaps. 2 and 4; *The Life,* Chap. 39; *The Way of Perfection,* Chap. 10.

[40]Cf. Council of Vienne, condemnation of the errors of the Beguards and Beguines (Denz. 471).

[41]Cf. Council of Trent, Decree on Justification, Chaps. 11 and 16 (Denz. 804 and 810) and canon 23 (Denz. 833); condemnation of the errors of Molinos, n. 56 (Denz. 1276).

Another question that arises in connection with the transforming union is that of the possibility of a vision or contemplation of the divine essence in this life. St. Thomas explicitly denies that it is possible for a soul to have the habitual vision of the divine essence in this life; he does admit, however, that through a stupendous miracle outside the ordinary providence of God a soul could receive a transitory communication of the light of glory (*lumen gloriae*), as he thinks was granted to Moses and St. Paul.[42] The only one who enjoyed the habitual vision of the divine essence in this life was Christ, who in his condition of Son of God was at the same time a wayfarer and a comprehensor.[43] A number of theologians likewise maintain that the beatific vision was granted in a transitory way to the Blessed Virgin in the culminating moments of her life. Apart from these cases, there is no certitude that anyone else was ever granted this exalted privilege. St. Teresa of Avila and St. John of the Cross speak of an intellectual vision of the Trinity whereby the Persons are known individually, but they both insist that this vision is effected by means of a created species and that the veil is never completely removed from the divinity.[44] The only certain conclusion that can be drawn is that the beatific vision does not form a part of the contemplative degrees of prayer which are proper to this life. Infused contemplation is of its very nature orientated to the beatific vision as its supreme analogate, just as sanctifying grace is orientated to eternal life, but the highest degree of contemplation which can be attained in this life is a prelude to the beatific vision.

THE VISION OF GOD

Perhaps no one has described as clearly as St. Teresa the marvelous effects which are produced in the soul by the transforming union or mystical marriage. We shall summarize her description of these effects as given in her *Interior Castle,* Seventh Mansions, Chapter 3:

EFFECTS OF UNION

1) *A forgetfulness of self* so complete that it seems as if the soul no longer existed. There is no longer any knowledge or remembrance of heaven or life or honor as regards the soul, so completely is it absorbed in seeking the honor of God. The soul lives in a state of forgetfulness so that it has no desire whatever in regard to self, but desires only to do what it can to promote the glory of God, and for this it would gladly lay down its life.

2) *A great desire to suffer,* but now the desire does not disturb the soul as it did previously. So great is the soul's longing that the will of God be done in it that it accepts whatever God wills as the best for it. If he

---

[42]Cf. *Summa,* I, q. 12, a. 11, ad 2; II-II, q. 175, aa. 3-6.
[43]Cf. *ibid.,* III, q. 9, a. 2; q. 10, aa. 1-4.
[44]Cf. St. John of the Cross, *The Living Flame of Love,* Chap. 4; St. Teresa of Avila, *Interior Castle,* Seventh Mansions, Chap. 1.

sends suffering, well and good; if not, the soul does not worry or fret about it as it did previously.

3) *Delight in persecution.* When the soul is persecuted, it experiences great interior joy and much more peace than formerly. It bears no enmity toward those who treat it badly or desire to do so. Rather, it conceives a special love for such persons, and if it were to see them in some affliction it would be deeply grieved and would do all in its power to relieve them. It loves to commend such persons to God, and would rejoice at relinquishing some of the favors it receives from God if it could bestow them on its enemies, and thus perhaps prevent them from offending God.

4) *Desire to serve God.* Whereas the soul formerly suffered because of its longing to die and to be with God, it now experiences a strong desire to serve God and to help any soul that it can. Indeed, it now desires not to die but to live for many years and to suffer the most severe trials if in this way it can be a means whereby God is praised. Its conception of glory is now connected in some way with helping Christ, especially when it sees how often people offend him and how few there are who are truly concerned about his honor.

5) *Detachment from everything created.* The desires of the soul are no longer for consolations, because the soul realizes that now the Lord himself dwells within it. As a result, the soul experiences a marked detachment from everything, and a desire to be alone, or to be occupied with something that will be beneficial to the soul. There is no more aridity or interior trial, but only a constant recollection in God and a tender love for him. There is no fear that this period of tranquility may be caused by the devil, because the soul has an unwavering certitude that it comes from God. This experience takes place in the very center of the soul and in the highest faculty, into which the devil cannot enter.

6) *Absence of ecstasies.* Upon reaching this state, the soul has no more raptures, or very seldom. The great weakness which formerly was the occasion for raptures has now given place to a great strength which has been granted by God. Nevertheless, the soul walks with great care and still does all in its power to strengthen itself with the help of God's grace. Indeed, the more it is favored by God, the more cautious it becomes and the more aware of its own littleness and humility.

IDEAL OF CHRISTIAN PERFECTION

Such is the bittersweet path which leads to the heights of contemplative prayer and the transforming union. It is the sublime ideal of Christian perfection, and it is offered to all souls in grace. When Jesus pronounced the precept: "You therefore are to be perfect, even as your heavenly Father is perfect" (Matt. 5:48), he was speaking to all souls without exception. The Christian life, if it is developed according to the supernatural powers that are inherent in it, will normally lead to the transforming union of charity, which is in turn the normal prelude to the beatific vision.[45]

> O souls created for these grandeurs and called to them! What do you do? With what do you occupy yourselves? Your desires are lowly things and your possessions are miseries. O wretched blindness of the eyes of your souls, which are blind to such great light and deaf to so clear a voice, not realizing that even as you seek grandeur and glory you remain wretched and lowly and have become ignorant and unworthy of such great blessings.[46]

---

[45]Cf. St. Teresa of Avila, *The Way of Perfection,* Chap. 19; *The Life,* Chap. 27; *Interior Castle,* Seventh Mansions, Chap. 2.

[46]St. John of the Cross, *Spiritual Canticle,* Stanza 39.

SECONDARY MEANS OF SPIRITUAL GROWTH

1: INTERNAL MEANS

Having discussed the fundamental means for the growth and development of the Christian life, both *ex opere operato* and *ex opere operantis,* we shall now consider certain secondary means which are of great practical importance. While they are not all of equal value, it will be evident that they do mutually assist each other. It should be kept in mind that they are only secondary means of growth in perfection, however, and therefore no one of them should be used to the exclusion of the basic and fundamental means already discussed.

These secondary means are of two classes, internal and external. The first group, which we shall treat in this chapter, includes the practice of the presence of God, the examination of conscience, the desire for perfection, conformity with the will of God, and fidelity to grace. The external secondary means will be discussed in the chapter which follows.

THE PRESENCE OF GOD

The practice of the presence of God consists in recalling as frequently as possible that God is present in all places, especially in the depth of the just soul, and consequently in doing all things in the sight of God. Sacred Scripture and tradition are unanimous in stressing the importance and sanctifying effect of the practice of the presence of God. "Walk in my presence and be perfect," God said to Abraham (Gen. 17:1). The one necessarily follows from the other, for if a person is convinced that God sees him, he will endeavor to avoid the slightest sin or imperfection and will strive to be as recollected as possible in God's presence. If properly used, this spiritual practice will keep the soul in a spirit of prayer and will lead it to contemplation and intimate union with God. St. Francis de Sales goes so far as to say that interior recollection accompanied by pious ejaculations can supply for any pious practice and that its absence cannot be remedied by any other.[1]

[1]*Introduction to the Devout Life,* Part II, Chap. 13.

GOD'S PRESENCE

It is a theological fact that we are constantly in God's presence, which admits of five distinct types. The *presence of immensity* flows from the divine attribute of the same name; it signifies that God is truly and intimately present to all things, and this in a threefold manner: by *essence, presence* and *power.* He is present by essence so far as he gives and preserves the existence of all things (creation and conservation), so that nothing could exist or continue to exist without God's presence. He is present by presence in the sense that absolutely nothing escapes his gaze but all things are naked and open to his eyes. He is present by power in the sense that all things are subject to his power. With one word he creates; with one word he could annihilate whatever he has created.

God's *presence by indwelling* is a special type of presence effected through grace and the operations which flow from grace, in virtue of which God is present to the just soul as a friend, enabling the soul to share in his own divine life.

God's *sacramental presence* is that which Christ enjoys in the Eucharist, so that he is truly present under the appearance of bread and wine. His presence there is *per modum substantiae,* as the theologians say, prescinding from space and extension.

God's *personal or hypostatic presence* is proper to Christ, the Second Person of the Trinity, so that the humanity of Christ subsists in the Person of the Word.

God's *presence by manifestation* signifies that which is proper to him in heaven. So far as we are concerned, however, we shall be aware of this manifestation only when we enjoy the beatific vision.

Of these five types of presence, those which most directly affect the practice of the presence of God are the first two, namely, the presence of immensity and the presence of indwelling. The first is verified of the soul at all times and under all conditions, even if the soul should be in the state of mortal sin. The second is also permanent and habitual, but it is found only in souls in the state of grace.

CONSEQUENCES OF GOD'S PRESENCE

The practice of the presence of God has several consequences which are of great importance for the spiritual life. The following are the principal ones:

1) *It urges us to avoid even the slightest deliberate fault.* If we are most careful of our behavior in the presence of superiors or persons of dignity lest we offend them, how much more so in the presence of God, who sees not only our external actions but our interior thoughts and movements.

2) *It impels us to do all things with the greatest possible perfection.* This is a natural consequence of great love, especially if one is performing an action in the very presence of the one he loves. Faithful observance of this norm of action is sufficient to lead a soul to the heights of sanctity. While it is

true that God does not demand perfection of us here and now, he does expect us to do the best we can at a given time.

3) *It enables us to observe modesty in our deportment at all times.* Whether alone or with others, a person who is constantly aware of God's presence will maintain a sense of Christian dignity in all his actions and in his very bearing. To this end, it is especially important that souls in the state of grace be conscious of the presence of God through the indwelling of the Trinity.

4) *It increases our fortitude in the struggles of the Christian life.* It is much more difficult to overcome obstacles and to suffer trials when one is alone. But God is always with us to animate our courage and to give us the positive assistance of his grace.

METHODS OF PRACTICE

There are two principal methods of practicing the presence of God. The first consists in a kind of exterior representation by which one visualizes God as ever watching us from above. We do not see him, but he is really there and we cannot do anything that escapes his divine gaze. This method of practicing the presence of God is greatly aided by the use of crucifixes and other religious symbols which are placed in a prominent place.

The second method is that of interior recollection. It requires that one live in an ever increasing awareness of God's presence in the soul, whether by immensity or by the indwelling. The result of this method is a more profound understanding of what Jesus meant when he said: "The kingdom of God is within you." It should be noted, however, that interior recollection should not be confused with egoistic introspection or a mechanical and lifeless observance of rigid rules of external behavior. Interior recollection is a turning inward of one's thoughts, not to seek self, but to seek God who is present to us. When properly used, interior recollection serves to unite the practice of the presence of God with a deep and intimate union with God. It is also, therefore, one of the necessary conditions for cultivating a deep and abiding spirit of prayer.

Other methods for practicing the presence of God have been proposed by various writers, which may prove helpful to one or another individual. Some of these secondary methods are: to see the hand of God in all the events of one's life, whether adverse or prosperous; to see God in all creatures (flowers, mountains, oceans, etc.); to see God in the person of one's superior and in one's neighbor; etc. The particular soul should try various methods and then select the one that is most helpful in cultivating the practice of the presence of God. It should be remembered that, however much one may try to keep himself constantly in the presence of God, he cannot achieve this in a complete and permanent manner until he has entered into the transforming mystical union, which is a prelude to the beatific presence of God in glory.

EXAMINATION OF CONSCIENCE

As its name indicates, the examination of conscience is an investigation of one's conscience in order to discover the good or evil acts which one has performed, and especially to verify one's basic attitude regarding God and one's personal sanctification. It should be evident that we are not here referring to the examination of conscience which is made prior to confession, which is simply a review and enumeration of one's sins. As a means to greater perfection, the examination of conscience should be made in view of one's further progress in holiness. It should take into account, therefore, the strength or weakness of one's virtues, as well as the number and frequency of one's sins. To place too great an emphasis on one's failings may result in meticulosity, anxiety, discouragement and even scrupulosity.

Spiritual writers are unanimous in stressing the importance of the examination of conscience as a spiritual exercise. Outstanding among them, of course, is St. Ignatius Loyola, who for a long time used no other methods of spiritual formation for his companions but the examination of conscience and the frequent reception of the sacraments. He attached such importance to this practice that in the Constitutions of the Society he never granted any dispensation from it.

KINDS OF EXAMINATION

St. Ignatius distinguishes two types of examination: general and particular.[2] The first is an over-all view of one's spiritual state and those things which would contribute to the improvement of one's spiritual life. The second is focused particularly on some definite vice which one is trying to eliminate or some virtue which one is trying to cultivate.

The *particular examen* has three steps or points. First, on arising in the morning, one resolves to correct the particular fault he is trying to eliminate, or to avoid failure in the practice of the particular virtue he is trying to cultivate. Secondly, after the noon meal one makes an examination of the faults committed during the morning and resolves to avoid them in the afternoon. Thirdly, after the evening meal one repeats the examination and resolution as at noon.

The general examination proposed by St. Ignatius has five points: 1) give thanks to God for benefits received; 2) beg the grace to know one's sins and to rid oneself of them; 3) a detailed examination, hour by hour, of one's thoughts, words and deeds; 4) beg pardon of God; 5) resolve to amend one's life and recite the Our Father. The general examen is made once a day, before retiring.

[2]*Spiritual Exercises,* nn. 24-43.

MAKING AN EXAMINATION

In order to obtain the maximum benefit from the examination of conscience, it is necessary to know how to practice it. We have already given the general directives in accordance with the teaching of St. Ignatius Loyola. Within this general framework, it seems to us that no one has succeeded in explaining the method of examination as simply and clearly as the anonymous author of *The Interior Life,* edited and adapted by Tissot. The following extract is a summary of the fundamental points:

1) One's spiritual exercises should be unified; otherwise they run the risk of being confined to some particular moment in the day, without exerting their influence throughout the entire day. The examination of conscience should be the bond of union for all one's spiritual exercises and the great means of achieving unity in one's spiritual life.

2) Philosophy teaches us that acts are transitory but habits are permanent. The act passes; the custom or habit remains. Hence we should especially examine our habits. The mere knowledge of our acts will not give us an intimate knowledge of our souls; through them alone we can never make a true examination of conscience in the full meaning of the word. What resides in the sanctuary of conscience is not our acts, which have already passed away, but our habits or dispositions of soul. If we have succeeded in knowing them, we have verified the true state of our souls, but not otherwise.

3) In order to know our souls it is necessary to ask ourselves this simple question: "Where is my heart?" Immediately we shall find the answer within ourselves. The question makes us look into the intimate depths of the soul and immediately the salient point stands out. One listens to the sound which comes from the soul, and at once the dominant note is heard. This is an intuitive and immediate function. It can be repeated many times throughout the day. There is no need for investigations, feats of memory, mathematical calculations. It is simply a rapid, all-inclusive glance which tells us at once the state of our souls. We seek to discover our fundamental disposition or attitude of soul. That is the mainspring of all our actions, and that is what must be corrected and made right if all else in our life is to go well.

4) The details and exact number of the external manifestations of our fundamental disposition of soul are of least importance. We don't waste time cutting the branches from a tree when we are going to cut down the whole tree. It is true that external acts reveal the internal condition, but we can discover this condition by looking at it directly instead of searching for it in the forest of external acts.

5) But if we attend exclusively to the principal interior disposition, shall we not lose sight of the other dispositions of soul, thus allowing them to grow in the darkness without paying any attention to them? There is no danger of this. The other dispositions of soul cannot emerge if one's whole soul is directed to God as a result of the examination. All of the secondary dispositions of soul are thereby subjected. Moreover, the dominant inclination or disposition of soul is not always the same; one's defects are manifested according to circumstances, and as soon as a disposition comes to the fore, the examination of conscience overcomes and subjects it.

6) But can we rest content with this glance? Does everything consist in seeing? By no means. It is necessary to rectify all disorders and to foster

all good movements and inclinations. The glance at one's state of soul should lead to contrition and resolution. Contrition corrects evil and resolution affirms good. Contrition looks to the past and resolution prepares for the future. Contrition should be inspired by the essential motive of our existence: the glory of God and the love of God for himself. Resolution should also lead us to the only things that are essential: knowledge of God, submission to his will, and conformity with the movement of his grace. The resolution should be a particular one which will touch the special point which dominates one's soul. It should rectify the tendency which leads farthest from God, or strengthen that which will bring one closest to God. It should place our hearts completely in the presence of the glory of God, under the will of God and in the grace of God.

7) There are, therefore, three steps in the examination of conscience: a glance at one's state of soul, contrition and resolution. All three can be utilized in the general and particular examens of which St. Ignatius speaks. In the general examen, the glance embraces first of all one's predominant disposition throughout the day. Then it can extend to the secondary dispositions which have been manifested but have not been predominant throughout the day. Contrition will then correct the evils and resolution will re-affirm the good. The particular examen is easier. As a matter of fact, it has already been done when one discovers his fundamental predominant disposition of soul. The morning examen should be used to assure one's proper orientation during the day and the avoidance of the evils to which one is most exposed.

8) In this way, the examination of conscience will give unity and consistency to all one's spiritual life. By means of it one can see and be illumined, one can avoid dangers and correct defects. It serves as a torch to light one's path and to reveal one's interior state, so that one cannot remain in evil but is obliged to advance in holiness.

CONCLUSION

There is no doubt that the faithful practice of examination of conscience will have profound effects on one's spiritual life. But in this, as in so many things, its efficacy depends to a great extent on perseverance. To omit the examination frequently or to make it in a purely mechanical fashion is to render it absolutely sterile. The soul that earnestly desires to become holy must be convinced that many of the other means of sanctification are frustrated if one does not make the daily examination of conscience.

THE DESIRE FOR PERFECTION

Of all the psychological factors which play a part in man's spiritual life, a prominent place must be given to the sincere desire for attaining perfection. It is said that when St. Thomas Aquinas was asked by one of his sisters what she should do to reach sanctity, he answered her in one brief sentence: "Will it."

Desire in general is a movement of the soul toward some absent good. It is impossible to desire evil precisely as evil, and it would be unreasonable to desire a good which is impossible of attainment.

ITS NATURE AND NECESSITY

The desire for perfection is an act of the will, under the influence of grace, which aspires unceasingly to spiritual growth until one reaches sanctity. It is an elicited act of the will, because goodness is the proper object of this faculty. It is under the influence of grace, because such a desire is manifestly supernatural and surpasses the exigencies and tendencies of pure nature. It must be constant in its aspiration for ever greater perfection, and it must not stop at any intermediate degree of perfection but must aspire to the heights of sanctity.

Sanctity is the supreme good which we can attain in this life. By its very nature it is something infinitely desirable, but since it is also an arduous and difficult good, it is impossible to tend toward it efficaciously without the strong impulse of a will which is determined to attain it at any cost. St. Teresa of Avila considers it of decisive importance "to have a great and very determined resolve not to stop until one reaches it,"[3] without reckoning the difficulties along the way, the criticism of those around us, the lack of health, or the disdain of the world. Therefore, only resolute and energetic souls, with the help of divine grace, will scale the heights of perfection.

QUALITIES OF DESIRE

In order that it will possess the greatest possible sanctifying efficacy, the desire for perfection should have the following qualities:

1) *It should be supernatural,* that is, it should flow from grace and be directed to the greater glory of God, the ultimate end of our existence. This means that the desire for perfection is a gift of God, for which we should petition humbly and perseveringly until we obtain it.

2) *It should be profoundly humble,* without reliance entirely on our own strength, which is weakness in God's sight, but placing our trust principally in him from whom all graces flow. Nor should we aspire to sanctity for any other motive than to love and glorify God. In the beginning, it is difficult to avoid every trace of presumption and egoism—which God sometimes punishes by allowing the most shameful falls so that the soul will see exactly what it is when he does not sustain it—but it is necessary to be constantly purifying one's intention and perfecting one's motives until they are directed only to the glory of God and conformity with his will.

3) *It should be filled with confidence.* This naturally follows from the preceding quality. Of ourselves we can do nothing, but all things are possible in him who strengthens us (Phil. 4:13). The Lord purposely places great obstacles before us in order to test our trust in him. Countless souls abandon

[3]*The Way of Perfection,* Chap. 21, n. 2; cf. also *The Life,* Chap. 13, n. 2.

the road to perfection in the face of obstacles because, becoming discouraged and lacking confidence in God, they think that sanctity is not for them. Only those who persevere in spite of hardships will receive the crown of victory.

4) *It should be the predominant desire.* This should be our most intense desire, since there is no greater good than the glory of God and, as a means to it, our own perfection. All other goods must be subordinated to this supreme good. Hence the desire for perfection is not simply one among many, but it must be the fundamental desire which dominates one's entire life. Those who wish to become saints must dedicate themselves to this task *professionally,* and this requires that they put aside anything that may prove an impediment. Many souls have failed in the pursuit of sanctity because, instead of giving themselves irrevocably to its pursuit, they have fluctuated between the things of God and the things of the world.

5) *It should be constant.* Numerous souls, on the occasion of some great event, such as the termination of a mission or retreat, reception of the religious habit or sacred orders, profession of vows, etc., experience a great spiritual impulse, as a result of which they resolve to dedicate themselves henceforth to the pursuit of sanctity. But they soon weary of the pursuit when they experience the first difficulties, and they either abandon the road to sanctity or the ardent desire becomes cool. Or sometimes they grant themselves vacations or pauses, under the pretext of resting a while to recover their strength. This is a great mistake, because the soul not only does not gain any strength but is greatly weakened. Later, when it wishes to renew its efforts, a greater effort is required to recapture the spiritual gains previously made. All this could have been avoided if the desire for perfection had remained constant, without undue violence or extremes, but also without respite or weakness.

6) *It should be practical and efficacious.* This is not a question of wishful thinking but of a definite determination which must be put into practice here and now, by using all the means at one's disposal for attaining perfection. It is easy to imagine that one has a desire for perfection because of occasional good intentions or certain noble sentiments experienced during prayer. But a desire is efficacious only when it is put into execution. To desire perfection in a theoretical way and to postpone one's efforts until some later date is to live in an illusion. The individual passes from one delay to another and life passes on, so that the person runs the risk of appearing before God with empty hands.

MEANS OF AROUSING DESIRE

Since the desire for perfection is of such great importance in the struggle for holiness, one should note carefully the following means for arousing this desire:

1) *To beg for it incessantly from God.* Since the desire is supernatural, it can come to us only from above.

2) *To renew it frequently.* It should be renewed daily at the most solemn moment of the day, namely, at the moment of Communion; at other times, on principal feasts, the monthly day of recollection, during the annual retreat, on special anniversaries.

3) *To meditate frequently on the motives which inspire this desire.* The principal motives are the following: a) our grave obligation to strive for perfection; b) consciousness that this is the greatest good we can seek in this life; c) awareness of the danger we risk if we do not truly strive to sanctify ourselves (mortal sin, loss of vocation, apostasy); d) recognition of the fact that the perfect imitation of Christ demands perfection and sanctity.

CONFORMITY TO GOD'S WILL

Perfect conformity to the divine will is a most efficacious means of sanctification. St. Teresa of Avila says in this regard that a person who begins the life of prayer must work and resolve and dispose himself with as much diligence as possible to make his will conformable to that of God; in this consists the greatest perfection that can be attained on the spiritual way.[4]

ITS NATURE

Conformity to the will of God consists in a loving, total and intimate submission and harmony of our will with that of God in everything he disposes or permits in our regard. When it reaches a perfect state it is known by the name of *holy abandonment to the will of God;* in its less perfect state it is called simply *Christian resignation.*

In order to understand this practice in an orthodox sense, it is necessary to keep in mind certain doctrinal points. In the first place, sanctity is the result of the action of God and the free co-operation of man. God is the director of the work of our sanctification, and therefore nothing should be done which is not in conformity with his plans and under the impulse of his grace.

Secondly, the will of God, most simple in itself, has various operations in regard to creatures, and these have been given different names by the theologians. The *absolute* will is that by which God wills a thing without any condition (creation of the world); the *conditional* will applies to that which God wills under some condition (salvation of a sinner if he repents). The *antecedent* will is that by which God wills something considered in itself (the salvation of all men); the *consequent* will is that by which God wills a thing in view of all its particular circumstances (the condemnation of a sinner who dies unrepentant).

[4] Cf. *Interior Castle,* Second Mansions, n. 8.

The divine will *of expression* refers to certain signs by which the will of God is known by man (precepts, prohibitions, events caused or permitted by God) and therefore is closely related to the virtue of obedience. The divine will *of good pleasure* is the internal act of the will of God which as yet has not been revealed and cannot be known by man (free future events, time of one's death, gift of final perseverance); hence it is closely related to the practice of abandonment to the will of God. The rule of life for the Christian should be one of complete obedience to the divine will of expression and total abandonment to the divine will of good pleasure.

Charity and abandonment

The basis of abandonment to the will of God is charity, because it belongs to love to unite the will of the lover to the will of the beloved, and perfect abandonment requires the complete surrender of our own will to that of God. It goes without saying that such perfect abandonment is found only in souls that are far advanced in perfection.

In order to attain this total abandonment, the following theological points should be meditated upon frequently:

1) Nothing happens that has not been foreseen by God from all eternity and willed or permitted by him.

2) God could not will or permit anything that is not in conformity with the purpose for which he created all things, namely, his own external glory.

3) All things contribute in some way to the good of those who love God and persevere in his love.[5]

4) Abandonment to the will of God does not excuse anyone from fulfilling the divine will of expression by obeying the precepts and commands of God, and then submitting themselves as regards all things else to the divine will of good pleasure, without any anxiety.[6]

ITS EXCELLENCE AND NECESSITY

From what has already been said, it should be evident that abandonment to the will of God is not only an excellent spiritual practice but a necessary one for the attainment of sanctity. Its excellence lies in its incomparable efficacy for removing the obstacles which impede the action of grace, for making one practice the virtues as perfectly as possible, and for establishing the absolute dominion of God over our will.

The necessity of practicing abandonment to the will of God is based upon the following points:

---

[5]Cf. Rom. 8:28.

[6]Cf. D. V. Lehodey, O.C., *Holy Abandonment* (New York: Benziger, 1934), Part II, Prol.; Part IV, Chap. 1; R. Garrigou-Lagrange, O.P., *Divine Providence* (St. Louis: Herder, 1937), Part II, Chap. 7; Part IV, Chap. 1.

INTERNAL MEANS

1) *Divine right.* As God's creatures, we are also his servants. He created us, he conserves us, he redeemed us, he has made us for himself. We do not belong to ourselves, but we are God's.[7] We are also his sons and friends through grace, but sons should be subject to their father and friends should be of one mind and one heart.

2) *Our utility.* Abandonment to God's will has a great sanctifying efficacy, and our sanctification is the greatest good which we could seek in this world.

3) *The example of Christ.* All during his life on earth Christ fulfilled the will of his heavenly Father. He proclaimed this by his actions and openly professed it in words. His last words from the cross were a submission and yielding of his whole being to the hands of his Father. Mary, too, handmaid of the Lord, practiced this total abandonment in imitation of her Son.

METHODS OF PRACTICE

Having traced the general lines of the practice of abandonment to the will of God, we shall now offer some concrete suggestions regarding the method of conforming one's will to that of God in the concrete circumstances of daily life. As regards the divine will of expression, we should conform ourselves to it by accepting and fulfilling whatever God requests of us through his laws, counsels, his church and the inspirations of actual grace. As regards the divine will of good pleasure, we should abandon ourselves in all confidence to the hidden designs of his providence. Let us now see how these two general norms can be put into practice.

Will of expression

St. Thomas says that the will of God can be manifested to us in five ways: 1) by doing something directly (*operatio*); 2) by allowing something to happen but not causing it (*permissio*); 3) by imposing his will through a precept (*praeceptum*); 4) by forbidding something (*prohibitio*); 5) by suggesting or persuading without commanding (*consilium*). St. Thomas then states that *operatio* and *permissio* refer to the present (*operatio* pertains to good and *permissio* pertains to evil); but the other three ways refer to the future (*praeceptum* to a future good, *prohibitio* to a future evil which is to be avoided, and *consilium* to the superabundance of a future good).

1) *Operatio.* God always positively wills whatever he makes or does of himself, because it is always referred to good and directed to his greater glory. Under this heading are included all the personal, domestic and social matters which have been disposed by God alone and do not depend on the will of man. Sometimes they are events which fill one with joy; at other times they are filled with bitterness and may cause great sorrow if one cannot see the loving hand of God, who ordains all things for

[7]Cf. I Cor. 6:19.

good and for his greater glory. Whatever God positively and directly wills is best for us, even if for the time being it causes pain and suffering. In the face of such happenings which are acts of God (incurable sickness, the death of loved ones, etc.), the only possible Christian attitude is: "Thy will be done." And if our love of God is strong enough to enable us to rise above simple resignation and through our pain or sorrow give thanks to God, we shall have reached the perfection of abandonment to the will of God.

2) *Permissio.* God never wills positively and directly that which he permits, because *permissio* refers to evil, which God cannot will as such. But in his infinite goodness and wisdom, God knows how to convert into good the evil which he permits, and that is why he permits it. The greatest evil ever committed was the crucifixion of Christ, but God ordained it to the great good of the redemption of the human race. Hence we manifest a lamentable shortsightedness when, in the evils which God permits to happen to us, we see only the secondary and immediate causes which have produced them and do not raise our eyes to heaven to adore the designs of God, who permits these things for our greater good. While it is true that God could not directly will the sinful actions of others which cause us suffering, he nevertheless permits them for our good. We must, therefore, strive to see in the injustice of men the justice of God which punishes us for our sins, and even his mercy which gives us an opportunity to make satisfaction for them.

3) *Praeceptum.* It is above all necessary to conform ourselves to the will of God as known through his precepts and laws. It would be a grave error to attempt to please God with works of supererogation freely selected by ourselves, and then disregard the laws which he has imposed on us directly or through his representatives. The first things that we should observe conscientiously if we wish to be perfectly subject to God's will of expression are his commandments, the laws of the Church, the commands of superiors and the duties of our state in life. We have a threefold obligation in regard to these various precepts: 1) to know what they are; 2) to love and respect them; 3) to fulfill them. "Not everyone who says to me, 'Lord, Lord,' shall enter the kingdom of heaven, but he who does the will of my Father in heaven" (Matt. 7:21).

4) *Prohibitio.* The first and most basic step toward conformity of one's will with that of God is to avoid most carefully all sin, however small. As St. Teresa says:

> May God deliver us from every deliberate sin, however small. All the more so since it is not a little thing, being set against so great a majesty and seeing that he is looking at us. This seems to me to be a deliberate sin, for it is as if one were to say: "Lord, although this offends you, I shall do it. I realize that you see it and I know that you do not wish it. I understand

all this, but I prefer to follow my own inclination and desire rather than your will." In a matter of this type it sems to me there is nothing little, however light the sin, but it is something great, and very great.[8]

But what is to be done if we fall into a grave sin? It is necessary to distinguish two aspects of the sin: the offense against God and the humiliation of the sinner. The first must be rejected completely, and one can never repent of it sufficently. The second can be accepted with penitence and gratitude, because one's humiliation through sin is a means of learning the significance of God's law.[9] As for those who lament their personal humiliation more than the offense against God, such purely human repentance can never produce truly supernatural fruit.

5) *Consilium.* The soul that wishes to attain perfect abandonment to the will of God must be disposed to practice the evangelical counsels. Religious make a vow to practice certain counsels in their daily life; lay persons are not called upon to do this, but they should observe the *spirit* of the counsels and carry them out in practice when the duties of their state in life permit. But it would be an error for the laity gratuitously to assume a manner of life which is proper to religious; the first duty of laymen—whether married or living singly in the world—is to fulfill the obligations imposed by their particular vocation.

Will of good pleasure

As regards the divine will of good pleasure, we have already observed that its decrees are completely unknown to us. We do not know what God has decreed for our future, but we do know some things for certain: that the will of God is the supreme cause of all things; that the divine will is essentially good and beneficent; that all things, whether adverse or prosperous, contribute to the good of those who love God.

What more could we ask in order to abandon ourselves entirely to God's will *de beneplacito*? This is the holy indifference which St. Ignatius establishes as the principle and foundation of the entire Christian life. By means of this holy indifference, says St. Ignatius, "it is necessary to make ourselves indifferent to all created things in everything that is granted to the liberty of our free will and is not prohibited, in such wise that we do not prefer health to sickness, wealth to poverty, honor to dishonor, a long life to a short life, and so likewise with everything else, but that we desire and choose that which best leads us to the end for which we were created."[10]

Holy indifference

Holy indifference is based upon the three theological principles which we have given above. It should be evident that, if the divine will is the supreme cause of everything that happens, and if the divine will is infinitely good, holy,

[8]*The Way of Perfection,* Chap. 41, n. 3.

[9]Cf. Ps. 118:71.

[10]*Spiritual Exercises,* n. 23. The indifference of which St. Ignatius speaks refers only to those things which do not fall under the divine will of expression. It is, therefore, a far cry from the heretical indifference proposed by the Quietists.

wise and powerful, then the more our wills conform to that of God, the more good, holy, wise and powerful they will be. Nothing evil can befall us, because the very evils which God permits to happen to us will contribute to our greater good if we know how to utilize them in the way which God desires.

But in order to understand the nature of holy indifference, the following basic principles should be kept in mind:

1) The purpose of holy indifference is to give oneself completely to God and to become utterly detached from self. It is not a purely stoical indifference to whatever befalls us, but an efficacious means of uniting our wills to that of God.

2) This indifference applies only to the superior part of the soul, for the inferior part or natural inclination cannot help but experience the blows of misfortune and suffering. It would be impossible to demand of our lower faculties that they remain insensate and indifferent, and therefore one should not be disturbed if he experiences the repugnance or revolt of nature, as long as the will accepts sufferings and trials as coming from the hand of God. This is amply verified in Christ's agony in Gethsemane and his words on Calvary.[11] It is in this sense also that certain expressions of the saints are to be understood: "To suffer, Lord, and to be despised for thee" (St. John of the Cross); "to suffer or to die" (St. Teresa of Avila); "not to die, but to suffer" (St. Magdalen of Pazzi). They were still human enough to suffer, but they wished to subject themselves to suffering in spite of the protests of their sense faculties.

3) Lastly, this indifference is not merely passive but truly active, although determined solely by the will of God. In those instances in which the divine will is made manifest (will of expression), the human will rushes forth to obey with generosity; in those cases in which the divine will is not yet manifested (will of good pleasure), the human will is perfectly disposed to accept and fulfill whatever God decrees as soon as his will becomes manifest. Holy indifference, it should be noted, ought to extend to all things in one's life, as is so beautifully explained by St. Francis de Sales.[12]

Would it be permissible to reach such a point of indifference that one is disinterested in his own salvation? By no means; this erroneous teaching of the Quietists has been expressly condemned by the Church.[13] God wills that all men be saved,[14] and he permits those to be condemned who have deliberately turned away from him and have died unrepentant.

---

[11]Cf. Lk. 12:50; Matt. 26:38, 27:46.
[12]Cf. *Treatise on the Love of God,* Bk. IX, Chap. 5.
[13]Condemnation of the errors of Molinos, n. 7 (Denz. 1227).
[14]Cf. I Tim. 2:4.

It is not that they could not have been saved, but they would not be saved. Hence to renounce one's own salvation under the pretext of practicing perfect abandonment to God's will would be in contradiction to God's will, as well as a violation of man's innate desire for perfect happiness. Moreover, since the glory of God is the prime motive for our existence, we should positively seek our own salvation, which is the perfect way in which we give glory to God.[15]

FRUITS OF ABANDONMENT

The fruits and blessings of complete abandonment to God's will are innumerable. In addition to those already mentioned, the following deserve to be noted:

1) It gives a sweet intimacy with God, such as a child experiences with its mother.

2) The soul travels with simplicity and freedom, desiring only what God wills.

3) The soul remains constant and serene in all events of life, because God wills or permits them.

4) The soul is filled with true joy which no one can destroy, because it wills whatever God wills.

5) It is a presage of a happy death if one remains faithful in abandonment to God's will.

FIDELITY TO GRACE

To understand the significance of fidelity to grace, it is necessary to recall what we have already explained concerning the nature and function of actual grace, which coincides with the inspiration of the Holy Spirit and to which the soul should give complete fidelity. Such is its importance for advancement in the spiritual life that we will closely examine its nature, its necessity, its sanctifying efficacy and the methods of practicing it.

ITS NATURE

Fidelity in general signifies the exact observance of the faith and loyalty which one person owes to another. In the middle ages the vassal was obliged to present himself to his lord and render homage to him, thereafter remaining

[15]When mystics explain that they would be willing to forego salvation and be condemned if thereby they could give glory to God, their words are to be understood as meaning that, were they to choose between their own perfect happiness and God's glory, they would choose the latter, even if it meant (*per impossibile*) that they would be deprived of the former.

subject to him and even signifying his subjection by adding the master's name at the end of his own. The same thing was true of many slaves, who took the names of their masters as their own family name. All of this has application to the practice of fidelity to grace, which is nothing other than loyalty or docility in following the inspirations of the Holy Ghost in any form in which they are manifested to us.

Divine inspirations

Inspirations, St. Francis de Sales points out, are all interior attractions, movements, reproaches and feelings of remorse, the lights and knowledge which God causes in us, in order to arouse us, impel us and draw us to virtue and to good resolutions.[16] Divine inspirations are produced in various ways. Even sinners receive them in order to be converted, but for the just soul, in whom the Holy Ghost dwells, it is perfectly connatural to receive inspirations at any moment. The Holy Spirit uses them to enlighten our minds so that we can see what we ought to do, and to move our will so that we shall desire to do it, as St. Paul says: "For it is God who of his good pleasure works in you both the will and the performance" (Phil. 2:13).

It is evident that the Holy Ghost works in us according to his will.[17] Sometimes he merely enlightens us, as when he gives us the knowledge by which we may resolve a doubt; at other times he only moves us, as when we perform some good action which we had already intended to do; again at other times, and this is most frequent, he both enlightens and moves us at the same time. At times he inspires us in the midst of some work or even distraction, sometimes during prayer, at the times of Communion, or in moments of recollection and fervor. He rules and governs the adopted sons of God in the ordinary events of daily life as well as in affairs of great importance. He does not always inspire us directly, however, but sometimes sends the inspirations through our guardian angel, a creature, a good book or a friend. Nevertheless, in the last analysis the Holy Ghost is always the principal author of the inspiration.

IMPORTANCE AND NECESSITY

It would be impossible to insist too strongly on the importance and necessity of fidelity to grace in order to advance on the way of perfection. It is, in a certain sense, the fundamental problem of the Christian life, because it determines whether one will make constant progress toward the heights of sanctity or will remain paralyzed and motionless. It could be said that practically the only task of the spiritual director is to lead the soul to a most exquisite and constant fidelity to grace. Without this, all other methods are doomed to failure. The profoundly theological reason for this can be found in the divine economy of actual grace, which maintains a strict relationship with the degree of the soul's fidelity.

---

[16]Cf. *Introduction to the Devout Life,* Part II, Chap. 18.

[17]Cf. Jn. 3:8.

INTERNAL MEANS

Actual grace

Theology teaches that actual grace is absolutely necessary for every salutary act. It is in the supernatural order what the previous divine motion is in the purely natural order, that is, it is absolutely indispensable so that a being in potency may pass into act. Without actual grace it is impossible to perform even the smallest supernatural action, even if the soul possesses sanctifying grace, the infused virtues and the gifts of the Holy Ghost.

Actual grace is continuously offered to us to assist us in the fulfillment of the duties of the moment. It is, therefore, extremely important that we respond to the actual grace that is given and co-operate generously with it. But this is not all. In the ordinary economy of divine providence, God subordinates consequent graces to those graces which have previously been given. In other words, infidelity to grace at a given time will be sufficient to deprive us of many other graces which God would have given to us if we had used the earlier gifts of grace. Only in eternity shall we see that a great number of frustrated saints were such because of their infidelity to actual grace. It should also be noted that we are not here speaking of serious sins, which cause the loss of habitual grace, but of those venial sins which, being fully deliberate, frustrated the action of the Holy Ghost by putting obstacles in the way of further progress toward perfection.[18]

SANCTIFYING EFFICACY

The evil effects which follow infidelity to grace should be sufficient to impress upon the soul the importance of being faithful to the graces which God gives, but it is also important that we understand the positive sanctifying value of fidelity to grace. We must rely on the inspirations and directions of the Holy Spirit if we are to purge ourselves of all evil and grow in goodness. Hence the whole process of growth in perfection depends upon one's fidelity to grace. We should strive to be so possessed by the Holy Ghost that he alone governs all of our faculties and regulates all of our interior and exterior movements. In this way we shall no longer live, but Christ will live in us, due to our faithful co-operation with all the actual graces which have been given us through the Holy Ghost. It may happen that an inspiration from God is met on our part with repugnance, doubt or difficulties, but it is necessary to overcome our unruly nature and to follow at any cost the inspirations that come to us from God. We can never reach perfection as long as we are governed and guided by a natural and human spirit, because perfection requires that God live in us and work through us according to his will.[19]

PRACTICE OF FIDELITY

The practice of fidelity to grace involves two aspects or elements, namely, the inspiration received from the Holy Ghost and our response to the inspira-

[18]Cf. R. Garrigou-Lagrange, O.P., *The Three Ages of the Spiritual Life* (St. Louis: Herder, 1947), I, Chap. 3.

[19]Cf. L. Lallemant, S.J., *Spiritual Doctrine,* IV, 2, aa. 1-2.

tion. As regards the inspiration, St. Thomas Aquinas, in commenting on the words of St. Paul to the effect that they who are moved by the Spirit of God are the sons of God (Rom. 8:14), says that they are ruled by the Holy Ghost so far as he enlightens them interiorly concerning that which they ought to do, and that the spiritual man is not only instructed by the Holy Spirit but is moved by him to do as he has been instructed. For that reason, St. Thomas continues, they are moved by a certain superior instinct and not simply by their own will, although this does not exclude the freedom of the will, because the Holy Ghost is the one who is the cause of man's free actions, according to the words of St. Paul: "For it is God who works in you both the will and the performance"[20] (Phil. 2:13).

Inspirations of the Holy Ghost

The inspiration of the Holy Ghost is to an act of virtue what temptation is to a sinful act. Man descends to sin by three steps: temptation, delectation, consent. The Holy Ghost proposes the virtuous act to the intellect and arouses the will; the just man accepts and approves the inspiration and then carries it out. Thus acts of virtue are produced under the impulse and direction of the Holy Ghost, and, in the measure that the soul is faithful to this impulse, it gradually acquires facility and delight in the practice of the virtue, and these are called the fruits of the Holy Ghost. Some of these fruits proceed from the soul with such perfection and sweetness that they bring a happiness to the soul which is a foretaste of the happiness of the life to come, and these are called the beatitudes. Possessing in our souls the gifts of the Holy Ghost, which are given in order to make us docile to the inspirations and movements of the Holy Ghost,[21] we have a kind of right to ask for these inspirations and to expect them. Indeed, the beautiful *Veni Creator Spiritus* is nothing other than a litany of petitions to the Holy Ghost, asking him to grant us his inspirations and his gifts.

Response to inspirations

As regards our response to the inspirations received from the Holy Ghost, three things are necessary: 1) attention to the inspirations; 2) discretion for distinguishing them from natural inclinations or movements from the devil; and 3) docility in carrying out the inspiration. We shall now explain each of these qualities in detail.

1) *Attention.* We should consider frequently that the Holy Ghost dwells within us through sanctifying grace.[22] If we were able to detach ourselves completely from all earthly things and withdraw to the silence and recollection of our own interior, we would undoubtedly hear the voice of God speaking within us. This is not a question of an extraordinary grace; it would be something completely normal and ordinary

---

[20]Cf. *In Epist. ad Rom.*, cap. 8, lect. 3.

[21]Cf. St. Thomas, *Summa,* I-II, q. 68, a. 1.

[22]Cf. I Cor. 6:19.

in a Christian life that is lived fully. Why then do we not hear the voice of the Holy Ghost? In the first place, because of our habitual dissipation. God is within us, but we live outside ourselves. The interior man, as Thomas à Kempis says, is recollected very quickly because he never diffuses himself completely to the exterior. The Holy Spirit himself says that he will lead us to solitude and will speak there to our hearts.[23]

God could speak to us in the depths of our souls and be heard above the noise of our distractions and attachments, but he does not choose to impose himself nor to take from us our own initiative. Consequently, God is not heard amidst the noise and distractions of a sensate soul. If he finds that a soul is occupied with many other earthly things, he stands at the door and waits. He does not force himself upon the soul; he does not enter if he is not wanted. And even if the soul is in the state of grace and enjoys the indwelling of the Trinity, God's presence is silent and hidden until the soul itself turns to him with love and attention.

Another reason why we do not hear the voice of God within us is our own sensuality. We are flesh and bone, and unless we are careful we shall have a taste only for the external and sensate things. The animal man, says St. Paul, does not perceive the things of the Spirit of God.[24] For that reason it is absolutely indispensable that we cultivate and preserve a spirit of mortification. The sensate man does not hear the voice of God; indeed, one of the first things that is lost by the person who gives himself over to the things of the world, and especially to sensual delight, is a taste for prayer and the things of God.

The third reason why we do not hear the voice of God is our own disordered affection. So weakened is human nature as a result of original sin that, even in seeking God, a man may deceive himself and actually seek himself. It is not at all unusual to find persons who are externally very pious and observant in their religious duties, but inwardly filled with egoism and self-complacency. The disorderliness of our affection is readily seen when it is a question of the passions of love and the bodily instincts, but we should not forget that the will itself can easily deviate from God and seek self as the object of love. Christ warned his followers several times that it is impossible to love God and a creature on the same level of love; one must necessarily be subordinated to the other. He likewise warned that he did not want a lukewarm and tepid love, but that he would vomit it out of his mouth.

It is easy to see, therefore, why those who seek themselves first, and even subordinate God to themselves, hear only the voice of their own

[23]Cf. Os. 2:14.
[24]Cf. I Cor. 2:14.

desires, while God remains silent. It follows that we must detach ourselves from every created affection and subordinate all things, including ourselves, to the God who dwells within us.

2) *Discretion.* The discernment of spirits is of great importance if one is to know for certain the spirit that moves him at a given moment. The following points will be of help in recognizing divine inspirations:

a) *The sanctity of the object of the inspiration.* The devil never inspires one to virtue and neither does human nature, as a rule, if it is a question of some virtuous act that is difficult.

b) *Conformity with one's state in life.* God does not generally inspire us to perform actions which are not in keeping with our state in life or particular vocation. Thus a cloistered monk would not likely be inspired by God to preach missions, nor a housewife and mother to attend church services at a time of the day when her duties required that she be at home with her husband and children. In this respect we must be cautious lest we try to do what we personally wish to do, and then justify it by calling it an inspiration from God.

c) *Peace and tranquility of soul.* St. Francis de Sales maintains that one of the best signs of the goodness and authenticity of an inspiration, and especially of an extraordinary one, is the peace and tranquility with which it is received, because God does not use violence but acts sweetly and gently.[25] This is another way of saying that one is not to presume that the inclination to perform some extraordinary action, such as changing one's vocation or state in life, is an inspiration from God unless there are sufficiently grave reasons for making the change. If, on the other hand, a soul is upset and perturbed by what it considers to be an inspiration from God, and if the soul is in all other respects a devout and balanced soul, it is not to be presumed that the inspiriation in question is from God.

d) *Humble obedience.* One who claims to be acting by divine inspiration and refuses to obey his superiors is an impostor, says St. Francis de Sales.[26] The first question which a spiritual director should ask in cases of doubt is whether or not the individual is obedient to the laws of God and the Church and the duties of his state in life. A disobedient spirit has been at the basis of a great number of apostates, heretics and fraudulent mystics.

e) *Judgment of the spiritual director.* In the ordinary events of everyday life it is not necessary to deliberate or seek counsel. As a

[25]Cf. *Treatise on the Love of God,* Bk. VIII, Chap. 12.

[26]*Op. cit.,* Bk. VI, Chap. 13.

rule, it suffices simply to choose that particular action which seems to be in conformity with the divine will and not be troubled by any scruples of conscience. In cases of doubt concerning matters of greater importance, however, one should always consult a spiritual director, one's superiors or someone who is in a position to be able to make a prudent decision.

3) *Docility.* This is a quality by which one follows the inspiration of grace promptly, without waiting for a second movement of grace. This, of course, applies only in those cases in which the divine inspiration is clear, because we have already stated that in doubtful cases it is necessary to deliberate or to consult someone in authority. The soul should always be disposed to fulfill the will of God at any given moment.

CONCLUSION

Cardinal Mercier was so convinced of the importance of the practice of fidelity to the inspirations of the Holy Spirit that he advised persons to spend five minutes each day in complete recollection in order to address the Holy Ghost in the following words: "O Holy Spirit, soul of my soul, I adore thee. Enlighten me, guide me, strengthen me, console me. Tell me what I ought to do. Give me thy commands. I promise to submit myself to whatever thou dost ask of me and to accept whatever thou dost permit to happen to me. Grant only that I may know thy holy will."

2: EXTERNAL MEANS

Having examined in some detail the internal secondary means of spiritual growth, we can now turn to a consideration of the external means, those which flow from influences exterior to our own soul. We shall briefly study three of these—the plan of life, spiritual reading and holy friendships—but spend considerably more time on the fourth, the principal and most important, which is spiritual direction.

PLAN OF LIFE

The plan of life is a somewhat detailed schedule of the occupations and practices of piety which an individual should perform during the day. As a rule, it should be approved by one's confessor or spiritual director. The advantage of some kind of plan or schedule for one's daily life is that it gives a constancy and regularity to one's efforts toward greater perfection. Without a schedule, one may lose much time, fall into a habit of indecision, neglect duties or fulfill them carelessly, or cultivate the defect of inconstancy of character. If, on the other hand, one has a fixed schedule of life, there is much less danger of vacillation and wasted time, of being caught unprepared by some unexpected event, and of falling away from the practices of piety which are necessary for the spiritual advancement of the individual. When one is faithful to a plan of life, it is much easier to supernaturalize all the activities of daily life, to reap the benefit of obedience to one's director, and to train one's will to be attentive to the duty of the moment.

PARTICULAR PLANS

It is of great importance, however, that the plan of life be adapted prudently to the individual in view of his particular vocation and duties of state in life. A plan of life that would be suitable for several classes of persons would lose its effectiveness by being too general. We shall mention briefly the requirements of a plan of life for persons in various vocations or states of life, namely, the laity, the diocesan priest and persons living in the religious life.

For the laity

Living as they do in the world, without a particular superior whom they are bound to obey in matters which touch their personal spiritual life, and without a rule to guide them in their efforts toward greater perfection, it is difficult for laymen to avoid at least some of the defects which are the result of the lack of a plan of life. They are more exposed to the danger of extreme individualism in their practices of piety, and they may easily fall into the custom of following their own personal tastes and inclinations rather than selecting those exercises which are most beneficial to them. It should be strongly emphasized that, although the laity have a great liberty as regards practices of piety and means of sanctification, they should take care to utilize the fundamental means of sanctification before selecting this or that secondary practice of piety. Thus the frequent use of the sacraments, devout attendance at Mass, fidelity in the practice of daily prayer, the performance of the works of mercy—these are basic practices which should play a dominant part in the spiritual life of the laity.

It is not unusual to find laymen put greater emphasis on certain private devotions or secondary means of sanctification and neglect those things which are of greater importance. Moreover, it frequently happens that laymen identify a plan of life with certain observances that are proper to the religious or priestly state. The life of the religious or the priest is not a life which is suited to the layman, and consequently it would be a serious error for a layman to attempt to live an adapted form of the religious life. The plan of life utilized by a husband or wife, a father or mother, or a member of the various professions in the world should be orientated to an ever increasing love of God but placed within the framework of the duties of the individual in his or her particular vocation or profession. For this reason it is of paramount importance that the confessor or spiritual director who approves the schedule or plan of life should understand very clearly what is involved in the life and duties of the particular layman and should eliminate any elements that would prove incompatible with the state of the layman. Perhaps the best rule to follow in drawing up such a plan of life would be to insure that nothing in the schedule would make it impossible or difficult for the individual to fulfill the duties of his or her vocation or profession.

For diocesan priests

The diocesan priest is sometimes exposed to the same dangers and difficulties that threaten the layman who has no definite plan of life. Much more than the religious priest, he must be in the world but not of the world. His apostolate is such that it keeps him in constant contact with the people, and for that reason his way of life is evident to all. He must, therefore, be conscious of his personal obligation to strive for holiness and to give good example to the faithful. It goes without saying that he needs some schedule or plan of life as an individual Christian, and also in view of the demands of his priestly apostolate.

In this respect, he must avoid the same mistake which the layman must avoid, namely, attempting to live a watered-down religious life. The diocesan priest is above all a man of the people, and while it may prove very satisfying to follow a plan of life which would provide several hours of recollection and solitude, he would run the risk of withdrawing too much from the people he has been sent to serve. At the other extreme, the diocesan priest without any plan of life is a constant contradiction in the eyes of his people, because they cannot understand how a priest could be a worthy priest and still give no sign of regularity in the practices of the spiritual life. A priest is expected to be a man of temperate and regular habits, to be available at all times for the needs of his people, to have that delicate sense of prudence which enables him to be in the world without becoming worldly.

The diocesan priest should seek to draw up a plan of life which enables him to dedicate himself completely to his apostolate and at the same time to utilize certain hours of the day for his own personal sanctification. Unlike the religious priest, the diocesan priest does not have a schedule of daily life provided for him by his superior or a religious rule; except for the demands of his ministry and the care of souls, he is left to himself as regards the schedule of his daily life.

For religious

Although persons living in religion have a definite schedule as regards community exercises, they also need a plan of life for their personal exercises. The community exercises usually follow a regular schedule, but they are held only at certain intervals in the day. While the community prayers and spiritual readings provide important material for meditation and private recollection, there is still the question of arranging those hours which are left to the personal initiative of the individual religious. It is a strange paradox to find in a religious house certain individuals who attend the community exercises regularly and perform their duties faithfully but use their free time to do absolutely nothing. It is as if they erroneously believed that they should do nothing except that which is explicitly demanded of them by their rule or their superior.

This is obviously a serious misunderstanding of the function of the vow of obedience, for it is precisely in those hours of freedom from explicitly commanded duties that the religious manifests the intensity of his desire to perfect himself. Many of the failures in religious life can be traced directly to the waste of time by those individuals who do only what they are commanded to do and then use the rest of the day for relaxation or pure idleness. The religious, therefore, whether living in a cloistered community or in one of the active institutes, will always have some free time which can be put to good use or simply wasted. It is for these free hours that the plan of life should provide, and it is in this area that the zealous religious will prudently arrange a schedule of life which allows for reasonable relaxation and at the same time prevent slothfulness.

EXTERNAL MEANS

QUALITIES OF A GOOD PLAN

If any plan of life is to serve its purpose, it is necessary that it be drawn up in view of one's vocation and the duties of his state in life. It is also a prudent practice to give the plan a period of trial rather than adopt it definitively and then later find it necessary to make changes. The first requisite, as we have already stated, is that the plan of life must be adapted to the duties of one's state, to one's profession or work, to one's disposition of spirit, to one's character and temperament, to one's strength of body, to the degree of perfection already attained, and to the attractions of grace. Moreover, the plan of life should be at once rigid and flexible. It needs a certain rigidity in order to give regularity and constancy to one's life; it must be flexible in order to allow for dispensations or adaptations when the need arises, or for substitutions and changes as one's needs vary.

While it would be pure slavery to impose a plan of life which would not allow for any dispensations or modifications, the individual who is following a given plan or schedule should be reasonably unwilling to excuse himself from observing it and should not be eager to make changes. If there is a reasonable cause for departing from the plan of life under given circumstances, the individual should not hesitate to do so, but one should never depart from the plan of life without a reasonable and justifying cause.

SPIRITUAL READING

The attentive and assiduous reading of spiritual books is an efficacious aid to the practice of prayer and the acquisition of knowledge of spiritual doctrine. This important practice should never be omitted from one's plan of life, and as much time as possible should be given to it. It is a laudable custom always to have at hand a book of spirituality which can be read from time to time as one's occupation permits. A good book will not only renew the desire to strive for greater perfection, but it will impart invaluable knowledge of the truth of the spiritual life. St. Teresa of Avila wisely advised her nuns that, if they could not find a director who could solve their doubts, they should seek a book which would explain the matter in question. In general, persons who do not find a suitable priest to direct them would do well to be faithful to the practice of daily spiritual reading.

SECONDARY MEANS

BOOKS TO READ

Not all spiritual books, however, have the same value or sanctifying efficacy. Objectively, Sacred Scripture should hold the first place, and especially those parts which are most instructive and doctrinal. Nevertheless, not all persons are able, for one reason or another, to obtain the maximum benefits from reading Sacred Scripture. This applies especially to the Old Testament, for there is no doubt that the New Testament, especially the gospels and the epistles, can be read by all with great benefit.

The lives of the saints can also be a source of edification and instruction, but here it is necessary to remark that one should be selective in the choice of biographies. If too much emphasis is placed on the extraordinary in the life of a given saint, the reader may be tempted to acquire a distaste for such books, or a feeling of incredulity regarding the veracity of such phenomena. What is worse, the reader may foolishly attempt to imitate particular details in the life of a saint who belongs to a different age, a distinct culture, or lived in a state of life which has little or nothing in common with that of the reader.

Doctrinal works

In general, one should select spiritual books which offer solid and practical doctrine regarding the Christian life. And since moods of the individual vary greatly, the book used at a given time is not always the one that is most beneficial at that time. Some books may be of great value in a particular period of a person's spiritual development but would cease to be of use later on. Other books would prove to be harmful to certain individuals because they are only beginners in the spiritual life, because of their lack of understanding of spiritual doctrine, or because of some particular defect at a given time. For example, it would be generally imprudent for young people or beginners to attempt to read the works of St. John of the Cross, Henry Suso or other authors who treat of the heights of the mystical life; it would be harmful for scrupulous persons to read books which treat of extraordinary phenomena or place great emphasis on the horror of sin and the fear of eternal damnation; and books which discuss miracles, diabolical influence and occult phenomena could be a source of error for persons who are uneducated in theology. In the matter of spiritual reading, it is generally safer and more beneficial to select those books which are less spectacular and more solid and doctrinal.

METHOD OF READING

Once a book has been selected for one's spiritual reading, it is of prime importance that it be read properly. Spiritual reading is not purely for reasons of study; it is an exercise of piety. While it is true that one derives much instruction through the reading of spiritual books, its ultimate purpose is to arouse one's love of God and to intensify one's desire for perfection. Hence the important thing is not to read many books but to assimilate what is read.

Sometimes it will be of great benefit to re-read certain sections of a book or to return again and again to the same book so that its doctrine can be deeply impressed upon one's mind and heart. The important thing to be kept in mind in regard to spiritual reading is that we should use a book as long as we need it and can derive benefit from it. Sometimes it is necessary to resist the temptation to change books frequently, without ever finishing any one book. It would be equally erroneous, however, to believe that one must necessarily finish every book that is started. If one begins a book which later proves unsatisfactory, the prudent thing to do would be to select a different book rather than waste time on something that is not beneficial. If the book is properly selected and properly read, the individual will easily pass from reading to prayer, and sometimes the two exercises will be so closely connected that he will not know when he ceased to read and began to pray.

HOLY FRIENDSHIPS

Father Lacordaire once said that true friendship is a rare and divine thing, a sure mark of a noble soul, and one of the greatest rewards of true virtue. We read in Sacred Scripture that a faithful friend is a powerful protector and that he who has found such a friend has found a treasure.[1] The truth of these statements is evident from daily experience. A virtuous friend is one of the greatest inspirations for the conquest of self and the practice of good.

True friendship is an alliance of souls who are united to do good. It is disinterested, generous, sincere and patient to the point of heroism. True friendship does not know the meaning of duplicity or hypocrisy; it does not deny the defects that exist in the friends, but it enables them to love each other in spite of their defects and weaknesses. Neither is it a sensual love, because the love of true friendship must be a love which seeks primarily, not the good of oneself, but the good of the other. That is why the love of friendship is synonymous with true charity.

VALUE OF FRIENDSHIP

There are three outstanding advantages which flow from a true and holy friendship. In the first place, a friend can be an intimate confidant to whom one can open his heart and receive advice and counsel when confronted with problems and doubts. Secondly, a friend can be a prudent and sympathetic corrector who will frankly point out one's defects and prevent many acts of

[1]Cf. Sirach 6:14-16.

imprudence. Thirdly, a friend will console in times of sorrow and will know how to select the proper words and remedies in times of trial.

If true friendship has been highly praised, even by pagan philosophers, as one of the greatest blessings in man's social life, it is reasonable to expect that it can be a powerful aid in the attainment of perfection. The struggle for perfection is the work of a lifetime, and it demands fidelity in the face of many obstacles. Even heroic souls have experienced the discouragement that comes from the recognition of the loftiness of the goal and the weakness of human nature. The love of a friend who has the same high ideals can be a source of encouragement and inspiration in times of darkness. Such a friendship was manifested time and again in the dark days of persecution in the early Church, and it can safely be surmised that many of the Christians who walked calmly to their death were inspired in no small measure by the example and the fraternal love of their fellow Christians. Indeed, even the persecutors were forced to exclaim: "These Christians, see how they love one another!" Through all the centuries of the Church's existence there have been outstanding examples of holy friendship in the lives of the saints.

DANGEROUS FRIENDSHIP

Since human love can so easily become tainted with selfishness and sensuality, however, it is necessary that one maintain a strict vigilance over oneself, lest one's love exceed the limits of virtue and become an occasion of evil. For if it is true that a good friend is a powerful stimulus to virtue, it is no less true that one of the most destructive forces in the Christian life is that of a sinful friendship. St. Francis de Sales warns that it happens frequently that a human friendship begins in a virtuous manner but that it imperceptibly but surely becomes mixed with sensual love and finally terminates in carnal love.[2]

For this reason it is extremely important that one know the signs by which one can determine whether a friendship is sensual. The first and most evident sign of a sensual friendship is that it is exclusive. This exclusiveness is frequently shown by the fact that the two friends withdraw from the company of others in order to be alone, are annoyed if others join their company, and are jealous of each other to the point of becoming angry if one sees the other in the company of a third party. Secondly, a sensual friendship is characterized by possessiveness, which may reach such a point that one cannot tolerate the absence of the other and seeks to prolong conversations and visits as much as possible. Thirdly, sensual friendships are obsessive. At the slightest provocation one's thoughts turn to the friend; on entering a room the first person sought is the friend; the imagination seems always to be

[2]Cf. *Introduction to the Devout Life,* Part III, Chap. 20.

focused on the face of the friend, and even in sleep the dreams are centered on the friend.

In order to avoid this type of friendship, which is so harmful to the spiritual life, the best remedy is to prevent such a friendship from developing. As soon as any of the signs have been noticed, one should react as he would to the symptoms of a disease. If, however, such a friendship has already been allowed to develop, it may be necessary to avoid any drastic and sudden measures but rather to let the friendship gradually cool until it is extinct. Spiritual directors and confessors who are prone to react violently to such friendships and to demand of their penitents an immediate and definitive break between the friends may unwittingly cause a psychological upheaval which is more serious than the disorder they hoped to cure.

SPIRITUAL DIRECTION

Spiritual direction is the art of leading souls progressively from the beginning of the spiritual life to the height of Christian perfection. It is an art in the sense that spiritual direction is a practical science which, under the guidance of supernatural prudence, applies to a particular case the principles of the theology of Christian perfection. It is orientated to the perfection of the Christian life, but this direction must be given progressively, that is, according to the strength and need of the soul at a given time. The direction should begin as soon as the soul has definitely resolved to travel along the road to Christian perfection and should continue through all the phases of that journey.

We shall discuss this important subject, after some preliminary considerations concerning the importance and necessity of spiritual direction, under two heads: the spiritual director, and the soul directed.

IMPORTANCE AND NECESSITY

The necessity of spiritual direction has been stressed by many theologians and spiritual writers.[3] St. Vincent Ferrer states in his *Treatise on the Spiritual Life* that Christ will not give his grace to anyone who has at hand someone capable of instructing and directing him but disdains this help in the belief that he is sufficient to himself and can provide for himself whatever is necessary for his salvation.

---

[3]Cf. St. John of the Cross, *The Living Flame of Love,* Canticle 3, n. 56; St. Teresa of Avila, *The Life,* Chap. 5; St. Francis de Sales, *Introduction to the Devout Life,* Bk. I, Chap. 4.

Although there is no text in Sacred Scripture which refers to this particular point, there are many references regarding the need to take counsel.[4] The mind of the Church can be seen in the following words of Pope Leo XIII, addressed to Cardinal Gibbons: "Moreover, it should be added that those who strive to sanctify themselves, by the very fact that they strive to follow a way that is little frequented, are more exposed to deceive themselves and therefore they, more than others, need a doctor and guide. And this method of procedure has always been seen in the Church. This doctrine was unanimously taught by all those who, in the course of centuries, flourished in wisdom and sanctity. And those who reject it shall not do so without temerity and danger."[5]

While it is true that individuals have attained sanctity without a spiritual director—which proves that spiritual direction is not absolutely necessary—the general rule is that those who have reached perfection have had the counsel and advice of a spiritual director. The road to Christian perfection is so beset with trials and pitfalls and darkness that, in the ordinary providence of God, spiritual direction of some kind is morally necessary for the attainment of Christian perfection.

THE DIRECTOR

Is it necessary that the spiritual director be a priest? We can answer without hesitation that normally the director should be a priest. There are many reasons for this. First of all, in the ordinary workings of divine providence the priest has the role of teacher, and he has both the theoretical and the practical knowledge required for the direction of souls. Secondly, the function of spiritual director is usually closely related to the office of confessor. Thirdly, because of the grace of the priesthood. Fourthly, the practice of the Church forbids any person who is not a priest, even religious superiors, to probe into matters of conscience.[6] Nevertheless, by way of exception, it is possible that in a particular case spiritual direction could be given by a prudent and experienced person who is not a priest. There is ample testimony in the history of the Church to justify such direction because of peculiar circumstances; for example, among the hermits in the desert and the primitive monks who were not priests, the direction given by St. Francis of Assisi, St. Ignatius Loyola before his ordination, St. Catherine of Siena and St. Teresa of Avila.

[4]Cf. Tob. 4:18; Eccles. 4:10, 32:23; II Cor. 5:20.
[5]Leo XIII, *Testem benevolentiae,* January 22, 1899.
[6]Cf. canon 530.

RECEPTION OF OFFICE

How does one receive the office of spiritual director? If it is a question of a priest, he receives the remote power from God and the Church when he is ordained to the priesthood and given the commission to sanctify souls through his priestly ministry. But the direction of a particular soul is based upon two essential factors: the free election of the one directed and the free acceptation by the director. No human power can oblige any individual to accept spiritual direction from a particular director. Even religious and seminarians retain their liberty when it is a question of the choice of a personal spiritual director. When the Church through a bishop assigns a particular priest to be confessor to religious, this is done simply to facilitate the weekly confession of the religious, but it in no way obligates any religious to take that priest as a spiritual director.[7] The office of confessor is not necessarily identified with the office of spiritual director, and it would require a special indult from the Holy See for any religious institute to obligate its members to accept a particular priest as spiritual director.

DIRECTION AND CONFESSION

On the part of the director, it should be observed that a pastor and those priests who are officially given the care of souls in a parish are bound in justice to hear the confessions of their subjects whenever they reasonably request it. In case of urgent necessity, all confessors are bound in charity to hear the confessions of the faithful, and in danger of death all priests are bound by this obligation.[8] Spiritual direction in the strict sense of the word, however, even in those cases in which it is given during sacramental confession, is a function completely distinct from the administration of the sacrament of penance. There is no divine or ecclesiastical law, therefore, which imposes upon any priest a strict obligation to accept the office of spiritual director. In justice a priest is always free to accept or to refuse such an office, although it is true that he would be performing an excellent act of charity if he were to accept the office. A priest's refusal to act as a spiritual director would never involve a violation of justice, although it may, in peculiar circumstances, be a sin against charity.

Since it frequently happens that spiritual direction is given during sacramental confession, it is necessary to point out the difference between confession and spiritual direction. The purpose of spiritual direction is to lead a soul to the perfection of the Christian life, and therefore the spiritual director is essentially a teacher, counselor and guide. The confessor is above all a judge who possesses power in the internal forum and can, within the limits of his jurisdiction, strictly obligate the penitent. His basic mission is to pardon sins in the name of God, and to do this it is sometimes necessary for him

[7]Cf. canons 519-523.
[8]Cf. canon 892.

to dispose the penitent for valid sacramental absolution. The spiritual director does not possess any jurisdiction in the internal forum; he cannot obligate the person directed unless the individual has voluntarily made a special vow of obedience to the director; nor does he have as his purpose the forgiveness of sin, but the gradual perfection of the soul in view of sanctity.

This raises the question of whether it is necessary or fitting that the spiritual director should also be the ordinary confessor of the one who is directed. The answer is that it is not strictly necessary, but it is fitting and convenient. It could not be said that one's spiritual director must of necessity be the confessor, because the two functions are distinct and separable. Moreover, it may happen that a priest is a good confessor but does not possess the qualifications necessary for the direction of a particular soul. But because of the intimate relation between the offices of confessor and spiritual director, it is most fitting that one and the same person fulfill both functions whenever possible. There are several reasons for this: it gives greater authority to the director; it makes it possible to give spiritual direction in the confessional; it enables the director to know the soul more perfectly.[9]

QUALITIES OF A DIRECTOR

We have mentioned that some priests may be qualified as confessors but would not be suitable as spiritual directors. This signifies that there are definite qualities required for the office of spiritual direction. Some of these qualities are essential to spiritual direction as such; others are required of the person who is to give the direction. The first may be called *technical* qualities, and the second may be considered as *moral* qualities.

TECHNICAL QUALITIES

Perhaps no writer has outlined with such clarity and precision the technical qualities of a good spiritual director as has St. Teresa of Avila.[10] She states that a good spiritual director should be learned, prudent and experienced. If the director does not possess all three qualities, St. Teresa maintains that he must at least be prudent and experienced. St. John of the Cross maintains that a director should be learned, prudent and experienced, thus agreeing with the statement of St. Teresa, and he places great emphasis on the importance of experience. Following the teachings of these two great masters of the spiritual life, we shall treat briefly of each of the *technical* qualities.[11]

---

[9]According to canon 891, a master of novices and his assistant and the rector of a seminary may be spiritual directors of their subjects, but they may not be the ordinary confessors.

[10]Cf. *The Life,* Chaps. 13, 16; *The Way of Perfection,* Chap. 5.

[11]These qualities will be considered objectively, as found in the ideal spiritual director. In fact, however, the perfect director is a rarity; anyone seeking a director should not expect to find a John of the Cross or a Francis de Sales.

Learning

1) *Learning.* The learning of a spiritual director should be extensive. In addition to a profound knowledge of dogmatic theology, without which he would be exposed to error in regard to matters of faith, and of moral theology, without which he could not even fulfill the office of confessor, the spiritual director should have a thorough knowledge of ascetical and mystical theology. He should know, for example, the theological doctrine concerning Christian perfection, especially regarding such questions as the essence of perfection, the obligation to strive for perfection, the obstacles to perfection, the role of purification, and the means of positive growth in virtue. He should have a detailed knowledge of the grades of prayer, the trials which God usually sends to souls as they advance from the lower to the higher degrees of prayer, and the illusions and assaults of the devil which souls may encounter. He also needs to be well versed in psychology so that he will have an understanding of various temperaments and characters, the influences to which the human personality is subjected, and the function of the emotions in the life of the individual. He should also know at least the basic principles of abnormal psychology and psychiatry so that he will be able to discern mental unbalance and nervous or emotional disorders.

A priest should realize that, if he is not competent to direct a particular soul, he should not attempt it but should advise the individual to go to some priest who possesses the necessary knowledge. For the direction of extraordinary or abnormal individuals, a greater knowledge than the ordinary is required, and one incurs a grave responsibility before God if he attempts to direct a soul when he lacks sufficient knowledge. In recent times, with the wider dissemination of knowledge of mental sickness, the priest must especially be warned that, as regards the field of psychiatry and the therapeutic methods proper to that branch of medicine, he is a mere "layman" and is incompetent to treat mental sickness. In spite of his personal inclinations or prejudice regarding psychiatry and psychiatrists, if he suspects that a penitent is suffering from a mental illness, he should direct that individual to a professional doctor of psychiatry, just as readily as he would expect a psychiatrist to refer spiritual problems to a clergyman.

Prudence

2) *Prudence.* This is one of the most important qualities for a spiritual director. It comprises three basic factors: *prudence in decisions, clarity in counseling,* and *firmness in exacting obedience.*

If a spiritual director lacks prudence, he is usually lacking in several other virtues as well. Prudence enables an individual to do the right thing under given circumstances. Spiritual direction is concerned, not with the general doctrine of spiritual theology, nor with theoretical situations that one may imagine, but with the individual soul placed in concrete circumstances at a given moment or in a given phase of spiritual growth.

Prudence in decisions

The director is not called upon to make decisions in regard to general doctrine; most people could find such answers in any standard manual of spiritual theology. The director's role is precisely to recognize the particular circumstances of a given situation and to give the advice or decision that is needed at that moment. In order that this decision be prudent, a good spiritual director must have the empathy by which he is able to place himself in the given circumstances and make the necessary decision against the background of orthodox doctrine. Of the various factors which militate against prudence in making decisions the following are especially common: lack of knowledge of the various states of the ascetical and mystical life, lack of understanding of human psychology, prejudice in regard to particular states of life or in regard to particular exercises of piety, lack of humility.

Clarity in advice

The second quality which should accompany prudence in the spiritual director is clarity in the advice which he gives to the one directed and in the norms of conduct which he gives to them. In order that he may be clear in his direction, he must possess clarity in his own mind. In speaking to the soul that he is directing he should avoid any vague or indecisive language, but always express himself in concrete and definite terms. He should resolve all problems with a yes or a no, and, if necessary, he should take the time for further thought and deliberation before making his decision. If a soul perceives that the director is not sure of himself, it will lose confidence in him, and his direction will lose all its efficacy. Moreover, the director should always be sincere and frank, without any regard for human respect or mundane motives. It would be a serious fault if a director were to avoid offending the person directed lest that person should go to some other priest for direction. Those priests who place great importance in attracting and retaining a large number of followers are, by that very fact, disposing themselves to failure as spiritual directors. The director should never forget that he is taking the place of Christ in dealing with the souls that come to him for spiritual help, and that he must therefore endeavor to treat those souls as Christ would treat them, that is, with kindness and understanding, but with firmness and utter frankness.

Firmness

The director must also take care that he does not become the one who is directed. Some persons are extremely competent in getting their own way in everything, and even the priest is in danger of falling under their power.[12] For that reason, once the director is certain of his decision and the course that should be followed, he should state his mind with unyielding firmness. Once the decision has been given, presupposing prudent deliberation, the director must never yield to the petitions or even the tears of the person directed. The individual must be convinced that there are only two alterna-

[12]Cf. St. John of the Cross, *The Dark Night,* Bk. I, Chaps. 2 and 3.

tives: to obey or to find another director. This is demanded by the dignity of the director and the good of the one directed. It is the only way in which a spiritual director can preserve his authority.

But the director should not forget that he should never demand of a soul anything that is incompatible with its state of life or vocation, its strength or present condition. He should realize that there are some things which can be demanded of advanced souls but could never be required of beginners; that some things would be perfectly fitting in dealing with a priest or religious but not with a lay person. Excessive rigor does nothing but frighten souls and cause them to abandon the road to perfection. There is, therefore, a world of difference between firmness in demanding obedience and an excessive rigidity which discourages the soul of the penitent.

Experience

3) *Experience.* This is one of the most precious qualities which a spiritual director can have. Even if he be less perfect in knowledge and somewhat deficient in prudence, experience can prove to be a means of supplementing these defects. This does not mean that the experience of the director must necessarily flow from his own spiritual life, for it is possible that he may obtain the benefits of experience from his observation and direction of others.

As regards the personal experience of the director, if it is a question of the guidance of the average Christian, he needs little more than the experience which any priest can obtain from the faithful fulfillment of his duties in the sacred ministry. If it is a question of advanced souls who have already entered the mystical stages of the spiritual life, it is most desirable that the priest himself have some experience of those higher stages. While it is true that a very delicate sense of prudence, coupled with competent knowledge of the mystical states, may suffice in the majority of cases, it is likewise true that, without any personal experience, the director could easily become confused and lose his way. The reason for this is that, when the gifts of the Holy Spirit begin to operate habitually in the soul of the mystic, there is such a complete and profound transformation that the director may not know the significance of these changes unless he himself has already experienced them to some degree. If, therefore, a spiritual director realizes that he does not have sufficient experience to guide a mystical soul, he should in all simplicity and generosity put that soul in the hands of another who is capable of directing it.

But personal experience alone is not sufficient to make a spiritual director as competent as he ought to be. There are many different paths by which the Holy Ghost can lead souls to the summit of sanctity. It would be a most serious mistake for a director to attempt to lead all souls along the same path and to impose on them his own personal experiences, however beneficial they may have been for himself. The spiritual director should never forget that he is merely an instrument in the hands of the Holy Spirit and that his work must be entirely subjected to the Holy Ghost. If, through a lack of an understanding of the variety of divine gifts and the multiplicity of roads to perfection, he were to force all souls to travel by the same road, he would not only cease to be a competent instrument, but would become a veritable obstacle to the workings of God in the soul. What a strange contradiction to find that the spiritual director, whose function is to lead souls to perfect union with God, actually ties the hands of God.

MORAL QUALITIES

The *moral* qualities which are indispensable for a good spiritual director are the following: piety, zeal for the sanctification of souls, good character, humility and disinterestedness.

Piety

It is easy to understand the necessity of piety in a spiritual director, and St. John of the Cross insists upon this quality with great emphasis.[13] The reason is that one cannot give what he does not have. If a spiritual director is lacking in the spirit of piety, he is incapacitated for leading his disciple to sanctity. It is true that sanctification is the work of God and that he does not depend essentially on human instruments, but at the same time it must be admitted that God ordinarily makes use of secondary causes, even in the work of the sanctification of souls.

The piety of the spiritual director should be permeated with the great truths of the Christian life. It should be eminently Christocentric and orientated absolutely to the glory of God. He should likewise be animated with a profound sense of our adoptive filiation so that he can see God above all as a loving Father who is pleased in his sons. He should have a most tender affection for Mary, the Mother of God and our mother. He should practice recollection and be completely detached from the things of the world. A director who is animated with these sentiments will be perfectly at home in the direction of souls. He will understand their language and will be able to communicate with them. His own experimental knowledge of God and divine things will give him an understanding which no acquired science could ever provide. There can be no doubt whatever that piety is the first and most basic moral quality which a good director of souls should possess.

Zeal for souls

The director's ardent zeal for the sanctification of souls is a natural consequence of his personal piety. Zeal, as St. Thomas explains, is an effect of intense love.[14] The love of God impels us to labor for the extension of his kingdom in souls, and the love of those souls enables us to forget ourselves so that we think of nothing but of sanctifying them in and for God. This is the zeal which urged St. Paul to become all things to all men in order to gain all and gave him that beautiful sympathy by which his whole being

[13]Cf. *The Living Flame of Love,* Canticle 3, n. 30.
[14]Cf. *Summa,* I-II, q. 20, a. 4.

was united with others in their joys and sufferings and sorrows.[15] Lacking this ardent zeal, spiritual direction will lose its power, because the director himself will have lost the stimulus for persevering in his efforts in spite of any difficulty, and the direction will become an oppressive burden to the director.

Goodness of character

Zeal, however, is always in danger of degenerating into a stubborn fanaticism which would be most harmful to the person who is being directed. For that reason it must be counterbalanced by a basic goodness and sweetness of character. The spiritual director should be animated by the very same sentiments which animated our Lord and Savior, Jesus Christ.[16]

The spiritual director should never forget that the effectiveness of his guidance will depend in no small measure on whether or not the person directed can see in him the understanding and compassion of Christ. The struggle for perfection is a most difficult task, especially in the beginning, and it is beset with indescribable trials when the soul advances into the dark night of the passive purgation. If the director is excessively rigorous and lacks compassion, this will suffice to discourage the soul and even cause it to abandon the work of its sanctification. The director needs sweetness and compassion especially in dealing with souls who are strongly tempted, who find it difficult to open their hearts to the director, or who are weak and inconstant by nature. For that reason the goodness and kindness of the spiritual director should enable him to be truly paternal in striving to form Christ in the souls whom God has entrusted to him.

Humility

The director likewise needs a profound humility, and this for three reasons. In the first place, God resists the proud and gives his grace to the humble.[17] Of what value is all human knowledge and wisdom if one is lacking in humility? Secondly, the spiritual director needs humility so that he will distrust himself when necessary and not rush forward to solve difficulties without reflection. Humility will cause him to study and meditate and to consult others more learned than himself. In this way he will avoid many of the mistakes and embarrassments which occur to those who are too proud to doubt themselves. Thirdly, humility in a director attracts souls, while pride repels them. In this respect also the director should imitate Christ, who said of himself that he is meek and humble of heart and that he seeks only the glory of his Father.[18]

Disinterestedness

Lastly, the director should love souls in a disinterested manner, that is, he should not seek to guide them because of any self-satisfaction or consolation that he would receive, but simply and solely to lead them to God. St. Augustine

---

[15]Cf. I Cor. 9:22; II Cor. 11:29.
[16]Cf. Phil. 2:5; Lk. 15:4; Matt. 12:20.
[17]Cf. I Pet. 5:5.
[18]Cf. Matt. 11:29; Jn. 8:50.

states emphatically that those who lead the sheep of Christ as if they were their own and not Christ's show that they love themselves and not the Lord. By means of this disinterested love the director will forestall many temptations that could arise in regard to pride and sensual affections, and he will also be able to respect the liberty of the souls he directs.

We have already stated that both the director and the soul directed enjoy complete freedom. If this freedom is to be respected, the spiritual director must never show any annoyance if a soul leaves his direction, and he should certainly not look upon other directors as his rivals or competitors. In order to preserve his detachment and disinterest, the spiritual director should never, under any circumstances, accept any gifts as a recompense for the work he has done for a particular soul, and he should never impose upon it any kind of sacrifice or mortification that is undertaken for his benefit.

Conclusion

Such are the principal moral qualities which should adorn the spiritual director. Precisely because there are so few who possess all these qualities, there are also few competent spiritual directors. St. John of the Cross and St. Francis de Sales have both stated that a good spiritual director is very rare;[19] yet it should not be thought that a person who is unable to find a perfect spiritual director will be unable to reach perfection. If the soul has an ardent desire for sanctification and strives faithfully to co-operate with all the graces which God bestows, it will not fail to reach sanctity, even if the spiritual director does not possess all the qualities which are necessary. Indeed, such a soul could possibly attain perfection even without a spiritual director. It is not the director who makes saints; sanctification is essentially the work of God and the co-operation of the soul.

DUTIES AND OFFICES

Having seen the various qualities which are required of the spiritual director, we shall now discuss the duties and the office of a spiritual director. We have already mentioned that the function of the confessor and that of the spiritual director are not the same, although spiritual direction is frequently given in the confessional. The following seem to us to be the principal duties of a spiritual director:

Knowledge

1) *To know the soul that is directed.* The director should have an intimate and profound knowledge of the person he is to direct, his character, temperament, good and evil inclinations, defects, likes and dislikes, powers and energy, etc. He should have a knowledge of the individual's past life, at least along general lines, so that he will know the principal sins the individual has committed, the vices to which he has been subjected and for how long, the means that were used to correct those vices and with what practical

[19]Cf. *The Living Flame of Love,* Canticle 3, n. 30; *Introduction to the Devout Life,* Part I, Chap. 4.

results, the graces received from God, the progress realized in virtue and by what means, the individual's present dispositions, the intensity of his desire to strive for perfection, the sacrifices he is willing to make in order to attain sanctity, the temptations which afflict him at the present time, and the obstacles and difficulties which he is experiencing.

Except in a rare case, however, the spiritual director should never demand a written account of a person's past life. Nothing should be put in writing, either by the director or the one directed. It is easy for a penitent to imagine that such written accounts may one day rank with the autobiographies of certain saints, and there is always the possibility that they may fall into the hands of the wrong persons. Moreover, it is usually difficult to understand perfectly and to judge accurately a written account of one's personal experiences. Hence all information given to the director should be given vocally. Unlike the confessor, who should normally believe whatever the penitent declares in the confessional, the spiritual director is not obliged to believe everything that he hears; indeed, there are occasions when he should examine and question the person before making any decision.

Instruction

2) *To give instruction.* The spiritual director is expected to instruct the person under his guidance in order to form a right conscience in the individual, thus making it possible for the individual to solve his own problems and difficulties whenever possible. Spiritual direction has as its goal the perfection of the individual, and the ideal is to enable the individual to walk or even to fly to the summit of sanctity. Like any form of counseling, spiritual direction should be given only when necessary. If the director dominates the conscience of the individual person excessively and makes that person come to him for decisions or permissions in unnecessary and sometimes foolish things, the subject becomes increasingly weaker and more dependent on the director. It is not unusual to find spiritual directors who violate this basic concept of direction and counseling and nullify any good they could accomplish by making themselves the focal point of all their direction. The director should also avoid any decisions that are not justified by sound theology. The only exception in regard to dogmatism would be in dealing with souls who are scrupulous or excessively curious, because with such persons the only method of treatment is to exact unquestioning obedience.

The instructions given by the director should avoid all controversial points in the theology of Christian perfection, all abstruse and disputed questions in speculative theology, and in general anything that would serve to sharpen the curiosity of the person directed without giving an understanding of spiritual matters. His instructions should be based on those fundamental points which are commonly accepted by all theologians rather than any particular devotion or spiritual exercise, which may be perfectly orthodox and commendable in itself but not suited to the taste or present need of the person directed. He will above all avoid any word or action which could be interpreted as disapproval or disdain of any other school of spirituality.

Encouragement

3) *To encourage the soul.* Few souls, even among those who are advanced, are so self-sufficient that they do not need to be encouraged. The spiritual director is not only called upon to give instructions and to solve difficulties, but he should be a true educator who makes a positive contribution to the spiritual formation of the soul which is under his direction. Sometimes the best possible way of contributing to this formation is by means of encouragement and stimulation. To that end, the director should endeavor to infuse in souls a healthy optimism which is founded on confidence in God and distrust of self. Souls must be made to realize that they are individually called to perfection and that they can attain it if they are faithful to the graces that God gives them. If they fail or become discouraged, the director should lift them up and make them see that discouragement at their failure can be more harmful to their spiritual life than the failure itself.

It would be impossible to measure the harm that is done to souls by severe and harsh treatment from the director at the precise moment in which the disheartened individuals need assistance and confidence and encouragement to resume the difficult journey toward perfection. Frequently there is nothing that so animates a soul as to be received with kindness and understanding, when it expected to be censured and scolded by the director.

Control

4) *To control the spiritual life of the person directed.* The soul should not take any important step without the approval of the spiritual director. The plan of life, the method of prayer, the practices of piety, the practice of mortification, the work of the apostolate, the material of the examination of conscience—all should be controlled by the spiritual director. But the direction should be limited strictly to those things which concern the soul's growth in holiness. The spiritual director should take scrupulous care that he does not become an intolerable burden to the person directed by interjecting his authority into those matters which are of petty consequence or are not related to the spiritual life.

By the same token, he should never allow the penitent to insert family matters, business affairs, human preoccupations, etc., into the interviews or conferences. As soon as he perceives that the person directed is beginning to wander from the matter that pertains to the spiritual life, he should immediately and definitively put an end to such discussion. In order to prevent any such digression, the spiritual director should always be in control of the conversation and should insist that all matters be discussed as briefly and as directly as possible. If from the very start of the spiritual direction he restricts the individual to a succinct discussion of the matter at hand, he will avoid wasting much precious time and will prevent the direction from degenerating into pious conversation or purely social visits.

5) *To correct defects.* The spiritual director will have to know how to unite sweetness of character with the obligation of correcting the fault of the person directed. Although the purpose of spiritual direction is eminently positive—to lead the soul to the height of perfection—he cannot achieve that goal without the negative aspect of uprooting defects. In the correction of imperfections he needs to consider not only moral defects but also psychological and temperamental disorders.

Correction

In other words, it does not suffice for the director to be concerned simply with the correction of voluntary faults; he must likewise understand and seek to remedy the psychological predispositions to vice which are found in the psychosomatic structure of the individual person. Thus the precipitation, inconstancy, superficiality, sensuality, etc., which predispose to various sins must be corrected, so that the personality can be integrated and properly disposed for the practice of virtue. As regards voluntary faults, the spiritual director will never allow the individual to excuse himself for his fall by blaming them on his temperament or some external circumstance.

The particular examen will be utilized as a means of discovering the occasions which provided the temptation and the causes which disposed for the deliberate fault. The director will be especially vigilant in suppressing the slightest movement of self-love in the person directed. Although he must avoid discouraging the individual, he must make the subject realize that voluntary imperfections are incompatible with the perfection of charity and that the ideal of the ascetical struggle is, in a sense, a return to the perfect integration of the human personality exemplified in our first parents.

Direction

6) *To direct by progressive stages.* Spiritual direction should be progressive and accommodated to the soul's degree of virtue, temperament, age and circumstances of life. If the direction given is far above the needs and capacities of the soul, the soul will become disheartened and discouraged, because more will be demanded of it than it is capable of doing. If, on the other hand, the soul has advanced beyond the type of direction that is given, the wings of the soul will be tied so that it cannot soar to God.

The director must, therefore, discern what are the needs of the soul at a given time, and then take care that the direction given will satisfy those needs. When he wishes to intensify the spiritual life of the soul, he should propose things by way of a trial or test, in order to see how the soul reacts. He need not and should not tell the soul that this is his method, but he should take every precaution not to hold the soul back when God wishes to lead it to a higher stage and not force the soul to a higher stage when it is not yet ready to make the step. Growth in the spiritual life, like any other kind of growth, must be gradual and continuous. In the natural order, things do not grow by leaps and starts but through a gradual evolution to full perfection. Consequently, the spiritual director should know the various steps which mark the phases of growth from the beginning of the ascetical life to the transforming union, and in dealing with particular individuals he should expect that they will not remain static in any given phase, but that they will progress in gradual stages from one phase of the spiritual life to another. And although it is true that God could take a soul in his arms, so to speak, and carry it from one stage of life to a much higher stage, this is not to be presumed in any given case, because it is not the ordinary working of God's grace. For that reason, the spiritual direction should grow in proportion as the directed person evolves from one phase to another.

Secrecy

7) *To observe secrecy.* The spiritual director is obligated to observe absolute secrecy in regard to the confidences which he has received from the persons he directs, not only because many of these things are in some way connected with the seal of confession, but also because the office of spiritual director obligates him to natural secrecy. The obligation to secrecy is especially important when it is a question of advanced souls who have experienced certain extraordinary phenomena and supernatural charisms. Although a director who comes into contact with such phenomena may have a strong inclination to discuss these things, he should remember that, as a rule, the narration of such things does nothing more than arouse morbid curiosity in others and dispose the director himself to feelings of pride and self-complacency.

THE SOUL DIRECTED

Since spiritual direction involves two persons, the success of the direction is not guaranteed by the mere fact that the director possesses all the necessary qualities and understands the purpose and function of spiritual direction. There are also definite requisites demanded of the soul that submits to the spiritual director, and these requisites flow, first of all, from the nature of spiritual direction itself and, secondly, from the relationship of the person directed with the spiritual director.

SPIRITUAL DIRECTION

As regards the direction itself, it cannot be successful unless the person directed possesses the following qualities:

Sincerity

1) *Sincerity.* This is the first and most important quality, because without it any kind of direction is impossible. The spiritual director has to know all: temptations and weaknesses, desires and resolutions, good and evil inclinations, difficulties and trials, success and failure, etc. If he is to guide the soul to greater perfection, his hands are tied unless he has sufficient knowledge of

the soul. Although the spiritual director need not also be the confessor, it would be impossible to give any spiritual direction if the director were to know nothing of the sins and imperfections of the individual.

One should reveal to the director whatever has any importance in regard to the spiritual life, but it is not necessary, and it would even be an abuse, to give him a detailed account of petty trifles and insignificant events. But what is revealed should be revealed with all frankness and sincerity, without condoning or excusing one's failures or exaggerating one's virtues.

Obedience

2) *Obedience.* The director does not possess any authority by which he can demand strict obedience. Spiritual direction is a matter of perfect liberty on the part of the director and the person directed. By the very fact that a person seeks the help of the director, however, the two are not on an equal footing, but the director is in a position of superiority as the master and guide.

Granted the voluntary submission of a person to the director, the director has a right to expect docility and obedience from the one who is directed. If these are lacking, there can be no spiritual direction. For that reason the director should demand obedience of the soul in all those things that pertain to the spiritual direction, and if this is not granted he should discontinue the direction. The soul should obey simply and without discussions or personal interpretations. And it should be noted that even worse than disobedience is the duplicity by which a soul would so ingratiate itself with the director that he would command it to do only the things which the soul wants to do. St. John of the Cross severely condemns this abuse.[20] This does not mean, however, that an individual may not take the initiative in order to make a manifestation of conscience or to point out particular difficulties or obstacles that the director perhaps did not see.

Vow of obedience

What is to be thought of the vow of obedience which some persons have taken to their spiritual director? In general, this is not advisable because of the disadvantages connected with it (i.e., too much responsibility for the director, anxiety for the person directed, too much passivity, unnecessary visits and interviews, etc.). In any case, the director should never take the initiative and suggest that a person make a vow of obedience to him, for this would be an abuse of his authority and his office. It would be an even greater abuse if a director were to add to the vow of obedience the promise never to change directors or never to consult anyone else.

But if an individual voluntarily and repeatedly requests permission to make a vow of obedience to the director (for an increase of merit), it could be permitted under the following circumstances: a) that the vow be made for a short period of time and then renewed if desired; b) that it be restricted to certain matters which are clearly stated, such as the time of prayer, the types

[20]Cf. *The Dark Night,* Bk. I, Chaps. 2 and 6.

of mortification, the work in the apostolate, etc.; c) that the person making the vow be perfectly normal, serene and balanced; d) that the vow may be revoked if any difficulties or anxieties arise.

What is to be done if a conflict arises between the commands of a lawful superior and those of a spiritual director? One must unhesitatingly obey the superior, even if he has taken a vow of obedience to his director. It should be noted that private vows taken by religious are null and void without the approval of their superiors.[21] And even if one has received permission of a religious superior to make a vow of obedience to one's director, the superior never loses the power over the subject which is the result of religious profession.[22]

Perseverance

3) *Perseverance.* The very nature of spiritual direction requires that the person directed should persevere in seeking the help and guidance of the director. Any spiritual direction or counseling is rendered sterile by the frequent change of directors, by absenting oneself for long periods, by the constant change of spiritual exercises and means of sanctification, or by letting oneself be led by a caprice of the moment instead of following the instructions received from the director. When serious reasons justify a change, a person should not hesitate to find a new director, but that is something quite distinct from the fickleness and inconstancy which is manifested by some persons in changing from one director to another under the slightest pretext.

Discretion

4) *Discretion.* The person receiving spiritual direction should never forget that, if the director is obliged to the seal of confession or to natural secrecy, the one receiving direction is obliged to observe silence concerning the director. As a general rule, a person should never reveal to others the particular admonitions or counsels which have been received from the spiritual director. Such advice is given to a particular person in view of particular circumstances and does not apply to other persons living in different circumstances. Many directors have suffered greatly as the result of the indiscretion of their penitents, and this is sufficient reason for a director to refuse to continue the direction of such a person.

SPIRITUAL DIRECTOR

The principal qualities required of the person directed in relation to the director are respect, confidence and supernatural love.

1) *Respect.* The person directed must see in the director, not merely a man who is gifted with certain qualities, but the lawful representative of God and of Christ. No matter what defects or perfections he may have in the natural order, he must be regarded with respect precisely as a director and guide of the spiritual life. This profound respect will be most useful, not only in fostering

[21]Cf. St. Thomas, *Summa,* II-II, q. 88, a. 6.
[22]Cf. *ibid.,* a. 8, ad 3.

the docility and obedience of the person directed, but also in serving as a brake to any excessive confidence or sensual affection toward the director.

2) *Confidence.* In addition to respect, there should be absolute confidence in the director. It should be a confidence which is truly filial, and so absolute that one can always be perfectly natural and frank when dealing with the director. If the person directed is timid and self-conscious, the spiritual direction will never be completely efficacious.

3) *Supernatural love.* Once a person has cultivated a filial confidence toward the director, it usually happens that a true love develops for the director. This is one of the most delicate problems in the relationship between the spiritual director and the person directed. It is not a purely theoretical question, but one that occurs with utmost frequency. There is nothing unlawful about a love for one's spiritual director as long as the love remains entirely on a supernatural level. The lives of the saints give countless cases in which there has been this type of holy love. The difficulty lies in keeping the love on a purely supernatural level.

The cause of the love may be any one of the many causes of love in general. It is not at all unlikely that, in many instances, the love of a woman for her spiritual director is purely natural, proceeding from the normal affinity that exists between a woman and a man. The love could also be the result of the spiritual relation, however, and in this case it is nothing more than a reaction to the paternal interest and affection which has been manifested by the director and a sense of gratitude for all that he has done for the individual. The danger that lies in the love or friendship between a director and a woman is augmented by the fact that the director necessarily must know about matters of conscience, temptations and even sins. Moreover, if the love for the director is purely natural, there is always the possibility of venial sins such as envy, jealousy, suspicion, scandal to others—not to mention the ever-present danger of sensual love. Even if a director is convinced that there is no danger to himself or his penitent, he must always be conscious of the danger of scandal to others. St. Teresa of Avila experienced an attachment to a spiritual director and has written some practical observations on this subject.[23]

As a consequence of all this, the person directed—and this applies especially to women—should make every effort to see the director as another Christ, to confer with him only when necessary, and scrupulously to avoid any manifestation of human affection.

Director's conduct

As regards the director, he must have a most delicate conscience and a refined prudence in these matters, without going to the extreme of being excessively timid, suspicious or gruff. If it is a question of a mutual sensible affection which is recognized by both parties, it would be more prudent for the in-

[23]Cf. St. Teresa, *The Life,* Chap. 24.

dividual directed to seek another spiritual director. The reason for this is not only the obvious danger that such a friendship may easily degenerate into sensual affection, but also that under those conditions it would be difficult to have true and efficacious spiritual direction.

If the director experiences a sensible affection for the person directed, he should examine it before God in order to discover whether such an affection disturbs his spirit, places him in danger of temptation, impedes the liberty which he should have as a spiritual director, or is the source of some other danger. In this case, without revealing his feelings to the person directed, he should find some reasonable cause for abandoning the direction. If, in spite of the sensible affection, he does not experience any danger of temptation or any obstacle to the direction, he may proceed with the direction, but always keeping a prudent vigilance over himself.

If, finally, the director realizes that his penitent has developed a sensible affection for him and he himself does not return that affection, he should examine whether or not such an affection is disturbing the peace of soul of, or provoking temptation for, the person directed. If so, he should advise and even command that the individual seek another spiritual director. If there is no danger that the affection of the penitent may degenerate into a sensual love, he may continue the direction of that individual, but he will be very careful, lest by some imprudent word or act he should augment that human affection.

SPECIAL QUESTIONS

We shall terminate the present chapter with a discussion of certain particular questions which may arise in the matter of spiritual direction.

CHOICE OF DIRECTOR

The first question concerns the choice of a spiritual director. Some persons are not in a position to choose their own director, for example, cloistered nuns or persons who do not have access to several priests. In such cases one must do as well as possible with the director at hand and trust in God to supply for any deficiencies in the director.

Apart from these particular cases, the choice of a spiritual director should be made in the following way. The first thing to be done is to ask God in prayer for the grace and light to proceed prudently in this important matter. Then one should investigate who among the available priests possesses the prudence and charity which are necessary for a good director. Under no circumstances should the choice be made because of one's natural inclinations toward a particular priest, although it should be recognized that it would be more difficult to open one's heart with confidence to a priest for whom one feels repugnance or antipathy. It is not advisable to ask the priest immediately to be the spiritual director, but one should test him for a time to see whether or not he will be able to fulfill the task of director. All things being equal, one should seek the holiest priest for ordinary cases and the most learned priest for extraordinary cases.[24] Once the choice has been made, a person should not easily change directors.

CHANGE OF DIRECTORS

But it may sometimes prove necessary for a person to seek a different spiritual director, although one should not readily or too easily believe that it is necessary to change directors. Some of the insufficient reasons for changing one's director are: inconstancy of character, which makes it impossible for the individual to persevere for a long time in the same spiritual exercises; pride, which causes the individual to seek out the priest who is most popular; excessive anxiety, which causes a person to go from one director to another, because none of them ever seem to be able to help the soul; a false sense of shame, which leads the individual to avoid the regular confessor when it is a matter of confessing certain humiliating faults; and injured feelings as a result of a disagreement with the director or a severe correction received from the director.

The reasons that are sufficiently serious for changing one's spiritual director can be listed under two heads: if the direction has become useless or harmful.

Useless direction

The spiritual direction becomes useless when, in spite of one's good will and sincere desire to advance in holiness, one does not feel toward the director the respect, confidence and frankness which are indispensable for the efficacy of the spiritual direction. It would also be a futile effort if one perceives that the director never dares to make corrections of one's defects, does not encourage progress in virtue, does not solve problems, and shows no special interest in the sanctification of the individual.

Harmful direction

The direction would be harmful if the person directed discovers that the director lacks the necessary knowledge, prudence and discretion; when he feeds the vanity and complacence of the individual, readily tolerates one's faults and imperfections, or judges things from a point of view that is too natural; when the director wastes time by frivolous conversations, or by asking questions out of simple curiosity, or in discussing matters which are not related to growth in holiness, or when one perceives that there has developed a strong sensible affection on the part of one or both; when the director imposes obligations that are beyond one's strength or incompatible with the duties of one's state in life, or wishes that the individual promise never to seek counsel from any other

[24]Cf. St. Teresa, *The Life,* Chap. 13; *The Way of Perfection,* Chap. 5; *Interior Castle,* Sixth Mansions, Chap. 8.

priest; when one perceives clearly that the advice given has been harmful instead of helpful. It should be noted, however, that one may easily be mistaken in making judgments concerning the competence of the director and the efficacy of the direction, and for that reason it is imperative that one deliberate before making a change in spiritual directors.

PLURALITY OF DIRECTORS

Would it be fitting to have several directors at the same time? Although there have been cases in which a person had several spiritual directors (for example, St. Teresa of Avila), in general it is not prudent or effective to do so. There is always the danger of a difference of opinion and a conflict as a result of discrepancy in the advice that is given. Nevertheless, it is perfectly compatible with the unity of direction to seek advice from other competent persons when an especially difficult or extraordinary problem arises. As we have already stated, the director himself, if he is prudent and humble, will take the initiative and advise the penitent to consult another person. But apart from these special cases, the unity of spiritual direction must always be preserved, especially when dealing with scrupulous persons, and this unity is best preserved by having one director.

WRITTEN DIRECTION

The last question to be answered in the matter of spiritual direction concerns direction given by mail. If it is a question of an isolated case in which an individual requests advice or the solution of a problem by mail, there is no reason why such direction should not be given in a letter, if one observes the necessary precautions which are required whenever confidential matters are discussed by letter. If advice is requested by persons who already have their own spiritual director, great caution should be observed, especially if one is not sure of the good faith and discretion of the person who is asking advice. Sometimes individuals seek an answer in writing from another priest in order to show this letter to their own director and confront him with advice that is contrary to that which he has given. If it is necessary for one priest to correct the advice given by another priest, this should always be done with utmost charity, and whenever possible it should be given as an amplification and further application of the advice already given rather than a complete and total rectification.

But what is to be said of spiritual direction which is given entirely by mail? It may happen in exceptional cases that it is the only way in which a person can receive spiritual direction, and even apart from these cases there are examples of direction by mail in the lives of the saints (for example, St. Francis de Sales and St. Paul of the Cross). But the disadvantages far outnumber the advantages of spiritual direction by letter. It is morally impossible for the director to acquire an intimate knowledge of the person directed unless there is oral communication between them. It is very difficult to express and describe one's interior life in writing; it is equally difficult to understand another person from a written account. Moreover, the spiritual director is not able to make corrections immediately, as he could do if the person were actually speaking to him. Another disadvantage is that letters may easily fall into the hands of others.

Practical conduct

In practice, the spiritual director should not be willing to accept the direction of a soul through correspondence unless he already knows the individual and the person has no other recourse. In the actual writing of letters, the director should never write a single line which would in any way constitute a violation of the seal of confession, and if he does receive such material in letters from the person directed, he should destroy the letter as soon as he has read it and should severely forbid the individual from writing such things in the future, under penalty of discontinuing the spiritual direction.

Whatever direction is given in writing should be brief and objective. The spiritual director should scrupulously avoid any terms of affection, pet names, excessively cordial salutations, and anything that smacks of sentimentality. Directors who have had experience in spiritual direction by mail have been most succinct in their answers, sometimes writing a few words on the letter itself and returning it to the sender without any signature.

If in some cases it is necessary to write at greater length, the director will confine himself to the problems or questions presented and to the instruction, exhortation or correction which the matter demands. He will observe the greatest prudence and delicacy, and never write anything in a letter which he would not wish his bishop or religious superior to read. He should always remember that, in spite of his own good will and zeal, there is always the danger of false interpretations and rash judgments. His letters should always be such that he never has anything to fear in this respect. Even in the case of accepting the direction of a soul by letter, the director must always give the penitent full liberty to consult other directors. Lastly, both he and the person directed must avoid any kind of secret or clandestine correspondence. If, in the case of a religious, the superior should forbid a subject to write to a spiritual director, this fact should be made known to higher authority, but the subject should never have recourse to a secret exchange of letters.

Letters and superiors

Does a religious superior have the right to read the letters of subjects when they deal with matters of conscience or spiritual direction? Ordinarily, no religious superior has this right, because the superior has no direct power over matters of conscience or the internal forum. But if a religious superior has sufficiently grave reasons to suspect that there is an abuse, or that the letters contain matters which have nothing to do with spiritual direction, the majority of authors maintain that a superior could read what is necessary to find out whether or not the letter is truly concerned with spiritual direction.

But the superior is bound to the most rigorous secrecy concerning the contents of the letter.

Some authors, on the other hand, teach that the superior should make known his or her suspicions to a higher authority and leave the matter in his hands; others affirm that the superior should destroy the letters without reading them, and then advise the subject so that recourse can be had, if desired, to a higher superior. Whatever the method of procedure in a particular case, superiors should keep in mind that it is a serious matter to probe into the consciences of their subjects and that, therefore, they need a sufficiently grave reason for reading letters in which such matters are discussed. For the peace of soul of the individual, for the unity of the community, for the preservation of confidence and respect from one's subjects, it would seem much more prudent for superiors to trust their subjects and to read their mail only when it is truly necessary.

MYSTICAL PHENOMENA

VII

1: BASIC NOTIONS

One of the most interesting of all the aspects of the theological study of mysticism is the consideration of those extraordinary phenomena which customarily seem to be present in the lives of all the great mystics. This is a difficult and delicate subject, however, and one that should be undertaken with great carefulness and discretion.

That our consideration of these interesting but difficult matters may be probing as well as solid, we shall proceed slowly, thoroughly and carefully. This initial chapter will take up certain basic notions essential for any proper appreciation of these phenomena, namely, the psychosomatic structure of the human person (his temperament and character) and the discernment of spirits. Indeed, knowledge of these two matters is necessary at every level of the spiritual life if one is properly to direct others (or be properly directed), but so pertinent is it for our present investigation that we have postponed its formal consideration until the present moment. Then, since one fully knows a thing only when its causes are known, we shall investigate in a second chapter the causes of extraordinary mystical phenomena. Finally, we shall study in some detail the phenomena themselves.

THE PSYCHOSOMATIC STRUCTURE

It is a truism in psychology that no two personalities are exactly alike. This being so, the perfection of charity will be manifested in different ways in different persons. A brief glance at the catalog of canonized saints will suffice to verify the fact that the perfect love of God and neighbor will be greatly modified by the psychosomatic structure of the individual saint. Thus, while all possessed heroic charity, there is a remarkable difference in the way in which this charity was carried into external practice in the lives of such saints as Augustine, Dominic, Francis Xavier, Peter Alcántara, Benedict Labre, Louis of France and John of the Cross.

MYSTICAL PHENOMENA

Differentiation

The same basic principle of differentiation must be applied to the mystical state, especially when it is a question of the extraordinary phenomena. While it is true that in many instances the only explanation for the occurrence of extraordinary phenomena is to be found in the will of God, who chooses according to his own hidden designs in the distribution of his gifts, one must also take into account the personality of the individual mystic in order to have a clearer understanding of the reason why certain manifestations occur. The psychosomatic structure can react only in a certain number of ways, and the reactions are further limited by the constitutional factors of the individual person. This is an evident fact in the operations of the various organs, cognitive powers and emotions when stimulated by their proper objects. The supernatural does not destroy the natural, but works through it in such a way that the human body-soul composite can be a help or a hindrance to the workings of grace. Hence it is of great importance to understand the manner in which man's psychosomatic structure concurs in the work of sanctification, although it does so on a purely natural plane as a dispositive cause or by the removal of obstacles (*removens prohibens*). We shall discuss the human personality under the twofold classification of temperament and character, which are the elements which constitute it.

TEMPERAMENT

There is a diversity of opinion among psychologists concerning the definition and classification of temperament. For our purposes we may define temperament as the pattern of inclinations which proceed from the physiological constitution of the individual. It is a dynamic factor which takes into account the manner in which the individual organic structure will react to stimuli of various kinds. Since it is rooted in the physiological structure, temperament is something innate and hereditary; it is that element of personality which makes the personality unique, since individuality is rooted in matter, and temperament is the natural inclination of the somatic structure. It is, therefore, something permanent and admits of only secondary modification; one's temperament can never be totally destroyed without destroying the individual. The axiom, "grace does not destroy nature but perfects it," has its most obvious application in the area of temperament.

Classification

The classification of the temperaments is nothing more than a handy framework which has been constructed according to the predominant characteristics of various physiological constitutions. It is by no means exclusive or definitive, nor does it signify that there are "pure" temperaments. As a matter of fact, individual persons generally manifest a combination of the characteristics of several temperaments. Whenever there are several elements combined in any composite, however, one or another will usually predominate at any given time, and in the matter of temperament we find that, although persons are usually a composite of many characteristics, one or another characteristic will specify the temperament. Bearing this in mind, we shall discuss the four temperaments according to the ancient classification of sanguine, melancholic, choleric and phlegmatic.

1) *Sanguine temperament.* A person of sanguine temperament reacts quickly and strongly to almost any stimulation or impression, but the reaction is usually of short duration. The stimulation or impression is quickly forgotten, and the remembrance of past experiences does not easily arouse a new response.

Good qualities

Among the good qualities of the sanguine temperament, we may list the following: affability and cheerfulness; sympathy and generosity toward others; sensitivity and compassion for the sufferings of others; docility and submission to superiors; sincerity and spontaneity. There may at times be a violent reaction to injuries received, but all is soon forgotten and no rancor remains. There is no obstinacy and stubbornness but the ability to act with complete self-detachment. Others are attracted by the individual's goodness of heart and contagious enthusiasm.

Sanguine persons usually have a serene view of life and are optimists; they are not discouraged by difficulties or obstacles but hope for a successful outcome in all their efforts. They are gifted with a great deal of common sense and a practical approach to life; they tend to idealize rather than criticize. Since they possess an affectionate nature, they make friends easily and sometimes love their friends with great ardor or even passion. Their intellects are alert and they learn quickly, although often without much depth. Their memory dwells on pleasant and optimistic things, and their imagination is active and creative. Consequently, they readily excel in art, oratory and the related fields, though they do not often attain the stature of the learned or the scholars. Sanguine persons could be superior types of individuals if they possessed as much depth as they do facility and if they were as tenacious in their work as they are productive of new ideas and projects. The following saints are examples of the sanguine temperament: St. Peter, St. Augustine, St. Teresa of Avila, St. Francis Xavier and St. Rose of Lima.

Defects of temperament

But each temperament will also be characterized by certain qualities which are dangerous and could become predispositions to evil. Thus the principal defects of the sanguine temperament are superficiality, inconstancy and sensuality. The first defect is due primarily to the ease and rapidity with which these persons conceive ideas and the creative activity of their imagination. While they appear to grasp in an instant even the most difficult problem or subject, they sometimes see it only superficially and incompletely. As a result, they run the risk of hasty judgments, of acting with insufficient reason, and of formulating inaccurate or false conclusions. They are more interested in breadth of knowledge than depth.

The inconstancy of the sanguine person is the result of the short duration of his impressions and reactions. He may pass quickly from joy to sorrow. He quickly repents of his sins but may return to them on the first occasion that presents itself. Being readily moved by the impression of the moment, he easily succumbs to temptation. As a rule he is not drawn to abnegation, sacrifice or any effort that is of long duration. For that reason he has great difficulty in observing custody of the external senses and the imagination and is easily distracted in prayer. His occasional periods of great fervor are often followed by discouragement and languor.

From the foregoing it is evident that sensuality finds easy access to the sanguine temperament. Such persons are easy victims of gluttony and lust. They may react strongly and with great sorrow after they have fallen, but they lack the energy and perseverance to fight against the inclinations of the flesh when the passions are again aroused. The entire organism is quickly alerted when the occasion is offered for sensual pleasure, and the strong tendency of the individual to sensuality causes the imagination to produce such phantasms very easily.

Control of temperament

The development and control of any temperament requires the fostering of its good qualities and the eradication or suppression of its defects. The sanguine person should utilize his good qualities, such as energy, affection, vivacity and sensitivity, but he should take care that these qualities are directed to objects that are good and wholesome. For him more than for any other person the advice of St. Augustine has special significance: "Choose wisely and then love with all your heart."

At the same time, he must fight against the evil inclinations of his sanguine temperament. To overcome superficiality he will acquire the habit of reflection and of thinking a matter through before he acts. This means that he has special need of deliberation or judgment as a subjective part of the virtue of prudence. Against his inconstancy he will strengthen his will to carry through resolutions that have been made and be faithful in the practice of prayer and the performance of good works, even in periods of aridity or in times of hardship and difficulty. The secondary helps which are of the greatest importance in this regard are a plan of life, followed conscientiously, and the daily examination of conscience, with self-imposed penances for failures. Sanguine persons sometimes need an expert spiritual director whom they should obey without question.

Lastly, sensuality must be combatted by constant vigilance and an unrelenting struggle. Above all, the sanguine person must flee immediately from the occasions of sin and take special care to observe a strict custody of the eyes. The custody of the external senses and the imagination should be further safeguarded by the practice of recollection and practices of mortification, for it would be futile to try to avoid sensuality if one were to leave the windows of the senses open to every kind of distraction and temptation.

2) *Melancholic temperament.* The melancholic temperament is weak as regards reaction to stimulus, and it is difficult to arouse; however, after repeated impressions the reaction is strong and lasting, so that the melancholic temperament does not forget easily.

Good qualities

As regards good qualities which serve as predispositions to virtue, persons of melancholic temperament are inclined to reflection, solitude, piety and the interior life. They are compassionate toward those who suffer, attracted to the corporal works of mercy, and able to endure suffering to the point of heroism in the performance of their duties. They have a sharp and profound intellect, and, because of their natural bent to solitude and reflection, they generally consider matters thoroughly in silence and tranquility. They may become detached and dry intellectuals, or contemplatives who are concerned solely with the things of God. They usually appreciate the fine arts but are more drawn to the sciences, especially the speculative sciences.

As regards their affective powers, when they love it is with difficulty that they detach themselves from the object of their love. They suffer greatly if others treat them with coldness or ingratitude. The power of their will is greatly affected by their physical strength and health. If their physical powers are exhausted, their will is weak and practically null, but if they are in good health and spirits they are energetic workers and joyful in spirit. They have great sobriety and continence because they seldom experience the disorderly passions which may torment the persons of a sanguine temperament. We may say in general that this temperament is opposed to the sanguine temperament as the choleric temperament is opposed to the phlegmatic temperament. Among the saints who possessed this particular temperament are St. John, the beloved disciple, St. Bernard, St. Louis Gonzaga and St. Thérèse of Lisieux.

Defects of temperament

The unfavorable traits of the melancholic temperament are the following: an exaggerated tendency to sadness and melancholy; an inclination to magnify difficulties and thus to lose confidence in self; excessive reserve and timidity, with a propensity to scrupulosity; lack of resolution. Persons of melancholic temperament do not show their feelings as do the sanguine; they suffer in silence because they find it difficult to reveal themselves. They always seem to see the difficult and pessimistic side of things. Many enterprises are never begun because of their lack of confidence and resolution.

Control of temperament

Those who are in charge of educating or training the melancholic temperament should keep in mind their strong tendency to concentrate excessively on themselves; otherwise there is danger of doing them an injustice or of treating them in a tactless manner. It is important to inculcate in these persons a strong confidence in God and in themselves, as well as a more optimistic view of life. Since they have good intellects and tend to reflection, they should be made to realize that there is no reason for them to be timid or irresolute. At all costs the director must destroy their indecision and cowardice and get them to make firm resolutions and to undertake projects with enthusiasm and optimism. Sometimes it is necessary to give them a special regimen of rest and nourishment and to forbid them to spend long hours in prayer and solitude or to observe fasts.

3) *Choleric temperament.* Persons of a choleric temperament are easily and strongly aroused, and the impression lasts for a long time. Theirs is the temperament which produces great saints or great sinners, and while all the temperaments can be utilized as material for sanctity, it seems that the largest number of canonized saints possessed a choleric temperament.

Good qualities

The good qualities of the temperament can be summarized as follows: great energy and activity; sharp intellect; strong and resolute will; good powers of concentration; constancy; magnanimity; and liberality. Choleric persons are practical rather than theoretical; they are more inclined to work than to think. Inactivity is repugnant to them, and they are always looking forward to the next labor or to the formulation of some great project. Once they have set upon a plan of work, they immediately set their hand to the task. Hence this temperament produces many leaders, superiors, apostles. It is the temperament of government and administration.

These persons do not leave for tomorrow what they can do today, but sometimes they may try to do today what they should leave for tomorrow. If difficulties or obstacles arise, they immediately set about to overcome them, and, although they often have strong movements of irascibility and impatience in the face of problems, once they have conquered these movements they acquire a tenderness and sweetness of disposition which are noteworthy. The saints who possessed a choleric temperament are numerous, but we shall mention only St. Paul, St. Jerome, St. Ignatius Loyola, St. Francis de Sales.

Defects of temperament

The tenacity of the choleric temperament sometimes produces the following evil effects: hardness, obstinacy, insensibility, anger and pride. If choleric persons are resisted, they may easily become violent, cruel, arrogant, unless the Christian virtues moderate these inclinations. If defeated by others, they may nurture hatred in their hearts until they have obtained their vengeance. They easily become ambitious and seek their own glory. They have greater patience than do the sanguine, but they may lack delicacy of feeling, are often insensitive to the feelings of others, and therefore lack tact in human relations. Their passions, when aroused, are so strong and impetuous that they smother the more tender emotions and the spirit of sacrifice which springs spontaneously from more sympathetic hearts. Their fever for activity and their eagerness to execute their resolutions cause them to disregard others, to thrust all impediments aside, and to give the appearance of being heartless egoists. In their treatment of others they sometimes display a coldness and indifference which reaches the point of cruelty. The only rights which they acknowledge are the satisfaction and attainment of their desires. It is evident from the foregoing that, if the choleric person pursues the path of evil, there is no length to which he will not go in order to achieve his goal.

Control of temperament

Choleric persons can be individuals of great worth if they succeed in controlling and guiding their energies. They could arrive at the height of perfection with relative facility. In their hands even the most difficult tasks seem to be brought to an easy and ready solution. Therefore, when they have themselves under control and are rightly directed, they will not cease in their efforts until they have reached the summit. They must be taught to keep themselves under the reins of self-mastery, not to act with precipitation, but to mistrust their first inclinations. Above all, they need to cultivate true humility of heart, to be compassionate to the weak and the uninstructed, not to humiliate or embarrass others, not to exert their own superiority, and to treat all persons with tenderness and understanding. In a word, they should be taught how to be detached from self and to manifest a generous love toward others.

4) *Phlegmatic temperament.* The phlegmatic is rarely aroused emotionally, and if so, only weakly. The impressions received usually last for only a short time and leave no trace.

Good qualities

The good characteristics of the phlegmatic person are that he works slowly but assiduously; he is not easily irritated by insults, misfortunes or sickness; he usually remains tranquil, discreet and sober; he has a great deal of common sense and mental balance. He does not possess the inflammable passions of the sanguine temperament, the deep passions of the melancholic temperament, or the ardent passions of the choleric temperament. In his speech he is orderly, clear, positive and measured, rather than florid and picturesque. He is more suited to scientific work which is the fruit of long and patient research and minute investigation than to original productions. He has a good heart, but it seems to be cold. He would sacrifice to the point of heroism if it were necessary, but he lacks enthusiasm and spontaneity because he is reserved and somewhat indolent by nature. He is prudent, sensible, reflexive and works with a measured pace. He attains his goals without fanfare or violence because he usually avoids difficulties rather than attacking them. Physically the phlegmatic is usually of robust build, slow in his movements, and possesses an amiable face. St. Thomas Aquinas seems to have possessed the best qualities of the phlegmatic temperament.

Defects of temperament

The defective qualities of the phlegmatic temperament are as follows: Their slowness and calmness cause these persons to lose many good opportunities because they delay so long in putting works into operation. They are not too interested in events that take place around them, but they tend to live by and for themselves, almost to the point of egoism. They are not suitable for government and administration. They are not usually drawn to corporal penances and mortification, as St. Teresa points out,[1] and there is no fear that they will kill themselves by penance and self-abnegation. In extreme cases they become so lethargic and insensible that they become completely deaf to the invitation or command that would raise them out of their stupor.

Control of temperament

The phlegmatic can avoid the bad effects of his temperament if he is inculcated with deep convictions and if he demands of himself methodical and constant efforts toward greater perfection. He will advance slowly, to be sure, but he will advance far. Above all, he must not be allowed to become indolent and apathetic but should be directed to some lofty ideal. He, too, needs to gain control of himself, not as the choleric, who must restrain and moderate himself, but to arouse himself and put his dormant powers to good use.

Conclusion

Having seen a brief description of the four basic temperaments, we repeat that none of these temperaments actually exists in a "pure" state. The reader himself may be aware that the complete portrait of his own temperament has not been found in any one of the four temperaments but that he possesses characteristics of several. This explains to a large extent why there are so many different opinions and theories in psychology on the question of temperaments. Nevertheless, each person will exhibit sufficient predominant qualities of a given temperament so that he can be classified under that particular type.

If we were to attempt to delineate the perfect temperament, we would select the best qualities of each temperament, taking care that they are not mutually exclusive. Thus we would take from the sanguine his sympathy, generous heart and vivacity; from the melancholic, the depth and delicacy of feeling; from the choleric, his inexhaustible energy and tenacity; and from the phlegmatic, his self-control, prudence and perseverance. In striving for this ideal which nature herself does not grant to anyone, we enter upon the problem of the ascetical struggle, which involves the difficult task of the formation of character.

CHARACTER

The temperament of an individual is a pattern of tendencies and inclinations which flow from the physiological structure or constitution of an individual; for that reason it is largely the result of hereditary factors. But character, on the contrary, is the pattern of habits which are the result of education, personal

[1]Cf. *Interior Castle,* Third Mansions, Chap. 2.

effort and environmental factors. Rather than physiological at basis, as is temperament, character is psychological, and while the temperament as such is immutable, it can be modified by character. Consequently, temperament is the material out of which character is made, much in the same way as the clay or marble or wood will be the material out of which a particular statue is fashioned. It is the character which gives the formal distinction to the personality.

Causes of character

We have mentioned three factors as causes of character, namely, education, personal effort and environmental factors. Under *education* we would include all those factors which, from the birth of an individual to the maturation of character (usually between the ages of 26 to 30), have influenced his attitudes and habits of life. During the early years, which extend from infancy to the beginning of formal education and even beyond, the child will be greatly affected by such factors as nationality, religious training, parental discipline and instruction, etc. Once the child begins his formal education, the school assumes a major role in the formation of character, especially if it is a school in which there is insistence on moral instruction and discipline. During these years and through the 'teen years the educational influence can usually be broken down into several categories: family, school, church and associates. Although the effects of these educative factors are not always immediately evident in the young, they leave impressions which form attitudes and value judgments which come into play when the individual reaches maturity and takes his place as a responsible member of society.

As regards the *environmental factors,* they are almost too numerous to mention, and they exert an especially strong influence on the individual during his formative years. The influence of example on children is too obvious to be denied. While the most forceful environmental influences are to be found in the lives of other human beings, such commonplace things as nutrition, climate, neighborhood environment and home life also exert a subtle but definite influence. Here again, the effects are not immediately evident in a growing child, but environment during youth is responsible to a large extent for those attitudes and evaluations which are most deeply rooted in the personality.

By *personal effort* as a cause of character we mean especially the deliberate acts of the will whereby, through the repetition of acts, certain habits are formed and developed until they become a second nature. This is by far the most important factor in the formation of character, and it is so potent an instrument that it can modify, correct or nullify the effects of education and environment. Man is master of himself by means of his free will, and he is responsible for the formation of his character by reason of the fact that any acquired habit is ultimately traced back to a deliberate choice of action which was repeated until the habit was formed. In this sense we can say that, whereas temperament is to a large extent what our ancestors have made us, character is what we have made ourselves. In its moral aspect a character will be good or evil according to whether the habits which predominate in an individual are virtues or vices. Consequently, the formation of character is closely associated with the psychology of habit formation and the theology of the virtues and vices. A man has the power within himself to become a sinner or a saint, but whatever his choice he will have to exert personal effort to achieve his goal.

Perfect character

According to the ancient philosophers, the life of virtue was a guarantee of the life of happiness and perfection. The same thing is true in reference to the ideal character: in the purely natural order it requires the balance and integration which is provided by the moral and intellectual virtues. For the perfect Christian, however, there is further required, as a superstructure built upon the natural foundation, the theological and moral infused virtues, as well as the gifts of the Holy Ghost.

To put the matter another way, we may say that from the psychological aspect the perfect character requires a clear, penetrating and broad intellect, assisted by a retentive memory, a firm and persevering will, and a delicate and well-controlled sensibility. From the moral point of view there is further required a right and certain conscience, self-possession through a properly orientated will, goodness of heart which manifests itself through affability, generosity, sympathy and self-detachment, and perfect composure or modesty of dress and action which reveals the balance and equilibrium of the internal man.

From what has been said, it should be evident that it is no easy task to form a perfect character. It is for many the work of a lifetime, for although the majority of persons are set in their characters before they reach the age of thirty, it is most rare that any character does not suffer modification and alteration during the entire lifetime of the individual. In the formation of character we would stress the necessity of proper education, good will and the assiduous cultivation of those virtues which pertain to the state and duties of life of the individual person.

DISCERNMENT OF SPIRITS

It is indispensable both for the direction of souls and for the study of extraordinary mystical phenomena to be able to distinguish between the various spirits or impulses under which individual persons act or are acted upon. Unless one is able to determine whether or not a given person is acting under the spirit of God, the spirit of darkness or the aberrations of his own illusions, it will be practically impossible to avoid error and even tragic mistakes.

BASIC NOTIONS

The spirit of an individual refers to his internal inclination or propensity to good or evil, and it manifests itself with such regularity that it must be considered as a personal trait. Thus, if a person has a propensity to prayer, he is said to possess the spirit of prayer; if he has a tendency to arguments and altercations, he is said to possess a spirit of contradiction, etc. Understood in this sense, the spirit of a person is usually the result of both temperament and character.

But it is also possible for an individual to come under the influence of a spirit which is extrinsic to his personality, whether from God or the devil, and for that reason it is the function of the discernment of spirits to judge whether a given act or repetition of acts flows from the spirit of the individual, the spirit of God or the diabolical spirit.

There are two types of discernment of spirit: acquired and infused. Acquired discernment of spirits is a special art which is complementary to ordinary spiritual direction and can be cultivated by all who use the proper means; infused discernment of spirits is a charismatic gift or *gratia gratis data* which is granted by God to certain individuals. We shall discuss infused discernment of spirits in its proper place under the *gratiae gratis datae;* for the time being we merely state that the charismatic gift of discernment is infallible because it is the result of an interior movement or inspiration received from the Holy Ghost, who cannot err. But it is extremely rare, and not even all the saints possessed it.

ACQUIRED DISCERNMENT

Acquired discernment, on the other hand, is not infallible, and it presents many great difficulties, although it is absolutely necessary for a good spiritual director. It stands to reason that, if a director is ignorant of the various spirits that may be the cause of the acts and movements of the soul and if he is unable to decide the particular spirit that motivates a given soul, he will be unable to determine which movements should be suppressed and which should be fostered and developed. St. John of the Cross and Father Scaramelli place great stress on the importance of discernment, pointing out that the possibility of error and tragic misguidance of souls is greatly augmented when acquired discernment is lacking and that the priest who presumes to take charge of the direction of souls without such knowledge is guilty of temerity.[2] It is, therefore, important to examine carefully the various means to be used in order to acquire the art of discernment of spirits.

Means of acquisition

1) *Prayer.* This is the most important and fundamental means. Although we are speaking of an acquired art, personal effort would avail nothing without the special assistance of the Holy Spirit through the virtue of prudence and the gift of counsel. Hence it is not only a question of the constant practice of

[2]Cf. St. John of the Cross, *The Living Flame of Love,* Stanza 3; J. B. Scaramelli, S.J., *Directorium Asceticum* (New York: Benziger), Chap. 4.

prayer, but the particular petition by which the director requests of God the prudence necessary for the direction of souls in general and the light to be able to discern the will of God for some particular soul at a given time. It does not suffice to possess a theoretical knowledge of the spiritual life and the ways to perfection; one needs in addition to know the practical and concrete application of these principles in particular cases. It is certain that God will answer these prayers with special graces which he gives to all rightly disposed souls so that they may fulfill their duties.

2) *Study.* The spiritual director likewise needs a vast amount of knowledge which is acquired through faithful study. He should be familiar with the general principles of spiritual theology as contained in Sacred Scripture, speculative theology, the masters of the spiritual life and the lives of the outstanding saints. He should be especially careful not to restrict himself to a particular "school" or method of spirituality, for while it is true that the individual soul will necessarily follow a particular path or way, the spiritual director must rise above this exclusive spirit and possess a broad and sympathetic understanding of the variety of schools and methods of the spiritual life. St. John of the Cross speaks with unusual severity when discussing those spiritual directors who know only one path to perfection and strive to force all the souls under their direction to follow that same path.[3]

3) *Personal experience.* Self-knowledge is a basic requirement for any kind of direction of others. While it is true that each person has his unique traits and characteristics, there is also a common pattern which is possessed by all, and, unless one understands himself, it will be very difficult, if not impossible, to understand others. Under this same heading we may include that sympathy or rapport which flows from an understanding of one's own virtues and defects and the ability to place oneself in the position and circumstances in which others find themselves, according to the statement of St. Paul: "There, but for the grace of God, go I." Moreover, if the spiritual director himself is not striving for greater perfection and has not attained some degree of virtue and self-mastery, it is not likely that he will be able to direct others or even understand their condition, especially when they enter upon the higher stages of the spiritual life. In this sense holiness of life is a most desirable trait in a spiritual director and is of inestimable value in acquiring the art of discernment of spirits.

4) *Removal of obstacles.* Under this heading we may place any of the defective qualities which are an impediment to the understanding and direction of souls. One of the greatest obstacles is the spirit of self-sufficiency which prevents the director from seeking the advice of those who are more learned or more experienced than himself. God refuses his graces to those who are

[3]Cf. *The Ascent of Mount Carmel,* Prol.; Bk. II, Chap. 18; *The Living Flame of Love,* Stanza 3. Cf. also St. Teresa, *The Life,* Chap. 34.

proud, and grants them to the humble. Secondly, the director must avoid at all costs an excessive attachment to the one he is directing, for this attachment will cloud his judgment and cause him to be too sympathetic. He must strive to be as objective as possible and to maintain a strict sense of reserve in regard to his own person and a cautious vigilance as regards the one being directed. He will avoid the inclination to judge according to purely human standards and will be guided at all times by supernatural prudence. He will never be precipitous in his decisions but will subject them to mature reflection, without excessive cavilling.

DIVERSE SPIRITS

As regards the diverse spirits, St. Bernard enumerates six: divine, angelic, diabolical, carnal, mundane and human.[4] All these, however, can be summarized under three headings: *the divine spirit, the human spirit* and *the spirit of the devil.* God always inclines us to the good, working either directly or through secondary causes; the devil always inclines us to evil, working by his own power or through the allurements of the things of the world; the human spirit may be inclined to evil or to good, depending upon whether the individual follows right reason or his own concupiscence.

Due to the basic indifference of many purely natural inclinations, it is evident that they may be utilized for good and for evil and that, while grace does not destroy nature but perfects and supernaturalizes it, the devil avails himself of human weakness and the effects of original sin to further his evil aims. Moreover, it may happen that in one and the same inclination or action the various spirits are intermingled, thus making it more difficult to discern which spirit has the predominance at a given time. It is evident that the spirit of God and the spirit of the devil cannot be operating at one and the same time, since they tend to opposite goals, but God can direct or intensify a naturally good inclination, or the devil may exercise his power to divert those inclinations to evil. Even when it is evident that the divine spirit predominates in a given action, therefore, it does not follow that all the antecedent or consequent movements and inclinations are likewise divine and supernatural. It frequently happens that purely human and natural movements introduce themselves, consciously or unconsciously, and cause the action to lose some of its supernatural purity. This is one of the factors which makes it almost impossible for the director or theologian to discern clearly the divine element in extraordinary mystical phenomena.

Moreover, it is not at all unusual in the lives of mystics that their mystical and truly supernatural operations are interrupted by purely natural activities or that, with God's permission, a diabolical influence is introduced. It is not easy to determine when the action of God terminates and when the natural

[4]St. Bernard, *Sermo de discretione spirituum.*

or diabolical movement begins.[5] If the director is familiar with the signs of the various spirits, however, he will have sufficient grounds for making a prudent judgment in each case. It will not always be a situation in which one spirit is operating exclusively, but even if there is a mixture of several spirits, one or another will always predominate.

SIGNS OF THE VARIOUS SPIRITS

The following characteristics are general signs of the various spirits. When we treat of the mystical phenomena in particular we shall have occasion to speak of some of these characteristics in greater detail.

Signs of the divine spirit

1) *Truth*. God is truth and cannot inspire anything but truth in a soul. If a person believed to be inspired by God, therefore, maintains opinions which are manifestly against revealed truth, the infallible teaching of the Church, or proven theology or philosophy or science, it must be concluded that the individual is deluded by the devil or is the victim of his own imagination or faulty reasoning.

2) *Gravity*. God is never the cause of things that are useless, futile, frivolous or impertinent. When his spirit moves a soul it is always for something serious and beneficial.

3) *Enlightenment*. Although one may not always understand the meaning of an inspiration from God, the effect of any divine movement or impulse is always enlightenment and certitude rather than darkness and confusion. This is true both as regards the effects on the individual who receives the inspiration and its effects on others.

4) *Docility*. Souls that are moved by the spirit of God, recognizing their own ignorance and weakness with all humility, accept cheerfully the advice and counsel of their directors or others who have authority over them. This spirit of obedience, docility and submission is one of the clearest signs that a particular inspiration or movement is from God. This is especially true in the case of the educated, who have a greater tendency to be attached to their own opinions.

5) *Discretion*. The spirit of God makes the soul discreet, judicious, prudent and thoughtful in all its actions. There is nothing of precipitation, lightness, exaggeration or impetuosity; all is well balanced, edifying, serious and full of calmness and peace.

6) *Humility*. This is one of the most certain signs of the spirit of God. The Holy Spirit always fills the soul with sentiments of humility and self-effacement. The more lofty the communications from on high, the more profoundly the soul inclines to the abyss of its own nothingness. "Behold the handmaid of the Lord; be it done to me according to thy word" (Lk. 1:38).

---

[5]Cf. St. Ignatius Loyola, *Spiritual Exercises,* II, 5 and 8.

7) *Peace.* St. Paul speaks frequently of the peace that comes from God (Rom. 15:33; Phil. 4:9), and Jesus mentions peace as one of the manifestations of his spirit (Jn. 14:27). This is a quality which always accompanies communications from God, and when they are received, especially in prayer, the soul experiences a profound and stable serenity in the depths of its spirit.

8) *Confidence in God.* This is a counterpart and necessary consequence of true humility. Recognizing that of itself it can do nothing, as St. Paul says, the soul throws itself on the power and mercy of God with a childlike trust. Then it learns that it can do all things in him (Phil. 4:13).

9) *Flexibility of will.* This sign consists primarily in a certain promptness of the will to subject itself to the inspirations and invitations of God. Secondarily it consists in a facility in following the advice and counsel of others, especially if they are superiors, confessors or spiritual directors. It is opposed to the rigid and unyielding will which is characteristic of those who are filled with self-love.

10) *Purity of intention.* The soul seeks only the glory of God in all that it does and the perfect fulfillment of the will of God, without human interest or motivation out of self-love.

11) *Patience in suffering.* Suffering is frequently the best touchstone for revealing the true worth of an individual. No matter what the source of the suffering or whether it is justly received or not, the soul bears it with patience and equanimity and uses it as a means of further perfection. But this sign is not to be confused with the stoicism and insensivity of those who are cold and phlegmatic by nature.

12) *Self-abnegation.* The words of Christ himself are sufficient evidence that this is a sign of the spirit of God: "If anyone will come after me, let him take up his cross and follow me" (Matt. 16:24).

13) *Simplicity.* Together with veracity and sincerity, this characteristic is never lacking in those who are truly motivated by the spirit of God. Any duplicity, arrogance, hypocrisy or vanity must be attributed rather to the spirit of the devil, the father of lies.

14) *Liberty of spirit.* First of all, there is no attachment to any created thing and not even to the gifts received from God. Secondly, all is accepted from the hands of God with gratitude and humility, whether it be a question of consolation or trial. Thirdly, while all duties and spiritual exercises are performed with promptness and punctuality, the soul is ready to leave even the most consoling and profitable exercise as soon as the charity of God calls it elsewhere. Liberty of spirit enables the soul to live in a state of constant joy and eagerness for the things of God.

15) *Desire to imitate Christ.* St. Paul says that it is impossible to have the spirit of God without having the spirit of Christ (Rom. 8:9). For that reason

St. John of the Cross states that the soul which aspires to perfection must have a desire to imitate Christ in all things by conforming its life as much as possible to his.[6]

16) *Disinterested love.* We mean by this kind of love all the characteristics which St. Paul attributes to true charity (I Cor. 13:4-7). St. Augustine said of this type of love: "Love with the love of charity and do what you will; you will not sin. . . . Whatever proceeds from interior charity cannot but be good."[7]

Signs of the diabolical spirit

The devil may disguise himself as an angel of light and inspire actions which at the beginning are good, in order thus to conceal his true motives and goals. For that reason the director of souls must proceed with great caution, remembering that what is begun as good may become evil if deviations are not corrected. Even the most amazing mystical phenomena are no proof of themselves that the spirit of God is at work in the soul; it is necessary to judge from the fruits that are produced rather than from the phenomenon in question.

Since the signs of the spirit of the devil will be directly opposed to the signs of the spirit of God, we shall merely enumerate these manifestations so that the director will have at hand a ready reference.

1) *Spirit of falsity.* Sometimes lies are covered and concealed by truths so that they will more readily be accepted.

2) *Morbid curiosity,* love of novelty and attachment to useless details which kill true devotion and solid piety.

3) *Confusion,* anxiety and darkness of spirit.

4) *Obstinacy.* Stubbornness is one of the surest signs of a diabolical spirit.

5) *Constant indiscretion.* Whatever goes against the duties of one's state of life, even if it be a question of exercises of piety, is a result of self-will or the spirit of the devil. The same is true of those persons who habitually go to extremes, for example, in matters of penance or activity.

6) *Spirit of pride and vanity.*

7) *Restlessness and unnecessary anxiety.*

8) *False humility.* Usually this is merely a disguise for self-love and pride.

9) *Despair,* lack of confidence and discouragement.

10) *Presumption,* vain security and unfounded optimism.

11) *Disobedience* and hardness of heart.

12) *Selfish motives,* such as self-complacency, vanity, desire to be esteemed.

13) *Impatience* in suffering and stubborn resentment.

14) *Rebellion of the passions* or violent inclinations to evil.

15) *Hypocrisy,* duplicity and simulation.

16) *Attachment to created things* or sensible consolations.

17) *Neglect of the imitation of Christ.*

---

[6]Cf. *The Ascent of Mount Carmel,* Bk. I, Chap. 13.

[7]St. Augustine, *In Epist. I S. Joannis,* tr. 7.

18) *Feigned charity,* fanatical zeal and scrupulous observance of the law. Many of the extreme reformers and defenders of the letter of the law fall under this category.

Once the spiritual director is assured that a person is under the influence of a diabolical spirit, he should concentrate his efforts on the following: 1) make the individual realize that he is a toy of the devil and that he must take arms against the enemy; 2) encourage the individual to pray earnestly to God for the grace to overcome the assaults of the devil; 3) advise the person to act quickly and with true disdain of the devil as soon as his influence is exercised, trying to perform the contrary acts to that which is suggested or felt.

Signs of the human spirit

These have been clearly enumerated by Thomas à Kempis in *The Imitation of Christ,* Bk. III, Chap. 54. His words should be pondered carefully, for he explains in a masterly fashion the struggle between grace and the human spirit, wounded by sin and inclined to its own interests and comforts.[8]

The human spirit is always inclined to its own satisfactions; it is a friend of pleasure and an enemy of suffering of any kind. It readily inclines to anything that is compatible with its own temperament, its personal tastes and caprices, or the satisfaction of self-love. It will not hear of humiliations, penance, renunciation or mortification. If any director or confessor goes against its own inclinations, he is immediately branded as inept and incompetent. It seeks success, honors, applause and pastimes. It is always a great promotor of anything that will arouse admiration or notoriety. In a word, the human spirit neither understands nor cares for anything except its own egoism.

Judgment

It is sometimes difficult in practice to judge whether given manifestations proceed from the devil or from a purely human and egoistic spirit, but it is always relatively easy to distinguish between these two and the spirit of God. It will be possible in most cases, therefore, to determine that a given spirit could not possibly be from God and that it must be combatted, even if one is not sure whether it is in fact from the devil or the human ego.

The following contrasts may serve as general rules for distinguishing between the diabolical and the human spirit. Natural impulses and inclinations are spontaneous; they can usually be traced back to some natural cause or disposition; the stimulation of the senses acts upon the interior powers, and they often persist in spite of prayer.[9] Diabolical impulse or suggestion, on the other hand, is usually violent and difficult to prevent; it arises unexpectedly or with the slightest provocation; a mental suggestion excites the senses and disappears as a rule with prayer. Self-denial and rectitude of intention are excellent remedies against the spirit of egoism.

---

[8]Cf. also F. W. Faber, *Growth in Holiness* (Baltimore: Murphy).

[9]For example, temptations against purity are not always dispelled by prayer.

DOUBTFUL SPIRITS

Father Scaramelli dedicates an interesting chapter to what he calls the effects of doubtful or uncertain spirits, meaning that these effects are not to be taken as conclusive manifestations of a particular spirit but that they may be the result of any one of the three.[10] In this respect the spiritual director and confessor will do well to keep in mind the admonition of Pope Benedict XIV when writing on the beatification and canonization of the servants of God: if there is a possible natural or diabolical explanation for a given phenomenon, it cannot be presumed that it is supernatural in origin.

The following are the principal *doubtful* cases listed by Father Scaramelli:

1) To aspire to some other state in life after having made a prudent and deliberate selection.

2) To be attracted to rare phenomena or to singular exercises which are not proper to one's state in life. When God desires such things he will give unmistakable proof of his will; the test is obedience and humility.

3) To seek the extraordinary in the practice of virtues, such as the "holy foolishness" of some of the saints who so acted under an impulse from the Holy Ghost.

4) An inclination to practice extreme corporal penances. God has demanded them of some souls, but this practice is not in the workings of ordinary providence.

5) A taste for sensible consolations in the practice of prayer or the exercise of the virtues. The desire for continual spiritual consolations is even more doubtful, since the spirit of God breathes where and when he wills.

6) The "gift of tears" or the strong inclination to concentrate on the sorrowful and penitential aspects of religion.

7) The exclusive devotion to some particular mystery or pious exercise, which easily leads to a distortion of orthodox theology.

8) Great extraordinary favors such as revelations, visions, stigmata, when they occur in a person of little sanctity. Although the extraordinary phenomena and *gratiae gratis datae* do not necessarily presuppose sanctity or even the state of grace, God does not ordinarily grant these gifts except to his servants and friends.

CONCLUSION

By way of conclusion, we again warn directors and confessors to proceed with great caution in making judgments in those matters involving the discernment of spirits. It is extremely easy to err. In cases of extraordinary phenomena, it should be noted that, as a rule, when these things proceed from God, the soul first experiences great fear and humility and then peace and consolation. If they come from the devil they usually begin with feelings of sensible consolation and satisfaction, but later they cause confusion, anxiety and restlessness.

[10] Cf. *op. cit.*, Chap. 10.

Lastly, in regard to the rather frequent inclination which some persons experience to change their state of life (and usually to go to a higher and stricter form of life), the director will bear in mind that it is quite possible that such a desire actually proceeds from God but without God's wanting the person actually to change his state in life. For example, a priest who is actively engaged in the apostolate may experience a strong desire to spend more time in prayer and solitude. In trying to understand the reason for this strong inclination, he may erroneously judge that it is God's will that he enter the Carthusians or the Trappists. Such is not necessarily the case, however, for it may well be that the only thing that God is asking of the priest is that he be less involved in the whirlpool of activity and that he dedicate more time each day to prayer and recollection.[11] As a final word on this common problem, we would state the following as a general rule for the solution of such cases. If the individual has prayerfully and seriously selected the state of life in which he is, he must present a serious positive cause for changing his state of life; otherwise, the will of God for him is the state of life in which he is. Another practical test is to see whether the individual is performing the duties of his present state in life with all fidelity; if not, he should not even think of changing to another state.

[11]Cf. Francis Trochu, *The Insight of the Curé d'Ars* (London: Burns, Oates and Washbourne, 1934), Chap. 15.

2: CAUSES OF MYSTICAL PHENOMENA

It is a basic principle in philosophy and science that we do not possess truly scientific knowledge of any fact or phenomenon unless we know the causes. Unless we go beyond the field of particulars we cannot have scientific knowledge. Now the extraordinary mystical phenomena can be attributed to one of three causes: natural, supernatural or preternatural. There is no other possible origin for any extraordinary phenomenon because these three causes embrace all the possible explanations. If the given phenomenon proceeds from God, it is supernatural in origin; if it proceeds from the devil, it is produced by a preternatural cause; if it is the result of a psychosomatic condition in the patient or some external physical power, it is classified under a natural cause.

FUNDAMENTAL CONCEPTS

It is necessary, therefore, to investigate these three types of causality before we treat of the extraordinary mystical phenomena in particular. First, however, it will be helpful to clarify the three notions: natural, supernatural and preternatural.

1) *Natural.* The word "nature" may be used in various senses: 1) to designate the essence of a concrete or particular thing (individual sense); 2) to signify all things in the visible created universe (collective sense); 3) to specify the essence of a thing as the radical principle of all its actions and passions (dynamic sense). As we use the word, it may have any one of the foregoing meanings, but especially the second and third. Accordingly, natural causes will include the following elements: that which constitutes the essence of a visible created thing; the powers or energies which naturally emanate from the essence of the concrete thing, including occult natural powers; whatever the created essence can produce by its own powers; the various effects which one natural agent can produce on another; whatever a concrete created individual thing requires for the full development of its perfection in the natural order.

2) *Supernatural.* In general, the supernatural signifies that which transcends the natural in any of the accepted meanings of nature and natural. Thus

the supernatural transcends the essence of the individual created being, all the laws of nature taken collectively, and the particular powers of an individual being as well. The supernatural can never be an exigency of the natural, but it can perfect the natural and complement it if gratuitously granted by God. In other words, the supernatural does not contradict or destroy the natural, but the natural has what the philosophers call an obediential potency or non-repugnance as regards the supernatural.

The supernatural is exactly what its name indicates: *above* the natural; it should never be understood as *contra naturam.* Hence the supernatural is never a matter of violence, since God works in creatures according to the natures which he implanted in them or according to that ontological necessity of creatures to obey their creator.[1] Neither should the supernatural be confused with the free, the artificial or the fortuitous. While it is true that the latter differ from the natural in the sense that they are not necessitated to one thing, they are nevertheless contained within the order of natural causality and, therefore, are essentially distinct from the supernatural.

Division of supernatural

The basic division of the supernatural is that of *absolutely* supernatural and *relatively* supernatural, and the former is again divided into the *substantially* supernatural and the *modally* supernatural. The absolutely supernatural (*simpliciter*) signifies that which surpasses the power of any creature that does or could exist. The relatively supernatural (*secundum quid*) is that which exceeds the powers of a particular creature but not of all creation. Thus what surpasses human power could well be connatural to an angel, and yet it would be supernatural in relation to the human being. This sense of the supernatural also includes the preternatural, as we shall see.

The division of the supernatural into substantial (*quoad substantiam*) and modal (*quoad modum*) was established by the theologians to explain the distinction between the supernaturality of miracles and the supernaturality of mysteries. Supernatural *quoad substantiam* does not refer to a supernatural substance only; it may apply to that which is substantial and uncreated, such as the Trinity, or to that which is accidental and created, such as grace; rather, it refers to that which is *essentially* supernatural, in the sense that it exceeds the causality and the essence of every being that is or could be created. It refers either to the divine nature in itself or to a participation in the divine nature precisely as divine.

The supernatural *quoad modum,* on the other hand, is essentially and entitatively natural, but it has been produced in a supernatural manner or is directed to the supernatural end in a supernatural way. An example of the first would be the gift of prophecy; an example of the second would be a natural act ordained by charity to a supernatural end.

---

[1]Cf. St. Thomas, III *Contra Gentiles,* Cap. 100.

Following John of St. Thomas we offer the following schema of the absolutely supernatural:[2]

- Supernatural *quoad substantiam* (by reason of formal cause)
  - uncreated (God and the person of Christ)
  - created (*lumen gloriae,* habitual and actual grace, infused virtues and gifts of the Holy Ghost)
- Supernatural *quoad modum* (by reason of extrinsic causes)
  - by reason of the end: a natural act ordained to a supernatural end
  - by reason of the efficient cause
    - miracle *quoad substantiam*
    - miracle *quoad subjectum*
    - miracle *quoad modum*

3) *Preternatural.* Theologians generally refer to the preternatural as the supernatural *secundum quid* or the relatively supernatural. It is outside the visible natural order, but it does not transcend the natural order absolutely or *simpliciter.* To put it another way, it transcends the powers of a given creature but not the powers of all creation, as does the absolutely supernatural.

Consequently, there is a great difference between the truly supernatural and the preternatural, and it would be better for reasons of clarity not to use the expression "relatively supernatural" when speaking, for example, of diabolical influence. Moreover, one must be careful not to confuse the preternatural with the supernatural *quoad modum,* for although they are both entitatively natural, the mode or manner in which an effect is produced in the case of the supernatural *quoad modum* is something which surpasses the powers of all creatures that do or could exist. For this reason the supernatural *quoad modum* is placed as a division of the absolutely supernatural. Hence the supernatural *quoad modum* is always a true miracle, whereas the preternatural phenomenon, although it may surpass the powers of a human being, is nevertheless within the power of an angel or a devil. It does not surpass the entire order of creation. On the other hand, we do not refer to telepathy, extrasensory perception or the phenomena of spiritualism as preternatural but as paranormal, since these phenomena lie even within the visible natural order.

[2] *De gratia,* Disp. XX, a. 1, sol. arg. 4; cf. also R. Garrigou-Lagrange, O.P., *De revelatione* (Paris: Lethielleux, 1926), p. 95.

SUMMARY

It should be evident that the foregoing distinctions are of great importance when attempting to diagnose the cause of a given extraordinary phenomenon. Many unusual events may seem at first glance to be truly mystical and supernatural phenomena because they obviously surpass the powers of human beings, but on closer examination they prove to be the result of diabolical powers and are not, therefore, truly supernatural at all. We shall use the term preternatural to refer to diabolical interventions in the visible universe, and we shall restrict the word natural to designate only those phenomena which proceed from the ordinary laws of the universe in the visible order.

GOD AS THE CAUSE OF MYSTICAL PHENOMENA

The only true cause of authentic mystical phenomena, whether ordinary and concomitant or extraordinary and gratuitous, is God himself as author of the supernatural order. Since the mystical state is essentially constituted by the operation of the gifts of the Holy Spirit and since God is the primary mover in the operation of the gifts, it follows that all truly mystical phenomena must be attributed to God. But the identification of such extraordinary mystical phenomena becomes exceedingly difficult when we consider that the human organism may present identically the same external manifestations as a result of natural or diabolical causes. The reason for this, as we have already stated, is that the psychosomatic structure can react in only a set number of ways, and for that reason the phenomena themselves are not always sure indications of their origin. The most general principle that can be used is that any phenomenon which does not violate any moral law or involve a contradiction could possibly have God as its cause. It frequently happens, therefore, that the most that can be concluded as regards a given phenomenon is the mere possibility of a truly supernatural cause, and if one arrives only at a possibility, one cannot conclude with certainty that the phenomenon is to be attributed to God.

GRATUITOUS GRACES

The majority of the authentic extraordinary mystical phenomena can be classified under the *gratiae gratis datae*. We say the majority and not all, because, as we shall see when we treat of the phenomena in particular, some of them seem to be the result of the sublime degree of spirituality in a soul at a given time and others appear to be extraordinary effects of the working of the gifts of the Holy Spirit which appeared in some but not in all mystics. In this matter one must always be wary of restricting God's power. The Spirit breathes where he will.

MYSTICAL PHENOMENA

Their nature

In his first letter to the Corinthians (12:4-6), St. Paul states that there are diverse gifts of God but that God is one in himself. All that we have received in both the natural and the supernatural order we have received from God, so that we could speak of all these things as *gratiae gratis datae.*[3] But theologians reserve the term *gratiae gratis datae* for a special type of graces called charisms. Unlike the *gratia gratum faciens* (habitual grace) a *gratia gratis data* has as its immediate purpose, not the sanctification of the one who receives it, but the spiritual benefit of others. It is called *gratis data* not only because it is above the natural power of man but because it is something outside the realm of personal merit.[4] With this distinction in mind, we may list the following conclusions regarding the *gratiae gratis datae*:

1. The *gratiae gratis datae* do not form part of the supernatural organism of the Christian life as do sanctifying grace and the infused virtues and gifts of the Holy Ghost, nor can they be classified under actual grace.
2. They are what we may call "epiphenomena" of the life of grace and may even be granted to one who lacks sanctifying grace.
3. They are not and cannot be the object of merit, whether condign or congruous, but are strictly gratuitous (*gratis datae*).
4. They are not habits, as are sanctifying grace and the infused virtues and the gifts, but they are received in the soul by way of a transitory movement.
5. They are not intrinsically supernatural (*quoad substantiam*) but only extrinsically (*quoad modum*), inasmuch as their efficient cause and purpose are supernatural. In themselves, however, they are formally natural.
6. Since they do not form part of the supernatural organism, they are not contained in the virtualities of sanctifying grace, and hence the normal development of the life of grace could never produce or demand them.
7. The *gratiae gratis datae* require in each instance the direct and extraordinary intervention of God in a miraculous way.

DIRECTIVE NORMS

From these conclusions concerning the nature of the *gratiae gratis datae* we can formulate the following norms which will serve as a guide for the spiritual director:

1) It would be temerarious in the normal course of events to desire or to ask God for *gratiae gratis datae.* They are not necessary for salvation nor for sanctification, and they require a miraculous intervention of God. Far more precious is an act of love than to raise the dead to life.

2) In the event that God does grant a *gratia gratis data,* it is not required that a person be in the state of grace; much less can the gratuitous grace be taken as a sign that the individual is a saint.

---

[3]Cf. St. Thomas, *Summa,* I-II, q. 111, a. 4.

[4]Cf. *ibid.,* a. 1.

3) The *gratiae gratis datae* do not sanctify the one who receives them, and if one in mortal sin were to receive one of these graces, he could possibly remain in his sinful state even after the gratuitous gift or charism had been received.

4) These graces are not given primarily for the benefit of the individual who receives them but for the good of others and for the edification of the Church.

5) Since the *gratiae gratis datae* are something independent of sanctity, it is not necessary that all the saints should have received them. St. Augustine gives the reason for this when he says that they were not given to all the saints lest weak souls should be deceived into thinking that such extraordinary gifts were more important than the good works which are meritorious of eternal life.[5]

Secondary effects

But one should not exaggerate this doctrine. It is true that sanctifying grace is of itself ordained to the sanctification of the person who receives it and that the gratuitous graces or charisms are ordained primarily to the good of others. Nevertheless, from the theological point of view any grace from God is ordained ultimately to eternal salvation, either intrinsically or by a special disposition of God. God works in such a way that some things are effected through secondary causes, as generally happens with the *gratiae gratis datae*. But it may happen that some of the effects of sanctifying grace redound to the benefit of one's neighbor and some of the effects of the charisms are profitable to the individual who receives the special graces. Hence the *gratiae gratis datae* may secondarily or by redundance be beneficial to the one who receives them; it depends upon the spirit with which such gifts are accepted.[6]

We have said that the *gratiae gratis datae* do not necessarily require the state of sanctifying grace in the person who receives them but that God could grant them even to a person in the state of mortal sin. This is true, although it is very rare that this would happen, as Suárez points out.[7] Some authors, such as López Ezquerra,[8] have maintained that there are two types of *gratiae gratis datae*: those which are primarily for the benefit of others (discretion of spirits, gift of tongues, curing the sick, etc.) and those which are especially directed to the benefit of the one who receives them, although they are not necessary for sanctification nor do they fall within the normal development of the spiritual life (visions, revelations, locutions, etc.). The more certain conclusion in this matter would seem to be that some of the *gratiae gratis datae* are definitely a source of benefit to the one who receives them and that these graces are normally found only in persons of superior virtue.

---

[5]Cf. St. Augustine, *De divers. quaest.* 83, q. 79.
[6]Cf. Suárez, *De gratia,* prol., cap. 4, n. 7.
[7]Cf. *ibid.,* n. 11.
[8]Cf. *Lucerna mystica,* tr. 4, c. 1, n. 6.

KINDS OF GRACES

Having discussed the nature of the *gratiae gratis datae,* we now come to the enumeration of these graces. Most of the ancient theologians accepted the names and classification of the *gratiae gratis datae* as they were given by St. Paul (I Cor. 7-11), but modern theologians and exegetes generally maintain that St. Paul did not intend to give a complete and rigorous enumeration of them all and was referring especially to the charisms which God bestows on those who are engaged in the apostolate and ministry of the Church. There are other charisms which are not enumerated by St. Paul and pertain to the extraordinary mystical phenomena, as we shall see later. There is no necessary contradiction between the modern and the ancient theologians, however, for the ancients merely set out to explain the classification of St. Paul, without explicitly stating that the enumeration was complete.[9]

We shall describe each of the charisms mentioned by St. Paul, but we remind the reader that this is by no means a complete and exhaustive enumeration of the *gratiae gratis datae.*

Gifts conferring divine knowledge

1) *Faith.* It should be evident that as a charism faith is distinct from the theological virtue of the same name, but theologians do not agree on the exact signification of this gift. According to St. John Chrysostom, Cajetan, Salmerón and Vázquez, it refers to the faith that works miracles, as referred to by Christ (Matt. 17:19) and St. Paul (I Cor. 13:2). Others define it as an intrepid heroism for confessing, preaching and defending the truths of faith and the constancy to hold to the faith in times of persecution. Still others maintain that it signifies a gift whereby one is able to expound the mysteries of faith with great exactitude and clarity. St. Thomas teaches that it is a profound certitude regarding the truths of faith which enables an individual to expound and persuade others concerning these truths.[10] If understood in this sense, the charism of faith is a miraculous illumination of the mind, seconded by the ability to convince others. But since this could be effected by one of the gifts of the Holy Ghost, it is necessary to find the precise differentiation between the charism of faith, the supernatural virtue of faith and the gift of understanding. Suárez points out that, whereas the theological virtue of faith is a permanent habit, the charism of faith is a transitory movement of the Holy Spirit from which results the gift of eloquence.[11] We would further add that the activity of the infused virtues and the gifts of the Holy Spirit tend primarily (though not necessarily exclusively) to the perfection of the individual who acts through them, whereas the charism of faith is primarily for

[9]Cf. St. Thomas, *Summa,* I-II, q. 111, a. 4, where he groups all the gifts named by St. Paul around the instruction of the faithful in divine things.

[10]*Ibid.,* ad 2.

[11]Cf. M. J. Ribet, *La mystique divine distinguée des contrefaçons diaboliques et des analogies humaines,* III, 5, n. 6.

the instruction and conversion of others. It will often be difficult in practice to distinguish between the activity of a charism and the activity of the gifts of understanding and wisdom.

2) *Utterance of wisdom.* Wisdom is taken here to signify the *scientia sapida* of divine things, and in this respect it is similar to the gift of the Holy Ghost. It differs from the gift, however, in the fact that, whereas the gift imparts this savory knowledge to the individual, the charism enables the individual to impart something of this savor to others and thus persuade and move and inspire them.[12] This charism is characteristic of the apostles, such as St. Paul, and for that reason some theologians identify this charism with the gift of the apostolate.

3) *Utterance of knowledge.* This is the charism whereby the individual is able to impart to others the truths of faith by means of demonstrations, analogies and examples in order to show their harmony and beauty. Such a one is able to impart an understanding of the truths of God even to the uneducated so that they can grasp and retain them. St. Augustine, however, teaches that this charism pertains to the explanation of those things that deal with morality and good works.[13] The same relation exists between the gift of the Holy Ghost called knowledge and the charism of knowledge as exists between the gift of wisdom and the charism of wisdom: the gift is primarily for the soul that receives it, the charism is directed to the good of others. This charism is commonly characteristic of doctors, a title and office which in the primitive Church were distinct from the ordinary ministry. According to Suárez, one can consider the charisms of wisdom and knowledge as essentially the gifts of the Holy Ghost of the same name, which become charisms when they are extended to the spiritual profit of others.[14]

Gifts confirming one's doctrine

4) *Gift of healing.* This charism includes all those miraculous events which have as their object the health of the body. It is the power of curing the sick by means that are beyond the powers of nature. It is one of the types of the gift of miracles, but it merits special mention because of the importance which men attach to the health and well-being of their bodies. Another distinction offered is that the gift of healing has for its primary purpose the welfare of the individual who is healed, whereas the gift of miracles in general is ordained primarily to the glory of God or the manifestation of his power.[15]

5) *Working of miracles.* As we have already stated, the charism of the working of miracles pertains to miracles of the physical order and includes

[12]Cf. St. Thomas, *Summa,* II-II, q. 177, aa. 1-2.
[13]Cf. *De Trinitate,* Lib. XII, c. 14.
[14]Suárez, *De gratia,* prol. 3, c. 5, n. 8.
[15]Cf. St. Thomas, *ibid.,* q. 178, a. 1, ad 4; Salmanticenses *Arbor praedicament. virtutum,* 17, n. 166.

the gift of healing as a species. Any miraculous event which occurs as proof of doctrine, a manifestation of holiness or for the glory of God would be classified under this title.[16] Some theologians make further classifications under the gift of healing and the working of miracles, to the extent that they posit various charisms for particular kinds of sickness or various types of miracles in general.[17]

6) *Prophecy*. This is one of the most important of all the *gratiae gratis datae*.[18] It is an intellectual miracle which embraces a double aspect: intellectual knowledge and the manifestation of this knowledge. It is not habitual but is received in a transitory manner. Although any type of knowledge could be the subject matter of prophetic revelation, properly speaking we use the term to designate the knowledge of future contingent events—not that the prophet will know *all* future contingencies, but only those which are communicated to him from God.

The prophet's mind can be instructed by God in two ways: by the explicit revelation, or by a mysterious prophetic instinct to which the human mind is subjected without being aware of it. The prophet has absolute certainty about those things which come to him by explicit revelation; but the individual cannot be certain, as regards the things known through the prophetic instinct, whether the knowledge is from God or from his own mind. This second situation makes it possible for errors to be found in material which for other reasons seems to be the result of prophetic illumination, and if the prophecy is truly from God, there could be no error. Moreover, the prophecy concerning future contingencies, since it is above all natural powers, can only be verified as a result of divine illumination, given either directly by God or through the instrumentality of an angel. And since true prophecy is supernatural, no previous disposition is required in the intellect of the one who receives it. Moreover, since prophecy is an intellectual gift, it could be granted to one in the state of mortal sin.

The devil, however, could never be the cause of true prophecy of future contingencies, since these are above his power of knowledge. Yet it could happen that a seer who is under the influence of the devil could *per accidens* foretell the truth about some future contingency. The prophet does not necessarily understand that which he reveals through the power of God, for in many instances he is merely an instrument of revelation used by God.

7) *Discernment of spirits*. This is the gift of distinguishing the various causes or spirits which produce given effects. In the primitive Church this charism often accompanied the gift of prophecy. We have already indicated

---

[16]Cf. M. J. Ribet, *op. cit.*, III, c. 5, n. 8; St. Thomas, *ibid.*, q. 178.

[17]Cf. Beraza, *De gratia Christi*, n. 23.

[18]For a complete treatment, cf. St. Thomas, *ibid.*, qq. 171-74.

the means by which a certain degree of proficiency in discernment can be acquired; we are here treating of that power of discernment which comes from a divine source and is a *gratia gratis data.* The charism is especially evident in the lives of St. Philip Neri, St. Joseph Cupertino, St. John Vianney and St. Rose of Lima. It should be noted, however, that even in the natural order it may happen that certain individuals possess a high degree of discernment, intuition and empathy which make them amazingly accurate in determining whether a given spirit is natural, diabolical or divine.

Gifts for proposing doctrine

8) *Gift of tongues.* This charism admits of a variety of manifestations. Ordinarily it consists in an infused knowledge of previously unknown languages. It may be the ability to speak or to understand a strange language. Sometimes it is manifested in a truly amazing manner, as when a speaker is understood by people of various languages, each in his own language. The most noteworthy example of the gift of tongues is that which took place on the first Pentecost, when the apostles spoke in various languages. It also occurred in the lives of St. Dominic and St. Vincent Ferrer.

9) *Interpretation of tongues.* The gift of tongues was often accompanied by the interpretation of tongues, although they are enumerated by St. Paul as two distinct gifts. In the early Church those who explained to others in their own language the words uttered by those who had the gift of tongues were called interpreters. This gift may also be utilized in the exposition of the writings of St. Paul and others, or in the translation of various writings into other languages.

CONCLUSION

Such are the marvelous charisms as St. Paul understood them, although most likely it was not his intention to give a complete enumeration. When we consider the particular extraordinary mystical phenomena we shall have occasion to see more clearly the importance of the charisms in explaining these phenomena. For the time being, we shall consider the other two causes which are capable of producing apparently mystical phenomena: nature and the devil.

PURELY NATURAL CAUSES

Nature often causes strange phenomena which are easily confused with extraordinary mystical manifestations, with the result that there is a danger of confusing two orders in themselves utterly distinct. The supernatural begins where the natural ends, and if the dividing line between the two were clearly defined, there would be no problem whatever in identifying the true cause of a given phenomenon. Unfortunately, such is not the case, for although it is certain that nature has its definite limitations and fixed laws, our imperfect knowledge of the power and laws of nature makes it easy for us to attribute to a supernatural cause that which is in reality the result of a natural but as yet unknown cause.

Moreover, it frequently happens that in a given action or phenomenon there may be a blending of natural and supernatural elements in one and the same manifestation. Sometimes, indeed, the theologian or spiritual director must frankly admit that he cannot determine with certainty what is the cause of a particular phenomenon; he must patiently wait to see the effects or fruits that are produced and use that as his criterion for judging whether or not the case is truly mystical in origin.

But while we do not know with certainty all that nature is capable of producing, we can know what nature could never possibly do. In other words, we have as our basic norm the principle of contradiction, which often leaves us with nothing more certain by way of conclusion than mere possibility or evident impossibility. In any event, the following rule must be followed most strictly: *one may not definitely attribute to a supernatural cause that which could possibly have a natural (or diabolical) explanation.* Thus two extremes will be avoided, namely, to see the supernatural or miraculous in every unusual phenomenon or to refuse to recognize anything but the natural or preternatural in any kind of phenomenon.

PRINCIPAL CAUSES

The natural causes may be grouped under the following general headings: *physiological or constitutional factors, imagination, depressive states* and *illness,* especially mental and nervous disorders. We shall discuss briefly the more immediate and direct factors which may produce certain extraordinary phenomena which closely resemble the truly mystical phenomena.

Physiological factors

By way of a prenote, we should recall the teaching of psychology concerning the intimate relationship and mutual interaction between the soul and the body. It is a fact of experience that ideas, judgments, volitions can cause profound transformations in man's somatic structure, for good or evil, and that the health or sickness of the body can in turn facilitate or obstruct the operations of the spiritual faculties. Moreover, the somatic structure, since it is organic, is so necessitated in its functions that it can react in only a limited number of ways. That is the basic reason why it is often so difficult to determine whether a particular unusual phenomenon is supernatural or natural in origin (we might say, natural but paranormal). It is also the reason why the theologian, doctor, psychiatrist or spiritual director must in each instance make a careful and exact examination of the constitutional factors of the individual.

The following physiological elements are of special importance in this examination:

1) *Temperament.* Of the four basic temperaments the melancholic temperament is most prone to illusion in mystical matters. By nature such persons tend to extreme introversion and extravagances of the imagination. It is not difficult to see how their excessive detachment from their surroundings could easily lead to something similar to ecstasy and their vivid imaginations could produce what would appear to be supernatural revelations and visions. St. Teresa of Avila has some practical advice for religious superiors concerning the treatment of melancholy subjects.[19]

The choleric temperament, which is extremely impressionable, may give rise to the same illusions. A sudden and intense stimulation will sometimes cause a kind of hysteria in which the imagination runs riot and the sense of judgment is completely unbalanced. On the other hand, if the individual is already in a state of extreme excitation, the most commonplace event may be exaggerated out of all proportion because the person is already predisposed to see the unusual and extraordinary in his surroundings.

Since the person of sanguine temperament is inclined to sensate pleasure and bodily satisfactions, he will more readily be deceived regarding those mystical phenomena of the affective order. It is not difficult to see how such a person would be prone to imagine that he is experiencing mystical touches, divine caresses or consoling visions and revelations when in a state of religious fervor.

But we must beware of exaggeration in the judgment of such individuals, for although the director will be doubly cautious in dealing with these temperaments, he would be mistaken to conclude that all such persons are victims of illusion and that no person of the above temperaments could ever experience truly mystical phenomena. No temperament is an obstacle to the *gratiae gratis datae;* God gives his gifts as he pleases. Here again we should note the importance of the distinction between concomitant mystical phenomena and extraordinary mystical phenomena, for the concomitant phenomena would usually be expected to follow the constitutional predisposition of the subject, since they are within the normal development of the supernatural organism.

2) *Sexual differences.* Women in general are more easily subject to illusion in mystical matters because their psychological structure predisposes them to a greater interest in religion, the practice of piety and ardent love. Their somatic structure makes them more passive than active and more accessible to movements of sentiment than to movements of reason. They go to God more easily, but at the same time they can be weak, inconstant, highly imaginative and sentimental. For that reason

[19]Cf. *The Book of Foundations,* Chap 7.

it is a general rule of spiritual direction that any kind of mystical phenomena is to be discounted in a woman until there is evident proof that she is solidly grounded in virtue. Above all, the director will be extremely reticent in making a judgment or will be careful not to let the individual know that he believes that she is receiving mystical favors. St. Teresa of Avila has some sound advice on this point.[20]

On the other hand, it must be admitted that in the history of spirituality the women have far outnumbered the men in the reception of extraordinary mystical phenomena, and we would have to admit that the weaker sex is also the more devout sex, because women generally are vastly superior to men in their abnegation and generosity in the service of God.[21]

3) *Age*. The human organism also manifests certain weaknesses and predispositions by reason of age. The periods of greatest weakness are those of infancy and old age. Through the childhood phase the individual is easily impressed by external stimuli and reacts strongly to anything that has an emotional overtone. There is also a vivacity of imagination which gradually declines as the use of reason becomes more predominant. In old age the body and its faculties again return to a period of weakness; the intellect is not so easily controlled by the will, the imagination again becomes active, the affective movements are for the most part centered around the ego. While no age is completely exempt from illusions in mystical matters, those who are young and impressionable offer the greatest possibility of exaggeration and misjudgment. This is true also of beginners or novices in the practice of prayer, the religious life and the exercises of virtue and piety. But no age is excluded from mystical communications; Scripture itself gives us examples of the young and the old who were favored with divine manifestations of one sort or another: Joseph, Jacob, Samuel, Daniel, St. John, the beloved disciple.[22]

The imagination

The imagination is one of man's most beneficial faculties, and it can also be one of the most harmful. It has the power of evoking past phantasms, of creating new images, of exerting a tremendous influence on the intellect and the will. Although it is an organic faculty localized in the brain, it is also the point of contact with the operation of man's spiritual powers. It is a mysterious link between the two worlds of the material and the spiritual. Localized as it is in the cerebrum, the healthy condition of that organism will have a direct bearing on the perfection of the activity of the imagination. If it escapes from

---

[20]Cf. *ibid.*, Chap. 8.

[21]Cf. J. G. Arintero, O.P., *The Mystical Evolution in the Development and Vitality of the Church* (St. Louis: Herder, 1949), II, pp. 298-303.

[22]Cf. Gen. 37:7, 49:1; I Kings 3; Dan. 1; Apoc. 1:9-11.

the control of the will it can be as capricious as the pages of a book which are left to the mercy of the wind.

It is evident that the imagination is often the source of many illusions in the spiritual life. Not that the imagination as such is in error, for in performing its function of recalling or creating phantasms it does not of itself have the power to say whether the particular phantasms truly exist in the order of reality or are purely fictitious and artificial. The error comes from the judgment of the individual who takes as true that which is merely a phantasy.

In order that spiritual directors may have a handy guide for discernment, they would do well to bear in mind the following principles:

1) The imagination does not create images in the proper sense of the word. It has three functions: a) to receive the sensations from the *sensus communis* (unifying sense) and to retain them when the sensible object is absent; b) to recall and reproduce phantasms already acquired; c) to unite them in themselves and with the sensations of the external senses and the *sensus communis* so that the simple sensation is converted into a perception. Hence the creative imagination, as it is called, merely combines partial or complete phantasms into a new pattern, but there is nothing in the imagination which was not previously received through the external senses and *sensus communis.*

The imagination is, therefore, limited to the recall or arrangement of phantasms already received, and it can contain nothing that was not received from the exterior world of reality. Thus if we encounter a person who spontaneously speaks or reads or writes a language with which he has never had any contact whatever, it must be concluded that this feat could not possibly be the result of his imagination. We are in the presence of a phenomenon which surpasses the natural powers of the imagination; the cause, therefore, must be either supernatural or preternatural.

2) The imagination cannot surpass the laws of nature. Instantaneous cures of organic lesions, fractures and mutilations cannot in any way be attributed to the imagination. If the cure cannot possibly be explained by the laws of nature, there must be a superior cause at work.[23]

Depressive states

The generic title, depressive states, covers a number of natural causes which may lead to illusion in the spiritual life. Sadness is one of the greatest enemies of the human spirit, both in the natural and the supernatural orders.

[23]The theologian, physician and psychiatrist will be extremely cautious in making judgments on sudden cures from mental illness, nervous disorders and transferred or sympathetic pains. It should be evident that, if certain illnesses may be induced by the imagination, they may be cured by that same faculty. For example, the sudden cure from paralysis of the entire body or of some organ of the body is frequently purely natural in its cause and may not be classified as miraculous, even if it occurs at some famous shrine where true miracles have occurred.

Its natural consequence is that it makes the individual excessively introspective, self-centered and anxious about himself. This may easily lead, in turn, to all sorts of illusions, whether regarding mystical phenomena or one's associations with others. Since we are concerned only with mystical phenomena, we shall enumerate the three chief causes of depressive states of spirit in this connection:

1) *Excessive intellectual labor* sometimes causes such a detachment from exterior things that a kind of alienation of spirit results. The remarkable detachment and absorption of scientists, artists and professors is the result of their intense concentration on the matter at hand. If the suspension of the external powers or the alienation from one's surroundings can be explained naturally, therefore, it may never be identified as a case of mystical alienation or rapture. We shall have occasion to point out the particular differences between mystical and supernatural alienation of the faculties and that which is from natural causes when we treat of the extraordinary mystical phenomena in particular.

2) *Badly regulated mental prayer* may also produce certain effects which are similar to those experienced by the great contemplative mystics. If the mental prayer is intense and prolonged, the truths of meditation may become so vivid that one takes them for realities of the sensible order, celestial visions, diabolical manifestations, etc. Likewise, intense and exclusive meditation on the Passion could cause the external signs of the stigmata or sympathetic pains. St. Teresa warns that women are more often subject to illusions of this type and that sometimes it may be necessary for the spiritual director to forbid the individual to practice mental prayer for a time.[24]

3) *Excessive austerities,* which lead to exhaustion of the body and a weakening of the sensitive faculties, may produce all kinds of illusions that are mistakenly attributed to a supernatural cause. Long periods of fasting or corporal penances carried to extremes will so sharpen the activity of the imagination and the memory that the individual readily reaches a point at which the world of dreams and illusions is taken for reality. It should be noted that moderate fasting is a boon to the functioning of the imagination and memory and the activity of the intellect, but once the body and its organic powers have been weakened, the sense faculties of cognition escape from the control of reason and cast the individual into the world of dream images. St. Teresa of Avila has some practical advice for spiritual directors on this point.[25]

Illness

Illnesses of certain kinds are also predispositions to illusion in mystical matters, and it is often an area of much dispute between doctors and theologians

---

[24]Cf. *The Book of Foundations,* Chap. 7.

[25]Cf. *ibid.* Chap. 6.

when what has been taken as a truly mystical phenomenon is declared to be the consequence of some bodily or mental illness. Here above all it is necessary that both doctors and theologians remember that, whereas the external manifestations of nervous and mental illnesses and those of true mystical states may be identical, the causes are utterly distinct, although sometime there may be a strange and perplexing admixture of the two orders. Consequently, the most that can be relied upon as a rule of discernment in many cases is to judge by the fruits or effects.

CAUSES OF MYSTICAL PHENOMENA

Admittedly, it is no easy matter to say whether St. Paul, St. Catherine of Siena, St. Simon Stylites, St. Teresa of Avila, St. Peter Alcántara and St. Magdalen of Pazzi at any time in their lives manifested the symptoms of some kind of illness. Neither is it derogatory of the sanctity of an individual to admit that some of the manifestations of neurosis, psychosis or diabolism cannot in themselves be distinguished from extraordinary mystical phenomena. But the similarity of the external manifestations does not suffice as a basis for concluding that the manifestations in question all proceed from the same cause, no more than the external act of virtue authorizes us to conclude that the person in question truly possesses the virtue.

The theologian, physician and psychiatrist, therefore, will do well to proceed with all caution in these matters and to assist each other with information from their respective fields. It is just as unfounded for the theologian to think that his theological knowledge alone will enable him to discern spirits as it is for the physician or psychiatrist to deny the possibility of supernatural influence in human affairs. When we treat of the extraordinary phenomena in particular we shall have the opportunity to offer certain detailed rules whereby one can attain at least a morally certain judgment in many cases.

DIABOLICAL INFLUENCE

THEOLOGICAL DOCTRINE

The study of the preternatural is so vast and complicated that a thorough treatment of the subject would take us far beyond the scope of the present work. We shall content ourselves with an enumeration of the main points of theological doctrine concerning diabolical influence and refer the reader to other works which treat of this subject in greater detail.[26]

1) It is *de fide* that devils exist, that is, a number of angels who were created good by God but became evil through their own sin.[27]

[26]Cf. *Satan,* ed. by Bruno de Jésus-Marie, O.C.D. (New York: Sheed and Ward, 1952).

[27]Cf. Matt. 25:41; II Pet. 2:4; Fourth Lateran Council (Denz. 428).

2) With God's permission the devils can exercise an evil influence over men, even to the extent of invading and tormenting them in a bodily manner.[28]

3) In the midst of the assaults of the devil the human will always remains free, because the will can be moved only in two ways: by the individual himself or by God. The most that any other extrinsic power can do is to persuade, and this is what the devils do.[29]

4) The good angels and devils can intrinsically act upon the imagination and other internal and external senses because these are all organic powers and the devil has power to exercise his influence on anything material.[30]

5) The devils cannot work true miracles, because by definition a miracle surpasses the power of all created nature. But since the angelic powers far surpass human powers, the devils can perform prodigious feats which arouse man's admiration so far as they exceed the power or knowledge of human beings.[31]

DIABOLICAL LIMITATIONS

By reason of some contradiction involved or because they surpass the power of an angelic being, the devils *cannot* do the following:

1) Produce any kind of truly supernatural phenomenon, because the supernatural by definition exceeds all natural created powers.

2) Create a substance, because creation requires an infinite power and no creature of any kind can be used even as an instrument of creation.[32]

3) Raise a dead person to life, although he could produce the illusion of doing so.

4) Instantaneously cure wounds, fractures, lesions, etc., because this is something only the Creator could do.

5) Instantaneously transport a body from one place to another without passing through the intervening space, although the devil can do so himself as a pure spirit and can transport bodies with great rapidity.[33]

6) Make truly prophetic predictions, since the devil does not by his own powers of intelligence know future contingencies, although he knows so many things in their causes that it may appear to human beings that what was predicted was a true prophecy.

7) Know the secrets of a person's mind and heart, since the devil does not by his own power have access to the human intellect and will. Because of

---

[28]Cf. Eph. 6:11-12; I Thess. 3:5; I Pet. 5:8-9.
[29]Cf. St. Thomas, *Summa,* I, q. 111, a. 2.
[30]Cf. *ibid.,* aa. 3-4.
[31]Cf. *ibid.,* q. 114, a. 4.
[32]Cf. *ibid.,* q. 45, a. 5.
[33]Cf. *ibid.,* q. 53, a. 2.

his superior intelligence, however, he can conjecture much more easily, and can know the temperament and character of individuals as well as the numerous circumstances of their life.

8) Produce in human beings extraordinary phenomena of the purely intellectual or volitional type, because he does not have free access to the human intellect and will.[34]

DIABOLICAL FALSIFICATION

The above are the principal things which the devils are unable to do, and they should be kept in mind when evaluating mystical phenomena which involve the miraculous, or the activity of the human intellect and will. The following mystical phenomena, however, can be falsified by the devil.

With God's permission the devil can do any of the following:

1) Produce corporeal or imaginative visions (but not intellectual visions).

2) Falsify ecstasy.

3) Produce rays of light in the body and sensible heat (there have been examples of "diabolical incandescence").

4) Cause sensible consolations and tenderness.

5) Instantaneously cure strange sicknesses which have been caused by diabolical influence, although according to Tertullian these were not authentic sicknesses in the first place and it is not so much a cure as it is that the devil ceases to torment the individual.[35]

6) Produce the stigmata and all other kinds of bodily extraordinary phenomena, and any phenomena dealing with physical objects, such as crowns, rings, etc.

7) Simulate miracles and the phenomena of levitation, bilocation and compenetration of bodies.

8) Cause persons or objects to disappear from sight by placing an obstacle in the line of vision or acting directly on the sense of sight; simulate locutions by means of sound waves or immediate action on the sense of hearing.

9) Produce bodily incombustibility by interposing some medium between the fire and the body of the individual.

To summarize: All the phenomena which result from the activity of any natural power or physical law, even if the human being is unable to produce them, can be produced by diabolical power, with God's permission. Whatever the activity of diabolical powers, however, it will never surpass the natural order. As we have already explained, we speak of the preternatural in relation to a given phenomenon which surpasses human power but can be produced by the devil.

[34]Cf. *ibid.*, q. 111, aa. 1-2.
[35]Cf. Tertullian, *Apolog.*, c. 22.

3: EXTRAORDINARY PHENOMENA

In proceeding to a study of the extraordinary mystical phenomena, it is important that we establish a scientific criterion for the classification and division of these phenomena. We have already explained that the essence of the mystical activity of the soul consists in the operations of the gifts of the Holy Ghost, *per modum actus* for the mystical act and habitually for the mystical state. We have also described the concomitant or ordinary phenomena of the mystical state and have linked them to the various grades of prayer through which certain souls pass in their ascent to the perfection of charity.

Since charity is the essence of the perfection of the Christian life, it should follow that whatever phenomena, concomitant or extraordinary, occur in the mystical life will be directed primarily and finally to the will, which is the faculty in which charity is radicated. Nevertheless, we have demonstrated that, whereas man's active purgation usually begins with the purgation of the external powers and only gradually ascends to the purification of the spiritual faculties of intellect and will, the action of God upon the soul, at least as regards the progress through the various grades of prayer, begins with the spiritual faculties and works down through the inferior powers. We shall, therefore, treat of the extraordinary mystical phenomena in that same order, namely, phenomena of the intellectual order, of the affective order and of the bodily order.

This does not mean, however, that there is a chronological order in which extraordinary mystical phenomena occur in the life of a mystic. God is perfectly free to distribute his gifts as he pleases, and it may be that he gives one phenomenon to this individual, another to the other individual, and none at all to a third. Above all, it should be clearly understood that the very word "extraordinary" signifies that these phenomena are in no way contained within the normal development of the mystical life nor do they of themselves prove that the individual is a mystic, for they could occur in persons who are not even in the state of grace. They are strictly gratuitous phenomena or *gratiae gratis datae*. Nor, we repeat, do all such manifestations proceed from a supernatural cause; many of them could be due to a mental, physical or nervous disorder, or they could be caused by diabolical power. On the other hand, when any of the following phenomena have God as their cause, they are usually found to occur in persons of holy life.[1]

COGNITIVE PHENOMENA

VISIONS

A vision is the supernatural perception of an object which is naturally invisible to man. We say "supernatural" to distinguish true visions from the illusions or hallucinations which proceed from natural causes or the fraudulent visions produced by diabolical power. St. Augustine is the author of the classical division of visions into corporeal, imaginative and intellectual.[2]

Kinds of visions

1) A *corporeal* vision is one in which the bodily eyes perceive an object which is normally invisible to the sense of sight. It is also called an apparition. The object of a corporeal vision need not be a concrete object or a true human body; it suffices that it be perceived by the sense of sight. Thus a corporeal vision of the Blessed Virgin does not necessarily mean that Mary herself has appeared in her own body, but it could be a mere representation of Mary by means of light rays or some vaporous substance.

The apparition may be caused in two ways, according to Vallgornera:[3] 1) by a physical form which impresses its image on the retina of the eye and causes the sensation of vision; 2) by the action of an external agent on the organ of sight, producing a visual image which would be normally effected by any body that is visible to the eye and actually present to the perceiver.

2) The *imaginative* vision is the representation of an image supernaturally produced in the imagination and presented to the intellect with as much clarity as are externally existing objects in the physical order. It can be produced in three ways: 1) by the recall of sense impressions already received through the external sense; 2) by a new arrangement of phantasms already acquired and conserved in the imagination; 3) by entirely new phantasms impressed upon the imagination by a supernatural power. This type of vision often occurs during sleep, and if it occurs during waking hours it is usually accompanied by an alienation of the external senses so that the visionary does not confuse the vision with that which is perceived through the external

[1]For further discussion and details on this matter see Zsalt Aradi, *The Book of Miracles* (New York: Farrar, Strauss, 1956); J. G. Arintero, O.P., *op. cit.*, Vol. II; Reginald Omez, *Psychical Phenomena* (New York: Hawthorn Books, 1958); Herbert Thurston, S.J., *The Physical Phenomena of Mysticism* (London: Burns, Oates, 1952).

[2]Cf. *De Gen. ad lett.*, Lib. II, c. 7, n. 16.

[3]Vallgornera, *Mystica theologia,* q. 3, dist. 5, a. 1.

senses. The vision may be a representation of Christ or some saint, or it may be purely symbolic.

3) The *intellectual* vision is a simple intuitive knowledge supernaturally effected without the aid of any sensible image or impressed species in the internal or external senses. As a rule, the object of the intellectual vision is something that surpasses the natural powers of the intellect, although this is not necessarily the case. The impression may last for hours or days or even months, whereas the lower types of vision are usually of short duration. It produces marvelous effects in the soul, such as great light, peace, a desire for heavenly things, etc. It may occur during sleep, during ecstasy or when a person is awake, but only God can cause it. Sometimes it is so ineffable that the individual is powerless to describe or explain it. One of the outstanding characteristics of the intellectual vision is the certitude which it imparts to the visionary.[4]

Objects of vision

Having considered the various types of supernatural visions, it remains to discuss the objects that may be represented in such visions. We may state as a general principle that the object of a supernatural vision may be anything at all that exists: God, Christ, Mary, the blessed, angels, devils, the souls in purgatory—any living being, or even an inanimate object. According to the teaching of St. Thomas and theologians generally, the apparitions of Christ, Mary and the blessed are not produced by their bodily presence but are merely *representative* visions effected through the instrumentality of angels.[5] The reason given for this is that it is metaphysically impossible for a body to be in two distinct places at the same time circumscriptively; hence it would seem necessary for Christ or Mary or a saint to leave heaven in order to appear on earth in an apparition. Nevertheless, St. Thomas does state that Christ appeared in his own body to St. Paul.[6] If this be so, it does not mean that Christ's physical body was actually present in two places at the same time, for even Christ cannot do that which is metaphysically impossible; rather, it means that Christ did not leave heaven to appear to St. Paul but that wherever Christ is, there is heaven and the beatific vision.[7] The same thing would seem to be true proportionately of Mary and the blessed, namely, that Mary could appear bodily in a vision and the soul of a blessed could be truly present in an apparition, for heaven or the state of glory consists essentially in the face-to-face vision of God, and this does not require that the comprehensor be localized in place. Nevertheless, the majority of theologians maintain that we should normally presume that corporeal apparitions are effected through the instrumentality of angels.

---

[4]Cf. St. Teresa, *The Life,* Chap. 27.
[5]Cf. St. Thomas, *Quodlibet.,* III, a. 2; *IV Sent.,* dist. 44, sol. 3, ad 4.
[6]Cf. *Summa,* III, q. 57, a. 6, ad 3.
[7]Cf. *ibid.,* q. 9, a. 2.

The apparitions which represent the divinity should usually be considered to be, as St. Teresa states, "some kind of representation."[8] They are not to be presumed, therefore, to be intuitive visions of the divine essence, for this is reserved for the state of glory. Nevertheless, St. Thomas admits that Moses and St. Paul received an intuitive vision of the divine essence through the transitory communication of the *lumen gloriae.*[9] There is no contradiction involved here, for the human intellect has an obediential potency to the reception of the *lumen gloriae,* and therefore God could grant it *per modum actus* even to a wayfarer. To those who maintain that the reception of the *lumen gloriae* in this life would result in the death of the individual, we answer that the same God who would communicate this light would also have the power to sustain the body during this experience. But the general norm to be followed is that we should not attribute a phenomenon to a higher order if it can be explained by a lower order. Hence the presumption in visions of the divine essence is that the apparition is by way of representation and not a transitory beatific vision.

There is no great difficulty in explaining the apparitions of angels or demons. These are pure spirits and a spirit is where it acts. Moreover, a spirit has the power, with God's permission, of assuming some material substance with which to represent itself even to the bodily eye, whether that substance be a body or light rays or some kind of cloud or vapor.[10] If the souls of the dead (whether blessed, in purgatory or in hell) were to appear in bodily form, the explanation would be the same as that given for angelic apparitions, since the separated souls are pure spirits and the bodies they once possessed are now reduced to dust.[11] As to the apparition of persons still living on earth or of inanimate objects, we are faced with an apparent bilocation, and therefore we shall treat of the matter under that heading.

Rules of discernment

Supernatural visions belong to the *gratiae gratis datae* and fall under the rules generally given in regard to charisms. They are not a proof of sanctity; they are normally intended primarily for the good of others, although they usually exert a beneficial influence on the one who receives them; they are not to be sought; they are in no way necessary to salvation or sanctification.[12]

As for the discernment or judgment of visions, the intellectual vision is the easiest to detect, although the spiritual director has nothing more for a basis of judgment than the certitude and conviction experienced by the visionary that the vision was from God. Since the intellect cannot be acted

---

[8]Cf. *Interior Castle,* Seventh Mansions, Chap. 1.

[9]*Summa,* II-II, q. 175, a. 3.

[10]Cf. St. Thomas, *ibid.,* I, q. 51, a. 2, ad 3.

[11]Cf. *ibid.,* q. 51, a. 2, ad 2; *Suppl.,* q. 69, a. 3.

[12]Cf. St. John of the Cross, *The Ascent of Mount Carmel,* Bk. II, Chap. 11; St. Teresa of Avila, *The Life,* Chap. 28; *Interior Castle,* Sixth Mansions, Chap. 8.

upon immediately by the devil, an intellectual vision could never be caused by diabolical power. The greatest difficulty lies in the discernment and verification of the imaginative and corporeal visions. Here there is always the possibility of diabolical influence, and sometimes the only criterion is to judge by the fruits or effects which the visions cause in the visionary. At first the visions which come from God cause fear in the soul, and this later gives place to love, humility and peace. The soul's energies are increased, and it gives itself more generously to the practices of virtue. Visions which are diabolical in origin begin with sweetness and peace but soon fill the soul with turbulence, presumption and pride. Visions caused by one's own imagination lead to vanity, curiosity, superficial virtue and contradiction in the descriptive account of the experience.

LOCUTIONS

Although it frequently happens that visions are accompanied by locutions, it is possible for either to occur without the other. A locution is an affirmation or statement supernaturally effected. Like visions, it admits of three types: auricular, imaginative and intellectual.

Kinds of locutions

1) *Auricular* locutions are words perceived by the bodily sense of hearing by reason of supernaturally produced acoustical vibrations. In themselves they may be produced by God, by angels or by demons. They may also be produced by natural causes, whether physical or psychic. They sometimes seem to proceed from a bodily vision, the Blessed Sacrament, a religious image such as a crucifix, or some other article which is used as an instrument.

2) *Imaginative* locutions are words perceived in the imagination and may occur either during sleep or in waking hours. They may proceed from God, the devil or natural causes. The best rule of discernment is the effects produced in the soul. If they are from God, they cause humility, fervor, desire for self-immolation, obedience, desire to perform perfectly one's duties of state. If they proceed from the devil they cause dryness, inquietude, insubordination, etc. The locutions that proceed from the individual himself do not usually produce any noteworthy effects.

3) *Intellectual* locutions are words perceived directly by the intellect, and the activity is similar to that by which angels would communicate ideas to each other. Two elements concur in this type of locution: the pre-existing or infused intelligible species, and the supernatural light which illumines and clarifies them. It is beyond the power of the devil to produce a truly intellectual locution, for he cannot operate on the human intellect directly. St. John of the Cross divides the intellectual locutions into three types: successive, formal and substantial.[13]

---

[13] Cf. *The Ascent of Mount Carmel,* Bk. II, Chaps. 28-31.

1) At first glance the *successive* locutions would seem to be a purely human dialogue because, as St. John of the Cross points out, the individual seems to be formulating the ideas and reasoning things out. But in reality it is the Holy Spirit who aids the soul to produce and form its concepts; thus it is an activity in which both the soul and the Holy Ghost play a part. These locutions are called successive because they are not the result of an instantaneous and intuitive enlightenment; on the contrary, God instructs the soul through successive reasonings. So far as it is an intellectual locution, there cannot be any error in substance or principle; if there is error, it is the result of concepts or reasonings of the human intellect in its own operation. There may be, however, certain illusions or deceptions as a result of the activity of the imagination. It can never be directly caused by the devil because he cannot act immediately on the human intellect.

2) The *formal* locutions are perceived by the intellect as evidently coming from another. The human intellect contributes nothing of itself, and, therefore, they may come upon the soul whether it is recollected or distracted or engaged in some other occupation, unlike the successive locutions which always refer to that which the individual is considering. The soul cannot help but receive these locutions, and it always understands them clearly. If the locutions pertain to future events, they are always fulfilled, although the individual should be cautious and fearful of deception by the devil. It is true that the devil cannot intervene directly on the human intellect, but he may act upon the imagination and thereby attempt to deceive or mislead the soul. St. John of the Cross says that these locutions can hardly be distinguished by their effects.[14]

3) The *substantial* locutions are basically the same as the formal locutions but with this difference: that which is stated in the locution is effected immediately. For example, if God says to the soul, "Be humble," it at once feels the inclination to prostrate itself before his divine majesty; if he says, "Peace be with you," the soul is immediately calm and tranquil. There is no room for error or deception in the substantial locutions because they are similar to the creative word of God, such as "let there be light." The effects so far surpass human and diabolical power that there can be no doubt as to their supernatural origin. The soul at this point needs but leave itself in the hands of God, whose words are works, as St. Teresa says.[15]

Theological nature

Since locutions are so closely associated with visions, we repeat what we said about visions, namely, that those phenomena do not pertain to the normal development of sanctifying grace and charity but are *gratiae gratis datae* in

[14]Cf. *ibid.*, Bk. II, Chap. 30.
[15]Cf. *The Life*, Chap. 25.

the strict sense. Locutions pertain reductively to the charism of prophecy. Nevertheless, it should be noted that locutions, and especially the substantial locutions, bring many blessings and fruits to the soul that receives them. Regardless of the profit to the individual, however, locutions should never be sought, because of the dangers and illusions to which they may expose the soul, with the exception of the substantial locutions, of which St. John of the Cross says: "Blessed is the soul to whom the Lord speaks the substantial locution. Speak, Lord, for thy servant heareth."[16]

REVELATIONS

Revelation is the supernatural manifestation of a hidden truth or divine secret for the general good of the Church or the benefit of some individual. The veil which hides the secret or hidden truth may be removed supernaturally by means of a vision, a locution or a prophetic instinct. All divine revelation presupposes the gift of prophecy, and its interpretation requires the discernment of spirits.

Kinds of revelations

Revelations are divided into public and private, depending upon whether the revelation is for the benefit of all the faithful or one or another individual. Public revelations are the basis and deposit of our faith, and the Church is the guardian and official interpreter of these revelations. It is commonly taught in theology that public revelation closed with the death of the last apostle. All revelations made since that time are classed as private revelations, even if they pertain to matters that are spiritually beneficial to the Church in general. Since public revelation belongs to the study of apologetics and dogmatic theology, we shall restrict ourselves to the consideration of private revelations.

Authors of spiritual theology usually divide private revelations into *absolute*, *conditioned* and *denunciatory* revelations, depending upon whether the revelation is a simple statement of a truth or mystery, a conditioned statement, or a threat of punishment. The denunciatory revelation may also be conditioned, as in the case of the prophecy of Jonas concerning the destruction of Ninive. If revelations refer to the future they are ordinarily called *prophecy*, although prophecy as such abstracts from time and place.

Revelations concerning the future may be *perfect* or *imperfect*, depending upon whether the seer has a full and clear knowledge of that which he transmits or whether he either does not know the meaning, as in the case of a revelation made through symbols, or he does not realize the mission or purpose for which the revelation was given. The last is also called the *prophetic instinct*, as was exemplified in Caiphas when he predicted that Christ would die for all the people.[17] Perfect revelations concerning the future are received

[16]Cf. *The Ascent of Mount Carmel*, Bk. II, Chap. 31.

[17]Jn. 11:49-52; cf. St. Thomas, *Summa*, II-II, q. 171, a. 5.

by means of visions and divine locutions, and ordinarily they are effected through the ministry of angels.[18] Imperfect revelations concerning the future merely presuppose an interior movement or an inspiration which is more or less conscious.

Private revelations

There have always been persons gifted with prophecy, as is testified by Scripture and the processes of canonization of the servants of God. To question the possibility of prophecy and private revelation would be to question the power of God and the holiness of the Church. Nevertheless, private revelations do not pertain to the deposit of faith, which consists of the truths contained in Scripture and Tradition under the vigilance of the Church. Yet if, after a prudent judgment, it is determined that a given revelation is authentic, the one who has received the revelation should accept it in the spirit of faith. It is disputed among the theologians whether this act of faith is an act of divine faith; it seems to us that it is.

Moreover, if a private revelation contains a message for others and it has been accepted as an authentic revelation, those persons also have an obligation to accept the truth of the revelation and act upon it. For all others, however, nothing more is required than a pious belief, even when the Church has given her negative approval to a revelation by stating that there is nothing contained in it that is contrary to faith and morals. The Church in approving a private revelation does not intend to guarantee the authenticity of the revelation; she simply examines the content of the revelation and states whether or not the faithful may accept it without danger to faith or morals. It would be reprehensible, nevertheless, if one were to contradict or ridicule a private revelation after the Church had given this negative approbation.[19]

Difficulties of private revelations

It sometimes happens that an individual who has received an authentic revelation does not report the revelation accurately, and this may be due to several reasons. If the revelation is extended to other matters which are closely related but were not actually revealed, the revelation has been falsified. It may also happen that, if an individual has been preoccupied with some theological question or already has an extensive knowledge of the matter in the revelation, he may unwittingly add to or alter the revelation. When there is a mixture of the human and the divine it becomes extremely difficult to discern one from the other. At other times the alteration of the revelation may be due to scribes, editors, translators, etc.[20] Another difficulty lies in the interpretation of private revelations, even when they have been transmitted

---

[18]Cf. St. Thomas, *ibid.*, q. 172, a. 2.

[19]For a more detailed treatment, cf. J. Aumann, O.P., "The Credibility of Private Revelations," *Cross and Crown*, X (1958), pp. 326-36.

[20]It is interesting to note that the revelations dictated by St. Catherine of Siena are in complete agreement with the doctrine of St. Thomas Aquinas, while those of Venerable Mary of Agreda seem to favor the teachings of Scotus.

accurately. Moreover, when it falls to others to interpret revelations and they themselves are not the recipients, God does not necessarily give the required light to these persons, or he may deliberately let them fall into error as a punishment.[21]

At this point we repeat again what we have said concerning visions and locutions, namely, that these phenomena are *gratiae gratis datae,* and, therefore, they neither presuppose sanctity in the individual nor are they within the normal development of the supernatural life. Revelations are properly classified, according to St. Paul, under prophecy. Revelations and prophecies have been of great spiritual profit to individual seers, and yet they are not to be desired or prayed for. There is always a great danger to the individual soul in the matter of revelation, and St. John of the Cross states that it would be at least a venial sin to ask God for revelations.[22]

Rules of discernment

The following norms are offered as rules by which the spiritual director may be guided in the discernment of spirits so far as it pertains to revelations and prophecies:

1) Any revelation contrary to dogma or morals must be rejected as false. God does not contradict himself.

2) Any revelation contrary to the common teaching of theologians or purporting to settle an argument among the schools of theology is gravely suspect. Most authors maintain that it must be rejected, but Pope Benedict XIV, while referring to both opinions, does not settle the question.[23]

3) If some detail or other in a revelation is false, it is not necessary to reject the entire revelation; the remainder may be authentic.

4) The fact that a prophecy is fulfilled is not of itself a conclusive proof that the revelation was from God; it could have been the mere unfolding of natural causes or the result of a superior natural knowledge on the part of the seer.

5) Revelations concerning merely curious or useless matters should be rejected as not divine. The same is to be said of those which are detailed, lengthy and filled with a superfluity of proofs and reasons. Divine revelations are generally brief, clear and precise.

6) The person who receives the revelation should be examined carefully, especially as to temperament and character. If the person is humble, well-balanced, discreet, evidently advanced in virtue, and enjoys good mental and physical health, there is good reason to proceed further and to examine the revelation itself. But if the individual is exhausted with excessive mortifications, suffers nervous affliction, is subject to periods of great exhaustion or

---

[21]Cf. St. John of the Cross, *The Ascent of Mount Carmel,* Bk. II, Chaps. 18-20.
[22]Cf. *ibid.,* Bk. II, Chap. 24.
[23]Cf. Pope Benedict XIV, *op. cit.,* Lib. III, cap. ult.

great depression, or is eager to divulge the revelation, there is cause for serious doubt.

7) Lastly, the principal rule of discernment is to judge the revelation by the fruits it produces in the soul of the individual, yet always understanding that the revelation as such is a charism and, therefore, primarily for the good of others and, moreover, that it is always possible for an individual to use the gifts of God to his own spiritual detriment.

READING OF HEARTS

This phenomenon consists in a knowledge of the secrets of hearts, supernaturally communicated by God. The grace is given not only for the good of others but sometimes for the spiritual benefit of the recipient. It has nothing to do with the natural dispositons of the individual nor the grade of holiness attained by the individual. Many saints received this charism, among them St. Thomas Aquinas, St. Philip Neri, St. Joseph Cupertino, St. John of God, St. Rose of Lima and St. John Vianney.

Its nature

The certain and infallible knowledge of the secrets of hearts is completely supernatural and cannot in any way be attained by human nature or the devil. The reason for this is that the human intellect and will are not accessible to any other human being or any angelic power; God and the individual alone have free access to the secrets of one's own heart. It is not at all impossible, however, for the angels and certain human beings to be able to possess a conjectural knowledge concerning the secrets of hearts, but this would not surpass the powers of created nature. Thus certain gifted persons of experience are able to observe and rightly interpret the facial expressions, gestures and attitudes of others, to such an extent that they seem to possess a clear and certain knowledge of matters which would normally be beyond the power of the average human being.

If this sort of insight is possible to men, with all the more reason would it be possible to devils or good angels, whose intellects are far superior to our own. But this type of knowledge, however astounding, is not to be considered as a true reading of hearts, which is a *gratia gratis data*. As such, it can be given to persons who are not themselves holy, although generally this particular phenomenon is not granted to evil persons or sinners. Consequently, a person of depraved life who claims a knowledge of the secrets of hearts is either a transitory instrument in the hands of God or, what is more likely, deceived by the devil, or a victim of his own malice.

HIEROGNOSIS

This phenomenon refers to the ability to recognize immediately any person, place or thing that is holy, blessed or consecrated and to distinguish it from those things that are not. Catherine Emmerich possessed this gift to a high degree, as did St. Catherine of Siena, St. Frances of Rome and St. Lydwina.

Hierognosis transcends the powers of nature and cannot be explained naturally or preternaturally. There is no way in which one could distinguish a blessed or consecrated article from those which are not holy objects. But it should be noted that, whereas many mystics have manifested an almost magnetic attraction for holy objects, the devil or those under his power have manifested the greatest revulsion or horror when any blessed article is brought near them. Nevertheless, the spiritual director should observe the greatest caution in attaching any importance to this negative sign, because there may be simulation and also because some persons under the influence of the devil have not reacted in any way toward holy objects.

Some theologians have considered that certain mystics have reached such a connaturality with things divine and such an affinity for sacred objects that they are, so to speak, predisposed to reverberate spontaneously in the presence of such objects. This may be so, although it would be difficult to explain how a person like the famous Louise Lateau could have reacted in this way during ecstasy. This last case seems to indicate that, at least in some cases, the gift or phenomenon of hierognosis is not within the normal development of the supernatural life of grace but that it is a true charism and *gratia gratis data*. But if this be true, how does it fulfill the requisite that such graces be primarily for the good of others? The obvious answer is that the purpose would be to demonstrate to others the great reverence that is due to any sacred object or person. Like the reading of hearts, hierognosis would be placed under discernment of spirits in the classification of St. Paul.[24]

AFFECTIVE PHENOMENA

The two outstanding mystical phenomena of the affective order are ecstasy and flames of love. But ecstasy is not a *gratia gratis data* nor an extraordinary phenomenon. We have already treated of ecstasy as a concomitant phenomenon which normally accompanies the prayer of ecstatic union. Therefore, we shall discuss only the flames of love.

FLAMES OF LOVE

This phenomenon is usually regarded as an external manifestation of the mystic's intense love of God. It consists in a burning sensation in the body, or even the scorching of the clothing, especially in the vicinity of the heart. It admits of three grades or degrees: 1) *simple interior heat*—an extraordinary

[24]There are numerous other phenomena of the cognoitive order, but we shall refer the reader to detailed studies on the subject made by Thurston, Aradi and Weisinger.

heat perceived in the area of the heart and sometimes spreading throughout the entire body; 2) *intense ardors*—the heat reaches such an intensity that cold applications must be used to assuage the burning sensation; 3) *material burning*—the heat reaches such a point of intensity that the clothing of the mystic is scorched.

There is no doubt that the explanation of this phenomenon offers difficulties, and yet it should be understood that the first and second degree could result from natural causes, and that all three degrees, with God's permission, could be caused by a diabolical power. Hence this phenomenon is not of itself a proof of sanctity or the mystical state. Thus the astounding cases of St. Philip Neri and St. Paul of the Cross would have to be studied in the light of other circumstances in order to verify whether or not this phenomenon was caused supernaturally. The history of spirituality is filled with strange occurrences which externally seem to be identical with the phenomena in the lives of many of the saints and mystics.

BODILY PHENOMENA

STIGMATA

The stigmata is the spontaneous appearance in the body of wounds which resemble the wounds of Christ crucified. They usually appear in the hands, feet and side, though sometimes there are also wounds in the head, as from a crown of thorns, and wounds over the entire surface of the body, resembling the wounds of the scourging. The wounds may be visible or invisible, permanent or periodic, and transitory, simultaneous or successive. It almost always occurs in ecstatics and is often preceded by physical and moral suffering. Tanquerey states that the absence of such suffering would be an unfavorable symptom, because in a true mystic the stigmata is a sign of union with the crucified Christ and a participation in his sufferings.[25] The first ecstatic to be recognized as such in the history of spirituality is St. Francis of Assisi, who received the stigmata on Mount Alvernia on September 17, 1224. It is possible that there were other stigmatics before the time of St. Francis, and it is certain that there have been many since his time.[26]

[25]A. Tanquerey, S.S., *The Spiritual Life* (Westminster: Newman, 1948), p. 714.

[26]In 1894 Dr. Imbert-Gourbeyre listed 321 stigmatics in the history of spirituality, but in the second edition of this work, *La estigmatisation,* in 1898 he published a letter from a correspondent who claimed that he had not compiled a complete listing. Of the listing in 1894 the distribution among religious orders was as follows: Dominicans, 109; Franciscans, 102; Carmelites, 14; Ursulines, 14; Visitandines, 12; Augustinians, 8; Cistercians, 5; Benedictines, 4; Jesuits, 3; Theatines, 3; Trinitarians, 2; Jeronymites, 2; Conceptionists, 2; various religious orders, 13; laymen, 28.

The question arises as to whether or not St. Paul suffered the stigmata, because of his statement in his Epistle to the Galatians (6:17) that he bore the stigmata of Christ. According to Père Lagrange, the word "stigmata" as used by St. Paul referred to the brands or tattoos which marked slaves and soldiers, and St. Paul uses the word to signify that he bore the marks of the sufferings which he had endured for the sake of Christ. Hence all the authors begin the list of stigmatics with the name of St. Francis and omit St. Paul entirely.[27]

Explanation of stigmatism

The Rationalists commonly deny that any such phenomenon as the stigmata is truly supernatural; they attribute the manifestation to mental disorder, auto-suggestion or self-hypnosis. Even in the time of Pope Benedict XIV there were authors who attributed the phenomenon of stigmatization in St. Francis to his active imagination and excessive concentration on the passion of Christ. The modern Rationalists generally assert that the persons who have borne the marks of the stigmata have been persons who were temperamentally and constitutionally predisposed to neuroses of various kinds. They also point out that the majority of the stigmatists practiced extreme corporeal penances and lived in a contemplative type of life which fostered excessive introspection. Their ardent longing to be united with Christ in his sufferings would be sufficient, so they maintain, to produce the bodily signs of the crucifixion.

Two extremes must be avoided in attempting to evaluate the stigmata: to assign too readily a supernatural cause for every such visible manifestation, and to see every such phenomenon as a purely psychosomatic disorder. The Church has accepted relatively few cases of stigmatization as authentic and has always demanded more proof than the mere appearance of visible signs in the body.

The evidence

On the other hand, there is historical evidence that certain Mohammedans, yogis and Brahmanists have produced marks on the body by auto-suggestion. There is also clinical proof that a German by the name of Arthur Otto Mook, a non-practicing Protestant, bore all the wounds of the stigmata. His condition was kept secret for several years but was finally made public in 1949.

Modern psychiatrists would surely admit that the human imagination is powerful enough to produce pains and wounds in the body. After the war there were many examples of men who suffered from physical wounds which were not inflicted in battle but were the result of their own imagination and powers of concentration; men who willed not to be cured so that they would not have to return to battle; men who suffered the sympathetic pains of wounds which they had witnessed in their comrades. It would seem, therefore, that if a person willed to suffer the passion of Christ and had a vivid imagination and strong powers of concentration that he could produce bodily

[27]Cf. M. J. Lagrange, O.P., *Epître aux Galates,* c. 6, v. 17.

wounds by auto-suggestion or self-hypnosis. A German psychiatrist claims to have done just this with a Lutheran girl.

But we find in the history of authentic stigmatics that they were often taken by surprise by the stigmata, that they sought to conceal it, and they asked God to remove the visible signs. While we must admit that a pathological mental state could produce the marks of the stigmata, the true stigmatization in a mystic must proceed from a supernatural cause. If the stigmata in a given case is truly supernatural, it must be classified as a *gratia gratis data* but with a purifying effect on the stigmatist. It enables the mystic to be more intimately configured with Christ. It can be understood in some cases, not only as a filling up to that which is wanting to the sufferings of Christ (Col. 1:24), but a means whereby "victim souls" have an opportunity to suffer for others. Yet the stigmata cannot be taken as a proof of sanctity, because it is a *gratia gratis data* and also because there have been so few stigmatics among the canonized saints.

Guiding norms

Granted the difficulty in discerning the true cause of a stigmata, the following norms may serve as a guide for distinguishing between true and apparent mystical stigmatization:

1) The marks of the true stigmata are usually located in the places in which tradition places the five wounds suffered by Christ; pathological wounds are not uniformly localized.

2) Usually the wounds of the true stigmata bleed on the days or at times when the passion of Christ is commemorated; not so with the pathological.

3) The true stigmata never suppurates, and the blood is always clean and pure, nor can the wounds be healed by natural medication.

4) The flow of blood is so great at times that it cannot be explained naturally.

5) The stigmata is usually found in persons who practice the virtues to a heroic degree and have a tender love of Christ in his passion, and it usually occurs during periods of ecstasy or prayer.

6) The appearance of the true stigmata is usually instantaneous whereas in pathological cases it often appears gradually.

Stigmata and the devil

But is it not possible that the stigmata could be caused by the devil? The devil, with God's permission, could produce the marks of the stigmata, for he can act upon man's body and external senses. He could also be responsible for the stigmata produced by the imagination, for he can have access to that faculty if God allows. He could also prompt an individual to simulate the stigmata, as happened in the case of a Dominican nun in Lisbon during the lifetime of Louis of Granada. Here, as in all the phenomena, we repeat again the basic norm for spiritual directors: if a person claims to have received the stigmata from God and even shows the signs of the wounds in hands and feet and side, and if at the same time that person does not give evidence of a high degree of virtue in the performance of the duties of state in life, then that person is to be judged a fraud or the victim of illusion.[28]

TEARS OF BLOOD AND BLOODY SWEAT

As the names imply, these two phenomena consist in an effusion of blood from the pores of the skin, especially on the face and forehead, or a bloody effusion from the eyes after the manner of tears. The most outstanding example of the bloody sweat is that of Christ in the Garden, but it is very rare in the history of the saints. Even more rare is the phenomenon of tears of blood. St. Lutgard (1182-1246) is reputed to have suffered the bloody sweat, as did Blessed Christina (1242-1312), Magdalen Morice (1736-1769), Mary Dominica Lazzari (1815-1848) and Catherine Putigny (1803-1885). There are only two recorded cases of the tears of blood: Rosa Maria Andriani (1786-1845) and Theresa Neumann.

There are cases in medical history of the bloody sweat, called in medicine *hematidrosis*. Many theories have been proposed in the attempt to give a medical explanation, ranging from hemophilia to the imagination and the organic effects of fear and courage. Whatever the medical explanation, it must be admitted that the bloody sweat can be caused by natural or diabolical powers. If it is truly supernatural it would have to be classified as a *gratia gratis data,* because of itself it does not sanctify the patient. But it would seem more prudent to work on the presumption that these phenomena of the blood have a natural explanation in a particular case.

EXCHANGE OF HEARTS

From all appearances this phenomenon consists in the extraction of the heart of the mystic and the substitution of another, presumably the heart of Christ. It is recorded in the lives of St. Catherine of Siena, St. Lutgard, St. Gertrude, St. Magdalen of Pazzi, St. Margaret Mary Alacoque, St. Catherine de Ricci, St. Michael de los Santos and several others. After the phenomenon occurs, the mystic often bears a wound and then a scar over the place in which the substitution of hearts was made.

How explain this strange phenomenon? It can hardly be doubted to have occurred, granted the testimony that is given in the lives of so many of the saints. The only plausible explanation is that it is strictly miraculous. The difficulty revolves around the apparent substitution of the heart of Christ for the heart of a human being. Pope Benedict XIV gave the most plausible theological explanation when he stated in his eulogy of St. Michael de los Santos that the exchange of hearts was a mystical and spiritual exchange.

[28]Of three contemporary stigmatists—Padre Pio, Theresa Neumann and Arthur Otto Mook—there is no history of nervous or mental disorder in the case of Padre Pio, but the cases of Theresa Neumann and Arthur Mook are amazingly similar as regards previous illness.

The Sacred Congregation of Rites approved this interpretation when it stated in the words of the Office of the Saint: "Hunc servum suum fidelem, peculiari voluit illustrare prodigio, quo ipse divini sui cordis mysticam commutationem cum corde illius inire dignatus est."[29] But since this phenomenon is a physical and corporeal one, it could also be simulated by the devil, with God's permission, or it could be the result of hallucination.

INEDIA OR ABSOLUTE FASTING

This phenomenon consists in the total abstinence from nourishment for a length of time beyond the natural powers. It was a noteworthy phenomenon in the lives of Blessed Angela de Foligno, St. Catherine of Siena, St. Lydwina, Louise Lateau and many others, and it is claimed to have been authenticated in the case of Theresa Neumann.

It is medically certain that the human body cannot exist beyond a certain period without nourishment. While there are some cases in medical history in which individuals have existed for almost 80 days without any solid food, but only on liquids, the point would be reached at which no human being could survive. How, then, can one explain the phenomenon in the lives of some saints who lived for months or entire years without food? Not only did they not lose weight, but they manifested great energy, mental balance and astounding activity.

It should be noted that the Church has never used inedia as a sole rule for the canonization of a saint. There is always the possibility here of diabolical intervention or the action of some unknown power and law of nature. But if it can ever be sufficiently verified that the inedia is of supernatural origin, it must be considered a suspension of the natural law and a presage, as it were, of the glorified body.

PROLONGED ABSENCE OF SLEEP

It is recorded of many saints that they took no sleep for long periods of time, or that they lived on scarcely any sleep at all. Some of the more well-known instances are found in the lives of St. Macarius, St. Lydwina, St. Peter Alcántara, St. Rose of Lima, St. Catherine de Ricci. This phenomenon surpasses the natural order, for sleep is one of the body needs without which the individual cannot survive. The organism must repair its strength if life is to be preserved. A person may reduce himself to an absolute minimum in this regard, but he cannot exclude rest entirely. The rest may be obtained by actual sleep, or by relaxation and inactivity of the body, or even during a mystical ecstasy in which all the faculties are suspended. Hence while it may be admitted that in some cases of absence of sleep there may have been a miracle involved, it is also possible that sufficient rest was gained in certain periods so that the body was able to survive, as St. Teresa seems to indicate

[29]Cf. *Breviarium Romanum,* July 5, lectio VI.

in the case of St. Peter Alcántara.[30] We do not intend to assume a purely rationalistic attitude in this matter, but merely to avoid multiplying miracles without sufficient reason. It should also be noted that up to a certain point the devil could intervene in the matter of living without sleep or rest.

AGILITY This phenomenon consists in the apparently instantaneous transfer or movement of a material body without seeming to pass through the intervening space. Many instances are recorded in the lives of the saints: St. Philip Neri, St. Peter Alcántara, St. Anthony of Padua, St. Martin de Porras, etc. There are also accounts of this phenomenon recorded in Scripture, for example, the deacon Philip (Acts 8:39-40) and Habacuc (Dan. 14:33-39).

As far as is known at the present time, the phenomenon surpasses the powers of nature and would have to be attributed to a supernatural or preternatural cause. If it were caused by the devil, it would be only apparently instantaneous, for although he has the agility of a spirit, if he were to transport a physical body, it would have to pass through the intervening space, even if the speed of the movement were faster than the human eye could detect.

If the agility were the result of a supernatural power, it would either be through the instrumentality of a good angel (and then the same explanation would prevail as in the case of a diabolical power), or else God could give to the individual person the power to move with the rapidity of light or electricity. In the latter case the phenomenon would be strictly a *gratia gratis data* and, according to some theologians, would be something of an anticipated agility of the glorified body. As such it would be strictly miraculous.

BILOCATION This is one of the most stupendous of all the extraordinary mystical phenomena, and one of the most difficult to explain. It consists in the apparently simultaneous presence of a physical body in two distinct places at the same time. The most noteworthy cases in hagiography are those of St. Clement, St. Francis of Assisi, St. Anthony of Padua, St. Lydwina, St. Francis Xavier, St. Martin de Porras, St. Joseph Cupertino, St. Alphonsus Liguori and Venerable Mary of Agreda.

It is philosophically repugnant that a material body should be in two distinct places at the same time by a circumscriptive presence.[31] Although this statement is denied by the followers of Leibniz as well as by Suárez and Bellarmine, we maintain that bilocation which would result in the circumscriptive presence of a material body in two distinct places is a contradiction in terms.[32] Hence it could not even be effected by a miracle.

[30]Cf. *The Life,* Chap. 27.

[31]Cf. St. Thomas, *Summa,* I, q. 67, a. 2.

[32]Cf. Suárez, *De Eucharistia,* dist. 48, sect. 5, n. 4; Bellarmine, *De Sacramento Eucharist.,* Lib. III, cap. 3.

If, therefore, it appears that a body is in two distinct places at the same time, the true and physical body is present in one of the places and in the other place it is only apparently present by means of a representation of some kind. But granted that this be true, what is the cause of the representation by means of a vision or phantasm? We conclude that such a representation could be produced supernaturally, preternaturally or naturally.

In case of a bilocation supernaturally caused, the person is physically present in one place (e.g., St. Martin in Lima) and miraculously represented by a sensible representation in the other term of the bilocation (e.g., St. Martin seen at the same moment in Mexico City). How is the representation effected? First of all, in the example cited, the physical body of St. Martin could be either at Lima or at Mexico City. If it is truly at Mexico City, there is also involved the phenomenon of agility. The representation will be at the terminus from which the physical body moved to the place where it now is actually present. The representation could be effected in any of the ways in which a vision or apparition could be effected, e.g., a true physical body in the likeness of St. Martin assumed by an angel, or a spiritual apparition after the manner of an intellectual, imaginative or corporeal vision. In the latter case the phenomenon of bilocation would be reduced to the phenomenon of a vision.[33]

If the phenomenon of apparent bilocation is effected through diabolical power, with God's permission, it is merely a case of the devil using light rays, vapor or a material substance to simulate the physical body of the person involved. There is no difficulty in affirming this, since the devil has power to make use of material substances.

Is it at all possible that by some natural power as yet unknown a given person could project, as it were, a phantasm or representation of himself to another place? Or is it possible that through some type of telepathy certain persons could see an individual in a distant place while the person remains in another location? We must confess that as yet there is nothing scientifically certain but that we should not close the door on a possible natural explanation, especially in view of the great strides that have been made in recent years in parapsychology.

LEVITATION

As its name indicates, this phenomenon refers to the suspension of a material body in the air without any visible support, in opposition to the law of gravity. There are numerous examples of this phenomenon in the lives of the

[33]In writing of her own bilocation whereby she was at once present in Spain and in the New World, Venerable Mary of Agreda wrote: "What seems more certain to me regarding the manner in which it occurred is that an angel appeared there in my likeness and preached and catechized the Indians and that the Lord showed me here [in Spain] during prayer what was happening there."

saints, e.g., St. Francis of Assisi, St. Catherine of Siena, St. Philip Neri, St. Peter Alcántara, St. Teresa of Avila, St. John of the Cross, St. Francis Xavier, St. Paul of the Cross, St. Thomas of Villanova and especially St. Joseph Cupertino. Generally the levitation occurs during ecstasy, which admits of various types: if the elevation is slight, *ascensional ecstasy;* if the elevation is great, *ecstatic flight;* if there is a rapid movement or gliding above the earth, *ecstatic march.* In the case of Venerable Mary of Agreda, her body seemed to lose all weight during levitation, so that if one breathed on it, it moved like a feather in the breeze.

The traditionally accepted statements on this phenomenon are those of Pope Benedict XIV: 1) levitation cannot be explained by natural causes; 2) levitation does not surpass the powers of angels or devils; 3) when truly supernatural, levitation is a kind of anticipated participation in the agility of a glorified body. Nevertheless, this phenomenon can easily be falsified, as we suspect has often occurred in spiritualistic séances. There are also authentic case histories in pathology in which there has been an apparent levitation, as in certain instances of hysterical seizures.[34] Although the devil cannot work a true miracle, it is possible for him, with God's permission, to make use of invisible powers in order to suspend a material body in the air or to cause it to levitate and move above the earth.

PENETRATION OF BODIES

The phenomenon whereby one material body apparently passes through another material body is recorded of Christ after his resurrection (John 19:20-26) and of St. Dominic and St. Raymond Pennafort.

It has generally been held that the compenetration of material bodies is philosophically repugnant and, therefore, physically impossible. This is based on the teaching that materials are naturally impenetrable intrinsically. It is also admitted that external impenetrability, however, which follows from the distribution of parts of quantity in place, can be suspended miraculously, as occurs in the Eucharist. Hence theologians commonly state that compenetration of bodies is effected miraculously by God as an anticipated participation in the subtlety of a glorified body. And since this phenomenon involves a miracle, it could never be produced naturally or preternaturally. As in the case of bilocation, however, it would be more prudent to suspend judgment in the light of modern scientific investigations concerning the nature and properties of the quantity and dimensions of physical bodies.

MYSTICAL AUREOLES

This phenomenon consists in the resplendent light which irradiates at times from the bodies of mystics, especially during contemplation or ecstasy. There are countless cases recorded: Moses, St. Louis Bertrand, St. Ignatius Loyola,

[34]For detailed descriptions of these medical cases and spiritualistic manifestations, see the reference readings listed in footnote 1.

St. Francis de Paula, St. Philip Neri, St. Francis de Sales, St. Charles Borromeo and St. John Vianney. It is considered by some authors to be an anticipation of the radiant splendor of the glorified body.

Illumination and phosphorescence have been witnessed in certain plants and insects and minerals as well as in the bodies of persons during spiritualistic séances. One of the noteworthy differences between the truly mystical aureole and the luminosity of the spiritualists is that the former seems to radiate from the body of the mystic, whereas the latter appears above or around the body. It is also possible for the devil to produce such rays of light, since it is something that is basically material. If the luminosity of persons of great sanctity is verified as supernatural in origin, it would seem to be either the effect of the intense supernaturalization of the soul or an anticipation of the clarity which that body will emit in the state of glory.

SUPERNATURAL ODOR

This is a phenomenon in which the body of a saint or the tomb emits a sweet odor. Frequently it is an odor which cannot be compared to any known perfume. Among the numerous cases in history we may mention St. Lydwina, St. Catherine de Ricci, St. Philip Neri, St. Gerard Majella, St. John of the Cross, St. Francis de Paula, St. Rose of Viterbo, St. Gemma Galgani and especially St. Joseph Cupertino. Of the saints whose relics have emitted a sweet odor we list St. Francis of Assisi, St. Dominic, St. Thomas of Villanova, St. Thomas Aquinas, St. Rose of Lima, St. Raymond Pennafort, St. Teresa of Avila, St. Frances of Rome.

Pope Benedict XIV declared that, whereas it may happen that a given body may not smell badly, it is not likely that a human body will smell sweetly, and especially when it is dead, whether corrupt or not; hence any sweet perfume which proceeds from it would have to be produced by supernatural powers and be classified as miraculous. But it could be caused by diabolical power, since the devil has power to act upon the external senses. It is recorded of Blessed Jordan of Saxony that the devil once caused his hands to emit a sweet perfume which filled the entire convent, but when Blessed Jordan learned through prayer the true cause of this phenomenon and that the devil's intention was to arouse vainglory, the perfume ceased. When the perfume is truly of supernatural origin, it is considered to be an anticipation of the sweet odor that will most likely emanate from the glorified body.

INCOMBUSTIBLE BODIES

It has been recorded of numerous saints that their bodies or some material object connected with them would not burn when placed in or over the flames of a fire (St. Polycarp, St. Peter Igneus, St. Dominic, St. Francis of Paula, St. Catherine of Siena). In general, the incombustibility of bodies may be truly supernatural, preternatural or due perhaps to some unknown power of nature which is possessed by certain individuals. Cases of spiritualism abound in which persons were able to hold in their hands red-hot coals and even put them on the top of their heads or those of others without being burned or the hair being singed. While it is true that many of the incidents in the lives of holy persons are obviously miraculous and must therefore be attributed to the direct intervention of God, the question in general must remain open as far as any natural explanation is concerned in the case of spiritualists and freaks of nature.

BODILY ELONGATION

This phenomenon has been witnessed not only in the lives of a few saints (Blessed Stephana Quinzani, Sister Veronica Laparelli, and the partial elongation of St. Catherine of Genoa), but also in certain spiritualists. Although in the latter case one must suspect tricks or diabolical intervention, if it occurs in the life of a mystic there is always a question as to its purpose. The fact remains that in these cases the body or limb of the individual has visibly elongated to proportions far beyond the normal. It is another strange phenomenon which we prefer to leave as an open question until more detailed studies have been made.

OTHER PRODIGIES

Other phenomena are well attested in the history of the saints. Incorruptibility of the body is a relatively common phenomenon in hagiography, and we mention only a few examples: St. Francis de Sales, St. John of God, St. Frances of Rome, St. John Capistrano, St. Francis of Paula, St. Paul of the Cross, St. Pius V, St. Philip Neri, St. Ignatius Loyola, St. Rose of Lima, St. Joseph Cupertino, St. Teresa of Avila. The bodies of these persons were found to be either temporarily or permanently incorrupt.

The absence of *rigor mortis* has been verified in the following instances: St. Raynerius of Pisa, St. Francis of Assisi, Blessed Peter of Luxembourg, St. Maria della Passione, St. Louis Bertrand, St. Peter Claver. Medical authorities have stated that *rigor mortis* is absolutely certain to set in sooner or later, although there may be a variation of a few hours one way or the other. In view of this, the phenomenon of the complete absence of any rigidity in the bodies of the deceased saints offers a curious problem. It could be from a supernatural or a preternatural cause, and perhaps in some instances there may possibly be a natural explanation. But the phenomenon itself is not sufficient as proof of sanctity.

Many of the accounts of corpses shedding blood are of ancient origin. It is stated that blood flowed from the dead bodies of St. Ambrose, SS. Gervase and Protase, SS. Marcellinus and Peter, St. Godric of Finchale, St. Catherine of Bologna, St. Francis di Geronimo, St. Nicholas of Tolentino. The blood prodigy of St. Januarius is a special case and is known to all.

What is to be said about these various prodigies relating to corpses? The truth of the matter is that very little can be said definitively. Granted that any one of them could possibly be supernatural in origin because of a divine intervention, or that any of them could, with God's permission, be the work of the devil, it is much more scientific and prudent to withhold judgment in most instances. Possibly in some future day the scientists will be able to give a natural explanation for many of these strange occurrences which in many cases seem to have no purpose from a spiritual point of view.

CONCLUSION

In discussing the extraordinary phenomena in particular we have tried to avoid any premature judgments but have attempted to hold fast to the principle that no phenomenon should be attributed to a superior cause if it can be explained by an inferior one. We have not listed each and every phenomenon; for that we refer the reader to the more detailed studies in books which treat specifically of occult phenomena. Neither have we given a definitive judgment in each instance, for we believe it much wiser to leave a question open when there is still room for doubt or hope of a natural explanation at some future date. Nevertheless, there are more than sufficient extraordinary and truly miraculous phenomena on record to show us that God is truly wonderful in his saints.

Mirabilis est Deus in sanctis suis!

SUBJECT INDEX